VISUAL BASIC® 5 DATABASE HOW-TO

THE DEFINITIVE DATABASE PROBLEM-SOLVER

Dennis Kennedy, Joe Garrick, Bill Harper, Jason T. Roff

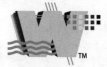

Waite Group Press™
A Division of
Macmillan Computer
Publishing
Corte Madera, CA

Publisher: Mitchell Waite
Associate Publisher: Charles Drucker
Executive Editor: Susan Walton
Acquisitions Editor: Rebekah Darksmith
Project Development Editor: Laura E. Brown
Content Editor: Russ Jacobs
Technical Editor: Chris Stone
Production Editor: Cheri Clark
Copy Editors: Mitzi Foster and Kristen Ivanetich
Managing Editor: Brice Gosnell
Indexing Manager: Johnna L. VanHoose
Resource Coordinators: Deborah Frisby and Charlotte Clapp
Software Specialist: Dan Scherf
Production Manager: Cecile Kaufman
Production Team Supervisor: Brad Chinn
Cover Designer: Sestina Quarequio
Book Designer: Jean Bisesi
Production: Carol Bowers, Mona Brown, Bruce Clingaman, Ayanna Lacey, Gene Redding

Printed in the United States of America
97 98 99 • 10 9 8 7 6 5 4 3 2 1

Library of Congress Cataloging-in-Publication Data
Visual Basic 5 database how-to / Dennis Kennedy... [et al.].
     p.   cm.
     Includes index.
     ISBN 1-57169-104-9
     1. Database management.   2. Microsoft Visual Basic. I. Kennedy,
Dennis, 1969–.
QA76.9.D3V567 1997   97-34130
     005.75'6--dc21   CIP
International Standard Book Number: 1-57169-104-9

DEDICATION

To Polly.
—Dennis Kennedy

To Connor, Logan, and Quinn. One day you'll look at this technology and laugh.
—Joe Garrick

To Mom and Dad—If it were not for your love and support, I would not be who I am. To Kimberly—If it were not for your love and support, I would not have a reason to be.
—Jason T. Roff

Starting his programming career at an early age writing game routines on a Commodore 64, **Dennis Kennedy** has since participated in application designs ranging from client/server suites at some of the country's largest insurance corporations to smartcard programs for cutting-edge development firms. Recently relocated to Bellevue, Washington, he now serves as a systems design consultant for several firms, as well as spending much of his free time programming freelance. When not programming, Dennis spends the rest of his free time, apparently, chiding his two ferrets.

Joe Garrick got hooked on programming, and BASIC in particular, 15 years ago when he brought down an IBM mainframe with a 10-page BASIC program (it was actually a compiler error that caused the crash, but the hook was set). Today, Joe is a programmer, database developer, e-mail administrator, network supervisor, and all-around "computer guy" for a small consulting company in Minneapolis, Minnesota. You can reach Joe by e-mail at `jgarrick@citilink.com` or visit him on the Web at `http://www.citilink.com/~jgarrick/vbasic/`.

Bill Harper is a founder of Solutions TeleComputing in Hanover, New Hampshire. Solutions TeleComputing develops multimedia database imaging and interactive voice response systems for jails, telephone companies, and emerging tele-medicine technologies. In addition to his development experience, Bill has spent more than 15 years in software development management, training, and consulting, including experience with a Big Six accounting firm, a major computer vendor, and a large telephone company. He holds bachelor's and master's degrees from the Massachusetts Institute of Technology and can be reached on the Internet at `Bill.Harper@Valley.Net`.

Jason T. Roff graduated from the University at Albany, in New York, with a degree in Computer Science with Applied Mathematics. After graduation, Jason began working for the Blockbuster Entertainment Group in Fort Lauderdale, Florida. Here, Jason developed client/server applications in Visual Basic and C/C++ that were used to manage Blockbuster franchise stores. Currently, Jason works for Isogon Corporation, a company that provides asset management solutions to Fortune 500 companies. For Isogon Corporation, Jason develops C/C++ client/server applications that are designed to run on heterogeneous networks. Jason is to be married to Kimberly A. McGowan in August of 1998.

TABLE OF CONTENTS

CONTENTS

ACKNOWLEDGMENTS

First and foremost, to the CIGNA Provider Workbench team. Also, to RHI Consulting, The Pathways Group, and Critical Path Technical Services for their patience and support during my writings. And a special acknowledgment to Chris Bielak, Joe Levesque, Gale & Kim Fulton, and Gene Tellier—without them, I'd probably be less sane than I am now…I think.

—Dennis Kennedy

Many people at Waite Group Press worked hard to make this book happen. I want to thank Laura Brown and the rest of the staff for their efforts. I also want to thank all of the people who helped me to learn enough about databases and programming to write about them. Rick and Hal Walters, Julie Zapp, and others put their faith in me to develop their software and databases and allowed me to learn while doing it. Tim Gray, Randy Birch, Shafayat Kamal, and many other Net friends, along with Rick Dill and all of the regulars at the VB and Database programming chat on MSN, all provided invaluable help and friendly, thought-provoking discussions. Many thanks to all of you. Most of all, I owe a great debt to my family. My sons, Connor, Logan, and Quinn, provided many smiles (and a few gray hairs) during this process. My wife and best friend, Carlene, and her mom, Mary, kept life moving forward while I had my fingers on the keyboard. I thank you all for your patience and support.

—Joe Garrick

I would like to thank Jeffrey Pincus, the engineer who turned a grape box into a stereo, for all the help he has given me throughout the writing of this book. I would also like to thank the DelBuono brothers, John, Anthony, and Charles, who together are probably considered the highest authority on Visual Basic, golf, and barbecuing in southern Florida. There is nothing these three men can't do. Special thanks to John for all his help and support. To the one who supported me through everything every night as I paced the driveway of my Boynton Beach residence, I would like to thank Mary Ellen—no other person knows how to say such kind words. Finally, I would like to thank my grandfather…I'd like to think you would have been proud.

—Jason T. Roff

INTRODUCTION

About This Book

Database programming and Visual Basic have been synonymous since the release of Visual Basic 3.0, which incorporated the Microsoft Access Jet database engine. The database arsenal of tools increased in power and complexity with the release of Visual Basic 4.0 and the addition of Remote Data Object technology, allowing even ODBC databases to be easily and efficiently handled.

Now, with the release of Visual Basic 5.0 and the addition of even more database programming capability, the Visual Basic arena has become larger than ever. Projects that were previously the realm of other, more arcane languages are now within reach. Not easy reach, though. With the addition of all this database power comes a bewildering array of objects, properties, and methods from which the Visual Basic database programmer can now choose. And with the technology moving at warp speed, that choice can be difficult.

That's why this book was created. *Visual Basic 5 Database How-To* gives an in-depth view of each major method of data access, with real-life examples with which to work. Like all books in the Waite Group's successful How-To series, *Visual Basic 5 Database How-To* emphasizes a step-by-step problem-solving approach to Visual Basic programming. Each How-To follows a consistent format that guides you through the issues and techniques involved in solving a specific problem. Each section contains the steps to solve a problem, as well as a discussion of how and why the solution works. In most cases, you can simply copy the provided code or objects into your application and be up and running immediately. All the code described in the book is available on the accompanying CD-ROM.

The book's concepts and examples are useful to Visual Basic programmers of all skill levels. Each How-To is graded by complexity level, with information on additional uses and enhancements to fit your needs exactly. Additionally, each chapter contains an introduction that summarizes each How-To and covers the chapter's techniques and topics so that you can zero in on just the solution you need without having to go through hundreds of pages to find it.

What You Need to Use This Book

First and foremost, you need Visual Basic 5.0. Some of the code works with Visual Basic 4.0, but we have introduced the most up-to-date capabilities of Visual Basic 5.0 to take advantage of new features, such as RDO 2.0 and ADO. We use the Enterprise Edition of Visual Basic, so the book is applicable to every database developer; but almost all chapters will work with the Professional Edition as well.

We avoid using unsupported controls or tools; all controls and objects are available in Visual Basic Enterprise, and almost all are available in Visual Basic Professional. However, a wide array of third-party tools, such as custom controls and Visual Basic add-ins, is readily available, and these tools are extremely useful for speeding your development timeline.

CHAPTER 1

ACCESSING A DATABASE WITH BOUND CONTROLS

1

ACCESSING A DATABASE WITH BOUND CONTROLS

How do I...

The Microsoft Jet database engine, supplied with Visual Basic, gives you the ability to access many types of databases—Microsoft Access databases; other PC-based databases such as dBASE, FoxPro, Paradox, and Btrieve; and any relational database that supports the Open Database Connectivity (ODBC) standard. Visual Basic provides two basic techniques for working with the Jet database engine: the data control and data access objects. The data control requires less code, but data access objects are much more flexible. This chapter shows you how to use the data control to perform common database operations. Chapter 2, "Accessing a Database with Data Access Objects," describes the use of data access objects.

VISUAL BASIC TERMINOLOGY PRIMER

If you're new to database programming, many Visual Basic terms might be new to you. Visual Basic works with all databases through a *recordset* consisting of all the records in a table or all the records satisfying a particular SQL (Structured Query Language) SELECT statement. A SELECT statement asks the database to retrieve specified database fields from one or more database tables in which record fields meet certain criteria. SQL itself is discussed in Chapter 3, "SQL." The programmer's interaction with the person behind the keyboard is through *visual controls* placed on the form for data entry, command buttons, menus, labels, pictures, and so on. The most common controls are *text boxes* for entering data, *command buttons* for getting the program to do useful work, *menus*, and *labels* to describe the other controls. *List boxes* and *combo boxes* allow the program to provide multiple selections for text entry to the person in front of the screen.

Most visual controls, including text, list, and combo boxes, can be *bound* to a data source for automatic display of data or have a special *data-bound* version. *Binding* is the process of connecting the data in a visual control to a field in a recordset. The most common binding method is the *data control*. The data control has a visual interface to support data movement through the records, and a recordset object to manage the interface to the database engine. The data control *component* also supports several *methods* and *properties* for programmatic or design-time control. A component is simply a "piece part" used to build a Visual Basic application. A method is equivalent to a function call to the component to get the component to do useful work. A property is a data element of the component that helps control its behavior. For example, the data control has a DatabaseName property to tell it where the database can be found and a Move method to move the visual control around on the form. In addition, the data control *exposes* all the methods and properties of its contained recordset object.

All the examples in this chapter use existing Microsoft Access database files delivered with Visual Basic (later chapters demonstrate how to create a database with Visual Basic). The techniques, however, apply to all the databases that Visual Basic can access through the Jet engine. In addition, the Enterprise Edition *remote data control* uses very similar techniques for direct use with ODBC databases. The remote data control bypasses the Jet engine and usually delivers faster performance than access through the Jet engine.

1.1 Browse a Recordset Using Bound Controls

One of the most fundamental operations in database work is the ability to browse through records in an existing database and modify data. In this How-To, you'll use the data control, bind its fields to some text boxes, and write one line of executable code to browse a database.

1.2 Validate Data Entered into Bound Controls

People make data entry errors, and an industrial-strength application anticipates and traps those errors. This How-To shows how to trap and respond to entry errors when you're using the data control and bound visual controls.

1.3 Allow Users to Undo Changes They've Made in Bound Controls

Sometimes people catch their own mistakes. In this How-To, you'll learn how to enable them to undo those mistakes when the application uses the data control.

1.4 Add and Delete Records Using Bound Controls

A database is fairly useless without some means of adding and deleting records. In this How-To, you'll see how to implement record additions and deletions with bound controls.

1.5 Create and Use Bound Lists

One way to reduce data entry errors—and make people's lives a bit easier—is to provide people with lists from which they can choose appropriate values for database fields. Visual Basic 5 provides the DBCombo and DBList controls that make this easy to do. In this How-To, you'll use the DBCombo control to display suggested field values.

1.6 Display Many Detail Records for a Single Master Record

Frequently, you need to work with related records at the same time in a master-detail relationship. You might want to show an invoice header and all its detail lines or show all the orders for a particular product. This How-To shows the use of the DBGrid control to place multiple detail records on a form for each master record.

1.7 Change Data in Data-Bound Grid Cells from Code

The master-detail grid looks great, but some applications require the capability to expand and edit grid data from the main form. This How-To walks through a form that edits DBGrid data from the form's code.

1.8 Gracefully Handle Data Control Errors

Whenever you're working with disk files, unanticipated errors can occur. Your Visual Basic database program should handle errors gracefully. This How-To shows how.

FINDING THE SAMPLES

All the How-To's in this book have been delivered on the accompanying CD-ROM. After you install the source code, you will find a directory for each chapter, and within that directory, a directory for each How-To. The steps of each How-To start with an opportunity to preview the completed How-To from your installation directory. If you decide to work through a How-To in its entirety, we assume that you are working in a separate work area on your computer.

COMPLEXITY
BEGINNING

1.1 How do I...
Browse a recordset using bound controls?

Problem

I need to see the records in a database, but I don't want to write a lot of code. How can I do this with Visual Basic?

Technique

The Visual Basic data control object, in conjunction with data-bound controls, allows you to browse records in a supported database without writing a single line of code.

To use the data control, place it on your form and set two properties: `DatabaseName`, which specifies the database to which it will be linked, and `RecordSource`, which designates the source of data within the database. Add a text box to your form for every database field you want to access from the `RecordSource`, and bind each text box to the data control object and `RecordSource` field.

COMPATIBLE DATABASES

Databases that are compliant with the Visual Basic data control—and with Visual Basic data access objects, discussed in Chapter 2—include Microsoft Access, dBASE, FoxPro, Paradox, Btrieve, and any other database products that support the Open Database Connectivity (ODBC) standard. Most relational database products for desktop systems and multiuser systems support ODBC. The examples throughout this book use Microsoft Access databases, except for those in Chapter 6, "External ISAM Database Files," Chapter 7, "Connecting to an ODBC Server," and Chapter 8, "SQL Server Databases," which relate specifically to other database products. Virtually all the examples in the book (except for those in Chapters 6 through 8) can be applied to any of the database products.

When you work with Microsoft Access databases, the `DatabaseName` is the name of a Microsoft Access database file. When you work with other database products, what constitutes "the database" depends on the type of database—for dBASE, Paradox, and FoxPro databases, for example, the `DatabaseName` is the name of the directory in which data files are stored. The `RecordSource` can also be a table or a SQL `SELECT` statement. Microsoft Access also allows you to specify the name of a query stored within the database as the `RecordSource`. (See the Table of Contents of this book for other chapters detailing the specifics of your database.)

The data control not only provides the link between your form and the database, but also provides tools for navigating through the database. Figure 1.1 shows a data control. The Next Record and Previous Record buttons move you through the database one record at a time. The First Record and Last Record buttons move you quickly to the beginning or end of the database.

Steps

To preview this How-To, open the project BrowseBound.VBP in the Chapter01\HowTo01 directory. Change the `DatabaseName` property of the data control `datEmployees` to point to the copy of NWind.MDB installed on your system (probably in the directory where VB5.EXE is installed). Then run the project. The form shown in Figure 1.2 appears. Use the buttons on the data control to view records in the Titles table of NWind.MDB.

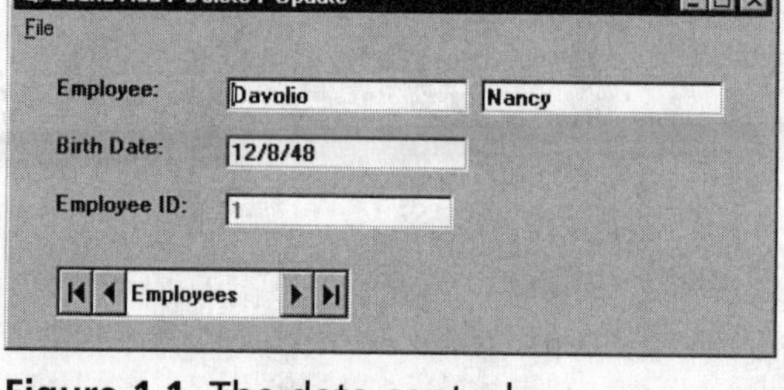

Figure 1.1. The data control.

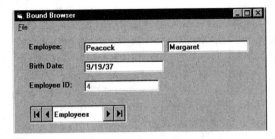

Figure 1.2. The Bound Browser form.

1. Create a new project in your work area called BrowseBound.VBP. Use
Form1 to create the objects and properties listed in Table 1.1, and save
the form as BrowseBound.FRM. Substitute the path to your copy of
NWIND.MDB for the `DatabaseName` property of `datEmployees`.

Table 1.1. Objects and properties for the Bound Browser form.

OBJECT	PROPERTY	SETTING
Form	Name	Form1
	Caption	"Bound Browser"
Data	Name	datEmployees
	Caption	"Employees"
	DatabaseName	"C:\VB5\NWIND.MDB"
	RecordSource	"Employees"
TextBox	Name	txtEmpLastName
	DataField	"LastName"
	DataSource	"datEmployees"
TextBox	Name	txtEmpFirstName
	DataField	"FirstName"
	DataSource	"datEmployees"
TextBox	Name	txtBirthDate
	DataField	"BirthDate"
	DataSource	"datEmployees"
TextBox	Name	txtEmployeeId
	DataField	"EmployeeID"
	DataSource	"datEmployees"
	Enabled	False
Label	Name	Label1
	Caption	"Employee:"
Label	Name	Label2

OBJECT	PROPERTY	SETTING
	Caption	"Birth Date:"
Label	Name	Label3
	Caption	"Employee ID:"

2. Use the Visual Basic menu editor to create the menu shown in Table 1.2.

Table 1.2. Menu specifications for the Bound Browser.

CAPTION	NAME	SHORTCUT KEY
&File	mnuFile	
----E&xit	mnuFileExit	

3. Enter the following code as the `Click` event for `mnuExit`:

```
Private Sub mnuFileExit_Click()
    Unload Me
End Sub
```

How It Works

When the application starts, the data control opens the NWind.MDB database, creates a *recordset* from the Titles table, and displays values from the first record of the recordset in the form's *bound controls*. A recordset is a Visual Basic object used to manipulate the contents of a database. Bound controls are visual interface controls such as text boxes that people can see on the screen, but that are also linked, or bound, to fields managed by a data control's recordset. Recordsets provide methods for moving between records as well as for adding, updating, and deleting records. When people click on one of the data control's record navigation buttons, the data control positions the record pointer to the selected record and updates the bound controls with the values from the new record.

Under the covers, the data control is working hard. We see a screen form with text boxes. Figure 1.3 shows the main interactions between bound text boxes, the data control, and the data control's recordset. Every time the data control moves to a different record, it checks for changed data between the bound controls and the recordset fields. If changes are found, the data control moves the data to the fields and performs an automatic update to the recordset and the underlying database. Finally, the data control retrieves the desired record from the database and copies the field data to text controls for display. In the remainder of this chapter, we'll explore the data control's events and methods to build solid applications with very little work.

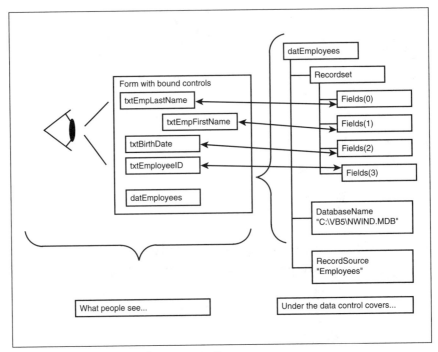

Figure 1.3. Under the data control's covers.

Comments

This is truly code-free development. The only executable line of code closes the application. However, this is a very limited application—there's no way to validate entries, add records, or delete records. To perform those operations, some code is needed—not a lot of code, but some code nonetheless. The following How-To's show how to add those functions to this simple beginning.

COMPLEXITY
BEGINNING

1.2 How do I...
Validate data entered into bound controls?

Problem

The data control and bound controls provide low-code database access. But I need to verify that entered form data is valid before I update the database. How can I check entered data when I'm using bound controls?

Technique

Each time you change the current record in a recordset attached to a data control—by moving to a different record, deleting the current record, or closing the recordset—Visual Basic triggers the data control's `Validate` event. You can write an event subroutine to check any changes made to data in bound controls.

The `Validate` event subroutine receives two arguments:

✔ `Action`, an integer which describes the event that caused the `Validate` event.

✔ `Save`, a Boolean value that is `True` if data in any bound control has changed, and `False` if the data hasn't changed.

In your event subroutine, you can check the value of `Save`. If it is `True`, you can then check each entry to verify that it falls within the bounds of what is legal in your application. If any entry is not legal, you set the `Action` argument to the built-in constant `dbDataActionCancel`, which cancels the event that caused the `Validate` event. For example, if the `Validate` event was triggered by clicking on the data control to move to a different record, setting `Action` to `dbDataActionCancel` cancels the `Move` event and leaves the data control positioned on the original record. Your `Validate` event subroutine should also display a problem message so that the entry can be corrected.

Steps

Open the project ValidateBound.VBP in the Chapter01\HowTo02 directory to preview the results of this How-To. Change the `DatabaseName` property of the data control `datEmployees` to point to the copy of NWind.MDB installed on your system (probably in the directory where VB5.EXE is installed). Then run the project. A form similar to that shown previously in Figure 1.2 appears. Use the buttons on the data control to view records in the Employees table of NWind.MDB. Select all the text in the Employee and Birth Date boxes and delete it; then try to move to another record. You'll see an error message like the one shown in Figure 1.4, informing you that you must enter a last name, first name, and birth date. Choose the File | Exit menu option to close the project.

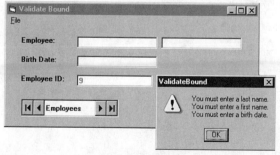

Figure 1.4. The Validate Bound form.

1. Create a new project called ValidateBound.VBP in your work area. Use
Form1 to create the objects and properties listed in Table 1.1, and save the
form as ValidateBound.FRM. (Note that this is the same form used for
How-To 1.1.) Substitute the path to your copy of NWind.MDB for the
DatabaseName property of datEmployees. Use the Visual Basic menu
editor to create the menu shown in Table 1.2.

2. Add the file clsUtility.cls to your project from the Chapter01\HowTo02
directory by selecting Project | Add File from the main menu or by
pressing Ctrl+D on the keyboard. Use the file common dialog to select
the file.

3. Add the following code to the declarations section of Form1. The Utility
class is used to tie MsgBox strings together gracefully.

```
Private Utility As New clsUtility
Private mblnValidationFailed As Boolean
```

4. Enter the following code into Form1 as the Validate event for the
datEmployees data control. This code checks to make sure that valid data
have been entered into all controls. If there are any invalid data, the
subroutine displays an error message, cancels the Validate event, and sets
the form-level variable mblnValidationFailed to True.

```
Private Sub datEmployees_Validate(Action As Integer, Save As Integer)
    Dim strMsg As String
    Dim enumMsgResult As VbMsgBoxResult

    If Save = True Or Action = vbDataActionUpdate _
    Or Action = vbDataActionUnload Then
        ' One or more bound controls has changed or the form
        ' is being unloaded, so verify that all fields have
        ' legal entries. If a field has an incorrect value,
        ' append a string explaining the error to strMsg and
        ' set the focus to that field to facilitate correcting
        ' the error. We explain all errors encountered in a
        ' single message box.
        strMsg = ""
        If txtEmpLastName.Text = "" Then
            Utility.AddToMsg strMsg, "You must enter a last name."
            txtEmpLastName.SetFocus
        End If
        If txtEmpFirstName.Text = "" Then
            Utility.AddToMsg strMsg, "You must enter a first name."
            txtEmpFirstName.SetFocus
        End If
        If Not IsDate(txtBirthDate.Text) Then
            Utility.AddToMsg strMsg, "You must enter a birth date."
            txtBirthDate.SetFocus
        Else
            If CDate(txtBirthDate.Text) >= Date Then
                Utility.AddToMsg strMsg, _
                    "Birth date must be in the past."
```

```
            txtBirthDate.SetFocus
        End If
    End If

    If strMsg <> "" Then
        ' We have something in the variable strMsg, which
        ' means that an error has occurred. Display the
        ' message. The focus is in the last text box where
        ' an error was found.
        MsgBox strMsg, vbExclamation
        ' Cancel the Validate event
        Action = vbDataActionCancel
        ' Deny form Unload until fields are corrected
        mblnValidationFailed = True
    Else
        mblnValidationFailed = False
    End If
    End If
End Sub
```

5. Enter the following code into `Form1` as the `Unload` event. If the `Validate` event has set the `UpdateCancelled` flag, this procedure cancels the `Unload` event.

```
Private Sub Form_Unload(Cancel As Integer)

    ' Don't allow the unload until the data is validated.
    If mblnValidationFailed Then Cancel = True
End Sub
```

6. Enter the following code as the `Click` event for `mnuExit`:

```
Private Sub mnuExit_Click()
    Unload Me
End Sub
```

How It Works

Each time the `Validate` event is called, the contents of the controls are checked to make sure that they contain valid data. If they do not, the `Validate` event is cancelled. This prevents the record from being saved with invalid data. The validation event procedure makes use of a "helper" utility class to gracefully append multiple messages from each error check to the displayed results. Displaying all validation errors at once is a good design technique because it reduces frustration for the person at the keyboard.

When the form is unloaded, the contents of bound controls are automatically saved through the data control. And that means that the `Validate` event gets called. If a control has invalid data, the `Validate` event is cancelled, but that does not in itself cancel the `Form Unload` event. Therefore, the `Validate` event sets a form-level flag variable, `mblnValidationFailed`, which the `Form Unload` procedure checks. If `mblnValidationFailed` is true, the `Form Unload` event is cancelled and the application does not terminate.

Comments

The validating browse form helps control data entry errors, but it is unforgiving without a cancellation option to undo form changes. After a field has been changed on this form, valid data must be entered before the user can change records or exit the application. Clearly, there should be a better way—and there is.

COMPLEXITY
BEGINNING

1.3   How do I...
Allow users to undo changes they've made in bound controls?

Problem

I want my form to have the capability to undo changes made to a record before the record is saved. How can I accomplish this when I'm using bound controls?

Technique

Your form gains the capability to undo changes to the current record by using the **Update Controls** method of the data control. This method causes Visual Basic to reread the current record from the database file and refresh the value of each bound control with the respective field value from the database. Simply execute this method, and any bound control changes are overwritten with the original data from the database.

Steps

Open the project UndoBound.VBP to preview this How-To. Change the **DatabaseName** property of the data control **datEmployees** to point to the copy of NWind.MDB installed on your system (probably in the directory where VB5.EXE is installed). Then run the project. The form shown in Figure 1.5 appears. Use the buttons on the data control to view records in the Employees table of NWind.MDB. Make a change in a record. Before you move to another record, select Edit | Undo. You'll see your changes "backed out" of the form.

1. Create a new project called UndoBound.VBP. Use **Form1** to create the objects and properties listed in Table 1.1, and save the form as UndoBound.FRM. (Note that this is the same form used for How-To's 1.1 and 1.2.) Substitute the path to your copy of NWind.MDB for the **DatabaseName** property of **datEmployees**. Use the Visual Basic menu editor to create the menu shown in Table 1.3.

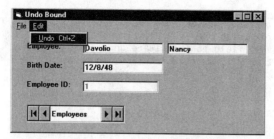

Figure 1.5. The Undo Bound form.

Table 1.3. Menu specifications for UndoBound.FRM.

CAPTION	NAME	SHORTCUT KEY
&File	mnuFile	
----E&xit	mnuFileExit	
&Edit	mnuEdit	
----&Undo	mnuEditUndo	Ctrl+Z

2. Add the file clsUtility.cls to your project from the Chapter01\HowTo03 directory by selecting Project | Add File from the main menu or by pressing Ctrl+D on the keyboard. Use the file common dialog to select the file.

3. Add the following code to the declarations section of **Form1**:

```
Private Utility As New clsUtility
Private mblnValidationFailed As Boolean
```

4. Enter the following code into **Form1** as the **Validate** event for the **datEmployees** data control. (Note the changes from How-To 1.2 highlighted in bold.) This code checks to make sure that valid data have been entered into all controls. If there are any invalid data, the subroutine displays an error message and asks for an OK or a Cancel response. An OK response cancels the **Validate** event and sets the form-level variable **mblnValidationFailed** to True. A Cancel response retrieves the database values to the bound form controls and backs out the changes.

```
Private Sub datEmployees_Validate(Action As Integer, Save As Integer)
    Dim strMsg As String
    Dim enumMsgResult As VbMsgBoxResult


    If Save = True Or Action = vbDataActionUpdate _
    Or Action = vbDataActionUnload Then
        ' One or more bound controls has changed or the form
        ' is being unloaded, so verify that all fields have
```

continued on next page

continued from previous page

```
' legal entries. If a field has an incorrect value,
' append a string explaining the error to strMsg and
' set the focus to that field to facilitate correcting
' the error. We explain all errors encountered in a
' single message box.
strMsg = ""
If txtEmpLastName.Text = "" Then
    Utility.AddToMsg strMsg, "You must enter a last name."
    txtEmpLastName.SetFocus
End If
If txtEmpFirstName.Text = "" Then
    Utility.AddToMsg strMsg, "You must enter a first name."
    txtEmpFirstName.SetFocus
End If
If Not IsDate(txtBirthDate.Text) Then
    Utility.AddToMsg strMsg, "You must enter a birth date."
    txtBirthDate.SetFocus
Else
    If CDate(txtBirthDate.Text) >= Date Then
        Utility.AddToMsg strMsg, _
            "Birth date must be in the past."
        txtBirthDate.SetFocus
    End If
End If

If strMsg <> "" Then
    ' We have something in the variable strMsg, which
    ' means that an error has occurred. Display the
    ' message. The focus is in the last text box where
    ' an error was found
    enumMsgResult = MsgBox(strMsg, vbExclamation + vbOKCancel + _
        vbDefaultButton1)

    If enumMsgResult = vbCancel Then
        ' Restore the data to previous values using the
        ' data control
        datEmployees.UpdateControls
        ' Allow form unload.
        mblnValidationFailed = False
    Else
        ' Cancel the Validate event
        Action = vbDataActionCancel
        ' Deny form unload until fields are corrected
        mblnValidationFailed = True
    End If
Else
    mblnValidationFailed = False
End If
End If
End Sub
```

5. Enter the following code into Form1 as the Unload event. (This code is the same as that for the identically named procedure in How-To 1.2.) If the Validate event has set the UpdateCancelled flag, this procedure cancels the Unload event.

```
Private Sub Form_Unload(Cancel As Integer)
    ' Don't allow the unload until the data is validated or the
    ' update is cancelled
    If mblnValidationFailed Then Cancel = True
End Sub
```

6. Enter the following code as the `Click` event for `mnuEditUndo`:

```
Private Sub mnuEditUndo_Click()

    ' Undo all pending changes from form by copying recordset
    ' values to form controls
    datEmployees.UpdateControls

End Sub
```

7. Enter the following code as the `Click` event for `mnuExit`. (This code is the same as that for the identically named procedure in How-To 1.2.)

```
Private Sub mnuExit_Click()
    Unload Me
End Sub
```

How It Works

The `mnuEditUndo_Click` procedure allows for removing any pending changes from the database by using the data control's `UpdateControls` method. This method takes the copy of the field data from the data control's recordset and "updates" the displayed bound controls. Remember from Figure 1.3 that there are constantly two copies of all data in a data control application—the copy on the screen fields (in the bound controls) and the copy in the data control's recordset fields. Data is moved from the bound controls to the recordset fields during an update but only after validation is successful. So no matter how much the data on the screen has changed, nothing happens until the recordset gets updated. (In this application so far, a recordset is updated only when the data control is moved from one record to another.)

Another useful enhancement in this version of the program is the use of a Cancel response from the validation error message box to refresh the screen display automatically without making the person outside the glass make a menu selection. The modified error message box is shown in Figure 1.6. If the response indicates a cancellation, the validation is cancelled and the data values are restored from the database to the bound controls.

The validation event procedure (in step 4) makes extensive use of Visual Basic constants such as `vbDataActionCancel` and `vbCancel` rather than numeric constants to improve the ability of programmers to understand the code. Values for constants can easily be found by pressing the F2 key from within Visual Basic to bring up the Object Browser window from which constants can be copied and pasted into your code. Declaring `enumMsgResult` as a `VbMsgBoxResult` type

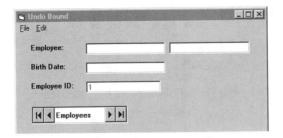

Figure 1.6. The Cancel button added to an error message box.

shows the use of strong typing to help make the program's meaning clearer to subsequent programmers.

Comments

Even though we can update, validate, and undo changes to our employee records, we still can't hire or fire anyone. Let's complete the core application by adding the add and delete functions.

COMPLEXITY
BEGINNING

1.4 How do I...
Add and delete records using bound controls?

Problem

How do I add and delete records when I'm using bound controls?

Technique

To add a record to the recordset of a data control, use the AddNew method of the recordset established by the data control. Visual Basic sets all bound controls to their default values (as determined by the table definition in the database you're accessing) and makes the new record the current record. After all data has been entered into the bound controls, Visual Basic creates a new record in the table and fills it with the values from the controls. Visual Basic knows that data entry is complete when you move to a different record, you add another new record, or your code executes the recordset's `Update` method. All records get added to the end of the data control's recordset.

If you make changes to an existing record and then unload the form, Visual Basic automatically updates the recordset with your changes. When you add a record, enter data into the record, and then either add another record or move to an existing record, Visual Basic automatically saves the new record. However, if you add a record, enter data into the new record, and then unload the form—before you move to another record—Visual Basic does not automatically save the new record. If you want to save the new record, you can invoke the `Recordset` object's `Update` method from the form's `Unload` event. The `Update` method saves the data in the form's bound controls to the corresponding fields in the recordset.

To delete the currently displayed record from the database, use the data control recordset's `Delete` method. Visual Basic deletes the current record from the database. Visual Basic does not, however, move to a new record or update the controls. You must do this through your code, by using one of the four `Move` methods: `MoveFirst`, `MoveLast`, `MovePrevious`, or `MoveNext`. If you do not move to a new record after executing the `Delete` method, there will be no current record. Visual Basic will, therefore, generate an error when you try to perform any operation on the current record.

Steps

Preview the project AddDeleteBound.VBP. Change the `DatabaseName` property of the data control `datEmployees` to point to the copy of NWind.MDB installed on your system (probably in the directory where VB5.EXE is installed). Then run the project. The form shown in Figure 1.7 appears. Select Data | Add Record. Enter some representative values into the fields. Move to another record or select Data | Save Record from the main menu. Move to the last record in the recordset by clicking the >| button on the data control. You should see the

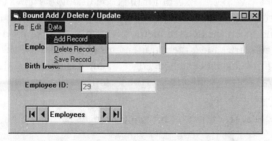

Figure 1.7. The Bound Add/Delete/Update form.

record you just added. Select Data | Delete Record. Move to the last record in the recordset again. The record you added should be gone.

1. Create a new project called AddDeleteBound.VBP. Use **Form1** to create the objects and properties listed in Table 1.1, and save the form as AddDeleteBound.FRM. Substitute the path to your copy of NWind.MDB for the **DatabaseName** property of **datEmployees**. You might find it easier to start from the UndoBound.VBP form from How-To 1.3. Use the Visual Basic menu editor to create the menu shown in Table 1.4.

Table 1.4. Menu specifications for the Bound Add/Delete form.

CAPTION	NAME	SHORTCUT KEY
&File	mnuFile	
----E&xit	mnuFileExit	
&Edit	mnuEdit	
----&Undo	mnuEditUndo	Ctrl+Z
&Data	mnuData	
----&Add Record	mnuDataAdd	
----&Delete Record	mnuDataDelete	
----&Save Record	mnuDataSave	

2. Add the file clsUtility.cls to your project from the Chapter01\HowTo03 directory by selecting Project | Add File from the main menu or by pressing Ctrl+D on the keyboard. Use the file common dialog to select the file.

3. Add the following code to the declarations section of **Form1**:

```
Private Utility As New clsUtility
Private mblnValidationFailed As Boolean
```

4. Add the following code as the **Validate** event of the data control **datEmployees**. (This code is the same as that for the identically named procedure in How-To 1.3, except for the code in bold.) The **Validate** event is called every time the current record changes, when the form is unloaded, and when the **Update** method is invoked. This procedure verifies that all entries meet the requirements of the application when data in bound controls have been changed. If an entry is incorrect, the routine cancels the **Validate** event and sets the form-level flag variable **mblnValidationFailed**.

```
Private Sub datEmployees_Validate(Action As Integer, Save As Integer)
    Dim strMsg As String
    Dim enumMsgResult As VbMsgBoxResult
```

```
If Save = True Or Action = vbDataActionUpdate _
Or Action = vbDataActionUnload _
Or Action = vbDataActionAddNew Then
    ' One or more bound controls has changed or the form
    ' is being unloaded, so verify that all fields have
    ' legal entries. If a field has an incorrect value,
    ' append a string explaining the error to strMsg and
    ' set the focus to that field to facilitate correcting
    ' the error. We explain all errors encountered in a
    ' single message box.
    strMsg = ""
    If txtEmpLastName.Text = "" Then
        Utility.AddToMsg strMsg, "You must enter a last name."
        txtEmpLastName.SetFocus
    End If
    If txtEmpFirstName.Text = "" Then
        Utility.AddToMsg strMsg, "You must enter a first name."
        txtEmpFirstName.SetFocus
    End If
    If Not IsDate(txtBirthDate.Text) Then
        Utility.AddToMsg strMsg, "You must enter a birth date."
        txtBirthDate.SetFocus
    Else
        If CDate(txtBirthDate.Text) >= Date Then
            Utility.AddToMsg strMsg, "Birth date must be in the past."
            txtBirthDate.SetFocus
        End If
    End If

    If strMsg <> "" Then
        ' We have something in the variable strMsg, which means that
        ' an error has occurred. Display the message. The focus is in
        ' the last text box where an error was found
        enumMsgResult = MsgBox(strMsg, vbExclamation + vbOKCancel + _
                vbDefaultButton1)

        If enumMsgResult = vbCancel Then
            ' Restore the data to previous values using the data
            ' control
            datEmployees.UpdateControls
            mblnValidationFailed = False
        Else
            ' Cancel the Validate event
            Action = vbDataActionCancel
            ' Deny form Unload until fields are corrected
            mblnValidationFailed = True
        End If
    Else
        ' Allow form unload
        mblnValidationFailed = False
        ' Disable the Save menu
        mnuDataSave.Enabled = False
    End If
End If
End Sub
```

5. Enter the following code as the `Click` method of the Edit | Undo menu item. If the user chooses Undo while adding a new record, the subroutine uses the Recordset object's `CancelUpdate` method to cancel the pending `AddNew` operation. If the menu item is clicked while the user is editing an existing record, the procedure updates the form's controls by filling them with the current values from the recordset.

```
Private Sub mnuEditUndo_Click()

    ' Undo all pending changes from form by copying recordset values
    ' to form controls
    datEmployees.UpdateControls

    If datEmployees.Recordset.EditMode = dbEditAdd Then

        ' Disable the menu save and cancel the update
        datEmployees.Recordset.CancelUpdate
        mnuDataSave.Enabled = False
    End If

End Sub
```

6. Add the following code as the `Click` event of the Data menu's Add Record item. This subroutine uses the `Recordset` object's `AddNew` method to prepare the form and the recordset for the addition of a new record.

```
Private Sub mnuDataAdd_Click()

    ' Reset all controls to the default for a new record
    ' and make space for the record in the recordset copy
    ' buffer.
    datEmployees.Recordset.AddNew

    'Enable the Save menu choice
    mnuDataSave.Enabled = True

    ' Set the focus to the first control on the form
    txtEmpLastName.SetFocus
End Sub
```

7. Add the following code as the `Click` event of the Data menu's Delete Record item. The procedure confirms that the user wants to delete the record and then deletes it. It then ensures that the record pointer is pointing at a valid record.

```
Private Sub mnuDataDelete_Click()
    Dim strMsg As String

    'Verify the deletion.
    strMsg = "Are you sure you want to delete " _
            & IIf(txtEmpLastName.Text <> "", txtEmpLastName.Text, _
                "this record") & "?"
    If MsgBox(strMsg, vbQuestion + vbYesNo + vbDefaultButton2) = vbYes Then
```

```
        ' We really want to delete
        datEmployees.Recordset.Delete

        ' Make a valid record the current record and update the display.
        datEmployees.Recordset.MoveNext

        ' If we deleted the last record, move to the new last record
        ' because the current record pointer is not defined after
        ' deleting the last record, even though EOF is defined.
        If datEmployees.Recordset.EOF Then datEmployees.Recordset.MoveLast
    End If
End Sub
```

8. Add the following code as the **Click** event of the Data menu's Save Record item. The Save Record subroutine uses the **Update** method of the **Recordset** object to write the values in the form's bound controls to their respective fields in the recordset. The **If** statement prevents performing a recordset **Update** without a preceding **AddNew** or **Edit**.

```
Private Sub mnuDataSave_Click()

    ' Invoke the update method to copy control contents to
    ' recordset fields and update the underlying table
    datEmployees.Recordset.Update
    If datEmployees.Recordset.EditMode <> dbEditAdd Then

        ' If we added move to the new record
        datEmployees.Recordset.MoveLast
    End If

End Sub
```

9. Add the following code as the **Click** event of the File menu's Exit item. (This code is the same as that for the identically named procedure in How-To 1.2.)

```
Private Sub mnuFileExit_Click()
    Unload Me
End Sub
```

10. Add the following code as the form's **Unload** event. If the data currently in the bound controls is invalid, the procedure cancels the **Unload** event. If the data is valid and an add record operation is in progress, the code invokes the **Update** event to save the data.

```
Private Sub Form_Unload(Cancel As Integer)

    ' Don't allow the unload until the data is valid or the
    ' update is cancelled
    If mblnValidationFailed Then Cancel = True

End SubEnd Sub
```

How It Works

The addition of record addition and deletion has made the data control program more complex, but it now looks like a real database application. The addition of a Data menu allows the person at the keyboard to explicitly control the data control's recordset activities through the appropriate click procedures. The **Data Add Record** procedure (step 6) adds a new, blank record to the data control's recordset. The data control is automatically positioned on the new record. The **Data Save** procedure (step 8) updates the recordset and moves to the last record (the new record) if the current action is a record addition. The Data Save Record menu choice is also managed explicitly by the program during record additions to provide clear feedback from the programmer about what is happening within the program.

Notice in the record deletion processing (step 7) that we have to manage the deletion of the last record carefully because the recordset object does not handle all changes gracefully. In particular, deleting the last record can leave the recordset with "No current record." In this state, any update actions (potentially caused by a record movement) can cause an error in your application.

Comments

A Visual Basic data control maintains a record pointer into its **RecordSource**. The record pointer keeps track of where you are within the **RecordSource**. The record pointer always points to the current record—except when you move past the end or the beginning of the **RecordSource**.

You can move past the end of the **RecordSource** by clicking the Next Record button when the record pointer is positioned on the last record; similarly, you can move past the beginning of the **RecordSource** by clicking the Previous Record button when you are on the first record. The record pointer then points at a special location, known as the end of the file (EOF) or beginning of file (BOF). When you are on EOF or BOF, there is no current record. If you try to delete or edit the record when you are on EOF or BOF, Visual Basic generates an error message. EOF and BOF are useful when you use data access objects for checking to see when you've reached the end or beginning of a **RecordSource**; but when you use the data control, you generally don't want to stay on EOF or BOF.

For this reason, Visual Basic gives you a choice of what to do when your data control reaches EOF or BOF. You execute this choice by setting the **BOFAction** and **EOFAction** properties. The possible settings for each property are shown in Table 1.5.

Table 1.5. The EOFAction and BOFAction properties of the data control.

PROPERTY	DESCRIPTION	RESULT
BOFAction	0 - MoveFirst (default)	Positions the record pointer on the first record.
	1 - BOF	Positions the record pointer on BOF.
EOFAction	0 - MoveLast (default)	Positions the record pointer on the last record.
	1 - EOF	Positions the record pointer on EOF.
	2 - AddNew	Adds a new record at the end of the RecordSource and positions the record pointer on it.

The Visual Basic data control does not handle empty recordsets well; trying to move to another record generates an error. The only thing you can do with a bound, empty recordset is to add a new record. When you open an empty recordset, its EOF property is initially True. If you have the data control's EOFAction property set to AddNew, when you open an empty recordset Visual Basic immediately adds a record. This is a low-cost, no-code way to prevent empty recordset errors when working with bound controls.

COMPLEXITY
INTERMEDIATE

1.5 How do I...
Create and use bound lists?

Problem

Many tables in my database have fields that are related to other tables. I need to restrict entry into these fields to values that exist in the related tables. At the same time, I'd like to make it easy to select valid entries for these fields. How do I accomplish this when I'm using bound controls?

Technique

Assume that you have a warehouse application. You have two tables, Products and Categories. The Products table defines available products:

```
ProductID
ProductName
SupplierID
CategoryID
QuantityPerUnit
UnitPrice
UnitsInStock
```

| UnitsOnOrder |
| ReorderLevel |
| Discontinued |

The Category table defines product categories and is related to the Product table via the `CategoryID` field:

| CategoryID |
| CategoryName |
| Description |
| Picture |

You have a form that displays basic product information from the Products table and its related Category. Because almost everybody has trouble remembering customer ID numbers, you want to provide the capability to designate the category by name. With a `DBCombo` or `DBList` control, people can choose a category name and have the control insert the category ID number corresponding to that category name into the Products table.

The `DBList` and `DBCombo` controls both display values in a list format. The `DBList` control creates a list box, with several lines always visible. The `DBCombo` control can create a drop-down list. They are both bound controls. Unlike with most bound controls, however, you bind them not to a single data control but to two data controls. The first data control maintains the recordset represented by the form as a whole—the data records you are browsing or editing. The second data control refers to the validation recordset, the recordset that is displayed in the list box or combo box. (You normally make the second data control—the data control that displays the values in the list—invisible, because people do not need to access it.)

In the example, one data control is linked to the Products table—the table into which category ID numbers are inserted. The other data control is linked to the Categories table—the source of the list. The table that is the source of the list must include both the information to be displayed (in this case, the information in the `CategoryName` field) and the value to be inserted into the other table (in this case, the `CategoryID`).

You link the `DBCombo` or `DBList` control to its recordsets by setting five properties. Two properties describe the recordset to be updated; they are shown in Table 1.6. The other three properties define the recordset that comprises the list; these appear in Table 1.7.

Table 1.6. DBList/DBCombo properties that describe the recordset to be updated.

PROPERTY	DESCRIPTION
DataSource	Name of the data control with the recordset to be updated
DataField	Name of the field to be updated

Table 1.7. `DBList/DBCombo` properties that create the list.

PROPERTY	DESCRIPTION
RowSource	Name of the data control that provides the values to display in the list
ListField	Name of the field with the values to display in the list
BoundColumn	Name of the field with the value to be inserted in the table being updated

---

DBCOMBO STYLE

If you set the `Style` property of the `DBCombo` control to `2` (Dropdown List), the control acts exactly like a `DBList` control—except, of course, that it displays only a single item until you drop it down. You can't add new items to the list through the control.

If you want to give the user the opportunity to add new items, set the `Style` to `0` (Dropdown Combo) or `1` (Simple Combo). Your code will need to handle the addition of the user's entry to the underlying row source—the control does not do this automatically for you.

Steps

Open the project ListBound.VBP to preview this How-To. Change the `DatabaseName` property of the data control `datEmployees` to point to the copy of NWind.MDB installed on your system (probably in the directory where VB5.EXE is installed). Then run the project. The form shown in Figure 1.8 appears. Select Data | Add Record, and enter some representative values into the fields. Use the drop-down list to enter the publisher. When you move to another record, your new record is automatically saved.

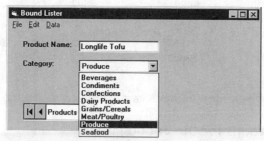

Figure 1.8. The Bound Lister form.

1. Create a new project called ListBound.VBP. Use Form1 to create the objects and properties listed in Table 1.8, and save the form as LISTBND.FRM. Substitute the path to your copy of NWind.MDB for the DatabaseName property of datEmployees and dtaPublishers.

Table 1.8. Objects and properties for the Bound Lister form.

OBJECT	PROPERTY	SETTING
Form	Name	Form1
	Caption	" Bound Lister "
Data	Name	datProducts
	Caption	"Products"
	DatabaseName	"C:\Vb5\Nwind.mdb"
	RecordSource	"Products"
Data	Name	datCategories
	Caption	"Categories"
	DatabaseName	"C:\Vb5\Nwind.mdb"
	RecordSource	"Categories"
TextBox	Name	txtProductName
	DataField	"ProductName"
	DataSource	"datProducts"
DBCombo	Name	dbcCategory
	BoundColumn	"CategoryID"
	DataField	"CategoryID"
	DataSource	"datProducts"
	ListField	"CategoryName"
	RowSource	"datCategories"
Label	Name	Label2
	Caption	"Category:"
Label	Name	Label1
	Caption	"Product Name:"

2. Use the Visual Basic menu editor to create the menu shown in Table 1.9.

Table 1.9. Menu specifications for the Bound Lister.

CAPTION	NAME	SHORTCUT KEY
&File	mnuFile	
----E&xit	mnuFileExit	
&Edit	mnuEdit	

CAPTION	NAME	SHORTCUT KEY
----&Undo	mnuEditUndo	Alt+Backspace
&Data	mnuData	
----&Add Record	mnuDataAdd	
----&Delete Record	mnuDataDelete	
----&Save Record	mnuDataSave	

3. Add the following code to the declarations section of Form1:

```
Private Utility As New clsUtility
Private mblnValidationFailed As Boolean
```

4. Add the following code as the Validate event of the data control datProducts. (This code is very similar to the Validate Event code for How-To 1.4 with the exceptions of data control name and actual field-checking logic.) The Validate event is called every time the current record changes, when the form is unloaded, and when the Update method is invoked. This procedure verifies that when data in bound controls have been changed, all entries meet the requirements of the application. If an entry is incorrect, the routine cancels the Validate event and sets the form-level flag variable mblnValidationFailed.

```
Private Sub datProducts_Validate(Action As Integer, Save As Integer)
    Dim strMsg As String
    Dim enumMsgResult As VbMsgBoxResult

    If Save = True Or Action = vbDataActionUpdate _
    Or mblnValidationFailed Or Action = vbDataActionAddNew Then
        ' One or more bound controls has changed or a previous validation
        ' failed, so verify that all fields have legal entries. If a field
        ' has an incorrect value, append a string explaining the error to
        ' strMsg and set the focus to that field to facilitate correcting
        ' the error. We explain all errors encountered in a single message
        ' box.
        strMsg = ""
        If txtProductName.Text = "" Then
            Utility.AddToMsg strMsg, "You must enter a Product name."
            txtProductName.SetFocus
        End If

        If strMsg <> "" Then
            ' We have something in the variable strMsg, which means that
            ' an error has occurred. Display the message. The focus is in
            ' the last text box where an error was found
            enumMsgResult = MsgBox(strMsg, vbExclamation + vbOKCancel + _
                vbDefaultButton1)

            If enumMsgResult = vbCancel Then
                'Restore the data to previous values using the data control
                datProducts.UpdateControls
```

continued on next page

continued from previous page

```
                    mblnValidationFailed = False
                Else
                    ' Cancel the Validate event
                    Action = vbDataActionCancel
                    ' Deny form Unload until fields are corrected
                    mblnValidationFailed = True
                End If
            Else
                mblnValidationFailed = False
            End If
        End If
    End If
End Sub
```

5. Enter the following code as the `Click` method of the Edit | Undo menu item. (This code is very similar to that for the identically named procedure in How-To 1.4 except for the reference to a different data control.) The procedure updates the form's controls by filling them with the current values from the recordset. If someone chooses Undo while adding a new record, the subroutine uses the `Recordset` object's `CancelUpdate` method to cancel the pending `AddNew` operation and turns off the data save menu item.

```
Private Sub mnuEditUndo_Click()

    ' Undo all pending changes from form by copying recordset values
    ' to form controls
    datProducts.UpdateControls

    If datProducts.Recordset.EditMode = dbEditAdd Then

        ' Disable the menu save and cancel the update
        datProducts.Recordset.CancelUpdate
        mnuDataSave.Enabled = False
    End If

End Sub
```

6. Add the following code as the `Click` event of the Data menu's Add Record item. (This code is very similar to that for the identically named procedure in How-To 1.4.) This subroutine uses the Recordset object's `AddNew` method to prepare the form and the recordset for the addition of a new record. It also enables the data save menu.

```
Private Sub mnuDataAdd_Click()

    ' Reset all controls to the default for a new record
    ' and make space for the record in the recordset copy
    ' buffer.
    datProducts.Recordset.AddNew

    'Enable the Save menu choice
    mnuDataSave.Enabled = True
```

```
' Set the focus to the first control on the form
txtProductName.SetFocus
End Sub
```

7. Add the following code as the `Click` event of the Data menu's Delete Record item. (This code is very similar to that for the identically named procedure in How-To 1.4.) The procedure confirms that someone wants to delete the record, then deletes it. It then ensures that the record pointer is pointing at a valid record.

```
Private Sub mnuDataDelete_Click()
    Dim strMsg As String

    'Verify the deletion.
    strMsg = "Are you sure you want to delete " _
            & IIf(txtProductName.Text <> "", txtProductName.Text, _
                "this record") & "?"
    If MsgBox(strMsg, vbQuestion + vbYesNo + vbDefaultButton2) = vbYes Then

        ' We really want to delete
        datProducts.Recordset.Delete

        ' Make a valid record the current record and update the display.
        datProducts.Recordset.MoveNext

        ' If we deleted the last record, move to the new last record
        ' because the current record pointer is not defined after
        ' deleting the last record, even though EOF is defined.
        If datProducts.Recordset.EOF Then datProducts.Recordset.MoveLast
    End If
End Sub
```

8. Add the following code as the `Click` event of the Data menu's Save Record item. (This code is very similar to that for the identically named procedure in How-To 1.4.) The **Save Record** subroutine uses the **Update** method of the **Recordset** object to write the values in the form's bound controls to their respective fields in the recordset.

```
Private Sub mnuDataSave_Click()

    ' Invoke the update method to copy control contents to
    ' recordset fields and update the underlying table
    datProducts.Recordset.Update
    If datProducts.Recordset.EditMode <> dbEditAdd Then

        ' If we added move to the new record
        datProducts.Recordset.MoveLast
    End IfEnd Sub
```

9. Add the following code as the `Click` event of the File menu's Exit item. (This code is the same as that for the identically named procedure in How-To 1.4.)

```
Private Sub mnuFileExit_Click()
    Unload Me
End Sub
```

10. Add the following code as the form's `Unload` event. (This code is the same as that for the identically named procedure in How-To 1.4.) If the data currently in the bound controls is invalid, the procedure cancels the `Unload` event.

```
Private Sub Form_Unload(Cancel As Integer)

    ' Don't allow the unload until the data is valid or the
    ' update is cancelled
    If mblnValidationFailed Then Cancel = True
End Sub
```

How It Works

When the form is loaded, the combined actions of `datCategories` and `dbcCategories` fill the Category combo box with a list of category names from the Categories table in NWind.MDB. When a category is chosen from the list, the category ID associated with the chosen category is inserted into the `CategoryID` field in the Products table.

Unlike the unbound list box and combo box controls, their bound cousins `DBList` and `DBCombo` do not have a `Sorted` property. If you want to provide a sorted list, therefore, you must make sure that the recordset providing the list itself is sorted on the appropriate field. You can accomplish this by setting the `RecordSource` property of the data control named in the `DBList` or `DBCombo`'s `RowSource` property to a SQL statement with an `ORDER BY` clause. In the example cited in the "Technique" section of this How-To, you could provide a sorted list of customers by setting the `RecordSource` property of the data control to this:

```
SELECT * FROM Categories ORDER BY CategoryID
```

With the `DBList` and `DBCombo`, you can designate how the list reacts to characters typed at the keyboard when the control has the focus. If the control's `MatchEntry` property is set to `vbMatchEntrySimple`, the control searches for the next match for the character entered using the first letter of entries in the list. If the same letter is typed repeatedly, the control cycles through all the entries in the list beginning with that letter. If you set the `MatchEntry` property to `vbMatchEntryExtended`, the control searches for an entry matching all the characters typed by the user. As additional characters are typed, the search is further refined.

Comments

The `DBCombo` and `DBList` controls are powerful additions to your programming arsenal, but be careful about the performance implications in everyday use. Each `DBCombo` and `DBList` control requires a data control, and the data control is a fairly large bit of code. In one experiment, replacing eight **DBCombo** controls with plain **Combo Box** controls loaded from a database reduced the form load time by more than 40 percent.

COMPLEXITY
INTERMEDIATE

1.6 How do I...
Display many detail records for a single master record?

Problem

I want to display product inventory and order detail information for a displayed product. How do I build a form to display "master-detail" information showing products and order quantities?

Technique

A "master-detail" display is frequently used to show a hierarchical relationship between two tables such as invoice headers and invoice lines. In this How-To, we build a form to display all the orders for a particular product. Assume that you have a warehouse application. The Product table contains the following fields:

ProductID
ProductName
SupplierID
CategoryID
QuantityPerUnit
UnitPrice
UnitsInStock
UnitsOnOrder
ReorderLevel
Discontinued

The Order Detail table defines the quantity of product included on each order:

OrderID
ProductID
UnitPrice
Quantity
Discount

You have a form that displays product and stock information together with order quantities for the displayed product. This master-detail relationship requires two data controls to display a single product and multiple order lines. The master data control has a recordset tied to the Product table, and the detail recordset is tied to the Order Details table. Master table information is usually displayed in text boxes or other appropriate controls; detail information is displayed in a `DBGrid` control.

The `DBGrid` control displays multiple rows from a recordset in a scrolling table that looks much like a spreadsheet. The `DBGrid` control allows recordset scrolling, column width changes, display formatting, and other useful capabilities. It is most useful as a display-only tool, but the `DBGrid` control can provide recordset maintenance functions as well. Table 1.10 describes important properties that control `DBGrid` runtime behavior.

Table 1.10. Important `DBGrid` design-time properties.

PROPERTY	DESCRIPTION
AllowAddNew	Controls ability to add new records (default is `False`)
AllowDelete	Controls ability to delete records displayed by the grid (default is `False`)
AllowUpdate	Controls ability to update records through the grid (default is `True`)
ColumnHeaders	Controls display of column headers (default is `True`)

You specify a recordset at design time for `DBGrid` so that you can design the initial column layout and formatting. The `DBGrid` can retrieve the field names from a linked recordset at design time to populate the initial column display. You then edit the column properties to set headers, formats, and default values.

Steps

Open the project GridLister.VBP to preview this How-To. Change the `DatabaseName` property of the data controls `datProducts` and `datOrderDetails` to point to the copy of NWind.MDB installed on your system (probably in the directory where VB5.EXE is installed). Then run the project. The form shown in Figure 1.9 appears. Navigate through the records using the product data control. Observe how the order detail information changes. Experiment with the grid's sliders to control the data display. Use the mouse to select rows or columns. Drastically change a column's display width, and observe how the horizontal scrollbar appears and disappears.

1. Create a new project called GridLister.VBP. Use **Form1** to create the objects and properties listed in Table 1.11 and save the form as GridLister.FRM. Substitute the path to your copy of NWind.MDB for the `DatabaseName` property of `datProducts` and `datOrderDetails`.

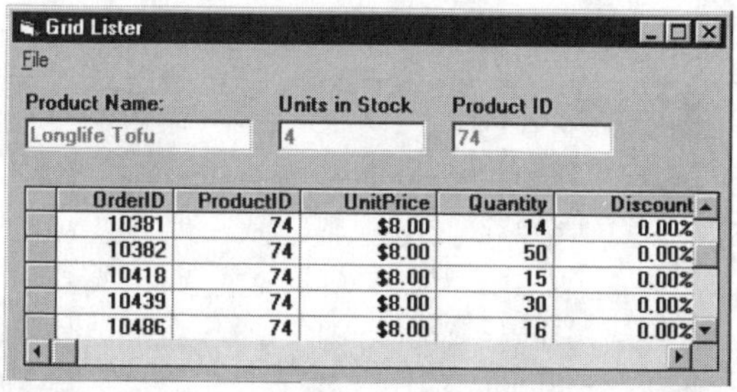

Figure 1.9. The Grid Lister form.

Table 1.11. Objects and properties for the Grid Lister form.

OBJECT	PROPERTY	SETTING
Form	Name	Form1
	Caption	"Grid Lister"
TextBox	Name	txtProductName
	DataField	"ProductName"
	DataSource	"datProducts"
TextBox	Name	txtUnitsInStock
	DataField	"UnitsInStock"
	DataSource	"datProducts"
TextBox	Name	txtProductId
	DataField	"ProductID"
	DataSource	"datProducts"
Data	Name	datProducts
	Caption	"Products"
	Connect	"Access"
	DatabaseName	"C:\vb5\Nwind.mdb"
	RecordSource	"Products"
Data	Name	datOrderDetails
	Caption	"Order Details"
	DatabaseName	"C:\vb5\Nwind.mdb"
	RecordSource	"Order Details"
	Visible	False
DBGrid	Name	dbgOrderDetails
	AllowAddNew	False
	AllowDelete	False
	AllowUpdate	False
	DataSource	"datOrderDetails"

continued on next page

continued from previous page

OBJECT	PROPERTY	SETTING
Label	Name	Label1
	Caption	"Product Name:"
Label	Name	Label2
	Caption	"Units in Stock"
Label	Name	Label3
	Caption	"Product ID"

2. Use the Visual Basic menu editor to create the menu shown in Table 1.12.

Table 1.12. Menu specifications for the Grid Lister.

CAPTION	NAME	SHORTCUT KEY
&File	mnuFile	
----E&xit	mnuFileExit	

3. Use the `DBGrid` design-time controls to define the columns. Right-click the grid to display the menu shown in Figure 1.10, and then select the Retrieve Fields option. The `DBGrid` column information will be retrieved from the `datOrderDetails` recordset. Right-click the `DBGrid` again and select Edit to make on-screen modifications to column widths and row heights.

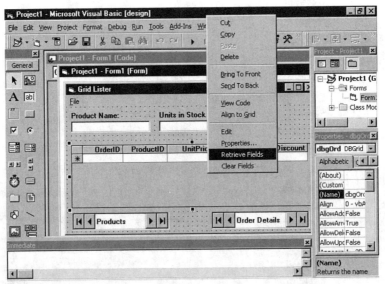

Figure 1.10. The `DBGrid` right-click design-time menu.

4. Right-click the DBGrid and select the Properties menu item to adjust the column formats. Figure 1.11 shows the Columns tab of the DBGrid design-time properties page.

5. Add the following code to the Reposition event of the data control datProducts:

```
Private Sub datProducts_Reposition()
    Dim strSql As String

    If datProducts.Recordset.RecordCount = 0 Then

        ' Don't re-query the Order Details if there are
        ' no products displayed.
        Exit Sub
    End If

    ' Re-query the Order Detail grid by SQL SELECT statement.
    ' The WHERE clause picks up only the order details for
    ' the displayed product.
    strSql = "SELECT * FROM [Order Details] WHERE ProductID = " _
        & datProducts.Recordset.Fields("ProductID")

    ' Assign the desired SQL statement as the record source.
    datOrderDetails.RecordSource = strSql

    ' Re-query the database to bring new data to the recordset.
    datOrderDetails.Refresh

    ' Set the default value for ProductID for any possible future
    ' Order Details inserts to the displayed product ID.
    dbgOrderDetails.Columns("ProductID").DefaultValue = _
        datProducts.Recordset.Fields("ProductID")

End Sub
```

6. Add the following code as the Click event of the File menu's Exit item. (This code is the same as that for the identically named procedure in How-To 1.5.)

```
Private Sub mnuFileExit_Click()
    Unload Me
End Sub
```

How It Works

When the form is loaded, the datProducts data control retrieves the first Products record and fires the Reposition event. The event procedure creates a SQL statement to query only those order detail records we want to see by use of a WHERE clause.

```
SELECT * FROM [Order Details] WHERE ProductID = <displayed product ID>
```

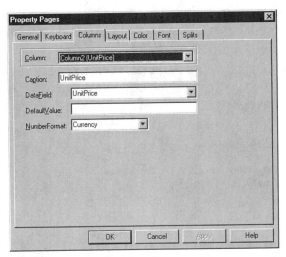

Figure 1.11. The DBGrid design-time properties.

When the data control is refreshed, the DBGrid is populated with only the order detail records for the displayed product. A more complicated SQL statement (see Chapter 3, "SQL") could also retrieve the order number and customer information for display on the form.

Comments

The DBGrid is a powerful control well worth exploring in the Visual Basic 5 help files and books online. It provides powerful display capabilities as well as add, update, and delete capabilities. When your program is running, people can resize columns and rows to suit their display needs.

The DBGrid is also useful as the display for a master query in any database that requires logical partitioning. A multiple warehouse inventory application might use a DBGrid to select a "master" warehouse before browsing through "detail" items in order to limit inventory item display to a particular location. Logical partitioning is often required in service bureau applications to prevent making incorrect changes to a person's account. Telephone companies and Internet service providers frequently need to see individual accounts but restrict the view to a particular corporate customer. The DBGrid can help partition at the high level and provide "drill-down" through hierarchies.

COMPLEXITY
INTERMEDIATE

1.7 How do I...
Change data in data-bound grid cells from code?

Problem

I want to display product inventory and order detail information and allow editing of just the quantity-ordered information. How do I edit a single DBGrid cell?

Technique

Assume that you have the same warehouse application as you did in How-To 1.6. Product information and Order Detail information are stored in two different tables, the structures of which are also shown in the preceding How-To. You have a form that displays product and stock information together with order quantities for the displayed product. Your management wants to have a secure editing function to allow adjustment of order quantities for particular products.

The DBGrid control can allow data updates, but all columns shown on the grid then become available for updates. We don't want to let the warehouse supervisor adjust prices or discounts, only the order quantity. We will have to directly manipulate the DBGrid cells to update just the order quantity.

Steps

Open the project GridChange.VBP. Change the DatabaseName property of the data controls datProducts and datOrderDetails to point to the copy of NWind.MDB installed on your system (probably in the directory where VB5.EXE is installed). Then run the project. The form shown in Figure 1.12 appears. Navigate through the product records and observe how the order detail information changes. Highlight an order detail row, enter a new quantity in the text box, and press the Change Qty command button. The quantity will be updated in the DBGrid and the underlying recordset and database table.

1. Create a new project called GridChange.VBP. Use Form1 to create the objects and properties listed in Table 1.13, and save the form as GridChange.FRM. Substitute the path to your copy of NWind.MDB for the DatabaseName property of datProducts and datOrderDetails.

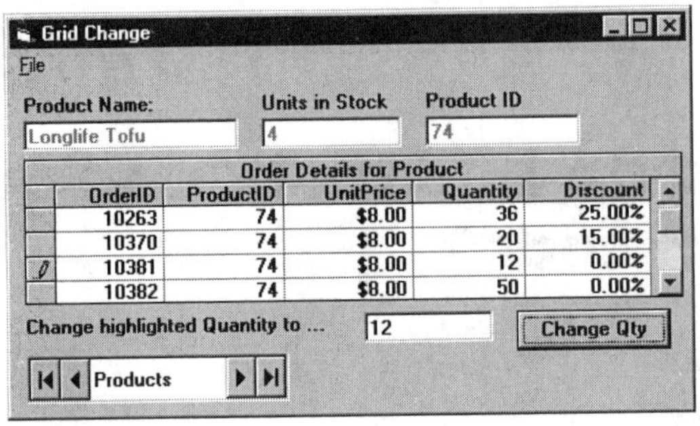

Figure 1.12. The Grid Change form.

Table 1.13. Objects and properties for the Grid Lister form.

OBJECT	PROPERTY	SETTING
Form	Name	Form1
	Caption	"Grid Lister"
TextBox	Name	txtProductName
	DataField	"ProductName"
	DataSource	"datProducts"
TextBox	Name	txtUnitsInStock
	DataField	"UnitsInStock"
	DataSource	"datProducts"
TextBox	Name	txtProductId
	DataField	"ProductID"
	DataSource	"datProducts"
TextBox	Name	txtChangeQuantity
	DataField	" "
	DataSource	" "
Data	Name	datProducts
	Caption	"Products"
	Connect	"Access"
	DatabaseName	"C:\vb5\Nwind.mdb"
	RecordSource	"Products"
Data	Name	datOrderDetails
	Caption	"Order Details"
	DatabaseName	"C:\vb5\Nwind.mdb"
	RecordSource	"Order Details"
	Visible	False

OBJECT	PROPERTY	SETTING
DBGrid	Name	dbgOrderDetails
	AllowAddNew	False
	AllowDelete	False
	AllowUpdate	False
	DataSource	"datOrderDetails"
Label	Name	Label1
	Caption	"Product Name:"
Label	Name	Label2
	Caption	"Units in Stock"
Label	Name	Label3
	Caption	"Product ID"

2. Use the Visual Basic menu editor to create the menu shown in Table 1.14.

Table 1.14. Menu specifications for the Grid Lister.

CAPTION	NAME	SHORTCUT KEY
&File	mnuFile	
----E&xit	mnuFileExit	

3. Use the DBGrid design-time controls to define the columns. Right-click the grid to display the menu shown earlier in Figure 1.10, and then select Retrieve Fields. The DBGrid column information will be retrieved from the datOrderDetails recordset. Right-click the DBGrid again and select Edit to make on-screen modifications to column widths and row heights.

4. Right-click the DBGrid and select the Properties menu item to adjust column formats.

5. Add the following code to the Reposition event of the data control datProducts:

```
Private Sub datProducts_Reposition()
    Dim strSql As String

    If datProducts.Recordset.RecordCount = 0 Then

        ' Don't re-query the Order Details if there are
        ' no products displayed.
        Exit Sub
    End If

    ' Re-query the Order Detail grid by SQL SELECT statement.
```

continued on next page

continued from previous page

```
' The WHERE clause picks up only the order details for
' the displayed product.
strSql = "SELECT * FROM [Order Details] WHERE ProductID = " _
    & datProducts.Recordset.Fields("ProductID")

' Assign the desired SQL statement as the record source.
datOrderDetails.RecordSource = strSql

' Re-query the database to bring new data to the recordset.
datOrderDetails.Refresh

' Set the default value for ProductID for any possible future
' Order Details inserts to the displayed product ID.
dbgOrderDetails.Columns("ProductID").DefaultValue = _
    datProducts.Recordset.Fields("ProductID")

End Sub
```

6. Add the following code as the `Click` event of `cmdChangeGridCell`. This code validates the entered amount as a positive number and updates the displayed grid cell.

```
Private Sub cmdChangeGridCell_Click()

' Change the selected grid cell value to the entered value
If Not IsNumeric(txtChangeQuantity.Text) Then
    MsgBox "Change quantity must be a positive number", vbInformation
ElseIf CInt(txtChangeQuantity.Text) < 0 Then
    MsgBox "Change quantity must be a positive number", vbInformation
Else
    dbgOrderDetails.Columns("Quantity").Text = txtChangeQuantity.Text
End If

End Sub
```

7. Add the following code as the `Click` event of the File menu's Exit item. (This code is the same as that for the identically named procedure in How-To 1.5.)

```
Private Sub mnuFileExit_Click()
    Unload Me
End Sub
```

How It Works

When the Change Qty button is pressed, the event procedure validates the entered number and updates the cell value in the grid. The heart of the code is the following statement:

```
dbgOrderDetails.Columns("Quantity").Text = txtChangeQuantity.Text
```

The data contents of the **DBGrid** control can be directly addressed just as the data contents of any other visual control can be. The currently selected grid row is available to have its columns directly manipulated by code. The data control will update the recordset field and table when the record pointer is repositioned.

Comments

Another useful `DBGrid` trick with a bound grid is to make the data control visible and allow recordset movement with the data control. The `DBGrid` automatically shows database positions. The `DBGrid` can also be used as a record selector because it can function as a multicolumn list box.

COMPLEXITY
INTERMEDIATE

1.8 How do I...
Gracefully handle database errors?

Problem

When I access a database through Visual Basic, I have limited control over the environment. Someone might move a database file or another program might have made unexpected changes to the database. I need my programs to be able to detect errors that occur and handle them in the context of the program. How do I accomplish this task with Visual Basic?

Technique

When an error occurs during execution of a Visual Basic program, control passes to error-handling logic. If you have not made provisions in your program to trap errors, Visual Basic calls its default error-handling process. When a compiled Visual Basic program is running, the default error-handling process displays a message describing the cause of the error—sometimes a helpful message, but often not—and terminates the program.

That's never a good solution, but fortunately Visual Basic gives you a choice. You can build error-trapping and error-handling logic into your Visual Basic code. Every Visual Basic program should make provisions for trapping and handling errors gracefully, but it's especially important in database work, in which many potential error conditions can be expected to exist at runtime.

Trapping Errors

Visual Basic error-trapping is accomplished through the `On Error` statement. When an `On Error` statement is in effect and an error occurs, Visual Basic performs the action specified by the `On Error` statement. You therefore avoid Visual Basic's default error-handling behavior.

An **On Error** statement is "in effect" when it has been executed before the occurrence of the error in the same function or subroutine where the error occurred, or in a function or subroutine that called the function or subroutine where the error occurred. For example, assume that you have these five subroutines (subroutines are used here for the example; exactly the same principles apply for functions):

```
Sub First()
    .
    .
    .
    Second
    Third
    .
    .
    .
End Sub

Sub Second()
    'On Error Statement here
    .
    .
    .
End Sub

Sub Third()
    'On Error Statement here
    .
    .
    Fourth
    Fifth
    .
    .
    .
End Sub

Sub Fourth()
    .
    .
    .
End Sub

Sub Fifth()
    'On Error Statement here
    .
    .
    .
End Sub
```

The subroutine **First** calls the subroutines **Second** and **Third**. The subroutine **Third** calls the subroutines **Fourth** and **Fifth**. **Second, Third,** and **Fourth** have **On Error** statements; **First** does not. If an error occurs during the execution of **First**, Visual Basic will use its default error-handling, because no **On Error** statement has been executed. This will be true even after the calls to

Second and Third have completed; the On Error statements in Second and Third have no effect on the procedure that calls them.

If an error occurs during the execution of Second, Visual Basic will take whatever action is specified by the On Error statement at the beginning of Second. Likewise, if an error occurs during Third, the error-handling specified by Third applies.

What happens if an error occurs during Fourth? There is no On Error statement in Fourth. However, because Fourth is called by Third, and because there is an On Error statement in Third (that is executed before Fourth is called), an error in Fourth will cause the error-handling specified by the On Error statement in Third to execute.

Fifth is also called by Third, but Fifth has an On Error statement of its own. If an error occurs in Fifth, the error-handling specified in its local On Error statement overrides that specified in Third's.

The On Error Statement

These are the two forms of the On Error statement that you will use routinely:

```
On Error Goto label

On Error Resume Next
```

The On Error Goto label form tells Visual Basic this: When an error occurs, transfer execution to the line following the named label. A label is any combination of characters that starts with a letter and ends with a colon. An error-handling label must begin in the first column, must be in the same function or subroutine as the On Error statement, and must be unique within the module. In the code that follows the label, you take whatever action is appropriate to deal with the specific error that occurred. Most of the time, you will use the On Error Goto label form of the On Error statement because you normally want to respond in a predetermined way to errors.

On Error Resume Next tells Visual Basic this: If an error occurs, simply ignore it and go to the next statement you would normally execute. Use this form when you can reasonably expect an error to occur but are confident that the error will not cause future problems. For example, you might need to create a temporary table in your database. Before you create the temporary table, you need to delete any existing table with the same name, so you execute a statement to delete the table. If you try to delete a table that does not exist, Visual Basic will create an error. In this case, you don't care that the error occurred, so you insert an On Error Resume Next statement before the delete table statement. After the delete table statement, you would probably insert an On Error Goto label statement to restore the previous error-handling routine.

Determining the Error Type

Errors generated by Visual Basic or the Jet database engine are associated with error numbers. There are hundreds of error types, each with a specific error number. When an error occurs, Visual Basic puts the error number into the **Number** property of the **Err** object. You can determine the error that occurred by looking at that property.

After you know the error type, you can take a specific action based on the error type. This is most often accomplished through a **Select Case** statement.

Assume that your application will be used in a multiuser environment, and that you need to trap errors caused by more than one user working with the same record at the same time. (A full list of trappable data access object errors can be found in Visual Basic Help file JetErr.HLP, located in the VB5 Help directory.) In your error-handling routine, you might include code similar to what's shown in Listing 1.1.

Listing 1.1. Multiuser error handler.

```
Select Case Err.Number

  Case 3197

    ' Another user has updated this record since the last time
    ' the Dynaset was updated. Display a meaningful error message
    ' and give the user the chance to overwrite the other user's
    ' change.

    strMsg = "The data in this record have already been modified "
    strMsg = strMsg & " by another user. Do you want to overwrite "
    strMsg = strMsg & " those changes with your own?"

    If MsgBox(strMsg, vbQuestion + vbYesNo + vbDefaultButton2) = vbYes Then

        ' The user said yes, so reexecute the Update method.
        ' This time it should "take."

        Resume

    Else

        ' The user said no, so refresh the dynaset with the
        ' current data and display that data. Then display a
        ' message explaining what's happened.

        rs.Requery
        DisplayRecord
        strMsg = "The current values of the record are now displayed."
        MsgBox strMsg, vbInformation

        ' Exit from the procedure now to bypass the code after
        ' the End Select statement.

        Exit Sub

    End If

  Case 3020
```

```
' The user clicked Update without previously having clicked
' Edit. The default error message is "Update without AddNew
' or Edit." Create an error that is more meaningful in the
' current context. (The message gets displayed after the
' End Select statement).

    strMsg = "You must click Edit before you click Update!"

Case 3260

    ' Another user has the page locked. Create a meaningful
    ' message. (The message gets displayed after the End Select
    ' statement.)

    strMsg = "Locking error " & Str$(Err) & " on Update."
    strMsg = strMsg & " Optimistic locking must be enabled!"

Case Else

    ' An unanticipated error, so just pass through Visual Basic's
    ' message.

    strMsg = Err.Description

End Select

    MsgBox strMsg, vbExclamation
```

Determining the Error Location

If your error-handler needs to determine where in the code the error occurs, you can use old-fashioned line numbers. When an error occurs, the built-in `Erl` function returns the line number of the line that generated the error. If the line that generated the error has no number, the `Erl` function returns the line number of the most recent numbered line. If there are no numbered lines preceding the line that caused the error, `Erl` returns `0`.

THE ERR OBJECT

The `Err` object incorporates the functionality of the `Err` statement, `Err` function, `Error` statement, `Error` function, and `Error$` function from earlier versions of Visual Basic. (These older techniques are still supported for purposes of backward compatibility in Visual Basic 5.0.)

Terminating an Error Handler

Error-handling code must terminate with a statement that clears the error. If it does not, the error handler itself will generate an error when it reaches the next `End Sub`, `End Function`, or `End Property` statement. The statements listed in Table 1.15 are those that clear an error.

Table 1.15. Statements that clear an error.

STATEMENT	EFFECT
Resume Next	Resumes execution at the line that follows the line that generated the error
Resume	Reexecutes the line that generated the error
Resume *label*	Resumes execution at the line following the named label
Resume *number*	Resumes execution at the line with the indicated number
Exit Sub	Exits immediately from the current subroutine
Exit Function	Exits immediately from the current function
Exit Property	Exits immediately from the current property
On Error	Resets error-handling logic
Err.Clear	Clears the error without otherwise affecting program execution
End	Terminates execution of the program

OPENING NWIND.MDB FOR HOW-TO'S

In many of the How-To's that use data access objects to work with NWIND.MDB, you will see directions to add READINI.BAS to the project. (READINI.BAS is a module that is installed in the main VB5DBHT directory.) In the code for the project, you will see the following lines:

```
' Get the database name and open the database.
strName = strNWindDb()
Set db = DBEngine.Workspaces(0).OpenDatabase(strName)
```

strNWindDb() is a function in READINI.BAS that reads the VB5DBHT.INI file and returns the fully qualified filename (that is, the directory, path, and name) of NWIND.MDB. The code assigns that fully qualified filename to the string variable strName and uses strName as the argument to the OpenDatabase method.

Steps

Open and run the project Errors.VBP. Three errors will occur in succession. For each, the message box reporting the error gives you the error number, error description, and line number where the error occurred. Figure 1.13 shows the first of these errors.

1. Create a new project called Errors.VBP. Use **Form1** to create the objects and properties listed in Table 1.16, and save the form as Errors.FRM.

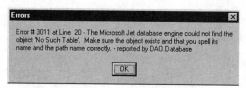

Figure 1.13. One of the errors.

Table 1.16. Objects and properties for the Errors form.

OBJECT	PROPERTY	SETTING
Form	Name	Form1
	Caption	"Errors"

2. Add the file READINI.BAS to your project from the Chapter01\HowTo08 directory.

3. Add the following code as the **Load** event of **Form1**. This code generates three errors. Line 20 generates an error because there is no such table as No Such Table. Line 40 generates an error because there is no such field as **No Such Field**. Line 60 generates an error because the **Year Published** field requires a numeric value. Each error causes execution to branch to the label **LoadError**. The code beginning with **LoadError** displays an informative message and then executes a **Resume Next**. The **Resume Next** transfers execution back to the line following the line that caused the error.

```
Private Sub Form_Load()
    Dim dbErrors As Database
    Dim strDbName As String
    Dim rsTest As Recordset
    Dim strTmp As String

    On Error GoTo LoadError

 ' Get the database name and open the database.
    strDbName = strNWindDb()        ' NWindPath is a function in READINI.BAS
10  Set dbErrors = DBEngine.Workspaces(0).OpenDatabase(strDbName)

    ' This statement will cause an error, because there's no such table
    ' as No Such Table.
20  Set rsTest = dbErrors.OpenRecordset("No Such Table", dbOpenTable)

    ' There is a table named Products, so this one should work.
30  Set rsTest = dbErrors.OpenRecordset("Products", dbOpenTable)

    ' There's no such field as No Such Field, so here's another error.
40  strTmp = rsTest![No Such Field]

    ' This causes an error because UnitPrice only takes currency values.
```

continued on next page

continued from previous page

```
50  rsTest![UnitPrice] = "XYZ"

    ' Finally!
60  End

Exit Sub

LoadError:
    MsgBox "Error #" & Str$(Err.Number) & " at Line " & Str$(Erl) & _
          " - " & Err.Description & " - reported by " & Err.Source
Resume Next

End Sub
```

How It Works

This simple example merely shows the error-handling logic that is possible using Visual Basic. The key to this sample is the use of the **MsgBox** function to show the various **Err Object** properties on the screen. Meaningful error handling has to be written into your application as you discover the most common problems with your applications.

Comments

The improvements in DAO error messages in Jet 3.5 (the version shipping with Visual Basic 5) eliminate much of the error discovery process of previous Visual Basic versions, but don't be surprised if you get some unexplainable errors. We can't assume that anything as complex as the data control will always behave the way we would have written it, so we sometimes have to learn parts of the data control's behavior through a process of discovery. The best way to trap elusive errors is to eliminate controls from your form and code from your program until the errors stop occurring. The last thing deleted before the program worked again is, no matter how unlikely, the part of the code or control causing the problem. The multiple cascading of events between the data control, its recordset object, and your event handlers can have unforeseen consequences that result in inexplicable errors. The most common of these data control errors is referencing invalid recordset fields during a reposition event because the recordset has moved to the "No current record" area.

CHAPTER 2
ACCESSING A DATABASE WITH DATA ACCESS OBJECTS

2

ACCESSING A DATABASE WITH DATA ACCESS OBJECTS

How do I...

53

The data control provides a means of quickly developing database applications with little or no code, but it limits your access to the underlying database. The Microsoft Jet database engine exposes another method of working with databases: data access objects (DAO). Although using DAO requires more coding than using the data control, it offers complete programmatic access to everything in the database and significantly greater flexibility. This chapter shows you how to use Jet data access objects to perform common database operations.

All the examples in this chapter use Microsoft Access (.MDB) database files. The Jet engine can also access other PC-based databases such as dBASE, FoxPro, Paradox, and Btrieve, as well as Open Database Connectivity (ODBC) data sources. The techniques shown can be used with any database that Visual Basic can access through Jet. Chapter 6, "External ISAM Database Files," shows how to access dBASE and other ISAM databases, and Chapters 7, "Connecting to an ODBC Server," and 8, "SQL Server Databases," show how to access ODBC and SQL Server databases.

2.1 Browse and Update a Recordset with Data Access Objects

Browsing and updating records are two of the most basic database operations. In this How-To, you will use unbound controls and data access objects to browse and update a recordset.

2.2 Validate Data Entered into Data Access Objects

Users make data entry errors, and robust applications anticipate and trap those errors. This How-To shows how to trap and respond to user errors when you're using data access objects.

2.3 Allow Users to Undo Changes They've Made in Data Access Objects

Users expect to be able to undo changes they make while they are working. In this How-To, you will learn to enable users to undo changes using data access objects and unbound controls.

2.4 Add and Delete Records Using Data Access Objects

Inserting and deleting records are common database activities. In this How-To, you will learn to use data access objects to add and delete records.

2.5 Use Unbound Controls to Update Fields in Data Access Objects

Simple text boxes are not the only user interface tools available when you're using unbound controls. In this How-To, you will build a generic form that can run an ad hoc query, display the results, and allow the user to select a record.

2.6 Find Records Using Index Values in Data Access Objects

Indexes can substantially speed up access to records. This How-To shows how you can leverage indexes for performance.

2.7 Determine How Many Records Are in a Dynaset- or Snapshot-Type Recordset

If you need to know how many records are in your recordset, this How-To will show you how to get that number.

2.8 Handle Data Access Object Errors

Although Jet is a robust database engine, a lot of things can go wrong when working with a database. This How-To shows you how to handle data access object errors gracefully.

COMPLEXITY
BEGINNING

2.1 How do I...
Browse and update a recordset with data access objects?

Problem

Bound recordsets with data controls are fine for many purposes, but the data control has significant limitations. I can't use indexes with bound controls, and I can't refer to the data control's recordset if the data control's form is not loaded. How can I browse a recordset without using bound controls?

Technique

Visual Basic and the Microsoft Jet database engine provide a rich set of data access objects that gives you complete control over your database and provide capabilities beyond what you can accomplish with bound controls.

If you've worked with other databases, and in particular Structured Query Language (SQL), you might be accustomed to dividing the database programming language into Data Definition Language (DDL) and Data Manipulation Language (DML). Although Jet provides programmatic access to both structure and data, DAO makes no clear distinction between the two. Some objects, such as the Recordset, are used strictly for data manipulation, whereas others, such as the TableDef object, act in both data definition and data manipulation roles. Figure 2.1 shows the DAO hierarchy.

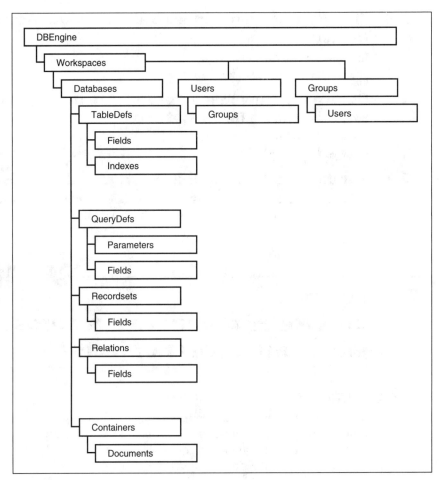

Figure 2.1. The data access object hierarchy.

In most cases, you will be using DAO to manage data. There are four general types of data operations:

- ✔ Retrieve records
- ✔ Insert new records
- ✔ Update existing records
- ✔ Delete records

DAO provides the recordset object for retrieving records and both the recordset object and the `Execute` method for inserting, updating, and deleting records.

Before you can do anything useful with DAO, you need to open a database. In most cases, this is as simple as using the `OpenDatabase` method of the default workspace. The following code fragment shows some typical code used to open an Access .MDB file and create a recordset:

```
' Declare database variable
Dim db As Database
Dim rs As Recordset

' Open a database file and assign it to db
Set db = DBEngine.Workspaces(0).OpenDatabase(App.Path & "\MyDB.MDB")

' Create a recordset
Set rs = db.OpenRecordset("MyQuery", dbOpenDynaset, , dbOptimistic)
```

If you are working with a secured database, you will need to take a few extra steps to provide a valid user name and password to the database engine so that a secured workspace object can be created. Refer to Chapter 12, "The Windows Registry and State Information," for more information.

Moving Within an Unbound Recordset

When you use the data control on a bound form, you rarely have to code move operations. The user clicks on the navigational buttons, and the data control executes a move internally. Only in the case of a delete do you need to code a move operation (see How-To 1.4).

When you use unbound controls, you must refresh the data displayed on the form with your code. The recordset object provides four methods to facilitate this task: `MoveFirst`, `MovePrevious`, `MoveNext`, and `MoveLast`.

When you use `MovePrevious`, you should always check to make sure that the movement has not placed the record pointer before the first record in the recordset. Do this by checking the value of the recordset's `BOF` property. If `BOF` is `True`, you're not on a valid record. The usual solution is to use `MoveFirst` to position the pointer on the first record. In like manner, when you use `MoveNext`, you should check to make sure that you're not past the last record in the recordset by checking the `EOF` property. If `EOF` is `True`, use `MoveLast` to move to a valid record. It's also a good idea to ensure that the recordset has at least one record by making sure that the value of the recordset's `RecordCount` property is greater than zero.

Updating Records

You can update the values in table-type or dynaset-type recordsets. Updating records in a recordset is a four-step procedure:

1. Position the record pointer to the record you want to update.

2. Copy the record's values to an area of memory known as the copy buffer by invoking the recordset object's **Edit** method.

3. Change the desired fields by assigning values to the **Field** objects.

4. Transfer the contents of the copy buffer to the database by invoking the recordset object's **Update** method.

Steps

Open and run the project HT201.VBP. The form shown in Figure 2.2 appears. Use the navigation buttons at the bottom of the form to browse through the records in the recordset. You can change the data by typing over the existing values.

1. Create a new project called HT201.VBP. Use **Form1** to create the objects and properties listed in Table 2.1, and save the form as HT201.FRM.

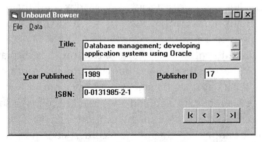

Figure 2.2. The Unbound Browser form.

Table 2.1. Objects and properties for Form1.

OBJECT	PROPERTY	SETTING
Form	Name	Form1
	Caption	"Unbound Browser"
CommandButton	Name	cmdMove
	Caption	"¦<"
	Index	0
CommandButton	Name	cmdMove
	Caption	"<"
	Index	1
CommandButton	Name	cmdMove
	Caption	">"
	Index	2
CommandButton	Name	cmdMove
	Caption	">¦"
	Index	3
TextBox	Name	txt
	Index	0
TextBox	Name	txt
	Index	1
TextBox	Name	txt
	Index	2
TextBox	Name	txt
	Index	3
Label	Name	Label1
	Caption	"&Title"
Label	Name	Label2
	Caption	"&Year Published"
Label	Name	Label3
	Caption	"&ISBN"
Label	Name	Label4
	Caption	"&Publisher ID"

2. Create the menu shown in Table 2.2.

Table 2.2. Menu specifications for Form1.

CAPTION	NAME	SHORTCUT KEY
&File	mnuFile	
----E&xit	mnuFileExit	
&Data	mnuData	
----&Save Record	mnuDataSaveRecord	Ctrl+S

3. Add READINI.bas to your project. READINI.bas looks for a file named VBDBHT.ini in the Windows directory with the following text:

```
[Data Files]
BIBLIO=<path to biblio directory>
```

The path should point to the Chapter 2 subdirectory of the directory where you installed the files from the CD setup program. The standard module uses the `GetPrivateProfileString` API function to obtain the path to the sample database.

You can also use the copy of Biblio.mdb that was installed with Visual Basic, although it is possible that there are differences in the file. If your copy has the same database structure, you can update the .ini file to point to your existing copy and delete the copy in the Chapter 2 subdirectory.

4. Add a class module to the project, name it `CTitles`, and save the file as HT201.CLS.

5. Add the following code to the declarations section of `CTitles`. Several private variables are declared, including database and recordset object variables, a flag to track changes to the record, strings to hold the property values, and public enumerations for record movement and class errors.

```
Option Explicit

' The CTitles class provides a light wrapper
' around the database and record for the
' Titles table in the Biblio database

' Note: It's up to the client to save

' Database and recordset objects
Private mdb As Database
Private mrs As Recordset

' Flags
' dirty flag
Private mblnIsDirty As Boolean
```

```
' Fields
' title
Private mstrTitle As String
' year - note use of string for
' assignment to text box
Private mstrYearPublished As String
' ISBN number
Private mstrISBN As String
' PubID - also a string
Private mstrPubID As String

' Move method constants
Public Enum CTitlesMove
    FirstRecord = 1
    LastRecord = 2
    NextRecord = 3
    PreviousRecord = 4
End Enum

' Error constants
' Note: RaiseClassError method provides the strings
' because you cannot assign a string to an Enum
Public Enum CTitlesError
    ErrInvalidMoveType = vbObjectError + 1000 + 11
    ErrNoRecords = vbObjectError + 1000 + 12
End Enum
```

ENUMERATIONS

Enumerations are a new feature in Visual Basic 5.0 that allow you to define publicly available constants within a class module. If you did any work with class modules in Visual Basic 4.0, you might have been frustrated by the need to provide a standard "helper" module for any class that used public constants. This type of workaround has been replaced with public enumerations. Note, however, that you can assign only long integer values in an enumeration. There is no means of making string or other types of constants public in classes.

6. Add the `Class_Initialize` and `Class_Terminate` event procedures to CTitles. `Class_Initialize` opens the database and creates a recordset, generating an error if there are no records. `Class_Terminate` closes the object variables opened by `Class_Initialize`.

```
Private Sub Class_Initialize()

    ' open the database and recordset

    Dim strDBName As String

    ' Get the database name and open the database.
```

continued on next page

continued from previous page

```
        ' BiblioPath is a function in READINI.BAS
        strDBName = BiblioPath()
        Set mdb = DBEngine.Workspaces(0).OpenDatabase(strDBName)

        ' Open the recordset.
        Set mrs = mdb.OpenRecordset( _
            "Titles", dbOpenDynaset, dbSeeChanges, dbOptimistic)

        ' Raise an error if there is no data
        If mrs.BOF Then
            RaiseClassError ErrNoRecords
        End If

        ' fetch the first record to the properties
        GetCurrentRecord

End Sub
Private Sub Class_Terminate()
' cleanup - note that since a Class_Terminate error
' is fatal to the app, this proc simply traps and
' ignores any shutdown errors
' that's not a great solution, but there's not much
' else that can be done at this point
' in a production app, it might be helpful to log
' these errors

        ' close and release the recordset object
        mrs.Close
        Set mrs = Nothing
        ' close and release the database object
        mdb.Close
        Set mdb = Nothing

End Sub
```

7. Add the private `RaiseClassError` method to `CTitles`. This is a simple switch that sets the `Description` and `Source` properties for errors raised by the class.

```
Private Sub RaiseClassError(lngErrorNumber As CTitlesError)
' Note: DAO errors are passed out as-is

    Dim strDescription As String
    Dim strSource As String

    ' assign the description for the error
    Select Case lngErrorNumber
        Case ErrInvalidMoveType
            strDescription = "Invalid move operation."
        Case ErrNoRecords
            strDescription = _
                "There are no records in the Titles table."
        Case Else
            ' If this executes, it's a coding error in
            ' the class module, but having the case is
            ' useful for debugging.
```

```
                    strDescription = _
                        "There is no message for this error."
            End Select

            ' build the Source property for the error
            strSource = App.EXEName & ".CTitles"

            ' raise it
            Err.Raise lngErrorNumber, strSource, strDescription

    End Sub
```

8. Add the `GetCurrentRecord` method. This procedure fetches the data from the recordset and writes the values to the private module-level variables used by the property procedures.

```
Private Sub GetCurrentRecord()
' Get current values from the recordset

    ' a zero length string is appended to
    ' each variable to avoid the Invalid use of Null
    ' error if a field is null
    ' although current rules don't allow nulls, there
    ' may be legacy data that doesn't conform to
    ' existing rules
    mstrISBN = mrs![ISBN] & ""
    mstrTitle = mrs![Title] & ""
    mstrYearPublished = mrs![Year Published] & ""
    mstrPubID = mrs![PubID] & ""

End Sub
```

9. Add the private `UpdateRecord` method. This procedure writes the module-level variables to the recordset. The error handler in this procedure clears any changes that were made to the field values.

```
Private Sub UpdateRecord()
' DAO Edit/Update
On Error GoTo ProcError

    ' inform DAO we will edit
    mrs.Edit
    mrs![ISBN] = mstrISBN
    mrs![Title] = mstrTitle
    mrs![Year Published] = mstrYearPublished
    mrs![PubID] = mstrPubID
    ' commit changes
    mro.Update
    ' clear dirty flag
    mblnIsDirty = False

    Exit Sub

ProcError:
    ' clear the values that were assigned
```

continued on next page

continued from previous page

```
' and cancel the edit method by
' executing a moveprevious/movenext
mrs.MovePrevious
mrs.MoveNext
' raise the error again
Err.Raise Err.Number, Err.Source, Err.Description, _
    Err.HelpFile, Err.HelpContext

End Sub
```

10. Add the `Property Let` and `Property Get` procedures for the `Title`, `YearPublished`, `ISBN`, and `PubID` properties of the class. The `Property Get` procedures simply return the values of the module-level variables. The `Property Let` procedures assign the new values to the module-level variables and set the `mblnIsDirty` flag.

```
Public Property Get Title() As String

    Title = mstrTitle

End Property
Public Property Let Title(strTitle As String)

    mstrTitle = strTitle
    ' set the dirty flag
    mblnIsDirty = True

End Property
Public Property Get YearPublished() As String

    YearPublished = mstrYearPublished

End Property
Public Property Let YearPublished(strYearPublished As String)

    mstrYearPublished = strYearPublished
    ' set the dirty flag
    mblnIsDirty = True

End Property
Public Property Get ISBN() As String

    ISBN = mstrISBN

End Property
Public Property Let ISBN(strISBN As String)

    mstrISBN = strISBN
    ' set the dirty flag
    mblnIsDirty = True

End Property
Public Property Get PubID() As String

    PubID = mstrPubID
```

```
End Property
Public Property Let PubID(strPubID As String)

    mstrPubID = strPubID
    ' set the dirty flag
    mblnIsDirty = True

End Property
```

11. Add the `IsDirty` **Property** `Get` procedure. This property returns the current value of the `mblnIsDirty` flag. Note that this is a read-only property. There is no corresponding **Property** `Let` procedure.

```
Public Property Get IsDirty() As Boolean
' pass out the dirty flag

    IsDirty = mblnIsDirty

End Property
```

12. Add the `Move` method. This method moves the current pointer for the recordset based on the `lngMoveType` parameter. The values for `lngMoveType` are defined by the `CTitlesMove` enumeration in the header section. This method is a simple wrapper around the various move methods of the underlying recordset object.

```
Public Sub Move(lngMoveType As CTitlesMove)
' Move and refresh properties

    Select Case lngMoveType
        Case FirstRecord
            mrs.MoveFirst
        Case LastRecord
            mrs.MoveLast
        Case NextRecord
            mrs.MoveNext
            ' check for EOF
            If mrs.EOF Then
                mrs.MoveLast
            End If
        Case PreviousRecord
            mrs.MovePrevious
            ' check for BOF
            If mrs.BOF Then
                mrs.MoveFirst
            End If
        Case Else
            ' bad parameter, raise an error
            RaiseClassError ErrInvalidMoveType
    End Select

    GetCurrentRecord

End Sub
```

MORE ON ENUMERATIONS

Declaring the `lngMoveType` parameter as `CTitlesMove` instead of as a long integer illustrates another benefit of using enumerations. If a variable is declared as the type of a named enumeration, the code editor will provide a drop-down list of available constants wherever the variable is used.

---

13. Add the `SaveRecord` method. This method tests the `mblnIsDirty` flag and updates the current record if necessary.

```
Public Sub SaveRecord()
' save current changes

    ' test dirty flag
    If mblnIsDirty Then
        ' update it
        UpdateRecord
    Else
        ' record is already clean
    End If

End Sub
```

14. Add the following code to the declarations section of `Form1`. A private object variable is created for the `CTitles` class, as well as constants for the control arrays and a status flag used to prevent the `txt_Change` events from writing the property values in the class during a refresh of the data.

```
Option Explicit

' CTitles object
Private mclsTitles As CTitles

' These constants are used for the various control arrays
' command button constants
Const cmdMoveFirst = 0
Const cmdMovePrevious = 1
Const cmdMoveNext = 2
Const cmdMoveLast = 3
' text box index constants
Const txtTitle = 0
Const txtYearPublished = 1
Const txtISBN = 2
Const txtPubID = 3

' refresh flag
Private mblnInRefresh As Boolean
```

15. Add the `Form_Load` event procedure. `Form_Load` creates the `mclsTitles` object and loads the first record. If an error occurs, the error handler displays a message and unloads the form, terminating the application.

```
Private Sub Form_Load()
' create the mclsTitles object and display the first record
On Error GoTo ProcError

    Dim strDBName As String

    Screen.MousePointer = vbHourglass

    ' create the CTitles object
    Set mclsTitles = New CTitles

    ' fetch and display the current record
    GetData

ProcExit:
    Screen.MousePointer = vbDefault
    Exit Sub

ProcError:
    ' An error was generated by Visual Basic or CTitles.
    ' Display the error message and terminate gracefully.
    MsgBox Err.Description, vbExclamation
    Unload Me
    Resume ProcExit

End Sub
```

16. Add the `Query_Unload` event procedure. This saves the current record before unloading the form. If an error occurs, the error handler gives the user the option of continuing (with loss of data) or returning to the form.

```
Private Sub Form_QueryUnload(Cancel As Integer, UnloadMode As Integer)
On Error GoTo ProcError

    Screen.MousePointer = vbHourglass

    ' save the current record
    mclsTitles.SaveRecord

ProcExit:
    Screen.MousePointer = vbDefault
    Exit Sub

ProcError:
    ' an error here means the record won't be saved
    ' let the user decide what to do
    Dim strMsg As String

    strMsg = "The following error occurred while attempting to save:"
strMsg = strMsg & vbCrLf & Err.Description & vbCrLf
    strMsg = strMsg & "If you continue the current operation, " _
    strMsg = strMsg & "changes to your data will be lost."
    strMsg = strMsg & vbCrLf
    strMsg = strMsg & "Do you want to continue anyway?"
```

continued on next page

continued from previous page

```
    If MsgBox(strMsg, _
        vbQuestion Or vbYesNo Or vbDefaultButton2) = vbNo Then
        Cancel = True
    End If
    Resume ProcExit

End Sub
```

17. Add the `cmdMove_Click` event procedure. This event saves the current record, requests the record indicated by the `Index` parameter from the `mclsTitles` object, and refreshes the form.

```
Private Sub cmdMove_Click(Index As Integer)
' move to the desired record, saving first
On Error GoTo ProcError

    Screen.MousePointer = vbHourglass

    ' save the record
    mclsTitles.SaveRecord

    ' move to the indicated record
    Select Case Index
        Case cmdMoveFirst
            mclsTitles.Move FirstRecord
        Case cmdMoveLast
            mclsTitles.Move LastRecord
        Case cmdMoveNext
            mclsTitles.Move NextRecord
        Case cmdMovePrevious
            mclsTitles.Move PreviousRecord
    End Select

    ' refresh display
    GetData

ProcExit:
    Screen.MousePointer = vbDefault
    Exit Sub

ProcError:
    MsgBox Err.Description, vbExclamation
    Resume ProcExit

End Sub
```

18. Add the `txt_Change` event procedure. This event writes the control values to the properties unless the `mblnInRefresh` flag is set. The flag tells the event procedure that the form is being refreshed and the property values in `mclsTitles` do not need to be set.

```
Private Sub txt_Change(Index As Integer)
' update property values if required
On Error GoTo ProcError

    Dim strValue As String
```

```
    Screen.MousePointer = vbHourglass

    ' fetch the value from the control
    strValue = txt(Index).Text

    ' check first to see if we're in a GetData call
    ' assigning the property values while refreshing
    ' will reset the dirty flag again so the data will
    ' never appear to have been saved
    If Not mblnInRefresh Then
        ' update the clsTitles properties
        Select Case Index
            Case txtTitle
                mclsTitles.Title = strValue
            Case txtYearPublished
                mclsTitles.YearPublished = strValue
            Case txtISBN
                mclsTitles.ISBN = strValue
            Case txtPubID
                mclsTitles.PubID = strValue
        End Select
    End If

ProcExit:
    Screen.MousePointer = vbDefault
    Exit Sub

ProcError:
    MsgBox Err.Description, vbExclamation
    Resume ProcExit

End Sub
```

19. Add the `mnuFileExit_Click` event. This procedure unloads the form. The rest of the unload logic is contained in the `QueryUnload` event procedure.

```
Private Sub mnuFileExit_Click()

    ' shut down
    ' work is handled by the Query_Unload event
    Unload Me

End Sub
```

20. Add the `mnuData_Click` and `mnuDataSaveRecord_Click` event procedures. The `mnuData_Click` event toggles the enabled flag for the `mnuDataSaveRecord` menu control, based on the `IsDirty` flag of the `mclsTitles` object. The `mnuDataSaveRecord_Click` procedure saves the current record.

```
Private Sub mnuData_Click()
' set enabled/disabled flags for menu commands
On Error GoTo ProcError
```

continued on next page

continued from previous page

```
    Screen.MousePointer = vbHourglass

    ' save enabled only when dirty
    mnuDataSaveRecord.Enabled = mclsTitles.IsDirty

ProcExit:
    Screen.MousePointer = vbDefault
    Exit Sub

ProcError:
    MsgBox Err.Description, vbExclamation
    Resume ProcExit

End Sub

Private Sub mnuDataSaveRecord_Click()
On Error GoTo ProcError

    Screen.MousePointer = vbHourglass

    ' save it
    mclsTitles.SaveRecord

    ' refresh display
    GetData

ProcExit:
    Screen.MousePointer = vbDefault
    Exit Sub

ProcError:
    MsgBox Err.Description, vbExclamation
    Resume ProcExit

End Sub
```

21. Add the private `GetData` procedure. `GetData` is used to refresh the controls, based on the property values in `mclsTitles`, and sets the `mblnInRefresh` flag so that the properties aren't changed again by `txt_Change`.

```
Private Sub GetData()
' display the current record

    ' set the mblnInRefresh flag so that the txt_Change event
    ' doesn't write the property values again
    mblnInRefresh = True

    ' assign the values to the controls from the properties
    txt(txtTitle).Text = mclsTitles.Title
    txt(txtYearPublished).Text = mclsTitles.YearPublished
    txt(txtISBN).Text = mclsTitles.ISBN
    txt(txtPubID).Text = mclsTitles.PubID
```

```
' clear the refresh flag
mblnInRefresh = False

End Sub
```

How It Works

When the form loads, it creates the object variable for the CTitles class and displays the first record. The user can navigate among the records by clicking the move buttons, and the logic in the form and the CTitles class will save changes if the record is dirty.

With placement of the data management logic in the class module and the user interface logic in the form, a level of independence between the database and the user interface is created. Several different forms can be created that all use the same class without duplicating any of the data management logic. Additionally, changes made to the underlying database can be incorporated into the class without requiring changes to the forms based on it.

Comments

The beauty of encapsulating all the data access code in a class module isn't fully revealed until you have an application that allows the user to edit the same data using more than one interface. If, for example, you display a summary of detail records in a grid and also provide a regular form for working with the same data, most of the code for managing that data will be shared in the class modules. Each form that presents the data will only need to have code that controls its own interface.

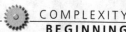

COMPLEXITY
BEGINNING

2.2 How do I...
Validate data entered into data access objects?

Problem

I need to verify that data entered is valid before I update the database. How can I do this with data access objects and unbound controls?

Technique

Databases, tables, and fields often have various business rules that apply to the data. You can apply rules by writing code to check the values of the data in unbound controls before you write the changes to the underlying tables.

Class modules are most often used to handle the data management logic for unbound data—adding a layer of separation between the database schema and the user interface logic. Normally, class modules should not handle any user interaction (unless of course the class is specifically designed to encapsulate user interface components), so instead of generating messages, classes raise errors if a validation rule is violated. The error is trapped by the user interface and handled in whatever manner is appropriate.

Steps

Open and run HT202.VBP. Tab to the Year Published text box, delete the year, and attempt to save the record. Because the year published is required, an error message is displayed, as shown in Figure 2.3. Experiment with some of the other fields to examine other rules and the messages that are displayed.

1. Create a new project called HT202.VBP. This project adds to the project developed for How-To 2.1 by adding validation code to the **CTitles** class module. The form and the READINI.bas module for this project are unchanged from the previous How-To, with the exception of the form caption, which was changed to Validating Browser. Changes to the class module are shown in the steps that follow.

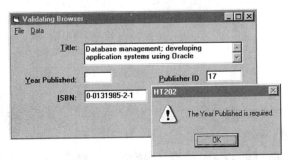

Figure 2.3. The Validating Browser form.

2. Add the following code to the declarations section of the class module. The modified enumeration, shown in bold, defines the errors that can be raised by the class. The rest of the declarations section is unchanged from the previous How-To.

```
Option Explicit

' The CTitles class provides a light wrapper
' around the database and record for the
' Titles table in the Biblio database

' Database and recordset objects
Private mdb As Database
Private mrs As Recordset

' Flags
' dirty flag
Private mblnIsDirty As Boolean

' Fields
' title
Private mstrTitle As String
' year - note use of string for
' assignment to text box
Private mstrYearPublished As String
' ISBN number
Private mstrISBN As String
' PubID - also a string
Private mstrPubID As String

' Move method constants
Public Enum CTitlesMove
    FirstRecord = 1
    LastRecord = 2
    NextRecord = 3
    PreviousRecord = 4
End Enum

' Error constants
' Note: RaiseClassError method provides the strings
' because you cannot assign a string to an Enum
Public Enum CTitlesError
    ErrMissingTitle = vbObjectError + 1000 + 1
    ErrMissingYear = vbObjectError + 1000 + 2
    ErrMissingISBN = vbObjectError + 1000 + 3
    ErrInvalidYear = vbObjectError + 1000 + 4
    ErrMissingPubID = vbObjectError + 1000 + 5
    ErrNonNumericPubID = vbObjectError + 1000 + 6
    ErrRecordNotFound = vbObjectError + 1000 + 10
    ErrInvalidMoveType = vbObjectError + 1000 + 11
    ErrNoRecords = vbObjectError + 1000 + 12
End Enum
```

3. Modify the `RaiseClassError` procedure as shown. This is a simple switch that sets the `Description` and `Source` properties for errors raised by the class. There are several new cases in the `Select Case` block dedicated to assigning descriptions to validation errors.

```
Private Sub RaiseClassError(lngErrorNumber As CTitlesError)
' Note: DAO errors are passed out as-is

    Dim strDescription As String
    Dim strSource As String

    ' assign the description for the error
    Select Case lngErrorNumber
        Case ErrMissingTitle
            strDescription = "The Title is required."
        Case ErrMissingYear
            strDescription = "The Year Published is required."
        Case ErrMissingISBN
            strDescription = "The ISBN number is required."
        Case ErrInvalidYear
            strDescription = "Not a valid year."
        Case ErrMissingPubID
            strDescription = "The Publisher ID is required."
        Case ErrNonNumericPubID
            strDescription = "The Publisher ID must be numeric."
        Case ErrRecordNotFound
            strDescription = "The record was not found."
        Case ErrInvalidMoveType
            strDescription = "Invalid move operation."
        Case ErrNoRecords
            strDescription = _
                "There are no records in the Titles table."
        Case Else
            ' If this executes, it's a coding error in
            ' the class module, but having the case is
            ' useful for debugging.
            strDescription = "There is no message for this error."
    End Select

    ' build the Source property for the error
    strSource = App.EXEName & ".CTitles"

    ' raise it
    Err.Raise lngErrorNumber, strSource, strDescription

End Sub
```

4. Add the `IsValid` property. This property takes an optional argument, `blnRaiseError`, which defaults to `False` and controls the procedure logic. If the flag is `True`, an error is generated if a validation rule is violated. Code within the class sets the flag to `True` so that errors are raised when rules are violated. Forms would normally ignore this optional parameter and simply test for a `True` or `False` value in the property.

```
Public Property Get IsValid _
  (Optional blnRaiseError As Boolean = False) As Boolean
' test the data against our rules
' the optional blnRaiseError flag can be used to have the
' procedure raise an error if a validation rule is
' violated.

    Dim lngError As CTitlesError

    If mstrISBN = "" Then
        lngError = ErrMissingISBN
    ElseIf mstrTitle = "" Then
        lngError = ErrMissingTitle
    ElseIf mstrYearPublished = "" Then
        lngError = ErrMissingYear
    ElseIf Not IsNumeric(mstrYearPublished) Then
        lngError = ErrInvalidYear
    ElseIf mstrPubID = "" Then
        lngError = ErrMissingPubID
    ElseIf Not IsNumeric(mstrPubID) Then
        lngError = ErrNonNumericPubID
    End If

    If lngError <> 0 Then
        If blnRaiseError Then
            RaiseClassError lngError
        Else
            IsValid = False
        End If
    Else
        IsValid = True
    End If

End Property
```

5. Modify the `SaveRecord` method to call `IsValid`. This method tests the `mblnIsDirty` flag and updates the current record if necessary. Before `UpdateRecord` is called, the procedure calls the `IsValid` procedure, setting the `blnRaiseError` parameter to `True` so that any rule violations are raised as errors in the form. The only differences between this version of `SaveRecord` and the version shown in How-To 2.1 are the call to `IsValid` and the relocation of the call to `UpdateRecord` so that it is called only if `IsValid` returns `True`.

```
Public Sub SaveRecord()
' save current changes

    ' test dirty flag
    If mblnIsDirty Then
        ' validate, raise an error
        ' if rules are violated
        If IsValid(True) Then
            ' update it
            UpdateRecord
```

continued on next page

continued from previous page

```
            End If
    Else
            ' record is already clean
    End If

End Sub
```

How It Works

Data validation logic is handled entirely within the `CTitles` class—no special coding is required in the form beyond normal error handlers that trap errors and display a simple message about the error. The rules applied for validation can be as simple or as complex as the application requires.

Only minor modifications to the class were required to implement data validation. The error enumeration and the corresponding `RaiseClassError` procedure were expanded to include validation errors, the `IsValid` procedure was added to perform the validation tests, and a few lines of code were changed in the `SaveRecord` procedure.

Comments

Not all database rules require you to write code to perform data validation. The Jet database engine can enforce some or possibly all of your rules for you using the properties of tables and fields or relational constraints. How-To 4.5 will show you how to use these objects and properties to supplement or replace validation code.

COMPLEXITY
BEGINNING

2.3   How do I...
Allow users to undo changes they've made in data access objects?

Problem

Users sometimes make data entry errors while working. How can I allow users to undo changes they've made to data in unbound controls using data access objects?

Technique

A few additional lines of code in the class module handling data management for your database can implement an undo feature. Because data is not updated in bound controls until you explicitly update it with your code, you can restore the original values by reloading them from the underlying recordset. The class module handles restoring the original values from the recordset and assigning them to the property values. The form only needs to read the data from the property procedures and write the property values to the controls.

Steps

Open and run the project HT203.VBP. The form shown in Figure 2.4 appears. Change the data in any control on the form, and use the Undo command on the Edit menu to restore the original value.

1. Create a new project called HT203.VBP. This project is based on the example developed for How-To 2.1 and also includes the READINI.bas module and CTitles.cls module. Menu controls and supporting code have been added to the form developed for How-To 2.1 to support the undo operation, and a public method has been added to the class module. If you have worked through How-To 2.1, you can copy or modify your existing files. If not, refer to the steps in that example to create the foundation for this project.

2. Change the caption of Form1 to Undo Browser, and add the menu shown in Table 2.3.

Table 2.3. Menu specifications for the Edit menu.

CAPTION	NAME	SHORTCUT KEY
&Edit	mnuEdit	
----&Undo	mnuEditUndo	Ctrl+Z

NOTE

By convention, the Edit menu is placed to the immediate right of the File menu.

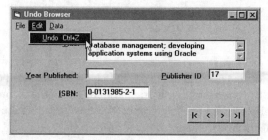

Figure 2.4. The Undo Browser form.

3. Add the mnuEdit_Click and mnuEditUndo_Click events to Form1. The mnuEdit_Click event checks the current record state and toggles the enabled property of the mnuEditUndo control, based on the value of the IsDirty property of mclsTitles. The mnuEditUndo_Click procedure calls the UndoRecord method of the mclsTitles object and refreshes the form. This is the only new code in the form.

```
Private Sub mnuEdit_Click()
' enable/disable undo command based on current dirty flag
On Error GoTo ProcError

    Screen.MousePointer = vbHourglass

    ' toggle based on dirty flag
    mnuEditUndo.Enabled = mclsTitles.IsDirty

ProcExit:
    Screen.MousePointer = vbDefault
    Exit Sub

ProcError:
    MsgBox Err.Description, vbExclamation
    Resume ProcExit

End Sub
Private Sub mnuEditUndo_Click()
' undo changes
On Error GoTo ProcError

    Screen.MousePointer = vbHourglass

    ' undo changes
    mclsTitles.UndoRecord

    ' refresh the display
    GetData

ProcExit:
    Screen.MousePointer = vbDefault
    Exit Sub

ProcError:
    MsgBox Err.Description, vbExclamation
    Resume ProcExit

End Sub
```

4. Add the UndoRecord method to the CTitles class. UndoRecord clears the mblnIsDirty flag and restores the original values from the recordset to the private variables used for the property procedures by calling the GetCurrentRecord procedure.

```
Public Sub UndoRecord()
' clear changes and refresh properties
```

```
' clear dirty flag
' but do not clear new flag
mblnIsDirty = False
' refresh the current values from the recordset
GetCurrentRecord

End Sub
```

How It Works

Each of the property procedures that represent fields in the `CTitles` class sets the module-level `mblnIsDirty` flag. This flag is then used to toggle the `enabled` property of the Undo command on the Edit menu. When the user selects Undo, the form calls the `UndoRecord` method of the class and refreshes the controls on the form. The `UndoRecord` method needs only to restore the private module-level variables with the data that is still unchanged in the recordset.

Comments

The standard text box control supports a field-level Undo capability with the built-in context menu. By adding some code, you could also implement a field-level Undo command for any field you display, regardless of the type of control that is used.

COMPLEXITY
BEGINNING

2.4 How do I...
Add and delete records using data access objects?

Problem

Viewing and editing existing records are only half of the jobs my users need to do. How do I add and delete records using unbound controls and data access objects?

Technique

The recordset object provides the `AddNew` and `Delete` methods for inserting and deleting records. When you are using unbound controls on a form, adding a record is a five-step process:

1. Clear (and if necessary save) the current record so that the user can enter data for the new record.

2. Call the `AddNew` method of the recordset.

3. Write the values from the controls to the fields.

4. Call the `Update` method of the recordset.

5. Restore the record pointer to the newly added record.

Deleting a record is a two-step process:

1. Call the `Delete` method of the recordset.

2. Move to a valid record and display it.

ADD AND DELETE USER INTERFACES

Microsoft Access and (if properly configured) the data control allow users to add new records by navigating to the end of the recordset and clicking the Next Record button. Although this two-step procedure might seem obvious to most programmers and database developers, it is not at all obvious to most users. Users will be looking for something clearly labeled as a command that will give them a new record to work with. Rather than emulate this confusing idiom, this example uses a New Record command on the Data menu.

The same reasoning applies to deleting records. Provide a clearly labeled menu command or button the user can click to perform a delete.

In short, don't aggravate your customers (the users) by burying common operations with obscure procedures in the interface.

Steps

Open and run the project HT204.VBP. To add a new record, select the Data | New Record menu command, as shown in Figure 2.5. To delete a record, choose the Delete Record command.

1. Create a new project called HT204.VBP. This project is based on the example developed for How-To 2.1. Only the changes to that project are described here. Refer to the steps in the original project for the complete details of creating the form, the `CTitles` class module, and the READINI.bas module.

2. Change the caption of `Form1` to Add and Delete, and add the New Record and Delete Record commands (shown in bold) to the Data menu as shown in Table 2.4.

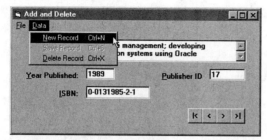

Figure 2.5. The Add and Delete form.

Table 2.4. Menu specifications for Form1.

CAPTION	NAME	SHORTCUT KEY
&File	mnuFile	
----E&xit	mnuFileExit	
&Data	mnuData	
----&New Record	mnuDataNewRecord	Ctrl+N
----&Save Record	mnuDataSaveRecord	Ctrl+S
----&Delete Record	mnuDataDeleteRecord	Ctrl+X

3. Modify the `Form_Load` event procedure to allow the user to create a new record if the table is empty when the form is initially loaded. Only the code in the error handler has changed.

```
Private Sub Form_Load()
' create the mclsTitles object and display the first record
On Error GoTo ProcError

    Dim strDBName As String

    Screen.MousePointer = vbHourglass

    ' create the CTitles object
    Set mclsTitles = New CTitles

    ' fetch and display the current record
    GetData

ProcExit:
    Screen.MousePointer = vbDefault
    Exit Sub

ProcError:
    ' An error was generated by Visual Basic or CTitles.
    ' Check for the "No Records" error and if so
    ' just provide a new record.
    Select Case Err.Number
        Case ErrNoRecords
```

continued on next page

continued from previous page

```
                mclsTitles.NewRecord
                Resume Next
        Case Else
            ' Some other error
            ' Display the error message and terminate gracefully.
            MsgBox Err.Description, vbExclamation
            Unload Me
            Resume ProcExit
    End Select

End Sub
```

4. Add the event procedures for mnuData_Click and its submenu items mnuDataNewRecord_Click, mnuDataSaveRecord_Click, and mnuDataDeleteRecord_Click. The mnuData_Click event toggles the enabled flag for the mnuDataSaveRecord menu control, based on the IsDirty flag of the mclsTitles object. The mnuDataNewRecord_Click event calls the NewRecord method of the mclsTitles object. The mnuDataSaveRecord_Click procedure saves the current record by calling the mclsTitles.SaveRecord method. The DeleteRecord method of mclsTitles is called by mnuDataDeleteRecord_Click. A special trap is used in the error handler. If the delete leaves the recordset empty, a new record is created.

```
Private Sub mnuData_Click()
' set enabled/disabled flags for menu commands
On Error GoTo ProcError

    Screen.MousePointer = vbHourglass

    ' save enabled only when dirty
    mnuDataSaveRecord.Enabled = mclsTitles.IsDirty

ProcExit:
    Screen.MousePointer = vbDefault
    Exit Sub

ProcError:
    MsgBox Err.Description, vbExclamation
    Resume ProcExit

End Sub
```

The mnuData_Click event procedure is unchanged from the example in How-To 2.1.

```
Private Sub mnuDataNewRecord_Click()
' set up a new record
On Error GoTo ProcError

    Screen.MousePointer = vbHourglass

    ' save existing first
```

```
    mclsTitles.SaveRecord

    ' get a new record
    mclsTitles.NewRecord

    ' refresh display
    GetData

ProcExit:
    Screen.MousePointer = vbDefault
    Exit Sub

ProcError:
    MsgBox Err.Description, vbExclamation
    Resume ProcExit

End Sub

Private Sub mnuDataSaveRecord_Click()
On Error GoTo ProcError

    Screen.MousePointer = vbHourglass

    ' save it
    mclsTitles.SaveRecord

    ' refresh display
    GetData

ProcExit:
    Screen.MousePointer = vbDefault
    Exit Sub

ProcError:
    MsgBox Err.Description, vbExclamation
    Resume ProcExit

End Sub

Private Sub mnuDataDeleteRecord_Click()
' delete the current record
On Error GoTo ProcError

    Screen.MousePointer = vbHourglass

    mclsTitles.DeleteRecord

    ' refresh display
    GetData

ProcExit:
    Screen.MousePointer = vbDefault
    Exit Sub

ProcError:
    Select Case Err.Number
```

continued on next page

continued from previous page

```
        Case ErrNoRecords
            ' last record was deleted
            ' Create a new record
            mclsTitles.NewRecord
            Resume Next
        Case Else
            ' inform
            MsgBox Err.Description, vbExclamation
            Resume ProcExit
    End Select

End Sub
```

5. Revise the declarations section of **CTitles** to include the new `mblnIsNew` flag, shown in bold in the following listing. This flag is `True` if the current data is a new record and `False` if it is an existing record.

```
Option Explicit

' The CTitles class provides a light wrapper
' around the database and record for the
' Titles table in the Biblio database

' Note: It's up to the client to save

' Database and recordset objects
Private mdb As Database
Private mrs As Recordset

' Flags
' dirty flag
Private mblnIsDirty As Boolean
' new record flag
Private mblnIsNew As Boolean

' Fields
' title
Private mstrTitle As String
' year - note use of string for
' assignment to text box
Private mstrYearPublished As String
' ISBN number
Private mstrISBN As String
' PubID - also a string
Private mstrPubID As String

' Move method constants
Public Enum CTitlesMove
    FirstRecord = 1
    LastRecord = 2
    NextRecord = 3
    PreviousRecord = 4
End Enum

' Error constants
' Note: RaiseClassError method provides the strings
```

```
' because you cannot assign a string to an Enum
Public Enum CTitlesError
    ErrInvalidMoveType = vbObjectError + 1000 + 11
    ErrNoRecords = vbObjectError + 1000 + 12
End Enum
```

6. Create the `AddNewRecord` method. This sub does the real work of inserting the record into the database. First the `AddNew` method is called, then the values from the properties are written to the fields, and finally the `Update` method is called to commit the changes. After a record is inserted using `AddNew` and `Update`, the current record is undefined. Setting the recordset's `Bookmark` property to the special `LastModified` bookmark restores the current record pointer to the new record.

```
Private Sub AddNewRecord()
' DAO AddNew/Update

    ' inform DAO we are going to insert
    mrs.AddNew
    ' write the current values
    mrs![ISBN] = mstrISBN
    mrs![Title] = mstrTitle
    mrs![Year Published] = mstrYearPublished
    mrs![PubID] = mstrPubID
    ' update the record
    mrs.Update
    ' return to the new record
    mrs.Bookmark = mrs.LastModified
    ' clear new flag
    mblnIsNew = False
    ' clear dirty flag
    mblnIsDirty = False

End Sub
```

7. Add the `IsNew` property. This flag indicates whether the current record is a new record (one that has not been added to the recordset) by returning the value of the private `mblnIsNew` flag.

```
Public Property Get IsNew() As Boolean
' pass out the new flag

    IsNew = mblnIsNew

End Property
```

8. Add the `NewRecord` method. This method clears the current values of the private variables used for the field properties and sets the `mblnIsNew` flag used by the `IsNew` property.

```
Public Sub NewRecord()
' clear the current values for an insert
' NOTE: the flags work so that if a new
```

continued on next page

continued from previous page

```
' record is added but not changed, you
' can move off of it or close with no
' prompt to save

    ' assign zero-length strings to the properties
    mstrISBN = ""
    mstrTitle = ""
    mstrYearPublished = ""
    mstrPubID = ""
    ' set the new flag
    mblnIsNew = True

End Sub
```

9. Add the `DeleteRecord` method. `DeleteRecord` calls the `Delete` method of the recordset object and then uses the `MovePrevious` method to reset the current record to a valid record pointer. If `MovePrevious` takes the recordset to `BOF` (before the first record), a `MoveFirst` is executed.

```
Public Sub DeleteRecord()
' DAO delete

    ' delete the record
    mrs.Delete
    ' clear new and dirty flags
    mblnIsDirty = False
    mblnIsNew = False

    ' reposition to a valid record
    mrs.MovePrevious
    ' check for BOF
    If mrs.BOF Then
        ' could be empty, check EOF
        If Not mrs.EOF Then
            mrs.MoveFirst
        Else
            ' empty recordset, raise error
            ' the client must decide how to
            ' handle this situation
            RaiseClassError ErrNoRecords
        End If
    End If

    GetCurrentRecord

End Sub
```

10. Add the `SaveRecord` method. This method tests the `mblnIsDirty` flag and updates the current record if necessary. If the record is new, the data is committed to the table using the `AddNewRecord` procedure. Existing records are updated using the `UpdateRecord` procedure.

```
Public Sub SaveRecord()
' save current changes
```

```
' test dirty flag
If mblnIsDirty Then
    ' test new flag
    If mblnIsNew Then
        ' add it
        AddNewRecord
    Else
        ' update it
        UpdateRecord
    End If
Else
    ' record is already clean
End If

End Sub
```

How It Works

The `CTitles` class handles all the data processing with the database engine and provides a lightweight wrapper around the `AddNew`, `Update`, and `Delete` methods of the `Recordset` object. The form exposes these features in the user interface by providing menu commands for each data operation and handling save and error-trapping logic.

Encapsulating all the recordset management logic in the class module means that all of that code can be easily reused in other forms based on the same data.

Comments

A complete application might not necessarily have a one-to-one correspondence between tables and class modules. The classes should reflect the object model for the application and its data, not the database schema itself. The database underlying a complex application might have tables that are not reflected in the object model, such as tables used only for supplying lookup values to lists, or tables that are not directly represented, such as junction tables in many-to-many relationships.

COMPLEXITY
INTERMEDIATE

2.5 How do I...
Use unbound controls to update fields in data access objects?

Problem

Using data access objects to build data entry forms with unbound controls works well in most situations, but sometimes the data is difficult for the user to work with. I need to extend the user interface of my application to provide alternative methods of finding and choosing records.

Technique

The nature of database applications is that users must often deal with less-than-obvious values such as foreign keys and coded data. Instead of forcing the user to remember arbitrary key values and data codes, you can alter the user interface to provide lists of values rather than simple text boxes.

> **NOTE**
> Chapter 4, "Designing and Implementing a Database," discusses foreign keys and table relationships.

Foreign key values can represent a special problem because the lookup tables for the keys are often quite large. Populating a list with all the available values can seriously damage the performance of the application. Additionally, because this is such a common operation, a generic tool for working with this type of data will save significant coding effort.

Using a simple form and a `ListView` control, you can build a generic tool that can display the results of an ad hoc query and return a key value for the record selected by the user.

Steps

Open and run the project HT205.VBP. Select Data | Find Publisher and enter `Waite`. Click OK to display the results. The form shown in Figure 2.6 appears.

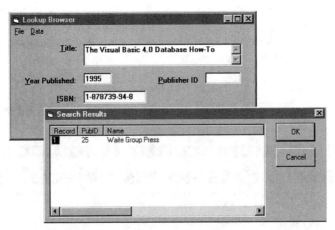

Figure 2.6. The Lookup Browser form.

1. Create a new project called HT205.VBP. This example extends the project developed for How-To 2.1 to provide a means for the user to search for an identifier value for a publisher. Refer to the steps in How-To 2.1 for complete details on building the base application. Only the changes to the original project are shown in the steps that follow.

2. Change the caption of `Form1` to Lookup Browser. Modify the Data menu as shown in Table 2.5, adding the Find Publisher command (shown in bold).

Table 2.5. Menu specifications for `Form1`.

CAPTION	NAME	SHORTCUT KEY
&File	mnuFile	
----E&xit	mnuFileExit	
&Data	mnuData	
----&Save Record	mnuDataSaveRecord	Ctrl+S
----&Find Publisher	**mnuDataFindPublisher**	**Ctrl+F**

3. Add the following code to `Form1` as the `mnuDataFindPublisher_Click` event. This event uses an input box and the `FSearchResults` form to build and display the results of an ad hoc query. The user is prompted to enter all or part of the name of a publisher. The value entered is used to build a SQL statement that is passed to the `FSearchResults` form. The `FSearchResults` form handles the balance of the selection process and sets its `KeyValue` property before it returns control to the `mnuDataFindPublisher_Click` event.

```
Private Sub mnuDataFindPublisher_Click()
' Use the FSearchResults form to find a pub id
On Error GoTo ProcError

    Dim strPrompt As String
    Dim strInput As String
    Dim strSQL As String
    Dim fSearch As FSearchResults

    strPrompt = "Enter all or the beginning of the publisher name:"
    strInput = InputBox$(strPrompt, "Search for Publishers")
    If strInput <> "" Then
        ' search
        strSQL = "SELECT * FROM Publishers " & _
            "WHERE Name LIKE '" & strInput & "*';"
        Set fSearch = New FSearchResults
        ' Note: Search method does not return
        ' until the user dismisses the form
        fSearch.Search "PubID", strSQL, Me
        If Not fSearch.Cancelled Then
            txt(txtPubID).Text = fSearch.KeyValue
```

continued on next page

continued from previous page

```
        End If
    End If

ProcExit:
    ' release the search form reference
    Set fSearch = Nothing
    Exit Sub

ProcError:
    MsgBox Err.Description, vbExclamation
    Resume ProcExit

End Sub
```

4. Create a new form, name it **FSearchResults**, and save the form. Table 2.6 shows the objects and properties for the form.

Table 2.6. Objects and properties for the FSearchResults form.

OBJECT	PROPERTY	VALUE
ListView	Name	lvwResults
	View	3 - lvwReport
	LabelEdit	1 - lvwManual
CommandButton	Name	"cmd"
	Index	0
	Caption	"OK"
	Default	True
CommandButton	Name	"cmd"
	Index	1
	Caption	"Cancel"
	Cancel	True

5. Add the following code to the declarations section of **FSearchResults**. The two constants are used for the index to the command button control array. The **mblnCancelled** flag is used to indicate that the user chose the Cancel button. The **mvntKeyValue** holds the value (typically the primary key field, but any field can be specified when the **Search** method is called) for the key field. The **mintItemIdx** holds the index to the **SubItems** collection of the listview control for the key value.

```
Option Explicit

' This form will run an ad hoc query and
' display the results in the list view control

' command button array constants
Const cmdOK = 0
```

```
Const cmdCancel = 1

' cancel property
Private mblnCancelled As Boolean
' selected key value
Private mvntKeyValue As Variant
' subitem index for key value
Private mintItemIdx As Integer
```

6. Add the `cmd_Click` event procedure for the command button control array. This event procedure sets the private flag indicating whether the user chose OK or Cancel and hides the form. Because the form is displayed modally, control returns to whatever procedure created the form after this procedure exits.

```
Private Sub cmd_Click(Index As Integer)

    If Index = cmdOK Then
        mblnCancelled = False
    Else
        mblnCancelled = True
    End If

    Me.Hide

End Sub
```

7. Add the `lvwResults_ItemClick` event procedure. When Visual Basic fires the `ItemClick` event for a listview control, it passes the clicked `ListItem` object as a parameter. The `mintItemIdx` variable set by the `Search` method is used to retrieve the value of the key field from the `SubItems` collection and assign it to the `mvntKeyValue` variable, where it can be read by the `KeyValue` property procedure.

```
Private Sub lvwResults_ItemClick(ByVal Item As ComctlLib.ListItem)
On Error GoTo ProcError

    mvntKeyValue = Item.SubItems(mintItemIdx)

ProcExit:
    Exit Sub

ProcError:
    MsgBox Err.Description, vbExclamation
    Resume ProcExit

End Sub
```

8. Add the `Cancelled` and `KeyValue` property procedures. Each procedure returns the values assigned to the module-level variables. These properties are checked by the procedure that created the instance of the form to see what button the user chose and the key value of the record selected.

```
Public Property Get Cancelled()

    Cancelled = mblnCancelled

End Property

Public Property Get KeyValue() As Variant

    KeyValue = mvntKeyValue

End Property
```

9. Add the following code to **FSearchResults** as the **Search** method. The method takes three parameters: a key field name used to return a value in the **KeyValue** property, a SQL statement used to create the list of results, and a parent form reference used by the **Show** method. The method builds the results list by first creating a recordset object based on the SQL statement provided. If there are records to display, it iterates the **Fields** collection of the recordset to generate a set of column headers for **lvwResults** (determining the index of the key field in the process). After the column headers for the list have been created, the method enters a **Do** loop and iterates the records in the recordset. For each record, the fields are iterated and their values are placed into the appropriate **SubItem** of the listview. In addition to the list of fields, the **lvwResults** listview control also shows the ordinal position in the results for each record.

```
Public Sub Search( _
    strKeyField As String, _
    strSQLStatement As String, _
    frmParent As Form)
' run the specified query and populate the
' listview with the results

    Dim strDBName As String
    Dim lngOrdRecPos As Long
    Dim db As Database
    Dim rs As Recordset
    Dim fld As Field

    strDBName = BiblioPath()
    Set db = DBEngine(0).OpenDatabase(strDBName)
    Set rs = db.OpenRecordset(strSQLStatement, _
        dbOpenDynaset, dbReadOnly)

    ' test for no records
    If Not rs.EOF Then
        ' create the ordinal position column
        lvwResults.ColumnHeaders.Add , "Ordinal", "Record"
        ' set width
        lvwResults.ColumnHeaders("Ordinal").Width = 600
        ' create the columns in the listview
        For Each fld In rs.Fields
            lvwResults.ColumnHeaders.Add , fld.Name, fld.Name
```

```
                    ' best guess column width
                    lvwResults.ColumnHeaders(fld.Name).Width _
                        = 150 * Len(fld.Name)
                    If fld.Name = strKeyField Then
                        ' mark the item index for later retrieval
                        mintItemIdx = fld.OrdinalPosition + 1
                    End If
                Next     ' field
                ' populate the list
                Do
                    ' increment the ordinal position counter
                    lngOrdRecPos = lngOrdRecPos + 1
                    ' add the item
                    lvwResults.ListItems.Add _
                        lngOrdRecPos, , CStr(lngOrdRecPos)
                    ' add the fields to the rest of the columns
                    For Each fld In rs.Fields
                        lvwResults.ListItems(lngOrdRecPos). _
                        SubItems(fld.OrdinalPosition + 1) = _
                        fld.Value & ""
                    Next     ' field
                    ' go to next record
                    rs.MoveNext
                Loop While Not rs.EOF
                ' clean up
                rs.Close
                Set rs = Nothing
                db.Close
                Set db = Nothing

                ' show modally
                Me.Show vbModal, frmParent
            Else
                ' no data, treat as a cancel
                mblnCancelled = True
                MsgBox "No matching records found.", vbInformation
                Me.Hide
            End If

    End Sub
```

How It Works

The **FSearchResults** form provides a generic tool for running an ad hoc query, displaying its results, and returning a key value selected by the user. The benefit of using a generic search form is that the form can be easily reused in any situation in which this type of lookup is required. This form can be added with minimal impact on the original design or performance of the main data entry form, but it still provides the user with a more advanced method of entering the **PubID** foreign key field.

The form works by filling a listview control using a completely generic population routine in the **Search** method. When the user selects a record and dismisses the form by clicking OK, a private module-level variable retains the selected item, which can then be read from the **KeyValue** property.

Comments

Over time, you might build a significant library of generic components such as this lookup form. If the tools are properly designed and not coupled too tightly to any particular application or database, you might be able to bundle them together in an ActiveX DLL, which can then be included in future applications without the need to return to the source code.

COMPLEXITY
BEGINNING

2.6 How do I...
Find records using index values in data access objects?

Problem

I know that indexes can be used to speed up database operations. How can I take advantage of indexes in my application?

Technique

When a table-type recordset has a current index (either the primary key or another index you have designated), you can use the **Seek** method to find records based on the indexed values. To use the **Seek** method, you provide it with an argument that matches each field in the index. When the **Seek** method executes, if it finds at least one record matching the index values, it positions the record pointer to the first matching record and sets the **NoMatch** property of the recordset to **False**. If it does not find a matching record, it sets the **NoMatch** property to **True**; the current record is then undefined, which means that you can't be sure where the record pointer is pointing.

When you use **Seek**, you specify not only the values for the key index fields but also the comparison criterion that **Seek** is to use. You provide the comparison criterion as the first argument to the **Seek** method, and you provide it as a string value. In the great majority of cases, you will specify that **Seek** is to match the index value exactly; you do this by specifying a comparison criterion of =. You can also specify < > for not equal, > for greater than, < for less than, >= for greater than or equal to, or <= for less than or equal to.

Steps

Open and run the project HT206.VBP. Use the Index command on the Data menu to select the ISBN index. Browse forward in the recordset a few records, and copy the ISBN number from the form to the clipboard. Using the MoveFirst button, return to the first record; then select Data | Seek to display the input box shown in Figure 2.7. Paste the value you copied into the input box, and click OK. The record with the matching ISBN number is displayed.

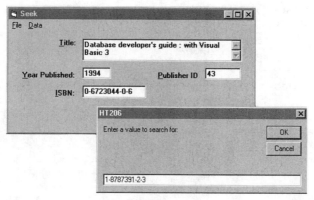

Figure 2.7. The Seek form.

1. Create a new project called HT206.VBP. This example adds the capability to find records using the `Seek` method to the basic browser application developed in How-To 2.1. The form and class module contain minor changes and some added code to support the seek operation. The READINI.bas module is unchanged. Only the code that has been added or modified for this project is shown in the steps that follow.

2. Change the caption of `Form1` to Seek, and modify the Data menu as shown in Table 2.7. The Index command, its submenu items, and the Seek command (all shown in bold) are new in this project.

Table 2.7. Menu specifications for `Form1`.

CAPTION	NAME	SHORTCUT KEY
&File	mnuFile	
----E&xit	mnuFileExit	
&Data	mnuData	
----&Save Record	mnuDataSaveRecord	Ctrl+S
----&Index	mnuDataIndex	
--------&ISBN	mnuDataIndexName	
--------&Title	mnuDataIndexName	
----&Seek	mnuDataSeek	

3. Modify the declarations section of `Form1` as shown. Index constants have been added for the `mnuDataIndexName` control array.

```
Option Explicit

' CTitles object
Private mclsTitles As CTitles
```

continued on next page

continued from previous page

```
' These constants are used for the various control arrays
' command button constants
Const cmdMoveFirst = 0
Const cmdMovePrevious = 1
Const cmdMoveNext = 2
Const cmdMoveLast = 3
' text box index constants
Const txtTitle = 0
Const txtYearPublished = 1
Const txtISBN = 2
Const txtPubID = 3

' index constants
Const idxISBN = 0
Const idxTitle = 1

' refresh flag
Private mblnInRefresh As Boolean
```

4. Modify the mnuData_Click event procedure to toggle the enabled flag for the mnuDataSeek menu control if an index has been chosen.

```
Private Sub mnuData_Click()
' set enabled/disabled flags for menu commands
On Error GoTo ProcError

    Screen.MousePointer = vbHourglass

    ' seek enabled only if index is set
    If Len(mclsTitles.IndexName) Then
        mnuDataSeek.Enabled = True
    Else
        mnuDataSeek.Enabled = False
    End If

ProcExit:
    Screen.MousePointer = vbDefault
    Exit Sub

ProcError:
    MsgBox Err.Description, vbExclamation
    Resume ProcExit

End Sub
```

5. Add the following code to Form1 as the mnuDataIndexName_Click and mnuDataSeek_Click events. The mnuDataIndexName_Click procedure assigns the index to use for the seek operation and manages the check marks on the menu. The mnuDataSeek_Click procedure prompts the user for search criteria and attempts to locate the value provided by calling the Seek method of mclsTitles.

```
Private Sub mnuDataIndexName_Click(Index As Integer)
' set the current index
On Error GoTo ProcError
```

```
        Screen.MousePointer = vbHourglass

        ' set the index
        Select Case Index
            Case idxISBN
                ' assign the index
                mclsTitles.Index = IndexISBN
                ' set up menu check marks
                mnuDataIndexName(idxTitle).Checked = False
                mnuDataIndexName(idxISBN).Checked = True
            Case idxTitle
                ' assign the index
                mclsTitles.Index = IndexTitle
                ' set up menu check marks
                mnuDataIndexName(idxTitle).Checked = True
                mnuDataIndexName(idxISBN).Checked = False
        End Select

        ' refresh display
        GetData

ProcExit:
        Screen.MousePointer = vbDefault
        Exit Sub

ProcError:
        MsgBox Err.Description, vbExclamation
        Resume ProcExit

End Sub

Private Sub mnuDataSeek_Click()
' seek a record
On Error GoTo ProcError

        Dim strMsg As String
        Dim strResult As String

        Screen.MousePointer = vbHourglass

        ' prompt for a value
        strMsg = "Enter a value to search for:"
        strResult = InputBox$(strMsg)

        ' seek for the record
        mclsTitles.SeekRecord strResult

        ' refresh display
        GetData

ProcExit:
        Screen.MousePointer = vbDefault
        Exit Sub

ProcError:
        MsgBox Err.Description, vbExclamation
```

continued on next page

continued from previous page
```
    Resume ProcExit

End Sub
```

6. Modify the declarations section of the **CTitles** class to include the new enumeration for the index and to modify the error enumeration for new error messages.

```
Option Explicit

' The CTitles class provides a light wrapper
' around the database and record for the
' Titles table in the Biblio database

' Database and recordset objects
Private mdb As Database
Private mrs As Recordset

' Fields
' title
Private mstrTitle As String
' year - note use of string for
' assignment to text box
Private mstrYearPublished As String
' ISBN number
Private mstrISBN As String
' PubID - also a string
Private mstrPubID As String

' Move method constants
Public Enum CTitlesMove
    FirstRecord = 1
    LastRecord = 2
    NextRecord = 3
    PreviousRecord = 4
End Enum

' Index constants
Public Enum CTitlesIndex
    IndexISBN = 0
    IndexTitle = 1
End Enum

' Error constants
' Note: RaiseClassError method provides the strings
' because you cannot assign a string to an Enum
Public Enum CTitlesError
    ErrRecordNotFound = vbObjectError + 1000 + 10
    ErrInvalidMoveType = vbObjectError + 1000 + 11
    ErrNoRecords = vbObjectError + 1000 + 12
    ErrInvalidIndex = vbObjectError + 1000 + 13
End Enum
```

7. Change the `Class_Initialize` procedure so that a table-type recordset is created rather than a dynaset-type recordset. Only the table-type recordset supports the `Seek` method. The only thing required to change to a table-type recordset is to change the `dbOpenDynaset` constant to `dbOpenTable`.

```
Private Sub Class_Initialize()

    ' open the database and recordset

    Dim strDBName As String

    ' Get the database name and open the database.
    ' BiblioPath is a function in READINI.BAS
    strDBName = BiblioPath()
    Set mdb = DBEngine.Workspaces(0).OpenDatabase(strDBName)

    ' Open the recordset.
    Set mrs = mdb.OpenRecordset( _
        "Titles", dbOpenTable, dbSeeChanges, dbOptimistic)

    ' Raise an error if there is no data
    If mrs.BOF Then
        RaiseClassError ErrNoRecords
    End If

    ' fetch the first record to the properties
    GetCurrentRecord

End Sub
```

8. The `RaiseClassError` procedure has had new sections added to the `Select...Case` block for the newly added errors.

```
Private Sub RaiseClassError(lngErrorNumber As CTitlesError)
' Note: DAO errors are passed out as-is

    Dim strDescription As String
    Dim strSource As String

    ' assign the description for the error
    Select Case lngErrorNumber
        Case ErrRecordNotFound
            strDescription = "The record was not found."
        Case ErrInvalidMoveType
            strDescription = "Invalid move operation."
        Case ErrNoRecords
            strDescription = "There are no records " _
                & "in the Titles table."
        Case ErrInvalidIndex
            strDescription = "Invalid Index Name."
        Case Else
            ' If this executes, it's a coding error in
            ' the class module, but having the case is
            ' useful for debugging.
            strDescription = "There is no message for this error."
```

continued on next page

continued from previous page

```
    End Select

    ' build the Source property for the error
    strSource = App.EXEName & ".CTitles"

    ' raise it
    Err.Raise lngErrorNumber, strSource, strDescription

End Sub
```

9. Add the `IndexName` and `Index` properties. The `IndexName` property is used to determine the current index for the recordset. The `Index` property changes the index based on the value provided in the `lngIndex` parameter.

```
Public Property Get IndexName() As String

    IndexName = mrs.Index

End Property

Public Property Let Index(lngIndex As CTitlesIndex)
' unlike the field values, this is validated when assigned

    Dim vntBookmark As Variant

    ' save a bookmark
    vntBookmark = mrs.Bookmark
    ' assign the index
    Select Case lngIndex
        Case IndexISBN
            mrs.Index = "PrimaryKey"
        Case IndexTitle
            mrs.Index = "Title"
        Case Else
            ' invalid, raise an error
            RaiseClassError ErrInvalidIndex
    End Select

    ' return to old record
    mrs.Bookmark = vntBookmark

End Property
```

10. Add the `SeekRecord` method. This method stores a bookmark and seeks the value passed in the `strValue` parameter. If a matching record is found, it is fetched. If no matching record is found, the saved bookmark is used to restore the record pointer to the original position.

```
Public Sub SeekRecord(strValue As String)
' seek to the indicated record based on the current index

    Dim vntBookmark As Variant

    ' mark the current record
```

```
vntBookmark = mrs.Bookmark
' seek, the first operator is the comparison,
' the following represent the field(s) in the index
mrs.Seek "=", strValue
' check for match
If Not mrs.NoMatch Then
    ' found it, now fetch it
    GetCurrentRecord
Else
    ' not found, return to prior location
    mrs.Bookmark = vntBookmark
    ' raise the not found error
    RaiseClassError ErrRecordNotFound
End If

End Sub
```

How It Works

The `Seek` method takes two or more parameters. The first parameter specifies the comparison operator (normally =), and the following parameters are the values for the fields in the index. The `Index Property Let` procedure in the `CTitles` class allows you to assign the current index for the recordset, and `SeekRecord` will search for a value. Both procedures use bookmarks to store and, if necessary, return to the original record.

Comments

You cannot set indexes or use the `Seek` method with dynaset- or snapshot-type `Recordset` objects. To find a record in a dynaset or snapshot recordset, use one of the `Find` methods: `FindFirst`, `FindNext`, `FindPrevious`, or `FindLast`. Because these methods do not use indexes, they are much slower than `Seek` operations with table-type recordsets. You also cannot use `Seek` on remote server tables, because these cannot be opened as table-type recordsets.

In most cases, it is much faster to create a new dynaset- or snapshot-type recordset than to use either a `Find` method or the `Seek` method. You do this by building a SQL statement that includes a `WHERE` clause specifying the records you want to retrieve. If the database engine can find a useful index for the query, it will use that index to speed up the query.

See Chapter 3, "SQL," for details on creating SQL statements and Chapter 4 for more information on choosing and defining indexes.

COMPLEXITY
BEGINNING

2.7 How do I...
Determine how many records are in a dynaset- or snapshot-type recordset?

Problem

I need to know how many records are in a recordset I've created. For table-type recordsets, this is easy—I just use the value of the `RecordCount` property. But when I try this with a dynaset- or snapshot-type recordset, I can't predict what value will be returned. Sometimes, it's the correct count, but other times it's not. How can I reliably determine the number of records in a dynaset- or snapshot-type recordset?

Technique

The system tables in a Microsoft Access database include information about the number of records in every table in the database. As records are added or deleted, the table is continuously updated by the Jet engine. You can determine the number of records in the table at any time by checking the `RecordCount` property of the `TableDef`. Unlike a table, dynaset- and snapshot-type recordsets are temporary recordsets. You can't obtain a record count by checking a `TableDef`.

You can retrieve the `RecordCount` property of a dynaset- or snapshot-type recordset, but the value it returns depends on several factors in addition to the number of records actually in the recordset. The only way the Jet engine has to determine how many records are in a dynaset- or snapshot-type recordset is by counting them. To count them, it has to move through the records, one by one, until it reaches the end of the recordset. When the Jet engine creates a dynaset- or snapshot-type recordset, however, it does not automatically count the records because counting the records in a large recordset could take a long time. If you retrieve the `RecordCount` property immediately after you create a dynaset- or snapshot-type recordset, therefore, you're guaranteed to get back one of two values—`0` if the recordset is empty or `1` if the recordset has at least one record.

To get an accurate count, your code must tell the Jet engine to count the records. Do this by executing the recordset's MoveLast method. After a MoveLast, you can retrieve the RecordCount with the confidence that the value is accurate. In the case of a dynaset-type recordset, if you add or delete records, the Jet engine keeps track of them for you, and any subsequent looks at RecordCount will give you the correct current count.

Steps

Open and run the project HT207.VBP. You will see the form shown in Figure 2.8. This form shows the number of records in the BIBLIO.MDB Authors table. The first box reports the number of records reported immediately after Authors is opened as a table-type recordset. The second box shows the number of records reported immediately after a dynaset is opened with the SQL statement SELECT Au_ID FROM Authors—a statement that returns a dynaset consisting of the entire table, the same set of records that is in the table-type recordset reported in the first box. The third box shows the record count from the dynaset after its MoveLast method has been used. Note that the first and third boxes have the same number (which might be different on your system). The second box, reporting the dynaset record count before the MoveLast, shows a count of 1.

1. Create a new project called HT207.VBP. Create the objects and properties listed in Table 2.8, and save the form as HT207.FRM.

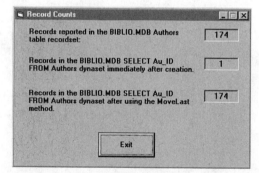

Figure 2.8. The Record Counts form.

Table 2.8. Objects and properties for Form1.

OBJECT	PROPERTY	SETTING
Form	Name	Form1
	Caption	"Record Counter"
CommandButton	Name	cmdExit
	Cancel	True
	Default	True
	Caption	"Exit"
Label	Name	lblTable
	Alignment	2 (Center)
	BorderStyle	1 (Fixed Single)
Label	lblDynasetCreate	Name
	Alignment	2 (Center)
	BorderStyle	1 (Fixed Single)
Label	lblDynasetMoved	Name
	Alignment	2 (Center)
	BorderStyle	1 (Fixed Single)
Label	Name	Label1
	Caption	"Records reported in the BIBLIO.MDB Authors table recordset:"
Label	Name	Label2
	Caption	"Records in the BIBLIO.MDB SELECT Au_ID FROM Authors dynaset immediately after creation."
Label	Name	Label3
	Caption	"Records in the BIBLIO.MDB SELECT Au_ID FROM Authors dynaset after using the MoveLast method."

2. Add READINI.BAS to your project.

3. Add the `Form_Load` event procedure. `Form_Load` opens the database, opens table and dynaset recordsets, and gets record counts for both recordsets. It then uses `MoveLast` to go to the end of the dynaset and gets the record count again. Finally, it inserts each of the record counts into label controls on the form.

```
Private Sub Form_Load()
On Error GoTo ProcError

    Dim strDBName As String
```

```
Dim strSQL As String
Dim db As Database
Dim rsTable As Recordset
Dim rsDynaset As Recordset

' Get the database name and open the database.
' BiblioPath is a function in READINI.BAS
strDBName = BiblioPath()

Set db = DBEngine.Workspaces(0).OpenDatabase(strDBName)
Set rsTable = db.OpenRecordset("Authors", dbOpenTable)
lblTable = rsTable.RecordCount

strSQL = "SELECT Au_ID FROM Authors"
Set rsDynaset = db.OpenRecordset(strSQL, dbOpenDynaset)
lblDynasetCreate = rsDynaset.RecordCount
rsDynaset.MoveLast
lblDynasetMoved = rsDynaset.RecordCount

ProcExit:
    On Error Resume Next
    ' clean up
    rsDynaset.Close
    rsTable.Close
    db.Close
    Exit Sub

ProcError:
    MsgBox Err.Description
    Resume ProcExit

End Sub
```

4. Insert the following code as the `Click` event of `cmdExit`:

```
Private Sub cmdExit_Click()
    Unload Me
End Sub
```

How It Works

The table-type recordset allows you to check the `RecordCount` property immediately after it is created, but with a snapshot- or dynaset-type recordset, you must first access all the records before you can get an accurate count. This is typically done via the `MoveLast` method.

Comments

One common reason for wanting an accurate record count is to use the count as the control for a `For...Next` loop to cycle through the entire recordset, as in this code fragment:

```
myRecordset.MoveLast
n = myRecordset.RecordCount
```

continued on next page

continued from previous page

```
myRecordset.MoveFirst
for i = 1 to n
    ' do something
    myRecordset.MoveNext
next i
```

The difficulties with getting and keeping accurate record counts make it inadvisable to use code like that—especially in shared data environments where the record count of a table can change the instant after you've retrieved it. This fragment illustrates a more reliable way to accomplish the same goal:

```
myRecordset.MoveFirst
Do While Not myRecordset.EOF
    ' do something
    myRecordset.MoveNext
Loop
```

This loop executes until the last record in the recordset has been processed (when `myRecordset.EOF` becomes `True`), and it does not depend on a potentially unstable record count.

COMPLEXITY
INTERMEDIATE

2.8 How do I...
Handle data access object errors?

Problem

When I access a database through Visual Basic, I have limited control over the environment. A user might move a database file or another program might have made unexpected changes to the database. I need my programs to be able to detect errors that occur and handle them in the context of the program. How do I accomplish this task with Visual Basic?

Technique

When an error occurs in a Visual Basic program, control passes to error-handling logic. Unless you have enabled an error handler, Visual Basic uses its default handler, which displays a message about the error—one that is sometimes useful, but often not—and terminates the application.

Clearly, the default handling is not acceptable. Fortunately, Visual Basic provides tools you can use to build your own error traps and handlers. Although any Visual Basic application should trap and handle runtime errors, it is especially important in database applications in which many error conditions can be expected to occur. Visual Basic error-trapping is enabled with the `On Error` statement. There are two basic forms of the `On Error` statement:

```
On Error Goto label
On Error Resume Next
```

In the first form, when a runtime error occurs, Visual Basic transfers control of the application to the location specified by *label*. In the second form, Visual Basic continues execution with the line following the line where the error occurred. When an error trap is enabled and an error occurs, Visual Basic performs the action indicated by the most recent **On Error** statement in the execution path. Listing 2.1 shows a hypothetical call tree and several variations of how error handlers are enabled and activated.

Listing 2.1. Trapping errors.

```
Sub SubA()

    ...other code
    SubB

End Sub

Sub SubB()
On Error Goto ProcError

  SubC

ProcExit:
    Exit Sub

ProcError:
    MsgBox "Error: " & Err.Number & vbCrLf & Err.Description
    Resume ProcExit

End Sub

SubC

    ...other code
    SubD

End Sub

SubD()
On Error Resume Next

    ...code

End Sub
```

Understanding the path of execution in this code fragment is important to understanding how error handlers are activated:

✔ In SubA there is no error handler. If an error occurs before the call to SubB, Visual Basic's default handler displays a message and terminates the application.

✔ SubB uses the On Error Goto form. If an error occurs in this routine, control is transferred to the statement following the ProcError label.

✔ SubC has no error handler. However, when it is called from SubB, the error handler in SubB is still enabled, so an error in SubC also transfers control to the statement following the ProcError label in SubB.

✔ SubD uses the On Error Resume Next form. If an error occurs in this procedure, code within the procedure needs to detect and handle the error.

WARNING

Errors in Class_Terminate events and most form and control events are fatal to your application if they are untrapped, so it is especially important that you include error-handling logic in these procedures.

Errors generated by Visual Basic and by components of an application—including the Jet database engine—are associated with error numbers. You can obtain the error number, which tells you the nature of the error, by reading the Number property of the Err object. You can read additional information about the error from the Description property. After you know the type of error, you can take appropriate action to handle it. This is typically done with a Select Case block.

NOTE

For backward compatibility, Visual Basic still supports the outdated Err and Error statements and functions. However, any new code should use the Err object.

The code fragment in Listing 2.2 illustrates how you might handle some common errors that occur in a multiuser environment. (See Chapter 12 for a complete discussion of working with a multiuser database application.)

Listing 2.2. Error handling.

```
Sub DAOCode()
On Error Goto ProcError

    ...code

ProcExit:
    Exit Sub

ProcError
    Dim strMsg As String
    Select Case Err.Number
```

```
            Case 3197
                ' Another user changed the data since the last time
                ' the recordset was updated
                strMsg = "The data in this record was changed by " & _
                    "another user." & _
                    vbCrLf & "Do you want to overwrite those changes?"
                If MsgBox(strMsg, vbYesNo or vbQuestion or vbDefaultButton2) _
                    = vbYes _
        Then
                    ' VB only generates the error on the first attempt
                    ' Resume reexecutes the line that caused the error
                    Resume
                Else
                    ' refresh the existing data
                    rs.Requery
                    DisplayData
                    Resume ProcExit
                End If
            Case 3260
                ' locked by another user
                strMsg = "The record is currently locked by another user."
                ' control continues at end of block
            Case Else
                ' default
                strMsg = "Error: " & Err.Number & vbCrLf & Err.Description
        End Select

        MsgBox strMsg, vbExclamation

        Resume ProcExit

End Sub
```

An error handler must execute a statement that clears the error. Table 2.9 lists the methods of clearing an error.

Table 2.9. Statements that clear an error.

STATEMENT	EFFECT
Resume	Reexecutes the line that generated the error.
Resume Next	Resumes execution at the line that follows the line that generated the error.
Resume *label*	Resumes execution at the line following the named label.
Resume *number*	Resumes execution at the line with the indicated number.
Exit Sub	Exits immediately from the current subroutine.
Exit Function	Exits immediately from the current function.
Exit Property	Exits immediately from the current property.
On Error	Resets error-handling logic.
Err.Clear	Clears the error without otherwise affecting program execution.
End	Terminates execution of the program.

ERRORS IN CLASS MODULES

It is good programming practice to separate data management code in class modules from user interface code in forms. To maintain this separation, it is important that you do not simply display a message if an error occurs in a class module. There are two types of error situations that can occur in a class module.

A class can detect an error condition (such as the violation of a validation rule). In this case, the class module should call the `Raise` method of the `Err` object and set the `Number`, `Description`, `Source`, and—if a help file is available—the appropriate help properties.

A class can also trap errors raised by the database engine. These can be much more difficult to handle. The sheer number of possible errors makes it impractical in most applications to reassign and describe these errors, so most applications simply regenerate them.

In either case, the code in the class module should, if possible, attempt to correct the error before raising it.

Steps

Open and run the project HT208.VBP. Three errors will occur in succession. For each, the message reporting the error gives you the error number, error description, and line number where the error occurred. Figure 2.9 shows the first of these errors.

1. Create a new project called HT208.VBP. Use **Form1** to create the objects and properties listed in Table 2.10, and save the form as HT208.FRM.

Table 2.10. Objects and properties for Form1.

OBJECT	PROPERTY	SETTING
Form	Name	Form1
	Caption	"Errors"

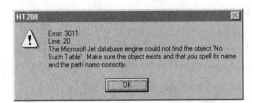

Figure 2.9. The HT208 error message.

2. Add the file READINI.BAS to your project.

3. Add the following code as the **Load** event of **Form1**. This code generates three errors. Line 20 generates an error because there is no such table as No Such Table. Line 40 generates an error because there is no such field as **No Such Field**. Line 60 generates an error because the **Year Published** field requires a numeric value. Each error causes execution to branch to the label **LoadError**. The code beginning with **LoadError** displays an informative message, then executes a **Resume Next**. The **Resume Next** transfers execution back to the line following the line that caused the error.

```
Private Sub Form_Load()
On Error GoTo ProcError

    Dim db As Database
    Dim dbName As String
    Dim rs As Recordset
    Dim s As String

    ' Get the database name and open the database.
    ' BiblioPath is a function in READINI.BAS
5   dbName = BiblioPath()
10  Set db = DBEngine.Workspaces(0).OpenDatabase(dbName)

20  Set rs = db.OpenRecordset("No Such Table", dbOpenTable)
30  Set rs = db.OpenRecordset("Titles", dbOpenTable)
40  s = rs![No Such Field]
50  rs.Edit
60  rs![Year Published] = "XYZ"
70  rs.Update
80  End

Exit Sub

ProcError:
    MsgBox "Error: " & Err.Number & vbCrLf & _
        "Line: " & Erl & vbCrLf & _
        Err.Description, vbExclamation
Resume Next

End Sub
```

NOTE

Line numbers are used here to help illustrate the error handler. Few programmers actually use them in production code, although they can be helpful for debugging.

How It Works

When Visual Basic encounters a runtime error, it transfers control of the application to the error-handling code you specify by using the On Error statement. You have a choice of inline handling using On Error Resume Next or centralized handling using On Error Goto. Either way, it's up to you to determine the type of error generated and the appropriate action to take for that error.

ERRORS COLLECTION

It is possible for a single statement in DAO code to generate several errors. You can examine these errors by iterating the DAO Errors collection, as shown in the following code fragment:

```
For Each Error In Errors
    Debug.Print Err.Number & " - " & Err.Description
Next ' Error
```

Comments

There are hundreds of potential runtime errors that can occur in a Visual Basic application, and you are unlikely to be able to anticipate all of them. With experience and careful coding, you can be prepared for the most common problems, but you should expect that from time to time your application will encounter a situation you did not explicitly plan for. What is important in this situation is for your general error-handling code to provide as much information as possible to the user and the opportunity to correct the problem.

You might also find it useful to write errors to a log file. Examining an error log will provide you with information you can use to build more robust error-handling procedures.

CHAPTER 3
SQL

3

SQL

How do I...

3.14 Create a new table with data from existing tables?
3.15 Modify a table's structure?
3.16 Create a crosstab query?

The Structured Query Language (SQL) is a standard language for defining and manipulating relational databases. Virtually all relational database products on the market today support SQL. The Jet database engine, the heart of Visual Basic and Microsoft Access, uses SQL as its primary definition and manipulation method.

For truly flexible, powerful database programming, SQL is a vital element. You *can* work with Visual Basic databases without SQL, of course; the Jet database engine provides a robust set of objects and capabilities to allow you to accomplish in Visual Basic almost anything that can be accomplished in SQL.

Because of the versatility of the Jet database engine, the benefits of SQL are not readily apparent. To help you visualize the power that SQL can add to your database applications, examine the following example. Assume that you want to delete all the records with a `ShipmentDate` earlier than January 1, 1993, from the Orders table in your ACCOUNTS.MDB database. Your program could delete the records this way by using Jet data access objects (commonly known as DAO objects):

```
Dim dbfAccounts as Database
Dim recOrders as Recordset
Set dbfAccounts = DBEngine.Workspaces(0).OpenDatabase("ACCOUNTS.MDB")
Set recOrders = dbfAccounts.OpenRecordset("Orders", dbOpenTable)
If recOrders.RecordCount > 0 Then
    recOrders.MoveFirst
    Do Until recOrders.EOF
        If recOrders("ShipmentDate") < #1/1/1993# Then recOrders.Delete
        recOrders.MoveNext
    Loop
End If
recOrders.Close
dbfAccounts.Close
```

Now, examine the following SQL example. (For an explanation of the `dbfAccounts.Execute` statement in this example, see How-To 3.13.)

```
Dim dbfAccounts as Database
Set dbfAccounts = DBEngine.Workspaces(0).OpenDatabase("ACCOUNTS.MDB")
dbfAccounts.Execute("DELETE Orders.* FROM Orders " & _
             "WHERE Orders.ShipmentDate < #1/1/1993#")
dbfAccounts.Close
```

Both examples achieve the same result. However, the SQL result not only uses less code, but also in most cases provides faster results than the Jet database example. The first example, employing data access object (DAO) techniques, is forced to retrieve the entire table and then check each record one by one, deleting it if needed. The second example, however, selects, checks, and deletes in one step, allowing the database, rather than Visual Basic, to manage the deletion.

Although the prospect of learning another language might be disquieting, you'll find that most SQL programming tasks can be accomplished with a very basic level of SQL training. The How-To's in this chapter illustrate the most important SQL statements and techniques. Furthermore, if you have a copy of Microsoft Access, you don't need to *learn* SQL to *use* SQL in Visual Basic. Access can write even the most difficult SQL for you, by way of the various query design tools and wizards packaged with the application.

3.1 Create Recordsets by Selecting Records from Single Tables

The SELECT statement is the basic building block for retrieving records from a database with SQL. In this How-To, you'll learn how to create a SELECT statement that specifies fields, records, and a sort order.

3.2 Select Unique Field Values in a SQL Query

The SELECT statement normally returns one record for every record in the source table that meets the designated criteria. This How-To shows you how to modify the basic SELECT statement to ensure that the resulting recordset contains no duplicated records.

3.3 Use Variables and Visual Basic Functions in a SQL Query

The choice between SQL and "regular" Visual Basic code is not an either-or proposition. You can combine Visual Basic variables with SQL statements to create a powerful data management environment. In this How-To, you'll extend the basic SELECT statement with variables.

3.4 Use Wildcards and Ranges of Values in a SQL Query

Much of the power of SQL comes from the many ways you can specify recordsets. This How-To demonstrates the use of wildcards and the Between operator in SQL SELECT statements.

3.5 Define and Use a Parameter Query

The optimization process Microsoft Access uses on queries is more effective if the query is stored in the database and used multiple times. That can be difficult, however, when the query's parameters change often. A parameter query can bridge that difficult gap to give you both speed and flexibility, and with a remarkable ease of programming. This How-To demonstrates how to create and use a parameter query involving a single parameter.

3.6 Create Recordsets by Joining Fields from Multiple Tables

A properly designed relational database splits data into multiple tables, then relates those tables through key fields. Visual Basic SQL can "cement" fields from multiple tables together into dynaset- and snapshot-type recordsets. This How-To shows the technique for joining fields from multiple tables into unified recordsets through SQL INNER JOIN operations.

3.7 Find Records in a Table Without Corresponding Entries in a Related Table

You might need to identify records that have no corresponding entries in a related table—perhaps you're looking for Customer table records with no records in the Orders table, for example. This How-To shows how to use a SQL OUTER JOIN statement to locate these orphans.

3.8 Retrieve Information Such as Counts, Averages, and Sums and Display Them by Binding Them to a Data Control

Sometimes you don't need the records themselves, but just some statistics on records that meet certain criteria. This How-To shows you how to use SQL aggregate functions in SELECT statements to retrieve record counts, averages, sums, and other statistics.

3.9 Create a Recordset Consisting of Records That Have Duplicate Values

It's often useful to find duplicated values in a table—for example, you might want to find all cases in which the same customer was invoiced more than once on the same day. This How-To shows how to find the duplicate values in a table.

3.10 Use Visual Basic Functions Within a SQL Statement

Although SQL is a flexible and powerful method of database manipulation, sometimes extra power is needed. Access and Visual Basic can make use of Visual Basic functions directly in a SQL query, ensuring your complete control over your data. This How-To illustrates how to employ Visual Basic functions in a SELECT query.

3.11 Make Bulk Updates to Database Records

In addition to SELECT statements, which retrieve recordsets from a database, SQL also provides a rich set of action statements. Action statements let you modify the contents of database tables. In this How-To, you'll see how to change values in existing records through SQL.

3.12 Create and Delete Tables

You can use SQL to create empty tables with a list of fields you specify. You can also use SQL to delete tables from your database. This How-To shows you how to accomplish both of these operations.

3.13 Append and Delete Records

Another type of action statement enables you to create a recordset, then append the records in that recordset to an existing table. In this How-To, you'll see how to accomplish this useful task, as well as how to delete records from a table.

3.14 Create a New Table with Data from Existing Tables

SQL action statements can also create new tables from records in existing tables. In this How-To, you'll create a new table from a recordset that you specify through SQL.

3.15 Modify a Table's Structure

SQL's capabilities don't stop at data manipulation. The data definition capabilities of SQL allow a great deal of control over a database's structure, as well as its data. This How-To demonstrates several ways a table can easily be modified with SQL statements.

3.16 Create a Crosstab Query

A crosstab report allows data to be cross-indexed in a compact, spreadsheet-like format. Once a difficult report to design, crosstab reports are now quick and easy. In this How-To, you'll receive an introduction in the ways of crosstab query design.

COMPLEXITY
BEGINNING

3.1 How do I...
Create recordsets by selecting records from single tables?

Problem

I want to select a subset of the records in a table, based on criteria I specify. I don't need to see all the fields for each record, but I do want to specify the order in which the records appear. How can I accomplish this task in Visual Basic by using SQL?

Technique

You create recordsets from data in tables through the SQL SELECT statement. You can embed the SQL statement in your Visual Basic code, or you can use it as the `RecordSource` for a data control.

The SQL SELECT Statement

A basic single-table SQL SELECT statement has four basic parts, as shown in Table 3.1. Parts 1 and 2 are required in every SELECT statement. Parts 3 and 4 are optional. If you omit Part 3, the record-selection criteria, your recordset will consist of all the records in the table. If you omit Part 4, the sort order, the records will be ordered as they are in the table.

Table 3.1. The four parts of a basic SQL SELECT statement.

PURPOSE	EXAMPLE
1. Specify which fields you want to see	SELECT [Name], [Telephone]
2. Specify the table	FROM [Publishers]
3. Specify the record-selection criteria	WHERE [State] = "NY"
4. Specify the sort order	ORDER BY [Name]

Combining the four example lines in the table produces this complete SQL SELECT statement:

```
SELECT [Name], [Telephone] FROM [Publishers] WHERE [State] = "NY" ORDER BY [Name]
```

This example is from the BIBLIO.MDB database supplied with Visual Basic. That database has a table named Publishers. Among the fields in the Publishers table are Name, Telephone, and State.

In the example, the field names and the table name are surrounded by square brackets, and the text NY is enclosed by quotation marks. These syntax requirements help the Jet database engine interpret the SQL statement. Table 3.2 lists the enclosure syntax requirements for SQL statements.

Table 3.2. The enclosure syntax requirements for SQL statements.

ELEMENT	ENCLOSURES	EXAMPLES	WHEN REQUIRED
Numeric data	None		
Text data	Single or double	"NY" or 'NY'	Always quotation marks
Date data	Pound signs	#6/11/1996#	Always
Field names	Square brackets	[Name], [Zip Code]	When name has spaces or punctuation
Table names	Square brackets	[Publisher Comments]	When name has spaces or punctuation

CAPITALIZATION DOESN'T MATTER

In the Table 3.1 example, the SQL keywords (SELECT, FROM, WHERE, and ORDER BY) appear in capital letters. This is a convention, and it is completely optional. Neither Visual Basic nor the Jet database engine cares about the capitalization of SQL keywords or about the capitalization of table names and field names.

Note that in the example from Table 3.1, the field and table names do not require the square brackets, because all the names consist of a single word with no spaces or punctuation characters. The brackets are optional when there are no spaces or punctuation.

Multiple Fields and Multiple Criteria

If you need more than one field in the returned recordset, specify the fields by separating the field names with commas. Do the same to designate multiple-field sorts. The following example returns three fields sorted first by the **State** field, then by the **City** field:

```
SELECT [Name], [City], [State], FROM [Publishers]
ORDER BY [State], [City]
```

Specify multiple criteria through the **AND** and **OR** keywords. Assume that you have a table consisting of invoices with the fields shown in Table 3.3.

Table 3.3. Fields for a hypothetical Invoices table.

FIELD	TYPE
Invoice Number	Numeric
Issue Date	Date
Amount	Currency
Customer Number	Numeric

You want to create a recordset consisting of invoices to customer number 3267 that were dated on or after August 1, 1995. Your SQL **SELECT** statement might look like this:

```
SELECT [Invoice Number], [Issue Date], [Amount] FROM [Invoices]
WHERE [Customer Number] = 3267 AND [Issue Date] >= #8/1/95#
ORDER BY [Issue Date]
```

Notice the use of the greater-than-or-equal-to operator (>=) in that statement. SQL comparison operators mimic those available in Visual Basic. Also notice that because the customer number is a numeric field, not a text field, the customer number is not enclosed in quotation marks.

In another situation, perhaps you want to find all invoices issued to customers 3267 and 3396. Your statement might be this:

```
SELECT [Invoice Number], [Issue Date], [Amount] FROM [Invoices]
WHERE [Customer Number] = 3267 OR [Customer Number] = 3396
ORDER BY [Issue Date]
```

You can combine **AND** and **OR** to select those invoices to customers 3267 and 3396 that were issued on or after August 1, 1995:

```
SELECT [Invoice Number], [Issue Date], [Amount] FROM [Invoices]
WHERE ([Customer Number] = 3267 OR [Customer Number] = 3396)
AND [Issue Date] >= #8/1/95# ORDER BY [Issue Date]
```

In the last example, the OR'd criteria are enclosed in parentheses. You do this to specify to the Jet engine the order in which it should evaluate the criteria. In this situation, "the ORs go together." You want to select the invoices that were sent to either customer after the specified date.

Using SQL Statements with the Data Control

When you use the data control, you set the control's RecordSource property to specify the records that the control will display. The RecordSource property can be set to a table, to a stored query, or to a SQL SELECT statement. When you use a SQL SELECT statement as the RecordSource, you can specify records within a table by criteria you specify, and you can specify the order in which the records are presented. Because you cannot use indexes with the data control, the ability to define the sort order is an important one.

Using SQL Statements with OpenRecordset

The Database object includes a method called OpenRecordset, with which you can create a dynaset or snapshot by using a SQL statement as the first argument. The SQL statement must be in the form of a string (that is, enclosed in quotation marks).

Assume that you have declared dbfTemp to be a Database object and recTemp to be a Recordset object and that you have set dbfTemp to point to a database. You can then create the recordset with the following statement (the statement must be all on one line, of course):

```
Set recTemp = dbfTemp.OpenRecordset("SELECT [Name], [Telephone] FROM [Publishers]⇐
WHERE [State] = 'NY' ORDER BY [Name]")
```

After this statement has executed, recTemp represents a set of records that meet the criteria specified in the SQL statement. You can use any of the Recordset object's methods to work with these records.

Notice in the previous example that because the entire SQL statement is enclosed in "double" quotation marks, the text data within the SQL statement requires "single" quotation marks. If the text being enclosed contains single quotation marks, you should use a pair of double quotation marks. For example, assume that you are looking for records in which the company name is Joe's Beanery. The WHERE clause in your SQL statement would be this:

```
WHERE [Company Name] = "'Joe's Beanery'"
```

You can also assign the **SELECT** statement to a string variable and then use the string variable as the argument to the **OpenRecordset** method. Assume that **sqlStmt** has been declared as a string and that the following assignment statement appears all on one line:

```
sqlStmt = "SELECT [Name], [Telephone] FROM [Publishers] WHERE [State] = 'NY'⇐
ORDER BY [Name]" Set recTemp = dbfTemp.OpenRecordset(sqlStmt)
```

Because SQL statements can get very long—and you can't use Visual Basic's line-continuation feature in the middle of a quoted string—assigning SQL statements to strings often produces more readable code. You can build the string with the concatenation operator:

```
sqlStmt = "SELECT [Invoice Number], [Issue Date], [Amount] FROM [Invoices]"
sqlStmt = sqlStmt & " WHERE ([Customer Number] = 3267 OR [Customer Number] = 3396)"
sqlStmt = sqlStmt & " AND {Issue Date] >= #8/1/95# ORDER BY [Issue Date]"
Set recTemp = dbfTemp.OpenRecordset(sqlStmt)
```

Steps

Open the project SELECT1.VBP. Change the **DatabaseName** property of the data control **Data1** to point to the copy of BIBLIO.MDB installed on your system (probably in the directory where VB.EXE is installed). Then run the project. The form shown in Figure 3.1 appears. Scroll the top list to see the publishers in the database. Scroll the bottom list to see the titles in the database.

1. Create a new project called SELECT1.VBP. Use **Form1** to create the objects and properties listed in Table 3.4, and save the form as SELECT1.FRM.

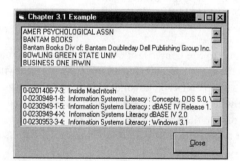

Figure 3.1. The main form for the Chapter 3.1 example.

Table 3.4. Objects and properties for the Simple SELECTer form.

OBJECT	PROPERTY	SETTING
Form	Name	Form1
	Caption	"Chapter 3.1 Example"
CommandButton	Name	cmdClose
	Caption	"Close"
	Default	True
ListBox	Name	lstTitles
Data	Name	dtaData
	Caption	"dtaData"
	RecordSource	"SELECT [Company Name] FROM [Publishers]
		WHERE STATE = 'NY' ORDER BY [Company Name]"
	Visible	False
DBList	Name	dlstPublishers
	RowSource	dtaData
	ListField	"Company Name"

2. Add the following code to the declarations section of **Form1**. Ensure that your **BIBLIO_PATH** constant points to the location of your copy of BIBLIO.MDB, shipped with Visual Basic.

```
Option Explicit

'Change the following to point to your copy of BIBLIO.MDB.
Private Const BIBLIO_PATH = "C:\Program Files\DevStudio\VB\⇐
Biblio.MDB"
```

3. Add the following code to the **Load** event of **Form1**. The **Form_Load** event will set the **dtaData** data control's **DatabaseName** property, allowing it to retrieve data. Then, a snapshot-type **Recordset** object containing records from the Titles table where the **[Years Published]** field is equal to **1993** or **1994** is created, and the titles are added to the **lstTitles** list box. More detail about types of recordsets is provided in Chapter 2, "Accessing a Database with Data Access Objects."

```
PPrivate Sub Form_Load()
    Dim dbfBiblio As Database, recSelect As Recordset
    Dim strSQL As String

    'Set up the error handler.
    On Error GoTo FormLoadError

        'Get the database name & open the database.
```

```
        dtaData.DatabaseName = BIBLIO_PATH
        dtaData.Refresh
        Set dbfBiblio = DBEngine.Workspaces(0).OpenDatabase(BIBLIO_PATH)

        'Open a snapshot-type recordset on the [Titles] table,
        ' selecting only those titles published in 1993 or 1994,
        ' sorting by the ISBN number. Note the use of the line
        ' continuation character (_), used throughout the
        ' examples, to make code more readable.
        strSQL = "SELECT [Title], [ISBN] FROM [Titles] " & _
            "WHERE [Year Published] = 1993 Or [Year Published] = 1994 " & _
            "ORDER BY [ISBN]"

        'Create the recordset.
        Set recSelect = dbfBiblio.OpenRecordset(strSQL, dbOpenSnapshot)

        'Iterate through the recordset until the end of the file
        '(EOF) is reached.  Display each record in the unbound
        'list box lstTitles.
        If recSelect.RecordCount > 0 Then
            recSelect.MoveFirst
            Do Until recSelect.EOF
                lstTitles.AddItem recSelect![ISBN] & ":  " & _
                recSelect![Title]
recSelect.MoveNext
            Loop
        End If
    Exit Sub

FormLoadError:
    'If an error occurs, display it with a MsgBox command.
    MsgBox Err.Description, vbExclamation
    Exit Sub
End Sub
```

4. Add the following code to the `Click` event of `cmdClose`. The code in the `cmdClose_Click` event will end the application.

```
Private Sub cmdClose_Click()
    End
End Sub
```

How It Works

This How-To displays two lists, each showing the records in a recordset generated by a SQL **SELECT** statement. The top list is a **DBList** control, bound to the data control **dtaData**. The SQL statement that generates the recordset is supplied as the **RecordSource** property of the data control. The bottom list is an unbound **ListBox**. Its recordset is generated by the **OpenRecordset** method called from the **Form_Load** event.

Comments

As basic as the code for this example might seem, it becomes the foundation for data access in Visual Basic using SQL. No matter which method you may use—data controls, data access objects, or some of the other methods we will explore—Structured Query Language is the foundation on which these methods stand.

COMPLEXITY
BEGINNING

3.2 How do I...
Select unique field values in a SQL query?

Problem

I know that records in my table contain duplicate values in a particular field. How can I create a list of the unique values in the field?

Technique

By default, a SQL statement returns one row for each row in the table that meets the criteria specified in the statement's **WHERE** clause. If this action results in duplicate rows, those duplications are reproduced in the output recordset. For example, assume that your company provides products in several colors but uses the same product number for all colors of an otherwise identical product. You might have a [Products] table with this structure:

```
Product Number      Color
AGD44523            Green
AGD44523            Red
AGD44527            Red
```

You have two records with the [Product Number] field equal to AGD44523, each with a different entry in [Color]. Query the table with this SQL statement:

```
SELECT [Product Number] FROM [Products]
```

Included in your resulting recordset will be two identical rows, each with the value AGD44523.

But perhaps you want a list of unique product numbers, with no duplication. You can tell the Jet engine to filter duplicates out of the resulting recordset by inserting the keyword **DISTINCT** immediately after the word **SELECT**. You would rewrite your SQL statement like this:

```
SELECT DISTINCT [Product Number] FROM [Products]
```

That statement would result in a recordset with just one occurrence of the value AGD44523.

WHEN SQL IS SLOWER

The question "When is SQL faster?" is a complex one. In most cases, SQL methods will be faster than traditional procedural approaches. If an operation is time-critical, it will probably pay you to benchmark both the SQL approach and the procedural approach before making a decision on which to use in your production code.

An important class of exceptions to the generalization that "SQL is usually faster" is random access into an indexed table using the Seek method when each Seek operation is followed by operations on a small number of records. This code fragment provides an example:

```
Set recSelect = dbfTest.OpenRecordset("MyTable", dbOpenTable)
recSelect.Index = "MyIndex"
recSelect.Seek "=", intSomeValue
If Not recSelect.NoMatch Then
    ' Perform an action on the record sought
End If
' If needed, perform another Seek, or close the recordset &
move on.
```

In these cases, the traditional procedural methods are usually faster than SQL statements.

Steps

The BIBLIO.MDB database (supplied with Visual Basic) contains multiple publishers from the same state. Open the project SELECT2.VBP and run it. Initially, the list box on the form is blank. Click the Show All button, and the form then looks as shown in Figure 3.2; notice the occurrence of multiple CA entries. Click the Show Unique button, and the form looks as shown in Figure 3.3, with only one entry for each state.

1. Create a new project called SELECT2.VBP. Use **Form1** to create the objects and properties listed in Table 3.5, and save the form as SELECT2.FRM.

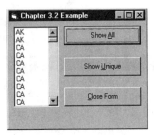

Figure 3.2. The main form after the Show All button is clicked.

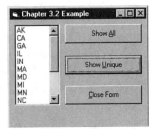

Figure 3.3. The main form after the Show Unique button is clicked.

Table 3.5. Objects and properties for the Distinct SELECTer form.

OBJECT	PROPERTY	SETTING
Form	Name	Form1
	Caption	"Chapter 3.2 Example"
CommandButton	Name	cmdClose
	Caption	"&Close Form"
CommandButton	Name	cmdShowUnique
	Caption	"Show &Unique"
CommandButton	CommandButton	cmdShowAll
	Caption	"Show &All"
Data	Name	dtaData
DBList	Name	dlstData
	DataSource	State
	RowSource	dtaData

2. Add the following code to the declarations section of Form1:

```
Option Explicit

'Ensure that the following points to your copy of BIBLIO.MDB.
Private Const BIBLIO_PATH = "C:\Program Files\DevStudio\VB\Biblio.MDB"
```

3. Add the following code to the Click event of cmdShowAll. This code builds a SQL statement that creates a recordset with one record for every [Publishers] table row with a non-NULL [State] field and passes the SQL statement to the RefreshControls subroutine.

```
Private Sub cmdShowAll_Click()
    Dim strSQL As String

    'Perform the simple SELECT query.  Note the lack of the
    'DISTINCT keyword (see the cmdShowUnique_Click event
    'for more info.)
    strSQL = "SELECT [State] FROM [Publishers] " & _
        "WHERE [State] IS NOT NULL " & _
        "ORDER BY [State]"

    'Set the RecordSource and refresh the data control & DBList control
    RefreshControls strSQL
End Sub
```

4. Add the following code to the Click event of cmdShowUnique. This code builds a SQL statement that creates a recordset with one record for every unique value in the [State] field of the [Publishers] table and passes the SQL statement to the RefreshControls subroutine.

```
Private Sub cmdShowUnique_Click()
Dim strSQL As String

    'Perform the SELECT DISTINCT query.  Since the DISTINCT keyword is
    'present, only the first instance of a given [State] value is
    'represented in the result set.
    strSQL = "SELECT DISTINCT [State] FROM [Publishers] " & _
        "WHERE [State] IS NOT NULL " & _
        "ORDER BY [State]"

    'Set the RecordSource and refresh the data control & DBList control
    RefreshControls strSQL
End Sub
```

5. Create the RefreshControls subroutine by entering the following code into Form1. This routine assigns the SQL statement received as the argument to the RecordSource property of the data control. It then refreshes the data control and the bound list box.

```
Private Sub RefreshControls(strSQL as string)
    dtaData.RecordSource = strSQL
    dtaData.Refresh
    dlstData.Refresh
End Sub
```

6. Add the following code to the Click event of cmdClose:

```
Private Sub cmdClose_Click()
    End
End Sub
```

How It Works

The RecordSource property of the data control dtaData is set to an empty string in the Properties window. At form load, therefore, the Recordset object of dtaData will be empty, and it will remain empty until the RecordSource property is set to something that will return a valid recordset and the data control is refreshed. Because the DBList control is bound to the data control, it will be empty while the data control remains empty.

The Click routines of cmdShowAll and cmdShowUnique both perform the same basic function: they build a SQL statement to select the [State] field from the [Publishers] table, then pass the SQL statement to the RefreshControls subroutine. The difference in the Click routines is that cmdShowUnique includes the DISTINCT keyword in its SELECT statement and, therefore, returns only one record for each unique [State] value in the table.

Comment

In addition to the DISTINCT keyword described in this How-To, the Jet database engine also supports DISTINCTROW operations. When you use DISTINCTROW rather than DISTINCT, the database engine looks not just at the fields you've specified in your query but at entire rows in the table specified by the query. It returns one record in the dynaset for each unique row in the table, whether or not the output recordset row is unique.

Here's a simple example to illustrate the difference. Assume that the table [Cities] consists of these records:

```
CITY         STATE
Chicago      IL
Rockford     IL
Madison      WI
Madison      WI
Dubuque      IA
```

Here are two SQL queries:

```
SELECT DISTINCT [State] FROM [Cities]

SELECT DISTINCTROW [State] FROM [Cities]
```

The first SQL statement would return the following recordset. The DISTINCT statement ensures that each row in the output recordset is unique.

```
IL
WI
IA
```

The second SQL statement would return the following recordset. The IL entry appears twice because there are two unique records in the underlying table with a value of IL in the [State] field. The WI entry, on the other hand, appears only once because there is only one unique record in the underlying table.

IL
IL
WI
IA

In a well-designed database, a table will have no duplicate records because each record will have a primary key—and primary keys are, by definition, unique. If you have primary keys on all your tables, therefore, you have no need for DISTINCTROW.

COMPLEXITY
INTERMEDIATE

3.3 How do I...
Use variables and Visual Basic functions in a SQL query?

Problem

SQL SELECT statements are useful tools. But if I have to hard-code the criteria into the statement, it limits my flexibility because I can't change the criteria at runtime. I'd like to be able to use variables in the criteria clauses of my SELECT statements or—even better—use Visual Basic functions that return values. How can I accomplish this?

Technique

The SQL statement that you pass to the OpenRecordset method of the Database object or that you assign as the RecordSource property of a data control is a string. Because it is a string, you can insert the values of variables into it using Visual Basic's concatenation operator. You can use the same technique to insert the value returned by a call to a function (a built-in Visual Basic function or one you write yourself) into the string.

Steps

Open the project SELECT3.VBP and then run the project. The form shown in Figure 3.4 appears. Scroll the top list to see the publishers in the database. Click on a publisher, and the titles for that publisher appear in the bottom list. Enter a year in the Year Published box, and click on a publisher to restrict the display to titles published by a specific publisher in a specific year.

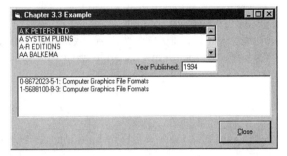

Figure 3.4. The Variable SELECTer form at startup.

1. Create a new project called SELECT3.VBP. Use **Form1** to create the objects and properties listed in Table 3.6, and save the form as SELECT3.FRM.

Table 3.6. Options and properties for the Variable SELECTer form.

OBJECT	PROPERTY	SETTING
Form	Name	Form1
	Caption	"Chapter 3.3 Example"
CommandButton	Name	cmdClose
	Caption	"Close"
	Default	True
ListBox	Name	lstTitles
Data	Name	dtaData
	Caption	"dtaData"
	RecordsetType	Snapshot
	RecordSource	"SELECT [Company Name] FROM [Publishers] ORDER BY [Company Name]"
	Visible	False
DBList	Name	dlstPublishers
	RowSource	dtaData
	ListField	"Company Name"
Label	Name	lblYearPublished
	AutoSize	True
	Caption	"Year Published:"
TextBox	Name	txtYearPublished
	Text	""

2. Add the following code to the declarations section of **Form1**:

```
Option Explicit

Private Const BIBLIO_PATH = "C:\Program Files\DevStudio\VB\Biblio.MDB"
Dim dbfBiblio As Database
```

3. Add the following code to the **Load** event of **Form1**:

```
Private Sub Form_Load()
On Error GoTo FormLoadError
        'Set the data control & load the Database object dbfBiblio.
        dtaData.DatabaseName = BIBLIO_PATH
        dtaData.Refresh
        Set dbfBiblio = DBEngine.Workspaces(0).OpenDatabase(BIBLIO_PATH)
    On Error GoTo 0
Exit Sub

FormLoadError:
    MsgBox Err.Description, vbExclamation
    Exit Sub
End Sub
```

4. Add the following code to the **Click** event of **dlstPublishers**. When the user clicks on a publisher name, this subroutine opens a snapshot-type **Recordset** object created from the Titles table, selecting only those titles published by the selected publishing company and (if the user has entered a publication year in **txtYearPublished**) in the designated year. It sorts the records in the snapshot by the ISBN number.

The **WHERE** clause in the SQL statement includes the value returned from the function **GetPubID**. **GetPubID** returns a numeric value corresponding to the Publishers table's **PubID** field for the currently selected publisher in **dlstPublishers**. Its value can be inserted into the SQL string by concatenating the function call to the string.

If the user has entered a publication year into **txtYearPublished**, its value is assigned to the numeric variable **yrPublished**, then inserted into the SQL string by concatenating the variable **yrPublished** to the string. Note that both values added to the string (the return value of **GetPubID** and the value of **yrPublished**) represent numeric fields in the database. Therefore, neither value is delimited by quotation marks in the SQL statement.

```
Private Sub dlstPublishers_Click()
Dim recSelect As Recordset
    Dim strSQL As String
    Dim intYearPublished As Integer

    On Error GoTo PublishersClickError
        'Clear the list box
        lstTitles.Clear
```

continued on next page

continued from previous page

```
        'Confirm that the year is numeric; if so, set the
        'intYearPublished variable to its numeric value.
        If IsNumeric(txtYearPublished) Then intYearPublished = _
            Val(txtYearPublished)

        'Build the SQL statement
        strSQL = "SELECT [Title], [ISBN] FROM [Titles] " & _
            "WHERE [PubID] = " & GetPubID()

        'If the year published selection is greater than zero, modify the
        'SQL to search for it.
        If intYearPublished > 0 Then
            strSQL = strSQL & " AND [Year Published] = " & intYearPublished
        End If

        'Sort the results by the ISBN number.
        strSQL = strSQL & " ORDER BY [ISBN]"

        'Get the recordset from our SQL statement.
        Set recSelect = dbfBiblio.OpenRecordset(strSQL, dbOpenSnapshot)

        'If we have obtained results, add the ISBN & Title fields to the
        'list box.
        If recSelect.RecordCount > 0 Then
            recSelect.MoveFirst
            Do Until recSelect.EOF
                lstTitles.AddItem recSelect![ISBN] & ": " _
                & recSelect![Title]
                recSelect.MoveNext
            Loop
        End If
    On Error GoTo 0
Exit Sub

PublishersClickError:
    MsgBox Err.Description, vbExclamation
    Exit Sub
End Sub
```

5. Create the following function in **Form1**. This function creates a recordset consisting of the **PubID** field of the record from the Publishers table with the company name value of the current selection in the **dlstPublishers** list. (This code assumes that each record in Publishers has a unique company name.) It then returns the value of that **PubID** field. In the SQL statement, the value **dblPublishers.Text** is used as the criterion of the **WHERE** clause. Because this value is a string (text) value, it must be delimited by quotation marks in the SQL statement. A single pair of double quotation marks—one at the beginning of the variable name and one at the end—won't do because the entire SQL statement is in quotation marks. You could use single quotation marks, like this:

```
strSQL = strSQL & " WHERE [Company Name] = '" & dblPublishers.Text & "'"
```

That would work if you could be sure that the value `dblPublishers.Text` would never include an apostrophe. But because you can't be sure of that (in fact, BIBLIO.MDB does contain one publisher, O'Reilly & Associates, with an apostrophe), a double quotation mark is the safest course.

```
Function GetPubID() As Long
Dim recPubID As Recordset
    Dim strSQL As String

    'This subquery, once constructed, selects the publisher ID
    'given a company name.
    strSQL = "SELECT [PubID] FROM [Publishers] " & _
        "WHERE [Company Name] = """ & dblPublishers.Text & """"

    'Construct the recordset from our SQL statement.
    Set recPubID = dbfBiblio.OpenRecordset(strSQL, dbOpenSnapshot)

    'If we have a record, get the ID.  If not, return zero.
    If recPubID.RecordCount > 0 Then
        GetPubID = recPubID![PubID]
    Else
        GetPubID = 0
    End If
End Function
```

6. Add the following code to the `Click` event of `cmdClose`:

```
Private Sub cmdClose_Click()
    End
End Sub
```

How It Works

When the form loads, it opens the database by setting the value of the `Database` object variable `dbfBiblio` to BIBLIO.MDB. The `Publishers` list is a bound list and is filled on startup by the records specified in the `RecordSource` property of `Data1` (see How-To 3.1 for a discussion of this bound list and data control). The `Titles` list is initially empty, and it remains so until the user clicks on the name of a publisher. Then the `dlstPublisher_Click` event code fills the `Titles` list with the titles published by the selected publisher. It does this by building a SQL statement that includes the `PubID` of the selected publisher. If the user has entered a year in the Year Published text box, its value is appended to the `WHERE` clause as an additional criterion.

Because the `dlstPublishers` list does not include the `PubID` field, its `Click` event needs to retrieve the value of the `PubID` field for the selected record. It does this by a call to the `GetPubID` function. `GetPubID` returns a numeric value, which is inserted directly into the SQL string.

Comment

You can also use built-in Visual Basic functions in your SQL statement. The functions are evaluated at runtime and their return values inserted into the SQL statement passed to the Jet engine. For example, if you have an integer variable named `intIndex`, you could embed the built-in `Choose` function within a SQL statement like this:

```
strSQL = SELECT * FROM Orders WHERE [Delivery Service] = '" & _
Choose(intIndex, "Speedy", "Rapid", "Quick", "Rabbit", "Tortoise") & "'"
```

COMPLEXITY
BEGINNING

3.4 How do I...
Use wildcards and ranges of values in a SQL query?

Problem

I need to create recordsets where the records returned fall within a range of values or contain certain text strings. How can I do this with SQL?

Technique

You might need to create recordsets that consist of records that fall within a range of values. Or perhaps you need to create recordsets consisting of records in which a given field contains a certain text string. You can accomplish both of these tasks with SQL.

Finding Records Within Criteria Ranges

You can use the standard comparison operators to find records that have a field value within a range of values. For example, to find all records in the Invoices table with `Invoice Date` values between January 1, 1996, and January 15, 1996, you could use this statement:

```
SELECT * FROM [Invoices]
WHERE [Invoice Date] >= #1/1/1996# AND [Invoice Date] <= #1/15/1996#
```

As an alternative, you can use the SQL `Between` operator. This statement returns the same recordset as the preceding one:

```
SELECT * FROM [Invoices]
WHERE [Invoice Date] Between #1/1/1996# AND #1/15/1996#
```

Using Wildcards in String Criteria

You can find records containing designated strings of text within text fields by using the wildcard characters * and ? with the SQL Like operator. The asterisk matches any combination of characters. The question mark matches a single character.

This statement retrieves all records that have the Company field beginning with mcgraw:

```
SELECT * FROM [Publishers] WHERE [Company] LIKE "mcgraw*"
```

This statement retrieves all records with the last name Hansen or Hanson:

```
SELECT * FROM [Authors] WHERE [Last Name] LIKE "hans?n"
```

You can use more than one wildcard character in a string. This statement retrieves all the records in which the [Company Name] field includes the word hill:

```
SELECT * FROM [Publishers] WHERE [Company Name] LIKE "*hill*"
```

Steps

Open and run the project SELECT4.VBP. The form shown in Figure 3.5 appears. Enter *visual basic* in the text box labeled Title includes text, and click the Look Up button. Enter 1992 and 1993 in the Published between boxes, and click Look Up again. Delete the values from the Published between boxes; then change the entry in the Title includes text box to visual basic* and click Look Up. Change the text in the Title includes text box to *visual basic and click Look Up.

1. Create a new project called SELECT4.VBP. Use Form1 to create the objects and properties listed in Table 3.7, and save the form as SELECT4.FRM.

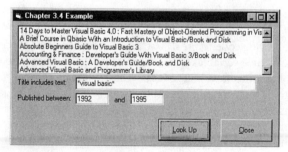

Figure 3.5. The Wildcard SELECTer form on startup.

Table 3.7. Options and properties for the Wildcard SELECTer form.

OBJECT	PROPERTY	SETTING
Form	Name	Form1
	Caption	"Chapter 3.4 Example"
ListBox	Name	lstTitles
TextBox	Name	txtPartialTitle
TextBox	Name	txtStartYear
TextBox	Name	txtEndYear
Label	Name	lblPartialTitle
	AutoSize	True
	Caption	"Title includes text:"
Label	Name	lblStartYear
	AutoSize	True
	Caption	"Published between:"
Label	Name	lblEndYear
	AutoSize	True
	Caption	"and"
CommandButton	Name	cmdLookup
	Caption	"&Look Up"
	Default	True
CommandButton	Name	cmdClose
	Caption	"&Close"

2. Add the following code to the declarations section of Form1:

```
Option Explicit

Private Const BIBLIO_PATH = "C:\Program Files\DevStudio\VB\Biblio.MDB"
```

3. Add the following code to the Click event of cmdLookup. This sets the values of the three variables to be inserted into the SQL statement to the contents of the three text boxes. It uses the IIf function to set the variables to default values if a text box is blank or if one of the year text boxes contains a non-numeric value. It then builds the SQL statement, inserting the variable values into the WHERE clause, opens the recordset, and fills the list with the recordset contents. (See How-To 3.3 for a discussion of using Visual Basic variables in SQL statements.)

```
Private Sub cmdLookup_Click()
Dim dbfBiblio As Database, recSelect As Recordset
    Dim strName As String, strSQL As String
    Dim strTitleText As String, strStartYear As String, strEndYear As String
```

```
On Error GoTo LookupError
    'Clear the list box
    lstTitles.Clear
    'Construct the search strings, using wildcards where appropriate.
    'For example, if the txtPartialTitle field is blank, the
    '* wildcard is substituted.
    strTitleText = IIf(txtPartialTitle <> "", txtPartialTitle, "*")
    strStartYear = IIf(IsNumeric(txtStartYear), txtStartYear, "1")
    strEndYear = IIf(IsNumeric(txtEndYear), txtEndYear, "9999")

    'Open the database
    Set dbfBiblio = DBEngine.Workspaces(0).OpenDatabase(BIBLIO_PATH)

    'Build the SQL statement, substituting our search strings, built
    'above,in the appropriate locations.
    strSQL = "SELECT [Title] FROM [Titles] " & _
        "WHERE [Title] LIKE '*" & strTitleText & "*' " & _
        "AND [Year Published] BETWEEN " & strStartYear & " AND " & _
        strEndYear & _
        " ORDER BY [Title]"

    'Construct the SQL statement.
    Set recSelect = dbfBiblio.OpenRecordset(strSQL, dbOpenSnapshot)

    'If we get results, load the Title field of each record into the
    'list box.
    If recSelect.RecordCount > 0 Then
        recSelect.MoveFirst
        Do Until recSelect.EOF
            lstTitles.AddItem recSelect![Title]
            recSelect.MoveNext
        Loop
    End If
    On Error GoTo 0
Exit Sub

LookupError:
    MsgBox Err.Description, vbExclamation
    Exit Sub
End Sub
```

4. Add the following code as the `Click` event of `cmdClose`:

```
Private Sub cmdClose_Click()
    End
End Sub
```

How It Works

The true action of this sample application occurs in the `cmdLookup_Click` event. After clearing the contents of the `lstTitles` list box, the code uses the values supplied in the text boxes to construct a SQL statement to run against the `dbfBiblio Database` object. If records were retrieved after the statement was run with the `OpenRecordset` method, the `lstTitles` list box is populated with the contents of the `[Title]` field from each record.

Comment

A Visual Basic database stores a date field as a number. In the WHERE clause of a SQL statement, you can treat it like a number; using the Between operator or comparison operators like > or < returns the results you would expect.

However, you can treat the date field like text in the WHERE clause of a SQL statement. This method enables you to use wildcard characters for any of the three values in a standard date.

For example, this WHERE clause returns all records with an invoice date in January 1996:

```
WHERE [Invoice Date] LIKE "1/*/1996"
```

The following WHERE clause returns all records with an invoice date in 1996:

```
WHERE [Invoice Date] LIKE "*/*/1996"
```

Notice that when you use the Like operator and wildcard characters, you delimit the date with quotation marks, not pound signs. Quotation marks tell the Jet database engine, "Treat this date like a string." The pound signs tell it, "Treat this date like a number."

COMPLEXITY
BEGINNING

3.5 How do I...
Define and use a parameter query?

Problem

I need to create recordsets with search criteria based on a parameter that will change often and reload quickly each time the parameter changes.

Technique

Normally, when using SQL to search for a specific value or values, you would specify which values you wanted in the statement. For example, to retrieve names and telephone numbers from the [Publishers] table in which the [State] field was equal to "NY", you would use this SQL statement:

```
SELECT [Name], [Telephone] FROM [Publishers] WHERE [State] = "NY" _
    ORDER BY [Name]
```

But this limits you. If you wanted all the names and telephone numbers from a different state, you would create a new query. There is, however, a faster way. A *parameter query* is a special SQL query in which replaceable parameters are used. Think of a parameter in SQL as a variable in Visual Basic. This allows your query to be flexible, and it also allows an increase in performance, because the

SQL precompiler doesn't have to completely build a new query every time you change a parameter.

To use a parameter in your SQL statement, you first have to specify the parameter, like declaring a variable in Visual Basic. This is done in the **PARAMETERS** section of your query, which usually precedes the **SELECT** statement. The declaration, as in Visual Basic, consists of a name and a data type, although the data types vary slightly from the names you might be accustomed to in Visual Basic. The **PARAMETERS** section is separated from the **SELECT** section by a semicolon (;) so that the SQL precompiler can tell the difference between the two sections.

To rewrite the preceding query for use with parameters, you might use something like this:

```
PARAMETERS prmState String; SELECT [Name], [Telephone] FROM [Publishers] _
    WHERE [State] = [prmState] ORDER BY [Name]
```

The parameter is substituted for the search value but in all other respects does not alter the SQL statement.

Steps

Open and run the project SELECT5.VBP. The form shown in Figure 3.6 appears. Enter NY in the State text box and click Search. Enter any other value in the State text box and click Search again.

1. Create a new project called SELECT5.VBP. Use **Form1** to create the objects and properties listed in Table 3.8, and save the form as SELECT5.FRM.

Table 3.8. Options and properties for the Parameter SELECTer form.

OBJECT	PROPERTY	SETTING
Form	Name	Form1
	Caption	"Chapter 3.5 Example"
Label	Name	lblParameter
	Caption	"State abbreviation:"
TextBox	Name	txtParameter
Label	Name	lblResults
	Caption	"Results:"
ListBox	Name	lstResults
CommandButton	Name	cmdSearch
	Caption	"&Search"
CommandButton	Name	cmdClose
	Caption	"&Close"

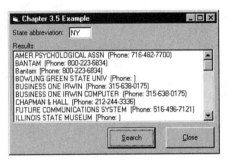

Figure 3.6. The main form for the Chapter 3.5 example on startup.

2. Add the following code to the declarations section of Form1:

```
Option Explicit

Private Const BIBLIO_PATH = "C:\Program Files\DevStudio\VB\Biblio.MDB"
Private mdbfBiblio As Database, mrecSelect As Recordset
Private mqdfTemp As QueryDef
```

3. Add the following code to the **Load** method of **Form1**. The **CreateQueryDef** method is used on the database to create a **QueryDef** object, which will hold our parameter query. Later, the **QueryDef** will be used to create a recordset for display.

```
Private Sub Form_Load()
    'Open a Database object first - the familiar BIBLIO.MDB
    Set mdbfBiblio - DBEngine.Workspaces(0).OpenDatabase(BIBLIO_PATH)

    'Use the CreateQueryDef method to create a temporary QueryDef object
    'that will store our parameter query.  The best way to use a parameter
    'query in DAO is with the QueryDef object.
    Set mqdfTemp = mdbfBiblio.CreateQueryDef("")

    'Set the SQL property to our parameter query SQL statement.
    mqdfTemp.SQL = "PARAMETERS pstrState String;SELECT " & _
        "[Name],[Telephone] " & _
        "FROM [Publishers] WHERE [State] = [pstrState] " & _
        "ORDER By [Name]"
End Sub
```

4. Add the following code to the **Click** event of **cmdSearch**. Now that we have a possible value for our parameter, we reference the **pstrState** parameter of the **QueryDef** object we created in the **Form_Load** routine. Then, using the **QueryDef**, we create a recordset. Now, the best part of this is when we change the parameter; instead of recreating the recordset, we use the **Requery** method provided by the **Recordset** object. Using this method is much faster, because the recordset has an existing connection to

the database and has its SQL already defined; we're just changing a
parameter.

```
Private Sub cmdSearch_Click()
    Dim lstrTemp As String

    'Set the parameter to the contents of our text box
    mqdfTemp![pstrState] = txtParameter.Text

    'If we haven't run this query yet, we'll need to
    'create it.  If we have, we don't need to create it,
    'just to requery it.
    If mrecSelect Is Nothing Then
        Set mrecSelect = mqdfTemp.OpenRecordset()
    Else
        mrecSelect.Requery mqdfTemp
    End If

    'Clear the list box
    lstResults.Clear

    'Populate the list box with names & phone numbers
    If mrecSelect.RecordCount > 0 Then
        mrecSelect.MoveFirst
        Do Until mrecSelect.EOF
            lstResults.AddItem mrecSelect![Name] & "  (Phone: " _
                & mrecSelect![Telephone] & ")"
            mrecSelect.MoveNext
        Loop
    End If
End Sub
```

5. Add the following code to the Click event of cmdClose:

```
Private Sub cmdClose_Click()
    End
End Sub
```

How It Works

When the application is started, Form1 loads. The Form_Load event creates a
Database object instance, then uses object's CreateQueryDef method to create a
temporary QueryDef object. At this point, our parameter query is created by
placing the SQL statement for the query into the SQL property of the newly
created QueryDef object.

When the cmdSearch_Click event is triggered, we first populate the
QueryDef's Parameter object with information from the txtParameter field.
Then, the routine checks whether the Recordset object it's about to populate is
set to Nothing. If so, the query hasn't been run yet, so the routine constructs a
Recordset object by running the OpenRecordset method from the QueryDef
object. If not, it uses the Requery method, which simply reexecutes the query
without having to make a new connection to the database, compile the SQL, and
so on.

After it does so, if the query has returned records, the `lstResults` list box is populated with the information.

Comment

One of the benefits of using a parameter query is the `Requery` method. The `Requery` method allows you to re-issue a query with different parameters; Access will actually reuse the existing connection, running the query faster. Also, the optimization engine built into Jet works best on static SQL (that is, SQL stored in the database, as opposed to the SQL statements stored in code), so you can get even more benefit from the use of a parameter query that is saved to a Microsoft Access database. For more information on how to use a stored parameter query, examine How-To 5.7 in Chapter 5 on Microsoft Access databases.

COMPLEXITY
INTERMEDIATE

3.6 How do I...
Create recordsets by joining fields from multiple tables?

Problem

I've designed my database using good relational database design principles, which means that I have data in multiple tables that are related through key fields. How can I use SQL to return recordsets with data from multiple tables in each recordset record?

Technique

In BIBLIO.MDB, the Publishers table contains information about publishers, and the Titles table contains information about titles. Each publisher is assigned a unique publisher ID, which appears in the `PubID` field in the Publishers table. In the Titles table, the publisher is indicated by the publisher number, as well as in a field named `PubID`. This relationship is shown in Figure 3.7. If you were using procedural coding and wanted to find the name of the publisher of a given title, you would find the title in the Titles table, store the value of the `PubID` for that title, and then find the matching `PubID` in the Publishers table.

This job is a lot easier with SQL. When you have a link such as that illustrated in Figure 3.7, you can use the keywords `INNER JOIN` in the `FROM` clause of a SQL `SELECT` statement to create a single recordset with fields from both tables. To continue the example, you could create a recordset with the `Title` field from the Titles table and the `Name` field from the Publishers table with this SQL statement:

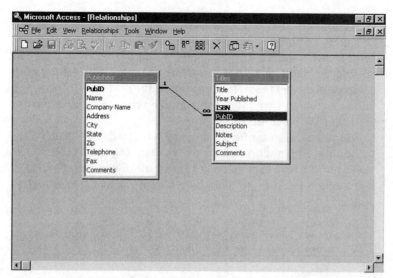

Figure 3.7. The BIBLIO.MDB Publishers and Titles table relationship.

```
SELECT Titles.Title, Publishers.Name
FROM Publishers INNER JOIN Titles ON Publishers.PubID = Titles.PubID
```

In a single-table **SELECT** statement, the **FROM** clause is simple—it just gives the name of the table. A multitable statement **FROM** clause consists of one (or more) subclauses, each based on an **INNER JOIN**. The syntax of each **INNER JOIN** is as follows:

```
<table 1 name> INNER JOIN <table 2 name>
ON <table 1 linking field name> = <table 2 linking field name>
```

Note that the field names in both the **SELECT** clause and the **FROM** clause are fully qualified with their table names, with the period operator separating the table name from the field name. Strictly speaking, this is necessary only when both tables have fields with identical names. In the example, the table names are required in the **FROM** clause because both tables have a field named **PubID**; they are optional in the **SELECT** clause because only the Titles table has a field named **Title** and only the Publishers table has a field named **Name**. It's good practice, however, to fully qualify all field names in multitable SQL statements. That not only makes the code easier to interpret but also makes it less likely that your code will be broken by subsequent changes to the structure of the database.

MULTIFIELD JOINS

It's quite common to have relationships based on multiple fields within each table. For example, assume that you have an Employees table and an Hours Worked table. You identify each employee by two fields, [Last Name] and [First Name]. Those two fields appear in each table and are used to link Employee records to Hours Worked records.

Code these multifield joins by creating an INNER JOIN subclause, with multiple ON expressions tied together with the AND keyword. Each ON expression links one pair of common fields. The FROM clause you'd use to link the tables in the example would be this:

```
FROM Employees INNER JOIN [Hours Worked]
ON Employees.[Last Name] = [Hours Worked].[Last Name]
AND Employees.[First Name] = [Hours Worked].    [First Name]
```

Steps

Open the project SELECT6.VBP. The form shown in Figure 3.8 appears. Use the data control's record navigation buttons to page through the records in the recordset.

1. Create a new project called SELECT6.VBP. Use Form1 to create the objects and properties listed in Table 3.9.

Table 3.9. Options and properties for the INNER JOINer form.

OBJECT	PROPERTY	SETTING
Form	Name	Form1
	Caption	"Chapter 3.6 Example"
TextBox	Name	txtYearPublished
	DataField	"Year Published"
	DataSource	"dtaData"
TextBox	Name	txtPublisher
	DataField	"Name"
	DataSource	"dtaData"
TextBox	Name	txtTitle
	DataField	"Title"
	DataSource	"dtaData"
CommandButton	Name	cmdClose
	Caption	"&Close"

OBJECT	PROPERTY	SETTING
Data	Name	dtaData
	Caption	"dtaData"
	RecordSource	"SELECT DISTINCTROW Titles.Title,
		Publishers.Name, Titles.[Year
		Published] FROM Publishers INNER JOIN
		Titles ON Publishers.PubID =
		Titles.PubID
		ORDER BY Titles.Title"
Label	Name	lblYearPublished
	AutoSize	True
	Caption	"Year Published:"
Label	Name	lblPublisher
	AutoSize	True
	Caption	"Publisher:"
Label	Name	lblTitle
	AutoSize	True
	Caption	"Title:"

2. Add the following code to the declarations section of **Form1**:

```
Option Explicit

Private Const BIBLIO_PATH = "C:\Program Files\DevStudio\VB\Biblio.MDB"
```

3. Add the following code as the **Load** event of **Form1**:

```
Private Sub Form_Load()
    'Set the DatabaseName for the data control.
    dtaData.DatabaseName = BIBLIO_PATH
End Sub
```

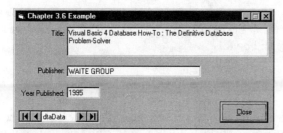

Figure 3.8. The Chapter 3.6 example form on startup.

4. Add the following code as the `Click` event of `cmdClose`:

```
Private Sub cmdClose_Click()
    End
End Sub
```

How It Works

This program makes use of the innate capabilities of bound controls (discussed in more detail in Chapter 1, "Accessing a Database with Bound Controls") to illustrate the use of an `INNER JOIN`. When the program is started, the `Form_Load` event will set the `DatabaseName` property of the `dtaData` data control to the location of BIBLIO.MDB. At that point, the `dtaData` data control will run the SQL statement stored in its `RecordSource` property. The rest will then be handled by the data control.

Comments

The `INNER JOIN` can be extremely useful in databases, but don't go "whole hog" with it. The more tables added to a `JOIN`, no matter what type, the slower the SQL statement will be to execute. Consider this a database developer's maxim: *Retrieve only the data you need; if you don't need it, don't include it.* That goes for `JOIN`s as well. If you don't need the table, don't `JOIN` it.

COMPLEXITY
ADVANCED

3.7 How do I...
Find records in a table without corresponding entries in a related table?

Problem

I have an Orders table and a Customers table, related on the `Customer Number` field. I'd like to find all the customers who have not placed an order in the past six months. How can I do this?

Technique

The `INNER JOIN`, discussed in the preceding How-To, allows you to find all the records in a table that have matching records in another table, when the two tables are related on a key field and when "matching" means that values in the key fields match. SQL also provides an outer join, which lets you list all the records in one of the related tables whether or not they have matching records in the other table.

For example, assume that you have two tables, Customers and Invoices, with these entries:

Customers Table

Customer Number	Customer Name
100	ABC Company
101	MNO Company
102	XYZ Company

Invoices Table

Customer Number	Invoice Date	Invoice Amount
102	12/12/1996	$589.31
100	12/15/1996	$134.76
102	12/22/1996	$792.13

Create a recordset using the following SQL statement with an INNER JOIN in the FROM clause:

```
SELECT Customers.[Customer Name], Customers.[Customer Number], _
    Invoices.[Customer Number], Invoices.[Invoice Date], _
    Invoices.[Invoice Amount]
FROM Customers INNER JOIN Invoices
ON Customers.[Customer Number] = Invoices.[Customer Number]
ORDER BY Customers.[Customer Number], Invoices.[Invoice Date]
```

Executing that statement returns this recordset:

Customers		Invoices		
Customer Name	Customer Number	Customer Number	Invoice Date	Invoice Amount
ABC Company	100	100	12/15/1996	$134.76
XYZ Company	102	102	12/12/1996	$589.31
XYZ Company	102	102	12/22/1996	$792.13

MNO Company, customer number 101, would not appear at all in the recordset, because there are no records in the Invoices table for customer number 101, and an INNER JOIN returns only records with matching key field values in both tables. But see what happens when you change the join type in the FROM to a LEFT JOIN, one of the two types of outer joins:

```
SELECT Customers.[Customer Name], Customers.[Customer Number], _
    Invoices.[Customer Number], Invoices.[Invoice Date], _
    Invoices.[Invoice Amount]
FROM Customers LEFT JOIN Invoices
ON Customers.[Customer Number] = Invoices.[Customer Number]
ORDER BY Customers.[Customer Number], Invoices.[Invoice Date]
```

Executing that SQL statement returns this recordset:

Customers		Invoices		
Customer Name	Customer Number	Customer Number	Invoice Date	Invoice Amount
ABC Company	100	100	12/15/1996	$134.76
MNO Company	101			
XYZ Company	102	102	12/12/1996	$589.31
XYZ Company	102	102	12/22/1996	$792.13

The recordset consists of all the records that the INNER JOIN version produced, plus one additional record for each record in the table on the left side of the FROM clause that has no matching records in the table on the right side of the FROM clause.

LEFT JOINS AND RIGHT JOINS

There are two outer joins: LEFT JOIN and RIGHT JOIN. The "direction" of the join refers to the relative position of the table names in the FROM clause of the SQL statement. A LEFT JOIN returns a record from the table on the left side of the FROM clause, whether or not a matching record exists on the right side. A RIGHT JOIN returns a record from the table on the right side of the FROM clause, whether or not a matching record exists on the left side. These two FROM clauses, therefore, have identical results:

```
FROM Customers LEFT JOIN Invoices
ON Customers.[Customer Number] = Invoices.[Customer Number]

FROM Invoices RIGHT JOIN Customers
ON Invoices.[Customer Number] = Customers.[Customer Number]
```

The "missing" fields on the right side of the recordset all have the value NULL. You can use that fact to modify the SQL statement to select only the records from the left table that do not have matching records in the right table:

```
SELECT Customers.[Customer Name], Customers.[Customer Number], _
    Invoices.[Customer Number], Invoices.[Invoice Date], _
    Invoices.[Invoice Amount]
FROM Customers LEFT JOIN Invoices
ON Customers.[Customer Number] = Invoices.[Customer Number]
WHERE Invoice.[Customer Number] IS NULL
ORDER BY Customers.[Customer Number], Invoices.[Invoice Date]
```

That statement returns this recordset:

```
              Customers                 Invoices
Customer Name  Customer Number  Customer Number  Invoice Date Invoice Amount
MNO Company          101
```

The field used in the WHERE clause can be any field from the right-side table, because all right-side fields will be NULL when there is no record to match a left-side table record.

Steps

Open the project SELECT7.VBP. The form shown in Figure 3.9 appears. The list shows all the publishers in the Publishers table that do not have entries in the Publisher Comments table.

1. Create a new project called SELECT7.VBP. Use **Form1** to create the objects and properties listed in Table 3.10.

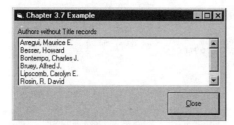

Figure 3.9. The Chapter 3.7 example
form on startup.

Table 3.10. Options and properties for the Outer JOINer form.

OBJECT	PROPERTY	SETTING
Form	Name	Form1
	Caption	"Chapter 3.7 Example"
Data	Name	dtaData
	Caption	"dtaData"
	RecordSource	"SELECT Publishers.[Company Name] FROM Publishers LEFT JOIN [Publisher Comments] ON Publishers.PubID = [Publisher Comments].PubID WHERE [Publisher Comments].PubID IS NULL ORDER BY [Company Name]"
	Visible	False
DBList	Name	dlstAuthors
	RowSource	dtaData
	ListField	"Author"
CommandButton	Name	cmdClose
	Caption	"&Close"
Label	Name	lblAuthors
	Caption	"Authors without Title records:"

2. Add the following code to the declarations section of Form1:

```
Option Explicit

Private Const BIBLIO_PATH = "C:\Program Files\DevStudio\VB\Biblio.MDB"
```

3. Add the following code to the **Load** event of **Form1**:

```
Private Sub Form_Load()
    'Set the DatabaseName of the data control.
    dtaData.DatabaseName = BIBLIO_PATH
End Sub
```

4. Add the following code as the **Click** event of **cmdClose**:

```
Private Sub cmdClose_Click()
    End
End Sub
```

How It Works

The **dtaData** recordset is built by the SQL statement:

```
SELECT Publishers.[Company Name]
FROM Publishers LEFT JOIN [Publisher Comments]
ON Publishers.PubID = [Publisher Comments].PubID
WHERE [Publisher Comments].PubID IS NULL
ORDER BY [Company Name]
```

The **WHERE** clause of that SQL statement creates a **LEFT JOIN** between the left-side table (Publishers) and the right-side table (Publisher Comments). Ignoring the **WHERE** clause for a moment, that **LEFT JOIN** would create a snapshot with one record for each record in the Publisher Comments table, plus one record for every record in the Publishers table that did not have a matching record in Publisher Comments.

The **WHERE** clause eliminates from the snapshot all records in which there is a Publisher Comment, because the **[Publisher Comments].PubID** field will not be **NULL** where there is a record in Publisher Comments. For snapshot records created by records in Publishers without matching records in Publisher Comments, **[Publisher Comments].PubID** is **NULL**; the **WHERE** clause causes these records to be included in the output snapshot.

Comments

As with the **INNER JOIN**, explained in the preceding How-To, this can be a powerful tool if used well. You should be encouraged strongly to experiment with the behavior of all sorts of joins—you might be surprised at what you get. Use this How-To's code as a basic example, and go from there, trying out different SQL joins, to "get a feel" for what to expect with other SQL queries involving **JOIN** statements.

3.8 How do I...
Retrieve information such as counts, averages, and sums and display them by binding them to a data control?

Problem

I'd like to extract descriptive statistics about the data in a table (for example, averages and sums or numeric fields, minimum and maximum values, and counts of records that meet certain criteria). How can I use SQL to accomplish this task?

Technique

SQL includes a rich set of aggregate functions—functions you can embed in SQL statements to return descriptive statistics about the data in your database. Table 3.11 lists the aggregate functions available and shows what each function returns. Note that all functions ignore **NULL** values in the recordset.

Table 3.11. SQL aggregate functions.

AGGREGATE	RETURNS FUNCTION
Sum	Sum of the values in a designated numeric field.
Avg	Average of the non-NULL values in a designated numeric field.
Count	Count of non-NULL values in one or more designated fields.
Min	Minimum value in a designated numeric or text field.
Max	Maximum value in a designated numeric or text field.
First	Value of a designated field in the first record in the recordset.
Last	Value of a designated field in the last record in the recordset.
StDev	Sample standard deviation of the non-NULL values in a designated field.
StDevP	Population standard deviation of the non-NULL values in a designated field.
Var	Sample variance of the non-NULL values in a designated field.
VarP	Population variance of the non-NULL values in a designated field.

The syntax for using these functions in the **SELECT** clause of a SQL statement is the same for all functions:

```
<functionname>(<fieldname>) AS <outputfieldname>
```

The *<fieldname>* is the name of the field in the table whose records you are examining. The *<outputfieldname>* is the name you give to the result column in the recordset created by the SQL statement. The two field names must be different, and the *<outputfieldname>* cannot duplicate the name of a field in any table referenced in the SQL statement.

For example, assume that you want to get a total of the **Invoice Amount** field for all Invoice Table records with **Invoice Dates** between January 1, 1996, and January 31, 1996. Your SQL statement could be this:

```
SELECT SUM([Invoice Amount]) AS SumOfInvoices
WHERE [Invoice Date] BETWEEN #1/1/1996# AND #1/31/1996#
```

That statement would return a recordset consisting of one record with one field, with a field name of **SumOfInvoices**. The field's value would be the total of all the invoices between the specified dates.

You can include more than one aggregate function in a SQL statement. The following statement would return a single record with two fields, **SumOfInvoices** and **AverageInvoice**. **SumOfInvoices** would be the sum of all invoices for the designated customer. **AverageInvoice** would be the average invoice amount for that customer (disregarding any fields for which the **Invoice Amount** is **NULL**).

```
SELECT SUM([Invoice Amount]) AS SumOfInvoices, AVG([Invoice Number]) as
AverageInvoice
WHERE [Customer Number] = 12345
```

Steps

Open the project SELECT8.VBP. The form shown in Figure 3.10 appears. The labels on the form show several statistics about the authors in the Authors table of BIBLIO.MDB.

1. Create a new project called SELECT8.VBP. Use **Form1** to create the objects and properties listed in Table 3.12. Save the form as SELECT8.FRM.

Figure 3.10. The main form for the Chapter 3.8 example on execution.

Table 3.12. Options and properties for the Author Statistics form.

OBJECT	PROPERTY	SETTING
Form	Name	Form1
	Caption	"Chapter 3.8 Example"
Data	Name	dtaData
	Caption	"dtaData"
	RecordSource	"SELECT Count(*) AS CountOfAuthor,
		Avg([Year Born]) AS [AvgOfYear Born],
		Min([Year Born]) AS [MinOfYear Born],
		Max([Year Born]) AS [MaxOfYear Born] FROM
		Authors"
	Visible	False
	RecordsetType	Snapshot
CommandButton	Name	cmdClose
	Cancel	True
	Caption	"&Close"
	Default	True
Label	Name	dlblCount
	BorderStyle	Fixed Single
	DataField	"CountOfAuthor"
	DataSource	"dtaData"
Label	Name	dlblMin
	BorderStyle	Fixed Single
	DataField	"MinOfYear Born"
	DataSource	"dtaData"
Label	Name	dlblMax
	BorderStyle	Fixed Single
	DataField	"MaxOfYear Born"
	DataSource	"dtaData"
Label	Name	dlblAvg
	BorderStyle	Fixed Single
	DataField	"AvgOfYear Born"
	DataSource	"dtaData"
Label	Name	lblCount
	AutoSize	True
	Caption	"Number of authors:"

continued on next page

continued from previous page

OBJECT	PROPERTY	SETTING
Label	Name	lblMin
	AutoSize	True
	Caption	"Earliest year born:"
Label	Name	lblMax
	AutoSize	True
	Caption	"Latest year born:"
Label	Name	lblAvg
	AutoSize	True
	Caption	"Average year born:"

2. Add the following code to the declarations section of Form1:

```
Option Explicit

Private Const BIBLIO_PATH = "C:\Program Files\DevStudio\VB\Biblio.MDB"
```

3. Add the following code to the Load event of Form1:

```
Private Sub Form_Load()
    'Set the DatabaseName of the data control.
    dtaData.DatabaseName = BIBLIO_PATH
End Sub
```

4. Add the following code as the Click event of cmdClose:

```
Private Sub cmdClose_Click()
    End
End Sub
```

How It Works

The data control creates a one-record recordset with this SQL statement:

```
SELECT Count(*) AS CountOfAuthor, Avg([Year Born]) AS [AvgOfYear Born],
Min([Year Born]) AS [MinOfYear Born], Max([Year Born]) AS [MaxOfYear Born]
FROM Authors
```

The single record contains four fields, each reporting one statistic about the records in the Authors table. The four bound labels on the form are each bound to one of the recordset fields.

Comment

The SQL statement used in the example for this How-To included this expression in its SELECT clause:

```
Count(*) as CountOfAuthor
```

Using the wildcard character * as the argument to the Count aggregate function indicates that you want the count of all the records in the table. You could achieve the same thing by using a field that you know to be non-NULL in every record (for example, the primary key of the table, which must by definition be non-NULL):

```
Count ([AuthorID]) as CountOfAuthor
```

However, it's better to use the wildcard character *, because the Jet database engine is optimized to perform Count queries with the wildcard. You get the same answer either way, but you get it faster with the wildcard.

COMPLEXITY
ADVANCED

3.9 How do I...
Create a recordset consisting of records that have duplicate values?

Problem

I need to create a recordset that shows records with duplicate values. How can I do this with SQL?

Technique

Three features of SQL—the GROUP BY clause, the HAVING clause, and SQL IN subqueries—facilitate the identification of duplicate values in a table.

The GROUP BY Clause

SQL provides the GROUP BY clause, which combines records with identical values into a single record. If you include a SQL aggregate function (such as COUNT) in the SELECT statement, the GROUP BY clause applies that function to each group of records to create a summary value.

For example, to return a recordset with one record for each unique state/city pair from the Publishers table in BIBLIO.MDB, you could use this SQL statement:

```
SELECT State, City, COUNT(*) AS CountByCityAndState FROM Publishers
GROUP BY State, City
```

The HAVING Clause

The HAVING clause is similar to the WHERE clause, but you use HAVING with GROUP BY. The argument to HAVING specifies which grouped records created by GROUP BY should be included in the output recordset. For example, this SQL statement

returns one record for each unique state/city pair from the Publishers table in
BIBLIO.MDB, restricting the records to those in which the state is **CA**:

```
SELECT [State],[City] FROM [Publishers]
GROUP BY [State],[City]
HAVING [State] = 'CA'
```

You can use **HAVING** with the aggregate **COUNT** function (see the preceding
How-To for information on aggregate functions) to restrict the output recordset
to records in which the values grouped by the **GROUP BY** clause have a specified
range of occurrences. This example selects only city/state pairs that occur more
than once in the table:

```
SELECT [State],[City] FROM [Publishers]
GROUP BY [State],[City]
HAVING COUNT(*) > 1
```

The **SELECT** and **GROUP BY** clauses in that example create a recordset to which
the **HAVING** clause applies the **COUNT** aggregate function. The **HAVING COUNT(*) >
1** clause eliminates from the final output recordset record groups that occur only
once.

You can use multiple criteria with the **HAVING** clause. This example selects
only city/state pairs that occur more than once in the table where the state is **CA**:

```
SELECT [State],[City] FROM [Publishers]
GROUP BY [State],[City]
HAVING COUNT(*) > 1 AND [State] = 'CA'
```

SQL IN **Subqueries**

An **IN** subquery is a **SELECT** statement nested inside the **WHERE** clause of another
SELECT statement. The subquery returns a set of records, each consisting of a
single field. The **WHERE** clause then compares a field from the "main" **SELECT**
statement to the field returned by the subquery. The resultant recordset consists
of those records from the main recordset where the main field equals the
subquery field.

Consider this simple **SELECT** query:

```
SELECT [City], [Company Name] FROM [Publishers]
ORDER BY [City]
```

That query creates a recordset consisting of one record for every record in the
[Publishers] table, sorted by [City]. Now add a **WHERE** clause containing an **IN**
subquery:

```
SELECT [City], [Company Name] FROM [Publishers]
WHERE [City] IN
        (SELECT [City] FROM [Publishers]
         GROUP BY [City]
         HAVING COUNT(*) > 1)
ORDER BY [City]
```

The subquery in the example is parenthesized and indented. (The
parentheses are required; the indenting is not.) The subquery returns one record

for every [City] value that occurs more than one time in the [Publishers] table. If a [City] value occurs only once, it is not included in the subquery output.

The WHERE clause of the main query compares the [City] field of every record in the table to the set of [City] values returned by the subquery. If there is a match, the record is included in the main query's output recordset. If there is no match, the record is excluded from the output recordset. Because the subquery [City] values include only those occurring more than once in the table, the WHERE clause includes in the output recordset only those records with a [City] value that occurs more than once.

If you need a recordset based on a single duplicated field, the last illustration is sufficient. If you need to compare multiple fields to find duplicate values, additional steps are required. For example, your [Publishers] table contains records in which the [City] field is duplicated but in which the [State] field differs, as in the following table:

```
CITY                STATE
Springfield         IL
Springfield         MA
Springfield         OH
```

(The BIBLIO.MDB database supplied with Visual Basic does not have any records in which this condition exists, but a real-life example might.)

Finding the true duplicates here requires additions to the subquery. The additions to the original subquery are shown here in bold.

```
(SELECT [City] FROM [Publishers] AS Tmp
GROUP BY [City], [State]
HAVING COUNT(*) > 1 AND [State] = Publishers.[State])
```

The addition of the State field to the GROUP BY clause creates a record for every unique combination of City and State; the three Springfields will now each appear in the recordset returned by the GROUP BY. The additional criterion State = Publishers.State in the HAVING clause compares the State field in each GROUP BY record output to the State field in the original Publishers table and selects only those in which the fields are equal; note that the table name on the right side of the equal sign is mandatory. Because of the additional criterion in the HAVING clause, it is necessary to assign the output of the subquery to a temporary variable—arbitrarily called Tmp, but any legal name that does not duplicate an existing field name will do.

You can use up to 10 criteria in a subquery. For additional criteria, simply append them to the GROUP BY clause with a comma and to the HAVING clause with the AND keyword.

Steps

Open and run the project SELECT9.VBP. The form shown in Figure 3.11 appears. The grid control on the form shows records from the Publishers table for which the city and state appear more than once in the table.

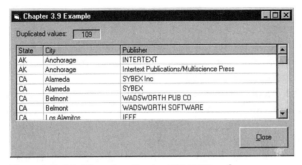

Figure 3.11. The duplicate SELECTer form on startup.

1. Create a new project called SELECT9.VBP. Use **Form1** to create the objects and properties listed in Table 3.13, and save the form as SELECT9.FRM.

Table 3.13. Objects and properties for the Duplicate SELECTer form.

OBJECT	PROPERTY	SETTING
Form	Name	Form1
	Caption	"Chapter 3.9 Example"
Label	Name	lblCount
	Alignment	2 - Center
	BorderStyle	1 - Fixed Single
Label	Name	lblDupValues
	Caption	"Duplicated values:"
Grid	Name	grdValues
	Cols	3
	FixedCols	0
	Scrollbars	2 - Vertical
CommandButton	Name	cmdClose
	Cancel	True
	Caption	"&Close"

2. Add the following code to the declarations section of **Form1**:

```
Option Explicit

Private Const BIBLIO_PATH = "C:\Program Files\DevStudio\VB\Biblio.MDB"
```

3. Enter the following code as the **Load** event for **Form1**. For the **Form_Load** event, the routine first creates a **Database** object. Then, it starts creating the SQL statement from the inside out, by first creating the subquery in the **strSubQuery** string and then "wrapping" the rest of the query around it inside the strSQL string. After execution, if records are present, the **grdValues** grid is configured and populated with the contents of the [State], [City], and [Company Name] fields.

```
Private Sub Form_Load()
    Dim dbfBiblio As Database, recSelect As Recordset
    Dim strSQL As String, strSubQuery As String
    Dim intCount As Integer, intGridRow As Integer

  ' Get the database name and open the database.
    Set dbfBiblio = DBEngine.Workspaces(0).OpenDatabase(BIBLIO_PATH)

  ' Build the subquery, starting with its SELECT statement.
    strSubQuery = "SELECT City FROM Publishers AS Tmp " & _
        "GROUP BY City, State " & _
        "HAVING COUNT(*) > 1 AND State = Publishers.State "

  ' Build the SQL statement
  ' Start by designating the fields to be included in the recordset
  ' and the WHERE IN clause
    strSQL = "SELECT City, State, [Company Name] FROM Publishers " & _
        "WHERE City IN (" & strSubQuery & ") " & _
        "ORDER BY State, City"

  ' Run the query.
    Set recSelect = dbfBiblio.OpenRecordset(strSQL, dbOpenSnapshot)

  ' Make sure the query returned at least one record
    If recSelect.RecordCount > 0 Then

        ' Get a count of records in the recordset and display it on the
        ' form.
        recSelect.MoveLast
        intCount = recSelect.RecordCount
        lblCount.Caption = intCount

        ' Initialize the grid
        With grdValues
            .Rows = intCount + 1
            .ColWidth(0) = 700: .ColWidth(1) = 2000: .ColWidth(2) = 4000
            .Row = 0: .Col = 0: .Text = "State"
            .Col = 1: .Text = "City"
            .Col = 2: .Text = "Publisher"
        End With

        'Populate the grid
        recSelect.MoveFirst
        For intGridRow = 1 To intCount
            With grdValues
                .Row = intGridRow
```

continued on next page

continued from previous page

```
                .Col = 0:  .Text = recSelect![State]
                .Col = 1:  .Text = recSelect![City]
                .Col = 2:  .Text = recSelect![Company Name]
            End With
            recSelect.MoveNext
        Next intGridRow
    End If
End Sub
```

4. Enter the following code as the `Click` event of `cmdClose`. This event ends the application.

```
Private Sub cmdClose_Click()
    End
End Sub
```

How It Works

The `Form_Load()` event subroutine creates a SQL statement, first by building the subquery, then by creating the main query with the inserted subquery. (Refer to the "Technique" section for an explanation of the syntax of the SQL statement.) The subroutine then executes the query and creates a `Recordset` object. If the recordset contains at least one record, the subroutine initializes the grid control and inserts each record into the grid.

Comment

If you insert the word `NOT` in front of the word `IN`, a `SELECT` statement containing an `IN` subquery returns a recordset consisting of records that do not meet the criteria of the subquery. Assume that you changed the query in the example by inserting the word `NOT`:

```
SELECT [City], [Company Name] FROM [Publishers]
WHERE [City] NOT IN
        (SELECT [City] FROM [Publishers] AS Tmp
         GROUP BY [City], [State]
         HAVING COUNT(*) > 1 AND [State] = Publishers.[State])
ORDER BY [City]
```

That query would produce a recordset consisting of those records with a city/state combination that occurred only once in the table.

COMPLEXITY
INTERMEDIATE

3.10 How do I...
Use Visual Basic functions within a SQL statement?

Problem

I need to create a recordset with special formatting based on the contents of a field, but I can't find any standard SQL function to use for the formatting.

Technique

One of the benefits of using the Jet database engine and data access objects is the capability of embedding VBA functions in Access SQL for various tasks that SQL by itself could not accomplish easily.

Steps

Open and run the project SELECT10.VBP. The form shown in Figure 3.12 appears. The grid control on the form shows records from the Publishers table, before and after the execution of the StrConv() function to convert the case from upper to proper case.

1. Create a new project called SELECT10.VBP. Use Form1 to create the objects and properties listed in Table 3.14, and save the form as SELECT10.FRM.

Table 3.14. Objects and properties for the Duplicate SELECTer form.

OBJECT	PROPERTY	SETTING
Form	Name	Form1
	Caption	"Chapter 3.10 Example"
Label	Name	lblPublishers
	Caption	"Publisher Names"
MSFlexGrid	Name	grdValues
	Cols	3
	FixedCols	1
	AllowUserResizing	1 - flexResizeColumns
	Scrollbars	2 - Vertical
	Width	5655
CommandButton	Name	cmdClose
	Cancel	True
	Caption	"&Close"

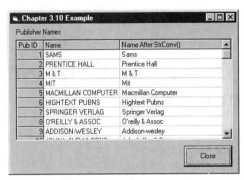

Figure 3.12. The Chapter 3.10 example
form, showing Publishers data.

2. Add the following statements to the declarations section of **Form1**. Ensure
that the **BIBLIO_PATH** constant is set to the location of BIBLIO.MDB on
your workstation.

```
Option Explicit

Private Const BIBLIO_PATH = "C:\Program Files\DevStudio\VB\Biblio.MDB"
```

3. Enter the following code as the **Load** event for **Form1**. As with the
preceding How-To, the event starts by creating a **Database** object, opening
BIBLIO.MDB for use. Then, a SQL statement is created, using the VBA
function **StrConv** to convert the string to proper case (the first letter of
each word is capitalized), as denoted by the second parameter in the
command. (For more information on the **StrConv** command, search for
StrConv in the Visual Basic 5 help index.) Note that the constant for the
second parameter, **vbProperCase**, was not used here—some constants
might not be accessible by the SQL precompiler used by the DAO library.

```
Private Sub Form_Load()
    Dim dbfBiblio As Database, recSelect As Recordset
    Dim strSQL As String
    Dim intCount As Integer, intGridRow As Integer

    Set dbfBiblio = DBEngine.Workspaces(0).OpenDatabase(BIBLIO_PATH)

    ' Build the query, starting with its SELECT statement.
    ' Note the StrConv() function; a VBA function, NOT a SQL function.
    strSQL = "SELECT Publishers.PubID, Publishers.Name, " & _
            "StrConv([Publishers].[Name],3) AS CheckedName " & _
            "FROM Publishers;"

    ' Run the query to create the recordset.
    Set recSelect = dbfBiblio.OpenRecordset(strSQL, dbOpenSnapshot)

    ' Make sure the query returned at least one record
```

```
If recSelect.RecordCount > 0 Then

    'Get the record count & display it on the form
    recSelect.MoveLast
    intCount = recSelect.RecordCount
    lblPublishers.Caption = "Publisher Names (" & CStr(intCount) & _
    "records)"

    'Initialize the grid
    With grdValues
        .Rows = intCount + 1
        .ColWidth(0) = 700: .ColWidth(1) = 2000: .ColWidth(2) = 4000
        .Row = 0: .Col = 0: .Text = "Pub ID"
        .Col = 1: .Text = "Name"
        .Col = 2: .Text = "Name After StrConv()"
    End With

    'Populate the grid
    recSelect.MoveFirst
    For intGridRow = 1 To intCount
        With grdValues
            .Row = intGridRow
            .Col = 0: .Text = recSelect![PubID]
            .Col = 1: .Text = recSelect![Name]
            .Col = 2: .Text = recSelect![CheckedName]
        End With
        recSelect.MoveNext
    Next intGridRow
    End If
End Sub
```

4. Enter the following code as the `Click` event of `cmdClose`:

```
Private Sub cmdClose_Click()
    End
End Sub
```

How It Works

The `Form_Load()` event subroutine creates a SQL statement, showing both the raw data in the `[Name]` field and the same data after processing by the `StrConv()` VBA function, using the `vbProperCase` option to "scrub" the raw data. The recordset data is placed directly into the grid with no further processing.

Comment

VBA functionality can expand DAO query power enormously, allowing for everything from math functions to string processing within the SQL. Rather than the tedious and time-consuming process of performing the same action by looping through a recordset and using the same VBA function to modify the data field by field, the ease of a single SQL statement is something that should strongly encourage you to experiment with VBA functions in Access SQL.

COMPLEXITY
INTERMEDIATE

3.11 How do I...
Make bulk updates to database records?

Problem

I need to make an identical change to a number of records that meet certain criteria. How can I accomplish this task with a single SQL statement?

Technique

In addition to **SELECT** queries, which create recordsets based on criteria you specify, SQL provides a group of action query statements. One type of action query is the **UPDATE** query, which makes specified changes to a set of records that meet designated criteria.

An **UPDATE** query contains the clauses shown in Table 3.15. The example shown in Table 3.15 increases the **[Price Each]** field by 3 percent for each record in the [Parts List] table that has a **[Part Number]** beginning with the string **"XYZ7"**.

Table 3.15. The UPDATE statement.

CLAUSE	PURPOSE	EXAMPLE
UPDATE	Names the table.	UPDATE [Parts List]
SET	Designates the fields to be updated and their new values.	SET [Price Each] = [Price Each] * 1.03
WHERE	Specifies the records to be updated.	WHERE [Part Number] LIKE "XYZ7*"

You run a SQL action query statement using the **Execute** method of the **Database** object. Assuming that you have a **Database** object **db**, you would run the query shown in the table using this Visual Basic code (the entire statement would normally appear on one line):

```
db.Execute("UPDATE [Parts List] SET [Price Each] = " & _
    "[Price Each] * 1.03 WHERE [Part Number] LIKE "XYZ7")
```

Steps

The BIBLIO.MDB file distributed with Visual Basic contains outdated information about four publishers. These publishers were formerly located on College Ave. in Carmel, IN. They have moved to an address in Indianapolis. The UPDATE.VBP project updates all four publishers' records to show their new address. It also provides the capability to restore the firms' original Carmel address.

Open the project UPDATE.VBP and then run the project. Click the Update button, and the form looks as shown in Figure 3.13. Click the Restore button, and the addresses change to show the Carmel address.

1. Create a new project called UPDATE.VBP. Use `Form1` to create the objects and properties listed in Table 3.16, and save the form as UPDATE.FRM.

Table 3.16. Objects and properties for the UPDATEr form.

OBJECT	PROPERTY	SETTING
Form	Name	Form1
	Caption	"UPDATEr"
CommandButton	Name	cmdClose
	Cancel	True
	Caption	"&Close"
CommandButton	Name	cmdRestore
	Caption	"&Restore"
CommandButton	Name	cmdUpdate
	Caption	"&Update"
ListBox	Name	lstData

2. Add the following statements to the declarations section of `Form1`:

```
Option Explicit

Private Const BIBLIO_PATH = "C:\Program Files\DevStudio\VB\Biblio.MDB"
Private dbfBiblio As Database
```

3. Add the following code as the `Click` event of `cmdUpdate`. This procedure builds a SQL **UPDATE** statement that changes the contents of the `[City]`, `[Address]`, and `[Zip]` fields for each record that meets the criteria. The

Figure 3.13. The main form for the Chapter 3.11 example, after the update.

criteria are the city being equal to "`Carmel`" and the address containing the strings "`11711`" and "`College`". The `LIKE` clause in the address is needed because BIBLIO.MDB, as supplied, uses a different form of the same address for each of the four publishers at 11711 N. College Ave.

The procedure executes the SQL statement, using the `Execute` method of the `Database` object. It then calls the `ListRecords` subroutine to display the records.

```
Private Sub cmdUpdate_Click()
Dim strSQL As String

    On Error GoTo UpdateError
        'Build the UPDATE statement.
        strSQL = "UPDATE Publishers " & _
            "SET City = 'Indianapolis', Address = '201 W. 103rd St.', " & _
            "Zip = '46290' " & _
            "WHERE ([City] = 'Carmel') AND (Address LIKE '*11711*College*')"

        'Execute the update query.
        dbfBiblio.Execute strSQL

        ListRecords "Indianapolis"
    On Error GoTo 0
Exit Sub

UpdateError:
    MsgBox Err.Description, vbExclamation
Exit Sub

End Sub
```

4. Add the following code as the `Click` event of `cmdRestore`. The `cmdRestore` routine reverses the action of `cmdUpdate`, using the same methodology.

```
Private Sub cmdRestore_Click()
Dim strSQL As String

    On Error GoTo RestoreError
        'Build the UPDATE statement.
        strSQL = "UPDATE Publishers " & _
            "SET City = 'Carmel', Address = '11711 N. College Ave.', " & _
            "Zip = '46032' " & _
            " WHERE ([City] = 'Indianapolis') AND " & _
                    "(Address = '201 W. 103rd St.')"

        'Execute the update query.
        dbfBiblio.Execute strSQL

        ListRecords "Carmel"
    On Error GoTo 0
Exit Sub
```

```
RestoreError:
    MsgBox Error$, vbExclamation
Exit Sub
End Sub
```

5. Create the subroutine ListRecords by entering the following code.
ListRecords builds a SQL SELECT statement that selects records based on
the city name passed as the parameter, and then lists those records in the
list box on the form.

```
Private Sub ListRecords(cityName As String)
    Dim recSelect As Recordset
    Dim strSQL As String, strAddress As String

    On Error GoTo ListError
        ' Set the correct street address based on the city name.
        strAddress = IIf(strCity = "Indianapolis", "201 W. 103rd St.", _
            "11711 N. College Ave.")

        ' Create the recordset for the list box.
        strSQL = "SELECT [Company Name], [Address], [City], " & _
            "[State], [Zip] " & _
            "FROM Publishers " & _
            "WHERE [City] = '" & strCity & "'" & "AND [Address] = '" & _
            strAddress & "'"

        'Construct the recordset.
        Set recSelect = dbfBiblio.OpenRecordset(strSQL, dbOpenSnapshot)

        'Clear the list box
        lstData.Clear

        'Show each record in the list box.
        If recSelect.RecordCount > 0 Then
            recSelect.MoveFirst
            Do
                lstData.AddItem Left$(recSelect![Company Name], 10) _
                    & ", " & recSelect![Address] & ", " & recSelect![City] _
                    & ", " & recSelect![State] & " " & recSelect![Zip]
                recSelect.MoveNext
            Loop While Not recSelect.EOF
        End If
    On Error GoTo 0
Exit Sub

ListError:
    MsgBox Err.Description, vbExclamation
Exit Sub
End Sub
```

6. Add the following code as the Click event of cmdClose:

```
Private Sub cmdClose_Click()
    End
End Sub
```

How It Works

Until either the Update or the Restore button is clicked, the form just lies in wait. If the Update button is clicked, the form executes a SQL statement, modifying any record the statement finds with specific [City] and [Address] field contents, changing the [City], [Address], and [Zip] fields. The Restore performs exactly the same action but reverses the actions taken by the Update button, searching for the newly altered records and restoring them to their previous values.

Comments

This method is usually the best way to make bulk updates to records in any database; it gets the database, rather than the calling application, to do the work, and usually in a more efficient fashion. But, as with any powerful tool, this method can be misused. Ensure that your WHERE clause incorporates *only* those records to be changed. Have too "loose" a selection, and records might be mistakenly altered, much too quickly for the error to be stopped. Be cautious, and your caution will serve you well.

COMPLEXITY
INTERMEDIATE

3.12 How do I...
Create and delete tables?

Problem

I need to create a temporary table, use it for a while, and then get rid of it. How can I accomplish this using SQL?

Technique

SQL provides two statements that allow you to create and delete tables. CREATE TABLE creates a new table, using a name and field list that you specify. DROP TABLE deletes a named table.

To create a table with CREATE TABLE, you need to pass it two arguments: the name of the table to be created and a field list, with the field list enclosed in parentheses. The field list consists of a set of field descriptions, separated by commas. Each field description has two parts: a field name and a data type. The field name and data type are separated by a space.

Execute the CREATE TABLE statement by passing it as the parameter of the Execute method of the Database object. The following Visual Basic statement creates a new table in the database represented by the Database object variable dbfTest. The new table is named My Parts and has two fields: [Part Name], which is a text field, and [Quantity], which is a long integer.

```
dbfTest.Execute("CREATE TABLE [My Parts] ([Part Name] TEXT, " & _
    "[Quantity] LONG)")
```

As with any table or field name, the brackets are required if the name contains a space, and they are optional if there is no space. The convention is to capitalize the data type, but this capitalization is not required.

The data type names used by the Jet database engine do not match exactly the names required by SQL. Table 3.17 shows the SQL data types and the corresponding Jet data type for each.

Table 3.17. SQL data types used by CREATE TABLE and their corresponding Jet database engine data types.

SQL DATA TYPE	EQUIVALENT JET DATA TYPE
BINARY	N/A—for queries on attached tables that define a BINARY data type
BIT	Yes/No
BYTE	Numeric—Byte
COUNTER	Counter
CURRENCY	Currency
DATETIME	Date/Time
SINGLE	Numeric—Single
DOUBLE	Numeric—Double
SHORT	Numeric—Integer
LONG	Numeric—Long
LONGTEXT	Memo
LONGBINARY	OLE objects
TEXT	Text

The DROP TABLE requires just one argument, the name of the table to be removed from the database. Like CREATE TABLE, the DROP TABLE statement is executed through the Execute method of the Database object. The following Visual Basic statement deletes the table My Parts from the database represented by dbfTest:

```
dbfTest.Execute("DROP TABLE [My Parts]")
```

Steps

The NEWTABLE.VBP project lets you create tables in BIBLIO.MDB and assign the table's fields using any data type. Open the project NEWTABLE.VBP and then run the project. The form shown in Figure 3.14 appears.

Click the List Tables button, and the form shown in Figure 3.15 appears. This form lists the tables currently in BIBLIO.MDB. Click Close to return to the Table Creator form.

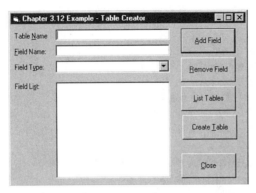

Figure 3.14. The Chapter 3.12 example main form at startup.

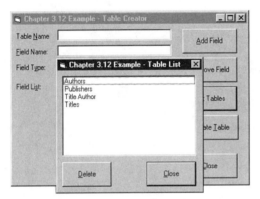

Figure 3.15. The Table List form, showing table names.

In the Table Name text box, type any legal table name. In the Field Name text box, type a field name; then select a field type from the drop-down list. Click Add Field to create the field. Create several additional fields; for each field, type a field name, select a field type, and click Add Field. When you have several fields defined, the form will look as shown in Figure 3.16. Click Create Table to add the table to BIBLIO.MDB. The table name and field names will disappear to ready the Table Creator form for creation of another table. You can click List Tables to see your table BIBLIO.MDB.

After you've created several tables, click List Tables. Select one of the tables you created and click Delete. (The program will not let you delete a table with data in it, so you will not be able to delete any of the original BIBLIO.MDB tables.) The table disappears from the table list.

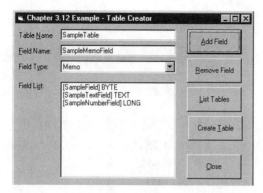

Figure 3.16. The Chapter 3.12 example main form, with new fields added.

1. Create a new project called NEWTABLE.VBP. Rename Form1 to frmMain, create the objects and properties listed in Table 3.18, and save the form as NEWTABLE.FRM.

Table 3.18. Objects and properties for the Table Creator form.

OBJECT	PROPERTY	SETTING
Form	Name	frmMain
	Caption	"Chapter 3.12 Example - Table Creator"
CommandButton	Name	cmdListTables
	Caption	"&List Tables"
CommandButton	Name	cmdCreateTable
	Caption	"Create &Table"
CommandButton	Name	cmdRemoveField
	Caption	"&Remove Field"
CommandButton	Name	cmdAddField
	Caption	"&Add Field"
	Default	True
CommandButton	Name	cmdClose
	Cancel	True
	Caption	"&Close"
ComboBox	Name	cboFieldTypes
	Style	2 - Dropdown List
ListBox	Name	lstFields
TextBox	Name	txtFieldName
TextBox	Name	txtTableName

continued on next page

continued from previous page

OBJECT	PROPERTY	SETTING
Label	Name	lblTableName
	Caption	"&Table Name:"
Label	Name	lblFieldName
	Caption	"&Field Name:"
Label	Name	lblFieldType
	Caption	"Field T&ype:"
Label	Name	lblFieldList
	Caption	"Field Li&st:"

2. Insert a new form into the project. Rename it `frmTableList`, create the objects and properties listed in Table 3.19, and save the form as TABLIST.FRM.

Table 3.19. Objects and properties for the Current Tables form.

OBJECT	PROPERTY	SETTING
Form	Name	frmTableList
	BorderStyle	3 - Fixed Dialog
	Caption	"Chapter 3.12 Example - Table List"
	MaxButton	False
	MinButton	False
CommandButton	Name	cmdDelete
	Caption	"&Delete"
CommandButton	Name	cmdClose
	Caption	"Close"
ListBox	Name	lstTables
	Sorted	True

3. Add the following statements to the declarations section of `frmMain`:

```
Option Explicit

Private Const IllegalCharacters = "[].!'"
Private Const FIELDNAME = 1
Private Const TABLENAME = 2

Private Const BIBLIO_PATH = "C:\Program Files\DevStudio\VB\Biblio.MDB"
```

4. Enter the following code for the **Form_Load** event for `frmMain`:

```
Private Sub Form_Load()

    'Fill the Field Type combo box.
    FillTypeList
End Sub
```

5. Create the `FillTypeList` subroutine in `frmMain` with the following code. This procedure fills the drop-down list with the available data types, using the Jet database engine names.

```
Sub FillTypeList()
'Fill the Field Type combo box with types of available fields
    With cboFieldTypes
        .AddItem "Counter"
        .AddItem "Currency"
        .AddItem "Date/Time"
        .AddItem "Memo"
        .AddItem "Number: Byte"
        .AddItem "Number: Integer"
        .AddItem "Number: Long"
        .AddItem "Number: Single"
        .AddItem "Number: Double"
        .AddItem "OLE Object"
        .AddItem "Text"
        .AddItem "Yes/No"
    End With
End Sub
```

6. Enter the following code as the `Click` event of `frmMain`'s `cmdListTables`. This subroutine displays the **List Tables** form modally.

```
Private Sub cmdListTables_Click()
    ' Display the Table List form modally.
    frmTableList.Show vbModal
End Sub
```

7. Enter the following code as the `Click` event of `frmMain`'s `cmdAddField`. The `cmdAddField` routine first calls the `LegalName` function to verify that the user has entered a legal field name and verifies that the user has selected a field type. It then translates the data type shown in the drop-down list from the Jet name to the SQL name. It formats the field name and data type and adds it to the field list. It then clears the field name and field type for entry of the next field.

```
Private Sub cmdAddField_Click()
Dim strFieldType As String

    'Check first if the Field Name text box contains a legal name
    If LegalName(FIELDNAME) Then
        'If it does, check if the Field Type has been selected.
        If cboFieldTypes.ListIndex > -1 Then
            'If both criteria are satisfied, store the SQL field type
            'in the strFieldType string.
```

continued on next page

continued from previous page

```
            Select Case cboFieldTypes.Text
                Case "Counter"
                    strFieldType = "COUNTER"
                Case "Currency"
                    strFieldType = "CURRENCY"
                Case "Date/Time"
                    strFieldType = "DATETIME"
                Case "Memo"
                    strFieldType = "LONGTEXT"
                Case "Number: Byte"
                    strFieldType = "BYTE"
                Case "Number: Integer"
                    strFieldType = "SHORT"
                Case "Number: Long"
                    strFieldType = "LONG"
                Case "Number: Single"
                    strFieldType = "SINGLE"
                Case "Number: Double"
                    strFieldType = "DOUBLE"
                Case "OLE Object"
                    strFieldType = "LONGBINARY"
                Case "Text"
                    strFieldType = "TEXT"
                Case "Yes/No"
                    strFieldType = "BIT"
            End Select

            'Add the new field to the Field List list box.
            lstFields.AddItem "[" & txtFieldName & "] " & strFieldType

            'Reset the Field Name and Field Type controls.
            txtFieldName = ""
            cboFieldTypes.ListIndex = -1
        Else
            MsgBox "You must select a field type.", vbExclamation
        End If
    End If
End Sub
```

8. Create the **LegalName** function in **frmMain** by entering the following code.
The function performs a number of checks to verify that the name entered
by the user as a table name or field name is acceptable to the Jet engine.
For each check, it generates a user-defined error if the name fails the test.
The error-handling code displays a message that explains to the user what
the problem is, then returns **False** to the calling routine. If the name
passes all the tests, the error-handling code is never called, and the
function returns **True**.

```
Function LegalName(intNameType As Integer) As Boolean
    Dim i As Integer
    Dim strObjectName As String
    Dim dbfBiblio As Database, tdfNewTable As TableDef

    On Error GoTo IllegalName
```

```
            'Depending on the type of name being checked, store either the
            'field or table name text box contents.
            If intNameType = FIELDNAME Then
                strObjectName = txtFieldName
            Else
                strObjectName = txtTableName
            End If


            'If blank, raise an error.
            If Len(strObjectName) = 0 Then Err.Raise 32767
            'If it has a leading space, raise an error.
            If Left$(strObjectName, 1) = " " Then Err.Raise 32766
            'If it contains any of the characters in the IllegalCharacters
            'constant, raise an error
            For i = 1 To Len(IllegalCharacters)
                If InStr(strObjectName, Mid(IllegalCharacters, i, 1)) > 0 _
                    Then Err.Raise 32765
            Next i
            'If it contains any ANSI character from Chr$(0) to Chr$(31),
            '(you guessed it) raise an error.
            For i = 0 To 31
                If InStr(strObjectName, Chr(i)) > 0 Then Err.Raise 32764
            Next i


            'Check if the field or table name already exists.  If so,
            'raise an error.
            If intNameType = FIELDNAME Then
                For i = 0 To lstFields.ListCount - 1
                    If strObjectName = lstFields.List(i) Then Err.Raise 32763
                Next i
            ElseIf intNameType = TABLENAME Then
                Set dbfBiblio = DBEngine.Workspaces(0).OpenDatabase(BIBLIO_PATH)
                For Each tdfNewTable In dbfBiblio.TableDefs
                    If tdfNewTable.Name = strObjectName Then Err.Raise 32762
                Next
            End If


            'If they've managed to get through all that validation, the function
            'should be True, to indicate success.
            LegalName = True
        On Error GoTo 0
    Exit Function

IllegalName:
    Dim strErrDesc As String, context As String

    'Note the use of an IIf statement to reduce code size.
    context = IIf(intNameType = FIELDNAME, "field name", "table name")

    'Build an error message based on the user-defined error that occurred.
    Select Case Err.Number
        Case 32767
            strErrDesc = "You must enter a " & context & "."
        Case 32766
            strErrDesc = "The " & context & " cannot begin with a space."
        Case 32765
```

continued on next page

continued from previous page

```
                strErrDesc = "The " & context & _
                    " contains the illegal character " & _
                    Mid(IllegalCharacters, i, 1) & "."
        Case 32764
                strErrDesc = "The " & context & _
                    " contains the control character " & _
                    "with the ANSI value" & Str$(i) & "."
        Case 32763
                strErrDesc = "The field name " & strObjectName & _
                    " already exists in the field name list."
        Case 32762
                strErrDesc = "The table name " & strObjectName & _
                    " already exists in the database " & BIBLIO_PATH & "."
        Case Else
                ' Visual Basic's default error message.
                strErrDesc = Err.Description
    End Select

    MsgBox strErrDesc, vbExclamation

    'The function indicates False, or failure.
    LegalName = False
Exit Function

End Function
```

9. Enter the following code as the **Click** event of **frmMain**'s **cmdRemoveField**. This procedure deletes the field selected by the user.

```
Private Sub cmdRemoveField_Click()
    ' If the user has selected a field, remove it from the list.
    ' Otherwise, just ignore the click.
    If lstFields.ListIndex > -1 Then lstFields.RemoveItem _
        lstFields.ListIndex
End Sub
```

10. Enter the following code as the **Click** event of **frmMain**'s **cmdCreateTable**. This procedure calls **LegalName** to verify that the table name is acceptable and verifies that the user has defined at least one field. It creates the field list for the SQL statement by reading through the data in **lstFields** and building a comma-delimited string from the entries in that list box. It then builds the SQL statement and uses the **Execute** method of the **Database** object to create the table.

```
Private Sub cmdCreateTable_Click()
    Dim strSQL As String, strFieldList As String
    Dim i As Integer
    Dim dbfBiblio As Database

    On Error GoTo CreateTableError
        Screen.MousePointer = vbHourglass

        If LegalName(TABLENAME) Then
            If lstFields.ListCount > 0 Then
                strFieldList = " (" & lstFields.List(0)
```

```
                    For i = 1 To lstFields.ListCount - 1
                        strFieldList = strFieldList & ", " & lstFields.List(i)
                    Next i
                    strFieldList = strFieldList & ") "
                    strSQL = "CREATE TABLE [" & txtTableName & "]" _
                            & strFieldList

                    Set dbfBiblio = _
                            DBEngine.Workspaces(0).OpenDatabase(BIBLIO_PATH)
                    dbfBiblio.Execute (strSQL)

                    Screen.MousePointer = vbDefault
                    MsgBox "Table created successfully."

                    txtTableName = ""
                    lstFields.Clear
                Else
                    Screen.MousePointer = vbDefault
                    MsgBox "You must define at least one field.", vbExclamation
                End If
            End If
        On Error GoTo 0
    Exit Sub

CreateTableError:
    Screen.MousePointer = vbDefault
    MsgBox Error$, vbExclamation
Exit Sub
End Sub
```

11. Enter the following code as the `Click` event of `frmMain`'s `cmdClose`. Unlike most of the `cmdClose_Click` events in previous How-To's, this has a bit more to it. If the user has entered a partial table definition (as determined by a table name or one or more created fields), a message box is presented to ask the user whether to abandon the current creation, and it requires a Yes or No answer. If the user answers Yes, the program is ended. If there is no partial table definition, the program ends without showing the message box.

```
Private Sub cmdClose_Click()
    Dim strErrDesc As String

    ' If the user has entered a partial table definition, make sure that the
    ' user wants to abandon it. If so, end the program.
    If txtTableName <> "" Or lstFields.ListCount > 0 Then
        strErrDesc = "Do you want to abandon operations on the " & _
                    "current table?"
        If MsgBox(strErrDesc, vbQuestion + vbYesNo + vbDefaultButton2) = _
                vbYes Then
            End
        End If
    Else
        ' No partial table definition, so just end the program
        End
    End If
End Sub
```

12. Switch to `frmTableList`. Enter the following code into the declarations section of `frmTableList`, modifying the path in the `Const` statement to point to your copy of BIBLIO.MDB.

```
Option Explici

Private Const BIBLIO_PATH = "C:\Program Files\DevStudio\VB\Biblio.MDB"
```

13. Enter the following code as `frmTableList`'s `Form_Load` event. This calls the `ListTables` subroutine, explained in the next step, to fill the `lstTables` list box with the database's tables.

```
Private Sub Form_Load()
    ' Fill the list box with the current non-system tables in BIBLIO.MDB.
    ListTables
End Sub
```

14. Create the `ListTables` subroutine in `frmTableList` by entering the following code. `ListTables` is called when the form loads and when the user deletes a table. It uses the `TableDefs` collection of the `Database` object to build a list of tables in the BIBLIO.MDB database. The `TableDefs` collection contains one record for each table in the database, including the (normally hidden) system tables. Because the `Name` property of all system table `TableDef` objects begins with the string `"MSys"`, this procedure assumes that any table starting with that string is a system table and ignores it. The names of all other tables get added to the `lstTables` list box.

```
Private Sub ListTables()
Dim dbfBiblio As Database, tdfTableList As TableDef

    On Error GoTo ListError
        Screen.MousePointer = vbHourglass
        'Clear the list box, then open the database.
        lstTables.Clear
        Set dbfBiblio = DBEngine.Workspaces(0).OpenDatabase(BIBLIO_PATH)
        ' Cycle through the table definitions in BIBLIO_PATH.
        ' If the table is a system table (name begins with MSys), ignore it.
        ' Otherwise, add it to the list.
        For Each tdfTableList In dbfBiblio.TableDefs
            If Left$(tdfTableList.Name, 4) <> "MSys" Then lstTables.AddItem _
                    tdfTableList.Name
        Next

        Screen.MousePointer = vbDefault
    On Error GoTo 0
Exit Sub

ListError:
    Screen.MousePointer = vbDefault
    MsgBox Err.Description, vbExclamation
    Unload frmTableList
Exit Sub
End Sub
```

15. Enter the following code as the Click event frmTableList's cmdDelete.
CREATE TABLE deletes a table whether or not the table contains data.
Because we do not want to delete any tables with data, this procedure
checks to make sure that the table is empty, then deletes it.

```
Private Sub cmdDelete_Click()
Dim dbfBiblio As Database

    On Error GoTo DeleteError
        Screen.MousePointer = vbHourglass
        'If a table is selected, then continue
        If lstTables.ListIndex > -1 Then
            'Confirm that the table has no records
            If TableIsEmpty() Then
                ' Delete the selected table from BIBLIO_PATH.
                Set dbfBiblio = _
                    DBEngine.Workspaces(0).OpenDatabase(BIBLIO_PATH)
                dbfBiblio.Execute ("DROP TABLE [" & lstTables.Text & "]")

                ' Display the modified list of tables.
                ListTables
                Screen.MousePointer = vbDefault
            Else
                'The table has records, so inform the user.
                Screen.MousePointer = vbDefault
                MsgBox lstTables.Text & " is not empty.", vbExclamation
            End If
        Else
            'No table has been chosen, so inform the user.
            Screen.MousePointer = vbDefault
            MsgBox "You have not selected a table to delete.", vbExclamation
        End If
    On Error GoTo 0
Exit Sub

DeleteError:
    Screen.MousePointer = vbDefault
    MsgBox Err.Description, vbExclamation
    Unload frmTableList
Exit Sub
End Sub
```

16. Create the TableIsEmpty function by entering the following code into
frmTableList. This function returns True if the table currently selected in
lstTables is empty.

```
Function TableIsEmpty() As Boolean
Dim dbfBiblio As Database, tdfTableList As TableDef

    On Error GoTo TableIsEmptyError
        Set dbfBiblio = DBEngine.Workspaces(0).OpenDatabase(BIBLIO_PATH)

        ' Cycle through the table definitions in BIBLIO_PATH.
        ' When the table currently selected in lstTables is found, check to
        ' see whether it has records. If it does not, return True;
```

continued on next page

continued from previous page

```
        ' otherwise, return False.
        For Each tdfTableList In dbfBiblio.TableDefs
            If tdfTableList.Name = lstTables.Text Then
                TableIsEmpty = IIf(tdfTableList.RecordCount = 0, _
                    True, False)
                Exit For
            End If
        Next
    On Error GoTo 0
Exit Function

TableIsEmptyError:
    MsgBox Err.Description, vbExclamation
    Unload frmTableList
Exit Function
End Function
```

17. Enter the following code as the `Click` event of `frmTableList`'s `cmdClose`:

```
Private Sub cmdClose_Click()
    Unload frmTableList
End Sub
```

How It Works

The `frmMain` form essentially builds a **CREATE TABLE** SQL statement by using the table name listed in the `lstTables` control, with the fields listed in the `lstFields` list box. This might seem greatly simplified, but it guides all the reasoning behind the code we've added in this How-To.

The main action occurs in the `cmdCreateTable_Click` event of `frmMain`. Here, based on the choices the user made regarding the name of the table and the name and type of the fields to be added, the **CREATE TABLE** SQL statement is concatenated and executed. The `cmdListTables` button is used to display a list of existing tables in the Access database, in case the user wants to rewrite an existing empty table (the `TableIsEmpty` function is used to ensure that valuable data is not overwritten; the program will destroy only an empty table). The `cboFieldTypes` combo box allows the program to filter the various field types in a manner accessible to the user.

Comments

One of the key notes to remember in this How-To is the destructive behavior of the **CREATE TABLE** statement, as mentioned in step 15. If a **CREATE TABLE** statement is issued defining a table with the same name as one that already exists in the Access database, it destroys the existing table. Although this behavior is not true across all database platforms, it's usually better to be safe than sorry and include a routine similar to the `TableIsEmpty` function in this How-To.

COMPLEXITY
INTERMEDIATE

3.13 How do I...
Append and delete records?

Problem

I have a table to which I'd like to add records that are built from records in other tables. I'd also like to delete records based on criteria I specify. How can I accomplish these tasks with SQL?

Technique

SQL provides two statements, the INSERT INTO and DELETE statements, that append records to a table and delete records from a table, respectively.

The INSERT INTO Statement

SQL's INSERT INTO statement is used to append records to an existing table. The INSERT INTO statement has three clauses, shown in Table 3.20.

Table 3.20. The syntax of the INSERT INTO statement.

CLAUSE	PURPOSE	EXAMPLE
INSERT INTO	Names the table and fields into which data are to be inserted.	INSERT INTO [Publisher Titles] ([Name], [Title])
SELECT	Names the fields from which data are to be taken.	SELECT Publishers.Name, Titles.Title
FROM	Names the table or other source of the data.	FROM Publishers INNER JOIN Titles ON Publishers.PubID = Titles.PubID

The INSERT INTO clause takes two parameters, the table name ([Publisher Titles] in the example) and the field names into which data are to be inserted. The field names are enclosed in parentheses and delimited by commas.

The SELECT clause consists of a list of fields from which the data to be inserted into the fields named in the INSERT INTO clause will be drawn. There must be a one-to-one correspondence between the fields in the INSERT INTO clause and the fields in the SELECT clause. If you have more INSERT INTO fields than SELECT fields, or vice versa, an error will result. If the field names are from multiple tables—as in the example—and if the names are ambiguous (that is, both tables have fields with the same names), then they must be qualified with the table names.

The FROM clause names the table or other source of the fields named in the SELECT clause. In the example, the FROM clause names not a single table, but a pair of tables linked by an INNER JOIN. (See How-To 3.6 for details on INNER JOINs.)

As with other SQL action queries, you run the INSERT INTO clause by using it as the argument for the Execute method of the Database object. To execute the query shown in the table against a database object represented by the variable dbfTest, you would create the following Visual Basic statement (note the continuation character):

```
dbfTest.Execute("INSERT INTO [Publisher Titles] ([Name], " & _
    "[Title]) SELECT Publishers.Name, " & _
    "Titles.Title FROM Publishers INNER JOIN Titles ON " & _
    "Publishers.PubID = Titles.PubID")
```

The DELETE Statement

Use the SQL DELETE statement to delete records from a table, based on criteria you specify in the DELETE statement. The DELETE statement has the syntax shown in Table 3.21.

Table 3.21. The syntax of the DELETE statement.

CLAUSE	PURPOSE	EXAMPLE
DELETE FROM	Names the table from which records are to be deleted.	DELETE FROM [Publisher Titles]
WHERE	Criteria that select records for deletion.	WHERE [Publication Date] <= 1990

Execute the DELETE statement by passing it as the parameter to the Execute method of the Database object. If you have a Database object variable named dbfTest, this Visual Basic statement executes the SQL shown in the table:

```
dbfTest.Execute("DELETE FROM [Publisher Titles] WHERE [Publication Date] <= 1990")
```

Steps

Open and run the project UPDATE.VBP. Click the Create Table button, then the Append Records button. These two actions create a table named [Publisher Titles], fill it with records, and display those records in the form, as shown in Figure 3.17. Notice the titles from Addison-Wesley on your screen (you might need to scroll down to see them.)

Click the Delete Records button. The Select Publisher form, shown in Figure 3.18, appears. Select Addison-Wesley and then click OK. The previous form reappears, with the list refreshed to show the records currently in the [Publisher Titles] table. Notice that the Addison-Wesley titles are missing.

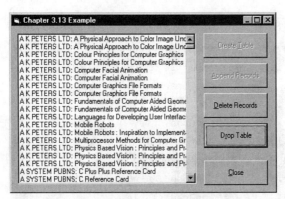

Figure 3.17. The Chapter 3.13 example
main form, showing appended records.

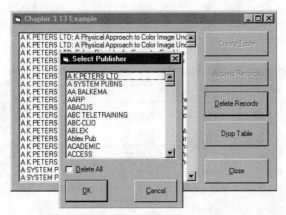

Figure 3.18. The Publisher List form,
showing publisher names.

1. Create a new project called APPEND.VBP. Rename Form1 to frmMain,
create the objects and properties listed in Table 3.22, and save the form as
APPEND.FRM.

Table 3.22. Objects and properties for the Append and Delete form.

OBJECT	PROPERTY	SETTING
Form	Name	frmMain
	Caption	"Chapter 3.13 Example"
ListBox	Name	lstData
	Sorted	True

continued on next page

continued from previous page

OBJECT	PROPERTY	SETTING
CommandButton	Name	cmdDeleteRecords
	Caption	"&Delete Records"
CommandButton	Name	cmdClose
	Caption	"&Close"
CommandButton	Name	cmdDropTable
	Caption	"D&rop Table"
CommandButton	Name	cmdAppendRecords
	Caption	"&Append Records"
CommandButton	Name	cmdCreateTable
	Caption	"Create &Table"

2. Insert a new form into the project. Rename it to `frmSelectPublisher`, create the objects and properties listed in Table 3.23, and save the form as PublisherSelect.FRM.

Table 3.23. Objects and properties for the Select Publisher form.

OBJECT	PROPERTY	SETTING
Form	Name	frmSelectPublisher
	BorderStyle	3 - Fixed Dialog
	Caption	"Chapter 3.13 - Publisher List"
	MaxButton	False
	MinButton	False
CommandButton	Name	cmdOK
	Caption	"&OK"
	Default	True
CommandButton	Name	cmdCancel
	Caption	"&Cancel"
CheckBox	Name	chkDeleteAll
	Caption	"&Delete All"
ListBox	Name	lstPublishers
	Sorted	True

3. Add the following statements to the declarations section of `frmMain`:

```
Option Explicit

Private Const BIBLIO_PATH = "C:\Program Files\DevStudio\VB\Biblio.MDB"
```

```
Private strPublisherToDelete As String Private dbfBiblio As Database
```

4. Enter the following code as in the **Load** event of **frmMain**. The **Form_Load**
code checks to see whether the [Publisher Titles] table exists in the
database and, if it exists, whether it has any records. It then enables and
disables the appropriate command buttons.

```
Private Sub Form_Load()
Dim tdfTable As TableDef
    Dim blnTableFound As Boolean

    On Error GoTo LoadError
        blnTableFound = False

        'Open the database.
        Set dbfBiblio = DBEngine.Workspaces(0).OpenDatabase(BIBLIO_PATH)
        'Iterate through the TableDefs collection.  If the table "Publisher
        'Titles" is found, configure the form's buttons appropriately.
        For Each tdfTable In dbfBiblio.TableDefs
            If tdfTable.Name = "Publisher Titles" Then
                blnTableFound = True
                cmdDropTable.Enabled = True
                cmdCreateTable.Enabled = False

                If tdfTable.RecordCount > 0 Then
                    cmdDeleteRecords.Enabled = True
                    cmdAppendRecords.Enabled = False
                    FillList
                Else
                    cmdDeleteRecords.Enabled = False
                    cmdAppendRecords.Enabled = True
                End If
                Exit For
            End If
        Next

        'If the table is not found, configure the form's buttons
        'appropriately.
        If blnTableFound = False Then
            cmdDropTable.Enabled = False
            cmdCreateTable.Enabled = True
            cmdAppendRecords.Enabled = False
            cmdDeleteRecords.Enabled = False
        End If
    On Error GoTo 0
Exit Sub

LoadError:
    MsgBox Err.Description, vbExclamation
    Unload Me
Exit Sub

End Sub
```

5. Create the `FillList` subroutine in `frmMain` by entering the following code. The `FillList` routine fills the list box `lstData` with the records from the [Publisher Titles] table.

```
Sub FillList()
Dim recSelect As Recordset
    Dim strSQL As String

    On Error GoTo FillListError
        'Clear the list box.
        lstData.Clear
        'Get all the records from the Publisher Titles table.
        Set recSelect = dbfBiblio.OpenRecordset("SELECT * FROM " & _
            "[Publisher Titles]", dbOpenSnapshot)

        'Put the records into the list box.
        If recSelect.RecordCount > 0 Then
            recSelect.MoveFirst
            Do Until recSelect.EOF
                lstData.AddItem recSelect![Name] & ": " & recSelect![Title]
                recSelect.MoveNext
            Loop
        End If
    On Error GoTo 0
Exit Sub

FillListError:
    MsgBox Err.Description, vbExclamation
Exit Sub
End Sub
```

6. Enter the following code as the `Click` event for `frmMain`'s `cmdCreateTable`. This code creates the [Publisher Titles] table. Refer to the previous How-To for information on the **CREATE TABLE** statement.

```
Private Sub cmdCreateTable_Click()
    Dim strSQL As String

    On Error GoTo CreateTableError
        'Build the CREATE TABLE statement.
        strSQL = "CREATE TABLE [Publisher Titles] " & _
            "([Name] TEXT, [Title] TEXT)"
        'Execute the statement.  Since it's an action query,
        'you don't use the OpenRecordset command.  It would
        'fail, since an action query does not return a recordset.
        dbfBiblio.Execute (strSQL)

        'Configure the form's buttons appropriately.
        cmdCreateTable.Enabled = False
        cmdDropTable.Enabled = True
        cmdAppendRecords.Enabled = True
    On Error GoTo 0
Exit Sub

CreateTableError:
```

```
    MsgBox Err.Description, vbExclamation
Exit Sub
End Sub
```

7. Enter the following code as the **Click** event for **frmMain**'s **cmdDropTable**. This code deletes the [Publisher Titles] table. Refer to the preceding How-To for information on the **DROP TABLE** statement.

```
Private Sub cmdDropTable_Click()
Dim dbName As String

    On Error GoTo DropTableError
        'Build & execute the DROP TABLE statement.
        dbfBiblio.Execute ("DROP TABLE [Publisher Titles]")

        'Configure the form's buttons appropriately.
        cmdDropTable.Enabled = False
        cmdCreateTable.Enabled = True
        cmdAppendRecords.Enabled = False
        cmdDeleteRecords.Enabled = False

        'Clear the list box.
        lstData.Clear
    On Error GoTo 0
Exit Sub

DropTableError:
    MsgBox Err.Description, vbExclamation
Exit Sub
End Sub
```

8. Enter the following code as the **Click** event for **frmMain**'s **cmdAppendRecords**. This command builds the SQL statement that will append the records to the database, then executes the statement. The SQL statement is identical to that shown in Table 3.20.

```
Private Sub cmdAppendRecords_Click()
    Dim strSQL As String

    On Error GoTo AppendRecordsError
        Screen.MousePointer = vbHourglass
        'Build the INSERT INTO statement
        strSQL = "INSERT INTO [Publisher Titles] ( [Name], Title ) " & _
            "SELECT Publishers.Name, Titles.Title " & _
            "FROM Publishers INNER JOIN Titles " & _
            "ON Publishers.PubID = Titles.PubID"

        'Execute the statement.
        dbfBiblio.Execute (strSQL)

        'Fill the list box via the FillList subroutine.
        FillList

        'Configure the form's buttons appropriately.
```

continued on next page

continued from previous page

```
        cmdDeleteRecords.Enabled = True
        cmdAppendRecords.Enabled = False

        Screen.MousePointer = vbDefault
    On Error GoTo 0
Exit Sub

AppendRecordsError:
    Screen.MousePointer = vbDefault
    MsgBox Err.Description, vbExclamation
Exit Sub
End Sub
```

9. Enter the following code as the **Click** event for **frmMain**'s
cmdDeleteRecords. This procedure deletes the designated records from
the database. It calls the **GetPublisher** function of **frmSelectPublisher**,
returning a value to be placed in **strPublisherToDelete**. Then it
examines the public variable **strPublisherToDelete**; if
strPublisherToDelete is an empty string, it indicates that the user wants
to cancel the deletion, so no records are deleted. If **strPublisherToDelete**
is "*****", the user wants to delete all the records. Otherwise,
frmSelectPublisher contains the name of the publisher whose titles the
user wants to delete. The procedure builds the appropriate SQL **DELETE**
statement, then executes the statement.

```
Private Sub cmdDeleteRecords_Click()
    Dim strSQL As String

    On Error GoTo DeleteRecordsError

    'Use the GetPublisher function on frmSelectPublisher to return
    'a publisher to delete.
    strPublisherToDelete = frmSelectPublisher.GetPublisher
    'If one is selected, then delete it.
    If strPublisherToDelete <> "" Then
        'Build the DELETE statement.
        strSQL = "DELETE FROM [Publisher Titles]"
        'If the publisher to delete isn't the * wildcard, then
        'modify the SQL to choose the selected publisher(s).
        If strPublisherToDelete <> "*" Then
            strSQL = strSQL & " WHERE [Publisher Titles].[Name] = " & _
                """" & strPublisherToDelete & """"
        End If

        'Execute the statement.
        dbfBiblio.Execute (strSQL)

        'Fill the list box.
        FillList
    End If

    cmdAppendRecords.Enabled = (lstData.ListCount = 0)
    cmdDeleteRecords.Enabled = (lstData.ListCount > 0)
```

```
Exit Sub

DeleteRecordsError:
    MsgBox Err.Description, vbExclamation
Exit Sub
End Sub
```

10. Enter the following code as the `Click` event for `frmMain`'s `cmdClose`:

```
Private Sub cmdClose_Click()
    End
End Sub
```

11. Switch to `frmPublisherSelect` and enter the following code into the declarations section. Modify the path in the `Const` statement to point to your copy of BIBLIO.MDB.

```
Option Explicit

Private Const BIBLIO_PATH = "C:\Program Files\DevStudio\VB\Biblio.MDB"

Private strPublisherToDelete As String
```

12. Enter the following code as the `Load` event for `frmSelectPublisher`. On loading, the form builds a recordset of publisher names in the [Publisher Titles] table through a SQL `SELECT` statement with the `DISTINCT` keyword. (See How-To 3.2 for information on the `DISTINCT` keyword.) It uses that recordset to fill the `lstPublishers` list box.

```
Private Sub Form_Load()
    Dim dbfBiblio As Database, recSelect As Recordset
    Dim strSQL As String

    On Error GoTo LoadError
        Set dbfBiblio = DBEngine.Workspaces(0).OpenDatabase(BIBLIO_PATH)
        strSQL = "SELECT DISTINCT [Name] FROM [Publisher Titles]"
        Set recSelect = dbfBiblio.OpenRecordset(strSQL)
        If recSelect.RecordCount > 0 Then
            recSelect.MoveFirst
            Do Until recSelect.EOF
                lstPublishers.AddItem recSelect![Name]
                recSelect.MoveNext
            Loop
        End If
    On Error GoTo 0
Exit Sub

LoadError:
    MsgBox Err.Description, vbExclamation
    strPublisherToDelete = ""
    Me.Hide
Exit Sub
End Sub
```

13. Enter the following code as the **Click** event for **frmSelectPublisher**'s **cmdOK**. This procedure sets the public variable **strPublisherToDelete**. If the user has clicked the Delete All button, **strPublisherToDelete** is set to the string **"*"**. Otherwise, **strPublisherToDelete** is set to the name of the selected publisher.

```
Private Sub cmdOK_Click()
If chkDeleteAll Then
        strPublisherToDelete = "*"
        Me.Hide
    ElseIf lstPublishers.ListIndex > -1 Then
        strPublisherToDelete = lstPublishers.Text
        Me.Hide
    End If
End Sub
```

14. Enter the following code as the **DblClick** event for **frmSelectPublisher**'s **lstPublishers**. This allows the program to call the **cmdOK_Click** event, preventing duplication of code. A double-click of the Publishers list brings about exactly the same result as if a publisher had been selected with a single left click, and the OK button had then been clicked.

```
Private Sub lstPublishers_DblClick()
    cmdOK_Click
End Sub
```

15. Enter the following code as the **Click** event for **frmSelectPublisher**'s **cmdCancel**. This code ensures that the **strPublisherToDelete** string is blank, preventing the calling form's code from inadvertently deleting a publisher. Note that the form is hidden (as opposed to unloaded) here. This form is called by the **GetPublisher** public function and is unloaded by that function.

```
Private Sub cmdCancel_Click()
    strPublisherToDelete = ""
    Me.Hide
End Sub
```

16. Enter the following code to create the **GetPublisher** method for **frmSelectPublisher**. This is a public function, allowing you to use this form like a dialog box, with the result of this function being sent back to the calling form. You will find that this method for using forms is preferable to the "one use" form in many situations, especially when a "generic" form is used for multiple purposes.

```
Public Function GetPublisher() As String
    Me.Show vbModal
    GetPublisher = strPublisherToDelete
    Unload Me
End Function
```

How It Works

When the `cmdCreateTable` button is clicked, a `CREATE TABLE` statement is executed (for more information on the `CREATE TABLE` statement, see the preceding How-To) to create an empty table in BIBLIO.MDB. The `cmdAppendRecords` button, once clicked, fills that empty table by executing the `INSERT...INTO` statement, creating the information from a `SELECT` query run on two other tables in the database. When the table is fully populated, the list box `lstTitles` is then filled from the new table's data via the `FillList` subroutine. The `cmdDeleteRecords` button, which deletes the newly created records, first calls the `GetPublisher` public function on the `frmSelectPublisher` form. The form presents a dialog box with options to delete either records from a single publisher or all publishers in the table. Based on this selection, the `GetPublisher` function returns either a publisher's name or the asterisk wildcard character. Using this information, the `cmdDeleteRecords` button builds and executes a `DELETE` statement. Last, but not least, the `cmdDropTable` button simply executes a `DROP TABLE` statement on the new table.

Comments

One of the more interesting capabilities of Visual Basic 5.0 (and 4.0, for that matter) is the capacity for public functions and subroutines on forms. This allows for a wide degree of flexibility in the way forms can be used, including the ability to use a form in a manner similar to that of, say, a common dialog, by calling a public function on the form. This functionality serves well in this How-To, because it makes the selection process for deletion of a group of records go much easier and "cleaner" in terms of design and user interface.

The `INSERT...INTO` and `DELETE` statements are useful for creating and emptying temporary tables. Temporary tables, although not always the most efficient way to go, do have their purposes, and these two new tools in your arsenal should go a long way toward their proper and efficient management.

COMPLEXITY

INTERMEDIATE

3.14 How do I...
Create a new table with data from existing tables?

Problem

I know I can use `CREATE TABLE` and `INSERT INTO` to create a table and add records to it. But in my application, I do this many times, and I'd like to accomplish it all with a single SQL operation. How can I do this?

Technique

The SELECT...INTO statement lets you create a new table with data from existing tables in a single operation. Its syntax is shown in Table 3.24. As with the INSERT...INTO and DELETE statements, both covered in the preceding How-To, this tool makes an excellent way to work with temporary tables.

Table 3.24. The syntax of the SELECT...INTO statement.

CLAUSE	PURPOSE	EXAMPLE
SELECT	Names the fields in the existing table that will be re-created in the new table.	SELECT Publishers.Name, Titles.Title
INTO	Names the new table.	INTO [Publisher Titles]
FROM	Names the table (or other source) of the data.	FROM Publishers INNER JOIN Titles ON Publishers.PubID = Titles.PubID

To run the SELECT...INTO query, use the Execute method of the Database object. The following Visual Basic statement (on one line) executes the query shown in the table on the database represented by the variable dbfTest:

```
dbfTest.Execute("SELECT Publishers.Name, " & _
    "Titles.Title INTO [Publisher Titles]" & _
    " FROM Publishers INNER JOIN Titles ON Publishers.PubID = Titles.PubID")
```

With the example presented previously, a new table, titled [Publisher Titles], is created in the database, constructed from information gleaned from two other tables, connected by an INNER JOIN. The difference between the SELECT...INTO command and the INSERT...INTO command is simple: the INSERT...INTO command creates new records and performs an INSERT on the existing recipient table, whereas the SELECT...INTO creates a new recipient table before performing an INSERT. The SELECT...INTO statement, because of this behavior, is the ideal method of creating a temporary table in one step. In the preceding How-To, we needed two steps—one to create the table, and one to add the records. SELECT...INTO combines these two steps into one, making it simpler to use and simpler to debug if problems arise. Note that the behavior on some databases differs as to exactly what happens when a SELECT...INTO statement is executed, with the recipient table being the same name as an existing table in the database. In a Microsoft Access 97 database, the SELECT...INTO command deletes the existing table first. Some databases, however, might trigger an error in performing this action. To examine this behavior, it is advised that you create a sample table with data, execute a SELECT...INTO statement with that sample table as recipient, and note the results.

Steps

Open and run the project MAKETABL.VBP. Click the Create Table button; the list box fills with the records added to the newly created table (Figure 3.19). Click the Drop Table button to delete the table.

1. Create a new project called MAKETABL.VBP. Use **Form1** to create the objects and properties listed in Table 3.25, and save the form as MAKETABL.FRM.

Table 3.25. Objects and properties for the Table Maker form.

OBJECT	PROPERTY	SETTING
Form	Name	Form1
	Caption	"Chapter 3.14 Example"
ListBox	Name	lstData
	Sorted	True
CommandButton	Name	cmdClose
	Caption	"&Close"
CommandButton	Name	cmdDropTable
	Caption	"D&rop Table"
CommandButton	Name	cmdCreateTable
	Caption	"Create &Table"

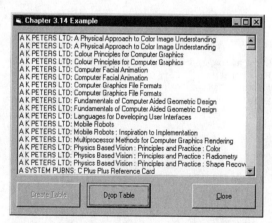

Figure 3.19. The Chapter 3.14 example form, with new table and records.

2. Add the following statements to the declarations section of **Form1**:

```
Option Explicit

Private Const BIBLIO_PATH = "C:\Program Files\DevStudio\VB\Biblio.MDB"
Private dbfBiblio As Database
```

3. Enter the following code as the **Load** event for **Form1**. On loading, this procedure looks for the [Publisher Titles] table in the database. If it finds the table, it fills the list box with the table's data and enables the Drop Table button. If it does not find the table, it enables the Create Table button.

```
Private Sub Form_Load()
Dim tdfTable As TableDef
    Dim blnTableFound As Boolean

    On Error GoTo LoadError
        blnTableFound = False
        'Open the database
        Set dbfBiblio = DBEngine.Workspaces(0).OpenDatabase(BIBLIO_PATH)

        'Check each table in the TableDefs collection; if the name matches,
        'then allow the user to drop the table, and populate the list box.
        For Each tdfTable In dbfBiblio.TableDefs
            If tdfTable.Name = "Publisher Titles" Then
                blnTableFound = True
                cmdDropTable.Enabled = True
                cmdCreateTable.Enabled = False
                FillList
                Exit For
            End If
        Next

        'If no table was found, allow the user to create the table.
        If blnTableFound = False Then
            cmdDropTable.Enabled = False
            cmdCreateTable.Enabled = True
        End If
    On Error GoTo 0
    Exit Sub

LoadError:
    MsgBox Err.Description, vbExclamation
    Unload Me
Exit Sub
End Sub
```

4. Create the **FillList** subroutine by entering the following code into **Form1**. This subroutine fills the list box with the contents of the [Publisher Titles] table.

```
Sub FillList()
Dim recSelect As Recordset
```

```
    Dim strSQL As String

    On Error GoTo FillListError
        'Clear the list box
        lstData.Clear

        'Get the [Publisher Titles] table in a recordset
        Set recSelect = dbfBiblio.OpenRecordset("SELECT * FROM " & _
            "[Publisher Titles]", dbOpenSnapshot)
        'If there are any records, fill the list box
        If recSelect.RecordCount > 0 Then
            recSelect.MoveFirst
            Do Until recSelect.EOF
                lstData.AddItem recSelect![Name] & ": " & recSelect![Title]
                recSelect.MoveNext
            Loop
        End If
    On Error GoTo 0
Exit Sub

FillListError:
    MsgBox Err.Description, vbExclamation
Exit Sub
End Sub
```

5. Enter the following code as the **Click** event for **cmdCreateTable**. This procedure builds the **SELECT...INTO** SQL statement, building the [Publisher Titles] table from the combination of the **[Name]** field from the [Publishers] table and the **[Title]** field from the [Titles] table, as described in the "Technique" section of this How-To. When built, it then executes the statement and calls the **FillList** subroutine to fill the list box on the form. Finally, this step enables the Delete Records button, because (hopefully) we now have records to delete.

```
Private Sub cmdCreateTable_Click()
Dim strSQL As String

    On Error GoTo CreateTableError
        Screen.MousePointer = vbHourglass

        'Build the SELECT INTO statement.
        strSQL = "SELECT Publishers.Name, Titles.Title " & _
            "INTO [Publisher Titles] " & _
            "FROM Publishers INNER JOIN Titles " & _
            "ON Publishers.PubID = Titles.PubID"

        'Create the new table by executing the SQL statement.
        dbfBiblio.Execute (strSQL)

        'Fill the list box with records.
        FillList

        'Set the command buttons.
        cmdCreateTable.Enabled = False
```

continued on next page

continued from previous page

```
        cmdDropTable.Enabled = True

        Screen.MousePointer = vbDefault
    On Error GoTo 0
Exit Sub

CreateTableError:
    Screen.MousePointer = vbDefault
    MsgBox Err.Description, vbExclamation
Exit Sub
End Sub
```

6. Enter the following code as the `Click` event for `cmdDropTable`. The routine executes a **DROP TABLE** statement against our newly created [Publisher Titles] table and reenables the Create Table button.

```
Private Sub cmdDropTable_Click()
On Error GoTo DropTableError
        'Execute the DROP TABLE statement
        dbfBiblio.Execute ("DROP TABLE [Publisher Titles]")

        'Set the command buttons
        cmdDropTable.Enabled = False
        cmdCreateTable.Enabled = True

        'Clear the list box.
        lstData.Clear
    On Error GoTo 0
Exit Sub

DropTableError:
    MsgBox Err.Description, vbExclamation
Exit Sub
End Sub
```

7. Enter the following code as the `Click` event for `cmdClose`:

```
Private Sub cmdClose_Click()
    End
End Sub
```

How It Works

When `Form1` loads, it first attempts to find the [Publisher Titles] table. If it finds the table, it loads the table's information into the list box by calling the `FillList` subroutine, disables the Create Table button, and then enables the Drop Table buttons. If it doesn't find the table, it enables the Create Table button and disables the Drop Table button.

If the Create Table button is enabled, when clicked it constructs and executes a **SELECT...INTO** statement, creating the [Publisher Titles] table and pulling in information from both the [Publishers] and the [Titles] table to populate it in one step. When completed, it loads the data into the list box by using the `FillList` subroutine.

The Drop Table button, if enabled, issues a DROP TABLE statement when clicked, destroying our [Publisher Titles] table in one fell swoop.

Comment

When you use SELECT...INTO to create the table, the fields in the new table inherit only the data type and field size of the corresponding fields in the query's source table. No other field or table properties are picked up from the existing table.

COMPLEXITY
INTERMEDIATE

3.15 How do I...
Modify a table's structure?

Problem

I need to be able to add or drop columns from a table without having to use Access or go through the lengthy process of working with TableDef and Field objects. Can I do this with a simple SQL statement?

Technique

The ALTER TABLE statement lets you add or drop columns or indexes as needed, with a single SQL operation. The syntax is explained in Table 3.26, with a sample statement.

Table 3.26. The syntax of the ALTER TABLE statement.

CLAUSE	PURPOSE	EXAMPLE
ALTER TABLE	Selects the table to be altered.	ALTER TABLE [Publisher Titles]
ADD COLUMN	Adds a column, defining its data type at the same time.	ADD COLUMN [Notes] MEMO NOT NULL

Several other keywords are used in the ALTER TABLE table. These are listed in Table 3.27.

Table 3.27. Additional syntax for the ALTER TABLE statement.

CLAUSE	PURPOSE	EXAMPLE
DROP COLUMN	Removes a column.	DROP COLUMN [Notes]
ADD CONSTRAINT	Adds an index to the table.	ADD CONSTRAINT [Key1] [Notes]
DROP CONSTRAINT	Removes an index.	DROP CONSTRAINT [Key1]

The `Execute` method is used on a `Database` object to perform an **ALTER TABLE** statement. The next example executes the queries shown in Table 3.26 on the database represented by the variable `dbfTest`:

```
dbfTest.Execute("ALTER TABLE [Publisher Titles] ADD COLUMN [Notes] MEMO NOT NULL")
```

Steps

Open and run the project ADDFIELD.VBP. Type a valid field name into the Field Name text box. Select a field type from the Field Type drop-down list and then click the Add Field button; the list box fills with the fields added to the newly created table (Figure 3.20). Highlight one of the newly created fields and click the Remove Field button to delete the field. Note that this example is similar in appearance to the example in How-To 3.12.

1. Create a new project called ADDFIELD.VBP. Use `Form1` to create the objects and properties listed in Table 3.28, and save the form as MAKETABL.FRM.

Table 3.28. Objects and properties for the Table Maker form.

OBJECT	PROPERTY	SETTING
Form	Name	Form1
	Caption	"Chapter 3.14 Example"
ListBox	Name	lstFields
	Sorted	True
Label	Name	lblTableName
	Caption	"Table &Name:"
Label	Name	lblFieldName
	Caption	"&Field Name:"
Label	Name	lblFieldType
	Caption	"Field T&ype:"
Label	Name	lblFieldList
	Caption	"Field Li&st:"
TextBox	Name	txtTableName
	Enabled	False
TextBox	Name	txtFieldName
ComboBox	Name	cboFieldType
	Style	2 - Dropdown List
CommandButton	Name	cmdClose
	Caption	"&Close"
CommandButton	Name	cmdAddField
	Caption	"&Add Field"

OBJECT	PROPERTY	SETTING
CommandButton	Name	cmdRemoveField
	Caption	"&Remove Field"

2. Add the following statements to the declarations section of `Form1`:

```
Option Explicit

Private Const BIBLIO_PATH = "C:\Program Files\DevStudio\VB\Biblio.MDB"

Private Const IllegalCharacters = "[].!'"
Private dbfBiblio As Database
```

3. Add the following statements to the `Load` event of `Form1`. The `FillTypeList` and `FillFieldList` routines, detailed next, are called to prepare the form for use.

```
Private Sub Form_Load()
    'Open the database
    Set dbfBiblio = DBEngine.Workspaces(0).OpenDatabase(BIBLIO_PATH)
    'Set the txtTableName control to the table that will be edited.
    txtTableName = "Title Author"
    'Fill the Field Type combo box
    FillTypeList
    'Fill the Field List list box
    FillFieldList
End Sub
```

4. Create the following subroutine in `Form1`. The `FillFieldList` subroutine will iterate through the `Fields` collection of the [Title Author] table, including the names and data types in the `lstFields` list box.

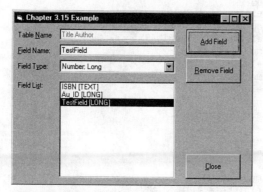

Figure 3.20. The Chapter 3.15 example main form on startup.

```
Sub FillFieldList()
    Dim tbfTemp As TableDef, fldTemp As Field
    Dim strFieldType As String

    'Iterate through the TableDefs collection of the database, searching
    'for the table name specified in the txtTableName edit control.
    For Each tbfTemp In dbfBiblio.TableDefs
        'If we find the table, iterate through the Fields collection,
        'adding each field and its field type to the Field List list box
        If tbfTemp.Name = txtTableName.Text Then
            For Each fldTemp In tbfTemp.Fields
                Select Case fldTemp.Type
                    Case dbBigInt
                        strFieldType = "BIGINT"
                    Case dbBinary
                        strFieldType = "BINARY"
                    Case dbBoolean
                        strFieldType = "BOOLEAN"
                    Case dbByte
                        strFieldType = "BYTE"
                    Case dbChar
                        strFieldType = "CHAR(" & fldTemp.FieldSize & ")"
                    Case dbCurrency
                        strFieldType = "CURRENCY"
                    Case dbDate
                        strFieldType = "DATE"
                    Case dbDecimal
                        strFieldType = "DECIMAL"
                    Case dbDouble
                        strFieldType = "DOUBLE"
                    Case dbFloat
                        strFieldType = "FLOAT"
                    Case dbGUID
                        strFieldType = "GUID"
                    Case dbInteger
                        strFieldType = "INTEGER"
                    Case dbLong
                        strFieldType = "LONG"
                    Case dbLongBinary
                        strFieldType = "LONGBINARY"
                    Case dbMemo
                        strFieldType = "LONGTEXT"
                    Case dbNumeric
                        strFieldType = "NUMERIC"
                    Case dbSingle
                        strFieldType = "SINGLE"
                    Case dbText
                        strFieldType = "TEXT"
                    Case dbTime
                        strFieldType = "TIME"
                    Case dbTimeStamp
                        strFieldType = "TIMESTAMP"
                    Case dbVarBinary
                        strFieldType = "VARBINARY"
                End Select
                lstFields.AddItem fldTemp.Name & " [" & strFieldType & "]"
```

```
            Next
        Exit For
        End If
    Next
End Sub
```

5. Create the following subroutine in **Form1**. The **FillTypeList** subroutine adds the various data types to the **cboFieldType** drop-down combo box.

```
Sub FillTypeList()
    'Fill the Field Type combo box with types of available fields
    With cboFieldTypes
        .AddItem "Counter"
        .AddItem "Currency"
        .AddItem "Date/Time"
        .AddItem "Memo"
        .AddItem "Number: Byte"
        .AddItem "Number: Integer"
        .AddItem "Number: Long"
        .AddItem "Number: Single"
        .AddItem "Number: Double"
        .AddItem "OLE Object"
        .AddItem "Text"
        .AddItem "Yes/No"
    End With
End Sub
```

6. Add the following code to the **Click** event of **cmdAddField**. The routine checks for a field name, ensures that the name is legal (no invalid characters, no leading spaces, and so on), determines its data type from the Field Type combo box, and finally builds the SQL needed to send the **ALTER TABLE** command to the database.

```
Private Sub cmdAddField_Click()
    Dim strFieldType As String, strSQL As String

    'Check first if the Field Name text box contains a legal name
    If LegalName(True) Then
        On Error GoTo BadAdd
            'If it does, check if the Field Type has been selected.
            If cboFieldTypes.ListIndex > -1 Then
                'If both criteria are satisfied, store the SQL field type
                'in the strFieldType string.
                Select Case cboFieldTypes.Text
                    Case "Counter"
                        strFieldType = "COUNTER"
                    Case "Currency"
                        strFieldType = "CURRENCY"
                    Case "Date/Time"
                        strFieldType = "DATETIME"
                    Case "Memo"
                        strFieldType = "LONGTEXT"
                    Case "Number: Byte"
                        strFieldType = "BYTE"
```

continued on next page

continued from previous page

```
                Case "Number: Integer"
                    strFieldType = "SHORT"
                Case "Number: Long"
                    strFieldType = "LONG"
                Case "Number: Single"
                    strFieldType = "SINGLE"
                Case "Number: Double"
                    strFieldType = "DOUBLE"
                Case "OLE Object"
                    strFieldType = "LONGBINARY"
                Case "Text (25 chars)"
                    strFieldType = "TEXT(25)"
                Case "Yes/No"
                    strFieldType = "BIT"
            End Select

            'Crate the ALTER TABLE statement
            strSQL = "ALTER TABLE [" & txtTableName.Text & _
                "] ADD COLUMN " _
                & "[" & txtFieldName & "] " & strFieldType
            'Execute the SQL
            dbfBiblio.Execute (strSQL)
            'Add the new field to the Field List list box.
            lstFields.AddItem txtFieldName & " [" & strFieldType & "]"

            'Reset the Field Name and Field Type controls.
            txtFieldName = ""
            cboFieldTypes.ListIndex = -1
        Else
            MsgBox "You must select a field type.", vbExclamation
        End If
        On Error GoTo 0
    End If
Exit Sub

BadAdd:
    MsgBox Err.Description, vbExclamation
End Sub
```

7. Create the `LegalName` function in `Form1` with the following code. This function checks for a valid field name containing at least one character, without trailing spaces, that doesn't contain an illegal character. If it passes all that, it performs one more check, depending on the value of `intAction`. If `intAction` is `True`, indicating that the field is to be added, the function checks whether a field already exists. If `intAction` is `False`, indicating that the field is to be deleted, it ensures that there is no data in the field anywhere in the table.

```
Function LegalName(intAction As Boolean) As Boolean
    Dim i As Integer
    Dim recNameCheck As Recordset

    On Error GoTo IllegalName
        'If blank, raise an error.
```

```
        If Len(txtFieldName.Text) = 0 Then Err.Raise 32767
        'If it has a leading space, raise an error.
        If Left$(txtFieldName.Text, 1) = " " Then Err.Raise 32766
        'If it contains any of the characters in the IllegalCharacters
        'constant, raise an error
        For i = 1 To Len(IllegalCharacters)
            If InStr(txtFieldName.Text, Mid(IllegalCharacters, i, 1)) _
                > 0 Then Err.Raise 32765
        Next i
        'If it contains any ANSI character from Chr$(0) to Chr$(31),
        '(you guessed it) raise an error.
        For i = 0 To 31
            If InStr(txtFieldName.Text, Chr(i)) > 0 Then Err.Raise 32764
        Next i

        If intAction Then
            'It's an add field; ensure that the name doesn't already exist.
            'If so, raise an error.
            For i = 0 To lstFields.ListCount - 1
                If txtFieldName.Text = lstFields.List(i) _
                    Then Err.Raise 32763
            Next i
        Else
            'It's a drop field; ensure that the field being erased contains
            ' no data. If so, raise an error
            Set recNameCheck = dbfBiblio.OpenRecordset("SELECT [" & _
                txtFieldName.Text & "] FROM [" & txtTableName.Text & _
                "] WHERE [" & txtFieldName.Text & "] IS NOT NULL")
            If recNameCheck.RecordCount Then Err.Raise 32762
        End If

        'If they've managed to get through all that validation, the function
        'should be True, to indicate success.
        LegalName = True
    On Error GoTo 0
Exit Function

IllegalName:
    Dim strErrDesc As String
    'Build an error message based on the user-defined error that occurred.
    Select Case Err.Number
        Case 32767
            strErrDesc = "You must enter a field name."
        Case 32766
            strErrDesc = "The field name cannot begin with a space."
        Case 32765
            strErrDesc = "The field name contains the illegal character " & _
                Mid(IllegalCharacters, i, 1) & "."
        Case 32764
            strErrDesc = "The field name contains the control character " & _
                "with the ANSI value" & Str$(i) & "."
        Case 32763
            strErrDesc = "The field name " & txtFieldName.Text & _
                " already exists in the field name list."
        Case 32762
            strErrDesc = "The field name " & txtFieldName.Text & _
```

continued on next page

continued from previous page

```
                          " has data; it cannot be deleted."
        Case Else
            ' Visual Basic's default error message.
            strErrDesc = Err.Description
    End Select

    MsgBox strErrDesc, vbExclamation

    'The function indicates False, or failure.
    LegalName = False
Exit Function

End Function
```

8. Add the following code to the **Click** event of **cmdRemoveField**:

```
Private Sub cmdRemoveField_Click()
    Dim strSQL As String, strTemp As String

    ' If the user has selected a field, remove it from the list.
    ' Otherwise, just ignore the click.
    If lstFields.ListIndex > -1 Then
        'Call the lstFields_Click event, to ensure that txtFieldName is
        'still populated. The user might have erased it after selecting a
        'field to delete.
        Call lstFields_Click
        If LegalName(False) Then
            'Build the ALTER TABLE statement
            strSQL = "ALTER TABLE [" & txtTableName.Text & _
                "] DROP COLUMN [" & _
                txtFieldName.Text & "]"
            'Execute the SQL
            dbfBiblio.Execute (strSQL)
            'Delete the field from the Field List
            lstFields.RemoveItem lstFields.ListIndex
        End If
    End If
End Sub
```

9. Add the following code to the **Click** event of **lstFields**. This code extracts the name of the field selected in **lstFields** and pass it to the **txtFieldName** text box.

```
Private Sub lstFields_Click()
    Dim strTemp As String

    'If a field has been selected, extract the field's name from
    'the list entry and display it in the txtFieldName control.
    If lstFields.ListIndex > -1 Then
        strTemp = lstFields.List(lstFields.ListIndex)
        strTemp = Left(strTemp, InStr(strTemp, "[") - 2)
        txtFieldName.Text = strTemp
    End If
End Sub
```

10. Add the following code to the `Click` event of `cmdClose`:

```
Private Sub cmdClose_Click()
    End
End Sub
```

How It Works

When `Form1` is loaded, it prepares for use by running the `FillTypeList` routine, which loads the `cboFieldTypes` combo box with the various field types allowed by Visual Basic, and the `FillFieldList` routine, which loads all the field information from a given table into the `lstFields` list box. The `Form_Load` event defaults the table name for this routine to the [Title Author] table.

Each time the user adds a field to the table, an `ALTER TABLE` statement is concatenated in the `cmdAddField_Click` routine. Several steps are performed to ensure that the entered field is valid and meets the criteria for the statement. The routine uses the `LegalName` function to determine whether the field name specified is legal for use—doesn't have any illegal characters, has at least one character, and doesn't start with a space (ASCII 32). After that step, the routine fetches the field's type from the `cboFieldTypes` combo box and translates the English-readable selection into a valid SQL data type. After the translation is complete, it builds and executes the `ALTER TABLE` statement, using the `ADD COLUMN` keywords to create the field. If run successfully, it adds the newly created field to the `lstFields` list box.

Removing a field, however, is much less involved. Given the selected field name from the `lstFields` list box, and after the `LegalName` function is called to ensure that the selected field contains no data, another `ALTER TABLE` statement is issued, this time utilizing the `DROP COLUMN` keywords to remove the field from the table. After execution is complete, the field is then removed from the `lstFields` list box.

Comments

The `ALTER TABLE` has different behaviors depending on the database platform. Microsoft SQL Server, for example, won't allow a field-level constraint (for example, restricting a field's data to a certain range of values) to be added to an already existing field. As with the `SELECT...INTO` statement (covered previously in How-To 3.14), the best way to ensure that you get a complete understanding of how the database reacts to the `ALTER TABLE` statement is to experiment and observe the results.

COMPLEXITY
ADVANCED

3.16 How do I...
Create a crosstab query?

Problem

I need to be able to supply a worksheet-style query showing cross-referenced information easily. How do I do this?

Technique

The new features of the Microsoft Jet 3.5 engine include the capability to create *crosstab*, or cross-tabulated, queries. Think of a crosstab query as a spreadsheet, with the information provided by the query read by referencing the row and column of the spreadsheet. For example, using our old familiar friend BIBLIO.MDB, we need to get a count of all the titles published since 1975, year by year, listed by publisher. Normally, this job would take a couple of queries, but the crosstab query allows us to use some SQL "sleight of hand" in performing this action by adding a couple of new SQL keywords to your arsenal.

In the following sample query, notice the **TRANSFORM** and **PIVOT** keywords. These new additions allow Jet 3.5 to construct a crosstab query.

```
TRANSFORM Count(Titles.Title) AS [TitlesCount] _
    SELECT Publishers.Name FROM Publishers INNER JOIN Titles ON _
    (Titles.PubID = Publishers.PubID) WHERE Titles.[Year Published] _
    > 1975 GROUP BY Publishers.Name
PIVOT Titles.[Year Published]
```

Table 3.29 lists the **TRANSFORM** and **PIVOT** keywords, used to create a crosstab query.

Table 3.29. The syntax of the crosstab query.

CLAUSE	PURPOSE	EXAMPLE
TRANSFORM	Selects the data to be shown in	TRANSFORM Count(Titles.Title)
	the body of the query.	AS [TitlesCount]
SELECT	In a crosstab query, this chooses	SELECT Publishers.Name FROM
	the row information for the query.	Publishers INNER JOIN Titles
		ON (Titles.PubID =
		Publishers.PubID) WHERE
		Titles.[Year Published] > 1975
PIVOT	Selects the column information	PIVOT Titles.[Year Published]
	for the query.	

To better understand the results of this query, visualize the results as a spreadsheet. The **SELECT** creates the rows of the spreadsheet; in the preceding example, a row is created for each publisher who has a title published after 1975. The **PIVOT** creates the columns of the spreadsheet; a column for each year a title was published after 1975 is created. The **TRANSFORM** statement creates the information on our spreadsheet where each row and column intersect—in the preceding query, a count of titles.

Steps

Open and run the project CROSSTAB.VBP. When the form appears, a grid displays the count of all the titles published after 1975, listed by publisher, as shown in Figure 3.21.

1. Create a new project called CROSSTAB.VBP. Use **Form1** to create the objects and properties listed in Table 3.30, and save the form as CROSSTAB.FRM.

Table 3.30. Objects and properties for the Crosstab form.

OBJECT	PROPERTY	SETTING
Form	Name	Form1
	Caption	"Chapter 3.16 Example"
Data	Name	dtaData
MSFlexGrid	Name	grdCrossTab
	DataSourcw	dtaData
Label	Name	lblCrossTab
	Caption	"Titles per year published after 1975,
		sorted by Publisher ID"
CommandButton	Name	cmdClose
	Caption	"&Close"

2. Add the following statements to the declarations section of **Form1**:

```
Option Explicit

Private Const BIBLIO_PATH = "C:\Program Files\DevStudio\VB\Biblio.MDB"
```

3. Add the following statements to the **Load** event of **Form1**. At this point, the event constructs the SQL statement used for our crosstab query (explained earlier in this How-To) and places it in the **RecordSource** property of the **dtaData** data control. After it's added, the data control is refreshed to execute the query and return the needed records, which will automatically display in the bound **MSFlexGrid** control, **grdCrossTab**.

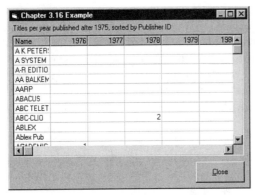

Figure 3.21. The Chapter 3.16 example main form, displaying crosstab data.

```
Private Sub Form_Load()
    Dim strSQL As String

    'Construct the crosstab query statement.  Note the use of several new
    'SQL keywords, including TRANSFORM and PIVOT.  These two keywords are
    'the building blocks of the crosstab query.
    strSQL = "TRANSFORM Count(Titles.Title) AS [TitlesCount] " & _
        "SELECT Publishers.Name FROM Publishers INNER JOIN Titles " & _
        "ON (Titles.PubID " & _
        "= Publishers.PubID) WHERE Titles.[Year Published] > 1975 " & _
        "GROUP BY Publishers.Name " & _
        "PIVOT Titles.[Year Published]"

    'Set up the data control
    With dtaData
        .DatabaseName = BIBLIO_PATH
        .RecordSource = strSQL
        .Refresh
    End With

End Sub
```

4. Add the following statements to the Click event of cmdClose:

```
Private Sub cmdClose_Click()
    End
End Sub
```

How It Works

When Form1 loads, it constructs the example crosstab query detailed earlier in the How-To. It then uses the dtaData data control to execute it and retrieve the records for display in grCrossTab.

Comment

The crosstab query is a powerful tool for generating tabular data, especially aggregate or arithmetically derived information such as counts or statistical data, for a quick summary. Normally, without the TRANSFORM or PIVOT keywords, performing a query like the one we used would require two or three queries and possibly a temporary table, making it a complex task not only to execute but also to maintain. A crosstab query takes all that work and hands it to the database to perform, making the tedious job of cross-indexing information that much faster and easier.

CHAPTER 4
DESIGNING AND IMPLEMENTING A DATABASE

4

DESIGNING AND IMPLEMENTING A DATABASE

How do I...

4.1 Create a new database?

4.2 Define tables and fields?

4.3 Define the primary key and other indexes?

4.4 Define relations between tables?

4.5 Use the Jet database engine to enforce business rules?

No amount of Visual Basic coding skill can overcome the problems of a poorly designed database. This chapter introduces some fundamental principles of relational database design. You'll see how you can use Visual Basic code to create databases and database objects, including tables, fields, indexes, and relationships. You'll also see how you can use the properties of these database objects to enforce business rules for your application.

4.1 Create a New Database

Creating a database with data access object (DAO) code can be done with a single method. This How-To shows you how.

4.2 Define Tables and Fields

Every database design starts with tables and fields. This How-To examines time-tested principles of table design and demonstrates how you can use DAO code to create your database objects.

4.3 Define the Primary Key and Other Indexes

Indexes are the key to establishing relationships between tables and improving database application performance. This How-To introduces several types of indexes and shows you how to create indexes with Visual Basic code.

4.4 Define Relations Between Tables

This How-To shows you how to use Visual Basic to create the relations for your database.

4.5 Use the Jet Database Engine to Enforce Business Rules

There are two ways to enforce business rules in your database applications. You can write Visual Basic code to enforce your rules, or you can build the rules right into the database schema. This How-To shows you how to use the properties of the objects in your database to enforce business rules.

COMPLEXITY
BEGINNING

4.1 How do I...

Create a new database?

Problem

My application needs to create a database at a location chosen by the user. How can I do this with Visual Basic?

Technique

The `CreateDatabase` method of the `Workspace` object will create a database and return a database object you can use in your application. The `CreateDatabase` method takes three arguments:

 `name`

The database name. VB will append "mdb" if you do not supply an extension. You can also use a UNC name in the form `\\server\share\path\file` if your network supports it.

✔ `locale`

The language used for the sort order. You can also use the `locale` argument to create a password-protected database by appending a password string to the `locale` constant. `locale` constants are shown in Table 4.1.

✔ `Option`

An optional constant or combination of constants you can use to specify a database version or to encrypt the database. If you want to specify a version and encrypt the database, use the bitwise `OR` operator to combine the constants. `Option` constants are shown in Table 4.2.

Table 4.1. Locale constants for the `CreateDatabase` method.

CONSTANT	COLLATING ORDER
dbLangGeneral	English, German, French, Portuguese, Italian, and Modern Spanish
dbLangArabic	Arabic
dbLangChineseSimplified	Simplified Chinese
dbLangChineseTraditional	Traditional Chinese
dbLangCyrillic	Russian
dbLangCzech	Czech
dbLangDutch	Dutch
dbLangGreek	Greek
dbLangHebrew	Hebrew
dbLangHungarian	Hungarian
dbLangIcelandic	Icelandic
dbLangJapanese	Japanese
dbLangKorean	Korean
dbLangNordic	Nordic languages (Microsoft Jet database engine version 1.0 only)
dbLangNorwDan	Norwegian and Danish
dbLangPolish	Polish
dbLangSlovenian	Slovenian
dbLangSpanish	Traditional Spanish
dbLangSwedFin	Swedish and Finnish
dbLangThai	Thai
dbLangTurkish	Turkish

Table 4.2. Option constants for the CreateDatabase method.

CONSTANT	DESCRIPTION
dbEncrypt	Creates an encrypted database.
dbVersion10	Creates a database that uses the Microsoft Jet database engine version 1.0 file format.
dbVersion11	Creates a database that uses the Microsoft Jet database engine version 1.1 file format.
dbVersion20	Creates a database that uses the Microsoft Jet database engine version 2.0 file format.
dbVersion30	(Default) Creates a database that uses the Microsoft Jet database engine version 3.0 file format (compatible with version 3.5).

Steps

Open and run HT401.VBP. Click the Create Database button. Choose a directory and filename using the common dialog and click Save to create the database, as shown in Figure 4.1.

1. Create a new Standard EXE project, and save it as HT401.VBP. Create the objects and properties listed in Table 4.3, and save the form as FCreateDB.frm.

Table 4.3. Objects and properties for the Database Creator form.

OBJECT	PROPERTY	SETTING
Form	Name	FCreateDB
	Caption	"Create Database"
CommonDialog	Name	dlgCreateDB
CommandButton	Name	cmdCreate
	Caption	"Create Database"

Figure 4.1. Creating a database.

2. Add `Option Explicit` to the declarations section.

3. Create the `GetDBName()` function. This function sets up the common dialog control with the appropriate filters and flags and returns the file selected by the user as the return value of the function.

```
Private Function GetDBName() As String
' Get the desired name using the common dialog
On Error GoTo ProcError

    Dim strFileName As String

    ' set up the file save dialog file types
    dlgCreateDB.DefaultExt = "mdb"
    dlgCreateDB.DialogTitle = "Create Database"
    dlgCreateDB.Filter = "VB Databases (*.mdb)|*.mdb"
    dlgCreateDB.FilterIndex = 1
    ' set up flags
    dlgCreateDB.Flags = _
    cdlOFNHideReadOnly Or _
    cdlOFNOverwritePrompt Or _
    cdlOFNPathMustExist
    ' setting CancelError means the control will
    ' raise an error if the user clicks Cancel
    dlgCreateDB.CancelError = True
    ' show the SaveAs dialog
    dlgCreateDB.ShowSave
    ' get the selected name
    strFileName = dlgCreateDB.filename
    ' dialog prompted for overwrite,
    ' so kill file if it exists
    On Error Resume Next
    Kill strFileName

ProcExit:
    GetDBName = strFileName
    Exit Function

ProcError:
    strFileName = ""
    Resume ProcExit

End Function
```

4. Create the `CreateDB()` procedure. This procedure takes a filename as a parameter and creates a database using the `CreateDatabase` method of the `Workspace` object.

```
Private Sub CreateDB(strDBName As String)
' create the database

    Dim db As Database

    ' if desired, you can specify a version or encrypt
```

continued on next page

continued from previous page

```
' the database as the optional third parameter to
' the CreateDatabase method
Set db = DBEngine(0).CreateDatabase(strDBName, dbLangGeneral)

End Sub
```

5. Add the following code as the cmdCreateDB_Click event procedure. This procedure calls the GetDBName function to obtain a filename and passes it to CreateDB to create the database.

```
Private Sub cmdCreateDB_Click()
On Error GoTo ProcError

    Screen.MousePointer = vbHourglass

    Dim strDBName As String

    strDBName = GetDBName()

    If Len(strDBName) > 0 Then
        CreateDB strDBName
    End If

ProcExit:
    Screen.MousePointer = vbDefault
    Exit Sub

ProcError:
    MsgBox Err.Description
    Resume ProcExit

End Sub
```

How It Works

Two simple procedures—GetDBName and CreateDB—do all the work. The first obtains a filename from the user via the common dialog control, and the second creates the database using the filename provided.

THE SQL *CREATE DATABASE* STATEMENT

Some database engines provide a CREATE DATABASE statement as a command in their SQL dialects. Jet, however, does not. Although you can create tables, fields, indexes, relationships, and queries using Jet SQL, you must use the CreateDatabase method to create the actual .mdb file.

Comments

You might be able to avoid creating a database in code by using a model database. If you will be distributing an application that will always use the same database structure, you can create an empty version of the database and have the setup program install the empty model.

Although this approach will work in many cases, two common scenarios preclude the use of this technique:

1. If the database schema is not constant, a model will serve little or no purpose.

2. If the database needs to be secured at the installation point, you will need to have your code create the database using the account that will be the database owner. Although you can change the owner of database objects, you cannot change the owner of the database itself. See Chapter 12, "The Windows Registry and State Information," for additional information about working with secured databases.

COMPLEXITY
BEGINNING

4.2 How do I...
Define tables and fields?

Problem

I need a database that is flexible, accurate, and reliable. How do I design my table and column structure to ensure that this is what I get?

Technique

RECORDS AND ROWS—FIELDS AND COLUMNS

The terms *row* and *record* are interchangeable, as are the terms *column* and *field*. Referring to tables in terms of rows and columns is the generally accepted terminology for most literature on database design and for most database engines, except Jet. The data access objects (DAO) model and most of the Visual Basic documentation use the terms *record* and *field*. This kind of variation in terminology doesn't stop at the database design level. Most server databases, for example, describe the data returned by a query as a result set, whereas the Jet engine names its object a Recordset. Don't let the terminology confuse you. Whether you are dealing with records, rows, columns, or fields, the concepts are still the same.

Building a database structure is a process of examining the data that is useful and necessary for an application, then breaking it down into a relatively simple row-and-column format. There are two points to understand about tables and columns that are the essence of any database:

✔ Tables store data about an object.

An object in this case could be something tangible like a physical object or intangible like an idea, but the primary consideration is that a table must contain data about only one thing.

✔ Columns contain the attributes of the object.

Just as a table will contain data about a single type of object, each column should contain only one item of data about that object. If, for example, you're creating a table of addresses, there's no point in having a single column contain the city, state, and postal code when it is just as easy to create three columns and record each attribute separately.

The simplest model for any database is a flat table. The trouble with flat files is that they waste storage space and are problematic to maintain. Table 4.4 shows a flat table design that could be used to store information about students and classes at a school.

Table 4.4. A flat table.

STUDENT	ADVISOR	COURSE1	DESCRIPTION1	INSTRUCTOR1	COURSE2	DESCRIPTION2	INSTRUCTOR2
B. Williams	H. Andrews	VB1	Intro to VB	C. MacDonald	DAO1	Intro to DAO	S. Garrett
L. Duncan	P. Lowell	DAO1	Intro to DAO	S. Garrett	SQL1	Jet SQL	K. Olson
H. Johnson	W. Smith	API1	API Basics	W. Smith	OOP1	VB Objects	T. Carter
F. Norris	J. Carter	VB1	Intro to VB	C. MacDonald	API1	API Basics	W. Smith

There are several problems with this flat table:

✔ Repeating groups

The course ID, description, and instructor are repeated for each course. If a student wanted to take a third course, you would need to modify the table design. Although you could add columns for Course3, Course4, and so on, no matter how many you added there could one day be a student who needed one more. Additionally, in most cases all the extra columns would be a waste of storage. What is required is a means of associating a student with any number of courses.

✔ Inconsistent data

If after entering the data you discover that the SQL1 course should be titled "Transact-SQL" rather than "Jet SQL," you would need to examine two columns in each row to make all the necessary changes. You should be able to update this by changing only a single entry.

✔ Delete anomalies

If you want to remove S. Garrett's Intro to DAO course from the course list, you would need to delete two students, two advisors, and one additional instructor to do it. The data for each of these objects (students, advisors, instructors, and courses) should be independent of each other.

✔ Insert anomalies

Say that the department head wants to add a new course titled "Advanced Client/Server Programming" but has not yet created a schedule or even assigned an instructor. What do you enter in the other columns to record this information? You need to be able to add rows for each of the objects independently of the others.

The solution to these problems is a technique known in relational database parlance as normalization. Normalization is the process of taking a wide table with lots of columns but few rows and redesigning it as several narrow tables with fewer columns but more rows. A properly normalized design allows you to use storage space efficiently, eliminate redundant data, reduce or eliminate inconsistent data, and ease the data maintenance burden.

Several forms of normalization will be discussed shortly, but there is one cardinal rule that absolutely must be followed:

YOU MUST BE ABLE TO RECONSTRUCT THE ORIGINAL FLAT VIEW OF THE DATA.

If you violate this rule, you will have defeated the purpose of normalizing the design.

NORMALIZATION IS *NOT* A PANACEA

Don't be misled into thinking that all database design woes can be cured with proper normalization. In fact, the opposite can be true. Taken to extremes, normalization can cause as many problems as it cures. Although you might be able to cure every type of data anomaly that could possibly occur, you will send performance on a downward spiral if your design requires more than two or three relational joins in a query to reconstruct a flat view of your data.

Consider this scenario:

You are designing a customer database. It's a well-known fact that in the United States a postal ZIP code defines a specific city and state, and that a nine-digit ZIP code defines a specific delivery point. You could, then, store only a ZIP code in the customer table and eliminate the city and state columns that would typically be required. However, then every time the city and state needed to be retrieved, the database engine would have to perform an additional join. This might or might not be acceptable in your situation.

continued on next page

continued from previous page

Now take this scenario to an additional level of detail. It's also true that although there are millions of people in the United States, there are a limited number of last names and first names, and only 26 possible middle initials. Theoretically, you could create a foreign key column in place of the normal last name column and do the same for the first name. This level of normalization, however, steps into the realm of the ridiculous. It's pointless complexity that adds no real benefit for data accuracy.

Forms of Normalization

Relational database theorists have divided normalization into several rules called normal forms:

✔ *First normal form*—No repeating groups.

✔ *Second normal form*—No nonkey attributes depend on a portion of the primary key.

✔ *Third normal form*—No attributes depend on other nonkey attributes.

Additionally, for a database to be in second normal form, it must be in first normal form, and so on. There are also fourth and fifth normal forms, but these are rarely applied. In fact, it might be practical at times to violate even the first three forms of normalization (see the sidebar "Normalization Is *Not* a Panacea").

First Normal Form

First normal form requires that a table not contain repeating groups. A repeating group is a set of columns like the `CourseID`, `Description`, and `Instructor` columns in Table 4.4. Repeating groups are removed by creating a separate table from the columns that repeat.

> **NOTE**
>
> If you have a set of columns with names that end in numbers, such as the `CourseID1` and `CourseID2` columns in the example, it's a clear sign that you have encountered repeating groups and need to think about removing the columns to a separate table.

Table 4.5 is a revised version of the sample table, with the repeating groups for the course moved to their own table. (Note that in this table and the following several tables, primary key columns have been put in bold type. The primary key concept is explained a little later in the chapter.)

Table 4.5. First normal form.

STUDENTS	STUDENTCOURSES
StID	**SCStID**
	SCCourseID
StName	SCCourseDesc
StAdvisorName	SCCourseInstrName

The repeating group has been eliminated by creating a second table. The student can now enroll in any number of courses (including no courses). Although the repeating group is gone, we can still reconstruct the original table by joining the two via the new `SCStID` column in the StudentCourses table. This column is a foreign key that matches the value of the `StID` column in the Students table.

TABLE AND COLUMN NAMING CONVENTIONS

A naming convention has been applied to these table and column names:

✔ Names are restricted to 30 characters and can contain only letters, numbers, and the underscore character. A letter must be the first character. The 30-character limit provides compatibility with Microsoft SQL Server. The other restrictions eliminate the need to use square brackets as delimiters around column names in SQL statements and VB code.

✔ Tables are named using the plural form of the objects they represent.

✔ Columns are named to represent the attribute they record.

✔ Each table is assigned a unique column name prefix. With the addition of a prefix to the column names, all columns within the name space of a database will have a unique name. This eliminates the need to fully qualify the column with the table name in SQL statements.

Naming conventions have an annoying tendency to start religious wars among programmers, but nearly all programmers will—perhaps grudgingly—admit their usefulness. You can adopt this convention or any other convention that suits you or your company. What's important is not the particular convention you choose but that you choose one and follow it faithfully.

Second Normal Form

Second normal form requires that no nonkey attributes depend on a portion of the primary key. To understand this rule, you need to understand the concept of a primary key. A primary key is a column or set of columns in a table that uniquely identifies a single record. The primary key for a table is most often an arbitrary value such as an autoincrement column (Jet refers to this as a counter), although the primary key can be any type of data.

> **NOTE**
>
> Proceed with caution if you decide to use anything other than an arbitrary value as the primary key for a table. Even seemingly reliable data such as a Social Security number can fail if used as a primary key. An arbitrary value provided by the database engine is guaranteed to be unique and independent of the data in the table.

Second normal form really applies only to tables in which the primary key is defined by two or more columns. The essence is that if there are columns that can be identified by only part of the primary key, they need to be in their own table. The StudentCourses table in Table 4.5 violates second normal form because the course information can be identified without using the SCStID column. Table 4.6 shows the same data, reorganized so that it meets the requirements for second normal form.

Table 4.6. Second normal form.

STUDENTS	STUDENTCOURSES	COURSES
StID	**SCStID**	**CourseID**
	SCCourseID	
StName		CourseDesc
StAdvisorName		CourseInstrName

The partial dependence on the primary key has been eliminated by moving the course information to its own table. The relationship between students and courses has at last revealed itself to be a many-to-many relationship. Each student can take many courses, and each course can have many students. The StudentCourses table now contains only the two foreign keys to **Students** and **Courses**.

Third Normal Form

Third normal form requires that no attributes depend on other nonkey attributes. This means that all the columns in the table contain data about the entity that is defined by the primary key. The columns in the table must contain data about only one thing. Like second normal form, this is used to remove columns that belong in their own table.

Table 4.7 shows a revised version of these tables with a few columns added that will help illustrate third normal form.

Table 4.7. Detail columns added.

STUDENTS	STUDENTCOURSES	COURSES
StID	**SCStID**	**CourseID**
	SCCourseID	
StFirstName		CourseDesc
StLastName		CourseInstrName
StAddress		CourseInstrPhone
StCity		
StState		
StZIP		
StAdvisorName		
StAdvisorPhone		

To complete the normalization, we need to look for columns that are not dependent on the primary key of the table. In the Students table, we have two data items about the student's advisor: the name and phone number. The balance of the data pertains only to the student and so is appropriate in the Students table. The advisor information, however, is not dependent on the student. If the student leaves the school, the advisor and the advisor's phone number will remain the same. The same logic applies to the instructor information in the Courses table. The data for the instructor is not dependent on the primary key `CourseID` because the instructor will be unaffected if the course is dropped from the curriculum (unless school officials fire the instructor when they drop the course). Table 4.8 shows the revised schema in third normal form.

Table 4.8. Third normal form.

STUDENTS	ADVISORS	INSTRUCTORS	STUDENTCOURSES	COURSES
StID	**AdvID**	**InstrID**	**SCStID**	**CourseID**
			SCCourseID	
StAdvID	AdvFirst	InstrFirst		CourseInstrID
StFirst	AdvLast	InstrLast		CourseDesc
StLast	AdvPhone	InstrPhone		
StAddress				
StCity				
StState				
StZIP				

The database is now in third normal form:

✔ It is in first normal form because there are no repeating groups in any table.

✔ It is in second normal form because it is in first normal form and because there are no nonkey attributes that depend on a portion of the primary key in any table.

✔ It is in third normal form because it is in first and second normal forms and because no attributes depend on other nonkey attributes in any table.

Advanced Design Techniques

In Table 4.8, you can see two types of relationships between tables:

✔ *One to many*, in which a row in one table can have zero or more related rows in another table. The relationship between advisors and students, for example, is a one-to-many relationship. Any advisor can have no students, one student, or more than one student.

✔ *Many to many*, in which rows in one table can have many related rows in a second table, and the second table can have many related rows in the first table. The relationship between students and courses is many to many. Each student can be enrolled in zero or more courses, and each course can have zero or more students enrolled.

There is a third possible type of relationship between tables: one to one. Table 4.8 reveals a possible use of a one-to-one relational design. Both the Advisors table and the Instructors table contain identical lists of columns. In a real-world database, each of these tables would contain additional columns specific to the role of advisor or instructor and additional information about the individual faculty member who had that role. If you examine Table 4.4, you will also notice that faculty members can act in both roles—as advisors and instructors. Table 4.9 shows a more detailed view of the advisor and instructor data.

Table 4.9. Advisors and instructors.

ADVISORS	INSTRUCTORS
AdvID	**InstrID**
AdvFirst	InstrFirst
AdvLast	InstrLast
AdvPhone	InstrPhone
AdvGradeLevel	InstrSpecialty

For this example, it is assumed that advisors handle students by grade level (undergraduate or graduate) and that instructors have a specialty area that they teach. For example, in a Computer Science department, an instructor might specialize in teaching classes related to a particular language.

Much of the data in these two tables is shared. You could duplicate the columns in both tables, or you could further subdivide these tables, as shown in Table 4.10.

Table 4.10. The school faculty.

FACULTY	ADVISORS	INSTRUCTORS
FacID	**AdvFacID**	**InstrFacID**
FacFirst	AdvGradeLevel	InstrSpecialty
FacLast		
FacPhone		

The columns that are shared by both tables have been removed to the Faculty table. The Advisors and Instructors tables now contain only a foreign key to the Faculty table and the columns that relate specifically to the role of advisor or instructor. The foreign key columns in this case also act as the primary key for these tables, because there must be one and only one row in the Faculty table for any advisor or instructor. This is a one-to-one relationship. The Advisors and Instructors tables define extensions to the Faculty table for subsets of the data in that table.

Designing the tables so that they use the shared Faculty table allows for the reuse of the code required to manage that data and common querying of all members of the school staff.

The design of the database for the mythical school is nearly complete, but there is still one missing set of data. All but the smallest of organizations will normally employ a hierarchical management structure. If the school is a large university, it will probably have several campuses, each of which will have several colleges. Each college will probably be further divided into several departments, and even those departments might be subdivided. The trouble with hierarchical organizations is that you often can't know in advance how many levels will exist within the hierarchy. There is, however, a solution to this problem. Table 4.11 expands the view of the faculty information.

Table 4.11. The school faculty.

FACULTY	DEPARTMENTS
FacID	**DeptID**
FacDeptID	DeptName
FacFirst	DeptParentDeptID
FacLast	
FacPhone	

A foreign key to the Departments table has been added to the Faculty table. This allows a faculty member to be assigned to a department. The Departments table has three columns: `DeptID`, the primary key; `DeptName`, the department name; and the key to establishing the hierarchical relationship, the `DeptParentDeptID` column. This column is a foreign key, but the key points back into the Departments table. This relationship might be easier to understand if you look at some sample data, as shown in Table 4.12.

Table 4.12. The Departments table.

DEPTID	DEPTNAME	DEPTPARENTDEPTID
1	Minnesota State University	NULL
2	Institute of Technology	1
3	College of Liberal Arts	1
4	College of Medicine	1
5	Department of Internal Medicine	4
6	Oncology Department	5

Looking at the sample data, you can see that the College of Medicine is directly under the University, the Department of Internal Medicine is under the College of Medicine, and the Oncology Department is under the Department of Internal Medicine. This type of structure can be reassembled as a flat table, using a self-join. In a self-join, a table is included twice in the same query.

NOTE

The `TreeView` control is an excellent choice as a tool for displaying hierarchical data.

Creating Tables and Fields with Visual Basic

A well-designed database schema is critical, but that's only half of the work of creating a database. You still need to create the actual database objects. You can use two methods to create database objects in a Jet database:

✔ SQL Statements

You can use SQL **CREATE TABLE** and **ALTER TABLE** statements to create tables. Using a SQL statement is fast and easy but limits the control you have over the database objects. Many of the properties available for tables and columns cannot be set using SQL alone. You can also use the SQL **DROP** statement to delete tables. Chapter 2, "Accessing a Database with Data Access Objects," provides detailed instructions for using SQL statements to create database objects.

✔ Data Access Objects

The `TableDef` object and `TableDefs` collection are used to create tables, and the `Field` object and `Fields` collection are used to create columns. In this How-To, you will use DAO code to create database objects. Using the `Delete` method of the `TableDefs` collection is also demonstrated.

Creating a table with DAO code is a three-step process:

1. Create the `TableDef` object by using the `CreateTableDef` method.

2. Create the `Field` objects by using the `CreateField` method, and add them to the `TableDef` object using the `Append` method.

3. Add the `TableDef` object to the collection by using the `Append` method.

Steps

Open and run project HT402.vbp. A sample database based on the tables shown in Table 4.8 and Table 4.10 has been created and saved as HT402.mdb. You can open the sample database and inspect it, or you can create a new database by using the File | New menu command and then creating the Students, Courses, and StudentCourses tables as shown in Table 4.8 and the Faculty, Advisors, and Instructors tables as shown in Table 4.10. To create the tables, select Table | Add. Figure 4.2 shows the `Create TableDef` form with the Students table in progress.

NOTE

This example and the two examples that follow in How-To 4.3 and How-To 4.4 use the Microsoft Windows Common Dialog 5.0, the Microsoft Windows Common Controls 5.0, and the Microsoft DAO 3.5 Object Library components.

1. Create a new project called HT402.vbp. Add BMain.bas to the project. This standard module contains procedures to open an existing database and create a new database. These procedures are based in large part on the example presented in How-To 4.1.

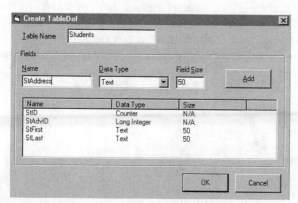

Figure 4.2. Creating the Students table.

2. Add frmMain.frm to the project. This is based on a form created by the VB Application Wizard. The wizard-generated code manages the split view for the tree and list panes of the main form. For simplicity, a considerable amount of the wizard-generated code was removed. The right pane supports only the report view, and all the toolbar buttons and menu controls were removed, along with their associated event procedures. Menu controls and associated code were then added for the File and Table menus. Table 4.13 shows the menu controls that were added for the example. In the declarations section, an object variable is declared for the **CDBExplorer** class:

```
Private mcdbExp As CDBExplorer
```

Table 4.13. Menu controls for frmMain.

NAME	CAPTION
mnuFile	&File
mnuFileOpen	&Open
mnuFileNew	&New
mnuFileBar1	-
mnuFileClose	&Close

NOTE

Due to space limitations, all the wizard-generated code that manages the split Explorer view for the left and right panes of the main form has not been included here.

3. The following code controls the File menu for the main form. The **mnuFileOpen_Click** and **mnuFileNew_Click** event procedures call routines in BMain.bas to open or create a database and then create and initialize the **mcdbExp** object variable. When initialized using the **ExploreDatabase** method, the **CDBExplorer** class accepts a database name, a reference to a **TreeView** control, and a reference to a **ListView** control as parameters. Code within the class then handles most of the management of the tree and list panes of the form.

```
Private Sub mnuFileOpen_Click()
' open a database
On Error GoTo ProcError

    Dim strDBName As String

    Screen.MousePointer = vbHourglass

    strDBName = GetOpenDBName(dlgCommonDialog)
```

```
   If Len(strDBName) Then
     Set mcdbExp = Nothing
     Set mcdbExp = New CDBExplorer
     mcdbExp.ExploreDatabase strDBName, tvTreeView, lvListView
   End If

   ' no node is selected by default, so we
   ' select the root node here
   SelectRootNode

ProcExit:
   Screen.MousePointer = vbDefault
   Exit Sub

ProcError:
   MsgBox Err.Description
   Resume ProcExit

End Sub

Private Sub mnuFileNew_Click()
' create a new database
On Error GoTo ProcError

   Dim strDBName As String

   Screen.MousePointer = vbHourglass

   ' get the filename
   strDBName = GetNewDBName(dlgCommonDialog)
   ' kill it if it exists
   ' note that GetDBName prompts to confirm overwrite
   On Error Resume Next
   Kill strDBName
   ' create the database
   CreateDB strDBName

   ' explore it
   Set mcdbExp = New CDBExplorer
   mcdbExp.ExploreDatabase strDBName, tvTreeView, lvListView

   SelectRootNode

ProcExit:
   Screen.MousePointer = vbDefault
   Exit Sub

ProcError:
   MsgBox Err.Description
   Resume ProcExit

End Sub

Private Sub mnuFileClose_Click()
   'unload the form
   Unload Me
End Sub
```

4. The following code passes the Expand and NodeClick events for the tree pane on to the **CDBExplorer** class:

```
Private Sub tvTreeView_Expand(ByVal Node As ComctlLib.Node)
' Expand the node
On Error GoTo ProcError

  Screen.MousePointer = vbHourglass

  ' the class does the work
  mcdbExp.ExpandNode Node

ProcExit:
  Screen.MousePointer = vbDefault
  Exit Sub

ProcError:
  MsgBox "Error: " & Err.Number & vbCrLf & Err.Description
  Resume ProcExit

End Sub

Private Sub tvTreeView_NodeClick(ByVal Node As ComctlLib.Node)
' Display the properties of the selected node in the listview
On Error GoTo ProcError

  Screen.MousePointer = vbHourglass

  ' the class does the work
  mcdbExp.ListProperties Node

ProcExit:
  Screen.MousePointer = vbDefault
  Exit Sub

ProcError:
  MsgBox "Error: " & Err.Number & vbCrLf & Err.Description
  Resume ProcExit

End Sub
```

5. Add the CDBExplorer.cls class module to the project. Code in this class module does most of the work of mapping database objects to nodes in the tree pane of the form. This was developed as a class module to provide a degree of isolation between the database engine and the user interface in the form. The class presents a hierarchical view of a database, including tables, fields, indexes, queries, and relationships in a tree.

The class works by examining the **Expand** and **NodeClick** events of a **TreeView** control. When a node in the tree is expanded, the class populates that branch of the tree (empty dummy nodes are initially written to unexpanded nodes so that the node will be expandable on the form). After a node is selected by the user, the class determines what database object is associated with the node by examining the position of the node in the tree and then displays the properties of the associated object in the list pane. The property list works by iterating the **Properties** collection common to all DAO objects (except collections) and adding them as items in the **ListView** control. In this How-To, **mnuTableAdd** and **mnuTableDelete** call the **AddTable** and **DeleteTable** methods of the class. These methods add or remove a **TableDef** object and refresh the **TableDefs** branch of the tree on **frmMain**.

```
Public Sub AddTable()

  Load frmCreateTableDef

  Set frmCreateTableDef.Database = mdb

  frmCreateTableDef.Show vbModal

  ' refresh the tabledefs node
  ExpandNode mtvw.Nodes("TableDefs")

End Sub

Public Sub DeleteTable(strTableDefName As String)

  ' delete the TableDef
  mdb.TableDefs.Delete strTableDefName

  ' refresh the tree
  ExpandNode mtvw.Nodes("TableDefs")

End Sub
```

NOTE

Due to the length of the code in the CDBExplorer class, it was not possible to present all of it here. Source code comments in the class and the CDBExplorer.html file included in the project as a related file on the CD-ROM provide additional details about the class.

6. Add a new form to the project and save it as frmCreateTableDef.frm. Add the objects and properties shown in Table 4.14. Except for **lblTableDefName**, **txtTableDefName**, and the **cmd** command button array, all controls should be drawn within the **fraFields** frame.

Table 4.14. `frmCreateTableDef` objects and properties.

OBJECT	PROPERTY	VALUE
Form	Name	frmCreateTableDef
	Caption	Create TableDef
	BorderStyle	3-Fixed Dialog
Label	Name	lblTableDefName
	Caption	&Table Name
TextBox	Name	txtTableDefName
Frame	Name	fraFields
	Caption	Fields
Label	Name	lblFieldName
	Caption	&Name
TextBox	Name	txtFieldName
Label	Name	lblFieldType
	Caption	&Data Type
ComboBox	Name	cboFieldDataType
	Style	2-Dropdown List
Label	Name	lblFieldSize
	Caption	Field &Size
TextBox	Name	txtFieldSize
CommandButton	Name	cmdAdd
	Caption	&Add
ListView	Name	lvwFields
CommandButton	Name	cmd
	Index	0
	Caption	OK
	Default	True
CommandButton	Name	cmd
	Index	1
	Caption	Cancel
	Cancel	True

7. Add the following code to the declarations section. The database object is used to create the `TableDef` object. The two constants are indexes into the `cmd` command button control array.

```
Option Explicit

' database object
Private mdb As Database
```

```
' command button array index constants
Private Const cmdOK = 0
Private Const cmdCancel = 1
```

8. Add the `Form_Load` event procedure. This procedure populates the field type list, sets up the list view headers, and disables the frame and OK button. The frame is enabled after a table name is provided. OK is enabled when a table name is provided and at least one field has been added to the field list.

```
Private Sub Form_Load()
' set up form
On Error GoTo ProcError

    Screen.MousePointer = vbHourglass

    ' set up fields controls
    cmdAdd.Enabled = False

    ' fill the data types combo
    With cboFieldDataType
        ' Note: not all field types are
        ' included here
        .Clear
        .AddItem "Boolean"
        .AddItem "Counter"
        .AddItem "Date/Time"
        .AddItem "Long Integer"
        .AddItem "Text"
        .AddItem "Memo"
    End With
    cboFieldDataType.Text = "Text"

    ' set up list view
    lvwFields.View = lvwReport
    With lvwFields.ColumnHeaders
        .Add , "Name", "Name"
        .Item("Name").Width = 2000
        .Add , "Type", "Data Type"
        .Add , "Size", "Size"
    End With

    ' disable the entire fields frame
    fraFields.Enabled = False

    ' disable OK button
    cmd(cmdOK).Enabled = False

ProcExit:
    Screen.MousePointer = vbDefault
    Exit Sub

ProcError:
    MsgBox "Error: " & Err.Number & vbCrLf & Err.Description
    Resume ProcExit

End Sub
```

9. Add the `cboFieldDataType_Click` procedure. This enables or disables the field size text box, depending on the type of field selected.

```
Private Sub cboFieldDataType_Click()

  If cboFieldDataType.Text = "Text" Then
    lblFieldSize.Enabled = True
    txtFieldSize.Enabled = True
  Else
    txtFieldSize.Text = ""
    lblFieldSize.Enabled = False
    txtFieldSize.Enabled = False
  End If

End Sub
```

10. Add the `cmdAdd_Click` event procedure. This procedure uses the data in the field name, data type, and size controls to add the field to the field list in the `ListView` control. It then enables the OK button and returns focus to the field name control.

```
Private Sub cmdAdd_Click()
' add to the listview
On Error GoTo ProcError

  Screen.MousePointer = vbHourglass

  Dim li As ListItem
  Dim strFieldName As String
  Dim strFieldDataType As String

  strFieldName = txtFieldName.Text
  strFieldDataType = cboFieldDataType.Text

  Set li = lvwFields.ListItems.Add _
    (, strFieldName, strFieldName)
  With li
    .SubItems(1) = strFieldDataType
    ' only add size if applicable
    If strFieldDataType = "Text" Then
      .SubItems(2) = txtFieldSize.Text
    Else
      .SubItems(2) = "N/A"
    End If
  End With

  ' prep for new entry
  txtFieldName.Text = ""
  txtFieldName.SetFocus

  ' enable the OK button
  cmd(cmdOK).Enabled = True

ProcExit:
  Screen.MousePointer = vbDefault
  Exit Sub
```

```
ProcError:
  MsgBox "Error: " & Err.Number & vbCrLf & Err.Description
  Resume ProcExit

End Sub
```

11. Add the `Change` event procedures for the `txtTableDefName` and `txtFieldName` controls. These enable or disable other controls on the form based on the current values.

```
Private Sub txtTableDefName_Change()
' Enable/disable controls

  cmd(cmdOK).Enabled = False
  fraFields.Enabled = False

  If Len(txtTableDefName) > 0 Then
    fraFields.Enabled = True
    If lvwFields.ListItems.Count > 0 Then
      cmd(cmdOK).Enabled = True
    End If
  End If

End Sub

Private Sub txtFieldName_Change()

  If Len(txtFieldName.Text) > 0 Then
    cmdAdd.Enabled = True
  Else
    cmdAdd.Enabled = False
  End If

End Sub
```

12. Add the `cmd_Click` event procedure. This procedure adds the table if OK is chosen or unloads the form if Cancel is chosen.

```
Private Sub cmd_Click(Index As Integer)
On Error GoTo ProcError

  Screen.MousePointer = vbHourglass

  Select Case Index
    Case cmdOK
      ' add the table
      AddTable
    Case cmdCancel
      ' just unload the form
  End Select

  Unload Me
```

continued on next page

continued from previous page

```
ProcExit:
  Screen.MousePointer = vbDefault
  Exit Sub

ProcError:
  MsgBox "Error: " & Err.Number & vbCrLf & Err.Description
  Resume ProcExit

End Sub
```

13. Create the AddTable procedure. AddTable creates the TableDef object, then extracts the field information from the ListView to create and add each Field object. After the fields have been added to the table, the table is added to the database using the Append method of the TableDefs collection.

```
Private Sub AddTable()

  Dim li As ListItem

  Dim td As TableDef
  Dim fld As Field
  Dim lngType As Long

  Dim strFieldName As String
  Dim strFieldDataType As String

  Set td = mdb.CreateTableDef(txtTableDefName.Text)

  ' add the fields
  For Each li In lvwFields.ListItems
    ' get the name
    strFieldName = li.Text
    ' get the data type
    strFieldDataType = li.SubItems(1)
    Select Case strFieldDataType
      Case "Boolean"
        lngType = dbBoolean
      Case "Counter"
        lngType = dbLong
      Case "Date/Time"
        lngType = dbDate
      Case "Long Integer"
        lngType = dbLong
      Case "Text"
        lngType = dbText
      Case "Memo"
        lngType = dbMemo
    End Select
    ' check field type
    If lngType = dbText Then
      ' text, create with size
```

```
     Set fld = td.CreateField _
       (strFieldName, dbText, CInt(li.SubItems(2)))
   Else
     ' other, create without size
     Set fld = td.CreateField(strFieldName, lngType)
     If strFieldDataType = "Counter" Then
       fld.Attributes = fld.Attributes Or dbAutoIncrField
     End If
   End If
   td.Fields.Append fld
   Set fld = Nothing
 Next  ' ListItem

 ' append the tabledef
 mdb.TableDefs.Append td

End Sub
```

14. Add the `Database` property. This is used by the `AddTable` procedure and must be set before the form is shown.

```
Public Property Set Database(db As DAO.Database)

  Set mdb = db

End Property
```

How It Works

The `AddTable` procedure in `frmCreateTableDef` is the critical procedure for this How-To. This routine creates the table using the name provided on the form, then iterates the items in the list to create and append the fields. When all the fields have been added, the table is appended to the database. The balance of the code on the form serves only to manage and coordinate the user interface.

Comments

Much of the code provided on the CD-ROM drives the main Explorer form and class module, but the code in `frmCreateTableDef` does all the work of creating a table and its fields. It is helpful, but not necessary, to fully understand the code in the class module and the wizard-generated code in the main form.

The sample application is not limited to creating the sample database described in this How-To. You can inspect or modify any Jet database using the project.

COMPLEXITY
BEGINNING

4.3 How do I...
Define the primary key and other indexes?

Problem

I know that a primary key is an important component in a proper relational database design and that indexes can significantly improve database performance. How do I choose fields to index and create the indexes for those fields?

Technique

Database indexes can be broadly grouped into two categories:

✔ *Constraints*—The primary key and other unique indexes place constraints on the data that can be entered into the columns bound to the indexes.

✔ *Performance Indexes*—Some, perhaps most, indexes are added strictly for performance reasons. An index speeds access to data by allowing the database engine to more quickly retrieve rows from the tables.

Many developers consider indexes, particularly indexes that act as constraints, to be part of the database schema or overall table design. In reality, however, indexes serve only to enforce the constraints that need to be applied to the data. It is the constraints, or rules, that form the database design. Indexes are a tool to implement those constraints. It is possible (although not recommended) to create tables that do not have primary keys or unique indexes and still have a fully functional relational design, but it is much more efficient to have the database engine enforce rules at that level.

Establishing indexes on tables is a two-step process. First you must determine what columns need to be indexed and the type of indexes the columns require, and then you need to create the indexes using the properties and methods provided by the database engine.

Constraints

In How-To 4.2, you learned about primary keys and relationships between tables, including one-to-many, many-to-many, and one-to-one relationships. Although you can create a table without a primary key, this technique is not recommended. In most situations, it is also recommended that an arbitrary value such as a number provided by the database engine be used as the primary key. For those tables that act as the junction table of a many-to-many relationship between tables, the combination of the two foreign key columns typically acts as the primary key. In a one-to-one relationship, the foreign key column alone is the primary key. Only one primary key can be defined for a table, although you can define additional unique indexes.

A primary key imposes some constraints on the data in the columns included in the index:

✔ Each entry in the index must be unique. For single-column indexes, every value in the table must be unique. In multiple-column indexes, each combination of values must be unique.

✔ Every column in the index must contain a value. You cannot have nulls in columns included in the primary key.

Indexing for Performance

In addition to imposing constraints on your data, indexes can be added strictly to improve performance. The database engine can optimize SELECT queries if it has useful indexes available. Determining what constitutes a useful index can be more of an art than a science, but the following guidelines are appropriate in most situations:

✔ Index foreign key columns. These are almost always excellent candidates for indexes.

✔ Index columns that are frequently used for restrictive criteria in the WHERE clause of SELECT queries.

✔ Index columns that are used for sorting in the ORDER BY clause of SELECT queries.

✔ If you frequently do multiple field sorts, create a multiple field index ordered using the same order used in the sort. Sorts are normally ascending but can be descending.

To obtain the best performance in your own applications, you should experiment with various indexing strategies and use profiling techniques to determine which indexes provide the greatest advantage.

WHEN NOT TO INDEX

Don't think that you can index every column to gain optimum performance. Although indexes accelerate data retrieval, they slow inserts, updates, and deletes because the database engine not only has to update the tables but also must update the indexes.

Additionally, the database engine might not find all indexes useful, especially on small tables. If you have tables with very few rows (such as lookup tables of coded values, tables of U.S. states, and the like), it is likely that the database engine can perform a

continued on next page

continued from previous page

table scan (read every row in the table) faster than it can find a row using an index.

Finally, there are situations that can force a table scan, in which case all indexes will be ignored.

Defining Indexes

Indexes are created by using the `CreateIndex` method of the `TableDef` object in a three-step process:

1. Call `CreateIndex` to create an `Index` object.

2. Create the fields in the index by using the `CreateField` method, and then use the `Append` method to add them to the `Fields` collection of the index.

3. Use the `Append` method of the `Indexes` collection to add the index to the `TableDef` object.

NOTE

If you think this process looks remarkably similar to that of creating a table using DAO code, you're right—the processes are nearly identical.

Steps

Open and run HT403.vbp. You can create the indexes shown in Table 4.15 by choosing the Index | Add command and using the form shown in Figure 4.3.

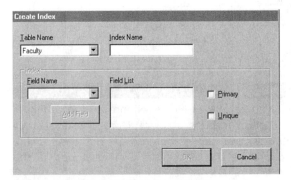

Figure 4.3. The Create Index form.

Table 4.15. Indexes in HT403.mdb.

TABLE	INDEX	PROPERTIES	FIELDS
Advisors	apkAdvisors	Primary	AdvFacID
Courses	apkCourses	Primary	CourseID
	idxCourseIstrID		CourseInstrID
Faculty	apkFaculty	Primary	FacID
	idxFacLast		FacLast
Instructors	apkInstructors	Primary	InstrFacID
StudentCourses	apkStudentCourses	Primary	SCStID
			SCCourseID
	idxSCStID		SCStID
	idxSCCourseID		SCCourseID
Students	apkStudents	Primary	StID
	idxStAdvID		StAdvID
	idxStLast		StLast
	idxStState		StState

The indexes shown in Table 4.15 are recommended based on the guidelines listed in this How-To. Each table has a primary key, all foreign key columns are indexed, and several additional columns that are likely candidates for use as query selection or sort columns are indexed.

INDEX NAMES

The following naming convention was used to determine the index names shown in Table 4.15:

✔ Primary keys are named using the prefix "apk" followed by the table name. This convention provides forward compatibility if the database is later upsized to a database server such as SQL Server or Oracle. With remote server tables, the Jet engine assumes that the first index in an alphabetical list is the primary key. The "apk" prefix places the primary key first in the list.

continued on next page

continued from previous page

✔ Unique nonprimary indexes use the prefix "udx" followed by the name of the indexed column or columns. (There are no unique, nonprimary indexes in Table 4.15.)
✔ Other indexes use the prefix "idx" followed by the column name or names.

This project is an extended version of the project developed in How-To 4.2. Code was added to the main form and class module to launch `frmCreateIndex`, which handles the balance of the code to create indexes.

1. Create a new Standard EXE project, and save it as HT403.vbp. Add BMain.bas to the project. This module contains code used to open or create a new database and is based largely on the code developed in How-To 4.1.

2. Add `frmMain` to the project. This form is based on an Explorer style form generated by the VB Application Wizard. The wizard form was modified for this project as described in How-To 4.2. In addition to the modifications added for How-To 4.2, the menu controls in Table 4.16 were added to create the Index menu.

Table 4.16. The Index menu controls.

NAME	CAPTION
mnuIndex	&Index
mnuIndexAdd	&Add
mnuIndexDelete	&Delete

3. Three event procedures support the Index menu. The top-level menu `mnuIndex_Click` event enables or disables the delete command based on the currently selected object. The add command calls on the services of the `CDBExplorer` class via the `mcdbExp` module-level object variable to create a new index, and the delete command uses the same object to delete an index.

```
Private Sub mnuIndex_Click()
On Error GoTo ProcError

    If mcdbExp Is Nothing Then
        ' no database open
        mnuIndexAdd.Enabled = False
        mnuIndexDelete.Enabled = False
    Else
        ' enable add
        mnuIndexAdd.Enabled = True
        ' only enable delete if an Index is selected
        If mcdbExp.NodeType(tvTreeView.SelectedItem) = _
            "Index" Then
```

```
      mnuIndexDelete.Enabled = True
    Else
      mnuIndexDelete.Enabled = False
    End If
  End If

ProcExit:
  Exit Sub

ProcError:
  MsgBox "Error: " & Err.Number & vbCrLf & Err.Description
  Resume ProcExit

End Sub

Private Sub mnuIndexAdd_Click()
On Error GoTo ProcError

  mcdbExp.AddIndex

ProcExit:
  Exit Sub

ProcError:
  MsgBox "Error: " & Err.Number & vbCrLf & Err.Description
  Resume ProcExit

End Sub

Private Sub mnuIndexDelete_Click()
' Note: mnuIndex_Click already determined
' that an index is selected in the tree
On Error GoTo ProcError

  Dim strTableDefName As String
  Dim strIndexName As String

  ' get the index name
  strIndexName = tvTreeView.SelectedItem.Text
  ' get its parent table name
  strTableDefName = tvTreeView.SelectedItem.Parent.Parent.Text

  mcdbExp.DeleteIndex strTableDefName, strIndexName

ProcExit:
  Exit Sub

ProcError:
  MsgBox "Error: " & Err.Number & vbCrLf & Err.Description
  Resume ProcExit

End Sub
```

4. Add the CDBExplorer.cls class module to the project. This is the same class as that developed in How-To 4.2, with methods added to support creating and deleting indexes. The class manages the population of the items in the tree and list views of the Explorer style main form. Additional information about the class module can be found in CDBExplorer.html, which is included as a related file in the project on the CD. The two procedures added to this class to support the creation and deletion of indexes are the **AddIndex** and **DeleteIndex** methods. **AddIndex** uses the **frmCreateIndex** form to create the index, but it first attempts to determine whether the current item in the tree is within the branch of a table. If so, it passes the table name to the index creation form, saving the user a step in data entry. The **DeleteIndex** method accepts a table name and an index name as parameters and constructs a call to the **Delete** method of the **Indexes** collection of the appropriate **TableDef** object. Both procedures also refresh the tree.

```
Public Sub AddIndex()

  Dim obj As Object

  Set obj = GetDAOObjectFromNode(mtvw.SelectedItem)

  Select Case TypeName(obj)
    Case "TableDef"
      ' initialize the form with a table name
      frmCreateIndex.Initialize mdb, obj.Name
    Case "Indexes"
      frmCreateIndex.Initialize _
        mdb, mtvw.SelectedItem.Parent.Text
    Case "Index"
      frmCreateIndex.Initialize mdb, _
        mtvw.SelectedItem.Parent.Parent.Text
    Case "Field"
      ' if it's a table field, get the table name
      ' the great-grandparent node tells the type
      If mtvw.SelectedItem.Parent.Parent.Parent.Text _
        = "TableDefs" Then
        ' get the name from the grandparent node
        frmCreateIndex.Initialize _
          mdb, _
          mtvw.SelectedItem.Parent.Parent.Text
      Else
        frmCreateIndex.Initialize mdb
      End If
    Case Else
      frmCreateIndex.Initialize mdb
  End Select

  frmCreateIndex.Show vbModal

  ' check cancel flag
  If Not frmCreateIndex.Cancelled Then
    ' expand the tabledef node
    ExpandNode _
      mtvw.Nodes(frmCreateIndex.TableDefName)
```

```
   ' now expand the index node for the tabledef
   ExpandNode _
     mtvw.Nodes(frmCreateIndex.TableDefName & "Indexes")
 End If

End Sub

Public Sub DeleteIndex( _
  strTableDefName As String, _
  strIndexName As String)

  ' delete the index from the indexes collection of the
  ' tabledef provided
  mdb.TableDefs(strTableDefName).Indexes.Delete strIndexName
  ' refresh the tree
  ExpandNode mtvw.Nodes(strTableDefName & "Indexes")

End Sub
```

5. Add a new form to the project, create the objects and properties shown in Table 4.17, and save the form as frmCreateIndex.frm.

Table 4.17. Objects and properties of `frmCreateIndex`.

OBJECT	PROPERTY	VALUE
Form	Name	frmCreateIndex
	Caption	Create Index
	BorderStyle	3-Fixed Dialog
Label	Name	lblTableDefName
	Caption	&Table Name
ComboBox	Name	cboTableDefName
	Style	2-Dropdown List
Label	Name	lblIndexName
	Caption	&Index Name
TextBox	Name	txtIndexName
Frame	Name	fraIndex
	Caption	Index

Draw the following controls within the `fraIndex` *frame:*

Label	Name	lblFieldName
	Caption	&Field Name
ComboBox	Name	cboFieldName
	Style	2-Dropdown List
CommandButton	Name	cmdAddField
	Caption	&Add

continued on next page

continued from previous page

OBJECT	PROPERTY	VALUE
Label	Name	lblFields
	Caption	Field &List
ListBox	Name	lstFields
CheckBox	Name	chkPrimary
	Caption	&Primary
CheckBox	Name	chkUnique
	Caption	&Unique

Draw the following two command buttons below the fraIndex *frame at the lower-right corner of the form:*

OBJECT	PROPERTY	VALUE
CommandButton	Name	cmd
	Index	0
	Caption	OK
	Default	True
CommandButton	Name	cmd
	Index	1
	Caption	Cancel
	Cancel	True

NOTE

Figure 4.3, which appears at the beginning of this section, shows the visual layout of the completed form.

6. Add the following code to the declarations section of the form. Several module-level variables are created. The database object mdb is used to create the index. The mblnCancel flag is used to mark that the user cancelled the addition of the index. Several flag variables are used to control when the OK button should be enabled or disabled—each of the flags must be true before OK can be enabled and the index created. The mstrTableDefName variable stores the name of the table where the index was created so that when control returns to the class module and the main form, the proper collection can be refreshed. Finally, the two constants are the indexes into the cmd command button control array.

```
Option Explicit

' database object
Private mdb As Database

' cancel flag
Private mblnCancel As Boolean
```

```
' flags for controlling the OK button
Private mblnHasTableDefName As Boolean
Private mblnHasIndexName As Boolean
Private mblnHasFields As Boolean

' tabledefname for property get
Private mstrTableDefName As String

' command button array constants
Private Const cmdOK = 0
Private Const cmdCancel = 1
```

7. Add the `Initialize` method. This procedure is used when the form is loaded, but before it is shown, to set up module-level variables and populate controls on the form.

```
Public Sub Initialize( _
  db As DAO.Database, _
  Optional strTableDefName As String = "")
' initialize the form
' NOTE: must be called before the form is shown

  Set mdb = db
  ' populate the table combo
  GetTables

  ' set an initial table name if provided
  If strTableDefName <> "" Then
    cboTableDefName.Text = strTableDefName
    ' fill the field list
    GetFields (strTableDefName)
  End If

End Sub
```

8. Add the public `TableDefName` and `Cancelled` properties. These are used after the form is dismissed and control returns to the main form and class to determine what, if any, branch of the tree needs to be refreshed.

```
Public Property Get TableDefName() As String

  TableDefName = mstrTableDefName

End Property
Public Property Get Cancelled() As Boolean

  Cancelled = mblnCancel

End Property
```

9. The `EnableOK` and `EnableIndex` procedures check several flags and enable or disable the OK button and the index frame, based on the current status of the form.

```
Private Sub EnableOK()

  If mblnHasTableDefName _
    And mblnHasIndexName And mblnHasFields Then
    cmd(cmdOK).Enabled = True
  Else
    cmd(cmdOK).Enabled = False
  End If

End Sub
Private Sub EnableIndex()

  If mblnHasTableDefName And mblnHasIndexName Then
    fraIndex.Enabled = True
  Else
    fraIndex.Enabled = False
  End If

End Sub
```

10. Add the `GetTables` and `GetFields` procedures. These routines populate
the table and field list combo boxes.

```
Private Sub GetTables()
' fill the table list combo

  Dim td As TableDef

  With cboTableDefName
    ' clear what (if anything) is there
    .Clear
    For Each td In mdb.TableDefs
      ' check for system table
      If (td.Attributes And dbSystemObject) = 0 Then
        ' not a system table, add it
        .AddItem td.Name
      End If
    Next  ' TableDef
  End With

End Sub
Private Sub GetFields(strTableDefName As String)
' fill the field list combo

  Dim fld As Field

  With cboFieldName
    ' clear it
    .Clear
    For Each fld In mdb.TableDefs(strTableDefName).Fields
      ' add it
      .AddItem fld.Name
    Next  ' Field
  End With

End Sub
```

11. Add the `Form_Load` event procedure. This routine performs some initial setup of the controls on the form.

```
Private Sub Form_Load()
' set up controls

  ' disabled until a name is set and
  ' at list one field is in the field list
  cmd(cmdOK).Enabled = False

  ' disabled until a field is chosen
  cmdAddField.Enabled = False

  ' disable the entire fraIndex frame
  ' until a table and index name are chosen
  fraIndex.Enabled = False

End Sub
```

12. The `Click` and `Change` event procedures for the table name, index name, field name, and check box controls set module-level variables and enable or disable the index frame and OK button, depending on the status of the data. Before the index frame is enabled, a table name and an index name must be provided. To create an index, at least one field must have been added.

```
Private Sub cboTableDefName_Click()
' set up controls and status

  ' copy it to the module-level variable
  ' for later property get
  mstrTableDefName = cboTableDefName.Text
  ' text it and set flags
  If mstrTableDefName <> "" Then
    ' enable the Index frame
    mblnHasTableDefName = True
  Else
    mblnHasTableDefName = False
  End If

  EnableIndex
  EnableOK

End Sub
Private Sub txtIndexName_Change()
' set control and status flags

  If txtIndexName.Text <> "" Then
    mblnHasIndexName = True
  Else
    mblnHasIndexName = False
  End If

  EnableIndex
  EnableOK
```

continued on next page

continued from previous page

```
End Sub
Private Sub cboFieldName_Click()
' enable/disable add field button

  If cboFieldName.Text <> "" Then
    ' enable the add field button
    cmdAddField.Enabled = True
  Else
    cmdAddField.Enabled = False
  End If

End Sub
Private Sub chkPrimary_Click()
' if it's primary, it must be unique
' set control status to indicate the
' user doesn't need to deal with the
' unique check box if primary is set

  If chkPrimary Then
    chkUnique = 1
    chkUnique.Enabled = False
  Else
    chkUnique.Enabled = True
  End If

End Sub
```

13. Create the **Click** event procedure for the **cmdAddField** button. This code adds the current field in the combo box to the list, removes it from the combo box, and returns the focus to the combo box.

```
Private Sub cmdAddField_Click()
' add to list and remove from combo

  lstFields.AddItem cboFieldName.Text
  cboFieldName.RemoveItem cboFieldName.ListIndex

  ' set status flag
  mblnHasFields = True

  EnableOK

  ' return to field name combo
  cboFieldName.SetFocus

End Sub
```

14. Add the **cmd_Click** event procedure. This procedure creates the index if the OK button is clicked, or it unloads the form (setting the **Cancelled** flag) if the Cancel button is clicked.

```
Private Sub cmd_Click(Index As Integer)
' add the index or unload the form
On Error GoTo ProcError
```

```
      Screen.MousePointer = vbHourglass

      Select Case Index
        Case cmdOK
          ' add the index
          CreateIndex
          ' set cancel flag
          mblnCancel = False
          Unload Me
        Case cmdCancel
          ' set cancel flag and unload
          mblnCancel = True
          Unload Me
      End Select

  ProcExit:
      Screen.MousePointer = vbDefault
      Exit Sub

  ProcError:
      MsgBox "Error: " & Err.Number & vbCrLf & Err.Description
      Resume ProcExit

  End Sub
```

15. Add the `CreateIndex` procedure. This code creates the `Index` object by reading the data entered on the form. The index is created by first calling the `CreateIndex` method, then looping through the fields in the list box, calling `CreateField` and `Append` for each. Finally, the `Append` method adds the index to the table.

```
Private Sub CreateIndex()
' create the index
' called only from cmd(cmdOK) click

    Dim td As TableDef
    Dim idx As Index
    Dim fld As Field
    Dim intListIndex As Integer

    ' get a reference to the tabledef and
    ' create the index
    Set td = mdb.TableDefs(cboTableDefName.Text)
    Set idx = td.CreateIndex(txtIndexName.Text)

    ' add the fields
    For intListIndex = 0 To lstFields.ListCount - 1
      lstFields.ListIndex = intListIndex
      Set fld = idx.CreateField(lstFields.Text)
      idx.Fields.Append fld
      Set fld = Nothing
    Next  ' item in list

    ' set primary or unique flags
```

continued on next page

continued from previous page

```
If chkPrimary = 1 Then
   idx.Primary = True
ElseIf chkUnique = 1 Then
   idx.Unique = True
End If

' append the index
td.Indexes.Append idx

End Sub
```

How It Works

Although additional code was added to the main Explorer form to coordinate the user interface, the `CreateIndex` procedure in `frmCreateIndex` does all the work of creating the `Index` objects in this example. The procedure extracts the data provided on the form to create an index, adds the fields from the list box, and then appends the index to the `Indexes` collection of the selected table.

The only information that must be provided to the form is supplied by the `Initialize` procedure as the `db` parameter. The optional `strTableDefName` parameter is a convenience added for the benefit of the users (so that they don't need to select the table name again if they have already chosen one on the Explorer form). Because the interaction between the forms takes place through a public interface, this form could be plugged into any database management application.

Comments

If you worked through this How-To and How-To 4.2, you probably discovered that the procedures for creating an index using DAO code are nearly identical to those for creating a table. As you will see in the next How-To, the procedure for creating a relation is also very similar.

ANOTHER WAY TO CREATE AN INDEX

You can use SQL statements rather than DAO code to create indexes for your tables. Constraints can be created using the CREATE TABLE statement or the ALTER TABLE...ADD CONSTRAINT statement. Indexes can also be created using the CREATE INDEX statement. SQL statements are simple to use and require only a single line of code to execute, but they do not expose all the available properties of an index. Chapter 2 provides the details of using SQL statements to create and manage database objects.

COMPLEXITY
BEGINNING

4.4 How do I...
Define relations between tables?

Problem

I know that if I define relations for my database, the Jet engine will enforce referential integrity. How do I define relations with Visual Basic?

Technique

Like indexes, defined relationships are a tool you can use to enforce rules and improve application performance. How-To 4.2 described the different types of relationships between tables: one-to-one, one-to-many, and many-to-many. Building the database schema with related tables is only the first step. You also need to enforce those relationships. The best way to do that is to let the database engine do it for you by creating `Relation` objects.

Defining a relation enforces three rules to maintain referential integrity between tables:

✔ No row on the many side of a relationship may reference a primary key value on the one side that does not exist.

✔ No row on the one side of a relationship can be deleted if there are related rows on the many side.

✔ The primary key values on the one side cannot be changed if related rows exist on the many side.

Creating the Relation

Creating a `Relation` object with DAO code is similar to creating a table or index. The creation is carried out in four steps:

1. Use the `CreateRelation` method to obtain a reference to a `Relation` object.

2. Assign the `Table` and `ForeignTable` properties.

3. Create and add each of the `Field` objects to the `Fields` collection of the `Relation` object. For each field, you must set the `Name` and `ForeignName` properties.

4. Add the `Relation` to the `Relations` collection of the database by using the `Append` method.

In addition to creating the relationship and adding the fields, you can specify some additional properties that affect how the database engine treats the relationship:

- ✔ *Cascading Updates*—If cascading updates are specified, changes to the primary key values on the one side of a relationship are propagated through the related records on the many side.

- ✔ *Cascading Deletes*—If cascading deletes are specified, deleting a record on the one side of a relationship will also delete all records on the many side.

BE CAREFUL WITH CASCADING UPDATES AND DELETES

The concept of specifying cascading updates and deletes seems powerful and convenient at first glance but can be dangerous if not used with caution. Consider the following scenario:

You have a lookup table of U.S. states that includes the state name and two-letter postal code. A unique index is defined on the postal code so that it can be used as the one side of a relationship. This table is then used to enforce that any value entered for a state as part of a set of address columns in another table is valid. This setup is good so far—the database engine will now validate any state postal code entered in the database. If, however, you created this relationship with cascading updates and deletes, you could inadvertently change every address in one state to another state with a single update or delete every address in a state with a single delete. If you were to run the query DELETE FROM States;, you would delete every row in your database that has a state column!

This is a somewhat contrived and extreme example. But the point is that by using cascading updates and deletes, you hand off work to the database engine, and you might forget later that the database engine is doing the work for you. An alternative to this approach is to define the relationship without specifying cascading updates or deletes. When you try to perform an operation that violates referential integrity constraints, a trappable error will be raised. You can then examine that error and decide whether to cancel the change or manually perform the cascade by running additional update or delete queries. See Chapter 3, "SQL," for additional information on building and executing update or delete queries.

In addition to specifying cascading updates and deletes, you can also indicate that the relationship is one-to-one or one-to-many. Don't let yourself be confused by the difference. One-to-one relationships are really just a special case of one-to-many relationships. Instead of allowing multiple rows on the many side, the database engine allows only one. Many-to-many relationships are defined using two one-to-many relationships.

Steps

Open and run project HT404.vbp. Open the database HT404.mdb. You can use the Relation | Add menu command to create the relationships shown in Table 4.18. Figure 4.4 shows the form used to create a relationship.

> **NOTE**
>
> File HT404A.mdb is identical to HT404.mdb except that all the relations have already been created for you. If you do not want to create all the relationships shown in the table, you can open HT404A.mdb and inspect the objects using the Explorer form.

Table 4.18. Relations in HT404.mdb.

NAME	TABLE	FOREIGN TABLE	FIELD NAME	FOREIGN NAME	TYPE	CASCADE
fkAdvFacID	Faculty	Advisors	FacID	AdvFacID	1-1	Deletes
fkInstrFacID	Faculty	Instructors	FacID	InstrFacID	1-1	Deletes
fkCourseInstrID	Instructors	Courses	InstrFacID	CourseInstrID	1-Many	N/A
fkSCStID	Students	StudentCourses	StID	SCStID	1-Many	N/A
fkSCCourseID	Courses	StudentCourses	CourseID	SCCourseID	1-Many	N/A
fkStAdvID	Advisors	Students	AdvFacID	StAdvID	1-Many	N/A

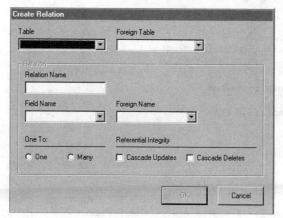

Figure 4.4. The Create Relation form.

1. Create a new Standard EXE project and save it as HT404.vbp. Add BMain.bas to the project. This module contains code derived from the example in How-To 4.1 used to open or create a database.

2. Add frmMain.frm to the project. This is the same form used for How-To 4.3. Add the menu controls shown in Table 4.19 for the Relation menu.

Table 4.19. The Relation menu controls.

NAME	CAPTION
mnuRelation	&Relation
mnuRelationAdd	&Add
mnuRelationDelete	&Delete

3. Three event procedures control the Relation menu. The top-level `mnuRelation_Click` event procedure determines which of the other menu controls should be enabled based on the currently selected object in the `TreeView` control on the form. The `Add` command uses the `mcdbExp` object to show the form used to create a relationship and update the `TreeView` control. The `Delete` command calls on the `DeleteRelation` method of the `mcdbExp` object to delete the currently selected relationship.

```
Private Sub mnuRelation_Click()
On Error GoTo ProcError

  If mcdbExp Is Nothing Then
    ' no database open
    mnuRelationAdd.Enabled = False
    mnuRelationDelete.Enabled = False
  Else
    ' enable add
    mnuRelationAdd.Enabled = True
    ' only enable delete if an Index is selected
    If mcdbExp.NodeType(tvTreeView.SelectedItem) = _
      "Relation" Then
      mnuRelationDelete.Enabled = True
    Else
      mnuRelationDelete.Enabled = False
    End If
  End If

ProcExit:
  Exit Sub

ProcError:
  MsgBox "Error: " & Err.Number & vbCrLf & Err.Description
  Resume ProcExit

End Sub
Private Sub mnuRelationAdd_Click()
On Error GoTo ProcError
```

```
    mcdbExp.AddRelation

ProcExit:
  Exit Sub

ProcError:
  MsgBox "Error: " & Err.Number & vbCrLf & Err.Description
  Resume ProcExit

End Sub

Private Sub mnuRelationDelete_Click()
On Error GoTo ProcError

  Dim strRelationName As String

  ' get the name
  strRelationName = tvTreeView.SelectedItem.Text

  mcdbExp.DeleteRelation strRelationName

ProcExit:
  Exit Sub

ProcError:
  MsgBox "Error: " & Err.Number & vbCrLf & Err.Description
  Resume ProcExit
End Sub
```

4. Add the class module CDBExplorer.cls to the project. This is the same
class module used in How-To 4.3, but with code added to support creating and deleting relationships in the database. The **AddRelation** method
loads, initializes, and shows **frmCreateRelation** and then refreshes the
node in the Explorer form tree for relationships. The **DeleteRelation**
method takes the name of a **Relation** object as a parameter and deletes
the **Relation** object from the **Relations** collection of the database.

```
Public Sub AddRelation()
' load the form to create a relation

  Load frmCreateRelation

  ' pass it the database reference
  Set frmCreateRelation.Database = mdb

  frmCreateRelation.Show vbModal

  ' refresh the tabledefs node
  ExpandNode mtvw.Nodes("Relations")

End Sub

Public Sub DeleteRelation(strRelationName As String)
```

continued on next page

continued from previous page

```
' delete a relation

  ' delete it
  mdb.Relations.Delete strRelationName
  ' refresh the relations node
  ExpandNode mtvw.Nodes("Relations")

End Sub
```

5. Add a new form to the project, create the objects and properties shown in Table 4.20, and save the form as frmCreateRelation.frm.

Table 4.20. Objects and properties of `frmCreateRelation`.

OBJECT	PROPERTY	VALUE
Form	Name	frmCreateRelation
	Caption	Create Relation
	Border Style	3-Fixed Dialog
Label	Name	lblTableDefName
	Caption	Table
ComboBox	Name	cboTableDefName
	Style	2-Dropdown List
Label	Name	lblForeignTableDefName
	Caption	Foreign Table
ComboBox	Name	cboForeignTableDefName
	Style	2-Dropdown List
Frame	Name	fraRelation
	Caption	Relation

Draw the following controls within the `fraRelation` *frame:*

Label	Name	lblRelationName
	Caption	Relation Name
TextBox	Name	txtRelationName
Label	Name	lblFieldName
	Caption	Field Name
ComboBox	Name	cboFieldName
	Style	2-Dropdown List
Label	Name	lblForeignName
	Caption	Foreign Name
ComboBox	Name	cboForeignName
	Style	2-Dropdown List
Label	Name	lblOneTo
	Caption	One To:

OBJECT	PROPERTY	VALUE
Line	Name	Line1
OptionButton	Name	optOneTo
	Caption	One
	Index	0
OptionButton	Name	optOneTo
	Caption	Many
	Index	1
Label	Name	lblReferentialIntegrity
	Caption	Referential Integrity
Line	Name	Line2
CheckBox	Name	chkRef
	Caption	Cascade Updates
	Index	0
CheckBox	Name	chkRef
	Caption	Cascade Deletes
	Index	1

Draw the following two command buttons at the bottom right of the form below the fraRelation *frame:*

CommandButton	Name	cmd
	Caption	OK
	Default	True
	Index	0
CommandButton	Name	cmd
	Caption	Cancel
	Cancel	True
	Index	1

Figure 4.4 shows the visual design of the form at runtime.

6. Add the following code to the declarations section of the form. Module-level variables are defined to store the database object, the table and foreign table names, and the field name and foreign name properties. There are also three pairs of constants defined as indexes into the three control arrays on the form.

```
Option Explicit

' database
Private mdb As Database

' table
```

continued on next page

continued from previous page

```
Private mstrTableDefName As String
' foreign table
Private mstrForeignTableDefName As String

' relation name
Private mstrRelationName As String
' field name
Private mstrFieldName As String
' foreign name
Private mstrForeignName As String

' control array constants
Private Const optOneToOne = 0
Private Const optOneToMany = 1

Private Const chkRefCascadeUpdates = 0
Private Const chkRefCascadeDeletes = 1

Private Const cmdOK = 0
Private Const cmdCancel = 1
```

7. Add the **Database** property procedure. This property is used to allow the **CDBExplorer** class to pass a database object to the form. After the database has been provided, the table and foreign table combo boxes are populated with lists of table names.

```
Public Property Set Database(db As DAO.Database)
' set database object and set up form

  ' assign the database object
  Set mdb = db

  ' populate the table combo boxes
  GetTables cboTableDefName
  GetTables cboForeignTableDefName

End Property
```

8. Add the **EnableOK** and **EnableRelation** procedures. These procedures examine the current state of the data on the form to determine whether the **fraRelation** frame and the OK button should be enabled or disabled.

```
Private Sub EnableOK()
' to create a relation, you need the following
' a table name
' a foreign table name
' a relation name
' a field name
' a foreign name for the field
' additionally, CreateRelation will fail if the
' field data types do not match correctly

  If mstrTableDefName = "" Or _
      mstrForeignTableDefName = "" Or _
```

```
        mstrRelationName = "" Or _
        mstrFieldName = "" Or _
        mstrForeignName = "" Then
      cmd(cmdOK).Enabled = False
    Else
      cmd(cmdOK).Enabled = True
    End If

End Sub
Private Sub EnableRelation()
' enable/disable the relation frame

    If _
        mstrTableDefName = "" Or _
        mstrForeignTableDefName = "" _
        Then
      fraRelation.Enabled = False
    Else
      fraRelation.Enabled = True
    End If

End Sub
```

9. Add the `GetTables` and `GetFields` procedures. These procedures populate a combo box with a list of tables or fields by examining the `TableDefs` collection of the database or the `Fields` collection of a table.

```
Private Sub GetTables(cbo As ComboBox)
' fill the table list combo

    Dim td As TableDef

    With cbo
      ' clear what (if anything) is there
      .Clear
      For Each td In mdb.TableDefs
        ' check for system table
        If (td.Attributes And dbSystemObject) = 0 Then
          ' not a system table, add it
          .AddItem td.Name
        End If
      Next  ' TableDef
    End With

End Sub
Private Sub GetFields(cbo As ComboBox, strTableDefName As String)
' fill the field list combo

    Dim fld As Field

    With cbo
      ' clear it
      .Clear
      For Each fld In mdb.TableDefs(strTableDefName).Fields
        ' add it
```

continued on next page

continued from previous page

```
      .AddItem fld.Name
    Next  ' Field
  End With

End Sub
```

10. Add the `Form_Load` event procedure. The relations frame and OK button are disabled by this procedure.

```
Private Sub Form_Load()
On Error GoTo ProcError

  ' disable the relations frame
  fraRelation.Enabled = False

  ' disable the OK button
  cmd(cmdOK).Enabled = False

ProcExit:
  Exit Sub

ProcError:
  MsgBox "Error: " & Err.Number & vbCrLf & Err.Description
  Resume ProcExit

End Sub
```

11. Add the `Click` event procedures for the `cboTableDefName` and `cboForeignTableDefName` combo box controls. These procedures store the values of the combo boxes in the module-level variables and call the `GetFields` procedure to populate the field lists. They then call both `EnableOK` and `EnableRelation` to enable or disable both the relationship frame container and the OK button.

```
Private Sub cboTableDefName_Click()
On Error GoTo ProcError

  Screen.MousePointer = vbHourglass

  mstrTableDefName = cboTableDefName.Text

  If mstrTableDefName <> "" Then
    GetFields cboFieldName, mstrTableDefName
  End If

  EnableOK
  EnableRelation

ProcExit:
  Screen.MousePointer = vbDefault
  Exit Sub

ProcError:
  MsgBox "Error: " & Err.Number & vbCrLf & Err.Description
```

```
      Resume ProcExit

End Sub

Private Sub cboForeignTableDefName_Click()
On Error GoTo ProcError

   Screen.MousePointer = vbHourglass

   mstrForeignTableDefName = cboForeignTableDefName.Text

   If mstrForeignTableDefName <> "" Then
     GetFields cboForeignName, mstrForeignTableDefName
   End If

   EnableOK
   EnableRelation

ProcExit:
   Screen.MousePointer = vbDefault
   Exit Sub

ProcError:
   MsgBox "Error: " & Err.Number & vbCrLf & Err.Description
   Resume ProcExit

End Sub
```

12. Add the `Click` events for the `cboFieldName` and `cboForeignName`
controls. The current values in the combo boxes are passed to the module-
level variables, and the `EnableOK` procedure is called to enable or disable
the OK button.

```
Private Sub cboFieldName_Click()
On Error GoTo ProcError

   mstrFieldName = cboFieldName.Text

   EnableOK

ProcExit:
   Exit Sub

ProcError:
   MsgBox "Error: " & Err.Number & vbCrLf & Err.Description
   Resume ProcExit

End Sub

Private Sub cboForeignName_Click()
On Error GoTo ProcError

   mstrForeignName = cboForeignName.Text

   EnableOK
```

continued on next page

continued from previous page

```
ProcExit:
  Exit Sub

ProcError:
  MsgBox "Error: " & Err.Number & vbCrLf & Err.Description
  Resume ProcExit

End Sub
```

13. Add the `txtRelation_Change` event. This procedure passes the contents of the text box to the module-level variable and calls the `EnableOK` procedure to enable or disable the OK button.

```
Private Sub txtRelationName_Change()
On Error GoTo ProcError

  mstrRelationName = txtRelationName

  EnableOK

ProcExit:
  Exit Sub

ProcError:
  MsgBox "Error: " & Err.Number & vbCrLf & Err.Description
  Resume ProcExit

End Sub
```

14. Add the `cmd_Click` procedure. This procedure either calls the `CreateRelation` procedure and unloads the form, or simply unloads the form.

```
Private Sub cmd_Click(Index As Integer)
' create the relation or unload
On Error GoTo ProcError

  Screen.MousePointer = vbHourglass

  Select Case Index
    Case cmdOK
      ' create relation and unload
      CreateRelation
      Unload Me
    Case cmdCancel
      ' just unload
      Unload Me
  End Select

ProcExit:
  Screen.MousePointer = vbDefault
  Exit Sub
```

```
ProcError:
  MsgBox "Error: " & Err.Number & vbCrLf & Err.Description
  Resume ProcExit

End Sub
```

15. Add the `CreateRelation` procedure. This procedure uses the steps described earlier in this How-To to create the `Relation` object, based on the values saved in the module-level variables. The procedure calls `CreateRelation`, creates and appends a `Field` object to the `Fields` collection, and finally uses the `Append` method to add the `Relation` object to the `Relations` collection.

```
Private Sub CreateRelation()
' create the relation
' called only from cmd(cmdOK) click event

  Dim rel As Relation
  Dim fld As Field
  Dim lngAttributes As Long

  ' set up attributes
  If optOneTo(optOneToOne) Then
    lngAttributes = dbRelationUnique
  End If
  If chkRef(chkRefCascadeUpdates) Then
    lngAttributes = lngAttributes Or dbRelationUpdateCascade
  End If
  If chkRef(chkRefCascadeDeletes) Then
    lngAttributes = lngAttributes Or dbRelationDeleteCascade
  End If
  ' create the relation
  Set rel = mdb.CreateRelation( _
      mstrRelationName, _
      mstrTableDefName, _
      mstrForeignTableDefName, _
      lngAttributes)
  Set fld = rel.CreateField(mstrFieldName)
  ' set the foreign name
  fld.ForeignName = mstrForeignName
  ' append the field to the relation
  rel.Fields.Append fld
  ' append the relation to the database
  mdb.Relations.Append rel

End Sub
```

How It Works

If you've worked through the previous examples, the method and the code used to create relationships will look quite familiar. Again, a single procedure—in this case, the `CreateRelation` procedure in `frmCreateRelation`—does all the real work of creating the relationship. Based on values entered by the user, the procedure creates the `Relation` object. It then adds the desired field and assigns the `ForeignName` property, and finally it appends the field and the relation to their respective collections. The rest of the code in the form coordinates the user interface.

> **NOTE**
>
> This example does not implement the capability to create relationships with multiple fields. If you need to create such a relationship, just repeat the code that creates and appends the field for each field in the relationship.

Comments

The Jet database engine also allows you to use SQL statements to create relationships between tables by using a **CONSTRAINT** clause in a **CREATE TABLE** or **ALTER TABLE** statement. See Chapter 3 for details on using SQL statements to create relationships.

COMPLEXITY
BEGINNING

4.5 How do I...
Use the Jet database engine to enforce business rules?

Problem

I need to make sure that certain rules are followed when data is entered into my database. How do I get the database engine to enforce these rules for me?

Technique

Various rules can be applied against tables and columns in a database:

✔ Values for columns can be restricted to a specific list of values, or the value can be restricted by a formula. For example, a numeric column can be required to be greater than zero.

✔ Columns can require an entry.

✔ Values for one column can be dependent on the values for another column.

The collective term for these types of restrictions on data is *business rules*. You can enforce rules in your database in two ways:

✔ Write Visual Basic code to examine the data and apply the rules before inserts, updates, or deletes are completed.

✔ Build the rules into the design of the tables and columns and let the database engine enforce them for you.

Although in certain situations the rules will be too complex to be entered using the available properties for `TableDef` and `Field` objects, you should allow the database engine to enforce as many of your rules as it is capable of enforcing.

If you have worked through the examples in How-To 4.2 through How-To 4.4, you have already been enforcing some simple rules in your database:

✔ When a column is defined, the data type restricts the data that can be entered in the column.

✔ Defining a primary key or unique index restricts the data in a column to unique entries.

✔ Defining a relationship between tables restricts the values in foreign key columns to the available values in the primary key from the table on the other side of the relationship.

In addition to these constraints on data, you can specify an additional property for tables and three additional properties for columns that further restrict the data that can be entered:

✔ The `Required` property for `Field` objects can be used to disallow `Null` values in the column. Setting this property to `True` means that a value is required.

✔ The `ValidationRule` property applies to both tables and columns and can be used to force the data to conform to an expression. The partner of the `ValidationRule` property is the `ValidationText` property. This property can be used to provide the text of the error message that is generated when the rule is violated.

✔ The `AllowZeroLength` property can be used to allow or disallow zero-length strings as valid entries for a column. The Jet engine treats zero-length strings and `Null`s separately. Developers can use the two to distinguish between values that are unknown (most often using `Null`) and values that are known to be nothing (using a zero-length string). For example, if a middle name column allows a zero-length string, a `Null` would indicate that the data was not available, whereas a zero-length string would indicate that the person has no middle name. Although this is a potentially useful tool, the subtle difference between these values will probably be lost on most users. Additionally, not all types of databases support this differentiation.

`Required` and `AllowZeroLength` are both Boolean properties. If the `Required` property is set to `True`, `Null` values will not be allowed. If the `AllowZeroLength` property is set to True, the column will allow a zero-length string as a valid value.

The ValidationRule property is a string and can be any valid Visual Basic expression. It cannot, however, contain a reference to a user-defined function, SQL aggregate functions, a query, or, in the case of a table, columns in another table.

The ValidationText property can be any string expression and is provided as the description of the trappable error that results when the rule is violated.

Steps

Open and run project HT405.vbp. The form shown in Figure 4.5 appears. Choose File | Open and open database HT405.mdb. This is the school database developed and refined in How-To 4.2 through How-To 4.4. Click the Add Rules button to apply the rules shown in Table 4.21 to the database.

Table 4.21. Business rules for HT405.mdb.

TABLE	FIELD	PROPERTY	VALUE
Advisors	AdvGradeLevel	Required	True
Advisors		ValidationRule	IN ('Freshman', 'Sophomore', 'Junior', 'Senior')
		ValidationText	Grade level must be Freshman, Sophomore, Junior, or Senior
Courses	CourseDesc	Required	True
Faculty	FacFirst	Required	True
	FacLast	Required	True
Students	StFirst	Required	True
Students	StLast	Required	True

Figure 4.5. The
Create Rules form.

In addition to the field-level rules in Table 4.21, the following rule applies to the Students table:

```
ValidationRule
  IIf(
    (
      (Not IsNull([StAddress])) Or
      (Not IsNull([StCity])) Or
      (Not IsNull([StState])) Or
      (Not IsNull([StZIP]))
    ),
    (
      IIf(
        (
          (Not IsNull([StAddress])) And
          (Not IsNull([StCity])) And
          (Not IsNull([StState])) And
          (Not IsNull([StZIP]))
        )
      ), True, False)
  ), True)
```

```
ValidationText
  If provided, the address must be complete.
```

This rather cumbersome-looking expression enforces the rule that if any of the address columns (**StAddress**, **StCity**, **StState**, **StZIP**) contains data, they all must contain data. Because Jet restricts the **ValidationRule** property to a single expression, the nested **IIf** statements must be used. The outer **IIf** returns **True** if any of the columns contains data; the inner **IIf** returns **True** only if they all contain data.

A MISLEADING STATEMENT IN THE HELP FILE

The following statement appears in the Visual Basic 5 help file topic for the ValidationRule property:

For an object not yet appended to the Fields collection, this property is read/write.

This would seem to imply that after the field has been created, the property can no longer be assigned. In fact, the ValidationRule and ValidationText properties for both tables and fields can be assigned after the objects have been created, and the Required property can be assigned after a field has been created—all as demonstrated in the sample application.

---

1. Create a new standard EXE project, and name it HT405.vbp.

2. Change the name of **Form1** to **frmMain**, and create the objects and properties shown in Table 4.22.

Table 4.22. Objects and properties for `frmMain`.

OBJECT	PROPERTY	VALUE
Form	BorderStyle	3-Fixed Dialog
	Caption	Create Rules
CommonDialog	Name	dlg
CommandButton	Name	cmdAddRules
	Caption	Add Rules
Menu	Name	mnuFile
	Caption	&File
Menu	Name	mnuFileOpen
	Caption	&Open
	Shortcut	Ctrl-O
Menu	Name	mnuFileBar
	Caption	-
Menu	Name	mnuFileExit
	Caption	E&xit
	Shortcut	Ctrl-Q

3. Add the following code to the declarations section of the form:

```
Option Explicit

Private mdb As Database
```

4. Add the `cmdAddRules_Click` event procedure. This procedure calls the `AddRules` subroutine described here.

```
Private Sub cmdAddRules_Click()
On Error GoTo ProcError

  Screen.MousePointer = vbHourglass

  AddRules
  MsgBox "Rules Added"
  cmdAddRules.Enabled = False

ProcExit:
  Screen.MousePointer = vbDefault
  Exit Sub

ProcError:
  MsgBox "Error: " & Err.Number & vbCrLf & Err.Description
  Resume ProcExit

End Sub
```

5. Add the `mnuFileOpen_Click` procedure. This procedure calls the `GetOpenDBName` function shown next, opens the database using the filename returned, and enables the `cmdAddRules` button.

```
Private Sub mnuFileOpen_Click()
On Error GoTo ProcError

  Dim strDBName As String

  Screen.MousePointer = vbHourglass

  ' use the common dialog to get the db name
  strDBName = GetOpenDBName(dlg)
  If Len(strDBName) Then
    Set mdb = DBEngine(0).OpenDatabase(strDBName)
    cmdAddRules.Enabled = True
  End If

ProcExit:
  Screen.MousePointer = vbDefault
  Exit Sub

ProcError:
  MsgBox "Error: " & Err.Number & vbCrLf & Err.Description
  Resume ProcExit

End Sub
```

6. Create the `mnuFileExit_Click` event. This procedure unloads the form, ending the application.

```
Private Sub mnuFileExit_Click()
On Error GoTo ProcError

  Screen.MousePointer = vbHourglass

  ' close the database and unload the form
  mdb.Close
  Unload Me

ProcExit:
  Screen.MousePointer = vbDefault
  Exit Sub

ProcError:
  MsgBox "Error: " & Err.Number & vbCrLf & Err.Description
  Resume ProcExit

End Sub
```

7. Create the `GetOpenDBName` function. This function sets up the common dialog control and returns the filename selected by the user as its return value.

```
Private Function GetOpenDBName(dlg As CommonDialog) As String
' Get the desired name using the common dialog
On Error GoTo ProcError

    Dim strFileName As String

    ' set up the file save dialog file types
    dlg.InitDir = App.Path
    dlg.DefaultExt = "mdb"
    dlg.DialogTitle = "Open Database"
    dlg.Filter = "VB Databases (*.mdb)¦*.mdb"
    dlg.FilterIndex = 1
    ' set up flags
    dlg.Flags = _
        cdlOFNHideReadOnly Or _
        cdlOFNFileMustExist Or _
        cdlOFNPathMustExist
    ' setting CancelError means the control will
    ' raise an error if the user clicks Cancel
    dlg.CancelError = True
    ' show the SaveAs dialog
    dlg.ShowOpen
    ' get the selected name
    strFileName = dlg.filename

ProcExit:
    GetOpenDBName = strFileName
    Exit Function

ProcError:
    strFileName = ""
    Resume ProcExit

End Function
```

8. Create the **AddRules** routine. This routine assigns the **Required**,
ValidationRule, and **ValidationText** properties described previously.
Each of the values is directly assigned to the property. The various
With...End With blocks add some efficiency by eliminating extra object
references.

```
Private Sub AddRules()

    Dim td As TableDef
    Dim fld As Field

    ' Advisors table
    ' AdvGradeLevel field
    Set fld = mdb.TableDefs("Advisors").Fields("AdvGradeLevel")
    With fld
        ' require entry
        .Required = True
        ' require a value in a list
        .ValidationRule = _
```

```
                "IN ('Freshman', 'Sophomore', 'Junior', 'Senior')"
    .ValidationText = _
                "Grade level must be Freshman, " & _
                "Sophomore, Junior or Senior"
End With
  Set fld = Nothing
  ' Courses table
  ' CourseDesc field
  mdb.TableDefs("Courses").Fields("CourseDesc").Required = True
  ' Faculty table
  Set td = mdb.TableDefs("Faculty")
  With td
    ' FacFirst required
    .Fields("FacFirst").Required = True
    ' FacLast required
    .Fields("FacLast").Required = True
  End With
  Set td = Nothing
  ' Students table
  Set td = mdb.TableDefs("Students")
  With td
    ' first and last names are required
    .Fields("StFirst").Required = True
    .Fields("StLast").Required = True
    ' table rule - if any part of the
    ' address is provided, all of it
    ' must be provided
    ' the outer IIf evaluates if any field is not null
    ' the inner IIf evalutates if all fields are not null
    .ValidationRule = _
      "IIf(" & _
        "(" & _
          "(Not IsNull([StAddress])) Or " & _
          "(Not IsNull([StCity])) Or " & _
          "(Not IsNull([StState])) Or " & _
          "(Not IsNull([StZIP])) " & _
        "), " & _
        "(IIf(" & _
          "(" & _
            "(Not IsNull([StAddress])) And " & _
            "(Not IsNull([StCity])) And " & _
            "(Not IsNull([StState])) And " & _
            "(Not IsNull([StZIP])) " & _
          "), " & _
          "True, False)" & _
        "), " & _
        "True)"
    .ValidationText = _
        "If provided, the address must be complete."
  End With
  Set td = Nothing

End Sub
```

How It Works

This How-To provides the final refinement to the database that has been developed throughout the chapter by adding some basic business rule enforcement at the level of the database engine. The rules are established by obtaining references to the appropriate table and field objects and setting the `ValidationRule`, `ValidationText`, and `Required` properties.

As you can see in the examples, it can be difficult to implement even relatively simple rules due to the limitations of these properties. Thus, you might need to supplement the properties provided by the database engine with additional validation code. Chapter 1, "Accessing a Database with Bound Controls," and Chapter 2, "Accessing a Database with Data Access Objects," provide additional information on using Visual Basic code to enforce rules on the data in your database.

Comments

Unless you specify otherwise, field validation rules are applied when the record is updated. If you want the rule to be applied as soon as the entry is applied to the field, set the `ValidateOnSet` property of the `Field` object to `True`.

MICROSOFT ACCESS DATABASES

5

MICROSOFT ACCESS DATABASES

How do I...

5.1 **Determine the number of records in a table and the table's created and last-modified dates?**

5.2 **Attach a table from another database file?**

5.3 **Import a text file?**

5.4 **Save graphics in a database file?**

5.5 **Make sure that an operation involving multiple tables is not left partially completed?**

5.6 **Compact a database or repair a corrupted database?**

5.7 **Use parameter queries stored in Microsoft Access databases?**

You can use Visual Basic with the Jet database engine to read, add, update, and delete records from various database types. You can work with PC-based indexed sequential access method (ISAM) databases such as dBASE, FoxPro, Paradox, and Btrieve. You can use Open Database Connectivity (ODBC) drivers to work with almost any database that supports SQL. Techniques for working with ISAM and ODBC databases are covered in Chapter 6, "External ISAM Database Files," and Chapter 7, "Connecting to an ODBC Server."

When you have a choice of database formats, you will find it easiest to work with Visual Basic's "native" database format, Microsoft Access. Because Visual Basic and Microsoft Access have been created to work in tandem, you have a rich feature set available to you. This chapter shows you how to use many of the unique features of Microsoft Access database files.

5.1 Determine the Number of Records in a Table and the Table's Created and Last-Modified Dates

A Microsoft Access database contains information about each table in the database—including, among other items, when the table was created, when it was last modified, and the number of records it currently contains. This How-To consists of a tool for extracting and displaying that information.

5.2 Attach a Table from Another Database File

In some cases, it is necessary or desirable to make the contents of a table available to more than one Microsoft Access database. A database can access a table from another database by attaching the table to itself. This How-To shows you how to attach Microsoft Access tables to Microsoft Access databases through Visual Basic.

5.3 Import a Text File

The source of your application's data might be files consisting of delimited ASCII or ANSI text. This How-To shows how to use Visual Basic classes and collections to convert text files into records that you can add to Microsoft Access tables.

5.4 Save Graphics in a Database File

The capability to store graphics in a database can be very useful, but sometimes challenging. This How-To explains two methods of saving graphics, as well as providing an example of one of them.

5.5 Make Sure That an Operation Involving Multiple Tables Is Not Left Partially Completed

A well-designed relational database uses multiple tables that are related together. A single "logical" add, delete, or update operation often requires making a change to more than one table. If an error occurs during a multitable operation, you generally want to abort the entire operation and return all the tables to the condition in which they existed at the start of the operation. This How-To shows how to use the transaction features of the Jet database engine to ensure the integrity of your tables.

5.6 Compact a Database or Repair a Corrupted Database

The Jet database engine has the capability to recover space after deletion of data, but it does not perform the operation automatically. The Jet engine also can repair certain types of database damage—but again, it will not make the attempt unless it is instructed to do so. This How-To shows how to use Visual Basic to initiate the Jet engine's database-compact and database-repair capabilities.

5.7 Use Parameter Queries Stored in Microsoft Access Databases

Microsoft Access queries can be designed to use replaceable parameters. A query with a replaceable parameter must be provided with a value for that parameter each time the query is run. This How-To shows how to use stored queries with replaceable parameters from Visual Basic.

COMPLEXITY
BEGINNING

5.1 How do I...
Determine the number of records in a table and the table's created and last-modified dates?

Problem

I have an application that periodically adds records to a table. No other user or application ever modifies this table. To make sure that I don't perform the same update twice, I'd like to check the current record count and the date the last changes were made to the table's recordset. How can I do this from Visual Basic?

Technique

The `TableDefs` collection of the `Database` object consists of `TableDef` objects, each of which represents one table from the database. The properties of the `TableDef` object describe the table. Table 5.1 lists the properties of `TableDef` objects applicable to native Microsoft Access database tables.

Table 5.1. Properties of a `TableDef` object applicable to Microsoft Access tables.

PROPERTY	DESCRIPTION
Attributes	Characteristics of the table, including whether the table is an attached table.
DateCreated	The date and time the table was created.
LastUpdated	The date and time the table was most recently changed.
Name	The name of the table.
RecordCount	The number of records in the table.
SourceTableName	The name of the base table, if the `TableDef` is for an attached table.
Updatable	Specification of whether `SourceTableName`, `ValidationRule`, and
	`ValidationText` properties of the `TableDef` can be modified.

continued on next page

continued from previous page

PROPERTY	DESCRIPTION
ValidationRule	An expression used to set the criteria for accepting a new record or a modification to an existing record.
ValidationText	The message returned if a change fails to meet the ValidationRule criteria.

Steps

The Table Status application displays four of the most useful properties for each user table in a database. Open and run TableData.VBP. You'll see a standard Windows File Open dialog box. Choose a Microsoft Access (*.MDB) file, and click OK. The form shown in Figure 5.1 appears with a list of the tables in the database shown in the list box. Select a table, and the table's creation date, last modification date, and current record count appear in the boxes on the form, similar to what's displayed in Figure 5.2.

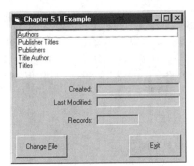

Figure 5.1. The main form for the Chapter 5.1 example, displaying the table list.

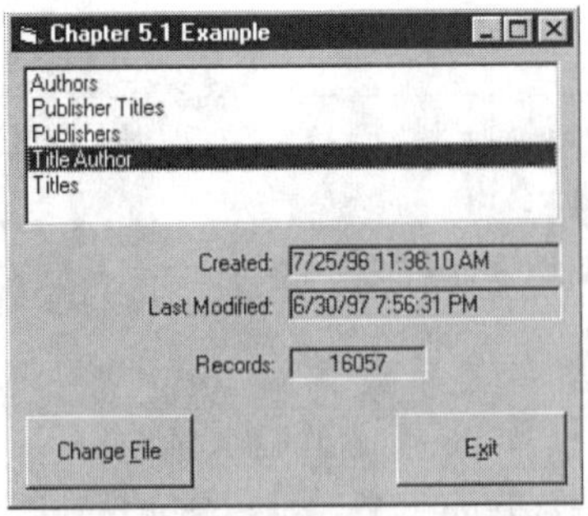

Figure 5.2. The main form, now showing table statistics.

1. Create a new project called TableData.VBP. Create the objects and properties listed in Table 5.2, and save the form as TableData.FRM.

Table 5.2. Objects and properties for the Table Status form.

OBJECT	PROPERTY	SETTING
Form	Name	Form1
	Caption	"Chapter 5.1 Example"
CommandButton	Name	cmdChangeFile
	Caption	"Change &File"
CommandButton	Name	cmdExit
	Cancel	True
	Caption	"E&xit"
ListBox	Name	lstTables
	Sorted	True
CommonDialog	Name	cdlTableData
	CancelError	True
	DefaultExt	"MDB"
	DialogTitle	"Database File"
	FileName	"*.MDB"
	Filter	"*.MDB"
Label	Name	lblCreated
	Alignment	2 (Center)
	BorderStyle	1 (Fixed Single)
Label	Name	lblModified
	Alignment	2 (Center)
	BorderStyle	1 (Fixed Single)
Label	Name	lblRecords
	Alignment	2 (Center)
	BorderStyle	1 (Fixed Single)
Label	Name	lblTableData
	Index	0
	Caption	"Created:"
Label	Name	lblTableData
	Index	1
	Caption	"Last Modified:"
Label	Name	lblTableData
	Index	2
	Caption	"Records:"

2. Add the following code to the declarations section of Form1. The Collection object created by the declaration is used by several procedures within the form, so it is declared at form level to give all the procedures access to it.

```
Option Explicit

Private colTableData As Collection
```

3. Add the following code to the Form_Load event of Form1. Form_Load just calls the GetDatabase subroutine, which controls the rest of the application.

```
Private Sub Form_Load()
    GetDatabase
End Sub
```

4. Create the GetDatabase subroutine with the following code. This procedure gets a database selection from the user, retrieves information from its nonsystem table definitions into clsTableStatus objects, and puts the clsTableData objects into colTableData. (The clsTableData class is discussed later in this section.) It then lists the table names in the form's list box.

```
Private Sub GetDatabase()
    Dim dbfTableData As Database
    Dim tdfTables As TableDefs, tdfSelectedTable As TableDef
    Dim objTable As clsTableData
    Dim strDatabaseName As String

    On Error GoTo NoDatabaseError
        'Call the ShowOpen method of the CommonDialog control, so the user
        'can select a database.
        cdlTableData.ShowOpen
        On Error GoTo GetDatabaseError
            strDatabaseName = cdlTableData.filename
            Screen.MousePointer = vbHourglass
            'Open the chosen database
            Set dbfTableData =
DBEngine.Workspaces(0).OpenDatabase(strDatabaseName, False, True)
                'Fetch the TableDefs collection & place in a local variable.  This
                'has the benefit of slightly faster processing
                Set tdfTables = dbfTableData.TableDefs
                'Set up the collection class we're using, so new instances of our
                'clsTableData class can be stored in it.
                Set colTableData = New Collection
                'For each TableDef in TableDefs, use the clsTableData to get
                'the needed info from the table, and place the table's name
                'and its index within the collection in the list box.
                For Each tdfSelectedTable In tdfTables
                    If Left$(tdfSelectedTable.Name, 4) <> "MSys" Then
                        Set objTable = New clsTableData
                        objTable.ExtractStatusData tdfSelectedTable
```

```
                    colTableData.Add objTable
                    With lstTables
                        .AddItem objTable.Name
                        .ItemData(lstTables.NewIndex) = colTableData.Count
                    End With
                End If
            Next
            'Now that it's not needed, close the database.
            dbfTableData.Close
        On Error GoTo 0
        Screen.MousePointer = vbDefault
    On Error GoTo 0
Exit Sub

NoDatabaseError:
    'If the user didn't select a database, end the application.
    End

GetDatabaseError:
    Screen.MousePointer = vbDefault
    MsgBox Err.Description, vbExclamation
    End
End Sub
```

5. Add the following code to the **Click** event of **lstTables**. When the user clicks on a table name in the list box, this procedure extracts the properties from the selected **clsTableData** object and displays those properties in the boxes on the form.

```
Private Sub lstTables_Click()
    Dim objTable As clsTableData, intPosition As Integer

    'Get the ItemData from the list, the index of the selected
    'clsTableData stored in our collection.
    intPosition = lstTables.ItemData(lstTables.ListIndex)

    'Using this index, fetch our selected instance of clsTableData.
    Set objTable = colTableData.Item(intPosition)

    'Read the properties of our class into the labels
    lblCreated = Format$(objTable.WhenCreated, "General Date")
    lblModified = Format$(objTable.WhenModified, "General Date")
    lblRecords = objTable.NumRecords
End Sub
```

6. Add the following code to the **Click** event of **cmdChangeFile**. This procedure first clears the data from the controls on the form and empties the **Collection** object. It then resets the common dialog default filename to *.MDB and calls **GetDatabase**.

```
Private Sub cmdChangeFile_Click()
    'Clear out the form, and flush the existing collection.
    lstTables.Clear
    lblCreated = "": lblModified = "": lblRecords = ""
```

continued on next page

continued from previous page

```
    Set colTableData = Nothing

    'Reset our CommonDialog control, and get another database.
    cdlTableData.filename = "*.MDB"
    GetDatabase
End Sub
```

7. Add the following code to the **Click** event of **cmdExit**:

```
Private Sub cmdExit_Click()
    End
End Sub
```

8. Insert a new class module into the project and name it **clsTableData**; then add the following code to the declarations section of the class module. The four private variables represent the properties of the class. As private class-module-level variables, they are accessible to all routines within the class but accessible to outside procedures only through the methods defined for the class.

```
Option Explicit

'Module-level variables used to hold property values.  They are not accessible,
'or not "exposed," outside of the class directly.  Property Get statements are
'used to "expose" this data to other objects that may request it.
Private mlngNumRecords As Long
Private mdatWhenModified As Date
Private mdatWhenCreated As Date
Private mstrName As String
```

9. Add the following code to **clsTableData** as the **ExtractStatusData** method. This public method sets the class properties to the values of the table definition object passed as an argument.

```
Public Sub ExtractStatusData(tblDef As TableDef)
    'This subroutine retrieves the property data from a given TableDef.
    mstrName = tblDef.Name
    mdatWhenModified = tblDef.LastUpdated
    mdatWhenCreated = tblDef.DateCreated
    mlngNumRecords = tblDef.RecordCount
End Sub
```

10. Add the following four **Property Get** methods to **clsTableData**. Each of these methods returns the value of a property to the requesting procedure.

```
Property Get Name() As String
    Name = mstrName
End Property

Property Get NumRecords() As Long
    NumRecords = mlngNumRecords
```

```
End Property

Property Get WhenModified() As Date
    WhenModified = mdatWhenModified
End Property

Property Get WhenCreated() As Date
    WhenCreated = mdatWhenCreated
End Property
```

How It Works

When the application's only form loads, it calls the `GetDatabase` procedure, which uses the Windows common dialog to get from the user the name of the database to be examined. It then opens the database and the `TableDefs` collection of the database, cycling through the `TableDefs` collection and examining each `TableDef` object in the collection to see whether it represents a system table or a user-defined table. If it is a user-defined table, `GetDatabase` creates a new `clsTableData` object and points the variable `objTable` to the object. The `clsTableData` object extracts four properties from the `TableDef` object. These `TableDef` properties become the properties of the `clsTableData` object. `GetDatabase` then adds the `clsTableData` object to the `colTableData`. When all the `TableDef` objects in the `TableDefs` collection have been examined, `GetDatabase` closes the database. It then cycles through the `clsTableData` objects in the `colTableData` and adds the name of each table in the collection to the list box.

When the user clicks on a table name in the list box, the `Click` routine extracts the information about the chosen table from the `clsTableData` object in `colTableData` and displays the information on the form.

Comment

Each Microsoft Access database includes a set of system tables that maintain information about the objects in the database. These tables all have names beginning with MSys. You can access some of these tables directly. The tables are not documented and, therefore, are subject to change in a new release of Access, so it's generally not a good idea to build an application that relies on direct access to the MSys tables. Fortunately, the `TableDefs` object described in this How-To gives you a documented way to get at much of the most useful information in these system tables, including status information on each table in the database.

5.2 How do I...
Attach a table from another database file?

Problem

My application has a Microsoft Access database file with several tables that it "owns." But it also needs to work with data in a table that resides in another Microsoft Access file, a table that my application must share with other applications. How can I use a table in a different Microsoft Access file?

Technique

A "database" in older PC database products such as dBASE, FoxPro, and Paradox products consists of multiple files—data files, index files, form files, report files, procedure files, and so on. Microsoft Access, on the other hand, uses a single file, into which it incorporates multiple objects—data objects (tables), queries, indexes, forms, reports, macros, and Access Basic code modules. The "database" is a single file.

In most situations, the Microsoft Access way is better. This method eases system administration and makes it less likely that a needed file will be inadvertently moved or deleted. But it's not an advantage when multiple applications each maintain separate databases—and, therefore, separate database files—and the applications also need to share some common data.

Microsoft Access provides the capability to share data between separate databases through the use of attached tables. Attaching a table creates a link between a database file and a table that physically resides in a different file. When you attach a table to a Microsoft Access database, you can treat that table very much like you treat the internal tables of the database—with a few restrictions.

The major restriction in working with attached tables is that you cannot use them with table-type recordsets—you can use only dynaset- or snapshot-type recordsets. Because you cannot work with attached table-type recordsets, you cannot use the **Seek** method to access data. The **Seek** method is usually the fastest way to randomly access data from a single table, so this might or might not be a significant restriction, depending on the needs of your application. (See the introduction to Chapter 3, "SQL," for a discussion of the conditions under which the **Seek** method provides faster access than the use of SQL **SELECT** queries.)

Attaching Tables

Each Microsoft Access database file contains a set of table definitions. When you create a **Database** object and connect a database file to that object, the file's table definitions constitute the `TableDefs` collection of the `Database` object. If tables have been attached to the database, the `TableDefs` collection includes `TableDef` objects for each attached table; one of the properties of the `TableDef` object indicates that it is an attached table. For more detailed information on the steps needed to attach a table in a Microsoft Access database, be sure to closely follow step 5 in this How-To.

Steps

Open the project ATTACH.VBP and then run the project. The form shown in Figure 5.3 appears. Click Attach a Table and a standard File Open dialog box appears. Select a Microsoft Access database file to which you want to attach a table (the destination file), and then select the source file for the table (you must select different files). After you have selected both files, the form shown in Figure 5.4 appears with a list of the tables in the source file. Select a table from the list and click OK. A message appears indicating successful attachment, and then the form shown in Figure 5.3 reappears.

Click Detach a Table and select the same file you used as the destination file when you attached a table. The form shown in Figure 5.4 appears again, this time listing the attached tables in the selected file. Select the table you just attached, and click OK.

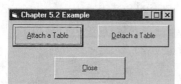

Figure 5.3. The project's main form.

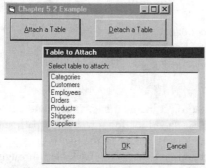

Figure 5.4. The project's Table to Attach form, showing table names.

1. Create a new project called ATTACH.VBP. Rename `Form1` to `frmAttach` and use it to create the objects and properties listed in Table 5.3. Save the form as frmAttach.FRM.

Table 5.3. Objects and properties for `frmAttach`.

OBJECT	PROPERTY	SETTING
Form	Name	frmAttach
	Caption	"Chapter 5.2 Example"
CommandButton	Name	cmdAttach
	Caption	"&Attach a Table"
CommandButton	Name	cmdDetach
	Caption	"&Detach a Table"
CommandButton	Name	cmdClose
	Caption	"&Close"
CommonDialog	Name	cdlFile

2. Add a new form to the project, and create the object and properties shown in Table 5.4.

Table 5.4. Objects and properties for `frmSelector`.

OBJECT	PROPERTY	SETTING
Form	Name	frmSelector
ListBox	Name	lstBox
Label	Name	lblList
	Caption	" "
CommandButton	Name	cmdOK
	Caption	"&OK"
	Default	True
CommandButton	Name	cmdCancel
	Cancel	True
	Caption	"&Cancel"

3. Add a new module to the project, name it **basAttach**, and add the following code. The `GetFileName` function, given a full path and filename string, extracts and returns just the name of the file. It does so in an inefficient but workable manner, by stepping backward through the string, checking each character until it finds a backslash. When the backslash is found, the function retrieves everything to the right of that backslash and returns it as the filename.

```
Public Function GetFileName(ByVal strFullPath As String) As String
    Dim I As Integer, strTemp As String

    If Len(strFullPath) Then
        For I = Len(strFullPath) To 1 Step -1
            If Mid(strFullPath, I) = "\" Then strTemp = _
            Right(strFullPath, Len(strFullPath) - I)
        Next
        If strTemp = "" Then strTemp = strFullPath
    End If

    GetFileName = strTemp
End Function
```

4. Add the following code to the declarations section of `frmAttach`. These constants will be used later for the `GetMDBFile` function.

```
Option Explicit

Const SOURCE_FILE = 1
Const DESTINATION_FILE = 2
Const DETACH_FILE = 3
```

5. Enter the following code in `frmAttach` as the `Click` event of `cmdAttach`. This routine gets the user's choices of the destination and source files for the table to be attached. It then gets the user's selection of the table to be attached. If a table is selected, it performs several steps—it creates a `TableDef` object with the name of the table to be attached, providing a `Connect` string with the name of the source database and then providing the `SourceTableName` property. All three items are needed to attach an external table. After all these items have been provided, the `Attach` method is called to attach the new `TableDef` to our `Database` object.

```
Private Sub cmdAttach_Click()
    Static strSourceFile As String, strDestFile As String
    Dim strTableName As String
    Dim dbfAttach As Database, tdfAttach As TableDef

    strDestFile = GetMDBFile(DESTINATION_FILE)

    If Len(strDestFile) Then strSourceFile = GetMDBFile(SOURCE_FILE)

    If Len(strSourceFile) Then
        'Call the custom method, Display, from frmSelector.  This
        'will return either "" or the name of a selected table.
        strTableName = frmSelector.Display(True, strSourceFile)
        On Error GoTo BadAttach
            If Len(strTableName) Then
                'If we have a table, let's attach it.
                Set dbfAttach = Workspaces(0).OpenDatabase(strDestFile)
                'Generate a TableDef object
                Set tdfAttach = dbfAttach.CreateTableDef(strTableName)
                'Provide the connection info
```

continued on next page

continued from previous page

```
                          tdfAttach.Connect = ";DATABASE=" & strSourceFile
                          'Provide the table's name
                          tdfAttach.SourceTableName = strTableName
                          'Append it to the database's TableDefs collection
                          dbfAttach.TableDefs.Append tdfAttach
                          'And it's good!
                          MsgBox "Table " & strTableName & " attached to " & _
                              GetFileName(strDestFile) & "."
                  End If
              On Error GoTo 0
          End If
  Exit Sub

  BadAttach:
      MsgBox Err.Description, vbExclamation
  End Sub
```

6. Enter the following code in `frmAttach` as the `Click` event of `cmdDetach`. This routine gets the user's choices of the file from which the table is to be detached, and then the user's selection of the table to be detached from the file. After these items are had, the routine finds the appropriate `TableDef` in our `Database` object and runs the `Delete` method to remove it from the database.

```
Private Sub cmdDetach_Click()
    Static strDetachFile As String
    Dim strTableName As String
    Dim dbfDetach As Database

    strDetachFile = GetMDBFile(DETACH_FILE)

    'Call frmSelector's Display method
    If Len(strDetachFile) Then strTableName = _
        frmSelector.Display(False, strDetachFile)

    On Error GoTo BadDetach
        If Len(strTableName) Then
            'If we have a table, then detach it.
            Set dbfDetach = Workspaces(0).OpenDatabase(strDetachFile)
            dbfDetach.TableDefs.Delete strTableName
            MsgBox "Table " & strTableName & " detached from " & _
                GetFileName(strDetachFile) & "."
        End If
    On Error GoTo 0
Exit Sub

BadDetach:
    MsgBox Err.Description, vbExclamation
End Sub
```

7. Enter the following code in `frmAttach` as the `GetMDBFile` subroutine. This subroutine is used for three related purposes: to get a source file for an attached table, to get a destination file for an attached table, and to get the file from which a table is to be attached. This subroutine uses the Windows File Open common dialog box for all three purposes. It sets the defaults for the common dialog to facilitate the opening of an existing Microsoft Access (MDB) file. If the user selects a file, the routine returns the name and path of that file. If the user does not select a file (that is, the user clicks Cancel when the common dialog box appears), the function returns an empty string.

```
Private Function GetMDBFile(intPurpose As Integer) As String
    On Error GoTo GetMDBFileError
        Select Case intPurpose
            Case SOURCE_FILE
                cdlFile.DialogTitle = "Select Source File For Attach"
            Case DESTINATION_FILE
                cdlFile.DialogTitle = "Select Destination File For Attach"
            Case DETACH_FILE
                cdlFile.DialogTitle = "Select Source File For Detach"
        End Select

        With cdlFile
            .DefaultExt = "*.MDB"
            .Filter = "Access Files *.MDB|*.MDB|All Files *.*|*.*"
            'The user must select an existing file.
            .Flags = cdlOFN_FILEMUSTEXIST
            .CancelError = True
            .filename = "*.MDB"
            .ShowOpen
        End With

        GetMDBFile = cdlFile.filename
    On Error GoTo 0
Exit Function

GetMDBFileError:
    Exit Function
End Function
```

8. Enter the following code in **frmAttach** as the **ExtractPath** function of **frmAttach**. This function extracts the pathname from a fully qualified filename (drive, path, and file) and returns the drive and path to the calling routine.

```
Private Function ExtractPath(fileName As String, fullPath As String)
    ExtractPath = Left$(fullPath, Len(fullPath) - (Len(fileName) + 1))
End Function
```

9. Enter the following code in **frmAttach** as the **Click** event of **cmdClose**:

```
Private Sub cmdClose_Click()
    End
End Sub
```

10. That completes `frmAttach`. Now turn your attention to `frmSelector` and add the following line to its declarations section:

```
Option Explicit
```

11. Add the following new function to `frmSelector`. This function is used for two purposes: to list the tables that are candidates for attachment and to list the already-attached tables. The method that displays `frmSelector` determines the reason for which the form is being displayed by providing a Boolean variable. This method, **Display**, sets the form's captions appropriately, then calls `ListTables` to fill the list box. The arguments to `ListTables` specify the file and what kind of tables to list.

```
Private Function ListTables(blnAttach As Boolean, strFileSpec As String) _
As Integer
    Dim dbfTemp As Database, tdfTemp As TableDef
    Dim intTablesAdded As Integer

    lstBox.Clear

    On Error GoTo ListTablesError
        Screen.MousePointer = vbHourglass
        Set dbfTemp = DBEngine.Workspaces(0).OpenDatabase(strFileSpec)
        intTablesAdded = 0

        For Each tdfTemp In dbfTemp.TableDefs
            If blnAttach Then
                If Left$(tdfTemp.Name, 4) <> "MSys" And _
                    tdfTemp.Attributes <> dbAttachedTable And _
                    tdfTemp.Attributes <> dbAttachSavePWD And _
                    tdfTemp.Attributes <> dbAttachExclusive Then
                        lstBox.AddItem tdfTemp.Name
                        intTablesAdded = intTablesAdded + 1
                End If
            ElseIf tdfTemp.Attributes = dbAttachedTable Or _
                tdfTemp.Attributes = dbAttachSavePWD Or _
                tdfTemp.Attributes = dbAttachExclusive Then
                    lstBox.AddItem tdfTemp.Name
                    intTablesAdded = intTablesAdded + 1
            End If
        Next

    Screen.MousePointer = vbDefault

    ListTables = intTablesAdded

Exit Function

ListTablesError:
    Screen.MousePointer = vbDefault
    MsgBox Err.Description, vbExclamation
    ListTables = 0
Exit Function

End Function
```

12. Enter the following code in `frmSelector` as the `Display` function. This is the public function that is called by `frmAttach` to provide a table name to attach or detach. The `blnAttach` Boolean determines the form's purpose when called; if `True`, it configures for attachment; otherwise, it configures for detachment. The `strFileSpec` is the name of the database that was provided in `frmAttach` via the `GetMDBFile` function.

```
Public Function Display(ByVal blnAttach As Boolean, _
   ByVal strFileSpec As String) As String

    With Me
        .Caption = "Table to " & IIf(blnAttach, "Attach", "Detach")
        .lblList = "Select table to " & IIf(blnAttach, "attach:", "detach:")
    End With

    If ListTables(blnAttach, strFileSpec) Then
        Me.Show vbModal
    Else
        MsgBox "There are no attached tables in " & GetFileName(strFileSpec) & "."
    End If

    If lstBox.ListIndex > -1 Then Display = lstBox.Text

End Function
```

13. Enter the following code in `frmSelector` as the `Click` event of `cmdOK`. If the user has made a selection, the routine hides the form. Because the form is opened modally, this allows the `Display` function to complete, passing back the selected table name.

```
Private Sub cmdOK_Click()
    If lstBox.ListIndex > -1 Then
        frmSelector.Hide
    Else
        MsgBox "You have not yet made a selection.", vbExclamation
    End If
End Sub
```

14. Enter the following code in `frmSelector` as the `DblClick` event of `lstBox`. If the user has made a selection, the routine updates the `Public` variable `TableName` and hides the form.

```
Private Sub lstBox_DblClick()
    cmdOK_Click
End Sub
```

15. Enter the following code in `frmSelector` as the `Click` event of `cmdCancel`. The user does not want to designate a table, so set the list box's `ListIndex` to -1 and then hide the form.

```
Private Sub cmdCancel_Click()
    lstBox.ListIndex = -1
    frmSelector.Hide
End Sub
```

How It Works

When the user clicks the Attach a Table button, the `Click` event uses the Windows File Open common dialog box to get the destination and source files for the attachment. It then calls the `Display` method of `frmSelector`, setting `blnAttach` to `True` to indicate that `frmSelector` is to display those tables eligible for attachment from the designated source file. When the user makes a selection in `frmSelector`, the subroutine creates a new `TableDef` object and appends it to the destination file's `TableDefs` collection.

When the user clicks Detach a Table, the `Click` event uses the Windows File Open common dialog box to the get file from which the table is to be detached. It then calls the `Display` method of `frmSelector` again, setting `blnAttach` to `False` to indicate that `frmSelector` is to display the attached tables in the designated file. When the user makes a selection in `frmSelector`, the subroutine removes the selected `TableDef` object from the designated file's `TableDefs` collection.

Comments

The capability to attach external tables opens a lot of possibilities for the Visual Basic database application developer. The DAO engine is capable of providing many services that would otherwise be inconvenient to duplicate with extensive ODBC-related code, with a familiar object hierarchy. Also, when one is dealing with importing and exporting data, the capability to attach tables comes in very handy, making a sometimes tedious process of reading from one database and writing to another a snap. At a client/server level, the flexibility granted by the capability to attach tables from several different external database platforms allows for an ease of data access, whether for mainframe databases, server databases, or even several locally accessed workstation databases, without needing to program for each database platform.

COMPLEXITY
INTERMEDIATE

5.3 How do I...
Import a text file?

Problem

I periodically get downloads from a mainframe database (or other source) as delimited text files that I need to import into my database. If I could be sure that users had Microsoft Access installed, my program could use OLE to invoke the import capability of Access, but some users might not have a copy of Access. How can I use Visual Basic to import text files into a database file?

Technique

Visual Basic has a rich variety of features for working with text files. You can employ these capabilities to open the text file and read the text data. From that point, the problem resolves to using the delimiters in the text file to split the text into records and fields and storing the data in the appropriate database tables. You need to be prepared to handle errors, both the normal data access errors and any errors that incorrect input text might cause.

Steps

This How-To imports text data from the text files VENDORS.DAT and INVOICES. DAT into a Microsoft Access database, ACCTSPAY.MDB. The text files use an end-of-line sequence (a carriage return followed by a line feed) as a record delimiter and a tab character as a field delimiter. The Vendors table in the ACCTPAY.MDB has the following fields, with [Vendor Number] as the primary key:

✔ Vendor Number

✔ Name

✔ Address

✔ FEIN (Federal Employer Identification Number, required for tax reporting purposes)

The Invoices table in the database has the following fields. The primary key is a composite of [Vendor Number] and [Invoice Number].

✔ Vendor Number

✔ Invoice Number

✔ Date

✔ Amount

The tables are related on the [Vendor Number] field; every record in the Invoices table must have a corresponding record in the Vendors table.

Open and run TextImport.VBP. You'll see the form shown in Figure 5.5. Click the Import Data button, and the application imports the contents of the text files VENDORS.DAT and INVOICES.DAT into the Vendors and Invoices tables of ACCTSPAY.MDB. Click List Vendors, and a list of the vendors imported appears in the list box at the top of the form. Select a vendor name; if any invoices for that vendor were imported, a list of the invoices appears in the grid control at the bottom of the form. With a vendor selected, click Vendor Details, and you'll see the vendor details form shown in Figure 5.6.

1. Create a new project called TextImport.VBP. Rename Form1 to frmVendorDetails, and then create the objects and properties listed in Table 5.5. Save the form as Vendors.FRM.

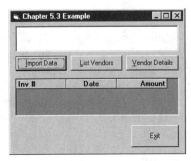

Figure 5.5. The program's
Text Import form on startup.

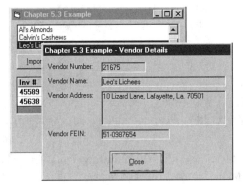

Figure 5.6. The program's Vendor
Details form, showing vendor
information.

Table 5.5. Objects and properties for the Vendor Details form.

OBJECT	PROPERTY	SETTING
Form	Name	frmVendorDetails
	Caption	"Chapter 5.3 Example - Vendor Details "
Label	Name	lblNumber
	BorderStyle	1 (Fixed Single)
	Caption	" "
Label	Name	lblName
	BorderStyle	1 (Fixed Single)
	Caption	" "
Label	Name	lblAddress
	BorderStyle	1 (Fixed Single)
	Caption	" "

OBJECT	PROPERTY	SETTING
Label	Name	lblFEIN
	BorderStyle	1 (Fixed Single)
	Caption	" "
Label	Name	lblVendor
	Index	0
	Caption	"Vendor Number:"
Label	Name	lblVendor
	Index	1
	Caption	"Vendor Name:"
Label	Name	lblVendor
	Index	2
	Caption	"Vendor Address:"
Label	Name	lblVendor
	Index	3
	Caption	"Vendor FEIN:"
CommandButton	Name	cmdClose
	Caption	"&Close"
	Default	True

2. Insert the following code into the `Click` event of `cmdClose` on `frmVendorDetails` (this is the only code needed for this form):

```
Private Sub cmdClose_Click()
    Unload frmVendorDetails
End Sub
```

3. Insert a second form into the project. Change its name to `frmMain`, and then create the objects and properties listed in Table 5.6. Save the form as TextImp.FRM.

Table 5.6. Objects and properties for the main Text Import form.

OBJECT	PROPERTY	SETTING
Form	Name	frmMain
	Caption	"Chapter 5.3 Example"
ListBox	Name	lstVendors
	Sorted	True
MSFlexGrid	Name	grdInvoices
	Cols	4
	Scrollbars	2 - flexScrollBarVertical

continued on next page

continued from previous page

OBJECT	PROPERTY	SETTING
CommandButton	Name	cmdImport
	Caption	"&Import Data"
CommandButton	Name	cmdListVendors
	Caption	"&List Vendors"
CommandButton	Name	cmdVendorDetails
	Caption	"&Vendor Details"
CommandButton	Name	cmdExit
	Cancel	True
	Caption	"Exit"

4. Insert the following code into the declarations section of `frmMain`. Edit the pathnames in the `Const` declarations to point to the locations of the indicated files on your system.

```
Option Explicit

'Change this constant to whatever path you have installed the
'CD contents into.

Const DATA_PATH = "C:\Program Files\VB5DBHT"

Private VendorFile As String, InvoiceFile As String, DatabaseFile As String
```

5. Add the following code to the `Load` event of `frmMain`. When the form loads, it calls the `InitializeGrid` subroutine to set up the grid, then deletes all existing data from the Vendors and Invoices tables in the database. You wouldn't ordinarily delete all the existing data before importing new data, but with this demonstration program this step is necessary if you want to run it more than once using the same input files. Otherwise, you'll get primary key errors when you try to add new records that duplicate existing primary key values.

```
Private Sub Form_Load()
    Dim dbfTemp As Database

    'Assign fully qualified pathnames to the form level data file variables.
    VendorFile = DATA_PATH & "\CHAPTER.04\VENDORS.DAT"
    InvoiceFile = DATA_PATH & "\CHAPTER.04\INVOICES.DAT"
    DatabaseFile = DATA_PATH & "\CHAPTER.04\ACCTSPAY.MDB"

    ' Initialize the grid control.
    InitializeGrid

    ' Delete any existing data in the Vendors and Invoices tables.
    Set dbfTemp = DBEngine.Workspaces(0).OpenDatabase(DatabaseFile)
    dbfTemp.Execute ("DELETE Vendors.* from Vendors")
    dbfTemp.Execute ("DELETE Invoices.* from Invoices")
End Sub
```

6. Create the following subroutine in frmMain. This code sets the grid column widths and alignments and inserts the column titles. Because the initial state of the grid (before a vendor is selected) shows no invoices, it is initialized with only the title row visible.

```
Private Sub InitializeGrid()

    With grdInvoices
        .ColWidth(0) = 0:
        .ColWidth(1) = 1300
        .ColWidth(2) = 1300
        .ColWidth(3) = 1300
        .ColAlignment(1) = flexAlignLeftCenter
        .ColAlignment(2) = flexAlignCenterCenter
        .ColAlignment(3) = flexAlignRightCenter
        .FixedAlignment(1) = flexAlignLeftCenter
        .FixedAlignment(2) = flexAlignCenterCenter
        .FixedAlignment(3) = flexAlignRightCenter
        .Row = 0
        .Col = 1: .Text = "Inv #"
        .Col = 2: .Text = "Date"
        .Col = 3: .Text = "Amount"
        .Rows = 1
    End With
End Sub
```

7. Add the following code to the Click event of cmdImport. This procedure imports vendor and invoice records from the text files named by the form-level variables VendorFile and InvoiceFile, respectively. As the procedure imports the file, it creates from each record an object of the class clsVendor or clsInvoice. (These classes are defined by vendor and invoice class modules, which are discussed later.) The cmdImport_Click subroutine then adds each clsVendor or clsInvoice object to a Collection object. One Collection object receives all the clsVendor objects, and a second Collection object receives all clsInvoice objects. After both collections have been built, the subroutine appends the objects in each collection to the Vendors or Invoices table, as appropriate.

The error handling in this subroutine requires comment. If the error is due to faulty input data, you want to give the user enough information to identify the specific record that caused the problem. For import data errors, therefore, the error message that will be displayed for the user is built into the body of the code. Error messages for errors encountered when importing vendors include the vendor number; those for errors encountered when importing invoices include both the vendor and the invoice numbers. Other types of errors, those not due to input data problems, get a standard error message built into the error-handling routine.

In this application, it's highly likely that you don't want to import some of the records—you want to import all of them or, if an error occurs, none of them. You accomplish this task by enclosing the code that actually appends the records to the database tables between **BeginTrans** and **CommitTrans** statements. This converts all the database modifications into a single atomic transaction. Any changes made within an atomic transaction (that is, changes made after **BeginTrans** and before **CommitTrans**) are not irrevocably committed to the database until **CommitTrans**. In this subroutine, if an error occurs between **BeginTrans** and **CommitTrans**, control is transferred to the error-handling routine, which executes a **Rollback** statement. The **Rollback** tells the Jet engine, "Back out all the changes made since the **BeginTrans** statement."

Rollback is executed only when the value of the Boolean variable **blnNeedRollback** is **True**. Initially, **blnNeedRollback** is **False** and is set to **True** at the beginning of the transaction in the statement immediately following **BeginTrans**. This provision is needed to ensure that **Rollback** doesn't get executed by an error that occurs before **BeginTrans**—because trying to execute a **Rollback** outside a transaction is itself an error.

```
Private Sub cmdImport_Click()
    Dim dbfTemp As Database, tblVendors As Recordset, tblInvoices As Recordset
    Dim objVendor As clsVendor, objInvoice As clsInvoice
    Dim colVendors As New Collection, colInvoices As New Collection

    Dim strInputLine As String, strErrMsg As String
    Dim blnNeedRollback As Boolean
    Dim intFileHandle As Integer

    On Error GoTo ImportTextError
        Screen.MousePointer = vbHourglass

        'Get the vendor text file, and create an instance
        'of objVendor for each line found in the text file,
        'passing the line to the DelimitedString property
        'of the instance of objVendor.
        intFileHandle = FreeFile
        Open VendorFile For Input As intFileHandle
        Do Until EOF(intFileHandle)
            Line Input #intFileHandle, strInputLine
            Set objVendor = New clsVendor
            objVendor.DelimitedString = strInputLine
            colVendors.Add objVendor
        Loop
        Close intFileHandle

        'Same as above, but with the invoice text file.
        intFileHandle = FreeFile:
        Open InvoiceFile For Input As intFileHandle
        Do Until EOF(intFileHandle)
            Line Input #intFileHandle, strInputLine
            Set objInvoice = New clsInvoice
```

```
            objInvoice.DelimitedString = strInputLine
            colInvoices.Add objInvoice
    Loop
    Close intFileHandle

    'Prepare for addition
    Set dbfTemp = DBEngine.Workspaces(0).OpenDatabase(DatabaseFile)
    Set tblVendors = dbfTemp.OpenRecordset("Vendors", dbOpenTable)
    Set tblInvoices = dbfTemp.OpenRecordset("Invoices", dbOpenTable)

    'This is where we start the transaction processing.  None of the
    'changes we make will be committed to the database until the
    'CommitTrans line, some lines below.
    Workspaces(0).BeginTrans
    blnNeedRollback = True

    'Iterate through our collection of clsVendor objects,
    'calling the StoreNewItem method and passing our newly opened
    'table.
    If colVendors.Count Then
        For Each objVendor In colVendors
            If objVendor.StoreNewItem(tblVendors) = False Then
                strErrMsg = "An error occurred while importing vendor #" & _
                CStr(objVendor.Number)
                Err.Raise 32767
            End If
        Next
    End If

    'Same as above, but for invoices. (Deja vu...?)
    If colInvoices.Count Then
        For Each objInvoice In colInvoices
            If objInvoice.StoreNewItem(tblInvoices) = False Or _
                objInvoice.VendorNumber = 0 Then
                strErrMsg = "An error occurred while importing invoice #" & _
                objInvoice.InvoiceNumber
                Err.Raise 32767
            End If
        Next
    End If

    'Here's where the data is committed to the database.
    'Had an error occurred, we would never reach this point;
    'instead, the Rollback command in our error
    'trapping routine would have removed our changes.
    Workspaces(0).CommitTrans

    Screen.MousePointer = vbDefault
    On Error GoTo 0
Exit Sub

ImportTextError:
    Screen.MousePointer = vbDefault
    If strErrMsg = "" Then strErrMsg = "The following error has occurred:" & ⇐
vbCr _
        & Err.Description
```

continued on next page

continued from previous page

```
    strErrMsg = strErrMsg & " No records have been added to the database."
    MsgBox strErrMsg, vbExclamation
    'Here's the Rollback method; if the blnNeedRollback variable
    'is still set to True, we undo our uncommitted changes.
    If blnNeedRollback Then Workspaces(0).Rollback
Exit Sub

End Sub
```

8. Add the following code to the **Click** event of **cmdListVendors**. This procedure lists the vendors in the database and in the list box on the form. It uses the **ItemData** property of the list box to attach the vendor number to the vendor name. Other procedures in the application use **ItemData** to uniquely identify the vendor.

```
Private Sub cmdListVendors_Click()
    Dim dbfTemp As Database, tblVendors As Recordset

    On Error GoTo ListVendorsError
    Set dbfTemp = DBEngine.Workspaces(0).OpenDatabase(DatabaseFile, False, True)
    Set tblVendors = dbfTemp.OpenRecordset("Vendors", dbOpenTable)
    If tblVendors.RecordCount <> 0 Then
        tblVendors.MoveFirst
        Do Until tbl.EOF
            lstVendors.AddItem tblVendors!Name
            lstVendors.ItemData(lstVendors.NewIndex) = tblVendors![Vendor Number]
            tblVendors.MoveNext
        Loop
    End If
    tblVendors.Close

Exit Sub

ListVendorsError:
    lstVendors.Clear
    MsgBox Err.Description
End Sub
```

9. Add the following code to the **Click** event of **lstVendors**. This procedure retrieves the vendor number from the selected item's **ItemData** value and passes that value to the **FillInvoiceList** routine, which fills the grid with invoices linked to this vendor.

```
Private Sub lstVendors_Click()
    FillInvoiceList lstVendors.ItemData(lstVendors.ListIndex)
End Sub
```

10. Create the **FillInvoiceList** subroutine by entering the following code into **frmMain**. This list box **Click** event calls **FillInvoiceList** when the user clicks on a vendor name. This subroutine fills the grid with information about the invoices for the selected vendor by creating a collection of all the invoice objects with vendor numbers that match the argument passed to the subroutine. It then cycles through the collection and adds each invoice to the grid.

```
Private Sub FillInvoiceList(intVendor As Integer)
    Dim dbfTemp As Database, recInvoices As Recordset
    Dim intRow As Integer, strSQL As String

    Dim colInvoices As New Collection, objInvoice As clsInvoice

    On Error GoTo FillInvoiceListError
        'Open the database & recordset used to fill the list box
        Set dbfTemp = DBEngine.Workspaces(0).OpenDatabase(DatabaseFile, _
            False, True)
        strSQL = "SELECT [Invoice Number] FROM Invoices " & _
            "WHERE [Vendor Number] = " & intVendor
        Set recInvoices = dbfTemp.OpenRecordset(strSQL, dbOpenSnapshot)

        If recInvoices.RecordCount > 0 Then
            recInvoices.MoveFirst
            Do Until recInvoices.EOF
                Set objInvoice = New clsInvoice
                If objInvoice.Retrieve(dbfTemp, intVendor, _
                    recInvoices("Invoice Number")) _
                    Then colInvoices.Add objInvoice
                recInvoices.MoveNext
            Loop

            grdInvoices.Rows = colInvoices.Count + 1

            For intRow = 1 To colInvoices.Count
                Set objInvoice = colInvoices(intRow)
                objInvoice.AddToGrid grdInvoices, intRow
            Next intRow
        Else
            grdInvoices.Rows = 1
        End If
    On Error GoTo 0
Exit Sub

FillInvoiceListError:
    grdInvoices.Rows = 1: lstVendors.ListIndex = -1
    MsgBox Err.Description, vbExclamation
Exit Sub

End Sub
```

11. Add the following code to the `Click` event of `cmdVendorDetails`. This procedure displays a form with information about the currently selected vendor in the list box. (See How-To 12.2 for an explanation of the `DBEngine.Idle dbFreeLocks` statement.)

```
Private Sub cmdVendorDetails_Click()
    Dim dbfTemp As Database
    Dim tblVendors As Recordset
    Dim intVendorNumber As Integer
```

continued on next page

continued from previous page

```
      On Error GoTo VendorDetailsError
          If lstVendors.ListIndex > -1 Then
              intVendorNumber = lstVendors.ItemData(lstVendors.ListIndex)
              Set dbfTemp = DBEngine.Workspaces(0).OpenDatabase(DatabaseFile, False,
True)
              Set tblVendors = dbfTemp.OpenRecordset("Vendors", dbOpenTable)

              tblVendors.Index = "PrimaryKey"
              tblVendors.Seek "=", intVendorNumber
              DBEngine.Idle dbFreeLocks

              With frmVendorDetails
                  .lblNumber = tblVendors![Vendor Number]
                  .lblName = IIf(IsNull(tblVendors!Name), "", tblVendors!Name)
                  .lblAddress = IIf(IsNull(tblVendors!Address), "",
tblVendors!Address)
                  .lblFEIN = IIf(IsNull(tblVendors!FEIN), "", tblVendors!FEIN)
              End With

              tblVendors.Close
              frmVendorDetails.Show vbModal
          Else
              Beep
              MsgBox "You haven't selected a vendor.", vbExclamation
          End If
      On Error GoTo 0
  Exit Sub

  VendorDetailsError:
      MsgBox Error(Err)
  Exit Sub

  End Sub
```

12. Add the following code to the **Click** event of **cmdExit**:

```
Private Sub cmdExit_Click()
    End
End Sub
```

13. Insert a new class module into the project. Name the module **clsVendor**. Each object of the **clsVendor** class will represent one vendor record.

14. Insert the following code into the declarations section of **clsVendor**. The class has five properties, maintained in five private variables, each starting with the prefix **prop**. One property, **propDelimitedString**, is set to the "raw" vendor data as read from the text file. The other four properties each hold a value that corresponds to a field in the Vendors table. Because these are private variables, they are not directly accessible to routines outside the class module, but can be accessed only through methods of the class.

```
Option Explicit

Private mintNumber As Integer
Private mstrCompany As String
Private mstrAddress As String
Private mstrFEIN As String
Private mstrDelimitedString As String
```

15. Create the following `Property Let` method in `clsVendor`. This method is passed a delimited string representing one vendor record. It stores the passed argument as the `DelimitedString` property by assigning it to the private variable `mstrDelimitedString`. The `Property Let DelimitedString` method also parses the string into fields and stores the individual field values as the appropriate object properties.

```
Property Let DelimitedString(strInput As String)
    Dim strDelimiter As String, strTextNumber As String
    Dim intEnd As Integer, intField As Integer, intStart As Integer
    Dim I As Integer

    strDelimiter = Chr$(9): mstrDelimitedString = strInput
    intStart = 1: intField = 1

    Do
        intEnd = InStr(intStart, strInput, strDelimiter)
        If intEnd = 0 Then intEnd = Len(strInput) + 1

        Select Case intField
            Case 1
                strTextNumber = ExtractField(intStart, intEnd)
                If IsNumeric(strTextNumber) Then
                    If strTextNumber >= 1 And strTextNumber <= 32767 Then
                        mintNumber = Val(strTextNumber)
                    Else
                        mintNumber = 0
                    End If
                Else
                    mintNumber = 0
                End If
            Case 2
                mstrCompany = ExtractField(intStart, intEnd)
            Case 3
                mstrAddress = ExtractField(intStart, intEnd)
            Case 4
                mstrFEIN = ExtractField(intStart, intEnd)
        End Select

        intStart = intEnd + 1: intField = intField + 1
    Loop While intEnd < Len(strInput) And intField <= 4
End Property
```

16. Create `ExtractField` as a private function in `clsVendor`. As a private function, it can be called only by other procedures within the class module. `ExtractField` returns a selection of text from the private variable `mstrDelimitedString`. The text to return is defined by the start and end positions received as arguments.

```
Private Function ExtractField(intStart As Integer, intEnd As Integer)
    ExtractField = Mid$(mstrDelimitedString, intStart, (intEnd - intStart))
End Function
```

17. Create the public method `StoreNewItem` in `clsVendor`. This method inserts the object into the database as a new record. It returns `True` if it successfully stores the object, `False` otherwise. `StoreNewItem` calls a private function, `WriteItem`, to actually assign property values to fields. Splitting the code into two functions allows the `WriteItem` code to be shared with another routine that would update an existing record. (This demonstration program does not include such a routine, but an actual application might.)

```
Public Function StoreNewItem(rs As Recordset) As Boolean
    On Error GoTo StoreNewError
        rs.AddNew
        If WriteItem(rs) Then
            rs.Update
        Else
            GoTo StoreNewError
        End If

        StoreNewItem = True
    On Error GoTo 0
Exit Function

StoreNewError:
    StoreNewItem = False
    Exit Function
End Function
```

18. Create the private function `WriteItem` in `clsVendor` with the following code. It assigns the current property values to the Vendor table fields in the current record. `WriteData` returns `True` unless an error occurs.

```
Private Function WriteItem(recTemp As Recordset) As Boolean
    On Error GoTo WriteItemError
        recTemp("Vendor Number") = mintNumber
        recTemp("Name") = mstrCompany
        recTemp("Address") = mstrAddress
        recTemp("FEIN") = mstrFEIN
        WriteItem = True
    On Error GoTo 0
Exit Function

WriteItemError:
    WriteItem = False
    Exit Function
End Function
```

19. Create the following four `Property Get` methods in `clsVendor`. These methods allow outside routines to access the values of the record represented by the object.

```
Property Get Number() As Integer
    Number = mintNumber
End Property

Property Get Company() As String
    Company = mstrCompany
End Property

Property Get Address() As String
    Address = mstrAddress
End Property

Property Get FEIN() As String
    FEIN = mstrFEIN
End Property
```

20. Insert a new class module into the project. Name the module `clsInvoice`. Each object of the `clsInvoice` class will represent one invoice record.

21. Insert the following code into the declarations section of `clsInvoice`. Like `clsVendor`, `clsInvoice` has five properties maintained in five private variables, each starting with the prefix **prop**. One property, `mstrDelimitedString` is set to the "raw" invoice data as read from the text file. The other four properties each contain a value that corresponds to a field in the Invoices table. Because these are all private variables, they are not directly accessible to routines outside the class module but can be accessed only through public methods of the class.

```
Option Explicit

Const FLD_VENNUMBER = 1
Const FLD_INVNUMBER = 2
Const FLD_DATE = 3
Const FLD_AMOUNT = 4

Private mintVendorNumber As Integer
Private mstrInvoiceNumber As String
Private mdatDate As Date
Private mcurAmount As Currency
Private mstrDelimitedString As String
```

22. Copy these four routines from the `clsVendor` class module and paste them into `clsInvoice`: Let DelimitedString, ExtractField, StoreNewItem, and WriteItem. (In the following steps, you will modify **Let Delimited String** and **WriteItem**. **ExtractField** and **StoreNewItem** require no modifications.)

23. In `clsInvoice`, modify the six program lines shown in bold in the following listing. (All the statements to be modified are in the `Select Case` structure.)

```
Property Let DelimitedString(strInput As String)
    Dim strDelimiter As String
    Dim intEnd As Integer, intField As Integer, intStart As Integer
    Dim I As Integer
    Dim strTextNumber As String

    strDelimiter = Chr$(9): mstrDelimitedString = strInput
    intStart = 1: intField = 1

    Do
        intEnd = InStr(intStart, strInput, strDelimiter)
        If intEnd = 0 Then intEnd = Len(strInput) + 1
        Select Case intField
            Case 1
                strTextNumber = ExtractField(intStart, intEnd)
                If IsNumeric(strTextNumber) Then
                    If strTextNumber >= 1 And strTextNumber <= 32767 Then
                        mintVendorNumber = Val(strTextNumber)
                    Else
                        mintVendorNumber = 0
                    End If
                Else
                    mintVendorNumber = 0
                End If
            Case 2
                mstrInvoiceNumber = ExtractField(intStart, intEnd)
            Case 3
                mdatDate = CDate(ExtractField(intStart, intEnd))
            Case 4
                mcurAmount = CCur(ExtractField(intStart, intEnd))
        End Select

        intStart = intEnd + 1: intField = intField + 1
    Loop While intEnd < Len(strInput) And intField <= 4
End Property
```

24. Make the four modifications shown in bold to the `WriteItem` function of `clsInvoice`:

```
Private Function WriteItem(recTemp As Recordset) As Boolean
    On Error GoTo WriteItemError
        recTemp("Vendor Number") = mintVendorNumber
        recTemp("Invoice Number") = mstrInvoiceNumber
        recTemp("Date") = mdatDate
        recTemp("Amount") = mcurAmount
        WriteItem = True
    On Error GoTo 0
Exit Function

WriteItemError:
```

```
        WriteItem = False
Exit Function

End Function
```

25. Create the public `Retrieve` method in `clsInvoice`. This method retrieves the invoice with the primary key values named in the arguments from the Invoices table and assigns the field values to the object's properties. It returns `True` if a corresponding record is located and successfully read, `False` otherwise.

```
Public Function Retrieve(dbfTemp As Database, VendorNumber As Integer, _
InvoiceNumber As String) As Boolean
    Dim recTemp As Recordset

    On Error GoTo RetrieveError
        Set recTemp = dbfTemp.OpenRecordset("Invoices", dbOpenTable, dbReadOnly)

        recTemp.Index = "PrimaryKey"
        recTemp.Seek "=", VendorNumber, InvoiceNumber
        DBEngine.Idle dbFreeLocks

        If Not recTemp.NoMatch Then
            mintVendorNumber = VendorNumber
            mstrInvoiceNumber = InvoiceNumber
            mdatDate = recTemp("Date")
            mcurAmount = recTemp("Amount")
            Retrieve = True
        Else
            Retrieve = False
        End If
    On Error GoTo 0
Exit Function

RetrieveError:
    Retrieve = False
Exit Function

End Function
```

26. Create the `AddToGrid` method in `clsInvoice`. This method receives a grid and grid row as its arguments and inserts the object's property values into the grid row.

```
Public Sub AddToGrid(grdTemp As MSFlexGrid, intGridRow As Integer)
    With grdTemp
        .Row = intGridRow
        .Col = 1: .Text = mstrInvoiceNumber
        .Col = 2: .Text = Format$(mdatDate, "Short Date")
        .Col = 3: .Text = Format$(mcurAmount, "Currency")
    End With
End Sub
```

27. Create the following four `Property Get` methods in `clsInvoice`. These public methods allow outside routines to access the values of the record represented by the object.

```
Property Get VendorNumber() As Integer
    VendorNumber = mintVendorNumber
End Property
Property Get InvoiceNumber() As String
    InvoiceNumber = mstrInvoiceNumber
End Property
Property Get InvoiceDate() As Date
    InvoiceDate = mdatDate
End Property
Property Get Amount() As Currency
    Amount = mcurAmount
End Property
```

How It Works

The `Form_Load` event of `frmMain` initializes the grid and deletes any existing values from the database tables. (As noted in the discussion for step 5, you probably would not delete the records in a real production application.) When the user clicks the Import Data button, the data is imported from the text files into objects of the `clsVendor` and `clsInvoice` classes, and these objects are collected into `Collection` classes. The contents of each `Collection` class are then written to the database tables.

The `cmdImport_Click` routine controls the import process and does that portion of the work that does not require knowledge of the structure of the database tables or the format of the individual records within the imported text strings. The processing that does require such knowledge is encapsulated into the objects by providing methods within the objects to perform the needed operations.

Each line in the vendor and invoice input files represents one record. The `cmdImport_Click` routine reads a line, creates a new `clsVendor` or `clsInvoice` object, and passes the record to the object through object's `Property Let DelimitedString` method. `Property Let DelimitedString` parses the text string into individual fields and assigns the field values to the object's property variables. Later, `cmdImport_Click` cycles through each of the collection objects and tells the object "Store yourself in the database" by invoking the object's `StoreNewItem` method.

When the user clicks the List Vendors button, `cmdListVendors_Click` gets the vendor list from the Vendors table and displays it in the list box. When the user then clicks on a vendor name, the list box `Click` routine passes the vendor number of the selected vendor to `frmMain`'s `FillInvoiceList` subroutine. `FillInvoiceList` creates a snapshot consisting of the invoice numbers of invoices for which the vendor numbers match the selected vendor. It then creates a `clsInvoice` object for each invoice, tells the object "Retrieve yourself from disk" by invoking the object's `Retrieve` method, and adds the invoice object to a `Collection` object. When all the matching invoices have been retrieved, the list box `Click` subroutine cycles through the collection, telling each invoice object in the collection, "Display yourself in this grid row."

Comment

A significant amount of code is duplicated, or duplicated with minor changes, between the two classes in this How-To. If Visual Basic were a full object-oriented programming language that supported class hierarchies with inheritance, this duplication would be unnecessary. The common code could be put into a parent object from which both `clsVendor` and `clsInvoice` would inherit. Each class would then add methods and override inherited methods as necessary to implement its unique needs.

Because Visual Basic doesn't have this feature, another approach would be to put the identical and nearly identical routines in code modules as `Public` procedures and let the class routines call them as needed. This option would certainly reduce code size, but it would also introduce two problems:

✔ Using `Public` procedures in code modules violates the object-oriented programmer's principle of encapsulation. Class methods have privileged access to the object's private data (that is, its properties). Converting class methods to `Public` procedures in a code module means that any data that the "methods" share can also be accessed by other routines in the same code module.

✔ The more a shared routine deviates from a common form, the harder it is to implement this option. In the example in this How-To, you have two record types, and each has four fields; so a four-option `Select Case` structure in the `Property Let DelimitedString` procedure fits both. What if you had 15 records, varying in size from 2 fields to 40? Yes, it could be done by passing parameters and lots of convoluted `If...Then` logic. No, you wouldn't want to write it, and you surely wouldn't want to maintain it.

The bottom line: If encapsulation and simple code are more important to you than the smallest possible code size, use the technique described in this How-To. If minimizing the amount of code is more important, consider using `Public` procedures in code modules.

5.4 How do I...
Save graphics in a database file?

Problem

I have an application that tracks employee information for generating company ID cards, and I need to include a picture of the employee in the database. How can I do this from Visual Basic?

Technique

There are two basic techniques, each with its benefits and detriments, for saving graphical data in a Microsoft Access database. One method, the easier but more limiting of the two, is to use a `PictureBox` control as a data-bound control, linking it to an `OLE Object` field in the Access database (the data type is represented by the constant `dbLongBinary`), allowing direct loading and saving of data to the database by use of the `LoadPicture` and `SavePicture` commands. This technique makes it simple to import pictures in common formats, such as the Windows bitmap (.BMP) format, the Graphic Interchange Format (.GIF) format, or the JPEG (.JPG) format, used by many graphics-processing software packages. However, the data is saved as raw binary information and is difficult to use outside of your application without allowing for an import/export feature in your Visual Basic code.

The second technique, which is more versatile but much more complex, is to use an OLE `Container` control as a data-bound control, linking it to an `OLE Object` field in a manner similar to that used by the `PictureBox` control discussed in the first technique. The data, however, is stored as an OLE object, available for export by any application that can employ OLE Automation techniques for importing the data. This technique has its own problems. The data is linked to a specific OLE class; your user might not be able to work with the data from another application if he does not have that specific OLE class registered by the external application. Also, it assumes that the external application, in most instances, will be used to edit the object; this adds overhead to your application that might not be needed.

The first technique previously described tends to be more commonly employed, but the second technique is used enough to make it worthwhile to provide further information on the subject. The Microsoft Knowledge Base, an excellent tool for programming research, provides several articles on the subject. Table 5.7 provides the names and article IDs of several relevant Knowledge Base entries.

Table 5.7. Knowledge Base entries.

ARTICLE ID	NAME AND DESCRIPTION
Q147727	"How To View Photos from the NWIND.MDB Database in VB 4.0." Although the article is for VB 4.0, its code is still up-to-date. The code provides a complete but complex method of loading the stored graphics in NWIND.MDB, a data-base provided with Visual Basic, into a `PictureBox` control with some API prestidigitation. Very educational.
Q103115	"PRB: Invalid Picture Error When Try To Bind Picture Control." If you have ever attempted to bind a `PictureBox` to an `OLE Object` database field and received this error, it's due to the fact that the control expects bitmap information, not an OLE object. The article explains in more detail.

Steps

Open and run PicLoad.VBP. You'll see a form appear, similar to the one displayed in Figure 5.7. Click the Load Picture button, and a File Open common dialog appears. Select a bitmap file, and click the Open button. That bitmap now displays in the center of the form, and it is added to the database. Move forward, then back, with the data control and the graphic reappears, loaded from the database.

1. Create a new project called PicLoad.VBP. Create the objects and properties listed in Table 5.8, and save the form as PicLoad.FRM.

Figure 5.7. The project's main form at startup.

Table 5.8. Objects and properties for the Picture Load form.

OBJECT	PROPERTY	SETTING
Form	Name	Form1
	Caption	"Chapter 5.4 Example"
Data	Name	dtaData
	Caption	"Publishers"
	RecordSource	"Publishers"
Label	Name	lblPublishers
	Caption	"Publisher: "
Label	Name	lblPublisherName
	Caption	" "
	BorderStyle	1 - Fixed Single
	DataSource	dtaData
	DataField	"Name"
PictureBox	Name	picPicture
	DataSource	dtaData
	DataField	"Logo"
CommandButton	Name	cmdLoad
	Caption	"&Load Picture"
CommandButton	Name	cmdClose
	Caption	"&Close"
	Cancel	True
CommonDialog	Name	cdlPicture
	Filter	"Bitmap files (*.bmp)|*.bmp|JPEG files (*.jpg, *.jpeg)|*.jpg;*.jpeg|GIF Files (*.gif)|*.gif|All Files (*.*)|*.*"
	DefaultExt	"BMP"
	Flags	&H1000

2. Add the following code to the declarations section of `Form1`:

```
Option Explicit

Const BIBLIO_PATH = "C:\Program Files\DevStudio\VB\Biblio.MDB"
```

3. Add the following subroutine to `Form1`. The `CheckForLogoField` subroutine checks our beloved BIBLIO.MDB and adds a new field to the Publishers table, called `Logo`. Our graphics loading and saving will be done from and to that field when run.

```
Private Sub CheckForLogoField()
    Dim dbfTemp As Database, tdfTemp As TableDef, fldTemp As Field
    Dim blnLogoFieldExists As Boolean

    On Error GoTo BadCheck
        Set dbfTemp = Workspaces(0).OpenDatabase(BIBLIO_PATH)
        For Each tdfTemp In dbfTemp.TableDefs
            If tdfTemp.Name = "Publishers" Then
                For Each fldTemp In tdfTemp.Fields
                    If fldTemp.Name = "Logo" Then
                        blnLogoFieldExists = True
                        Exit For
                    End If
                Next
                Exit For
            End If
        Next

        If blnLogoFieldExists = False Then
            If tdfTemp.Updatable Then
                Set fldTemp = New Field
                With fldTemp
                    .Name = "Logo"
                    .Type = dbLongBinary
                End With
                tdfTemp.Fields.Append fldTemp
            Else
                MsgBox "The database needs to be updated to Jet 3.0 format. " & _
                    "See How-To 5.7 for more information.", vbExclamation
            End If
        End If
    On Error GoTo 0
Exit Sub

BadCheck:
    MsgBox Err.Description, vbExclamation
    End
End Sub
```

4. Add the following code to the **Load** event of **Form1**. The form will, when loading, check the BIBLIO.MDB database for the existence of our graphics field via the **CheckForLogoField** subroutine, constructed in the preceding step.

```
Private Sub Form_Load()
    dtaData.DatabaseName = BIBLIO_PATH
    CheckForLogoField
End Sub
```

5. Add the following code to the **Click** event of **cmdLoad**. The **Load Picture** button uses the **CommonDialog** control **cdlPicture** to allow the user to select a graphics file to load into the database. When a file is selected, the **LoadPicture** method is used to copy the information from the file to the

PictureBox control, picPicture. Because picPicture is data-bound, the database field Logo now contains that graphics information. When the data control is moved to a different record, that information is committed to the database.

```
Private Sub cmdLoad_Click()
    On Error GoTo CancelLoad
        cdlPicture.ShowOpen
        On Error GoTo BadLoad
            picPicture = LoadPicture(cdlPicture.filename)
        On Error GoTo 0
    On Error GoTo 0
Exit Sub

CancelLoad:
    If Err.Number <> cdlCancel Then
        MsgBox Err.Description, vbExclamation
    Else
        Exit Sub
    End If

BadLoad:
    MsgBox Err.Description, vbExclamation
    Exit Sub
End Sub
```

6. Add the following code to the Click event of cmdClose:

```
Private Sub cmdClose_Click()
    End
End Sub
```

How It Works

When Form1 loads, it sets up the dtaData data control, using the BIBLIO_PATH constant to set the DatabaseName property and point it at BIBLIO.MDB. Then, using the CheckForLogoField routine, it confirms that the [Logo] field exists in the [Publishers] table; if not, it adds the field. Because the PictureBox control is bound to the data control, all aspects of displaying the data from the [Logo] field are handled as any other bound control, including field updates. The cmdLoad button allows new data to be added to the field using the LoadPicture method. Because the new data is added to the bound control, the loaded picture is saved to the database and is automatically displayed when the record is again shown.

Comment

The method previously detailed is quick to implement and makes ensuring security easy. The data stored in the Logo field is stored as raw binary data; as such, it's not recognized as an OLE object and is not easily edited. This is also the primary drawback to this method, making it less portable (not easily used by other applications). This method does conserves space, because the OLE object requires other information stored with it to describe what it is, how it can be processed, and so on. But for sheer flexibility, the OLE object approach is superior, and the articles mentioned in Table 5.8 should be reviewed. Be warned, however, that the information covered in those articles is advanced and should be reviewed only when you are confident in the use and understanding of the technique demonstrated in this How-To.

COMPLEXITY:
INTERMEDIATE

5.5 How do I...
Make sure that an operation involving multiple tables is not left partially completed?

Problem

I have an operation that requires several tables to be updated. Because of the nature of the operation, I want all the tables updated—or, if an error occurs, none of the tables to be updated. How can I ensure that only complete operations get applied to my database?

Technique

In database parlance, a *transaction* is a single logical operation that can involve multiple physical operations. Take, for example, a simple transaction in a banking environment, one in which money is withdrawn from a checking account and deposited to a savings account. If the money is withdrawn from the checking account but not applied to the savings account, the depositor will be unhappy. If the money is deposited to the savings account but never withdrawn from the checking account, the bank will be equally unhappy.

Various things might go wrong to cause the update to either account to fail. There might be a power failure or an error in the program. In a multiuser environment, the table representing one of the accounts might be locked by another user. Because it is important that both accounts be updated—or that neither account be updated—there needs to be some way to ensure that if any part of the transaction fails, the entire transaction is abandoned.

To tell Visual Basic and the Jet database engine to enforce transaction integrity, you enclose (or "wrap") all the program code implementing the transaction between two statements. The statement `BeginTrans` tells the database engine, "The transaction starts here. From here on, don't actually update the database. Make sure that it's possible to perform every operation I specify, but instead of actually changing the database, write the changes to a memory buffer." The statement `CommitTrans` tells the engine, "There have been no errors since the last `BeginTrans`, and this is the end of the transaction. Go ahead and write the changes to the database." The process of "making the changes permanent" is known as *committing* the transaction.

You can cancel the transaction in two ways. One method is to close the `Workspace` object without executing the `CommitTrans` statement—that automatically cancels the transaction. Another way, and the preferred way, is to execute a `Rollback` statement. `Rollback` simply tells the database engine, "Cancel the transaction."

The normal way to use these statements is to turn on error trapping before executing the `BeginTrans` statement. Wrap the operations that implement the transaction between a `BeginTrans...CommitTrans` pair. If an error occurs, execute the `Rollback` statement as part of your error routine.

Here's an example. Assume that `WithdrawFromChecking` is a subroutine that withdraws funds from a checking account, and that `DepositToSaving` deposits funds to a savings account. Both take two arguments: the account number and the amount.

```
Sub CheckingToSaving(strAccountNumber as String, curAmount as Currency)
    On Error Goto CheckingToSavingError
    BeginTrans
        WithdrawFromChecking strAccountNumber, curAmount
        DepositToSaving strAccountNumber, curAmount
    CommitTrans
Exit Sub
CheckingToSavingError:
    Rollback
    MsgBox Err.Description, vbExclamation
Exit Sub
End Sub
```

If an error occurs in either the `WithdrawFromChecking` routine or the `DepositToSaving` routine, the error trapping causes execution to branch to the `CheckingToSavingError` label. The code there executes the `Rollback` statement to terminate the transaction, displays an error message, and then exits from the subroutine. You can, of course, implement more sophisticated error handling, but the principle illustrated is the same—in the error routine, cancel the pending transaction with a `Rollback`.

Steps

Open and run the project TRANSACT.VBP. The form shown in Figure 5.8 appears. Enter the following record:

```
Author:         Bloom, Stuart        [type this in as a new entry]
Title:          Visual Basic 4.0 Database How-To
Publisher:      Waite Group Press     [select from the list]
ISBN:           0-0000000-0-0         [not the actual ISBN!]
Year Published:                       1995
```

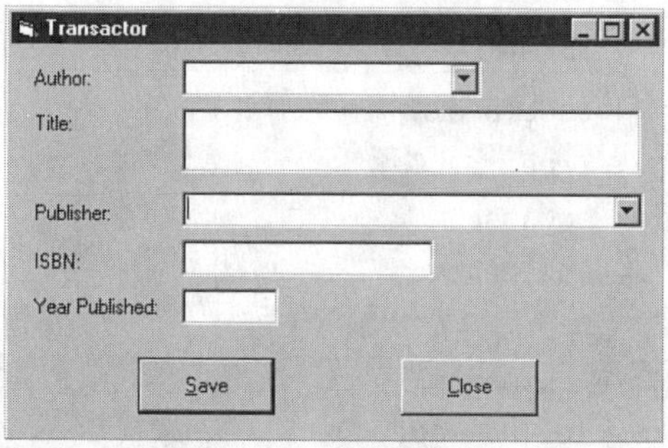

Figure 5.8. The project's main form on startup.

Click Save. The record is saved and the form is cleared, ready for another entry. Enter the same data again, this time choosing the author's name from the author list. Be sure to enter exactly the same ISBN. Click Save, and an error message should appear. The ISBN number is the primary key of the Titles table, and you cannot save two records with identical primary keys. Because this application uses the transaction protection features of the Jet engine and the error occurred within the transaction, no changes were made to the database.

1. Create a new project called Transact.VBP. Use `Form1` to create the objects and properties listed in Table 5.9, and save the form as TRANSACT.FRM.

Table 5.9. Objects and properties for the Transactor form.

OBJECT	PROPERTY	SETTING
Form	Name	Form1
	Caption	"Chapter 5.5 Example"
ComboBox	Name	cboAuthor
	Sorted	True
ComboBox	Name	cboPublisher
	Sorted	True
TextBox	Name	txtYearPublished
	Text	""
TextBox	Name	txtISBN
	Text	""
TextBox	Name	txtTitle
	Text	""
CommandButton	Name	cmdSave
	Caption	"&Save"
	Default	True

continued on next page

continued from previous page

OBJECT	PROPERTY	SETTING
CommandButton	Name	cmdClose
	Cancel	True
	Caption	"&Close"
Label	Name	lblTransact
	Index	0
	Caption	"Author:"
Label	Name	lblTransact
	Index	1
	Caption	"Title:"
Label	Name	lblTransact
	Index	2
	Caption	"Publisher:"
Label	Name	lblTransact
	Index	3
	Caption	"ISBN:"
Label	Name	lblTransact
	Index	4
	Caption	"Year Published:"

2. Add the following code to the declarations section of **Form1**:

```
Option Explicit

Const BIBLIO_PATH = "C:\Program Files\DevStudio\VB\Biblio.MDB"

Const AUTHOR_LIST = 1
Const PUBLISHER_LIST = 2
Private blnFormIsDirty As Boolean
Private blnRefillAuthorList As Boolean
Private blnRefillPublisherList As Boolean
```

3. Enter the following code as the **Load** event of **Form1**. The event makes use of the **FillList** subroutine, explained in the next step, to populate the Authors and Publishers combo boxes. It then sets the **blnFormIsDirty** variable to **False**, meaning that no data has yet been changed in the form.

```
Private Sub Form_Load()
    FillList AUTHOR_LIST: FillList PUBLISHER_LIST
    blnFormIsDirty = False
End Sub
```

4. Create the **FillList** subroutine in **Form1** with the following code. This subroutine, depending on the list type, retrieves a list of authors or publishers and loads them into their respective combo boxes.

```
Sub FillList(intListType As Integer)
    Dim cboTemp As ComboBox
    Dim dbfTemp As Database, recTemp As Recordset

    On Error GoTo FillListError

    Set dbfTemp = DBEngine.Workspaces(0).OpenDatabase(BIBLIO_PATH)

    Select Case intListType
        Case AUTHOR_LIST
            Set cboTemp = cboAuthor
            Set recTemp = dbfTemp.OpenRecordset("SELECT [Au_ID], " & _
                "[Author] FROM [Authors]")
        Case PUBLISHER_LIST
            Set cboTemp = cboPublisher
            Set recTemp = dbfTemp.OpenRecordset("SELECT [PubID], " & _
                "[Name] FROM [Publishers]")
    End Select

    cboTemp.Clear

    If recTemp.RecordCount Then
        recTemp.MoveFirst
        Do
            cboTemp.AddItem recTemp.Fields(1)
            cboTemp.ItemData(cboTemp.NewIndex) = recTemp.Fields(0)
            recTemp.MoveNext
        Loop Until recTemp.EOF
    End If
Exit Sub

FillListError:
    Dim strErrMsg As String

    strErrMsg = "Error while filling " & _
        IIf(intListType = AUTHOR_LIST, "Author", "Publisher") & " list."
    strErrMsg = strErrMsg & vbCr & Err.Number & " - " & Err.Description

    MsgBox strErrMsg, vbCritical
    End
End Sub
```

5. Create the **SaveRecord** function in **Form1** with the following code. **SaveRecord** creates a transaction by wrapping a series of database-updating statements between **BeginTrans** and **CommitTrans** statements. If an error occurs anywhere within the transaction, the **SaveError** error-handling routine is called. **SaveError** uses a **Rollback** statement to cancel the transaction, then informs the user of the specific error.

Errors can be generated by Visual Basic (or the Jet engine) for various reasons. To enable the display of an informative error message, line numbers are used within the transaction, and the error-handling routine uses these line numbers to tell the user where the error occurred.

The function also employs user-generated errors—the **Error** statement followed by an error number in the 32000 range. User-handler errors are set when the application detects that the user has entered data the application "knows" is incorrect—for example, if the user has failed to enter an author. These user errors have the same effect as the Visual Basic-generated errors: They call the error handler, which cancels the transaction. The error handler uses the user error number to display an informative error message; this lets the user correct the error and try to save again.

After **CommitTrans** has been executed, a different error routine must be used, because the original error routine contains a **Rollback** statement. The **CommitTrans** closes the pending transaction, and trying to execute a **Rollback** when there is no pending transaction will cause an error.

```
Function SaveRecord() As Boolean
    Dim lngAuthorID As Long, lngPublisherID As Long
    Dim dbfTemp As Database, recTemp As Recordset

    On Error GoTo SaveError
        Workspaces(0).BeginTrans

        If cboAuthor.ListIndex = -1 Then
            If cboAuthor.Text = "" Then Error 32767
1000        lngAuthorID = CreateAuthor(cboAuthor.Text)
            blnRefillAuthorList = True
        Else
            lngAuthorID = cboAuthor.ItemData(cboAuthor.ListIndex)
        End If

        If cboPublisher.ListIndex = -1 Then
            If cboPublisher.Text = "" Then Error 32766
1050        lngPublisherID = CreatePublisher(cboPublisher.Text)
            blnRefillPublisherList = True
        Else
            lngPublisherID = cboPublisher.ItemData(cboPublisher.ListIndex)
        End If

        If txtTitle <> "" And txtISBN <> "" Then
            Set dbfTemp = DBEngine.Workspaces(0).OpenDatabase(BIBLIO_PATH)

1100        Set recTemp = dbfTemp.OpenRecordset("Titles", dbOpenTable)
            With recTemp
                .AddNew
                ![PubID] = lngPublisherID
                ![ISBN] = txtISBN
                ![Title] = txtTitle
                ![Year Published] = txtYearPublished
                .Update
            End With

1150        Set recTemp = dbfTemp.OpenRecordset("Title Author", dbOpenTable)
            With recTemp
                .AddNew
                ![Au_ID] = lngAuthorID
```

```
                ![ISBN] = txtISBN
                .Update
            End With
        Else
            If txtTitle = "" Then Error 32765 Else Error 32764
        End If

        Workspaces(0).CommitTrans

    On Error GoTo SaveErrorNoRollback
        ClearForm
        blnFormIsDirty = False
        SaveRecord = True
    On Error GoTo 0
Exit Function

SaveError:
    Dim strErrMsg As String

    Workspaces(0).Rollback

    Select Case Err
        Case 32767
            strErrMsg = "You have not entered an author name"
        Case 32766
            strErrMsg = "You have not entered a publisher name"
        Case 32765
            strErrMsg = "You have not entered a title"
        Case 32764
            strErrMsg = "You have not entered an ISBN number"
        Case Else
            Select Case Erl
                Case 1000
                    strErrMsg = "Error " & Err.Number & " (" & Err.Description & _
                        "} encountered creating new Authors record."
                Case 1050
                    strErrMsg = "Error " & Err.Number & " (" & Err.Description & _
                        "} encountered creating new Publishers record."
                Case 1100
                    strErrMsg = "Error " & Err.Number & " (" & Err.Description & _
                        "} encountered creating new Titles record."
                Case 1150
                    strErrMsg = "Error " & Err.Number & " (" & Err.Description & _
                        "} encountered creating new Title Author record."
                Case Else
                    strErrMsg = Err.Description
            End Select
    End Select
    MsgBox strErrMsg, vbExclamation

    SaveRecord = False
Exit Function

SaveErrorNoRollback:
    MsgBox Err.Description, vbExclamation
Resume Next
End Function
```

6. Enter the following code in **Form1** as the **CreateAuthor** function. **CreateAuthor** creates a new record in the Authors table and returns the **Au_ID** assigned to the new author.

```
Function CreateAuthor(strAuthorName As String) As Long
    Dim dbfTemp As Database, recTemp As Recordset

    Set dbfTemp = DBEngine.Workspaces(0).OpenDatabase(BIBLIO_PATH)

    Set recTemp = dbfTemp.OpenRecordset("Authors", dbOpenTable)
    With recTemp
        .AddNew
        ![Author] = strAuthorName
        .Update
        .Bookmark = .LastModified
    End With

    CreateAuthor = recTemp![Au_ID]
End Function
```

7. Enter the following code in **Form1** as the **CreatePublisher** function. **CreatePublisher** creates a new record in the Publishers table and returns the **PubID** assigned to the new publisher.

```
Function CreatePublisher(strPublisherName As String) As Long
    Dim dbfTemp As Database, recTemp As Recordset
    Dim lngLastID As Long

    Set dbfTemp = DBEngine.Workspaces(0).OpenDatabase(BIBLIO_PATH)

    Set recTemp = dbfTemp.OpenRecordset("Publishers", dbOpenTable)
    With recTemp
        .Index = "PrimaryKey"
        .MoveLast
        lngLastID = ![PubID]
        .AddNew
        ![PubID] = lngLastID + 1
        ![Name] = strPublisherName
        .Update
    End With

    CreatePublisher = lngLastID + 1
End Function
```

8. Enter the following code in **Form1** as the **ClearForm** subroutine. **ClearForm** clears the text and combo boxes on the form. If the previous record resulted in a new author or publisher being added, **ClearForm** refreshes the appropriate combo box to put the new author or publisher into the list.

```
Sub ClearForm()

    If blnRefillAuthorList Then
        FillList AUTHOR_LIST
```

```
        blnRefillAuthorList = False
    Else
        cboAuthor.ListIndex = -1
    End If

    If blnRefillPublisherList Then
        FillList PUBLISHER_LIST
        blnRefillPublisherList = False
    Else
        cboPublisher.ListIndex = -1
    End If

    ' Clear the text boxes.
    txtTitle = ""
    txtISBN = ""
    txtYearPublished = ""
End Sub
```

9. Enter the following code into **Form1** as the **Click** event of **cmdClose**. If the form has an unsaved record, the subroutine gives the user a chance to save the record or cancel the close event.

```
Private Sub cmdClose_Click()
    If blnFormIsDirty Then
        Select Case MsgBox("Do you want to save the current record?", _
        vbQuestion + vbYesNoCancel)
            Case vbYes
                If SaveRecord() = False Then Exit Sub
            Case vbNo
                End
            Case vbCancel
                Exit Sub
        End Select
    End If
    End
End Sub
```

10. Enter the following five subroutines into **Form1** as the **Change** events for **txtISBN**, **txtTitle**, **txtYearPublished**, **cboAuthor**, and **cboPublisher**. Each of these event routines sets the **blnFormIsDirty** flag when the user types an entry into the control.

```
Private Sub txtISBN_Change()
    blnFormIsDirty = True
End Sub

Private Sub txtTitle_Change()
    blnFormIsDirty = True
End Sub

Private Sub txtYearPublished_Change()
    blnFormIsDirty = True
End Sub
```

continued on next page

continued from previous page

```
Private Sub cboAuthor_Change()
    blnFormIsDirty = True
End Sub

Private Sub cboPublisher_Change()
    blnFormIsDirty = True
End Sub
```

11. Enter the following two subroutines into **Form1**. These subroutines set the **blnFormIsDirty** flag when the user changes the entry in one of the combo boxes by selecting an item from the list.

```
Private Sub cboAuthor_Click()
    If cboAuthor.ListIndex <> -1 Then blnFormIsDirty = True
End Sub

Private Sub cboPublisher_Click()
    If cboPublisher.ListIndex <> -1 Then blnFormIsDirty = True
End Sub
```

How It Works

When the user clicks Save, the **cmdSave_Click** event calls **SaveRecord**, which does most of the work. If the user has entered a new author or new publisher (instead of selecting an existing item from the author or publisher list), **SaveRecord** calls a function (**CreateAuthor** or **CreatePublisher**) to create the new record. It then saves the record. If an error occurs (either a Visual Basic error or a user-generated error), the error handler in **SaveRecord** rolls back the transaction.

Comment

The main use of transactions is to maintain integrity when you're updating more than one table as part of a single logical operation. You can also use **BeginTrans**, **CommitTrans**, and **Rollback** when you're performing multiple operations on a single table and you want to make sure that all the operations are performed as a unit.

Transactions can also speed up some database operations. Under normal conditions, every time you use the **Update** method, the Jet engine writes the changes to disk. Multiple small disk writes can significantly slow down an application. Executing a **BeginTrans** holds all the operations in memory until **CommitTrans** executes, which can noticeably improve execution time.

The transaction features described in this How-To work when you are using Microsoft Access database files and most of the other file types supported by the Jet engine. Some database types—Paradox is one example—do not support transactions. You can check whether the database supports transactions by reading the **Transactions** property of the database object:

```
Dim dbfTemp as Database
Dim blnSupportsTransactions as Boolean
...
blnSupportsTransactions = dbfTemp.Transactions
...
```

Using the transactions statements `BeginTrans`, `CommitTrans`, and `Rollback` with a database that does not support transactions does not generate an error—but you need to be aware that you won't get the transaction integrity protection these statements would normally provide.

COMPLEXITY
BEGINNING

5.6 How do I...
Compact a database or repair a corrupted database?

Problem

I know that Microsoft Access provides the capability to make a database smaller by compacting it. Microsoft Access also lets me repair a database that has been corrupted. How can I perform these operations from my Visual Basic program?

Technique

When you delete data (or database objects) from a Microsoft Access database file, the Jet engine does not automatically shrink the size of the file to recover the no-longer-needed space. If the user deletes a significant amount of data, the file size can grow very large, with much of the space being wasted. You can use the `CompactDatabase` method of the `DBEngine` object to recover the space.

Occasionally, a database file can become corrupted by a General Protection Fault, a power failure, a bug in the database engine, or some other cause. Most corrupted databases can be restored by the `RepairDatabase` method of the `DBEngine` object.

Steps

Open the project REPAIR.VBP and run it. The form shown in Figure 5.9 appears. Choose Compact a database and click OK. The application asks you to designate an existing database and to supply a new filename for the compacted version of the database. When you have done so, the application compacts the database and displays a message indicating completion.

Choose Repair a database and click OK. The application asks you to designate a database to be repaired. When you have done so, the application repairs the database and displays a message indicating success.

Figure 5.9. The project's
main form on startup.

1. Create a new project called Repair.VBP. Use **Form1** to create the objects and
properties listed in Table 5.10, and save the form as Repair.FRM.

Table 5.10. Objects and properties for the Database Maintenance form.

OBJECT	PROPERTY	SETTING
Form	Name	Form1
	Caption	"Chapter 5.6 Example"
Frame	Name	grpOperation
	Caption	"Operation"
OptionButton	Name	optCompact
	Caption	"Compact a database"
OptionButton	Name	optRepair
	Caption	"Repair a database"
CommandButton	Name	cmdOK
	Caption	"OK"
	Default	True
CommandButton	Name	cmdClose
	Cancel	True
	Caption	"&Close"

2. Add the following code to the declarations section of **Form1**:

```
Option Explicit
```

3. Enter the following code into **Form1** as the **Click** event of **cmdOK**. The
setting of optCompact determines whether the user wants to compact or
repair the database. This procedure uses the Windows File Open common
dialog box to get the name of the file to compact or repair. In the case of a
compact operation, it then uses the File Save common dialog box to get
the name of the output file. It then uses the **DBEngine's** **CompactDatabase**
or **RepairDatabase** method to perform the operation.

```
Private Sub cmdOK_Click()
    Dim strInput As String, strOutput As String

    On Error GoTo OKError
        With cdlDatabase
            .DialogTitle = "Select File To " & _
                IIf(optCompact, "Compact", "Repair")
            .ShowOpen
        End With
        strInput = cdlDatabase.filename

        If optCompact Then
            With cdlDatabase
                .DialogTitle = "Repaired Filename"
                .filename = ""
                .ShowSave
            End With
            strOutput = cdlDatabase.filename
            Screen.MousePointer = vbHourglass
            DBEngine.CompactDatabase strInput, strOutput
            Screen.MousePointer = vbDefault
            MsgBox "Database " & strInput & " compacted to " & strOutput
        Else
            Screen.MousePointer = vbHourglass
            DBEngine.RepairDatabase strInput
            Screen.MousePointer = vbDefault
            MsgBox "Repair of " & strInput & " successful."
        End If
    On Error GoTo 0
Exit Sub

OKError:
    Screen.MousePointer = vbDefault
    If Err <> 32755 Then MsgBox Err.Description
Exit Sub
End Sub
```

4. Enter the following into Form1 as the Click event of cmdClose:

```
Private Sub cmdClose_Click()
    End
End Sub
```

How It Works

The cmdOK button supplies almost all the project's action. Depending on the selected option button, the cmdOK_Click event code first uses the CommonDialog control to retrieve the name of a valid Access database. After a name is returned, it issues either a CompactDatabase method or a RepairDatabase method, depending on the selected option button. If a CompactDatabase is required, the routine will again use the CommonDialog control to get the desired name for the compacted database. It has to do this because the CompactDatabase command cannot compact a database back into itself; it instead rebuilds the database from the ground up, so to speak, into another Access database file. The `RepairDatabase` method, however, does not write to another database file, and is instead called directly on the chosen database.

Comments

It is strongly recommended that `CompactDatabase` be performed on Access databases regularly, because it reclaims wasted space and re-indexes tables to allow for faster, more efficient use. `RepairDatabase`, on the other hand, should be used only when an Access database is indicated as corrupt. In Visual Basic, a trappable error is triggered when an Access database is corrupt, so automating this process is relatively easy.

COMPLEXITY
INTERMEDIATE

5.7 How do I...
Use parameter queries stored in Microsoft Access databases?

Problem

I'd like to use stored `QueryDef` objects to reduce the execution time for my program. But I need to change one or two values each time I run my SELECT query. How can I use stored queries with replaceable parameters from Visual Basic?

Technique

Microsoft Access provides the *parameter query* as a variation of the standard SELECT query. The definition of a parameter query specifies one or more *replaceable* parameters—values to be supplied each time the query executes. Each replaceable parameter is represented by a name, which is used much like a field name. The name can be any legal object name, provided that the name has not already been used as a field name in any of the tables in the query.

For example, you have a query that extracts information about customer accounts from several tables. Each time the query runs, it requires a value for the [Customer Number] field in the Customers table. If the name of the replaceable parameter was CustNum, the WHERE clause of the query would be this:

```
WHERE Customers.[Customer Number] = [CustNum]
```

When run from Microsoft Access, a parameter query pops up an input box for the user at runtime. The user types a value, and this value is used as the replaceable parameter. When you use a stored parameter query from Visual Basic, your code must provide the value for the replaceable parameter before you execute the query.

You provide the replaceable value through the QueryDef object. Each QueryDef object owns a Parameters collection, which consists of a set of Parameter objects, each with a name. When you assign a value to a Parameter object, the QueryDef object uses that as the replaceable value when you run the query.

Following is the full syntax for assigning a value to a QueryDef Parameter object (where myQueryDef is an object variable assigned to a QueryDef object and CustNum is the name of a Parameter object):

```
qdfTempQueryDef.Parameters("CustNum") = 141516
```

This can be abbreviated using the bang operator like so:

```
qdfTempQueryDef![CustNum] = 141516
```

The sequence for using a stored parameter query from your Visual Basic code, therefore, is this:

1. Declare the appropriate variables:

```
Dim dbfTemp as Database
Dim qdfTemp as QueryDef
Dim recTemp as Recordset
```

2. Set the Database and QueryDef variables to valid objects:

```
Set dbfTemp = DBEngine.Workspaces(0).OpenDatabase("ACCOUNTS.MDB")
Set qdfTemp = dbfTemp.OpenQueryDef("Customer Data")
```

3. Assign an appropriate value to each replaceable parameter of the QueryDef object. If the Customer Data QueryDef has two parameters, CustNum and Start Date, this would be your code:

```
qdfTemp![CustNum] = 124151
qdfTemp![Start Date] = #1/1/97#              ' the # signs delimit a date
```

4. Use the OpenRecordset method of the QueryDef object to create the recordset:

```
Set recTemp = qdfTemp.OpenRecordset()
```

Steps

Open and run the project ParameterQuery.VBP. The form shown in Figure 5.10 appears. Select a publisher and then click OK. Then the form shown in Figure 5.11 appears with the first record in BIBLIO.MDB belonging to that publisher. If the publisher has no titles in the database, the form is blank. Browse through the records by using the browse buttons. To select a different publisher, click the Publisher button.

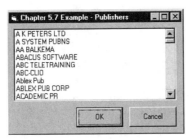

Figure 5.10. The project's
Publisher Parameters form,
showing publisher names.

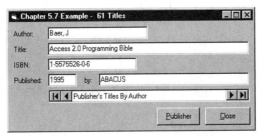

Figure 5.11. The project's Publisher Titles
form, showing publisher title information.

1. Create a new project called ParameterQuery.VBP. Rename `Form1` to
`frmMain`. Then create the objects and properties listed in Table 5.11, and
save the form as ParameterQuery.FRM.

Table 5.11. Objects and properties for the Query User form.

OBJECT	PROPERTY	SETTING
Form	Name	`frmMain`
	Caption	`"Publisher Information"`
Data	Name	`dtaData`
	Caption	`"Publisher's Titles By Author"`
TextBox	Name	`txtPublisher`
	DataSource	`dtaData`
	DataField	`"Name"`
TextBox	Name	`txtYearPublished`
	DataSource	`dtaData`
	DataField	`"Year Published"`

OBJECT	PROPERTY	SETTING
TextBox	Name	txtISBN
	DataSource	dtaData
	DataField	"ISBN"
TextBox	Name	txtTitle
	DataSource	dtaData
	DataField	"Title"
TextBox	Name	txtAuthor
	DataSource	dtaData
	DataField	"Author"
Label	Name	lblQuery
	Index	0
	Caption	"Author:"
Label	Name	lblQuery
	Index	1
	Caption	"Title:"
Label	Name	lblQuery
	Index	2
	Caption	"ISBN:"
Label	Name	lblQuery
	Index	3
	Caption	"Published:"
Label	Name	lblQuery
	Index	4
	Caption	"by:"
CommandButton	Name	cmdPublisher
	Caption	"&Publisher"
CommandButton	Name	cmdClose
	Cancel	True
	Caption	"&Close"

2. Add a new form to the project. Name it frmSelectPublisher. Create the objects and properties listed in Table 5.12, and save the form as Publishers.FRM.

Table 5.12. Objects and properties for the Query User form.

OBJECT	PROPERTY	SETTING
Form	Name	frmSelectPublisher
	Caption	"Chapter 5.7 Example - Publishers"
ListBox	Name	lstPublishers
CommandButton	Name	cmdOK
	Caption	"&OK"
	Default	True
CommandButton	Name	cmdCancel
	Cancel	True
	Caption	"&Cancel"

3. Enter the following code into the declarations section of frmMain:

```
Option Explicit

'NOTE:  The constant does NOT include the database name this time.
Const BIBLIO_PATH = "C:\Program Files\DevStudio\VB"
'Because the variable is public (exposed for use by other objects),
'the naming conventions for variables do not apply here - treat
'as a property.
Public SelectedPubID As Integer
```

4. Enter the following code into frmMain as its **Load** event. The
CheckDatabaseVersion routine, called in this event, ensures that the
BIBLIO.MDB database is Jet 3.0 compatible; if the database was created
with an earlier version of Access, there could be some difficulties.

```
Private Sub Form_Load()
    'Older versions of BIBLIO.MDB must be converted to the Jet 3.0 format
    'before a parameter query can be saved to it.
    CheckDatabaseVersion
    dtaData.DatabaseName = BIBLIO_PATH & "\Biblio.MDB"
    cmdPublisher_Click
End Sub
```

5. Enter the following code into frmMain as the **Click** event for
cmdPublisher. If a publisher's ID has been selected, the RunQuery
subroutine is called. If not, the form is still displayed, but with a different
title and no data.

```
Private Sub cmdPublisher_Click()
    frmSelectPublisher.Show vbModal

    If SelectedPubID > 0 Then
        RunQuery
    Else
        frmMain.Caption = "Chapter 5.7 Example - No Titles"
    End If
End Sub
```

6. Enter the following code into frmMain as the CheckDatabaseVersion subroutine. This subroutine checks the version of the Access database to ensure that it's compatible with Jet 3.0. It does so by creating a Database object, then checking the Version property, which supplies a formatted string indicating the major and minor number of the database version. If less than 3.0, the program uses the CompactDatabase method to convert the database to Jet 3.0 format, backing it up in the process just in case.

```
Private Sub CheckDatabaseVersion()
    Dim dbfTemp As Database, sngVersion As Single

    Set dbfTemp = Workspaces(0).OpenDatabase(BIBLIO_PATH & "\Biblio.MDB")
    'If the database's Version property is less than 3.0, then it needs
    'to be converted before we can save a parameter query to it from 32-bit
    'Visual Basic.
    sngVersion = Val(dbfTemp.Version)
    dbfTemp.Close: DBEngine.Idle dbFreeLocks

    If Val(sngVersion) < 3 Then
        'First, we'll back up the old database
        FileCopy BIBLIO_PATH & "\Biblio.MDB", BIBLIO_PATH & "\BiblioBackup.MDB"
        'Then, we'll use the CompactDatabase method to convert it to the
        'version 3.0 format
        CompactDatabase BIBLIO_PATH & "\Biblio.MDB", _
            BIBLIO_PATH & "\BiblioNew.MDB", , dbVersion30
        'Next, we'll delete the old database after we're sure the new one exists.
        If Len(Dir("BiblioNew.MDB")) Then Kill BIBLIO_PATH & "\Biblio.MDB"
        'Finally, we'll rename the new database to the old name, "Biblio.MDB".
        If Len(Dir(BIBLIO_PATH)) = 0 Then
            Name BIBLIO_PATH & "\BiblioNew.MDB" As BIBLIO_PATH & "\Biblio.MDB"
        End If
    End If
End Sub
```

7. Enter the following code into frmMain as the RunQuery subroutine. This subroutine searches for the query definition [Publisher's Titles By Author]. If it doesn't find what it's seeking, it creates the query and saves that query in BIBLIO.MDB. It next inserts the PubID code of the selected publisher into the Publisher parameter of the query definition. Then it runs the query and uses DisplayRecord to display the data.

```
Sub RunQuery()
    Dim dbfTemp As Database, recTemp As Recordset
    Dim qdfTemp As QueryDef
    Dim strSQL As String
    Dim blnFoundQuery As Boolean

    On Error GoTo QueryError
        Set dbfTemp = Workspaces(0).OpenDatabase(BIBLIO_PATH & "\Biblio.MDB")
        For Each qdfTemp In dbfTemp.QueryDefs
            If qdfTemp.Name = "Publisher's Titles By Author" Then
                blnFoundQuery = True
                Exit For
```

continued on next page

continued from previous page

```
                End If
        Next

        If blnFoundQuery = False Then
            strSQL = "PARAMETERS pintPubID Long; " & _
                "SELECT Authors.Author, Titles.Title, Titles.ISBN, " & _
                "Titles.[Year Published], Publishers.Name " & _
                "FROM (Publishers INNER JOIN Titles ON "
            strSQL = strSQL & "Publishers.PubID = Titles.PubID) INNER JOIN " & _
                "(Authors INNER JOIN [Title Author] ON " & _
                "Authors.Au_ID = [Title Author].Au_ID) ON " & _
                "Titles.ISBN = [Title Author].ISBN WHERE Publishers.PubID " & _
                "= pintPubID ORDER by Authors.Author;"
            Set qdfTemp = dbfTemp.CreateQueryDef("Publisher's Titles By " & _
                "Author", strSQL)
        Else
            Set qdfTemp = dbfTemp.QueryDefs("Publisher's Titles By Author")
        End If

        qdfTemp.Parameters![pintPubID] = SelectedPubID

        Set dtaData.Recordset = qdfTemp.OpenRecordset()
        If dtaData.Recordset.RecordCount > 0 Then
            frmMain.Caption = "Chapter 5.7 Example - " & _
                Str$(dtaData.Recordset.RecordCount) & _
                IIf(dtaData.Recordset.RecordCount = 1, " Title", " Titles")
        Else
            frmMain.Caption = frmMain.Caption = "Chapter 5.7 Example - No Titles"
        End If
    On Error GoTo 0
Exit Sub

QueryError:
    MsgBox Err.Description, vbExclamation
Exit Sub
End Sub
```

8. Enter the following code into **frmMain** as the **Click** event of **cmdClose**:

```
Private Sub cmdClose_Click()
    End
End Sub
```

9. Now that **frmMain** is complete, let's move on to **frmSelectPublisher**. Add the following code to its declarations section:

```
Option Explicit
```

10. Enter the following code as the **Load** event of **frmSelectPublisher**:

```
Private Sub Form_Load()
    Dim dbfTemp As Database, recTemp As Recordset
    Dim strSQL As String

    On Error GoTo LoadError
```

```
            Set dbfTemp = Workspaces(0).OpenDatabase(BIBLIO_PATH)
            strSQL = "SELECT [PubID], [Company Name] FROM [Publishers]"
            Set recTemp = dbfTemp.OpenRecordset(strSQL)

            If recTemp.RecordCount Then
                recTemp.MoveFirst
                Do Until recTemp.EOF
                    If Not IsNull(recTemp![Company Name]) Then
                        lstPublishers.AddItem recTemp![Company Name]
                    Else
                        lstPublishers.AddItem ""
                    End If
                    lstPublishers.ItemData(lstPublishers.NewIndex) = recTemp![PubID]
                    recTemp.MoveNext
                Loop
            Else
                MsgBox "There are no publishers in the database.", vbCritical
                End
            End If
        On Error GoTo 0
    Exit Sub

    LoadError:
        MsgBox Err.Description, vbCritical
        End
    End Sub
```

11. Enter the following code into `frmSelectPublisher` as the `Click` event of `cmdOK`. This routine gets the `PubID` of the selected publisher from the list box `ItemData` property and puts that value into the public variable `SelectedPubID`, then hides the form.

```
If lstPublishers.ListIndex > -1 Then
        frmMain.SelectedPubID = lstPublishers.ItemData(lstPublishers.ListIndex)
        Me.Hide
    Else
        MsgBox "You have not selected a publisher", vbExclamation
    End If
End Sub
```

12. Enter the following code into `frmSelectPublisher` as the `DblClick` event of `lstPublishers`:

```
Private Sub lstPublishers_DblClick()
    cmdOK_Click
End Sub
```

13. Enter the following code into `frmSelectPublisher` as the `Click` event of `cmdCancel`. This routine puts the value `0` into the public variable `SelectedPubID`, then hides the form.

```
Private Sub cmdCancel_Click()
    frmMain.SelectedPubID = 0
    Hide
End Sub
```

How It Works

When frmMain loads, it immediately generates a Click event for cmdPublisher to display the Select Publisher form. When the user makes a selection from the publisher list and clicks OK, the PubID of the selected publisher is used to set the Public variable SelectedPubID. The value of SelectedPubID is then used as the parameter passed to the [Publisher's Titles by Author] query definition. After its parameter has been set, the QueryDef is used to create the recordset of title information.

Comments

The parameter query allows for the flexibility of dynamically built SQL statements, but with the optimized speed of static SQL. One of the other benefits to using a parameter query is the Requery method, which allows you to reexecute a parameter query with different values; Access will actually reuse the existing connection, running the query faster. Also, the optimization engine built into Jet works best on static SQL (that is, SQL stored in the database, as opposed to the SQL statements stored in code), so you can get even more benefit from the use of a parameter query that is saved to a Microsoft Access database. For a similar example on the use of a parameter query, How-To 3.5 is another good reference, especially with the use of the Requery method.

CHAPTER 6
EXTERNAL ISAM DATABASE FILES

6

EXTERNAL ISAM DATABASE FILES

How do I...

6.1 **Access dBASE, FoxPro, and Paradox database files using the data control?**

6.2 **Access dBASE, FoxPro, and Paradox database files using data access objects?**

6.3 **Use indexes with dBASE, FoxPro, and Paradox files?**

6.4 **Access Excel worksheets using data access objects?**

6.5 **Access Btrieve files?**

As you have already found out in Chapter 2, "Accessing a Database with Data Access Objects," the Microsoft Jet Database Engine has built-in capabilities to handle Microsoft Access databases. There are many times, however, when we need to access other types of database files. Fortunately for us, the Microsoft Jet Engine 3.5 offers a long list of database files that we can access similarly to the way we interface to common Access databases. Files that are not Microsoft Access database files are considered *external* database files. Although there are limitations to accessing external database files, many useful methods and properties are still available to us.

External data files are split into two classifications: ISAM and ODBC. We will cover ISAM (Indexed Sequential Access Method) techniques to access ISAM databases in this chapter. ODBC (Open Database Connectivity) is covered in Chapter 7, "Connecting to an ODBC Server." ODBC databases can reside on a PC or on another computer platform.

Visual Basic uses the Jet database engine to access external ISAM databases. With Microsoft Jet, we can access many different ISAM formats. The formats covered in this chapter include dBASE databases (versions III, IV, and 5.0), Microsoft FoxPro databases (versions 2.0, 2.5, 2.6, and 3.0), Paradox databases (versions 3.x, 4.x, and 5.x), and Microsoft Excel Worksheets (versions 3.0, 4.0, 5.0, 7.0, and 8.0).

To access each of these formats, you must first have the proper IISAM (Installable ISAM) installed on your computer. For each IISAM driver, there is an entry in the Windows Registry. When the driver is initialized, settings are made, through the setup program, in the Windows Registry. You can install IISAMs by selecting the Custom Setup installation when you install Visual Basic. In addition to the previously listed formats, Btrieve database files, covered in How-To 6.5 of this chapter, are also supported, and it should be noted that the IISAM for accessing Btrieve databases is not included with Visual Basic, nor this book. If you want to access Btrieve databases, contact Btrieve for the proper IISAM.

Ways of Accessing ISAM Databases

You can access external databases in three ways, each with its own advantages and disadvantages:

✔ Use bound controls and the data control to access an external database. You do this by simply setting the Connect property of the data control to the proper ISAM type.

✔ Use DAO (Data Access Objects) to reference an external database by opening a database with the correct **Connect** string, depending on the desired ISAM type.

✔ Attach a table to a Microsoft Access database and use any of the recordset methods to reference the data.

The first option, using a data control, is shown in both How-To 6.1 and How-To 6.5. The second option, using DAO, is used in How-To's 6.2 and 6.3. Accessing an Excel worksheet using DAO is covered in How-To 6.4.

Many of the same choices that concern a programmer using an Access database are present when the programmer is deciding which technique to use when accessing an external ISAM data file. The data control offers simplicity when using data bound controls such as text boxes, but it lacks the capability to utilize indexes. Using DAO is more involved than using the data control, but it offers the greatest functionality, which includes indexes. Table 6.1 lists the objects that are not supported by external ISAM databases; Table 6.2 lists the methods that are either not supported or restricted when using external ISAM databases.

Table 6.1. Microsoft Access data access objects not supported by external ISAM files.

MICROSOFT ACCESS OBJECTS	EXTERNAL ISAM DATABASE
Container	Not supported
Document	Not supported
QueryDef	Not supported
Relation	Not supported

Table 6.2. Microsoft Access methods and external ISAM file restrictions.

MICROSOFT ACCESS METHODS	EXTERNAL ISAM DATABASE
CompactDatabase	Not supported
CreateDatabase	Not supported
CreateField	Supported only on new tables, not existing tables
CreateQueryDef	Not supported
OpenTable	Not supported on attached ISAM tables
RepairDatabase	Not supported
Seek	Not supported on attached ISAM tables

When to Use External ISAM Databases

When you are developing a new application or no longer need to keep the original format of an external database, it is a good idea to use a Microsoft Access database. By doing this, you will have the greatest control over your data from within your Visual Basic application. If, however, you have other applications that need to access external databases that you are working with, you might decide to keep these databases in their original format.

General Techniques for Accessing External ISAM Databases

The first thing that must be done when accessing any database is setting the database object. One difference when working with ISAM databases, as compared to Access databases, is the concept of a database name. With Access databases, you need to specify the complete path and database name in the **OpenDatabase** method for DAO or the **DatabaseName** property for a data control. The difference when using ISAM databases is that ISAM files require that you specify only the path of the database, without the filename. This is done in the **OpenDatabase** method (for DAO) or the **DatabaseName** property (for the data control). The actual database name, the filename, is used as the `Recordset` name in both access methods.

Another difference when working with ISAM databases is the use of IISAMs. With Access databases, this is not necessary, but when an external database is being used, the data control or DAO has no idea how the external file is accessed without a little help. This help comes from a DLL file specified in an IISAM, which resides in the Windows Registry. As stated earlier, Btrieve IISAMs are not included with Visual Basic and should be acquired through Btrieve. You can, however, install dBASE, Paradox, FoxPro, and Excel IISAMs using the Custom Setup installation of Visual Basic. To tell Visual Basic which driver you want to use at runtime, specify the ISAM type in the `Connect` property of your data control or `OpenDatabase` method.

Another important factor to consider is case-sensitive data sources. By default, FoxPro, dBASE, and Paradox databases are case sensitive when sorting and indexing. To change this behavior for Xbase databases (FoxPro and dBASE), set the `CollatingSequence` value in the `\HKEY_LOCAL_MACHINE\SOFTWARE\Microsoft\Jet\3.5\Engines\Xbase` key to `International`. A setting of `ASCII`, the default value for this key, allows Xbase databases to be case sensitive. For the non-Xbase databases (Paradox), check the `CollatingSequence` value in `\HKEY_LOCAL_MACHINE\SOFTWARE\Microsoft\Jet\3.5\Engines\Paradox` in the same manner. You can find more information on the Windows Registry in Chapter 12, "The Windows Registry and State Information."

In this chapter, we will explore external database connectivity using both bound data controls and DAO. After completing the How-To's in this chapter, you will have a complete understanding of accessing external databases using Visual Basic.

6.1 Access dBASE, FoxPro, and Paradox Database Files Using the Data Control

You can use the data control in Visual Basic to easily access dBASE, FoxPro and Paradox database files as if they were standard Microsoft Access databases, with a few restrictions. This How-To illustrates, through two variations of a project, how to reference dBASE and Paradox databases. It shows how you can view their content or add, edit, and delete records.

6.2 Access dBASE, FoxPro, and Paradox Database Files Using Data Access Objects

Although the data control is an easy method for accessing data in external ISAM files, it sometimes lacks the control that a programmer needs when manipulating records. This How-To presents a project that behaves exactly as the project in How-To 6.1 by using DAO (Data Access Objects) rather than a data control.

6.3 Use Indexes with dBASE, FoxPro, and Paradox Files

Using indexes with a Microsoft Access database offers faster and more efficient data access and sorting. These same techniques can be used to access external

ISAM database formats. This How-To demonstrates the use of indexes by building on the project in How-To 6.2. Here, indexes are used for seeking records and for sorting in recordset navigation.

6.4 Access Excel Worksheets Using Data Access Objects

An interesting capability of the Microsoft Jet engine is used to access Excel worksheets. In this How-To, we view and manipulate an Excel worksheet as if it were an ordinary database file.

6.5 Access Btrieve Files

Although Btrieve files are vastly different from the other ISAM databases we work with, namely Xbase databases, we can still access them as if they were of Jet database format. In this example, we access a Btrieve database and offer the capability to add, edit, and delete records, just as in the previous How-To's.

COMPLEXITY
BEGINNING

6.1 How do I...
Access dBASE, FoxPro, and Paradox database files using the data control?

Problem

I have existing dBASE, FoxPro, and Paradox database files that I want to access from my Visual Basic application. I use these files in other applications, so it is not practical to convert them to Access database files. How can I keep the format of these database files and still access them from my application?

Technique

As discussed earlier, there are different types of ISAM databases. The more common format, called Xbase, is used in dBASE III, IV, and 5.0, as well as FoxPro 2.0, 2.5, 2.6, and 3.0. These database formats use a default DBF file extension. Paradox, on the other hand, is a completely different format; it uses the extension DB. Although these databases are vastly different in structure, we can reference them both in an identical manner.

The introduction of this chapter talked about two unique steps involved in accessing external ISAM files using a data control as compared to referencing Microsoft Access Databases:

✔ Setting the **Connect** property of the data control with a valid ISAM type. In this How-To, the only differences between the two versions of the project will depend on this property. To make the dBASE version of the project, set the **Connect** property to dBASE 5.0; or, to make the Paradox version, set the **Connect** property to **Paradox 5.x;**. Assuming that the recordset structures in both of the databases used are identical, this will be the only change necessary to create two different projects.

✔ Ensure that the proper IISAM is installed in the Windows Registry for the external ISAM that is used in this project. Consult Table 6.3 for the proper keys and settings for the appropriate ISAM file to be used. These Registry settings replace the Microsoft Jet 2.5 need for INI files.

Table 6.3. Windows Registry settings from HKEY_LOCAL_MACHINE\SOFT-WARE\ for external ISAM files.

KEY	VALUE
\Jet\3.5\Engines\Xbase\Win32	"C:\WINDOWS\SYSTEM\MSXBSE35.DLL"
\Jet\3.5\Engines\Paradox\Win32	"C:\WINDOWS\SYSTEM\MSPDOX35.DLL"

Steps

The ISAM1 project allows you to view, add, edit, and delete records in a dBASE 5.0 database named CUSTOMER.DBF, which was installed when you installed the files from the distribution CD-ROM. Open and run ISAM1.VBP. The form shown in Figure 6.1 appears. You can navigate the dBASE 5.0 CUSTOMER.DBF database by using the VCR buttons of the data control on the form. You can add and delete records by clicking the appropriate buttons. To edit the current record, first click the Edit button and then edit the record. To save information after adding a new record, or editing the current one, click the move first or move last button (the button on the far left or the button on the far right of the data control) to successfully save the changes to the CUSTOMER database.

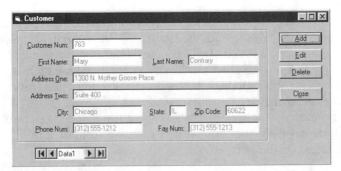

Figure 6.1. The Customer form.

If you get the error message `Can't find installable ISAM`, check to see whether the Registry entry matches that found in Table 6.3 and that the appropriate DLL actually resides in the Windows\System directory. If one of these is incorrect, reinstall Visual Basic with the Custom Setup installation option, being certain to install the appropriate IISAM.

1. If your Windows Registry does not match that of Table 6.3, install the appropriate IISAMs for use in this project.

2. Create a new project and call it ISAM1. Change the properties of **Form1** to those described in Table 6.4, and save it as ISAM1.FRM. If you are creating the Paradox version of this project, change the **Connect** property as shown in the table. Make sure that the **DatabaseName** property of the **Data1** data control is set to the correct path of the CUSTOMER database (remember not to include the filename in the **DatabaseName** property, just the path). *If you installed the files from the distribution CD-ROM, make sure that you change the* **DatabaseName** *property of the data control to the correct directory path of the CUSTOMER.DBF dBASE database file.* When creating the text boxes for this form, create a control array. This is the easiest way to carry out this task:

✔ Create the Customer Number text box.

✔ Set the appropriate properties of the Customer Number text box as shown in Table 6.4. Set the Index property to 0, which tells Visual Basic that this control is a part of a control array.

✔ Copy the control to the Clipboard.

✔ Paste the text box to the form and make it the First Name text box by changing the DataField property as shown in the table.

✔ Continue to paste text boxes onto the form until you have all 10 necessary text boxes. Take care to use the text boxes in the correct order (Customer Number, First Name, Last Name, Address One, Address Two, City, State, Zip Code, Phone, and Fax) so that the Index property of each is correct.

Table 6.4. Objects and properties for the Customer form.

OBJECT	PROPERTY	SETTING
Form	Name	frmISAM1
	Caption	"Customer"
Data Control	Name	Data1
	Caption	"Customer"
	Connect (for dBASE)	"dBASE 5.0;"
	Connect (for Paradox)	"Paradox 5.x;"
	DatabaseName	"C:\VB5DBHT\CHAPTER.06"
	RecordSource	"Customer"

continued on next page

continued from previous page

OBJECT	PROPERTY	SETTING
Frame	Name	fraRecord
	Caption	" "
Text box	Name	txtData
	Index	0
	DataField	"CUSTNUM"
	DataSource	"Data1"
Text box	Name	txtData
	Index	1
	DataField	"FIRSTNAME"
	DataSource	"Data1"
Text box	Name	txtData
	Index	2
	DataField	"LASTNAME"
	DataSource	"Data1"
Text box	Name	txtData
	Index	3
	DataField	"ADDRESS1"
	DataSource	"Data1"
Text box	Name	txtData
	Index	4
	DataField	"ADDRESS2"
	DataSource	"Data1"
Text box	Name	txtData
	Index	5
	DataField	"CITY"
	DataSource	"Data1"
Text box	Name	txtData
	Index	6
	DataField	"STATE"
	DataSource	"Data1"
Text box	Name	txtData
	Index	7
	DataField	"ZIPCODE"
	DataSource	"Data1"
Text box	Name	txtData
	Index	8

OBJECT	PROPERTY	SETTING
	DataField	"PHONE"
	DataSource	"Data1"
Text box	Name	txtData
	Index	9
	DataField	"FAX"
	DataSource	"Data1"
Command button	Name	cmdAdd
	Caption	"&Add"
Command button	Name	cmdEdit
	Caption	"&Edit"
Command button	Name	cmdDelete
	Caption	"&Delete"
Command button	Name	cmdClose
	Caption	"Cl&ose"
	Cancel	True
	Default	True
Label	Name	lblCustomerNum
	Caption	"&Customer Num:"
Label	Name	lblFirstName
	Caption	"&First Name:"
Label	Name	lblLastName
	Caption	"&Last Name:"
Label	Name	lblAddressOne
	Caption	"Address &One:"
Label	Name	lblAddressTwo
	Caption	"Address &Two:"
Label	Name	lblCity
	Caption	"&City:"
Label	Name	lblState
	Caption	"&State:"
Label	Name	lblZipCode
	Caption	"&Zip Code:"
Label	Name	lblPhoneNum
	Caption	"&Phone Num:"
Label	Name	lblFaxNum
	Caption	"Fa&x Num:"

3. Put the following declarations in the declarations section of the form:

```
Option Explicit

' form-level variable used to hold the recordset

Private rs As Recordset

' private constant values used to indicate whether to Enable or Disable
' the text boxes

Private Const ENABLE = True
Private Const DISABLE = False
```

4. Now code the Form_Activate event. This code sets the form-level variable, rs, to the data control Recordset property, allowing you to manipulate the recordset in your project. This code also initializes the text boxes on the form to disabled, not allowing the user to edit the current record as of yet. Finally, if the recordset is empty, the EmptyRecordset routine will be called. We will code this routine later.

```
Private Sub Form_Activate()

    ' set form-level variable to data controls recordset
    Set rs = Data1.Recordset

    ' set text boxes to disabled on startup
    SetTextBoxes DISABLE

    ' if both end of file and beginning of file, then the recordset
    ' is empty
    With rs
        If (.EOF And .BOF) Then EmptyRecordset
    End With

End Sub
```

5. Add the code for the Add and Edit command button Click events. In the cmdAdd_Click event, the program tells the recordset to add another record. It is unnecessary to set the recordset to edit mode in the cmdEvent_Click event because the recordset is by default in edit mode. In both events, the text boxes are set to enabled so that the user can edit their contents.

```
Private Sub cmdAdd_Click()

    ' add new record to recordset, automatically clears text boxes
    rs.AddNew

    ' enable text boxes to allow editing
    SetTextBoxes ENABLE

End Sub
```

```
Private Sub cmdEdit_Click()

    ' recordset is always in edit mode, no need to set it

    ' enable text boxes to allow editing
    SetTextBoxes ENABLE

End Sub
```

6. The record delete code is a bit more involved. First the program sets the text boxes to disabled. Next, the application asks the user whether she is sure that she wants to delete the record. If the answer is yes, the record is deleted. The code that follows the **Delete** method checks whether the record is the last one in the recordset, and if it is, the **EmptyRecordset** routine is called.

```
Private Sub cmdDelete_Click()

    Dim nResponse As Integer

    ' set text boxes to disabled if they were in edit mode
    If (txtData(0).Enabled) Then SetTextBoxes DISABLE

    ' ask the user if she is sure that she wants to delete the record
    nResponse = MsgBox( _
                "Are you sure you want to delete " & CustomerName & " ?", _
                vbYesNo + vbQuestion, _
                "Delete?")

    ' if the response is yes, then delete the record
    If (nResponse = vbYes) Then

        With rs

            ' delete and move to the next record
            .Delete
            .MoveNext

            ' if the record pointer is past the last record, move back one
            ' and check if there are no longer any records in the recordset
            If (.EOF) Then
                .MovePrevious
                If (.BOF) Then EmptyRecordset
            End If

        End With

    End If

End Sub
```

7. Enter the following code for the **cmdClose_Click** and **Form_Unload** events to properly end the program. Always use **Unload Me** instead of simply using the **End** command. This technique ensures that the program is terminated correctly. You also should always set all objects to nothing before ending the application, in this case, the recordset object variable, rs. By putting the code for this in the **Form_Unload** event, you are guaranteed that it will be executed even if the user does not close the application by using the Close button on the form.

```
Private Sub cmdClose_Click()

    ' always use Unload Me instead of End
    Unload Me

End Sub

Private Sub Form_Unload(Cancel As Integer)

    ' it is good practice to set the recordset to nothing
    ' this is the equivalent to closing the recordset
    Set rs = Nothing

End Sub
```

8. The following code ensures that the Customer Number entered on the form is indeed a number. If it is not a numeric value, the user is notified and the focus is set to the **txtData(0)** text box control, selecting the currently entered value for the user.

```
Private Sub txtData_LostFocus(Index As Integer)

    ' if the Customer Num text box just lost focus, check to see
    ' if the value entered is valid
    If (Index = 0) Then CheckValidCustomerNumber

End Sub

Private Sub CheckValidCustomerNumber()

    ' if the Customer Name is not numeric, then do not allow the
    ' user to continue
    If (Not IsNumeric(txtData(0))) Then

        MsgBox "The Customer Number must be numeric to continue.", _
               vbOKOnly, _
               "Invalid Customer Number"

        ' select the current value in the text box
        With txtData(0)
            .SelStart = 0
            .SelLength = Len(.Text)
        End With

        ' make sure that all text boxes are enabled
        SetTextBoxes ENABLE

    End If

End Sub
```

9. When the user is adding a new record or editing the current record, he must click either the move first or the move last button of the data control for the information to be saved. By placing the following code in the **MouseDown** event of the data control, you cause the text boxes to be set to disabled to give the appearance that edit mode is off:

```
Private Sub Data1_MouseDown(Button As Integer, _
                          Shift As Integer, _
                          X As Single, _
                          Y As Single)

    ' set text boxes to disabled if they were in edit mode
    If (txtData(0).Enabled) Then SetTextBoxes DISABLE

End Sub
```

10. Now type the code for setting the text boxes to the correct state. If the state is enabled, set focus to the first text box on the form. This text box corresponds to the **Customer Number** field.

```
Private Sub SetTextBoxes(StateIn As Boolean)

    Dim nCount As Integer

    ' set all text boxes to desired state (ENABLE or DISABLE)
    For nCount = 0 To 9
        txtData(nCount).Enabled = StateIn
    Next nCount

    ' if text boxes are set to ENABLE (edit mode), set focus to the first
    If (StateIn = ENABLE) Then txtData(0).SetFocus

End Sub
```

11. The next routine returns the customer name of the current record on the form. If no name is specified, "the current record" is returned. This routine is called from the **cmdDelete_Click** event when the user is asked whether he is sure he wants to delete a particular record.

```
Private Function CustomerName() As String

    ' make name: last name first, first name last
    CustomerName = Trim$(txtData(2)) & ", " & Trim$(txtData(1))

    ' if there is no name, return 'the current record'
    If (CustomerName = ", ") Then CustomerName = "the current record"

End Function
```

12. Finally, enter the code for the **EmptyRecordset** routine. This code notifies the user that there are no longer any records in the Customer database, and asks the user whether she wants to create a new record. If the answer

is yes, the program calls the **cmdAdd_Click** event; otherwise, the
application ends itself by calling the **cmdClose_Click** event.

```
Private Sub EmptyRecordset()

    Dim nResponse As Integer

    ' ask the user if they would like to add a new record to the
    ' recordset
    nResponse = MsgBox( _
                "There are no more records in the Customer Database, " _
              & "would you like to create a new one?", _
                vbYesNo + vbQuestion, "Empty!")

    ' if the response is yes then add a new record; otherwise, close the
    ' application now
    If (nResponse = vbYes) Then
        cmdAdd_Click
    Else
        cmdClose_Click
    End If

End Sub
```

How It Works

Using the data control provides simplicity in programming because we can
bound text boxes to its recordset. A problem that occurs with the data control,
however, is that it cannot handle an empty recordset. As a matter of fact, even
with DAO you cannot use most methods with an empty recordset. If you were
to click a navigation button on the data control with an empty recordset, you
would get a message **No Current Record**.

To avoid this problem, we check the recordset to ensure that we trap every
occurrence of an empty recordset. In the **Form_Activate** event, we check to see
whether the recordset **EOF** and **BOF** properties are both true. If this is the case, we
have an empty recordset, and we call the **EmptyRecordset** routine to gracefully
handle the event.

A recordset can also become empty if the user deletes a record, and this is
why in the **cmdDelete_Click** event we check to see whether the recordset is
empty. Again, if this event occurs, we call the **EmptyRecordset** routine to ask the
user what to do next.

Errors can also occur if we move before the beginning of a recordset or
beyond the end of a recordset. For this matter, the data control is designed to
automatically move to the first record if it has moved before that record or move
to the last record if it has moved beyond that point.

A nice thing about the data control is the bounding of other controls to the
recordset data as we did with the text boxes in this project. When the user
decides to add a new record, all we have to do is call the recordset's **AddNew**
method. With this method, the Microsoft Jet engine creates a new record at the

end of the recordset with blank fields. Because the record pointer is at a new field, with no information, the text boxes that are bound to the control are cleared. The recordsets `Delete` method, however, is not as clean. When we delete a record using this method, the deletion does not actually take place until we move the record pointer to a new record. In this case, we move to the next record. This technique works fine unless there is not a next record to move to (indicated by a `True` value for `rs.EOF`). In this case, we have to back up by moving to the preceding record instead. If this still isn't good enough (meaning that we are now at the beginning of the file), we have an empty recordset once again, and we have to handle it by calling `EmptyRecordset`.

Editing in a data control is extremely easy because the data control is always in edit mode. All we have to do is change the information in a text box and move the record pointer to another location for the information to take effect. This task is left to the user in this project and can be done with a click of the data control. To add to the professionalism of this project, we have added a little spice to the edit mode. Instead of simply allowing the user to edit the text boxes at any time, by default the text boxes are disabled. The user must click the Edit button, and then the code enables the text boxes. It looks more impressive than it actually is.

Comments

When you are working with various external database formats, you need to keep various considerations in mind. First, when deleting FoxPro and Paradox records, you must take extra steps to successfully ensure the removal of information from the database. Second, Paradox databases require that more than one physical file exist per database. Lastly, data conversion is important to keep in mind when talking about databases from different vendors.

Deleting FoxPro and Paradox Records

When you delete a record in either a FoxPro or a Paradox database, the file is not physically deleted but instead is marked for deletion. This is how database files can grow to an excessive size even if there are no records in the database. The only way to physically remove the records from these files is to compact the database. Unfortunately, we cannot do this with the Jet engine—it must be done with a FoxPro or Paradox application.

Just because the records still physically exist in the database after we marked them for deletion does not mean that they have to show up in your application. As a matter of fact, by default they don't. If for some strange reason you decide to include deleted records in your view of a recordset, you can change the default. This is done again, through the Windows Registry. To allow records marked for deletion in your dBASE database to appear in your recordset, set the `Deleted` value in the `\HKEY_LOCAL_MACHINE\SOFTWARE\Microsoft\Jet\3.5\ Engines\Xbase` key to `False`. Setting it to `True`, in turn, does not allow the records to be viewed. Because a FoxPro database is also in Xbase format, the same key and values are used in its case as well.

Working with Paradox Database Files

It is important to know that with Paradox files comes a PX index file. This file stores the primary key for the Paradox database. Even though you might not be using indexes when accessing a Paradox database, you still need this file. Microsoft Jet cannot open a Paradox database without it. The PX index file should be located in the same directory as the database DB file.

Paradox databases are a little more complicated than others when they are used over a file server. For this matter, when you link or open a Paradox recordset that is on a file server and is shared by other users, you must set the `PardoxNetPath` option in `\HKEY_LOCAL_MACHINE\SOFTWARE\Microsoft\Jet\3.5\Engines\Paradox` key to the path of the PARADOX.NET file when using Paradox 3.x, or of the PDOXUSRS.NET file when using Paradox 4.x.

Data Conversion

Because each database type is different and is developed by a different manufacturer, most of the time the data types do not correctly match up with Microsoft Jet data types. Table 6.5 shows the conversion types between dBASE/FoxPro, Paradox, and Microsoft Jet data types.

Table 6.5. Data conversions for ISAM database files.

DBASE/FOXPRO TYPE	PARADOX TYPE	MICROSOFT JET TYPE
Character	Alphanumeric	Text
Numeric, Float, Currency, Double	Number, Currency, BCD	Double
	Short Number	Integer
Logical	Logical	Boolean
Date, DateTime	Date, Time, Timestamp	Date/Time
Memo	Memo	Memo
OLE	OLE	Long Binary
Integer	Long	
	Binary	Byte
	Autoinc	AutoNumber

COMPLEXITY
BEGINNING

6.2 How do I...
Access dBASE, FoxPro, and Paradox database files using data access objects?

Problem

I know that I can access dBASE, FoxPro, and Paradox databases using the data control, but I need greater functionality that the data control does not offer. How can I use data access objects to access these foreign database files?

Technique

The techniques used to open dBASE, FoxPro, and Paradox databases are very similar to those used when opening a Microsoft Access database. If you already know how to do this, it is going to be very easy for you to adapt to opening external ISAM data files.

To open a Microsoft Access database, you specify the database filename with the path of the file in the `OpenDatabase` method. This is accomplished by setting the database object as follows:

```
Set db = DBEngine.Workspaces(0).OpenDatabase(MSACCESS.MDB, False, False)
```

Here, *MSACCESS*.MDB is a Microsoft Access database file which includes the entire path of the file. The second parameter, `False`, indicates that the database will be opened in shared mode. The last parameter, also `False`, indicates that the database will be opened with read/write access.

To open a recordset within a Microsoft Access database, you specify the table name, query definition, or SQL statement in the `OpenRecordset` method of the database object as done here:

```
Set rs = db.OpenRecordset(RecordSetName, dbOpenTable)
```

Here, *RecordSetName* is a valid table name. If you were to open a query definition or SQL statement, you would use the `dbOpenDynaset` or `dbOpenSnapshot` flags rather than the `dbOpenTable` flag shown previously. Regardless, the recordset name within the database is specified in the `OpenRecordset` method.

When you're opening a dBASE, FoxPro, or Paradox database with DAO and the Microsoft Jet, the story is a little different. It starts with the concept that a database is a path. Instead of indicating the file path and database name, as with a Microsoft Access database, you must specify only the data file path. In addition to this, in the `Connect` string of the `OpenDatabase` method, you must indicate what ISAM type the database is to use. This ISAM type can be any of the following: dBASE III;, dBASE IV;, dBASE 5.0;, FoxPro 2.0;, FoxPro 2.5;, FoxPro 3.0;, Paradox 3.x;, Paradox 4.x;, or Paradox 5.x;. Consider the following example:

```
Set db = DBEngine.Workspaces(0).OpenDatabase("C:\VB5DBHT\CUSTOMER", _
                            False, False, "Paradox 5.x;")
```

Notice that only the database path is specified as the first argument in the OpenDatabase method and that the connect string contains a valid ISAM data type, Paradox 5.x;.

If you need to add a password to the connect string, you would do so like this:

```
Set db = DBEngine.Workspaces(0).OpenDatabase("C:\VB5DBHT\CHAPTER.06", _
                            False, False, "Paradox 5.x; PWD=PASSWORD")
```

PASSWORD is a valid password for the current user.

With the information that we have given the database object so far, the Microsoft Jet can now figure out how to open the correct ISAM data file. To tell the Jet engine which file to open, you do so in the OpenRecordset method as shown here:

```
Set rs = db.OpenRecordset("CUSTOMER", dbOpenTable)
```

CUSTOMER is a valid Paradox 5.x data file located in the C:\VB5DBHT\ CHAPTER.06 directory. There is no need to specify a file extension of DB or DBF for either Xbase or Paradox because the Microsoft Jet knows what file you are looking for now.

Steps

Open and run ISAM2.VBP, which displays the form shown in Figure 6.2. Use the four navigation buttons in the lower-left of the form to view the different records in the recordset. To add a button, click the Add button. To edit or delete a record, display the correct record on the form and click the corresponding button.

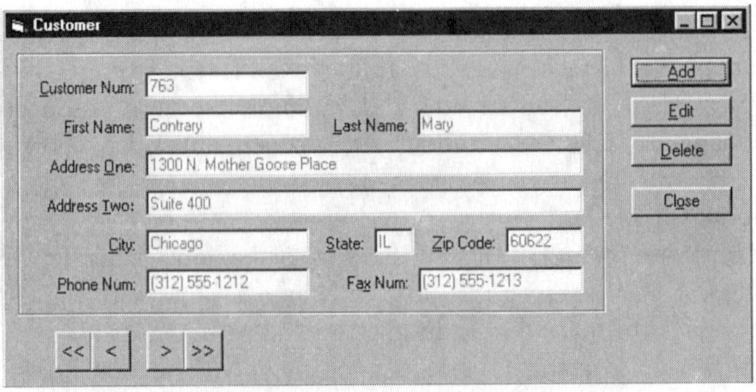

Figure 6.2. The ISAM2 project Customer form.

1. Make sure that the correct ISAM driver is installed in your Windows system directory and that the proper Windows Registry key points to the correct location of the DLL. For more information on IISAMs, see the beginning of this chapter and How-To 6.1.

2. Create a new project and call it ISAM2. Edit the objects and properties of the form as shown in Table 6.6. Make sure to create the four `cmdMove` buttons as a control array with indexes from **0** to **3**. When done, save the form as ISAM2.FRM.

Table 6.6. Objects and properties for the ISAM2 project.

OBJECT	PROPERTY	SETTING
Form	Name	frmISAM2
	Caption	"Customer"
Frame	Name	fraRecord
	Caption	" "
Text box	Name	txtData
	Index	0
Text box	Name	txtData
	Index	1
Text box	Name	txtData
	Index	2
Text box	Name	txtData
	Index	3
Text box	Name	txtData
	Index	4
Text box	Name	txtData
	Index	5
Text box	Name	txtData
	Index	6
Text box	Name	txtData
	Index	7
Text box	Name	txtData
	Index	8
Text box	Name	txtData
	Index	9
Command button	Name	cmdAdd
	Caption	"&Add"
Command button	Name	cmdEdit
	Caption	"&Edit"

continued on next page

continued from previous page

OBJECT	PROPERTY	SETTING
Command button	Name	cmdDelete
	Caption	"&Delete"
Command button	Name	cmdClose
	Caption	"Cl&ose"
	Cancel	True
	Default	True
Command button	Name	cmdMove
	Caption	"<<"
	Index	0
Command button	Name	cmdMove
	Caption	"<"
	Index	1
Command button	Name	cmdMove
	Caption	">"
	Index	2
Command button	Name	cmdMove
	Caption	">>"
	Index	3
Label	Name	lblCustomerNum
	Caption	"&Customer Num:"
Label	Name	lblFirstName
	Caption	"&First Name:"
Label	Name	lblLastName
	Caption	"&Last Name:"
Label	Name	lblAddressOne
	Caption	"Address &One:"
Label	Name	lblAddressTwo
	Caption	"Address &Two:"
Label	Name	lblCity
	Caption	"&City:"
Label	Name	lblState
	Caption	"&State:"
Label	Name	lblZipCode
	Caption	"&Zip Code:"
Label	Name	lblPhoneNum
	Caption	"&Phone Num:"
Label	Name	lblFaxNum
	Caption	"Fa&x Num:"

3. Enter the following variable and constant declarations in the declarations section of this project. The variables, **db** and **rs**, are the form-level variables for the database and recordset, respectively. These variables are accessible to all the routines in **frmISAM2**. The **m_bNeedToSaveRecord** Boolean variable stores a value indicating whether the current record is in edit mode. The **ENABLE** and **DISABLE** constants are used throughout the project to indicate whether the text boxes should be enabled or disabled.

```
Option Explicit

' form-level variables used to hold the database and recordset

Private db As Database
Private rs As Recordset

' form-level variable used to indicate if record is in edit mode

Private m_bNeedToSaveRecord As Boolean

' private constant values used to indicate whether to Enable and Disable
' the text boxes

Private Const ENABLE = True
Private Const DISABLE = False
```

4. Now add the following code for the **Form_Load** event. This code opens the database using the dBASE 5.0 **Connect** property and then opens the recordset using the CUSTOMER database file, as a table. The **DataPath** function is defined in the **INIFileReader** module, supplied with the installation CD-ROM, to define the location of the database.

```
Private Sub Form_Load()

    Dim sDBPath As String

    ' get path of database file
    sDBPath = DataPath & "\CHAPTER.06"

    ' open the database as a dBASE IV file, using database path
    Set db = DBEngine.Workspaces(0).OpenDatabase( _
            sDBPath, False, False, "dBase 5.0;")

    ' open the database file 'CUSTOMER' as a table
    Set rs = db.OpenRecordset("CUSTOMER", dbOpenTable)

End Sub
```

5. The code for the **Form_Activate** event checks whether the recordset is empty, calling **EmptyRecordset** if so. If there is at least one record in the recordset, the code will call the **DisplayCurrentRecord** to show the record.

```
Private Sub Form_Activate()

    ' if the recordset is empty, then call EmptyRecordset; otherwise,
    ' display the first record
    With rs
        If (.EOF And .BOF) Then
            EmptyRecordset
        Else
            DisplayCurrentRecord
        End If
    End With

End Sub
```

6. The code for the `cmdAdd_Click` event is more involved than that of
the code in How-To 6.1. First, if the application is in edit mode, the
program must save the current record. This is tested by checking the
`m_bNeedToSaveRecord` variable. After this is complete, the **AddNew** method
is called. Because we are not using the data control, the text boxes are not
automatically cleared for the new record, and therefore we must call the
`ClearTextBoxes` method. Next we set the flag to indicate that the
application is now in edit mode and enable the text boxes for editing.

```
Private Sub cmdAdd_Click()

    ' if the record needs to be saved before continuing, then do so
    If (m_bNeedToSaveRecord) Then SaveRecord

    ' set recordset to add a new record and clear the text boxes
    rs.AddNew

    ' clear the text boxes for new record
    ClearTextBoxes

    ' set flag to show that record must be saved
    m_bNeedToSaveRecord = True

    ' enable text boxes on form to allow editing
    SetTextBoxes ENABLE

End Sub
```

7. The code for the `cmdEdit_Click` event is very similar to that of
`cmdAdd_Click`. The only differences are that the recordset is set to edit
mode by calling the **Edit** method, and the text boxes are not cleared.

```
Private Sub cmdEdit_Click()

    ' if the record needs to be saved before continuing, then do so
    If (m_bNeedToSaveRecord) Then SaveRecord

    ' set recordset in edit mode
    rs.Edit
```

```
        ' set flag to show that record must be saved
        m_bNeedToSaveRecord = True

        ' enable text boxes on form to allow editing
        SetTextBoxes ENABLE

End Sub
```

8. Enter the `cmdDelete_Click` event code as shown next. In this routine, the text boxes are first disabled. Then if the current record has to be saved, the `SaveRecord` routine is called. The user is asked whether he is sure that he wants to delete the record, and if the answer is yes, the record is deleted. If the record was the last one in the recordset, the recordset is now empty, and `EmptyRecordset` is called. If records still remain, `DisplayCurrentRecord` is called because the record shown on the form is of the one that was deleted. The code moves to the next record if there is one; otherwise, to the previous record. Whichever one this is, it is displayed now.

```
Private Sub cmdDelete_Click()

    Dim nResponse As Integer

    ' set text boxes to disabled if they were in edit mode
    If (txtData(0).Enabled) Then SetTextBoxes DISABLE

    ' if the record needs to be saved before continuing, then do so
    If (m_bNeedToSaveRecord) Then SaveRecord

    ' ask the user if he is sure that he wants to delete the record
    nResponse = MsgBox( _
                "Are you sure you want to delete " & CustomerName & " ?", _
                vbYesNo + vbQuestion, _
                "Delete?")

    ' if the response is yes, then delete the record
    If (nResponse = vbYes) Then

        With rs

            ' delete and move to the next record
            .Delete
            .MoveNext

            ' if the record pointer is past the last record, move back one
            If (.EOF) Then .MovePrevious

            ' and check if there are no longer any records in the recordset
            If (.BOF) Then
                EmptyRecordset
            Else
                ' the recordset is not empty so show the current record
                DisplayCurrentRecord
```

continued on next page

continued from previous page
```
                End If

            End With

        End If

    End Sub
```

9. Now enter the code for the `cmdClose_Click` and `Form_Unload` events. This code properly ends the application by using `Unload Me` and ensures that the form-level object variables are set to nothing.

```
Private Sub cmdClose_Click()

    ' always use Unload Me instead of End
    Unload Me

End Sub

Private Sub Form_Unload(Cancel As Integer)

    ' it is good practice to set the recordset to nothing
    ' this is equivalent to closing the recordset and the database
    Set db = Nothing
    Set rs = Nothing

End Sub
```

10. Because we are not using the data control in this project, we must provide code for the navigation of the recordset. We do this with the four `cmdMove` buttons on `frmISAM2`. Enter the code for these buttons as shown next. The local constants defined correspond to each of the four buttons, representing their `Index` number. If the record has to be saved, `SaveRecord` is called, and the recordset is manipulated according to the button clicked. In the last two `If...Then` statements, the beginning-of-file (BOF) and end-of-file (EOF) are checked, as is the button clicked. The reason for this is that if the next button (">") is clicked at the end of a recordset, the recordset will be at the EOF, and must be moved back to the last record. This job is accomplished here. After the record position is changed, `DisplayCurrentRecord` is called to display the new record.

```
Private Sub cmdMove_Click(Index As Integer)

    ' local constants representing the navigation buttons on Form1
    Const MOVE_FIRST = 0
    Const MOVE_PREVIOUS = 1
    Const MOVE_NEXT = 2
    Const MOVE_LAST = 3

    ' if the record needs to be saved before continuing, then do so
    If (m_bNeedToSaveRecord) Then SaveRecord
```

```
' change position in the recordset, if MoveNext or MovePrevious
' has caused the record position to the EOF or BOF, then set the
' recordset to the Last or First record, respectively
If (Index = MOVE_PREVIOUS) Then rs.MovePrevious

If (Index = MOVE_NEXT) Then rs.MoveNext

If ((Index = MOVE_FIRST) Or (rs.BOF)) Then rs.MoveFirst

If ((Index = MOVE_LAST) Or (rs.EOF)) Then rs.MoveLast

' display the current record
DisplayCurrentRecord

End Sub
```

11. Enter the code to check for a valid **Customer Number** in the **txtData_LostFocus** event if the text box with an index of **0** was pressed. This text box corresponds to the **CUSTNUM** field in the recordset.

```
Private Sub txtData_LostFocus(Index As Integer)

' if the Customer Num text box just lost focus, check to see
' if the value entered is valid
If (Index = 0) Then CheckValidCustomerNumber

End Sub
```

12. The **SetTextBoxes** routine is used to set the text boxes to enabled or disabled, depending on whether the project is in edit mode. The **ClearTextBoxes** routine is used as it sounds, to clear the text boxes on the form when adding a new record. Both of these routines are coded as shown here:

```
Private Sub SetTextBoxes(value As Boolean)

Dim nCount As Integer

' set all text boxes to desired state (ENABLE or DISABLE)
For nCount = 0 To 9
    txtData(nCount).Enabled = value
Next nCount

' if text boxes are set to ENABLE (edit mode), set focus to the first
If (value = ENABLE) Then txtData(0).SetFocus

End Sub

Private Sub ClearTextBoxes()

Dim nCount As Integer

' clear all text boxes
For nCount = 0 To 9
```

continued on next page

continued from previous page

```
            txtData(nCount) = ""
    Next nCount

End Sub
```

13. The `DisplayCurrentRecord` routine takes the values from the current record and places them in the corresponding text boxes on the form. The text boxes are then disabled, and the **m_bNeedToSaveRecord** flag is set to `False`.

```
Private Sub DisplayCurrentRecord()

    Dim nCount As Integer

    ' set the text boxes to the correct field value
    ' by concatinating the empty string to the field value, NULL
    ' values will not cause errors
    For nCount = 0 To 9
        txtData(nCount) = "" & rs.Fields(nCount)
    Next nCount

    ' disable the text boxes from editing
    SetTextBoxes DISABLE

    ' no need to save record, we just got the new information
    m_bNeedToSaveRecord = False

End Sub
```

14. The following code saves the current record after checking for a numeric `Customer Number`. After the record is saved, it is displayed again with a call to `DisplayCurrentRecord`. When this routine is being called, the text boxes are disabled, prohibiting the user from making any changes to the record.

```
Private Sub SaveRecord()

    Dim nCount As Integer

    ' make sure that the Customer Num is valid
    CheckValidCustomerNumber

    ' set the fields to their text box values
    With rs

        For nCount = 0 To 9
            .Fields(nCount) = txtData(nCount)
        Next nCount

        ' make changes now by calling the Update method
        .Update

    End With
```

```
' display the current record
DisplayCurrentRecord

End Sub
```

15. Now enter the `EmptyRecordset` routine that asks the user whether she wants to add a new record. If the answer is yes, call the `cmdAdd_Click` event; otherwise, close the application by calling the `cmdClose_Click` event.

```
Private Sub EmptyRecordset()

    Dim nResponse As Integer

    ' clear the text boxes because recordset is empty
    ClearTextBoxes

    ' ask the user if she would like to add a new record to the
    ' recordset
    nResponse = MsgBox( _
                "There are no more records in the Customer Database, " _
            & "would you like to create a new one?", _
                vbYesNo + vbQuestion, "Empty!")

    ' if the response is yes, then add a new record; otherwise, close the
    ' application now
    If (nResponse = vbYes) Then
        cmdAdd_Click
    Else
        cmdClose_Click
    End If

End Sub
```

16. Now add the code to return the customer name of the current record in the recordset. As in How-To 6.1, this function returns the customer name if there is one; otherwise, it simply returns "the current record." This function is called from the `cmdDelete_Click` event when the user is being asked whether she wants to delete the record.

```
Private Function CustomerName() As String

    ' make name: last name first, first name last
    CustomerName = Trim$(txtData(2)) & ", " & Trim$(txtData(1))

    ' if there is no name, return 'the current record'
    If (CustomerName = ", ") Then CustomerName = "the current record"

End Function
```

17. To finish, enter the code for the `CheckValidCustomerNumber`, listed next. This routine checks to see whether a numeric value was entered for the customer number field.

```
Private Sub CheckValidCustomerNumber()

    ' if the Customer Name is not numeric, then do not allow the
    ' user to continue
    If (Not IsNumeric(txtData(0))) Then

        MsgBox "The Customer Number must be numeric to continue.", _
               vbOKOnly, _
               "Invalid Customer Number"

        ' select the current value in the text box
        With txtData(0)
            .SelStart = 0
            .SelLength = Len(.Text)
        End With

        ' make sure that all text boxes are enabled
        SetTextBoxes ENABLE

    End If

End Sub
```

How It Works

This How-To works almost identically to How-To 6.1, with a few exceptions. The most notable of these exceptions is that of displaying the records of the recordset. When you use the navigation buttons of a data control, the text boxes associated with the data control are automatically updated with the new records information. In this project, we implement our own navigation buttons because we are using DAO. When we move the record pointer to a new location, the old record remains displayed on-screen; therefore, we must update this information ourselves.

Our project calls the `DisplayCurrentRecord` routine in the `Form_Activate` event if the recordset is not empty. It also calls the `DisplayCurrentRecord` routine in the `cmdMove_Click` event when we move to a different record. Finally, we call this routine from the `cmdDelete_Click` routine when a record is deleted and should no longer be displayed on-screen.

To navigate through the CUSTOMER recordset, we have implemented a control array of command buttons to enable the user to move to the first record, the previous record, the next record, and the last record. A lot of responsibilities comes along with implementing this code "by hand." We must specify to move to the first record if we have moved to the beginning of the file and to move to the last record if we have moved to the end of the file. All of this checking is done automatically when the data control is used, but we have given up this luxury. The `BOF` and `EOF` properties of a recordset do not actually point to a record; they point to the location before the first and after the last, respectively.

In How-To 6.1, the user had to click either the move first or the move last VCR button on the data control to save edited information after invoking the

Edit or AddNew methods. In this How-To, we offer the luxury of clicking any button with the exception of Close, which acts as a cancel method, to save the current edited information. This is done with a check of the Boolean flag m_bNeedToSaveRecord in each of the command button Click events before continuing. If this flag is True, then the record is saved by calling the SaveRecord routine.

Again in this project, we disable the text boxes on the form so that the user cannot edit the currently selected record without clicking the Edit button. This ideology makes the program look more professional to the end user. When the Edit button is clicked, the record is saved if it was changed, and the Edit method of the recordset is called. The m_bNeedToSaveRecord flag is set to True so that the record will be saved before the display is changed later. Finally, the text boxes on the form are enabled for editing by calling SetTextBoxes with the argument ENABLE, a constant declared in the declarations section of this project.

Comments

When you use the data control in your Visual Basic application, you add a new record by calling the AddNew method of the data control. When you want to save the information for the record, you must click either the move first or the move last VCR buttons on the data control for your information to be saved. When you use data access objects in your Visual Basic application, you also use the AddNew method. The difference with DAO is that it is important to call the Update method before you move the record pointer of the recordset to successfully save your information.

COMPLEXITY
INTERMEDIATE

6.3 How do I...
Use indexes with dBASE, FoxPro, and Paradox files?

Problem

When I use dBASE, FoxPro, and Paradox database files, I want to locate particular records in a faster and more efficient manner than stepping through the records in the order in which they are stored in the database. How else can I locate particular records in a dBASE, FoxPro, or Paradox database file?

Technique

You already know that you can access a Microsoft Access database by using the Index property and the Seek method of a recordset. You can do the same with ISAM data files by using the Microsoft Jet engine. There are a couple of prerequisites to using indexes with an ISAM database, but after you get past them, you use the same procedures to set indexes and seek records as you would with a native Jet database.

When using Xbase data files (dBASE and FoxPro), you must have a setup information file for the use of indexes. This file has the extension INF. The first entry in this file is the ISAM type in brackets. In this case, we use [dBase 5.0]; however, you can easily change this to [FoxPro 3.0]. This file consists of a list of index files associated to a particular ISAM data file as shown here:

```
[dBase 5.0]
NDX1=CUSTNUM.NDX
NDX2=NAME.NDX
NDX3=STATE.NDX
NDX4=ZIPCODE.NDX
```

Here, *dBASE 5.0* is the desired ISAM to use when accessing these indexes. The prefix NDX# is an indication to the Jet engine that a dBASE index file follows. You can use the syntax

```
IDX1=CUSTNUM.IDX
```

for FoxPro ISAMs. In either case, for efficient use, the INF file should be located in the same directory as the database file itself.

After you have an INF file in the same directory as your ISAM database, you can continue to code your application as before. When you want to efficiently find a record based on an index, first set the **Index** property of the recordset, and then invoke the **Seek** method as shown here:

```
rs.Index = "CUSTNUM"
rs.Seek "=", CustNumber
```

CustNumber is a valid variable of the same type of the CUSTNUM index field. After this is done, you can check the NoMatch property of the recordset to see whether a valid record exists with your criteria. Consider the following piece of code:

```
If (rs.NoMatch) Then
    MsgBox "No record found."
Else
    DisplayCurrentRecord
End If
```

In this code, DisplayCurrentRecord is code that is to be run in the case of a match.

Steps

Open and run the ISAM3 project. You should see the form shown in Figure 6.3. This project has every feature that the project in How-To 6.2 did, with added functionality. This project offers the user the ability to seek records based on the indexes in the CUSTOMER data file. To search by an index, first select the index to use in the Index menu on the Customer form. After you have selected the proper index, click the Seek menu to enter values to search on based on your

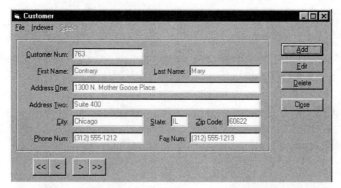

Figure 6.3. The Customer form of the ISAM3 project.

index choice. Changing the index also sorts the recordset based on your choice. You can return the recordset to its natural order by choosing Indexes | No Index from the menu. You can also view a list of indexes by choosing Index | View Indexes, revealing a list of the available indexes and their associated fields.

1. If you haven't done so already, check that the correct ISAM driver is installed in your Windows System directory and that the proper Windows Registry setting points to that driver. For information on installing ISAMs, see the beginning of this chapter and How-To 6.1.

2. Create a new project and call it ISAM3. Remove `Form1` from your project.

3. Copy ISAM2.FRM to ISAM3.FRM, and add this new file to your project. Rename the form `frmISAM3`. We will be using the same code as in ISAM2, with a few exceptions. These include menus, index functionality, and `Seek` methods.

4. Use the menu design window to create a menu for ISAM3.FRM with the captions and specifications shown in Table 6.7.

Table 6.7. Menu captions and specifications for `frmISAM3`.

CAPTION	NAME	INDEX
"&File"	mnuFile	
-"E&xit"	mnuFExit	
"&Indexes"	mnuIndexes	
-"&Customer Number"	mnuIIndex	0
-"Customer &Name"	mnuIIndex	1
-"&State"	mnuIIndex	2
-"&Zip Code"	mnuIIndex	3
-"N&o Index"	mnuIIndex	4

continued on next page

continued from previous page

CAPTION	NAME	INDEX
-"-"	mnuIBlank0	
-"&View Indexes"	mnuIViewIndexes	
"&Seek"	mnuSeek	

5. Add the form-level constants shown in bold to the declarations section of frmISAM3. These are used later in the project to represent the indexes of the indexes in the Index menu (got that?).

```
Option Explicit

' form-level variables used to hold the database and recordset

Private db As Database
Private rs As Recordset

' form-level variable used to indicate if record is in edit mode

Private m_bNeedToSaveRecord As Boolean

' private constant values used to indicate whether to Enable and Disable
' the text boxes

Private Const ENABLE = True
Private Const DISABLE = False

' private constant values for selected index

Private Const CUSTNUM = 0
Private Const CUSTNAME = 1
Private Const STATE = 2
Private Const ZIPCODE = 3
Private Const NO_INDEX = 4
```

6. Now add the last line in the Form_Load event next (shown in bold). This line initializes the CUSTOMER recordset to use no indexes.

```
Private Sub Form_Load()

    Dim sDBPath As String

    ' get path of database file
    sDBPath = DataPath & "\CHAPTER.06"

    ' open the database as a dBASE IV file, using database path
    Set db = DBEngine.Workspaces(0).OpenDatabase( _
            sDBPath, False, False, "dBase 5.0;")

    ' open the database file 'CUSTOMER' as a table
    Set rs = db.OpenRecordset("CUSTOMER", dbOpenTable)

    SetIndex NO_INDEX

End Sub
```

7. The following code, added to the `mnuFExit_Click` event, allows the user to exit the application from the File menu:

```
Private Sub mnuFExit_Click()

    ' exit the application
    cmdClose_Click

End Sub
```

8. The `mnuIIndex_Click` method returns an index to the menu item of its menu array. This array consists of the five possible index settings: `Customer Number`, `Customer Name`, `State`, `Zip Code`, and `No Index`. When the user selects an index from the menu, this code calls the `SetIndex` routine to take care of the details in selecting the new index. It is important to pass the `Index` variable to `SetIndex`, giving the routine the knowledge of which index to set.

```
Private Sub mnuIIndex_Click(Index As Integer)

    ' set the new index
    SetIndex Index

End Sub
```

9. Enter the following code for the `mnuIViewIndexes_Click` event. This routine uses the `TableDef` object of the database to read the collection of indexes included in the data file. The index names along with the fields that they represent are arranged in a local string that is passed to a `MsgBox` function, displaying them for the user to see.

```
Private Sub mnuIViewIndexes_Click()

    Dim nCurIndex As Integer
    Dim nNumIndexes As Integer
    Dim nIndNames As String

    ' access the table definitions of the CUSTOMER database
    With db.TableDefs("CUSTOMER")

        ' set number of indexes
        nNumIndexes = .Indexes.Count

        ' make sure that there is at least one index
        If (nNumIndexes > 0) Then

            ' loop through each index and add its information to the
            ' nIndNames string to be displayed

            For nCurIndex = 0 To nNumIndexes - 1

                With .Indexes(nCurIndex)
                    nIndNames = nIndNames _
```

continued on next page

continued from previous page

```
                                    & CStr(nCurIndex) & ": " _
                                    & .Name & " (" _
                                    & .Fields & ") " _
                                    & vbCr & vbCr

                End With

            Next nCurIndex

            ' show information
            MsgBox nIndNames, _
                    vbInformation, _
                    "CUSTOMER Table Index List"

        End If

    End With

End Sub
```

10. Enter the following code for the **mnuSeek_Click** event. This option is available only when the user has selected an index to seek by other than **No Index**. In this routine, the current index is retrieved through the **GetIndex** function defined later. Depending on this index, the application asks the user to enter a variable to seek by. In the case of the **Customer Name** index, two variables are necessary because the index is made up of the **LastName** and **FirstName** fields. If a record was found matching the criteria specified by the user, it is displayed; otherwise, a message notifying the user that a match was not found is displayed.

```
Private Sub mnuSeek_Click()

    ' local variables used to store values to be searched for
    Dim sSeekStr1 As String
    Dim sSeekStr2 As String

    Dim sMessage As String
    Dim nIndex As Integer

    ' get the current index and save it
    nIndex = GetIndex

    ' select appropriate sMessage for MsgBox and nIndex name
    Select Case nIndex

        Case CUSTNUM:
            sMessage = "Customer number to seek:"

        Case CUSTNAME:
            sMessage = "Customer last name to seek:"

        Case STATE:
            sMessage = "State to seek:"
```

```
        Case ZIPCODE
             sMessage = "Zip code to seek:"

    End Select

    ' ask the user for the search string
    sSeekStr1 = InputBox$(sMessage, "Customer List")

    ' if searching by customer name, must also ask for first name
    ' then seek record using values specified by user
    If (nIndex = CUSTNAME) Then

         sSeekStr2 = InputBox$( _
             "Customer First name to seek:", "Customer List")

         ' customer name uses two strings: First and Last
         rs.Seek "=", sSeekStr1, sSeekStr2

    Else

         ' all other indexes use one field in index
         rs.Seek "=", sSeekStr1

    End If

    ' notify the user if there are no matching records; otherwise,
    ' display the matching record
    If (rs.NoMatch) Then
        MsgBox "Record not found.", _
               vbExclamation, _
               "Customer List"
    Else
        DisplayCurrentRecord
    End If

End Sub
```

11. Enter the `GetIndex` routine shown next. This function walks through all
five possibilities of indexes selected. When a menu item with a check box
is encountered, the `GetIndex` function is assigned to its index number. We
ensure, in the `SetIndex` routine, that no more than one index is selected at
a time.

```
Private Function GetIndex() As Integer

    Dim nCount As Integer

    ' this code loops through all five possible indexes, and sets the
    ' Function to the index that was chosen
    For nCount = 0 To 4
        If (mnuIIndex(nCount).Checked) Then GetIndex = nCount
    Next nCount

End Function
```

12. Now enter the SetIndex routine. This is where the menu items' Check
properties, as well as the actual assignment of the index to the recordset,
are taken care of. Notice the code toward the bottom of this routine. If the
recordset supports bookmarks, which ours does, it saves the current
record position before setting the index. Afterward, the bookmark is set to
the old record. This ensures that the user still sees the same record on-
screen after selecting a new index. Without this code, it is possible that the
record pointer can move to a new location.

```
Private Sub SetIndex(Index As Integer)

    Dim vCurRecord As Variant
    Dim sIndName As String
    Dim nCount As Integer

    ' this loop sets all menu indexes to false, followed by setting the new
    ' index to checked
    For nCount = 0 To 4
        mnuIIndex(nCount).Checked = False
    Next nCount
    mnuIIndex(Index).Checked = True

    ' depending on the index number, choose the index name
    Select Case Index

        Case CUSTNUM:
            sIndName = "CUSTNUM"

        Case CUSTNAME:
            sIndName = "NAME"

        Case STATE:
            sIndName = "STATE"

        Case ZIPCODE
            sIndName = "ZIPCODE"

        Case NO_INDEX
            sIndName = ""

    End Select

    ' disable the seek option on the menu if no index has been chosen
    ' because the Seek method can only be used with indexes
    If (Index = NO_INDEX) Then
        mnuSeek.Enabled = False
    Else
        mnuSeek.Enabled = True
    End If

    ' this code changes the index of the recordset, but if the database
    ' supports bookmarks, it first saves the current record and reselects
    ' it after the change of indexes so that the user is still viewing the
    ' same record
```

```
With rs

    If (.Bookmarkable) Then vCurRecord = .Bookmark

    .Index = sIndName

    If (.Bookmarkable) Then .Bookmark = vCurRecord

End With

End Sub
```

How It Works

In this project, we implemented a menu to offer the user easy ways to exit the application, view indexes, set indexes, and seek by a particular chosen index. The other features, including navigation and modification of the recordset, were already included in How-To 6.2.

In the `mnuIViewIndexes_Click` event, a `TableDef` object of the database is used to reference the `Indexes` collection. With this collection, a string is created using the `Name` and `Fields` property of each index in the collection. This string is sent to a `MsgBox` function to display each index name and field list associated with it.

The `SetIndex` routine takes an index to a menu item as a parameter to set a new index. This new index can include the menu item represented by `No Index`. Selecting this index sets the recordset back to its default natural order by setting the `Index` property of the recordset to an empty string. Setting the index to any one of the valid indexes causes the recordset to be sorted on that index.

Finally, the `mnuSeek_Click` event is used to ask the user for proper values to seek for a record based on the index specified in the last call to `SetIndex`. This method of searching for particular records is much more efficient than using other methods such as `FindFirst`, which walks through every record in the recordset until something is found that matches its criteria. Using the `Seek` method utilizes the indexes that are a part of the database.

Comments

It should be noted that the `Seek` method can be used only when opening a recordset as a table (by using the `dbOpenTable` option). If you plan to use the `dbOpenDynaset` or `dbOpenSnapshot` options when opening a recordset, don't plan to use the `Seek` method. Unfortunately, because only recordsets opened as a table can use the `Seek` method, you cannot use the `Seek` method with attached tables. Attached tables cannot be opened as a table.

Using Indexes with Xbase Databases

As stated earlier in this section, you must have a correct INF file corresponding to your ISAM database file. You can not only specify ordinary index files in this INF file, but also specify unique indexes by using the prefix `U`, as shown here:

```
UNDX1=CUSTNUM.NDX      'for dBase

UIDX1=CUSTNUM.IDX      'for FoxPro
```

Here, `CUSTNUM`.NDX is a filename of a valid index file for a dBASE ISAM, or `CUSTNUM`.IDX is the filename of a valid index file for a FoxPro ISAM.

In addition to unique indexes, you can use the `MDX#` prefix when using dBASE IV and dBASE 5.0 multiple index files (files with the extension MDX). Consequently, FoxPro INF files can include combined index files (files with the extension of CDX) with the prefix of `CDX#`.

The best place to locate any ISAM INF file is in the same directory as the database itself. If this is not possible for some reason, you can alter the Windows Registry to tell the Jet engine to look in another location. You can do this for any Xbase ISAM by creating a new entry named `INFPath` as a string value in the `\HKEY_LOCAL_MACHINE\SOFTWARE\Microsoft\Jet\3.5\Engines\Xbase` key of the Windows Registry, containing the path of the INF file. For more information on the Windows Registry, see Chapter 12, "The Windows Registry and State Information."

Using Indexes with Paradox Databases

It is important to remember that with Paradox databases, a PX file must be associated with the database. This file contains the primary key of the Paradox database, which is necessary to simply access the data file. If a Paradox database has a PX file without a primary key, you cannot update it, nor view it in shared mode.

COMPLEXITY
INTERMEDIATE

6.4   How do I...
Access Excel worksheets using data access objects?

Problem

I have Excel worksheets that my company created. I need to incorporate this data into my own applications. I want to both display and manipulate the data from these Excel worksheets. How do I work with these Excel files in my Visual Basic projects?

Technique

By using the Microsoft Jet engine, you can access Excel worksheets as if they were actually Access databases. As with accessing other types of ISAM files with the Jet engine, there are a few restrictions with accessing Excel worksheets:

✔ You cannot delete rows.

✔ You cannot delete or modify cells that contain formulas.

✔ You cannot create indexes.

✔ You cannot read encrypted Excel files, even when using the correct password (`PWD` parameter) in the `Connect` string.

You can add records to a worksheet or edit standard cells (those without formulas).

When opening an ISAM database with the `OpenDatabase` method, you must provide a valid ISAM type. In addition to this, if you want to use the first row of the Excel document as field names, you can specify a parameter `HDR` equal to `Yes`. `HDR` stands for header. If you set `HDR` to `No`, the first row of the Excel worksheet is included as a record in the recordset, as in this example:

```
Set db = DBEngine.Workspaces(0).OpenDatabase("C:\VB5DBHT\" & _
                        "CHAPTER.06\EXCEL.XLS", _
                        False, False, "Excel 8.0; HDR=NO;")
```

Notice that when accessing Excel worksheets, unlike with other ISAM formats, you must specify the filename in the `OpenDatabase` method.

When opening a recordset from an Excel ISAM, you must specify the sheet name as the recordset name, followed by a dollar sign ($), as in this example:

```
WorkSheetName = "Sheet1"
Set rs = db.OpenRecordset(WorkSheetName & "$", dbOpenTable)
```

Here, `rs` is a recordset variable.

Steps

Open and run the ExcelDAO project. You should see a form that looks like the one shown in Figure 6.4. This application allows you to view a Microsoft Excel worksheet file in a list view control. If you click the Add or Edit buttons, the form expands, allowing you to edit the contents. Clicking OK or Cancel when editing a record either saves or discards your changes respectfully. By clicking the View in Excel button, you can view the worksheet in Microsoft Excel

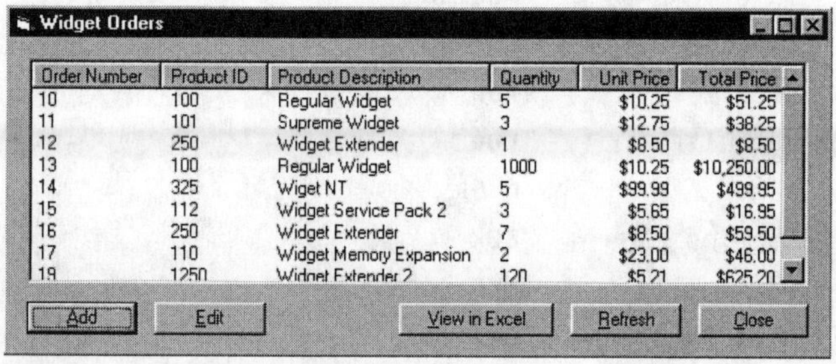

Order Number	Product ID	Product Description	Quantity	Unit Price	Total Price
10	100	Regular Widget	5	$10.25	$51.25
11	101	Supreme Widget	3	$12.75	$38.25
12	250	Widget Extender	1	$8.50	$8.50
13	100	Regular Widget	1000	$10.25	$10,250.00
14	325	Wiget NT	5	$99.99	$499.95
15	112	Widget Service Pack 2	3	$5.65	$16.95
16	250	Widget Extender	7	$8.50	$59.50
17	110	Widget Memory Expansion	2	$23.00	$46.00
19	1250	Widget Extender 2	120	$5.21	$625.20

Figure 6.4. The ExcelDAO project.

(assuming that you have Microsoft Excel; it is not included on the distribution CD-ROM with this book). If you make changes in Excel and click the Refresh button on the form, the list view control repopulates with the updates.

1. If you have not already installed the Excel IISAM, reinstall Visual Basic with the Custom Setup option, and specify the Excel IISAM in setup.

2. Create a new project and call it ExcelDAO.

3. Go to the Project | Components menu item in Visual Basic, and select Microsoft Windows Common Controls 5.0 from the list. This selection allows you to use the list view common control that comes with Windows 95.

4. Add the appropriate controls so that the form looks like that shown in Figure 6.5.

5. Edit the objects and properties of Form1, as shown in Table 6.8, and then save it as frmWidgetOrders.

Table 6.8. Objects and properties for the Widget Orders project.

OBJECT	PROPERTY	SETTING
Form	Name	frmWidgetOrders
	Caption	"Widget Orders"
	Height	3390
List view	Name	lstvWidgetOrders
	View	3 'vwReport
Command button	Name	cmdAdd
	Caption	"&Add"
Command button	Name	cmdEdit
	Caption	"&Edit"
Command button	Name	cmdView
	Caption	"&View in Excel"
Command button	Name	cmdRefresh
	Caption	"&Refresh"
Command button	Name	cmdClose
	Caption	"&Close"
	Cancel	True
	Default	True
Command button	Name	cmdOk
	Caption	"&Ok"
Command button	Name	cmdCancel
	Caption	"&Cancel"

OBJECT	PROPERTY	SETTING
Text box	Name	txtOrderNum
Text box	Name	txtProductID
Text box	Name	txtProductDesc
Text box	Name	txtQuantity
Text box	Name	txtUnitPrice
Label	Name	lblOrderNum
	Caption	"Order Num"
Label	Name	lblProductID
	Caption	"Product ID"
Label	Name	lblProductDesc
	Caption	"Product Description"
Label	Name	lblQuantity
	Caption	"Quantity"
Label	Name	lblUnitPrice
Caption	"Unit Price"	

6. Enter the following code in the declarations section of your project. The variables and constants included here are form level and can be accessed by any code within this form. The integer, m_nState, holds the value of one of the two constants defined. This variable states whether the user has selected to add a new record or edit the current one. The m_oSelItem object variable of type ComctlLib.ListItem is an object that holds the value of a selected item in the list view. The last two variables hold the path, filename, and worksheet name of the Excel file to be used in this project.

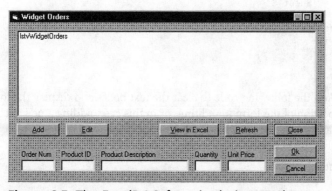

Figure 6.5. The ExcelDAO form in design mode.

```
Option Explicit

' form-level variables used to hold the database and recordset

Private db As Database
Private rs As Recordset

' form-level constant values used to indicate the current state

Private Const ADD_RECORD = 0
Private Const EDIT_RECORD = 1

' form-level variables used to save the current state, and selected
' list item

Private m_nState As Integer
Private m_oSelItem As ComctlLib.ListItem

' form-level variables used to store the file path and sheet name
' of the Excel file used in the app

Private m_sFilePath As String
Private m_sSheetName As String
```

7. Add the following code to the **Form_Activate** event to get the path and filename of the Excel XLS file to be used. This information is stored in the form-level variable **m_sFilePath**. The worksheet name is stored in the **m_sSheetName** form-level variable. Finally, the **PopulateListView** routine is called. This is where the file will be opened and read.

```
Private Sub Form_Activate()

    ' allow app to paint screen
    DoEvents

    ' get paths and names of files used in app
    m_sFilePath = DataPath & "\Chapter.06\WidgetOrders.xls"
    m_sSheetName = "Sheet1$"

    ' populate the list view control
    PopulateListView

End Sub
```

8. Add the following code to clear the text boxes and display the lower portion of the form for editing, or in this case, adding a new record. The last line of code sets the **m_nState** variable to **ADD_RECORD**, indicating that the user is adding a new record.

```
Private Sub cmdAdd_Click()

    ' clear all the text boxes
    txtOrderNum = ""
    txtProductID = ""
```

```
        txtProductDesc = ""
        txtQuantity = ""
        txtUnitPrice = ""

        ' show the bottom of the form and set the state to add so we know
        ' how to save the record later

        ShowBottomForm
        m_nState = ADD_RECORD

End Sub
```

9. The `cmdEdit_Click` event is used when the user wants to edit the current
record. The database will already be open from the `PopulateListView`
routine. This event walks through each record in the recordset until the
selected item's order number matches the record's order number. After the
record is found, the text boxes on the lower portion of the form are
populated with the values in the corresponding fields. The `Total Price`
field is left out because we are going to calculate it ourselves from the
given information. After the text boxes are populated, the form is
lengthened by the call to `ShowBottomForm`, and the `m_nState` variable is
set to `EDIT_RECORD`, indicating that the user has chosen to edit the current
record.

```
Private Sub cmdEdit_Click()

    ' we cannot use indexes with Excel files, so we must transverse the
    ' recordset until the record matches the selected item, then populate
    ' the text boxes with the records values
    With rs

        .MoveFirst

        While (.Fields("Order Number") <> m_oSelItem.Text)
            .MoveNext
        Wend

        txtOrderNum = .Fields("Order Number")
        txtProductID = .Fields("Product ID")
        txtProductDesc = .Fields("Product Description")
        txtQuantity = .Fields("Quantity")
        txtUnitPrice = .Fields("Unit Price")

    End With

    ' show the bottom of the form and set the state to editing so we know
    ' how to save the record later
    ShowBottomForm
    m_nState = EDIT_RECORD

End Sub
```

10. The `cmdView` command button allows the user to view the worksheet used in this project in Excel. To allow the user to view the file in Excel, the database must be closed first. This is done by setting the `rs` and `db` objects to nothing. The `Shell` command then calls Excel with the `m_sFilePath` variable, which holds the path and filename of the Excel worksheet. The `ExcelPath` function is included in the `ReadINIFile` module installed from the distribution CD-ROM.

```
Private Sub cmdView_Click()

    ' set the recordset and database to nothing because Excel will not be
    ' able to successfully open the file if not
    Set rs = Nothing
    Set db = Nothing

    ' open Excel with the file
    Shell ExcelPath & " " & m_sFilePath, vbNormalFocus

End Sub
```

11. If the user edits the worksheet in Excel while the Widget Orders project is open, the changes will not be apparent in the application. Use the Refresh button to repopulate the information from the worksheet. Enter the code for `cmdRefresh_Click`:

```
Private Sub cmdRefresh_Click()

    ' force a repopulation of the list view (use when the user has made
    ' changes in Excel to the file)
    PopulateListView

End Sub
```

12. Now enter the following code for the Close button and the `Form_Unload` event to successfully end the application:

```
Private Sub cmdClose_Click()

    ' always use Unload Me instead of End
    Unload Me

End Sub

Private Sub Form_Unload(Cancel As Integer)

    ' it is good practice to set all objects to nothing
    Set m_oSelItem = Nothing

    ' this is equivalent to closing the recordset and the database
    Set db = Nothing
    Set rs = Nothing

End Sub
```

13. The OK button is used to save the information after a user has edited the current record or added a new one. The event can determine the proper recordset method to use from the m_nState variable, either **AddNew** or **Edit**. The information for each field is saved, and the **Total Price** field is calculated from the **Unit Price** and the **Quantity**. After the save, the list view is repopulated, and the bottom of the form is hidden from the user. The code for the button is as follows:

```
Private Sub cmdOk_Click()

    ' edit or add new is confirmed, save the values of the text boxes
    ' this would be a good place to code validation for each field
    With rs

        If (m_nState = ADD_RECORD) Then
            .AddNew
        Else
            .Edit
        End If

        .Fields("Order Number") = txtOrderNum
        .Fields("Product ID") = txtProductID
        .Fields("Product Description") = txtProductDesc
        .Fields("Quantity") = txtQuantity
        .Fields("Unit Price") = txtUnitPrice
        .Fields("Total Price") = txtUnitPrice * txtQuantity

        .Update

    End With

    ' repopulate the listview with the changes, then hide the bottom of
    ' the form
    PopulateListView
    HideBottomForm

End Sub
```

14. The cmdCancel_Click event simply hides the bottom half of the form so that the user cannot edit the record. Because the recordset has not been set to **AddNew** or **Edit** yet, we need do nothing further.

```
Private Sub cmdCancel_Click()

    ' edit or add new was canceled, hide the bottom of the form
    HideBottomForm

End Sub
```

15. The following routines show the bottom of the form, hide the bottom of the form, and set the **Enabled** property of all input controls but the list view to the appropriate state:

```
Private Sub ShowBottomForm()

    ' lengthen the height of the form and enable the proper controls
    Me.Height = 4350
    SetObjects False

End Sub

Private Sub HideBottomForm()

    ' shorten the height of the form and enable the proper controls
    Me.Height = 3390
    SetObjects True

End Sub

Private Sub SetObjects(StateIn As Boolean)

    ' set Enabled property for controls on top of form
    cmdAdd.Enabled = StateIn
    cmdEdit.Enabled = StateIn
    cmdRefresh.Enabled = StateIn
    cmdView.Enabled = StateIn
    cmdClose.Enabled = StateIn

    ' set Enabled property for controls on bottom of form
    txtOrderNum.Enabled = Not StateIn
    txtProductID.Enabled = Not StateIn
    txtProductDesc.Enabled = Not StateIn
    txtQuantity.Enabled = Not StateIn
    txtUnitPrice.Enabled = Not StateIn
    cmdOk.Enabled = Not StateIn
    cmdCancel.Enabled = Not StateIn

End Sub
```

16. The `PopulateListView` routine is the core of this project because it opens the database and sets the worksheet to a recordset. This routine also reads the database `TableDefs` collection to define the column headers for the list view, as well as populate the entire list view with the recordset. This first part of the routine adds a column for each field in the `TableDefs(m_sSheetName).Fields` collection. The second part of the routine steps through each record in the recordset and adds a list item for each record. Enter the code for the `PopulateListView` routine:

```
Private Sub PopulateListView()

    Dim oField As Field
    Dim nFieldCount As Integer
    Dim nFieldAlign As Integer
    Dim nFieldWidth As Single
    Dim oRecItem As ListItem
    Dim sValFormat As String
```

```
' this might take a noticeable amount of time, so before we do anything
' change the mouse pointer to an hourglass and then hide the bottom of
' the form
Screen.MousePointer = vbHourglass
HideBottomForm

' open the database (this might already be open; however, if the user
' has just started the app or selected the 'View in Excel' button, then
' the database and recordset would be set to nothing
Set db = OpenDatabase(m_sFilePath, False, False, "Excel 8.0;HDR=YES;")
Set rs = db.OpenRecordset(m_sSheetName)

With lstvWidgetOrders

    ' clear the list view box in case this is a refresh of the records
    .ListItems.Clear

    ' using the For Each statement as compared to the For To statement
    ' is technically faster, as well as being easier to understand and
    ' use
    For Each oField In db.TableDefs(m_sSheetName).Fields

        ' align currency fields to the right, all others to the left
        nFieldAlign = IIf((oField.Type = dbCurrency), _
                    vbRightJustify, _
                    vbLeftJustify)

        ' our product description field is text, and the values in this
        ' field are generally longer than their field name, so increase
        ' the width of the column
        nFieldWidth = TextWidth(oField.Name) _
                    + IIf(oField.Type = dbText, 500, 0)

        ' add the column with the correct settings
        .ColumnHeaders.Add , , oField.Name, _
                        nFieldWidth, _
                        nFieldAlign

    Next oField

End With

' add the records
With rs

    .MoveFirst

    While (Not .EOF)

        ' set the new list item with the first field in the record
        Set oRecItem = lstvWidgetOrders.ListItems.Add(, , _
                                        CStr(.Fields(0)))
        ' now add the rest of the fields as subitems of the list item
        For nFieldCount = 1 To .Fields.Count - 1

            ' set a currency format for fields that are dbCurrency type
```

continued on next page

continued from previous page

```
                    sValFormat = IIf(.Fields(nFieldCount).Type = dbCurrency, _
                                "$#,##0.00", _
                                "")

            ' set the subitem
            oRecItem.SubItems(nFieldCount) = _
                        Format$("" & .Fields(nFieldCount), sValFormat)

        Next nFieldCount

        .MoveNext

    Wend

End With

' by setting the last record item to the selected record item form
' variable, we can assure ourselves that a record is selected for
' editing later
Set m_oSelItem = oRecItem

' remember to set object variables to nothing when you are done
Set oRecItem = Nothing
Set oRecItem = Nothing

Screen.MousePointer = vbDefault

End Sub
```

How It Works

In this project, an Excel worksheet file is opened and used to create a recordset object to populate a list view control. The code for accessing the recordset is the same as that of accessing Microsoft Access databases, using **AddNew** and **Edit** to alter the underlying ISAM data file. However, Excel worksheet rows cannot be deleted; therefore, the **Delete** method of a recordset is unavailable.

In the **PopulateListView** routine, the project uses the **TableDef** object of the database object to access the table definition of the Excel worksheet. Within this object, there is a collection of fields that the project loops through, adding a column header for each, using the fields' **Name**, **Width**, and **Align** properties.

After the column header collection of the list view is populated with the field names in the Excel worksheet, the list view control is populated with the records. Accessing these records is the same as accessing other Jet database records. A list item is set for each record with the first field of the record. After this, the subitems of the list item are populated with the remaining fields in the current record.

This application also uses a trick to gain more space when necessary. The form is elongated when either the Add button or the Edit button is clicked, allowing room for a record editing area. After the record is saved or canceled, the form resumes its normal size.

Another feature of this project is the ability to view the worksheet in Excel by using the **Shell** method to start another application. By using this option, the user can load a worksheet, edit its changes, and then switch to Excel to see the results. Even if the user changes the worksheet within Excel while the project is still running, as long as the file is saved and the user clicks the Refresh button, the list view control will be repopulated with the correct, up-to-date information.

Comments

It is possible to open ranges of an Excel worksheet using the Microsoft Jet Engine. To do this, replace the worksheet name in the **OpenRecordset** method with the range of cells you want returned, as in this example:

```
Set rs = db.OpenRecordset("B1:H12")
```

In this example, *"B1:H12"* is the range you want to create a recordset on, from the specified Excel worksheet.

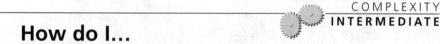

COMPLEXITY
INTERMEDIATE

6.5 How do I...
Access Btrieve files?

Problem

My company uses an accounts receivable program that stores all its data in Btrieve format. I need to access this data from my Visual Basic applications, and it is not practical to convert the files each time to an Access database. I know that I can access dBASE, FoxPro, and Paradox database files easily with a data control, but how do I do this with Btrieve files?

Technique

Btrieve is a database engine used to create and maintain indexed data files for use by applications written in a language such as C, Pascal, or Basic. Although you could write an application to access Btrieve database file via its application programming interface (API), it is much easier to use the Jet database engine to access the data as you would a Microsoft Access, dBASE, FoxPro, or Paradox database.

Figure 6.6 shows the components necessary for your Visual Basic application to use Btrieve files through the Jet database engine. Your application uses Visual Basic to access the Jet database engine, which in turn calls the routines in BTRV200.DLL to interfere with the runtime components of Btrieve, which are contained in WBTRCALL.DLL.

Data Definition Files

A Btrieve file contains the data and information it needs to create indexes to the data, but Btrieve regards the data itself as a stream of meaningless bytes with certain ranges within the stream defined to form indexes. A Btrieve file contains no information about the meaning of the data itself (meaning that no definitions of fields or data types are known). A Btrieve data file is, therefore, unlike Xbase or Paradox data files, which maintain complete information about data fields and data types. Applications that use the Btrieve data files, therefore, need a source of intelligence about the format and type of data in the Btrieve file.

This sort of intelligence comes from DDF files, or *data definition files*, which are binary files. The Jet engine requires two separate data definition files, FILE.DDF and FIELD.DDF. (The third data definition file shown in Figure 6.6 is required only if your program will create or delete Btrieve indexes.) FILE.DDF includes the fully qualified pathnames of all the files that make up a Btrieve database—the data files plus FIELD.DDF and INDEX.DDF. The second data definition file, FIELD.DDF, describes the fields within individual files.

DatabaseName

Like that of an Excel ISAM data file, the **DatabaseName** property with a Btrieve file does consist of the actual filename and the file directory path. For example, your **DatabaseName** property to the orders database FILE.DDF might be

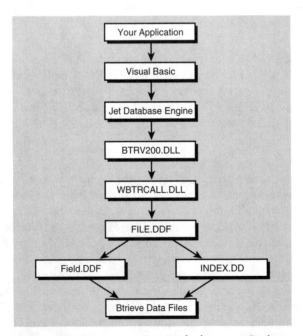

Figure 6.6. Components needed to use Btrieve data files.

`C:\VB5DBHT\FILE.DDF`. Because FILE.DDF contains not only the filenames but also their paths, the data files themselves can be in any directory, or can even be in more than one directory. However, the files must be in the directories named in FILE.DDF; if you move the files, you must update FILE.DDF, and you will need a DDF file utility program like Xtrieve or Ddtrieve to accomplish that task.

A Btrieve data file has no default extension, although convention tends to support both DAT and BTR as commonly used extensions.

BtrieveOptions in Initialization Files

BTRV200.DLL needs to have certain Btrieve options set to access Btrieve files. For version 5.1x, BTRV200.DLL looks in WIN.INI for the options setting. For version 6.x, it looks in either NOVDB.INI or BTI.INI. Whichever file is used, it should have a section with the following entry:

```
[BTRIEVE]
Options=/m:64 /p:4096 /b:16 /f:20 /l:40 /n:12 /t:C:\DB\BTRIEVE.TRN
```

Steps

Open and run the BtrieveDBC project. You should see the form shown in Figure 6.7. The BtrieveDBC project allows you to view, add, edit, and delete records from the Btrieve database, ORDERS. Click the Add button to clear the text boxes and add a new record. To edit or delete records, navigate to the desired record and then click the selected button. When saving changes to a new or an existing record, be sure to click either the move first or the move last button on the data control for your changes to take place.

1. If you have not already installed the Btrieve IISAM, either do it now or contact Btrieve for the correct IISAM. If you want to create this project using the Paradox version of the database, change the **Connect** property of the data control to **Paradox 5.x;**.

2. Start a new project and name it BtrieveDBC. Add the objects and properties listed in Table 6.9, and save it as Orders.frm.

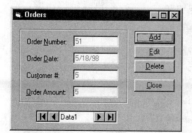

Figure 6.7. The BtrieveDBC project.

Table 6.9. Objects and properties for the BtrieveDBC project.

OBJECT	PROPERTY	SETTING
Form	Name	frmOrders
	Caption	"Orders"
Data control	Name	Data1
	Connect	"Btrieve;"
	DatabaseName	"C:\VB5DBHT\CHAPTER.06"
	RecordSource	"ORDERS"
Frame	Name	fraRecord
	Caption	""
Text box	Name	txtOrderNumber
	DataField	"Order Number"
	DataSource	"Data1"
Text box	Name	txtDateOrderd
	DataField	"Order Date"
	DataSource	"Data1"
Text box	Name	txtCustomerNumber
	DataField	"Customer Number"
	DataSource	"Data1"
Text box	Name	txtOrderAmount
	DataField	"Order Amount"
	DataSource	"Data1"
Command button	Name	cmdAdd
	Caption	"&Add"
Command button	Name	cmdEdit
	Caption	"&Edit"
Command button	Name	cmdDelete
	Caption	"&Delete"
Command button	Name	cmdClose
	Caption	"&Close"
	Cancel	True
	Default	True
Label	Name	lblOrderNumber
	Caption	"Order &Number:"
Label	Name	lblOrderDate
	Caption	"Order &Date:"

OBJECT	PROPERTY	SETTING
Label	Name	lblCustomerNumber
	Caption	"&Customer Number:"
Label	Name	lblQuantity
	Caption	"&Order Amount:"

3. Add the following code to the declarations section of your project. The **rs** object variable will represent the recordset of the data control and can be accessed by any code in the **frmOrders**. You could replace all instances of **rs** with **Data1.Recordset**, but using a form-level object variable increases readability and decreases maintenance.

```
Option Explicit

' form-level variable used to hold the recordset

Private rs As Recordset

' private constant values used to indicate whether to Enable or Disable
' the text boxes

Private Const ENABLE = True
Private Const DISABLE = False
```

4. Add the following code to the **Form_Activate** event to assign the **rs** object variable to the **Recordset** property of the **Data1** data control. The code then sets the text boxes to a default value of disabled and checks for an empty recordset by looking at the **EOF** and **BOF** recordset properties. If both of these properties are true, the record pointer does not point to a record, and the recordset is empty.

```
Private Sub Form_Activate()

    ' set form-level variable to data controls recordset
    Set rs = Data1.Recordset

    ' set text boxes to disabled on startup
    SetTextBoxes DISABLE

    ' if both end of file and beginning of file, then the recordset
    ' is empty
    With rs
        If (.EOF And .BOF) Then EmptyRecordset
    End With

End Sub
```

5. Now enter the code for the Add button here. The first thing this routine does is enable the text boxes for editing. After this, it calls the **AddNew**

method of the recordset, creating a new record at the end of the database and clearing all the bound text boxes. This routine also puts the current date into the **txtOrderDate** text box to help the user.

```
Private Sub cmdAdd_Click()

    ' enable text boxes to allow editing
    SetTextBoxes ENABLE

    ' add new record to recordset, automatically clears text boxes
    rs.AddNew
    txtOrderDate = Format$(Now, "MM/DD/YY")

End Sub
```

6. Because data controls are by default in edit mode, you need call no special method to begin an editing process. However, we have disabled the text boxes on the form to prevent the user from editing the record without first clicking the Edit button, shown here, to enable the text boxes.

```
Private Sub cmdEdit_Click()

    ' recordset is always in edit mode, no need to set it
    ' enable text boxes to allow editing
    SetTextBoxes ENABLE

End Sub
```

7. Clicking the Delete button causes a **cmdDelete_Click** event to occur. In this event, shown next, the user is asked whether he is sure that he wants to delete the current record. If the answer is yes, the record is deleted with the **Delete** method of the recordset. The changes to the recordset do not take place until the record pointer is changed, so the routine then moves to the next record. If no next record exists, the record pointer is set to the previous record. If there still is no record, there is an empty recordset and the **EmptyRecordset** routine is called. If a record does exist at the new record pointer location, it is automatically shown in the data bound text boxes.

```
Private Sub cmdDelete_Click()

    Dim nResponse As Integer

    ' set text boxes to disabled if they were in edit mode
    If (txtOrderNumber.Enabled) Then SetTextBoxes DISABLE

    ' ask the user if he is sure that he wants to delete the record
    nResponse = MsgBox( _
                "Are you sure you want to delete this record?", _
                vbYesNo + vbQuestion, _
                "Delete?")
```

```
        ' if the response is yes, then delete the record
    If (nResponse = vbYes) Then

        With rs

            ' delete and move to the next record
            .Delete
            .MoveNext

            ' if the record pointer is past the last record, move back one
            ' and check if there are no longer any records in the recordset
            If (.EOF) Then
                .MovePrevious
                If (.BOF) Then EmptyRecordset
            End If

        End With

    End If

End Sub
```

8. Enter the following code for the **Data1_MouseDown** event. This code changes the **Enabled** property to false when you click on the data control with the mouse.

```
Private Sub Data1_MouseDown(Button As Integer, _
                    Shift As Integer, _
                    X As Single, _
                    Y As Single)

    ' set text boxes to disabled if they were in edit mode
    If (txtOrderNumber.Enabled) Then SetTextBoxes DISABLE

End Sub
```

9. Now enter the **cmdClose_Click** and **Form_Unload** events to end the application. By placing the code for setting the recordset to nothing in the **Form_Unload** event, you are guaranteeing that it will be executed, even if the application is terminated by something other than the Close button.

```
Private Sub cmdClose_Click()

    ' always use Unload Me instead of End
    Unload Me

End Sub

Private Sub Form_Unload(Cancel As Integer)

    ' it is good practice to set the recordset to nothing
    ' this is the equivalent to closing the recordset
    Set rs = Nothing

End Sub
```

10. Enter the `SetTextBoxes` routine, which simply sets the value of the
`Enabled` property of the text boxes to a desired state. If they are enabled,
the focus is set to the first one, `txtOrderNumber`.

```
Private Sub SetTextBoxes(ValueIn As Boolean)

    txtOrderNumber.Enabled = ValueIn
    txtOrderDate.Enabled = ValueIn
    txtCustomerNumber.Enabled = ValueIn
    txtOrderAmount.Enabled = ValueIn

    ' if text boxes are set to ENABLE (edit mode), set focus to the first
    If (ValueIn = ENABLE) Then txtOrderNumber.SetFocus

End Sub
```

11. Finally, enter the code for the `EmptyRecordset` routine, which is called
when there are no longer any records left in the recordset:

```
Private Sub EmptyRecordset()

    Dim nResponse As Integer

    ' ask the user if he would like to add a new record to the
    ' recordset
    nResponse = MsgBox( _
                "There are no more records in the Orders Database, " _
              & "would you like to create a new one?", _
                vbYesNo + vbQuestion, _
                "Empty!")

    If (nResponse = vbYes) Then
        cmdAdd_Click
    Else
        cmdClose_Click
    End If

End Sub
```

How It Works

The four text boxes in this How-To are bound to the `Data1` data control and
react to the methods and properties that are set on that control. When a new
record is added by calling `AddNew`, the Jet engine creates an empty record at the
end of the recordset, and the text boxes are updated with the empty
information. When we navigate to a new record using the data control's VCR
buttons, the text boxes that are bound to the control change in accordance with
the recordset's record pointer.

It should be noted that although we accessed a Btrieve data definition file in
this How-To, the same techniques were used throughout this chapter regardless

of which ISAM data file was being used. This is the beauty of the Microsoft Jet engine.

Comments

Your Visual Basic program cannot use Btrieve data files without FILE.DDF and FIELD.DDF. Another data definition file, INDEX.DDF, may be present. INDEX.DDF maintains information about the indexes of the files named in FILE.DDF. If your application plans to add or remove indexes, these changes should be recorded in INDEX.DDF. You can control how your Visual Basic application uses INDEX.DDF through the `IndexDDF` property setting in the `[Btrieve ISAM]` section of VB.INI.

If the `IndexDDF` property in the `[Btrieve ISAM]` is `Require`, Visual Basic requires INDEX.DDF to be in the database directory with FILE.DDF and FIELD.DDF. If the property is `Maintain`, Visual Basic updates INDEX.DDF when an index is created or deleted and generates an error message if it cannot find INDEX.DDF. If the property is `Ignore` (which is the default), Visual Basic doesn't care whether the file exists and makes no attempt to update it.

NOTE

Btrieve is marketed and supported by Btrieve Technologies, Inc., 5918 West Courtyard Drive, Suite 400, Austin, TX 78730 (1-800-BTRIEVE).

Data Format Conversions

Btrieve supports a very large number of data formats. Table 6.10 lists these formats and shows how each is converted to a Visual Basic data type. Note that any Btrieve field that exceeds 255 bytes is treated as a Visual Basic Memo field.

Table 6.10. Btrieve to Visual Basic data conversions.

BTRIEVE DATA TYPE	VISUAL BASIC/MICROSOFT ACCESS DATA TYPE
Date, time	Date/Time
Float or bfloat (4-byte)	Number (FieldSize = Single)
Float or bfloat (8-byte), decimal, numeric	Number(FieldSize = Double)
Integer (1-, 2-, or 4-byte)	Number (FieldSize = Byte, Integer, or Long Integer)
Logical, bit	Yes/No
Lvar	OLE Object
Money	Currency
Note	Memo
String, lstring, zstring	Text

CHAPTER 7
CONNECTING TO AN
ODBC SERVER

7

CONNECTING TO AN ODBC SERVER

How do I...

The Open Database Connectivity (ODBC) standard has made accessing disparate database formats much easier than it was in older versions of Visual Basic. Starting with version 3.0, Visual Basic data access methods and properties include built-in support for ODBC data sources. This means you can use Visual Basic and ODBC together, either through the Jet database engine that comes with Visual Basic or through direct calls to the ODBC API, or by using both together.

When using Visual Basic to completely handle the connection to the ODBC system, you just make a few changes to the Visual Basic `OpenDatabase` method. This is the syntax of this statement:

```
Set database = workspace.OpenDatabase(dbname[, exclusive[, read-only[, _
    source]]])
```

The source argument is the main difference when you're using ODBC. In the How-To's throughout this chapter, you'll see how an ODBC connect string is used in the source to specify to which ODBC data source to connect. If you're not sure which data source you want to use, just make the source argument "ODBC" and Visual Basic will team up with ODBC and automatically present a list of the available data sources. Few things in Visual Basic are as straightforward as this.

You can perform a lot of ODBC tasks—including running SQL queries, retrieving results, looping through recordsets, and sending pass-through queries—in Visual Basic without getting any more involved in ODBC than making this change to the `OpenDatabase` method. Essentially, if Visual Basic has a data access method or property to do what you want, you almost always can use Visual Basic directly without knowing anything about ODBC beyond the existence of the data source you want to use.

ODBC can add a whole new dimension to your application's database access, going far beyond the functionality of Visual Basic's data access function. You can retrieve a wealth of information about a dataabase and manipulate it to your heart's—or client's—content.

Through the How-To's in this chapter, you'll get the details of using straight Visual Basic to access the ODBC API, using the ODBC API directly and bypassing Visual Basic, and combining the two techniques to get the job done.

The guiding philosophy of this chapter is that if there is a way to do it in Visual Basic, that's the way it should be done—unless there is a good reason not to do it that way. The main reason for going straight to the ODBC API is when Visual Basic can't perform the particular task by itself. But there are a few other reasons you'll see along the way.

Using Visual Basic and ODBC Together

If you are going to do any serious work with ODBC, get a copy of *Microsoft ODBC 3.0 Programmer's Reference and SDK Guide*, published by Microsoft Press. The SDK has all the detailed information you need and a list of all the ODBC functions. This section covers most of the details you'll need in order to use ODBC with Visual Basic.

The ODBC system has four components. Figure 7.1 shows the relationship of these four elements in a Visual Basic ODBC application.

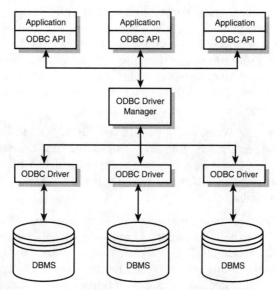

Figure 7.1. An overview of ODBC architecture.

✔ *Application:* This is your application program. Whether it makes calls through the Visual Basic data access methods and properties or makes direct calls to the ODBC API, the application sends SQL statements to ODBC and receives data as the results of those statements.

✔ *ODBC Driver Manager:* The ODBC Driver Manager is the layer of the ODBC system that sits between your application and the database driver. Some of the ODBC API calls are handled directly by the Driver Manager, but many are passed on to the driver. For some functions, the Driver Manager passes the call on to the driver if the function is implemented in the driver; if not, the Driver Manager handles the task itself.

✔ *Driver:* An ODBC driver is software, virtually always a dynamic link library (DLL), that handles the connection between the ODBC Driver Manager and the database server. A driver is usually written by the manufacturer of a database system, but many drivers are available from third parties.

✔ *Data source:* An installed database server that ODBC has associated with a particular ODBC driver and a specific database with its location on your local hard drive or network.

Following are a few other terms you'll encounter when reading about the ODBC system:

✔ *Connect string:* To make a connection to an ODBC data source, the ODBC system needs certain information. The first piece of information it always needs is the *data source name,* or DSN. This is the descriptive name ODBC uses to keep track of installed databases, and it is used any time you are presented with a list of data sources. The connect string varies by database, driver, and your network setup, but a typical string would be the data source name, user ID, password, and authorization string. The particular database server might have other required and optional items. In How-To 7.5, you'll see how to find out exactly what connect string a database requires.

✔ *Translator:* When you've worked with ODBC for a while, you'll probably encounter the term *translator*. A translator translates data flowing through the ODBC system. A common use is to translate between different character sets, such as between ASCII and EBCDIC on IBM mainframes and minis.

✔ *ODBC input and output buffers:* ODBC requires the use of input and output buffers to hold data it passes back and forth between the database and your application. The good news is that in most cases in Visual Basic, you won't be calling any ODBC API functions directly that need to have a buffer allocated. More good news is that a null pointer to a buffer sometimes works. The really good news is that Visual Basic, through the Jet engine, manages all this for you most of the time.

ODBC Handles

Before making any direct calls to functions in the ODBC API, you must allocate memory and receive a handle from ODBC for the particular operation. All this means is that ODBC is setting aside a small chunk of memory, through its DLL, to hold information about some aspect of the ODBC system. The handle is essentially a pointer in the Windows environment. As usual, if you are using ODBC through Visual Basic methods only, without direct calls to the ODBC API, you don't need to know or worry about handles at all.

Three handles are needed for calls to the different ODBC functions:

✔ *Environment handle (hEnv):* Your application needs to allocate and use one environment handle. The environment handle is used to manage the overall connection between your application and ODBC.

✔ *Connection handle (hDbc):* For each connection you make to a database, you must allocate and use one connection handle. Your application can have virtually any number of connection handles at any given time, and many databases can even have multiple simultaneous handles to a single data source.

✔ *Statement handle (hStmt):* For each SQL statement you send to a database, you must allocate and use a statement handle. The statement handle is how ODBC keeps straight what statement you are referring to for information. You can also have multiple statement handles active at any given time.

All ODBC handles must be released before terminating your application. Otherwise, there is no guarantee that the allocated memory will be released at the end of the application, and that is just not good Windows program manners! Eventually, the program will "leak" enough memory to cause performance problems with Windows, or even disrupt the operating system entirely.

The handles form a hierarchy. All connection handles in your application are associated with a single environment handle, and all statement handles are associated with one and only one connection handle. In general, all the lower-level handles in the hierarchy must be freed before the next handle up the hierarchy is freed. All the handles can be released and then reused.

ODBC API Conformance Levels

In response to the wide variety of database system capabilities available on every hardware and software platform, ODBC breaks its function list into three levels of conformance. A driver must support, at minimum, the Core level conformance to be considered an ODBC driver. ODBC also specifies SQL grammar conformance levels, which are not directly related to the API conformance level, as listed here:

✔ *Core:* The Core level is the minimum API conformance level a driver and database must support. This level corresponds to the X/Open and SQL Access Group Call Level Interface specification of 1992.

✔ *Level 1:* Conformance Level 1 adds significant functionality to ODBC's capabilities. All drivers that are used with Visual Basic's data access object must be Level 1 compliant, because Visual Basic assumes that certain services are available for it to use with the database. A Core level driver can be used, however, if you limit the use of ODBC strictly to direct Level 1 ODBC API calls.

✔ *Level 2:* Conformance Level 2 is the highest conformance level. It adds another large jump in functionality.

It is important to understand that just because a driver calls itself, say, a Level 1 ODBC driver doesn't necessarily mean that it supports *all* the options of *every* function at that level. The amount of support is usually tied directly to the capabilities of the underlying database, its limitations, and how aggressively a driver manufacturer is in building capabilities into a driver.

It is also very important to understand that there is no independent body that certifies a driver as meeting the requirements of an ODBC conformance level. The developer of each driver makes the conformance claim. Buyer beware!

The ODBC API: Visual Basic `Declare` Statements and ODBC Constants

Because ODBC is implemented in Windows as a dynamic link library, you must include a `Declare` statement for any ODBC functions you call from a Visual

Basic application. By requiring a `Declare` statement, Visual Basic knows what DLL file to load and the types of parameters each function uses so that it can perform type checking and flag any incorrect types you try to use in a function. The ODBCAPI.BAS file, on the accompanying disk, contains these ODBC `Declare` statements and other ODBC constants and user-defined types, ready to be copied to your application.

Debugging ODBC Applications

Even if you don't have access to the ODBC SDK, ODBC provides one valuable tool for debugging applications: the *trace log* (sometimes called the *trace file*). This is a log of all calls made by your application and Visual Basic through the ODBC system. The log can be quite educational about how ODBC works, and it lets you see exactly what is being done.

Data Type Conversions Between ODBC and Visual Basic

The correspondence between ODBC and Visual Basic data types is not one to one. Fortunately, with Visual Basic's slightly expanded list of data types, the correspondence is a bit closer. Table 7.1 lists the available ODBC data types and the Visual Basic equivalents.

Table 7.1. Data type conversions between ODBC and Visual Basic.

ODBC DATA TYPE	GRAMMAR LEVEL	VISUAL BASIC DATA TYPE
SQL_BIT	Extended	Boolean
SQL_TINYINT	Extended	Byte
SQL_SMALLINT	Core	Integer
SQL_INTEGER	Core	Long
SQL_BIGINT	Extended	No equivalent
SQL_REAL	Core	Single
SQL_FLOAT, SQL_DOUBLE	Core	Double
SQL_TIMESTAMP, SQL_DATE	Extended	DateTime
SQL_TIME	Extended	Time
SQL_CHAR	Minimum	String
SQL_VARCHAR	Minimum	String
SQL_BINARY	Extended	Binary
SQL_VARBINARY	Extended	Binary
SQL_LONGVARBINARY	Extended	Binary
SQL_LONGVARCHAR	Minimum	String
SQL_DECIMAL	Core	See Table 7.3
SQL_NUMERIC	Core	See Table 7.3

As reflected in Table 7.2, special handling is required for the SQL_DECIMAL and SQL_NUMERIC data types. Both data types supply a scale and precision to determine what range of numbers the fields can handle. Using this scale and precision, a good determination of variable scope can be made for Visual Basic. In addition, there are two exceptions to this rule, because SQL Server can employ a Currency field. ODBC interprets this with two different scope and precision combinations, as mentioned in Table 7.2.

Table 7.2. Numeric precision conversion between ODBC and Visual Basic.

SCALE	PRECISION	VISUAL BASIC DATA TYPE
0	1 to 4	Integer
0	5 to 9	Long
0	10 to 15	Double
0	16+	Text
1 to 3	1 to 15	Double
4	1 to 15	Double
4	16+	Text
4	10 or 19	Currency (SQL Server only)

ODBC data types correspond to the SQL grammar level that a driver and database support, similar to the conformance levels that ODBC's functions support. These are the SQL grammar conformance levels:

✔ *Minimum:* This is the minimum SQL grammar that a driver must support to be compliant with the ODBC standard. Only three data types are specified: SQL_CHAR, SQL_VARCHAR, and SQL_LONGVARCHAR. You won't be limited to these data types very often.

✔ *Core:* The Core SQL grammar expands the number of data types available to a far more workable number, and it includes many of the more common variable types.

✔ *Extended:* The Extended SQL grammar expands the list of variables to all the data types listed in Table 7.1. As with the Minimum level, you won't see a database that supports the full Extended level very often.

A database is not necessarily required to support all the data types at a given level, so an application should check to see what variables are available for a given data source by using the SQLGetTypeInfo function (an ODBC Conformance Level 1 function). See How-To 7.5 for a discussion of retrieving such information about an ODBC database.

ODBC Catalog Functions and Search Pattern Arguments

There are certain ODBC functions, called catalog functions, that return information about a data source's system tables or catalog. Most of the catalog functions are Conformance Level 2, so you probably won't encounter them when using Visual Basic and ODBC. Four of the functions, however, are Level 1: `SQLColumns`, `SQLSpecialColumns`, `SQLStatistics`, and `SQLTables`.

All the catalog functions allow you to specify a search pattern argument, which can contain the metacharacters underscore (_) and percent (%), as well as a driver-defined escape character. A *metacharacter* in this context is nothing more than a character that has a meaning other than just the character itself. Following is a detailed explanation of the search pattern characters:

✔ Use the underscore to represent any single character. This is equivalent to an MS-DOS question mark when searching for files.

✔ Use the percent character to represent any sequence of zero or more characters. This is analogous to the asterisk (*) in MS-DOS.

✔ The driver-defined escape characters allow you to search for one of the two metacharacters as a literal character (that is, to search for a string with either an underscore or a percent character in the string).

✔ All other characters represent themselves.

For example, to search for all items with a *P*, use the search pattern argument `%P%` To search for all table names having exactly four characters with a *B* in the second and last positions, use `_B_B`. Similarly, if the driver-defined escape character is a backslash, use `%\_\%` to find all strings of any length with an underscore in the second-to-last position and a percent in the last position of the string.

The driver-defined escape character can be found for any ODBC driver using the `SQLGetInfo` technique demonstrated in How-To 7.6.

Miscellaneous ODBC Topics

This section covers a few miscellaneous details that will make using ODBC and Visual Basic together a bit easier.

✔ Some ODBC databases support default drivers and data sources. A `[Default]` section in ODBCINST.INI (default driver) and/or ODBC.INI (default data source) is created during installation of the ODBC system or driver. In general, you won't want a default driver; you usually want to connect with one and only one specific data source and/or driver.

✔ If the driver uses a translator, it will be installed with the driver, and the usage should be transparent to you and your Visual Basic application.

✔ Get the *Microsoft ODBC 3.0 Programmer's Reference and SDK Guide*! If you are going to do any continuing work with ODBC at almost any level, buy the SDK. It has detailed references for all the functions, including various functions for installing ODBC drivers and systems. It also comes with some very useful debugging tools, including ODBC Test, which lets you interactively test various function calls, and ODBC Spy, which gives you a detailed record of which ODBC calls are being made. ODBC Spy also provides the capability to emulate either an application or a driver, letting you test applications without a driver. The SDK is highly recommended, and it is a must-have if you plan to develop your own drivers.

✔ In Windows NT and Windows 95, information on ODBC data sources, configuration, and tuning parameters is stored in the system registry, as is configuration information for Visual Basic. You should never need to modify that by hand, but if you do, at least now you know where to look.

✔ Any default installation of ODBC installs the ODBC Administrator. This is a handy utility you can use to set up drivers and data sources, as well as to get information about installed ODBC drivers. Everything that the ODBC Administrator does can be done in code with the ODBC API, but the utility simplifies some of the tasks.

Assumptions

This chapter assumes some things about what you are doing and the tools you are using:

✔ You are using ODBC version 2 or later. A lot of things changed between versions 1 and 2. You can take advantage of these changes even if you are working with a driver that supports only a previous version, as long as ODBC itself is the latest version.

✔ ODBC is installed on your development system. It would be quite difficult to develop ODBC applications with no access to ODBC.

✔ There are no heavy-duty data conversion issues. Most data conversions, if they go beyond those listed in Table 7.1 and 7.2, require some very specialized processing and will be very unusual. If you have such a situation, *definitely* get the ODBC SDK.

7.1 Use the ODBC Administrator to Maintain Data Sources

Under Windows 95 and Windows NT, ODBC data sources, explained in greater detail in this How-To, have become more complex entities, especially when it comes to issues such as security and network administration. This How-To explains how a simple Control Panel applet turns the administration of these data sources into a simple task.

7.2 Use ODBC with the Visual Basic Data Control

Using Visual Basic's data control to access ODBC demonstrates the power of both Visual Basic and ODBC. Accessing databases through ODBC without using the ODBC API is a simple matter, whether that data is on your own hard disk in a format Visual Basic doesn't directly support or half a world away on your network. This How-To shows how easy it is to make the connection.

7.3 Create an ODBC-Accessible Data Source Using
RegisterDatabase

Even though ODBC might install the driver you need for your application, a data source name must exist before the database can be used by any application. The RegisterDatabase method provides a way to enter a new data source if one doesn't exist (or even if it does!) so that your application can use the database through ODBC.

7.4 Prevent the Login Dialog Box from Being Displayed When I Open an ODBC Database

As long as you have the correct and complete connect string to feed to ODBC, you should be able to connect with any database to which you have access. But how do you discover the exact connect string for each database? ODBC provides the functionality and Visual Basic makes it easy to use it, as discussed in this How-To.

7.5 Determine What Services an ODBC Server Provides

Even though ODBC makes connecting with databases through a standard interface much easier, and it provides some of the services itself, it still relies on database systems to do most of the work. Not all databases are created equal, with equal capabilities. You'll discover how you can find out what services a database provides, all within your applications.

7.6 Use ODBCDirect to Connect to Database Servers

ODBCDirect is, like DAO and RDO, a new way to access databases. Unlike DAO and RDO, however, ODBCDirect is just a thin, but well-behaved, wrapper around the ODBC API. This How-To shows the first step in using this new technology by connecting to a data source and providing detailed information on the ODBCDirect Connection object.

COMPLEXITY
BEGINNING

7.1 How do I...
Use the ODBC Administrator to maintain data sources?

Problem

My Visual Basic program needs access to a Microsoft SQL Server database on another computer. How do I use the ODBC Administrator to connect to that database?

Technique

Visual Basic is a very powerful tool when it comes to quick database application development. At times, however, Visual Basic's native database tools are simply not enough, such as whenever a connection to SQL Server or Oracle databases is needed. ODBC makes the gap between Visual Basic and these databases easy to navigate, by providing a way to bridge the two resources with an ODBC connection.

ODBC connections usually start with a data source, an alias used by ODBC to refer an ODBC driver to a specified database so that an ODBC connection can happen. Although you can create an ODBC data source with code, it's much easier to use the ODBC Administrator, a tool specifically designed to perform data source–related tasks.

Data sources under Windows 95 and Windows NT are divided into three major types, as explained in Table 7.3. These three types make a difference in your application; the user DSN, for example, won't work with another user logged into the same machine. The system DSN assumes that all users on the same machine have security access, and the file DSN is used on a case-by-case basis.

Table 7.3. Data source name types.

TYPE	PURPOSE
System DSN	This DSN is usable by all users on a workstation, regardless of user security.
User DSN	The default, this DSN is usable only by certain users on a workstation (usually the user who created it).
File DSN	A "portable" data source, this DSN can be very useful with network-based applications. The DSN can be used by any user who has the correct ODBC driver(s) installed.

Steps

The ODBC Administrator is a Control Panel applet, so the first step is to locate the ODBC Administrator icon.

1. Double-click your Control Panel icon. You should see a window appear similar to the one shown in Figure 7.2. In that window, you should find an icon like the one highlighted in the figure.

2. Double-click the ODBC Administrator icon (usually titled "32bit ODBC") to start the Administrator applet. A dialog box similar to the one shown in Figure 7.3 should appear, displaying several property pages. The first three property pages deal with DSN (Data Source Name) entries, with each page representing a level of security. The User DSN property page provides ODBC access for a data source only for a given user on a given workstation; the System DSN allows ODBC access for a data source only for a given workstation, but for any user on that workstation. A File DSN entry is a file-based data source, usable by any and all who have the needed ODBC drivers installed, and it does not need to be local to a user or a workstation.

Also, you'll notice three more property pages. The ODBC Drivers property page allows the display of all installed ODBC drivers, including the version and file information. The Tracing property page offers the capability of tracking all ODBC activity for a given data source and saving it to a log file for debugging purposes. And, last of all, the About property

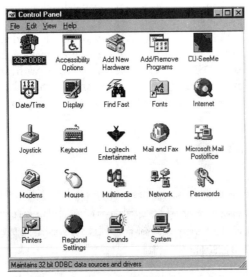

Figure 7.2. The Control Panel, with ODBC Administrator highlighted.

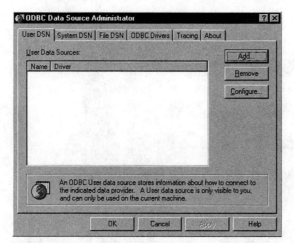

Figure 7.3. ODBC Administrator property pages.

page gives version and file information on the core components that compose the ODBC environment.

3. For your needs, you are going to create a User DSN. Click the Add button to start the process of adding a new data source. The first dialog box that appears gives you the list of available ODBC drivers from which to choose. One thing you'll want to note is the helpful information on each dialog box and property page, summarizing its purpose.

4. Select the Microsoft Access Driver from the list of drivers, and then click the Finish button. The next step is to provide the database-related information for the data source, and to that end a dialog box appears, similar to that displayed in Figure 7.4. The dialog box that appears is driver-specific; that is, if you had selected a different ODBC driver, you would probably have gotten a dialog box with a completely different set of properties.

5. Type `Biblio` in the Data Source Name field. Then click the Select button in the Database frame and choose your copy of BIBLIO.MDB. After this is done, click the OK button.

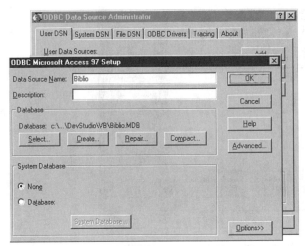

Figure 7.4. The ODBC Microsoft Access 97
Setup dialog box.

How It Works

Based on your selections, entries are added to the Registry by the ODBC Administrator (or to a file if you are creating a File DSN.) These Registry entries are vital to the ODBC drivers that require them; in many cases, the entries can determine not only the database that the driver will access, but also how and by whom it will be accessed. The only other recommended method for adding ODBC information to the Registry is the use of the `RegisterDatabase` method, which we'll cover later in this chapter. Avoid attempting to manually edit ODBC driver Registry entries without first researching the settings to ensure a full understanding of how they work.

Comments

Emphasis should be placed on the fact that each ODBC driver's setup dialog box will be different; if you're creating data sources by hand and using only one driver, this isn't a difficult thing to support. If, however, you really want to ensure a wide degree of compatibility for your programs, you might want to use the method detailed in How-To 7.3 to create your data sources. This technique uses the `RegisterDatabase` method to create data sources, and it can support a wide variety of options (even running "silently," displaying nothing to the user, if all the information needed for the data source is supplied).

COMPLEXITY
BEGINNING

7.2 How do I...
Use ODBC with the Visual Basic Data control?

Problem

I'm using the Visual Basic data control to process and display data in my application. But the data I need to access is on the network, in a format that Visual Basic doesn't directly support. How can I get the data and display it in a form? Can I use the data control?

Technique

The steps that are necessary to bind the Visual Basic data control and other bound controls are simple, not that much different from connecting to one of Visual Basic's native data formats using the Jet database engine. This How-To shows exactly what is necessary to set up the controls to make the connection.

Steps

Open the Person.VBP project file. Modify the project to use an existing ODBC data source, and then run the project. Use the Visual Basic data control's navigation buttons at the bottom of the form, as shown in Figure 7.5, to move through the database, and then click Quit when you are finished.

1. Create a new project, name it Person.VBP, and add a new form with property settings as listed in Table 7.4. Save the form as PERSON.FRM.

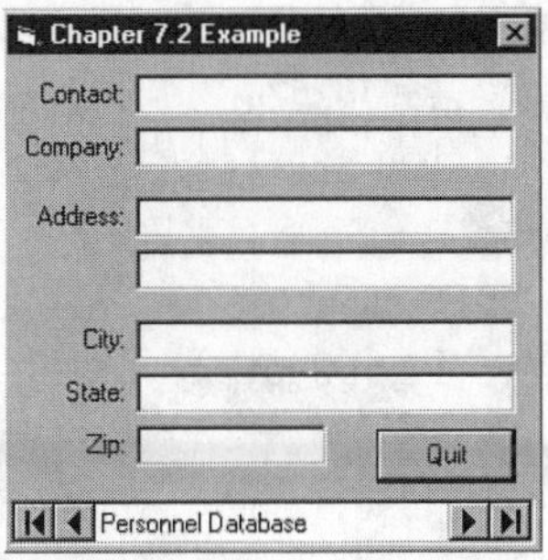

Figure 7.5. Chapter 7.2 example.

Table 7.4. Objects and properties for PERSON.FRM.

OBJECT	PROPERTY	SETTING
Form	Name	frmODBC
	Caption	"Chapter 7.2 Example"
	StartUpPosition	2 - CenterScreen
CommandButton	Name	cmdQuit
	Caption	"&Quit"
	Default	True
TextBox	Name	txtZip
	DataSource	"dtaData"
TextBox	Name	txtState
	DataSource	"dtaData"
TextBox	Name	txtCity
	DataSource	"dtaData"
TextBox	Name	txtAddress2
	DataSource	"dtaData"
TextBox	Name	txtAddress1
	DataSource	"dtaData"
TextBox	Name	txtName
	DataSource	"dtaData"
TextBox	Name	txtContact
	DataSource	"dtaData"
Data	Name	dtaData
	Align	2 - Align Bottom
	Caption	"Personnel Database"
	RecordSource	""
Label	Name	lblPerson
	Caption	"Zip:"
	Alignment	1 - Right Justify
	Index	5
Label	Name	lblPerson
	Alignment	1 - Right Justify
	Caption	"State:"
	Index	4
Label	Name	lblPerson
	Alignment	1 - Right Justify
	Index	3
	Caption	"City:"

OBJECT	PROPERTY	SETTING
Label	Name	lblPerson
	Alignment	1 - Right Justify
	Index	2
	Caption	"Address:"
Label	Name	lblPerson
	Alignment	1 - Right Justify
	Index	1
	Caption	"Company:"
Label	Name	lblPerson
	Alignment	1 'Right Justify
	Index	0
	Caption	"Contact:"

2. Add the following code to the declarations section of the form. Option Explicit tells Visual Basic to make sure that you declare all variables and objects before using them, to avoid naming problems.

```
Option Explicit
```

3. Add the following code to the form's Load event procedure. After centering the form, set the Connect and RecordSource properties of the data control, as well as the DataField properties of the text boxes that will hold the fields of the database. This step links each needed field with the text boxes that hold each record's data.

Change the data source name in the Connect property statement indicated to an available name in ODBC—or leave the DSN part of the Connect string out, and ODBC will prompt you for the information it needs. Also, set the SQL statement to a table in that data source, and change the text boxes to actual fields in that table.

```
Private Sub Form_Load()
    'Set up the form and connect to data source
    Dim dbfTemp As Database, recTemp As Recordset

    'Connect to the database
    'Change this to your data source
    dtaData.Connect = "ODBC;DSN=Personnel Database"

    'Set the data control's RecordSource property
    'Change this to your table name
    dtaData.RecordSource = "SELECT * FROM act"

    'Connect each of the text boxes with the appropriate fieldname
    txtContact.DataField = "Contact"
```

continued on next page

continued from previous page

```
    txtName.DataField = "Name"
    txtAddress1.DataField = "Addr1"
    txtAddress2.DataField = "Addr2"
    txtCity.DataField = "City"
    txtState.DataField = "State"
    txtZip.DataField = "Zip"
End Sub
```

4. Add the following code to the `Click` event of the `cmdQuit` command button. This is the exit point that terminates the program.

```
Private Sub cmdQuit_Click()
    End
End Sub
```

How It Works

The preceding code is all that is required to use ODBC with Visual Basic's data control. With the built-in navigation controls, you can move about the database.

Several important details are involved in setting up this procedure for use with ODBC. Note that in this How-To most of the setup and initialization is done in code, but you can easily set the properties of the data control and bound text boxes when designing the form and then simply load the form. In this case, Visual Basic will make the connection for you and display the data directly, and you won't need any code in the form's `Load` event. To ensure that this is done smoothly, follow the steps outlined here:

1. Leave the data control's `DatabaseName` property blank to use an ODBC data source. If you enter a database name here, Visual Basic attempts to open the database using its native data formats.

2. Set the `Connect` property of the data control to the connect string that ODBC needs to connect to the database. This is the same connect string that other How-To's in this chapter use for defining a `QueryDef`, in `RegisterDatabase`, and in setting up other uses of ODBC directly. You can also simply set this property to `ODBC`, and ODBC will prompt the user at runtime for information it needs in order to make the connection.

3. Set the data control's `RecordSource` property to the SQL statement you want to use to select the data from the database. This can be any SQL statement that creates a result set that Visual Basic can use to populate the bound text boxes.

4. Set each text box's `DataSource` to the name of the data control, `Data1` in this example. This is the normal Visual Basic way of binding a control to a data control. Remember too that you can have as many data controls on a form as you want, with different sets of controls bound to different bound controls and, therefore, to different databases.

5. Lastly, set each text box's `DataField` property to the particular field name in the result set of data records. This might be the name of the field in the database itself, but it is actually the name of the field that is returned in the result set. The two can be the same, but the SQL statement can rename the fields or even return calculated fields that don't exist in the database.

Comments

The method for ODBC access presented previously is usually the first, and simplest, method employed by programmers when delving into the ODBC library. You will find, however, that for more complex applications, your needs will quickly outstrip the capabilities of the data control. For a quick application or basic database access, though, this is a great way to start.

COMPLEXITY
BEGINNING

7.3 How do I...
Create an ODBC-accessible data source using `RegisterDatabase`?

Problem

ODBC provides a program, ODBC Administrator, to make manual changes to a data source, but how can I install a new ODBC data source name using code? I can't make the users of the application do it, and I can't expect them to have the information to give to ODBC. Does this mean that I have to make direct calls to the ODBC API?

Technique

The `RegisterDatabase` method of Visual Basic is a quick and easy way to register a new data source with ODBC. The method takes four arguments: `dbname`, `driver`, `silent`, and `attributes`, which are discussed more fully in the following text. After a data source name is created, it becomes available to any application using ODBC, whether it's a Visual Basic application or not.

Steps

Open the REGISTER.VBP file. The ODBC Data Sources form loads, shown in Figure 7.6, getting the list of currently installed drivers and data source names through direct calls to the ODBC system. Enter a name for the new data source, an optional description, and the driver that ODBC will use to connect with the database. Click the New Data Source command button to add it to the ODBC system. If any other additional information is needed to make a connection to the database, another dialog box appears, prompting for any missing items. The dialog box for adding a Microsoft Access data source is shown in Figure 7.4. The list of data sources is then updated so that it shows a current list of installed data sources.

1. Create a new project named REGISTER.VBP. Add the form ODBCErrors.FRM and the code module ODBC API Declarations.BAS, using Visual Basic's File | Add menu command. The code module contains all the declarations needed for the ODBC API functions and the constants used in many of the functions, and the form makes it easier to examine ODBC errors.

2. Make sure that the Microsoft Common Controls components are available to this project. To add, select the Project | Components menu item. When the dialog box appears, look for a component titled Microsoft Windows Common Controls 5.0, and ensure that it is checked. After it is checked, click OK. The ODBCErrors.FRM form uses the `TreeView` control to display ODBC errors in a hierarchical fashion.

3. Name the new project's default form `frmODBC`, and save the file as REGISTER.FRM. Add the controls shown in Figure 7.6, setting the properties as given in Table 7.5.

Table 7.5. Objects and properties for REGISTER.FRM.

OBJECT	PROPERTY	SETTING
Form	Name	frmODBC
	Caption	"ODBC Data Sources"
CommandButton	Name	cmdCreateDSN
	Caption	"&New Data Source"
Frame	Name	fraRegister
	Caption	"New Data Source"
TextBox	Name	txtDSNdesc
TextBox	Name	txtDSNname
ComboBox	Name	lstODBCdrivers
	Sorted	True
	Style	2 - Dropdown List
Label	Name	lblRegister
	Alignment	1 'Right Justify
	Index	2
	Caption	"Select ODBC Driver:"

OBJECT	PROPERTY	SETTING
Label	Name	lblRegister
	Alignment	1 'Right Justify
	Index	1
	Caption	"Description:"
Label	Name	lblRegister
	Alignment	1 'Right Justify
	Index	0
	Caption	"Name:"
CommandButton	Name	cmdQuit
	Caption	"&Quit"
ListBox	Name	lstODBCdbs
	Sorted	True
	TabStop	0 'False
Label	Name	lblRegister
	Index	3
	Caption	"Installed ODBC Data Sources:"

4. Put the following code in the declarations section of frmODBC. Option Explicit tells Visual Basic to check the variables for you. The dynamic arrays hold the information about installed drivers and data sources retrieved from calls to the ODBC API.

```
Option Explicit

'Dynamic arrays to hold data
Dim strDBNames() As String
Dim strDBDescs() As String
Dim strDvrDescs() As String
Dim strDvrAttr() As String
```

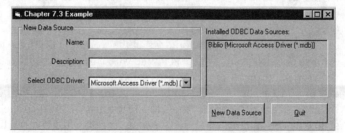

Figure 7.6. The project's ODBC Data Sources form, displaying the data source list.

5. Add the following code to the **Load** event of **frmODBC**. This code handles all the setup chores, including centering the form on the screen and allocating an ODBC environment handle. Each ODBC application that calls the API needs to have one, and only one, environmental handle. ODBC keeps track of what information goes where through the use of this handle, along with the connection and statement handles. The actual work of extracting the lists of data sources and drivers is handled in other procedures in this form, but called from here.

```
Private Sub Form_Load()
    'Allocate the ODBC environment handle
    If SQLAllocEnv(glng_hEnv) = SQL_SUCCESS Then
        'Load the current list of data sources to list box
        GetODBCdbs
        'Get the list of installed drivers
        GetODBCdvrs
        lstODBCdrivers.ListIndex = 0
        frmODBC.Show
        txtDSNname.SetFocus
    End If
End Sub
```

6. Insert the following procedures into **frmODBC**. The first procedure, **cmdCreateDSN_Click**, calls the procedure that validates data and actually creates the data source name in ODBC. The second procedure, **cmdQuit_Click**, creates an exit point in the application.

```
Private Sub cmdCreateDSN_Click()
    CreateNewDSN
End Sub

Private Sub cmdQuit_Click()
    End
End Sub
```

7. Add the following subroutine to **frmODBC**. Here is the first of two subroutines that extract the existing lists of data sources and drivers from ODBC. **GetODBCdbs** obtains the list of data source names and the descriptions of each, employing a function named **ODBCDSNList** in the ODBC API Declarations.BAS as a wrapper for the **SQLDataSources** API call. The **ODBCDSNList** function does all the work; the **Do While** loop extracts one data source name at a time with a call to **SQLDataSources**. If no error is returned from the function call, the data source name and its description are concatenated and added to the **lstODBCdbs** list box, showing all the data sources that are already installed. When the last data source has been returned to this function, the **SQLDataSources** function returns the **SQL_NO_DATA_FOUND** result, and the loop terminates. The function returns a variant array, if successful, or nothing if unsuccessful.

```
Private Sub GetODBCdbs()
    Dim varTemp As Variant, I As Integer

    lstODBCdbs.Clear
    'Call the ODBCDSNList function in ODBC API Declarations.BAS.
    varTemp = ODBCDSNList(glng_hEnv, True)

    'If the ODBCDSNList function returns an array, populate
    'the list box.
    If IsArray(varTemp) Then
        For I = LBound(varTemp) To UBound(varTemp)
            lstODBCdbs.AddItem varTemp(I)
        Next
    End If
End Sub
```

8. The next function, GetODBCdvrs, gets a list of the drivers that ODBC has installed. Put the following code in frmODBC. This function operates very similarly to GetODBCdbs, calling a function named ODBCDriverList, which loops through calls to the ODBC SQLDrivers function, returning one driver name at a time, and returning the names and descriptions in a local variant array to be added to the cboODBCdrivers drop-down list.

```
Private Sub GetODBCdvrs()
    Dim varTemp As Variant, I As Integer

    cboODBCdrivers.Clear
    varTemp = ODBCDriverList(glng_hEnv, True)

    'If the ODBCDriverList function returns an array,
    'populate the list box.  If not, let the user know.
    If IsArray(varTemp) Then
        For I = LBound(varTemp) To UBound(varTemp)
            cboODBCdrivers.AddItem varTemp(I)
        Next
    Else
        MsgBox "No ODBC drivers installed or available.", vbExclamation
    End If
End Sub
```

9. Add the following code to frmODBC. The CreateNewDSN procedure sets up and calls RegisterDatabase so that the new data source name is recorded in the ODBC system. The procedure first checks to make sure that a name is entered in the txtDSNname text box so that a descriptive name will be in the list (the description is optional). If all is well, the procedure assembles a set of variables to pass to RegisterDatabase. These are listed here:

✔ The new data source name

✔ The driver to be used to connect to the physical data

✔ Connection information

Before actually making the call to `RegisterDatabase`, the Visual Basic error handler is set to go to the `CantRegister` error-handling routine if there is any problem registering the data source. If there is an error, a `MsgBox` informs the user of what the trouble is and continues the procedure—giving the user the opportunity to rectify any problems and try again. If the error is anything other than error 3146, the error is passed on to the default Visual Basic error-handling routines.

```
Sub CreateNewDSN()
    'Add a new data source name to the ODBC system
    Dim strDSNname As String, strDSNattr As String, strDSNdriver As String
    Dim intResult As Integer, intSaveCursor As Integer

    If txtDSNname = "" Then
        MsgBox "You must enter a name for the new data source."
        txtDSNname.SetFocus
    Else
        intSaveCursor = Screen.MousePointer
        Screen.MousePointer = vbHourglass

        'Format the arguments to RegisterDatabase
        strDSNname = txtDSNname.text
        strDSNattr = "Description=" & txtDSNdesc.text
        strDSNdriver = cboODBCdrivers.List(cboODBCdrivers.ListIndex)

        On Error GoTo CantRegister
            'Trap any errors so we can respond to them
            DBEngine.RegisterDatabase strDSNname, strDSNdriver, False, strDSNattr
        On Error GoTo 0

        'Now, rebuild the list of data source names
        GetODBCdbs

        Screen.MousePointer = intSaveCursor
    End If

    Exit Sub

CantRegister:
    If Err.Number = 3146 Then
        'ODBC couldn't find the setup driver specified
        'for this database in ODBCINST.INI.
        MsgBox "Cannot find driver installation DLL.", vbCritical
        Resume Next
    Else
        MsgBox Err.Number, vbExclamation
    End If
End Sub
```

10. Add this code in the `Unload` event of `frmODBC`. This code makes cleanup calls to ODBC functions, releasing the memory and handles allocated to make the calls to the ODBC API. The first call is to `ODBCDisconnectDS`, which releases and then frees the connection handle and memory. The second call, **SQLFreeEnv**, releases the ODBC environment handle and memory.

```
Private Sub Form_Unload(Cancel As Integer)
    Dim intResult As Integer

    'Clean up the ODBC connections that we allocated
    'and opened.
    intResult = ODBCDisconnectDS(glng_hEnv, glng_hDbc, glng_hStmt)
    intResult = SQLCFreeEnv(ghEnv)
End Sub
```

How It Works

By providing the **RegisterDatabase** method, Visual Basic takes care of a lot of the details involved in establishing a new data source in ODBC. This is the syntax for the method:

```
DBEngine.RegisterDatabase dbname, driver, silent, attributes
```

The first argument is *dbname*. The Visual Basic help file describes *dbname* as "a string expression that is the name used in the **OpenDatabase** method that refers to a block of descriptive information about the data source." All true, of course, but *dbname* is just a descriptive name that you chose to call the data source. The name could reflect the origins of the data (such as being from an Oracle database) or the nature of the data (such as Corporate Marketing Research Data).

The *driver* argument is the name of the ODBC driver used to access the database. This is not the same as the name of the DLL file comprising the driver, but is instead a short, descriptive name that the author of the driver gave to it. SQL Server, Btrieve data, and Oracle are names of widely used drivers.

The third argument is *silent*. No, the argument isn't silent, but it is your opportunity to control whether ODBC prompts the user for more information when ODBC doesn't have enough information to make the requested connection. The options are **True** for no dialog boxes and **False** for ODBC to prompt for the missing information. If silent is set to True and ODBC can't make the connection because of a lack of information, your application will need to trap the error that will occur.

The fourth argument is *attributes*. Each database system that you connect to has its own requirements for the information it needs in order to make a connection. For some items, there is a default; for others there isn't. The more attributes you specify here, the fewer the user will need to specify. The *attributes* string is the string returned from the **Connect** property of the **Data** control, **Database**, **QueryDef**, or **TableDef** objects after a connection is made. In How-To 7.5, we discuss more fully this information and show a way to easily obtain the exact information needed to connect with a particular database. In fact, this How-To and How-To 7.5 can be effectively used together to give you all the information you need to make an ODBC connection.

Essentially, all `RegisterDatabase` does is add information to the ODBC.INI file usually located in your \WINDOWS directory—with some validation routines thrown in by ODBC. It checks to make sure that you provide all the information needed to make a connection and that the database is out there someplace and is accessible.

One error message that might be returned from ODBC when you use the `RegisterDatabase` method is `The configuration DLL ([`*file name*`]) for the [`*driver name*`] could not be loaded.` When you request that a new data source be established, ODBC looks in an ODBCINST.INI file, located in the same place as the ODBC.INI file, for the name of the DLL that contains the setup routines for that driver. Here are some sample lines for different drivers (there is additional information in each section for each driver):

```
[Microsoft Access Driver (*.mdb)]
Driver=C:\WINDOWS\SYSTEM\odbcjt16.dll
Setup=C:\WINDOWS\SYSTEM\odbcjt16.dll

[Microsoft Dbase Driver (*.dbf)]
Driver=C:\WINDOWS\SYSTEM\odbcjt16.dll
Setup=C:\WINDOWS\SYSTEM\oddbse16.dll

[SQL Server Driver]
Driver=C:\WINDOWS\SYSTEM\sqlsrvr.dll
Setup=C:\WINDOWS\SYSTEM\sqlsrvr.dll
```

As you can see, sometimes the setup driver is the same as the driver used for data access, but more commonly the two are different. If that driver is not available at the location specified, ODBC returns an error for the `RegisterDatabase` call.

Comments

One of the nice things about using ODBC is that it goes out of its way to give you the information you need in order to make the connections to databases. In this How-To, you have seen how ODBC prompts with its own dialog box if you don't give it enough information to make the connection. This is one area in which using Visual Basic to handle the conversation with ODBC doesn't hide any details from you. You'll see another example of using this ODBC feature to good advantage in How-To 6.5, in which the dialog box is used to construct connect strings that can be used directly in an application.

Perhaps, to state the obvious, it is necessary for the ODBC driver to be installed before `RegisterDatabase` is used. If this method only added entries to the .INI file, the driver wouldn't need to be installed before a data source was created using that driver. But because ODBC does some validation from Visual Basic in response to this method, the driver needs to be available along with the information stored in ODBC.INI and ODBCINST.INI by the driver setup program.

In response to the availability of `RegisterDatabase` in Visual Basic, it is logical to wonder whether there is an equivalent `UnRegisterDatabase` or `DeleteDatabase`. Alas, no. For that you would need to make a call to an

ODBC Installer DLL function, `SQLConfigDataSource`, available since ODBC version 1.0. Some other interesting installation functions that were introduced with version 2.0 (`SQLCreateDataSource`, `SQLGetAvailableDrivers`, `SQLGetInstalledDrivers`, and `SQLManageDataSources`) give finer control over the ODBC setup. These and other functions are used by driver manufacturers to install drivers and ODBC itself if necessary, but they can be used by any application. Information about these functions is available in the *Microsoft ODBC 3.0 Programmer's Reference and SDK Guide*.

Another Visual Basic property that is useful in connection with `RegisterDatabase` is the `Version` property. `Version` is a property of both the `Database` object and the `DBEngine` object. When returned from the `Database` object, `Version` identifies the data format version of the object, usually as a major and minor version number, such as 4.03. This gives you one more piece of information about the different components making up your applications.

COMPLEXITY
INTERMEDIATE

7.4 How do I...
Prevent the login dialog box from being displayed when I open an ODBC database?

Problem

I'm trying to use an ODBC driver to open a data source that is on the network, but the driver documentation is not very helpful regarding the information needed to make a connection. I need my application to make the connection (if it is at all possible) without requiring users to make decisions or respond to dialog boxes. How can I get the right connect string without wasting time by guessing? If the connection can't be made, why not?

Technique

As long as you are able to tell Visual Basic that you want to make some sort of connection through ODBC, all you need to do is make a call to Visual Basic's `OpenDatabase` method with certain default arguments. ODBC responds by prompting for information about what data source you want (from those data sources installed on the system). Then you can define a temporary `QueryDef`, make the connection, and examine the Visual Basic `Connect` property. The `Connect` property at that point contains the fully formed connect string required to make a connection to that data source. The string stored in the `Connect` property can be copied and used directly in future attempts to connect to the database.

Steps

Open and run the CONNECT.VBP Visual Basic project file. The Retrieve ODBC Connect String window opens, as shown in Figure 7.7. Click on the Connect to Data Source command button, and the ODBC SQL Data Sources window appears, prompting you to select an installed data source name. Visual Basic and ODBC obtains from that data source a list of available tables and puts them in the Tables Available list box on the main form. Either double-click on one of the tables or select one and click the Get Connect String command button. The application establishes a connection to that database table and returns the complete connect string, placing it in the Connect String text box, as shown in Figure 7.8. Click the Copy Connect String command button to put the string in the Windows clipboard, and then paste it into your application.

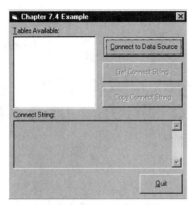

Figure 7.7. The project's main form on startup.

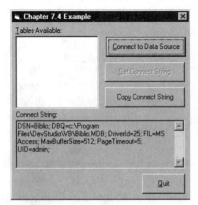

Figure 7.8. The project's main form, after ODBC connect string retrieval.

1. Create a new project named CONNECT.VBP. Add the form ODBCErrors.FRM and the code module ODBC API Declarations.BAS, using Visual Basic's File | Add menu command. The code module contains all the declarations needed for the ODBC API functions and the constants used in many of the functions.

2. Name the default form `frmODBC`, and save the file as CONNECT.FRM. Add the controls as shown in Figure 7.7, setting the properties as listed in Table 7.6.

Table 7.6. Objects and properties for CONNECT.FRM.

OBJECT	PROPERTY	SETTING
Form	Name	frmODBC
	Caption	"Chapter 7.4 Example"
CommandButton	Name	cmdCopyConnect
	Caption	"Cop&y Connect String"
	Enabled	0 - False
CommandButton	Name	cmdGetConnect
	Caption	"&Get Connect String"
	Enabled	0 - False
CommandButton	Name	cmdQuit
	Caption	"&Quit"
TextBox	Name	txtConnect
	MultiLine	True
	ScrollBars	2 - Vertical
	TabStop	False
CommandButton	Name	cmdConnect
	Caption	"&Connect to Data Source"
ListBox	Name	lstTables
	Sorted	True
Label	Name	lblConnect
	Index	0
	Caption	"Connect String:"
Label	Name	lblConnect
	Index	1
	Caption	"&Tables Available:"

3. Add the following code to the declarations section of `frmODBC`. `Option Explicit` tells Visual Basic to make sure that you declare all variables and objects before using them, to avoid naming problems.

```
Option Explicit

'Module level globals to hold connection info
Dim dbfTemp As Database, recTemp As Recordset
```

4. Add this code to the form's **Load** event. After the form is loaded, memory and a handle for the ODBC environment and connection are allocated. If either of these fails, there is no need to proceed, so the program is exited.

```
Private Sub Form_Load()
    'Log on to an ODBC data source
    'First, allocate ODBC memory and get handles
    Dim intResult As Integer

    'Allocate the ODBC environment handle
    If SQLAllocEnv(glng_hEnv) <> SQL_SUCCESS Then End

    intResult = SQLAllocConnect(glng_hEnv, glng_hDbc)
    If intResult <> SQL_SUCCESS Then
        intResult = frmODBCErrors.ODBCError("Dbc", glng_hEnv, & _
        glng_hDbc, 0, intResult, "Error allocating connection handle.")
        End
    End If

    frmODBC.Show
End Sub
```

5. Add the following code to the **Click** event of **cmdConnect**. Before you can get connection data, you need to select a data source name for the connection information you want. For this procedure, let the built-in ODBC dialog boxes do the work. The line

```
Set dbfTemp = OpenDatabase("", False, False, "ODBC;")
```

tells Visual Basic to open a database, but no information is given about which one, other than the fact that it is an ODBC database. ODBC responds by opening its Select Data Source dialog box for selection of a data source, as shown in Figure 7.9.

```
Private Sub cmdConnect_Click()
    'Connect to a data source and populate lstTables
    Dim I As Integer
    Dim strConnect As String
    Dim tbfTemp As TableDef

    Screen.MousePointer = vbHourglass
    lstTables.Clear

    On Error GoTo ErrHandler
        Set dbfTemp = OpenDatabase("", False, False, "ODBC;")
    On Error GoTo 0

    For Each tbfTemp In dbfTemp.TableDefs
```

```
            lstTables.AddItem tbfTemp.Name
        Next

        Screen.MousePointer = vbDefault

        If lstTables.ListCount Then
            cmdGetConnect.Enabled = True
        Else
            MsgBox "No tables are available. " & _
                "Please connect to another data source."
        End If

    Exit Sub

    ErrHandler:
        Screen.MousePointer = vbDefault
        Select Case Err.Number
            Case 3423
                'This data source can't be attached, (or the
                'user clicked Cancel, so use ODBC API
                APIConnect
            Case 3059
                'The user clicked on Cancel
                Exit Sub
            Case Else
                'The error is something else, so send it back to
                'the VB exception handler
                MsgBox Err.Number, vbExclamation
        End Select
    End Sub
```

After the user selects a data source name, the procedure loops through the **TableDefs** collection using a Visual Basic **For Each...Next** loop, retrieves the table name of each table available in that data source, and adds each table name to the **lstTables** list box. If a connection is made and any tables are available, the **cmdGetConnect** command button is **Enabled** for the next step, which is retrieving the connection information. The error-handling routine is important in this procedure, and is discussed with the **APIConnect** procedure code.

6. Add the following code to the **cmdGetConnect**'s **Click** event. This command button is enabled only when a connection is made and tables are available for selection. Assuming that a table name has been selected, a connection is made to that table by creating a dynaset. This makes the connection information available. The connection information is retrieved by copying the value of the dynaset's **Connect** property to the **txtConnect** text box, running it through the **AddSpaces** function as discussed in the following text. Finally, the **cmdCopyConnect** command button is enabled.

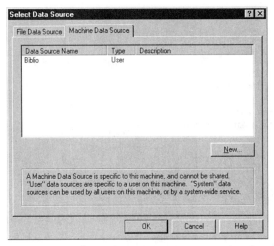

Figure 7.9. The Select Data Source selection dialog box.

```
Screen.MousePointer = vbHourglass
    txtConnect.text = ""

    If Len(lstTables.text) Then
        Set recTemp = dbfTemp.OpenRecordset(lstTables.text)
        txtConnect.text = AddSpaces(dbfTemp.Connect)
    Else
        MsgBox "Please select a table first."
    End If

    cmdCopyConnect.Enabled = True
    Screen.MousePointer = vbDefault
End Sub
```

7. Add the following code to **frmODBC**. When we receive the raw connect string back from ODBC after making the connection to the database table, it is strung together with no spaces, unless a space happens to be in any of the strings enclosed in quotation marks. Sometimes the connect string can become quite lengthy, so we use a text box with the **MultiLine** property set to **True**. But even with that, an unbroken string with no spaces can exceed any width we make the text box. So this function simply loops through the length of the string, replacing all the semicolon separators with a semicolon-space pair of characters. ODBC uses semicolons to separate the different phrases in a connect string.

```
Function AddSpaces(strC As String)
    Dim I As Integer
    Dim strNewStr As String, strNextChar As String
    Dim strNextChar As String
```

```
    For I = 1 To Len(strC)
        strNextChar = Mid$(strC, I, 1)
        If strNextChar = ";" Then
            strNewStr = strNewStr & strNextChar & " "
        Else
            strNewStr = strNewStr & strNextChar
        End If
    Next
    AddSpaces = strNewStr
End Function
```

8. Add the code for **cmdCopyConnect**'s **Click** event as shown here. This is added as a convenience for the programmer. When you have connected to the data source and have received the connect string, just click the Copy Connect String command button, and the full string is copied to the Windows Clipboard, ready to paste into your application.

```
Private Sub cmdCopyConnect_Click()
    'Select the text in txtConnect
    With txtConnect
        .SetFocus: .SelStart = 0: .SelLength = Len(txtConnect.text)
    End With

    ' Copy selected text to Clipboard.
    Clipboard.SetText Screen.ActiveControl.SelText
End Sub
```

9. Add the following code to the form's **Unload** event and the **cmdQuit** command button's event. The **cmdQuit** command button ends the program, triggering the form's **Unload** event. As usual for Visual Basic applications that make direct calls to the ODBC API, the code needs to clean up after itself, releasing the memory and handles needed for connection to ODBC.

```
Private Sub cmdQuit_Click()
    End
End Sub

Private Sub Form_Unload(Cancel As Integer)
    Dim intResult As Integer

    intResult = ODBCDisconnectDS(glng_hEnv, glng_hDbc, glng_hStmt)
    intResult = ODBCFreeEnv(glng_hEnv)
End Sub
```

10. Add the following code to the **DblClick** event procedure of the **lstTables** list box. This code simply adds the convenience of being able to double-click on a table in **lstTables** to retrieve the connect string, saving the work of also clicking the **cmdGetConnect** command button.

```
Private Sub lstTables_DblClick()
    cmdGetConnect_Click
End Sub
```

11. Last, but not least, add the following code to the code section of the form. Sometimes, it is necessary to handle errors generated by Visual Basic but caused by the ODBC system. This is one example of such a situation.

There are two sorts of Visual Basic errors that need to be handled in the `cmdConnect_Click` procedure. The first sort of error is when there is a problem making the connection to the data source, for any of a number of reasons (for example, the database is not available, the connection couldn't be made because of network traffic, and so on). One common error is attempting to open an ODBC database that is one of the databases Visual Basic handles natively, such as an Access .MDB file or one of the ISAM databases.

This is where the **APIConnect** procedure comes in. Even though the error is generated by the Visual Basic error handler, there is some reason lurking in ODBC for why the connection can't be made, and a call to the ODBC **SQLError** function will usually (but not always) give more information about the problem. **SQLError** doesn't always have information to give, for whatever internal reason. Basically, **APIConnect** just calls **SQLError** from within the error procedure, gets whatever additional information can be obtained, disconnects the ODBC connection (but not the handle—you might need that again for another attempt to make a connection), and returns to `frmODBC`.

```
Sub APIConnect()
    'Can't connect through VB, so go direct
    Dim intResult As Integer
    Dim strConnectIn As String
    Dim strConnectOut As String * SQL_MAX_OPTION_STRING_LENGTH
    Dim intOutCount As Integer

    strConnectIn = ""

    intResult = SQLDriverConnect(glng_hDbc, Me.hWnd, strConnectIn, _
        Len(strConnectIn), strConnectOut, Len(strConnectOut), _
        intOutCount, SQL_DRIVER_PROMPT)
    If intResult <> SQL_SUCCESS Then
        intResult = frmODBCErrors.ODBCError("Dbc", glng_hEnv, glng_hDbc, 0, _
            intResult, "Problem with call to SQLDriverConnect.")
        Exit Sub
    End If
    txtConnect.text = AddSpaces(strConnectOut)

    'Free the connection, but not the handle
    intResult = SQLDisconnect(glng_hDbc)
    If intResult <> SQL_SUCCESS Then
        intResult = frmODBCErrors.ODBCError("Dbc", glng_hEnv, glng_hDbc, 0, _
            intResult, "Problem with call to SQLDriverConnect.")
    End If

    cmdCopyConnect.Enabled = True
End Sub
```

The other error that must be handled is if the user clicks Cancel when ODBC's Select Data Source dialog box is shown. If this happens, the `Sub` procedure is exited and the user is returned to the main form.

How It Works

Three functions are available in the ODBC API for making a connection to a data source: `SQLConnect`, `SQLBrowseConnect`, and `SQLDriverConnect`. Although we can't easily know exactly how Visual Basic makes calls to ODBC functions to establish connections, it is enlightening to examine what is available in version 3 of ODBC. These functions are explained in more detail in Table 7.7.

Table 7.7. ODBC functions for establishing data source connections.

FUNCTION	VERSION	CONFORMANCE	PRIMARY ARGUMENTS
SQLConnect	1.0	Core	hDbc, data source name, user ID, authorization string
SQLDriverConnect	1.0	1	hDbc, Window handle (hwnd), connect string in, connect string out, completion option
SQLBrowseConnect	1.0	2	hDbc, connect string in, connect string out

`SQLConnect` is the standard way of connecting to an ODBC data source. All the arguments must be complete and correct because if anything is wrong, ODBC generates an error. If everything is right, a connection is established. Valid return codes are `SQL_SUCCESS`, `SQL_SUCCESS_WITH_INFO`, `SQL_ERROR`, and `SQL_INVALID_HANDLE`. Because this function is in the Core conformance level, all ODBC drivers are guaranteed to support it (or as guaranteed as it can be with drivers written by third-party developers attempting to adhere to a standard), so it is always available. The only flexibility that `SQLConnect` provides is when the specified data source name can't be found. In that case, the function looks for a default driver and loads that one if it is defined in ODBC.INI. If not, `SQL_ERROR` is returned, and more information about the problem can be obtained with a call to `SQLError`. This is the workhorse function of ODBC connections.

`SQLDriverConnect` offers a bit more flexibility for making ODBC connections. This function can handle data sources that require more information than the three arguments of `SQLConnect` (other than the connection handle `hDbc`, which all three functions require). `SQLDriverConnect` provides dialog boxes to prompt for any missing information needed for the connection, and it can handle connections not defined in the ODBC.INI file or registry. `SQLDriverConnect` provides three connection options:

✔ A connection string provided in the function call that contains all the data needed, including data source name, multiple user IDs, multiple passwords, and any other custom information required by the database.

✔ A connection string that provides only some of the data required to make the connection. The ODBC Driver Manager and the driver can prompt for any information that either of them needs in order to make the connection.

✔ A connection that is not defined in ODBC.INI or the registry. If any partial information is provided, the function uses it however it can.

When a connection is successfully made, the function returns SQL_SUCCESS and returns a completed connection string that can be used to make future connections to that database. It is a pretty safe bet that SQLDriverConnect is the function that Visual Basic uses when this How-To is employed to discover the connect string.

SQLDriverConnect can return SQL_SUCCESS, SQL_SUCCESS_WITH_INFO, SQL_NO_DATA_FOUND, SQL_ERROR, or SQL_INVALID_HANDLE. Valid choices for the completion option argument are SQL_DRIVER_PROMPT, SQL_DRIVER_COMPLETE, SQL_DRIVER_COMPLETE_REQUIRED, and SQL_DRIVER_NOPROMPT, as described here:

✔ SQL_DRIVER_PROMPT: This option displays dialog boxes (whether needed or not) to prompt for connection information. Any initial values included in the function call are used to fill in the appropriate controls in the dialog box.

✔ SQL_DRIVER_COMPLETE: If the connection information provided in the function call is sufficient to make the connection, ODBC goes ahead and makes the connection. If anything is missing, this option acts like SQL_DRIVER_PROMPT.

✔ SQL_DRIVER_COMPLETE_REQUIRED: This option is the same as SQL_DRIVER_COMPLETE, except that any information that is not needed to make the connection is grayed out in the dialog box.

✔ SQL_DRIVER_NOPROMPT: If the information in the connect string is sufficient to make the connection, it goes ahead and makes the connection. If anything is missing, no connection is made and the function returns SQL_ERROR.

The third function, SQLBrowseConnect, is perhaps the most interesting of the three functions. A call to this function initiates an interactive method of discovering what it takes to connect to a particular database. Each time SQLBrowseConnect is called, the function returns additional attributes that are needed to make a connection. An application making the call can parse out the resulting string containing missing attributes (which are marked as required or optional) and return successively more complete connect strings. Attributes that involve selection from a fixed list of items are returned as that full list so that an application can present a list box of choices to the user.

The bad news, for Visual Basic anyway, is that `SQLBrowseConnect` is a Conformance Level 2 function. Because Visual Basic is designed to require only Level 1 drivers, it doesn't have any functions that can directly use this function. But it is available to any application, including those written in Visual Basic, through direct calls to the ODBC API, if the driver supports Level 2 conformance.

Comments

As mentioned in the introduction to the chapter, you can't make an ODBC connection through an attached table to a database that Visual Basic natively supports, such as a Microsoft Access .MDB file or the ISAM databases Btrieve and dBASE. There normally isn't any reason to do so, although it can always be done using the ODBC API directly.

COMPLEXITY
ADVANCED

7.5 How do I...
Determine what services an ODBC server provides?

Problem

I'd like to be able to connect with the different data sources that are scattered throughout our network. But all the different drivers have different capabilities, even though they are all accessible through ODBC. How can I find out through code which services are available for each server, and keep the code as flexible and portable as possible?

Technique

In this example, we develop a useful ODBC viewer that gathers in one place much of the information needed to evaluate the data sources and drivers that are available to a particular workstation. The same techniques can be used whether the data is located on a single computer with one hard disk or connected to a network with data of widely varying formats on different hardware.

Steps

Open and run the Visual Basic SERVICES.VBP project. Select an ODBC data source name from the Installed ODBC Data Sources list, and then click the Get Functions command button. After a moment, a list of the functions that can be used with the data source appear in the bottom half of the form. Scroll through the list to see the functions available. Then, with the same data source highlighted, click the Get Properties command button. The Get ODBC Information window appears, as shown in Figure 7.10. Make the selections you want (from one to all the items in the list), and click the Get Info command button. The list of properties and their current values appears in the ODBC DSN Properties window, as shown in Figure 7.11.

1. Create a new project called SERVICES.VBP. Add the form ODBCErrors.FRM and the code module ODBC API Declarations.BAS using Visual Basic's File | Add menu command. The code module contains all the declarations needed for the ODBC API functions and the constants used in many of the functions, and the form allows for an easy-to-read display of ODBC errors.

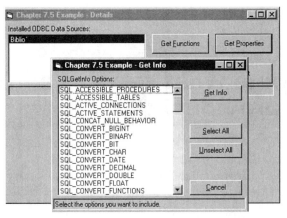

Figure 7.10. The project's Get Info form, showing the selected properties.

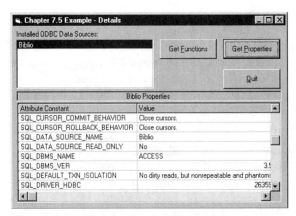

Figure 7.11. The project's Details form, showing the available functions.

2. Add a new form, frmODBC, and save the file as SERVICES.FRM. Add the controls shown in Figure 7.11, setting the properties as given in Table 7.8. The area under the Properties label is the MSFlexGrid control, grdResults.

Table 7.8. Objects and properties for SERVICES.FRM.

OBJECT	PROPERTY	SETTING
Form	Name	frmODBC
	Caption	"Chapter 7.5 Example - Details"
CommandButton	Name	cmdProperties
	Caption	"Get Properties"
CommandButton	Name	cmdFunctions
	Caption	"Get Functions"
CommandButton	Name	cmdQuit
	Caption	"Quit"
ListBox	Name	lstODBCdbs
	Sorted	True
Label	Name	lblGrid
	Caption	"Properties"
	BorderStyle	1 - Fixed Single
Grid	Name	grdResults
	Visible	False
	Scrollbars	2 - flexScrollBarVertical
	Highlight	0 - flexHighlightNever
Label	Name	lblServices
	Caption	"Installed ODBC Data Sources:"

3. Put the following code in the declarations section of the form. This code declares the dynamic array that will be used to hold the names of the data sources and drivers available to ODBC. Option Explicit tells Visual Basic to make sure that you declare all variables and objects before using them, to avoid naming problems.

```
Option Explicit

'Dynamic arrays to hold data
Dim strDBNames() As String
```

4. Add the following code to the form's Load event. First, the form is centered on-screen so that all the controls and information can be seen. Then, as with all applications that make direct calls to the ODBC API, the

ODBC wrapper functions are called to allocate memory and assign a handle for the ODBC environment and for the database connection. This is followed by a call to the GetODBCdbs Sub procedure, which will be discussed in the following text.

```
Private Sub Form_Load()
    'Log on to an ODBC data source
    'First, allocate ODBC memory and get handles
    Dim intResult As Integer

    'Allocate the ODBC environment handle
    If ODBCAllocateEnv(glng_hEnv) = SQL_SUCCESS Then
        'Load the current list of data sources to list box
        GetODBCdbs
        'Show the form
        frmODBC.Show
    Else
        End
    End If
End Sub
```

5. Add the following routine to frmODBC. This procedure extracts the existing lists of data sources and drivers from ODBC. GetODBCdbs obtains the list of data source names and the descriptions of each. The Do While loop extracts one data source name at a time with a call to SQLDataSources. If no error is returned from the function call, the data source name is added to the lstODBCdbs list box, showing all the data sources that are already installed. When the last data source has been returned to this function, the SQLDataSources function returns the SQL_NO_DATA_FOUND result, and the loop terminates.

```
Private Sub GetODBCdbs()
    Dim varTemp As Variant, I As Integer

    lstODBCdbs.Clear
    varTemp = ODBCDSNList(glng_hEnv, False)

    If IsArray(varTemp) Then
        For I = LBound(varTemp) To UBound(varTemp)
            lstODBCdbs.AddItem varTemp(I)
        Next
    Else
        MsgBox "No ODBC data sources to load!", vbCritical
        End
    End If
End Sub
```

6. Add the following routine to frmODBC. This procedure first determines whether a data source name has been selected in the lstODBCdbs list box. If none has been selected, a message box lets the user know that and then exits the procedure.

Assuming that a data source is selected, a call is made to **ODBCConnectDS** to allocate connection memory and a handle, which is required for a later call to **SQLGetFunctions**. If a connection is made successfully, the call to **SQLGetFunctions** is made, which does the actual work of retrieving the function list. The list is put into the **FuncList** array, which has 100 elements. An element of this array is set to true (**-1**) or false (**0**) if the referenced ODBC function is available with this data source. See the "How It Works" section for a discussion about how this array is used to identify available functions.

To set the number of rows in the **grdResults** grid, the number of array elements that are true needs to be counted. The first **For...Next** loop handles that, so that j is the number of true elements at the end of the loop. Then, after setting up the grid with the numbers of rows and columns to fit the data, the **intFuncList** array is looped through once again, to put the function names into each row of the grid.

```
Private Sub cmdFunctions_Click()
    Dim strDataSource As String
    Dim strUserName As String, strPassword As String
    Dim intResult As Integer, intErrResult As Integer
    ReDim intFuncList(100) As Integer
    Dim I As Integer, j As Integer

    'First, check to see if anything is selected
    'If not, notify user, then return to form.
    If lstODBCdbs.ListIndex >= 0 Then
        Screen.MousePointer = vbHourglass
        strDataSource = strDBNames(lstODBCdbs.ListIndex)

        If SQLAllocStmt(glng_hDbc, glng_hStmt) Then _
            intResult = ODBCConnectDS(glng_hEnv, glng_hDbc, _
                glng_hStmt, strDataSource, strUserName, strPassword)

        If intResult = SQL_SUCCESS Then _
            intResult = SQLGetFunctions(glng_hDbc, _
                SQL_API_ALL_FUNCTIONS, intFuncList(0))

        If intResult <> SQL_SUCCESS Then
            intErrResult = frmODBCErrors.ODBCError("Dbc", glng_hEnv, _
                glng_hDbc, 0, intResult, _
                "Error getting list of ODBC functions")
        Else
            'Run through the array and get the number of functions
            j = 0
            For I = 0 To 99
                If intFuncList(I) Then j = j + 1
            Next

            'Start by clearing the frmODBC grid
            With frmODBC.grdResults
                .Rows = j
                .Cols = 3
```

continued on next page

continued from previous page

```
                .FixedCols = 1
                .FixedRows = 0
                .ColWidth(0) = 8
                .ColWidth(1) = 0.65 * frmODBC.grdResults.Width
                .ColWidth(2) = 0.35 * frmODBC.grdResults.Width
            End With

            lblGrid.Caption = lstODBCdbs.text & ": " & Trim(Val(j)) & _
                " Functions"

            'Populate the grid with the function names
            j = 0
            For I = 0 To 99
                If intFuncList(I) <> 0 Then
                    With frmODBC.grdResults
                        .Row = j
                        .Col = 0: .text = j
                        .Col = 1: .text = ODBCFuncs(0, I)
                        .Col = 2: .text = ODBCFuncs(1, I)
                    End With
                    j = j + 1
                End If
            Next

            'Move to the top row
            frmODBC.grdResults.Row = 0
            frmODBC.grdResults.Col = 1

            'free the data source connection
            intResult = ODBCDisconnectDS(glng_hEnv, glng_hDbc, SQL_NULL_HSTMT)

            Screen.MousePointer = vbDefault
            frmODBC.grdResults.Visible = True
        End If
    Else
        MsgBox "Please select a data source name first.", _
            vbCritical, "ODBC Functions"
    End If
End Sub
```

7. Put the following code in the `cmdProperties_Click` event subroutine. After the program checks to make sure that a data source is selected, the program attempts to allocate a connection handle, then it loads the `frmGetInfo` form to continue obtaining information.

```
Private Sub cmdProperties_Click()
    Dim intResult As Integer
    If lstODBCdbs.ListIndex < 0 Then
        MsgBox "Please select a data source name first.", _
            vbCritical, "ODBC Properties"
    Else
        intResult = ODBCConnectDS(glng_hEnv, glng_hDbc, _
            glng_hStmt, lstODBCdbs.text, "", "")
```

```
        If intResult = SQL_SUCCESS Then Load frmGetInfo
    End If
End Sub
```

8. Enter the following two procedures to the code section of the form. The first procedure establishes a command button to quit the application. The Unload event then cleans up and releases the memory and handles that were needed for making calls to the ODBC API.

```
Private Sub cmdQuit_Click()
    End
End Sub

Private Sub Form_Unload(Cancel As Integer)
    Dim intResult As Integer

    intResult = ODBCDisconnectDS(glng_hEnv, glng_hDbc, glng_hStmt)
    intResult = ODBCFreeEnv(glng_hEnv)
End Sub
```

9. Add the following code to the code section of the form. This function provides a convenient way to convert some of the results of the properties to a more user-friendly and understandable form.

```
Private Function convCh(inChar As String, num As Variant)
    inChar = LTrim$(Left$(inChar, num))

    Select Case inChar
        Case "Y"
            convCh = "Yes"
        Case "N"
            convCh = "No"
        Case Else
            convCh = inChar
    End Select

End Function
```

10. Add a new form, frmGetInfo, and save the file as GETINFO.FRM. Add the controls shown in Figure 7.10, setting the properties as shown in Table 7.9.

Table 7.9. Objects and properties for GETINFO.FRM.

OBJECT	PROPERTY	SETTING
Form	Name	frmGetInfo
	Caption	"Chapter 7.5 Example - Get Info"
TextBox	Name	txtStatus
	Text	"Select the options you want to include."

continued on next page

continued from previous page

OBJECT	PROPERTY	SETTING
CommandButton	Name	cmdCancel
	Cancel	True
	Caption	"Cancel"
CommandButton	Name	cmdGetInfo
	Caption	"Get Info"
CommandButton	Name	cmdSelection
	Caption	"Unselect All"
CommandButton	Name	cmdSelection
	Caption	"Select All"
ListBox	Name	lstGetInfoData
	MultiSelect	Extended
	Sorted	True
Label	Name	lblGetInfo

11. Add the following line of code to the declarations section of the GETINFO.FRM form. `Option Explicit` tells Visual Basic to make sure that you declare all variables and objects before using them, to avoid naming problems.

```
Option Explicit
```

12. Add the following code to the form's `Load` event. The main job of this procedure is to load the `lstGetInfoData` list box with all the available ODBC functions. All the function names are loaded into the `ODBCGetInfo` array in the `LoadGetInfo Sub` procedure in ODBC API Declarations.BAS. That array is an array of `GetInfo` types, defined in ODBC API as this:

```
Type GetInfo
    InfoType As String
    ReturnType As String
End Type
```

The array has `SQL_INFO_LAST` number of elements, as defined in ODBC API Declarations.BAS in the declarations section:

```
Private Sub Form_Load()
    'Load the list box with the ODBCGetInfo array
    Dim I As Integer
    For I = 0 To SQL_INFO_LAST
        If ODBCGetInfo(I).InfoType <> "" Then
            lstGetInfoData.AddItem ODBCGetInfo(I).InfoType
        End If
    Next
    frmGetInfo.Show
End Sub
```

13. Add the following code to the **cmdGetInfo**'s **Click** event procedure.
Although this procedure looks foreboding, it is really doing only two main
jobs: getting a count and a list of the **SQLGetInfo** options that have been
selected in the list box, and then looping through to get their current
settings, populating the grid control on the **frmODBC** form with the results.
For more information on this procedure, review the "How It Works"
section later in this How-To.

```
Private Sub cmdGetInfo_Click()
    Dim intSelCount As Integer        'count of selected items
    Dim I As Integer, j As Integer

    Dim ri As Integer
    Dim rs As String * 255
    Dim rb As Long, rl As Long

    Dim lngInfoValue As Long
    Dim lngInfoValueMax As Integer, intInfoValue As Integer, _
        intResult As Integer
    Dim intConnIndex As Integer
    Dim strTemp As String, strID As String, strErrMsg As String
    Dim strRowData() As String

    lngInfoValueMax = 255

    'Get the number of rows selected and the type of data
    intSelCount = 0
    For I = 0 To lstGetInfoData.ListCount - 1
        If lstGetInfoData.Selected(I) Then
            ReDim Preserve strRowData(intSelCount + 1)
            strRowData(intSelCount) = lstGetInfoData.List(I)
            intSelCount = intSelCount + 1
        End If
    Next

    If intSelCount = 0 Then
        MsgBox "No attributes were selected. Please select " & _
            "at least one and try again.", vbExclamation
        Exit Sub
    End If

    'Start by clearing the frmODBC grid
    With frmODBC.grdResults
        .Rows = intSelCount + 1: .Cols = 3
        .FixedCols = 1: .FixedRows = 1
        .ColWidth(0) = 8
        .ColWidth(1) = 0.45 * frmODBC.grdResults.Width
        .ColWidth(2) = 0.55 * frmODBC.grdResults.Width
        .Row = 0
        .Col = 1: .text = "Attribute Constant"
        .Col = 2: .text = "Value"
    End With
    frmODBC.lblGrid.Caption = frmODBC.lstODBCdbs.text & " " & "Properties"
```

continued on next page

continued from previous page

```
    For I = 0 To intSelCount - 1
        With frmODBC.grdResults
            .Row = I + 1
            .Col = 0: .text = I + 1
            .Col = 1: .text = strRowData(I)
            .Col = 2
        End With

        'Get the index of ODBConn - have to do it this way
        'because there are gaps in the ODBC constants
        For j = LBound(ODBCGetInfo) To UBound(ODBCGetInfo)
            If strRowData(I) = ODBCGetInfo(j).InfoType Then Exit For
        Next

        'Format the data according the return type of
        'ODBCGetInfo
        Select Case Left$(ODBCGetInfo(j).ReturnType, 1)
            Case "S"      'String
                intResult = SQLGetInfo(glng_hDbc, j, ByVal rs, _
                    Len(rs), intInfoValue)
                If Len(Trim$(ODBCGetInfo(j).ReturnType)) > 1 Then
                    frmODBC.grdResults.text = SpecialStr(strRowData(I), _
                        Trim$(rs))
                Else
                    frmODBC.grdResults.text = Trim$(rs)
                End If
            Case "B"      '32-bit Bitmask
                intResult = SQLGetInfo(glng_hDbc, j, rb, 255, intInfoValue)
                frmODBC.grdResults.text = BitMask(rb)
            Case "I"      'Integer
                intResult = SQLGetInfo(glng_hDbc, j, ri, 255, intInfoValue)
                If Len(Trim$(ODBCGetInfo(j).ReturnType)) > 1 Then
                    frmODBC.grdResults.text = SpecialInt(strRowData(I), _
                        Trim$(ri))
                Else
                    frmODBC.grdResults.text = ri
                End If
            Case "L"      'Long
                intResult = SQLGetInfo(glng_hDbc, j, rl, 255, intInfoValue)
                If Len(Trim$(ODBCGetInfo(j).ReturnType)) > 1 Then
                    frmODBC.grdResults.text = SpecialLong(strRowData(I), _
                        Trim$(rl))
                Else
                    frmODBC.grdResults.text = rl
                End If
            Case Else
                'Error in array
                frmODBC.grdResults.text = "Error processing return value."
        End Select
        If intResult <> SQL_SUCCESS Then
            frmODBC.grdResults.text = "Error getting data."
        End If
    Next
    frmODBC.grdResults.Visible = True
```

```
        Unload Me
    End Sub
```

14. Add the code for **SpecialStr** to the code section of the module. This is the first of the "special" processing functions that make the results of the call to **SQLGetInfo** more meaningful. Most of the **Select Case** options simply convert a "Y" or "N" to "Yes" or "No." Another processing function, **SQL_KEYWORDS**, returns a long list of keywords that can be used. To keep things from getting too complex, this How-To just indicates that a list is available; the list could easily be put into a text box or list control to allow closer examination, or used by the application.

The return value of the **SpecialStr** function is the string that is actually displayed in the grid.

```
Private Function SpecialStr(Opt As String, RetStr As String)
    'Do any special processing required for a SQLGetInfo string
    Select Case Opt
        Case "SQL_ODBC_SQL_OPT_IEF"
            SpecialStr = IIf(RetStr = "Y", "Yes", "No")
        Case "SQL_COLUMN_ALIAS"
            SpecialStr = IIf(RetStr = "Y", "Yes", "No")
        Case "SQL_KEYWORDS"
            SpecialStr = "List of keywords."          '&&&
        Case "SQL_ORDER_BY_COLUMNS_IN_SELECT"
            SpecialStr = IIf(RetStr = "Y", "Yes", "No")
        Case "SQL_MAX_ROW_SIZE_INCLUDES_LONG"
            SpecialStr = IIf(RetStr = "Y", "Yes", "No")
        Case "SQL_EXPRESSIONS_IN_ORDERBY"
            SpecialStr = IIf(RetStr = "Y", "Yes", "No")
        Case "SQL_MULT_RESULT_SETS"
            SpecialStr = IIf(RetStr = "Y", "Yes", "No")
        Case "SQL_OUTER_JOINS"
            Select Case RetStr
                Case "N"
                    SpecialStr = "No outer joins."
                Case "Y"
                    SpecialStr = "Yes, left-right segregation."
                Case "P"
                    SpecialStr = "Partial outer joins."
                Case "F"
                    SpecialStr = "Full outer joins."
                Case Else
                    SpecialStr = "Missing data."
            End Select
        Case "SQL_NEED_LONG_DATA_LEN"
            SpecialStr = IIf(RetStr = "Y", "Yes", "No")
        Case "SQL_LIKE_ESCAPE_CLAUSE"
            SpecialStr = IIf(RetStr = "Y", "Yes", "No")
        Case "SQL_ACCESSIBLE_PROCEDURES"
            SpecialStr = IIf(RetStr = "Y", "Yes", "No")
        Case "SQL_ACCESSIBLE_TABLES"
            SpecialStr = IIf(RetStr = "Y", "Yes", "No")
        Case "SQL_DATA_SOURCE_READ_ONLY"
```

continued on next page

continued from previous page

```
            SpecialStr = IIf(RetStr = "Y", "Yes", "No")
        Case "SQL_PROCEDURES"
            SpecialStr = IIf(RetStr = "Y", "Yes", "No")
        Case "SQL_ROW_UPDATES"
            SpecialStr = IIf(RetStr = "Y", "Yes", "No")
        Case Else
            SpecialStr = "Missing special processing."
    End Select
End Function
```

15. Add the code for the `SpecialInt` function to the code section of the form. This function handles special integer return values from `SQLGetInfo`. In all of these special cases, the return value is an index to a keyword defined in ODBCAPI.BAS. Simply use a `Select Case` nested within the overall `Select Case` structure to translate the value into a more meaningful string.

```
Private Function SpecialInt(Opt As String, RetInt As Integer)
    'Do any special processing required for a SQLGetInfo integer
    Select Case Opt
        Case "SQL_CORRELATION_NAME"
            Select Case RetInt
                Case SQL_CN_NONE
                    SpecialInt = "Not supported."
                Case SQL_CN_DIFFERENT
                    SpecialInt = "Supported but names vary."
                Case SQL_CN_ANY
                    SpecialInt = "Any valid user name."
                Case Else
                    SpecialInt = "Missing data."
            End Select
        Case "SQL_NON_NULLABLE_COLUMNS"
            Select Case RetInt
                Case SQL_NNC_NULL
                    SpecialInt = "All columns nullable."
                Case SQL_NNC_NON_NULL
                    SpecialInt = "May be non-nullable."
                Case Else
                    SpecialInt = "Missing data."
            End Select
        Case "SQL_FILE_USAGE"
            Select Case RetInt
                Case SQL_FILE_NOT_SUPPORTED
                    SpecialInt = "Not a single tier driver."
                Case SQL_FILE_TABLE
                    SpecialInt = "Treats data source as table."
                Case SQL_FILE_QUALIFIER
                    SpecialInt = "Treats data source as qualifier."
                Case Else
                    SpecialInt = "Missing data."
            End Select
        Case "SQL_NULL_COLLATION"
            Select Case RetInt
                Case SQL_NC_END
                    SpecialInt = "NULLs sorted to end."
```

```
                Case SQL_NC_HIGH
                    SpecialInt = "NULLs sorted to high end."
                Case SQL_NC_LOW
                    SpecialInt = "NULLs sorted to low end."
                Case SQL_NC_START
                    SpecialInt = "NULLs sorted to start."
                Case Else
                    SpecialInt = "Missing data."
            End Select
        Case "SQL_GROUP_BY"
            Select Case RetInt
                Case SQL_GB_NOT_SUPPORTED
                    SpecialInt = "Group By not supported."
                Case SQL_GB_GROUP_BY_EQUALS_SELECT
                    SpecialInt = "All non-aggregated columns, no others."
                Case SQL_GB_GROUP_BY_CONTAINS_SELECT
                    SpecialInt = "All non-aggregated columns, some others."
                Case SQL_GB_NO_RELATION
                    SpecialInt = "Not related to select list."
                Case Else
                    SpecialInt = "Missing data."
            End Select
        Case "SQL_IDENTIFIER_CASE"
            Select Case RetInt
                Case SQL_IC_UPPER
                    SpecialInt = "Upper case."
                Case SQL_IC_LOWER
                    SpecialInt = "Lower case."
                Case SQL_IC_SENSITIVE
                    SpecialInt = "Case sensitive."
                Case SQL_IC_MIXED
                    SpecialInt = "Mixed case."
                Case Else
                    SpecialInt = "Missing data."
            End Select
        Case "SQL_QUOTED_IDENTIFIER_CASE"
            Select Case RetInt
                Case SQL_IC_UPPER
                    SpecialInt = "Upper case."
                Case SQL_IC_LOWER
                    SpecialInt = "Lower case."
                Case SQL_IC_SENSITIVE
                    SpecialInt = "Case sensitive."
                Case SQL_IC_MIXED
                    SpecialInt = "Mixed case."
                Case Else
                    SpecialInt = "Missing data."
            End Select
        Case "SQL_ODBC_API_CONFORMANCE"
            Select Case RetInt
                Case SQL_OAC_NONE
                    SpecialInt = "No conformance."
                Case SQL_OAC_LEVEL1
                    SpecialInt = "Level 1 supported."
                Case SQL_OAC_LEVEL2
                    SpecialInt = "Level 2 supported."
```

continued on next page

continued from previous page

```
                    Case Else
                        SpecialInt = "Missing data."
                End Select
            Case "SQL_CURSOR_COMMIT_BEHAVIOR"
                Select Case RetInt
                    Case SQL_CB_DELETE
                        SpecialInt = "Close and delete statements."
                    Case SQL_CB_CLOSE
                        SpecialInt = "Close cursors."
                    Case SQL_CB_PRESERVE
                        SpecialInt = "Preserve cursors."
                    Case Else
                        SpecialInt = "Missing data."
                End Select
            Case "SQL_CURSOR_ROLLBACK_BEHAVIOR"
                Select Case RetInt
                    Case SQL_CB_DELETE
                        SpecialInt = "Close and delete statements."
                    Case SQL_CB_CLOSE
                        SpecialInt = "Close cursors."
                    Case SQL_CB_PRESERVE
                        SpecialInt = "Preserve cursors."
                    Case Else
                        SpecialInt = "Missing data."
                End Select
            Case "SQL_TXN_CAPABLE"
                Select Case RetInt
                    Case SQL_TC_NONE
                        SpecialInt = "Transactions not supported."
                    Case SQL_TC_DML
                        SpecialInt = "DML statements only, DDL cause error."
                    Case SQL_TC_DDL_COMMIT
                        SpecialInt = "DML statements, DDL commit transaction."
                    Case SQL_TC_DDL_IGNORE
                        SpecialInt = "DML statements, DDL ignored."
                    Case SQL_TC_ALL
                        SpecialInt = "Both DML and DDL statements."
                    Case Else
                        SpecialInt = "Missing data."
                End Select
            Case "SQL_QUALIFIER_LOCATION"
                Select Case RetInt
                    Case SQL_QL_START
                        SpecialInt = "Start of name."
                    Case SQL_QL_END
                        SpecialInt = "End of name."
                    Case Else
                        SpecialInt = "Missing data."
                End Select
            Case "SQL_CONCAT_NULL_BEHAVIOR"
                Select Case RetInt
                    Case SQL_CB_NULL
                        SpecialInt = "Result is NULL valued."
                    Case SQL_CB_NON_NULL
```

```
                    SpecialInt = "Result is non-NULL concatenation."
                Case Else
                    SpecialInt = "Missing data."
            End Select
        Case Else
            SpecialInt = "Missing special integer processing."
    End Select
End Function
```

16. Add the code for the **BitMask** function to the code section of the form. One form of return value from the **SQLGetInfo** function is a 32-bit bitmask. A *bitmask* is a way of packing lots of information into a relatively compact variable, because each of the 32 bits can be "on" or "off" (1 or 0) to indicate the value of some option. This function simply converts the bitmask into a string of 32 1s and 0s to show their content. You could expand this function (in a way similar to the nested **Select Case SpecialInt** function) to test for the various values of the different options, and could present a list or otherwise use the information in your application.

In practical use in an application, you would be interested in checking for one or two characteristics contained in the bitmask and would check for that condition instead of just listing the contents of the bitmask.

```
Private Function BitMask(RetBit As Long)
    'Do processing required for a SQLGetInfo bit mask return
    Dim i As Long, bin As String
    Const maxpower = 30    ' Maximum number of binary digits supported.
    bin = ""   'Build the desired binary number in this string, bin.

    If RetBit > 2 ^ maxpower Then
        BitMask = "Error converting data."
        Exit Function
    End If

    ' Negative numbers have "1" in the 32nd left-most digit:
    If RetBit < 0 Then bin = bin + "1" Else bin = bin + "0"

    For i = maxpower To 0 Step -1
        If RetBit And (2 ^ i) Then    ' Use the logical "AND" operator.
            bin = bin + "1"
        Else
            bin = bin + "0"
        End If
    Next
    BitMask = bin ' The bin string contains the binary number.
End Function
```

17. Add the code for **SpecialLong** to the code section of the form. This is the last of the **Special** functions, and it is used with return type Long. The single case that must be handled here is for the

SQL_DEFAULT_TXN_ISOLATION attribute, and it is handled similarly to the SpecialInt function. The same nested Select Case structure has been used to allow easy expansion of this function for future versions of ODBC and handle the error condition if an unexpected Long is sent to the function.

```
Private Function SpecialLong(Opt As String, RetInt As Integer)
    'Do any special processing required for a SQLGetInfo long
    Select Case Opt
        Case "SQL_DEFAULT_TXN_ISOLATION"
            Select Case RetInt
                Case SQL_TXN_READ_UNCOMMITTED
                    SpecialLong = "Dirty reads, nonrepeatable, phantoms."
                Case SQL_TXN_READ_COMMITTED
                    SpecialLong = "No dirty reads, but nonrepeatable " & _
                        "and phantoms."
                Case SQL_TXN_REPEATABLE_READ
                    SpecialLong = "No dirty or nonrepeatable reads." & _
                        "Phantoms okay."
                Case SQL_TXN_SERIALIZABLE
                    SpecialLong = "Serializable transactions."
                Case SQL_TXN_VERSIONING
                    SpecialLong = "Serializable transactions with higher " & _
                        "concurrency."
                Case Else
                    SpecialLong = "Missing data."
            End Select

        Case Else
            SpecialLong = "Missing special Long processing."
    End Select
End Function
```

18. Add the code for the cmdSelection control array Click event. The Select All and Unselect All command buttons are provided for convenience in selecting items in the list. This procedure simply loops through the lstGetInfoData list box, selecting all items if the Index is 1 (Select All was clicked) and deselecting all items if the Index is 0 (Unselect All was clicked).

```
Private Sub cmdSelection_Click(Index As Integer)
    'Select all of the items in the list
    Dim I As Integer
    For I = 0 To lstGetInfoData.ListCount - 1
        lstGetInfoData.Selected(I) = (Index > -1)
    Next
End Sub
```

19. Add the code for the `cmdCancel Click` event. Even though `SQLGetInfo` uses an `hDbc` handle, the memory was allocated in the `frmODBC` form, so no special cleanup is needed in this form. Therefore, no form `Unload` procedure is required.

```
Private Sub cmdCancel_Click()
    Unload Me
End Sub
```

How It Works

The `SQLGetInfo` function is a versatile way to get lots of information about an ODBC data source. In a typical application, you would check for a small number of properties, or if a particular function is implemented, instead of retrieving bulk results as in this How-To, you would use the techniques shown here.

Step 13 of this How-To performs and deciphers the `SQLGetInfo` through a procedure that appears daunting, but in fact is really doing only two main jobs: getting a count and a list of the `SQLGetInfo` options that have been selected in the list box, and then looping through to get their current settings, populating the grid control on the `frmODBC` form with the results. Let's break this procedure down into more manageable chunks, because this procedure is important for you to understand.

After the variables used in the procedure are declared, the `lstGetInfoData` list box is looped through to find out what selections have been made by the user. For each selection, the `RowData` dynamic array is expanded by one element, and the name of the option is added. That way, the array will be fully populated with the names of the options selected. The variable `selCount` keeps a running count of how many options have been selected.

After that process is complete, the options are checked to see whether any were selected. If not, the user is asked to make at least one selection and then try again. There is no reason to proceed if there is nothing to do.

Next, the code clears the `grdResults` grid control in the `frmODBC` form, setting it up with three columns and rows equal to `intSelCount + 1`. One additional row is needed for column headings.

The real work of the procedure begins, looping through each of the options and actually making the call to the `SQLGetInfo` ODBC function. This function returns the current setting for the data source for a selected option. Two things make the code a bit more complex. First, an integer needs to be passed to `SQLGetInfo` representing an index into the attribute or option to be checked. To get that index, loop through the `ODBCGetInfo` array, comparing the `InfoType` member to the name in `strRowData`, until there is a match. Because the names in `strRowData` came from `ODBCInfo` in the first place, there will be a match somewhere.

The second complexity arises from the types of values returned from `SQLGetInfo`. Table 7.10 lists the possible return types.

Table 7.10. SQLGetInfo return types.

TYPE	INFOTYPE	DESCRIPTION
String	S	C type null-terminated string
Bitmask	B	32-bit, usually with multiple meanings
Integer	I	Standard Visual Basic 16-bit number
Long	L	Standard Visual Basic 32-bit number

The InfoType column refers to the InfoType member of the GetInfo structure defined in ODBCAPI.BAS. This is simply an arbitrarily chosen code for use in the Select Case in this procedure so that SQLGetInfo can be called with the right variable type to receive the results.

The InfoType member can be either one or two characters long. The second character, if present, means that some special processing is needed to make the result meaningful when it is put in the grid on the frmODBC form.

The Select Case structure then puts the results directly into the frmODBC grid.

Some of the property values returned might not be available, in which case the cmdGetInfo Click event procedure places a value of Error Getting Data in the results grid. You might get this result for many reasons, but the primary reason exposes one of the quirks of the ODBC system. Although ODBC has some rather specific demarcations between conformance levels (drivers must be at Conformance Level 1 to be usable with Visual Basic), there is no guarantee that a driver will implement all the functionality of a given function. SQLGetInfo is no exception to this rule, unfortunately.

One way to determine whether this is the case is to make a call to SQLError (or the ODBCError wrapper function) to obtain more information about the error. In any case, it is safe to assume in most cases that the particular attribute should not be used with the particular data source.

As noted in step 13 of this How-To, the syntax of the SQLGetInfo function is this:

```
SQLGetInfo(hDbc, fInfoType, rgbInfoValue, cbInfoValueMax, pcbInfoValue)
```

The arguments to the function are shown in Table 7.11.

Table 7.11. Arguments for the SQLGetInfo ODBC function.

ARGUMENT	DESCRIPTION
hDbc	Connection handle.
fInfoType	Type of information (in this How-To, from the ODBCGetInfo array).
rgbInfoValue	Variable of the proper type to store results.
cbInfoValueMax	Maximum length of the rgbInfoValue buffer.
pcbInfoValue	Total number of bytes available to return in rgbInfoValue.

The syntax of **SQLGetFunctions** is this:

```
SQLGetFunctions(hDbc, fFunction, pfExists)
```

The arguments to the function are shown in Table 7.12.

Table 7.12. Arguments for the **SQLGetFunctions** ODBC function.

ARGUMENT	DESCRIPTION
hDbc	Connection handle.
fFunction	The particular function, or in this How-To, SQL_API_ALL_FUNCTIONS.
pfExists	For SQL_API_ALL_FUNCTIONS, an array with 100 elements for output.

If you look at the contents of the ODBCAPI.BAS file, you'll see two functions, **LoadGetInfo** and **ODBCLoadFuncs**, that load global arrays with information about the **SQLGetInfo** property options and the list of functions available in ODBC. These two arrays are used to provide selection lists for the program in this How-To and to loop through to make the actual calls to **SQLGetInfo**. The **SQLGetInfo** function has many property options, too numerous to describe here—see the ODBC SDK for a more detailed description of the property options and information about in which ODBC version they first appeared.

What if a driver is written only to the Core conformance level? Well, in a way, that isn't a problem because you won't be using that driver with Visual Basic anyway: Visual Basic counts on Level 1 conformance to interact with ODBC. Running the program in this How-To will provide an ODBC error, and you are finished. You can still use the driver, but only by making direct calls to the ODBC API from Visual Basic. In that situation, you'll need to consult the driver's documentation to find out what it can and cannot do. As a practical matter, by far and away most drivers are at least at Level 1 conformance, so this will rarely be a problem.

The nice thing about the **SQLGetFunctions** function is that, even though it is a Conformance Level 1 function, it is implemented in the ODBC Driver Manager, which sits between all applications using ODBC and the ODBC driver. That way, if the driver doesn't implement **SQLGetFunctions**, the Driver Manager will still give a list. If the driver does implement the function, the Driver Manager passes the call to the driver.

Comments

The **SQLGetInfo** and **SQLGetFunctions** functions are an extremely important part of understanding the ODBC API. Before moving to another How-To, experiment with the use of these functions, especially between different ODBC drivers, to get a better understanding of how varied different drivers can be in terms of functionality.

COMPLEXITY
INTERMEDIATE

7.6 How do I...
Use ODBCDirect to connect to database servers?

Problem

My large application has been recently converted from DAO to ODBC, and the design specifications call for direct ODBC access. How can I get the power of ODBC with the ease of DAO programming in Visual Basic?

Technique

Well, we have good news. An extension of the DAO, called ODBCDirect, allows direct ODBC connection capability, with most of the flexibility of the DAO objects intact. ODBCDirect provides a **Connection** object, analogous to the DAO's **Database** object. It even has a **Database** property, to simulate the **Database** object for your needs. The **Connection** object is the most important piece of the ODBCDirect object hierarchy, so that is the area we will focus on for our example.

Steps

Open and run the ODBCDirect.VBP Visual Basic project file. Click the Open DSN button, and choose an ODBC data source. The form then opens a **Connection** object and displays the object's properties for the data source, similar to what's shown in Figure 7.12.

1. Create a new project, and save it as ODBCDirect.VBP.

2. Name the default form **Form1**, and save the file as TRANS.FRM. Add the controls shown in Figure 7.12, setting the properties as listed in Table 7.13.

Figure 7.12. Chapter 7.6 example.

Table 7.13. Objects and properties for the ODBCDirect form.

OBJECT	PROPERTY	SETTING
Form	Name	frmODBC
	Caption	"Chapter 7.6 Example"
TextBox	Name	txtProperties
	ScrollBars	2 - Vertical
	MultiLine	True
	Locked	True
	Font	Courier
	Font.Size	10
CommandButton	Name	cmdOpen
	Caption	"&Open DSN"
CommandButton	Name	cmdClose
	Caption	"&Close"
Label	Name	lblTables
	Caption	"No information available"

3. Add the following code to the declarations section of `Form1`:

```
Option Explicit
Dim conTemp As Connection
```

4. Add the following code to the form's **Load** event. The brevity of this routine doesn't explain its importance—the **DefaultType** property determines whether the DAO will construct a DAO or an ODBCDirect object. In this case, we are instructing the DBEngine that all objects created under it are ODBCDirect objects. If we planned to mix DAO and ODBCDirect access in the same application, we would perform this step at the workspace or database level, depending on our needs.

```
Private Sub Form_Load()
    'Notice the dbUseODBC parameter; this determines that DBEngine
    'will create an ODBCDirect workspace by default.
    DBEngine.DefaultType = dbUseODBC
End Sub
```

5. Add the following code to the **Click** event of **cmdOpen**. This routine first attempts to open an ODBCDirect **Connection** object, by forcing the user to select an ODBC driver from the ODBC Data Sources dialog box. After it is selected, the **Connection** object is created and its properties concatenated into the **txtProperties** text box for display.

```
Private Sub cmdOpen_Click()
    'Let's create a Connection object. This line will force
    'the ODBC driver to prompt the user.
    'The ODBCDirect Connection object is identical, in terms of
    'DAO object hierarchy, to the Database object.
    Set conTemp = Workspaces(0).OpenConnection("", , False, "ODBC;")
    'If open, let's get the TableDefs from the Database
    'property of the Connection object.
    If IsObject(conTemp) Then
        'Since the Connection object does not support a
        'Properties collection, we must iterate through
        'each property manually.
        lblTables = "Information   - ODBCDirect connection to " & _
            conTemp.Name & ":"
        With conTemp
            txtProperties = "Connect            " & .Connect
            ' Property actually returns a Database object.
            txtProperties = txtProperties & vbCrLf & _
                "Database[.Name]:  " & .Database.Name
            txtProperties = txtProperties & vbCrLf & _
                "Name:             " & .Name
            txtProperties = txtProperties & vbCrLf & _
                "QueryTimeout:     " & .QueryTimeout
            txtProperties = txtProperties & vbCrLf & _
                "RecordsAffected:  " & .RecordsAffected
            txtProperties = txtProperties & vbCrLf & _
                "StillExecuting:   " & .StillExecuting
            txtProperties = txtProperties & vbCrLf & _
                "Transactions:     " & .Transactions
            txtProperties = txtProperties & vbCrLf & _
                "Updatable:        " & .Updatable
        End With
    End If
End Sub
```

6. Add the following code to the **Click** event of **cmdClose**:

```
Private Sub cmdClose_Click()
    End
End Sub
```

How It Works

The DBEngine is initialized with the **dbUseODBC** flag, which tells DAO that all the workspaces, connections, and so on will be generated via ODBCDirect, rather than through the DAO. Note that it's not an "either-or" situation; the same property exists on **Workspace** objects. A **Workspace** object can be created, then flagged for use with ODBCDirect, so DAO and ODBCDirect workspaces can exist together. This, by the way, proves very useful for projects involving data conversion, or communication with server and mainframe databases. After the DBEngine is initialized and the user presses the Open DSN button, the

`Connection` object is created. After successful creation, the form prints each property of the `Connection` object (laboriously; the `Connection` object supports neither the `Properties` nor `TableDefs` collection) to the text box for your perusal.

The lack of a `TableDefs` collection can make it difficult to maneuver around a database, but this can be surmounted by workarounds. For example, Microsoft SQL Server allows a user to query the `SysTables` table, which maintains a list of tables in the database. It might take some doing, but workarounds can be found for many database systems to supply this information.

Comments

The ODBCDirect technology is being rapidly surpassed by the RDO (Remote Data Object) and newly released ADO (Active Data Object) object technologies, but it can still pack a punch. One good use of ODBCDirect is in the scaling of an application—if you see the need to move your DAO-based workstation application into the client/server arena, you can do so with a minimum of recoding and still apply the flexibility of ODBC at the same time with the use of ODBCDirect.

CHAPTER 8
SQL SERVER DATABASES

8

SQL SERVER
DATABASES

How do I...

If you're building large, high-volume database applications for many users, working with a database server such as Oracle, Sybase, or Microsoft SQL Server is probably in your future. This chapter focuses on Microsoft SQL Server. Although the techniques can often be applied to other server databases, each database can have its own particular feature set and SQL dialect.

Unless you've been away on a trip to another planet for the past couple of years, you've undoubtedly noticed that various new technologies have been introduced for accessing server databases. Developers now have a choice of using the Data control, the RemoteData control (RDC), Data Access Objects (DAO), Remote Data Objects (RDO), the Open Database Connectivity (ODBC) API, the VBSQL control and the native server API, or Microsoft's newest entries into remote server connectivity: ODBC Direct, OLEDB, and ADO. Each of these technologies can be a suitable candidate for any given task.

✔ *The Data Control*—This is the traditional entry point for new database developers and is often used for low-volume (and sometimes even high-volume) applications. However, the Data control is really best suited for access to desktop database engines like Jet. If you're scaling a database from Jet to SQL Server, the Data control will continue to work, but for optimum performance you should be thinking about using another data access strategy.

✔ *The RemoteData Control*—The RemoteData control (RDC) is the companion to the Data control for remote server databases. Although convenient for many applications, it imposes some of the same restrictions and lack of control that come with the Data control.

✔ *Data Access Objects*—DAO is the first step beyond the data control for most developers. It's a flexible and powerful object model for database application development. Using linked tables or SQL Passthrough, you can accomplish almost all server database tasks.

✔ *Remote Data Objects*—RDO is the remote server equivalent to DAO. It provides a similar (although not identical) object model but is optimized to work with intelligent server databases. Unlike DAO, which is bundled with the Jet engine, RDO does not contain a query engine; it expects all query processing to take place on the server. Because RDO is really just a thin object layer over the ODBC API, it exposes nearly all the capabilities of the database server with almost no impact on performance.

✔ *The ODBC API*—ODBC was designed to be a database independent server programming interface. Cumbersome and complex to work with, it is the data access strategy for the hard-core programmer. Despite its difficulties, it might offer a minor performance advantage over RDO.

✔ *VBSQL*—Built on DBLib, the native programming interface to SQL Server, VBSQL is a time-tested and reliable data access strategy. However, although other technologies have continued to advance, VBSQL has not and now has become an outdated technology. Many development shops are continuing to build new applications and update existing applications based on VBSQL despite its "lame duck" status—in part because it is still the only technology that provides access to all the features of SQL Server.

These are the new kids on the block:

✔ *ODBC Direct*—With the latest release of DAO, Microsoft unbundled the Jet engine from the object model. ODBC Direct uses the DAO model but sends queries directly through to the database server using RDO (and via the RDO proxy by ODBC) bypassing Jet entirely. This allows you to use existing DAO code (with minor modifications) but gain the performance benefits of RDO. The limitations of DAO, however, still apply, meaning that many server database features will be unavailable or difficult to work with.

✔ *OLEDB/ADO*—OLEDB is currently being touted as the new native interface to SQL Server. Flexible and powerful, this technology might meet its objective and become the universal data access technology, but at the moment it is new and unproven. Many development shops are unwilling to risk major client/server projects on technologies that are only a few months out of beta.

That's a wide array of choices—at times you might feel as if you've joined the technology-of-the-month club—but for most applications, RDO is probably the best option. RDO is now in its second release and is a proven technology. It offers the simplicity of a DAO-like object model but performance equal to the ODBC API or VBSQL. For those techniques available only with the ODBC API, RDO also exposes the necessary handles so you can go directly to the API when you need it.

Along with all the new data access technologies comes a plethora of SQL Server specific and general concepts and buzzwords. Rather than dealing with database files, SQL Server gives you database devices, dump devices, databases, transaction logs, and so on. Instead of a simple user and group list for security, you have logins, users, and groups that can be set up using standard, integrated, or mixed security models. The list goes on to concepts like n-tier design, the use of transaction servers and object brokers, Web connectivity technologies, and more. All this goes far beyond the scope of this chapter, and many excellent books have been written that address some or all of these tools and technologies. Fortunately, SQL Server also comes with excellent documentation.

NOTE

Consider yourself lucky if you have a seasoned dba (database administrator) on staff to help handle the details of creating devices, databases, users, and so forth for you on the server. A good dba can save you days or weeks of work. If you don't have a veteran dba available, dive into the SQL Server documentation. There's a lot to cover, but you will learn it in time. Rome wasn't built in a day, and your client/server application won't be either.

This chapter assumes that you have already successfully installed Microsoft SQL Server 6.5, the pubs sample database, Visual Basic 5.0 Enterprise Edition, and the SQL Server client utilities. You will need to have the authority necessary to create a database on your server or access to a dba who can do it for you. You will also need to be able to execute SQL statements on the server using either SQL Enterprise Manager or ISQL/w. Consult the SQL Server documentation for more information on the installation and use of these utilities.

8.1 Scale an Existing Microsoft Access Database to SQL Server

Database applications can take on a life of their own and outgrow their original designs. In this How-To, you learn how to transfer your database design and its data to SQL Server and adapt the existing application to work with the new server database.

8.2 Browse a SQL Server Database Using the RemoteData Control

This How-To introduces the most basic of operations on a database server: browsing the results of a query with the RemoteData control.

8.3 Add and Delete Records in a SQL Server Database Using the RemoteData Control

In this How-To, you learn to use the RemoteData control to perform inserts and deletes on the remote SQL Server database.

8.4 Connect to a SQL Server Database Using Remote Data Objects

Before you can do anything with remote server data, you must establish a connection to the server. This How-To shows you how to open an RDO Connection.

8.5 Browse Records in a SQL Server Database Using Remote Data Objects

The RemoteData control, like the Data control, has its limitations. In this How-To, you learn to use Remote Data Objects to read SQL Server data.

8.6   Add, Update, and Delete Records in a SQL Server Database Using Remote Data Objects

This How-To shows you how to insert, update, and delete records using RDO.

8.7   Execute a SQL Server Stored Procedure Using Remote Data Objects

Most server databases rely heavily on stored procedures for database operations. This How-To teaches you to execute a simple stored procedure that returns a result set.

8.8   Execute a Parameterized SQL Server Stored Procedure with Remote Data Objects

SQL Server stored procedures, like Visual Basic procedures, can have input and output parameters and return values. This How-To shows you how to execute a stored procedure with parameters.

8.9   Handle Remote Data Objects Errors

Despite your best efforts, things can go wrong on the remote database. In this How-To, you learn to trap and handle errors delivered to RDO by SQL Server.

COMPLEXITY
INTERMEDIATE

8.1   How do I...
Scale an existing Microsoft Access database to SQL Server?

Problem

My database application has outgrown my Access database. How can I scale the database to SQL Server without rewriting the entire application?

Technique

Database applications can have an uncanny ability to take on a life of their own. An application you created two years ago using an Access database and programmed with Data Access Objects (DAO) for two or three users might today be in use by two or three dozen users and contain scores or hundreds of megabytes of data.

With this many users and this much data, the Jet database engine begins to falter. Locking errors become routine, and database corruption problems are more and more frequent. Even without these kinds of severe errors, performance will become significantly degraded, and traffic will begin to overload the capacity of the network. This is the point when it's time to rethink the data access strategy and consider moving the database to a more robust database server such as SQL Server.

Two methods are available for you to transfer the design and data in your database to SQL Server:

✔ *The Microsoft Upsizing Wizard*—The wizard is a tool provided free of charge by Microsoft that can automatically transfer the structure and data in an Access database to SQL Server.

✔ *Roll your own*—In some cases, the wizard might not provide the results you need or might fail entirely. If that happens, you'll need to transfer the structure and the data yourself.

Using the wizard is a fairly straightforward process. Just answer its questions and keep going through the forms until you're done. This How-To will use the second approach. In either case, you might need to make some modifications to the application for it to work with the new server database.

A WORD ON WIZARDS

Tools are good things, but in some cases it might be better for you to forgo automated tools and do it yourself. Converting a database to SQL Server, especially if it is your first SQL Server database, might be one of these cases. You might be able to save some time by using the wizard if you're under a tight deadline, but eventually you'll need to understand how things work on the server anyway. The conversion is a good time to start learning.

Several steps are involved in manually transferring a database from Access to SQL Server:

1. Make a backup copy of your database. If you are working with a live database—and you probably will be—you might want to make several trial runs with copies of the master database file before you make the final conversion and bring the server database online for daily operations.

2. Find or create devices for the database and transaction log or have the dba create them for you. Devices are the rough equivalent of files in the file system.

3. Create the new, empty database on the server.

4. Duplicate the table structure on the server. Depending on the design and the data in your tables, you might be able to add foreign key constraints and engine-level rules at this time as well. However, if you added constraints or rules to your Access tables when the tables already had existing data, you might need to add rules later or the data transfer could fail due to rules violations.

5. Transfer the data. This is normally done by exporting the data to text files and then using the SQL Server Bulk Copy Program (BCP) to import the data. You can also skip forward at this point, link the server tables to your database, and use a series of INSERT queries (Append queries in Access terminology) to transfer the data. Either approach will work, but if you have a lot of data to move, the BCP approach is much faster. On the other hand, if the tables are relatively small, you can avoid (or at least postpone) the need to deal with the cryptic BCP syntax by linking the server tables and using INSERT queries. If you have more time to set up the conversion than to actually transfer the data, use BCP (you might be working with a live database that needs to be converted overnight and working correctly in the morning). If you don't have a lot of time to set up the conversion but it doesn't need to happen all at once, use linked tables and INSERT queries.

6. If necessary, apply rules and constraints either directly to the tables or by using insert, update, or delete triggers.

7. Add appropriate indexes to the tables. If you haven't worked with SQL Server before, you will be introduced here to a new type of index: the *clustered index*. In a clustered index, the rows in the table are stored as the leaf nodes of the index. This can provide a significant performance benefit if the right clustered index is chosen.

8. Delete your original tables and attach the new server tables as linked tables in your Access database. You can use Visual Basic code to do this, but it's much easier to use Access if you have it available. You will need to have configured an ODBC data source to complete this step.

9. If you used names in your Access tables that do not conform to SQL Server standards or if you renamed any of the objects on the server, you will need to create what is known as an *aliasing query* that maps the names of your server tables and columns to the old Access table and column names.

10. Make any modifications to the application necessary for it to work with the new server database. The most common cause of failures in existing code are the use of DAO and Jet specific techniques. The Seek method, for example, is not available for server tables.

11. Test the new application thoroughly to make sure everything works as expected. If you've encapsulated data access code into classes and compiled it into ActiveX components, you'll need to open those projects and examine that source code as well. At a minimum, test all data access routines and, if possible, test every line of code.

At this point, you can give yourself a small pat on the back. You've completed the *easy* part and will have a functional application running against a remote SQL Server database. However, your task is not complete because merely moving the database and getting everything to work right will give you an application designed for a desktop database running on a server database.

To fully realize the power of the remote database server, you'll need to start examining the design of the application, looking for areas where you can put the database server to better use. For example, you might have complex validation procedures in your application—procedures that could not be implemented by using Jet's simple `ValidationRule` properties but that could be done easily as Transact SQL (T-SQL) triggers or stored procedures.

There might be other complex logic in your application that could be moved to the server as well. Most large database applications rely heavily on stored procedures for data processing, and when you have completed the transfer, there will be none of these. Some databases provide no direct access to tables and gate all processing through stored procedures to provide better performance and tighter security.

Steps

There's no Visual Basic project associated with this How-To. All the steps are performed using SQL Enterprise Manager and Access. The Biblio.mdb sample database is an Access 7.0 file, but any 32-bit version of Access will work. Although it would be possible to set up the attached tables and transfer the data using only Visual Basic code, it is considerably easier and faster to use Access for this purpose.

> **NOTE**
>
> Be sure to make a fresh backup copy of your database before beginning the upsizing process if you are working with a production database.

1. Find or create devices on the SQL Server for your new database. SQL Server devices are essentially operating system files. To create a database device in SQL Enterprise Manager, browse to the folder labeled Database Devices, right-click the folder, and select New Device from the context menu. After upsizing, the Biblio database will require about 4MB of disk space. Normally, you would create separate devices for the database and the transaction log, although it is not required that you do so. For this How-To, create the devices shown in Table 8.1, using the dialog box shown in Figure 8.1.

Table 8.1. Biblio database devices.

NAME	SIZE
BiblioData	10MB
BiblioLog	10MB

NOTE

If you are low on free disk space on your SQL Server, you should be able to get by with 5MB devices. However, for a production database, it is advisable to add some room for growth.

2. Create the Biblio database. In SQL Enterprise Manager, right-click the Databases folder and select New Database from the context menu. Name the new database Biblio and use the two devices created in step 1 for the Data Device and Log Device. You can use all the available space on both devices for this database.

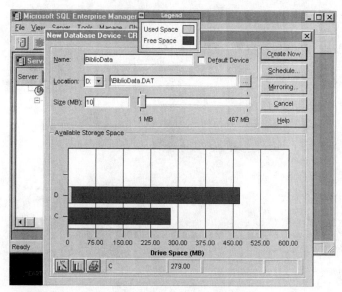

Figure 8.1. Creating the BiblioData device.

> **NOTE**
>
> If you've never worked with SQL Server before, the concept of preallocating space for devices and databases will be new to you. Access databases grow as they need to, but space for SQL Server databases must be allocated in advance. You can also resize existing databases or spread them across multiple devices, distributing the database over several physical disks.

3. Create the tables in the database by running a Transact-SQL (T-SQL) script. In SQL Enterprise Manager, open a new query window by selecting SQL Query Tool from the Tools menu. Load and run the script CreateTables.sql. The four **CREATE TABLE** statements create the tables in the database as well as define all the foreign key constraints (known in Access parlance as Relationships).

> **NOTE**
>
> T-SQL comments use C-style delimiters. /* indicates the beginning of a comment, and */ indicates the end. Line breaks are ignored in T-SQL scripts.

```
/* Create the tables in the Biblio sample database */
USE Biblio

/*
Authors table
Names mapped as follows
Au_ID - AuthID
Author - AuthName
Year Born - AuthYearBorn Note: Original name illegal in SQL Server
*/
PRINT 'Authors'
Go
CREATE TABLE Authors
   (
     AuthID INT IDENTITY NOT NULL
       CONSTRAINT apkAuthors PRIMARY KEY NONCLUSTERED,
     AuthName VARCHAR(50) NULL,
     AuthYearBorn SMALLINT NULL
   )
Go

/*
Publishers table
Names mapped as follows
PubID - PubID
Name - PubName
Company Name - PubCompName
Address - PubAddress
City - PubCity
```

```
State - PubState
Zip - PubZIP
Telephone - PubPhone
Fax - PubFax
Comments - PubComments
*/
PRINT 'Publishers'
Go
CREATE TABLE Publishers
  (
    PubID INT IDENTITY NOT NULL
      CONSTRAINT apkPublishers PRIMARY KEY NONCLUSTERED,
    PubName VARCHAR(5) NULL,
    PubCompName VARCHAR(255) NULL,
    PubAddress VARCHAR(50) NULL,
    PubCity VARCHAR(20) NULL,
    PubState VARCHAR(10) NULL,
    PubZIP VARCHAR(15) NULL,
    PubPhone VARCHAR(15) NULL,
    PubFax VARCHAR(15) NULL,
    PubComments TEXT NULL
  )
Go


/*
Titles table
Name mappings
Title - TitleName
Year Published - TitleYearPubl
ISBN - TitleISBN
PubID - TitlePubID
Description - TitleDesc
Notes - TitleNotes
Subject - TitleSubject
Comments - TitleComments
*/
PRINT 'Titles'
Go
CREATE TABLE Titles
  (
    TitleISBN VARCHAR(20) NOT NULL
      CONSTRAINT apkTitles PRIMARY KEY NONCLUSTERED,
    TitleName VARCHAR(255) NULL,
    TitleYearPubl SMALLINT NULL
      CONSTRAINT defTitleYearPubl DEFAULT 0,
    TitlePubID INT NOT NULL
      CONSTRAINT fkTitlePubID FOREIGN KEY
      REFERENCES Publishers(PubID),
    TitleDesc VARCHAR(50) NULL,
    TitleNotes VARCHAR(50) NULL,
    TitleSubject VARCHAR(50) NULL,
    TitleComments VARCHAR(50) NULL
  )
Go

/*
```

continued on next page

continued from previous page

```
TitleAuthors table
- Note name change from "Title Authors"
- space in name is illegal in SQL Server
Name mappings
ISBN - TAISBN
Au_ID - TAAuthID
*/
PRINT 'TitleAuthors'
Go
CREATE TABLE TitleAuthors
  (
    TATitleISBN VARCHAR(20) NOT NULL
      CONSTRAINT fkTATitleISBN FOREIGN KEY
      REFERENCES Titles(TitleISBN),
    TAAuthID INT NOT NULL
      CONSTRAINT fkTAAuthID FOREIGN KEY
      REFERENCES Authors(AuthID),
    CONSTRAINT apkTitleAuthors
      PRIMARY KEY CLUSTERED (TATitleISBN, TAAuthID)
  )
Go
PRINT 'Biblio Tables Created'
```

NOTE

If you are familiar with Jet SQL, you'll find T-SQL syntax for creating tables to be remarkably similar. In many cases, table creation scripts can be run against either type of database.

---

4. Create an ODBC data source using the 32-bit ODBC control panel applet. Use **Biblio** as the **Data Source Name** and **Database Name**, and enter the name of your SQL Server machine as the **Server**. See Chapter 7, "Connecting to an ODBC Server," for additional information on creating ODBC data sources.

5. Attach the newly created server tables to the original Biblio.mdb database using Microsoft Access. From the File menu, choose Get External Data and then Link Tables, or just right-click a blank area of the database window and choose Link Tables. Using the ODBC data source created in step 4, attach all four server tables. These will appear in the database window as dbo_Authors, dbo_Publishers, dbo_TitleAuthors, and dbo_Titles.

6. Transfer the data in the Authors Access table to the SQL Server Authors table. Before you can run this query, however, you need to inform SQL Server that you will be inserting existing values into an **IDENTITY** column. This is done using a SQL Passthrough query. Create a new query, select SQL Specific from the Query menu in query design view, and then choose Pass-Through. Open the query property sheet and set Returns Records to No; then enter and run the following SQL statement:

```
SET IDENTITY_INSERT Authors ON
```

Leave this query window open and create a new query. Enter and run the following SQL statement:

```
INSERT INTO dbo_Authors
  ( AuthID, AuthName, AuthYearBorn )
SELECT
  Authors.Au_ID, Authors.Author, Authors.[Year Born]
FROM Authors;
```

> **NOTE**
>
> It might take several minutes for this query to finish.

After this query has finished running, the Authors table on the SQL Server will be populated with the data in the Access table. You can now return to the pass-through query, change ON to OFF, and run the query to inform the SQL Server that you no longer need to insert values into the **IDENTITY** column in the Authors table.

> **NOTE**
>
> You should back up both the transaction log and the database on the SQL Server after each table is transferred.

7. Transfer the data in the Publishers table. Because this table also contains an **IDENTITY** column, you will need to repeat the pass-through queries run in step 6—changing the table name from Authors to Publishers—to inform SQL Server that you will once again be inserting existing values in an autonumber column. After you have run the pass-through query, run the following SQL statement:

```
INSERT INTO dbo_Publishers
  ( PubID, PubName, PubCompName, PubAddress, PubCity,
  PubState, PubZIP, PubPhone, PubFax, PubComments )
SELECT Publishers.PubID, Publishers.Name,
  Publishers.[Company Name], Publishers.Address,
  Publishers.City, Publishers.State, Publishers.Zip,
  Publishers.Telephone, Publishers.Fax, Publishers.Comments
FROM Publishers;
```

8. Transfer the data in the Titles table to SQL Server. This table does not use an **IDENTITY** column, so no pass-through queries are required. Create and run the following SQL statement to transfer the data in the table:

```
INSERT INTO dbo_Titles
  ( TitleName, TitleYearPubl, TitleISBN, TitlePubID,
  TitleDesc, TitleNotes, TitleSubject, TitleComments )
SELECT
  Titles.Title, Titles.[Year Published], Titles.ISBN,
  Titles.PubID, Titles.Description, Titles.Notes,
  Titles.Subject, Titles.Comments
FROM Titles;
```

> **NOTE**
>
> This is a fairly large table for this type of transfer. You might get a message from SQL Server that the query failed due to insufficient space in the transaction log. If this happens, truncate the log, increase its size, and try again.

9. Transfer the Title Author table by creating and running the following SQL statement:

```
INSERT INTO dbo_TitleAuthors
  ( TATitleISBN, TAAuthID )
SELECT
  [Title Author].ISBN, [Title Author].Au_ID
FROM [Title Author];
```

> **NOTE**
>
> You have now transferred all the structure and data from the original tables to the new SQL Server tables.

10. Make a fresh backup copy of Biblio.mdb and then delete the original Authors, Publishers, Title Author, and Titles tables.

11. Create an aliasing query for the Authors table to match the original column names to the new SQL Server column names using the following SQL statement. Aliasing queries are named using the original name of the Access tables so that queries, forms, reports, and code based on the tables will continue to work without modification.

```
SELECT
  dbo_Authors.AuthID AS Au_ID,
  dbo_Authors.AuthName AS Author,
  dbo_Authors.AuthYearBorn AS [Year Born]
FROM dbo_Authors;
```

12. Create an aliasing query for the Publishers table:

```
SELECT
  dbo_Publishers.PubID,
  dbo_Publishers.PubName AS Name,
  dbo_Publishers.PubCompName AS [Company Name],
  dbo_Publishers.PubAddress AS Address,
  dbo_Publishers.PubCity AS City,
  dbo_Publishers.PubState AS State,
  dbo_Publishers.PubZIP AS Zip,
  dbo_Publishers.PubPhone AS Telephone,
  dbo_Publishers.PubFax AS Fax,
  dbo_Publishers.PubComments AS Comments
FROM dbo_Publishers;
```

13. Create an aliasing query for the Titles table:

```
SELECT
  dbo_Titles.TitleISBN AS ISBN,
  dbo_Titles.TitleName AS Title,
  dbo_Titles.TitleYearPubl AS [Year Published],
  dbo_Titles.TitlePubID AS PubID,
  dbo_Titles.TitleDesc AS Description,
  dbo_Titles.TitleNotes AS Notes,
  dbo_Titles.TitleSubject AS Subject,
  dbo_Titles.TitleComments AS Comments
FROM dbo_Titles;
```

14. Create an aliasing query for the Title Author table:

```
SELECT
  dbo_TitleAuthors.TATitleISBN AS ISBN,
  dbo_TitleAuthors.TAAuthID AS Au_ID
FROM dbo_TitleAuthors;
```

15. In SQL Enterprise Manager, load and run the T-SQL script CreateIndexes.sql to create indexes for the Biblio database. These indexes were chosen based on little more than an educated guess on potential use of the columns. See Chapter 4, "Designing and Implementing a Database," for more information on choosing columns to index.

```
/* Create Indexes for the Biblio database */
USE Biblio
Go

PRINT 'Authors'
Go
CREATE CLUSTERED INDEX cdxAuthors ON Authors (AuthName)
Go

PRINT 'Publishers'
Go
CREATE CLUSTERED INDEX cdxPublishers ON Publishers (PubName)
Go
CREATE INDEX idxPubState ON Publishers (PubState)
Go

PRINT 'Titles'
Go
CREATE CLUSTERED INDEX cdxTitles ON Titles (TitleName)
Go
CREATE INDEX idxTitlePubID ON Titles (TitlePubID)
Go

PRINT 'TitleAuthors'
Go
CREATE INDEX idxTATitleISBN ON TitleAuthors (TATitleISBN)
Go
CREATE INDEX idxTAAuthID ON TitleAuthors (TAAuthID)
```

continued on next page

continued from previous page

```
Go

PRINT 'Done creating indexes.'
Go
```

How It Works

The general procedure for scaling a database to SQL Server from Access is to create a new empty database on the server, copy the structure, and then transfer the data. The Biblio sample is likely to be considerably less complex than any real production database that needs to be upsized, but the general idea is the same regardless of the size. The only real problems as the database to be scaled gets larger and more complex are the proper sequencing of data (so that foreign key constraints and rules can be enforced) and the time required for transferring the data. For larger databases, you will probably need to export the data from Access to text files and use SQL Server's BCP (Bulk Copy Program) applet to import the data. Using BCP allows you to import data without logging the operations (avoiding problems of filling the transaction log) and is considerably faster than the **INSERT** query approach shown in this How-To for large tables. For tables as small as those in the Biblio database, however, the **INSERT** query approach is sufficient.

Comments

Transferring the data, attaching the new server tables, and creating aliasing queries so that everything looks the same doesn't necessarily mean that everything will work right or that you will be getting the best performance from your database server. Some coding techniques (such as using the **Seek** method with table-type records) won't work, and some existing queries either won't work at all or will be processed entirely by Jet rather than run by the server.

The upsizing process as described here is the first of many steps in the transition from a desktop database such as Access to a server database and a true client/server application. You might need to update code in your application just to make things work as before, and you almost certainly will need to undertake some redesign to gain the maximum benefit from your investment in the server hardware and software.

COMPLEXITY
BEGINNING

8.2 How do I...
Browse a SQL Server database using the RemoteData control?

Problem

My data is on a SQL Server database. How do I access this data using the RemoteData control?

Technique

Accessing data from a SQL Server database need not be complex. With the RemoteData control (RDC), you can build a simple form based on SQL Server data in minutes. Building forms with the RDC is the ultimate in visual design—no code whatsoever is required.

Building a form with the RDC requires only a few simple steps:

1. Create an ODBC data source for your database.

2. Draw a RemoteData control on your form and set the `DataSourceName` and SQL properties.

3. Add controls to the form for the columns you need to display and set the `DataSource` and `DataField` properties.

That's all there is to it. The RDC handles everything else for you in conjunction with the ODBC drivers. Like the Data control, the RemoteData control handles updating the tables as well as providing navigation buttons for the rows in the query.

> **NOTE**
>
> This example and the rest of the examples in this chapter require that the pubs sample database be installed on your SQL Server and that an ODBC data source named pubs has been configured to connect to your server and the pubs sample database. See Chapter 7 for more information on configuring ODBC data sources.

Steps

Open and run project HT802.vbp. You can browse and update the rows returned by the query using the form shown in Figure 8.2.

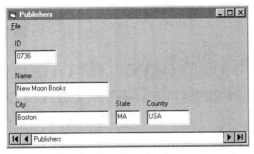

Figure 8.2. The Publishers form.

Depending on the configuration of your SQL Server and network, you might or might not be prompted to provide a user name and password when connecting to the server. All of these examples were created using integrated security, which uses your network logon to validate your connection to the database server. SQL Server integrated security is available only if the server is a member of a Windows NT domain.

1. Create a new Standard EXE project, add the Microsoft RemoteData Control 2.0 to the toolbox, and save the project as HT802.vbp. Change the name of `Form1` to `FMain` and create the objects and properties shown in Table 8.2.

Table 8.2. Objects and properties for `FMain`.

OBJECT	PROPERTY	VALUE
Form	Caption	Publishers
RemoteData Control	Name	rdc
	Caption	Publishers
	Align	2 - vbAlignBottom
	DataSourceName	pubs
	SQL	SELECT pub_id, pub_name,
		city, state, country
		FROM publishers
Label	Name	lbl
	Caption	ID
	Index	0

OBJECT	PROPERTY	VALUE
TextBox	Name	txtID
	DataSource	rdc
	DataField	pub_id
Label	Name	lbl
	Caption	Name
	Index	1
TextBox	Name	txtName
	DataSource	rdc
	DataField	pub_name
Label	Name	lbl
	Caption	City
	Index	2
TextBox	Name	txtCity
	DataSource	rdc
	DataField	city
Label	Name	lbl
	Caption	State
	Index	3
TextBox	Name	txtState
	DataSource	rdc
	DataField	state
Label	Name	lbl
	Caption	Country
	Index	4
TextBox	Name	txtCountry
	DataSource	rdc
	DataField	country

2. Using the menu editor, create the menu shown in Table 8.3.

Table 8.3. Menu controls for FMain.

NAME	CAPTION
mnuFile	&File
mnuFileExit	E&xit

3. Create the declarations section of the form:

```
Option Explicit
```

> **NOTE**
>
> You can and should set up Visual Basic to always use `Option Explicit` by checking the box marked Require Variable Declaration on the Editor tab of the Options dialog box.

4. Create the `mnuFileExit_Click` event procedure:

```
Private Sub mnuFileExit_Click()
  Unload Me
End Sub
```

How It Works

The RDC handles all the work for you in this application. When the application starts, the control opens a connection to the SQL Server, submits the query, and presents the results on the form. The navigation buttons provided by the control allow you to navigate among the rows returned by the query.

Comments

This simple application exemplifies the visual part of Visual Basic. The single line of executable code unloads the form and ends the program. Everything else required to enable live editing of data in the database is designed using visual tools.

COMPLEXITY

INTERMEDIATE

8.3 How do I...

Add and delete records in a SQL Server database using the RemoteData control?

Problem

My users need to be able to add and delete rows in my SQL Server tables as well as view and update existing rows. How do I add and delete rows using the RemoteData control?

Technique

Writing just a small amount of code allows you to implement the ability to insert and delete rows with the RemoteData control. The RemoteData control's `Resultset` object provides the `AddNew` and `Delete` methods. You can implement both with just a few lines of code and a user interface mechanism to invoke the procedures.

Inserting a row is a two-step process:

1. Call the `AddNew` method of the RemoteData control's `Resultset` to set the row buffer to a blank new row.

2. Call the `Update` method of the `Resultset` to insert the row into the table.

Deleting a row requires only a single call to the `Delete` method of the `Resultset`; but after the delete has been performed, the current row will be undefined, so you need to add code to move to a valid row. This example uses the Microsoft Access convention of moving to the previous row, but you could just as easily move to the next row.

Steps

Open and run project HT803.vbp. This is the same as the project created for How-To 8.2 with code and controls added to support inserts and deletes. You can browse, update, insert, and delete rows in the Publishers table using the RemoteData control's navigation buttons and the commands on the Data menu, as shown in Figure 8.3.

INSERTING AND DELETING ROWS IN THE PUBLISHERS TABLE

The Publishers table in the sample database has a rather unusual rule for the `pub_id` column:

```
(pub_id = '1756' or (pub_id = '1622' or
(pub_id = '0877' or (pub_id = '0736' or (pub_id = '1389'))))
or (pub_id like '99[0-9][0-9]'))
```

This rule requires that the `pub_id` value be one of the five specific values shown (1756, 1622, 0877, 0736, or 1389) or that it be a four-digit number between 9900 and 9999. Don't be surprised if you see strange-looking rules like this appearing from time to time. This sort of thing is occasionally necessary to maintain compliance with legacy code, data, or both.

If you add rows to the table while working with the sample application, you need to make sure the `pub_id` column meets this rule. In a production application, you would probably want to add code to automatically generate a valid value for this column.

Additionally, there are other tables in the database that contain foreign key references to the Publishers table, so you

continued on next page

continued from previous page

might not be able to delete some of the existing rows. A complete application based on the pubs database would need to implement methods of dealing with these foreign key references. Alternatively, you could write a delete trigger for the Publishers table that would delete any related rows in related tables.

1. Create a new Standard EXE project, add the Microsoft RemoteData Control 2.0 to the toolbox, and save the project as HT803.vbp.

2. FMain.frm is the same form developed for How-To 8.2. You can add the existing file from the previous How-To, or refer to Table 8.2 to add the RemoteData control, labels, text boxes, and refer to Table 8.3 to create the File menu controls.

3. Use the menu editor to add the menu controls for the Data menu as shown in Table 8.4.

Table 8.4. Specifications for the Data menu.

CAPTION	NAME	SHORTCUT KEY
&Data	mnuData	
&Save	mnuDataSave	Ctrl+S
-	mnuDataBar	
&New	mnuDataNew	Ctrl+N
&Delete	mnuDataDelete	

4. Add `Option Explicit` to the declarations section.

5. Create the `Form_Unload` event procedure. This procedure sets up an error handler and calls the `SaveRecord` procedure described in step 10.

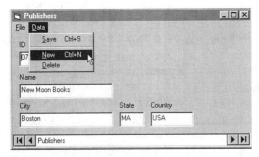

Figure 8.3. The Publishers form.

```
Private Sub Form_Unload(Cancel As Integer)
On Error GoTo ProcError

  SaveRecord

ProcExit:
  Exit Sub

ProcError:
  MsgBox Err.Number & vbCrLf & Err.Description
  Resume ProcExit

End Sub
```

6. Create the `mnuFileExit_Click` event procedure. This code is identical to the code in How-To 8.2.

```
Private Sub mnuFileExit_Click()
On Error Resume Next

  Unload Me
  If Err.Number <> 0 Then
    MsgBox Err.Number & vbCrLf & Err.Description
  End If

End Sub
```

7. Add code for the Data menu controls. The New, Delete, and Save commands call the corresponding **AddRecord**, **DeleteRecord**, and **SaveRecord** procedures described in steps 8, 9, and 10.

```
Private Sub mnuDataNew_Click()
On Error GoTo ProcError

  AddRecord

ProcExit:
  Exit Sub

ProcError:
  MsgBox Err.Number & vbCrLf & Err.Description
  Resume ProcExit

End Sub
Private Sub mnuDataDelete_Click()
On Error GoTo ProcError

  DeleteRecord

ProcExit:
  Exit Sub

ProcError:
  MsgBox Err.Number & vbCrLf & Err.Description
  Resume ProcExit
```

continued on next page

continued from previous page

```
End Sub
Private Sub mnuDataSave_Click()
On Error GoTo ProcError

  SaveRecord

ProcExit:
  Exit Sub

ProcError:
  MsgBox Err.Number & vbCrLf & Err.Description
  Resume ProcExit

End Sub
```

8. Create the `AddRecord` procedure. This procedure calls the `AddNew` method of the RemoteData control's `Resultset` to create the new record. The new row is inserted into the table later by the `SaveRecord` procedure.

```
Private Sub AddRecord()

  ' add it
  rdc.Resultset.AddNew
  txtID.SetFocus

End Sub
```

9. Add the `DeleteRecord` procedure. This procedure uses the `Delete` method of the RemoteData control's `Resultset` to remove the row from the table, then repositions the row pointer to a valid row in the table. The code first moves to the previous row, then checks for the beginning of the `Resultset` and, if necessary, moves to the first row.

```
Private Sub DeleteRecord()

  ' delete the row
  rdc.Resultset.Delete
  ' back up one row
  rdc.Resultset.MovePrevious
  ' check for beginning of set
  If rdc.Resultset.BOF Then
    rdc.Resultset.MoveFirst
  End If

End Sub
```

10. The `SaveRecord` procedure uses the `EditMode` property of the RemoteData control's `Resultset` to determine how to save the current row using a Select Case block. If the row has not been changed, no action is necessary. If an existing row has been changed, the `UpdateRow` method is used to commit the changes. New rows are added to the table by calling the `Update` method of the `Resultset`.

```
Private Sub SaveRecord()

  Select Case rdc.Resultset.EditMode
    Case rdEditNone
      ' clean record, do nothing
    Case rdEditInProgress
      ' the control handles regular edits
      rdc.UpdateRow
    Case rdEditAdd
      ' use the Update method of the
      ' resultset
      rdc.Resultset.Update
  End Select

End Sub
```

How It Works

This is a basic bound control application. The only thing that differentiates the techniques from an application based on the Data control is the use of the RemoteData control and a few minor variations in the code syntax. The control handles most of the work of displaying and updating data, with a little help from a few lines of code.

Comments

The RemoteData control is a convenient but limiting method of working with remote server databases. In the following How-To's, you'll learn to use Remote Data Objects to connect to and manage data in SQL Server databases.

COMPLEXITY
BEGINNING

8.4 How do I...
Connect to a SQL Server database using Remote Data Objects?

Problem

My application needs to connect to a SQL Server database without using the RemoteData control. How can I create a connection with Remote Data Objects?

Technique

If an ODBC data source has been configured, you can establish a connection to a SQL Server database with as little as a single line of code using the `OpenConnection` method of the `rdoEnvironment` object. By adding an extra line of code or two, you can also create a so-called "DSN-less" connection with no preconfigured ODBC data source name.

Using a preconfigured ODBC data source adds one additional required step in configuring the workstation but also allows you to share the connection among multiple applications. If you embed the connection information in the source code for the application, you eliminate one step in setting up the workstation. See Chapter 7 for more information on ODBC data sources.

The example that follows demonstrates both methods. Additionally, RDO 2.0 also allows you to create an **rdoConnection** object without an explicit physical connection to a remote database. After you have assigned the necessary properties to the **rdoConnection** object, use the **EstablishConnection** method to open the connection.

Steps

Open project HT804.vbp. Before running this project using a DSN-less connection, you will need to change the values used in creating the connect string in the **OpenConnection** routine to reflect the correct user name (**UID=**), password (**PWD=**), and SQL Server machine name (**SERVER=**). If you check the box marked Use pubs DSN, the application will open a connection using an ODBC data source named pubs (which you should have already created using the 32-bit ODBC control panel applet). If the check box is cleared, a DSN-less connection will be created. The connection form is shown in Figure 8.4.

1. Create a new Standard EXE project, add a reference to Microsoft Remote Data Object 2.0, and save the project as HT804.vbp.

2. Change the name of **Form1** to **FMain** and add the objects and properties shown in Table 8.5.

Table 8.5. Objects and properties for **FMain**.

OBJECT	PROPERTY	VALUE
CheckBox	Name	chkUseDSN
	Caption	Use pubs DSN
CommandButton	Name	cmdConnect
	Caption	Connect

Figure 8.4. The RDO connection form.

3. Add the following code to the declarations section. The module-level variable `mcon` is used later by the `OpenConnection` routine.

```
Option Explicit

Private mcon As rdoConnection
```

4. Create the `cmdConnect_Click` event procedure. This routine sets up an error handler, calls `OpenConnection`, and displays a message indicating the success or failure of the connection.

```
Private Sub cmdConnect_Click()
On Error GoTo ProcError

  If OpenConnection() Then
    MsgBox "Connection Opened"
  Else
    MsgBox "Connection Failed"
  End If

ProcExit:
  Exit Sub

ProcError:
  MsgBox Err.Number & vbCrLf & Err.Description
  Resume ProcExit

End Sub
```

5. Create the `OpenConnection` function. This function uses the value of the check box to determine whether it should use the pubs DSN or create a DSN-less connection, then calls the `OpenConnection` method of the default `rdoEnvironment` object to establish the connection to the remote server. The function returns true if the connection was successfully established.

```
Private Function OpenConnection() As Boolean
On Error GoTo ProcError

  Dim sConnect As String

  If chkUseDSN = vbChecked Then
    ' use pubs DSN
    Set mcon = rdoEnvironments(0).OpenConnection("pubs")
  Else
    ' use DSN-less connection
    sConnect = _
        "UID=sa;" & _
        "PWD=MyPassword;" & _
        "DATABASE=pubs;" & _
        "SERVER=MyServer;" & _
        "DRIVER={SQL SERVER};" & _
        "DSN='';"
```

continued on next page

continued from previous page

```
    Set mcon = rdoEnvironments(0).OpenConnection( _
        "", rdDriverNoPrompt, False, sConnect, rdAsyncEnable)
  End If

  OpenConnection = True

ProcExit:
  Exit Function

ProcError:
  OpenConnection = False
  Resume ProcExit

End Function
```

How It Works

A single line of code is all that's required to connect to a remote server. The `OpenConnection` method (or alternately the `EstablishConnection` method) connects you to the SQL Server database. You can then use the connection to execute SQL statements and create other RDO objects.

Comments

If you're familiar with the DAO object model, the `rdoConnection` object is the rough equivalent of the `Database` object. Many of the properties and methods are similar. In fact, you'll find the entire Remote Data Objects hierarchy very similar to the Data Access Objects hierarchy. The similarities in the two models not only make it easier to learn to use RDO but also make it easier to convert existing code from DAO to RDO.

COMPLEXITY
INTERMEDIATE

8.5 How do I...

Browse records in a SQL Server database using Remote Data Objects?

Problem

How can I use Remote Data Objects to browse rows in a SQL Server database?

Technique

Remote Data Objects (RDO) provides the `rdoResultset` object—similar to the DAO Recordset object—that you can use to capture and browse the results of a

SELECT query. If you've programmed with DAO, you'll find the rdoResultset familiar. The various Move methods work the same as the methods of the Recordset, and you still use AddNew, Edit, and Update to make changes to the data in a row. Many of the properties are also the same as those of the DAO Recordset. In fact, much of the code written for rdoResultsets is so similar that you could change the declaration and the Set statement and use your existing DAO code.

Despite the code similarities, there are differences in the techniques used to access SQL Server data with rdoResultsets:

✔ The SQL statements used to retrieve data must be written in syntax that the remote server will understand. Unlike DAO, which uses the Jet database engine, RDO does not have its own query processor. All processing takes place on the remote server.

✔ There are no Find methods. You are expected to run a new query and select only the rows you need if the criteria for searching the data changes. You can also move through the resultset testing for the desired values on individual rows and columns.

✔ There's no equivalent to the table-type recordset and its associated methods such as Seek.

✔ The types of rdoResultsets available are somewhat different from the types of Recordsets available. You can create a forward-only, keyset, dynamic, and static cursor.

✔ There are more locking strategies at your disposal. You can use read-only, pessimistic, optimistic based on row ID, optimistic based on row values, and batch updates.

✔ A single SQL Server query can return more than one set of results.

✔ You can't modify the structure of the database with RDO. SQL Enterprise manager provides visual tools for that purpose, and the Transact-SQL language also allows you to manipulate the database design.

A NOTE ON CURSORS

Don't be confused by all the new terminology. A *cursor* is essentially just a set of pointers to rows in a resultset that allows you to browse the results.

You create a resultset by using the OpenResultset method of an rdoConnection. You typically will provide a SQL statement to the method that specifies the rows to return. You can additionally specify the type of cursor which by default is forward-only, and the type of locking which by default is read-only.

After you have created the resultset, you can browse the rows using the various navigation methods: `MoveFirst`, `MovePrevious`, `MoveNext`, `MoveLast`, and Move. Like the DAO Recordset, the `rdoResultset` object provides the BOF and EOF properties that you can use to test for the ends of the resultset.

Values for individual columns in the rows retrieved are obtained from the `rdoColumns` collection. This is the default collection for a resultset. You can use the same syntax styles for columns in a resultset that you use for fields in a DAO recordset:

✔ `rdoResultset.rdoColumns("column0")`

✔ `rdoResultset("column0")`

✔ `rdoResultset!column0`

Depending on the query, the type of cursor, and the type of locking, the data might be read-only or might be updatable.

Steps

Before you can use this example, you need to install the States table in the pubs sample database. Using SQL Enterprise Manager or I-SQL/W, load the States.sql script, select the pubs database, and run the script. The script creates and populates the States table with a list of the 50 states in the U.S. as well as the District of Columbia and Puerto Rico. After you have installed this table, you can run the sample application.

Open and run project HT805.vbp. You can use the form shown in Figure 8.5 to browse and update the rows in the sample table from the pubs database. This project makes a simple extension to the project used for How-To 8.3. The text box used for the **state** column in the Publishers table has been replaced with a combo box that is populated with a list of state postal codes using a query and an rdoResultset object. This is a commonly implemented user interface convenience. Unless people work all day every day with a data entry application, few will remember the postal codes for all the states, so the combo box allows the user to pick a value from a list on the form.

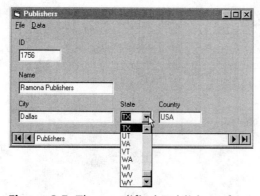

Figure 8.5. The modified Publishers form.

1. Create a new Standard EXE project, add a reference to Microsoft Remote Data Object 2.0, and save the project as HT805.vbp. Rename the default Form1 to FMain, save it as FMain.frm, and add the object and properties shown in Table 8.6. The menu controls for this example are identical to those in How-To 8.3.

Table 8.6. Objects and properties for FMain.

OBJECT	PROPERTY	VALUE
Form	Caption	Publishers
RemoteData Control	Name	rdc
	Caption	Publishers
	Align	2 - vbAlignBottom
	DataSourceName	pubs
	SQL	SELECT pub_id, pub_name,
		city, state, country
		FROM publishers
Label	Name	lbl
	Caption	ID
	Index	0
TextBox	Name	txtID
	DataSource	rdc
	DataField	pub_id
Label	Name	lbl
	Caption	Name
	Index	1

continued on next page

continued from previous page

OBJECT	PROPERTY	VALUE
TextBox	Name	txtName
	DataSource	rdc
	DataField	pub_name
Label	Name	lbl
	Caption	City
	Index	2
TextBox	Name	txtCity
	DataSource	rdc
	DataField	city
Label	Name	lbl
	Caption	State
	Index	3
ComboBox	Name	cboState
	DataSource	rdc
	DataField	state
Label	Name	lbl
	Caption	Country
	Index	4
TextBox	Name	txtCountry
	DataSource	rdc
	DataField	country

2. Add the following code to the declarations section. The `rdoConnection` object is used later to populate the state combo box.

```
Option Explicit

Private mcon As rdoConnection
```

3. Create the `Form_Load` event procedure. This procedure calls the `OpenConnection` procedure to connect to the remote server and then calls `GetStates` to populate the combo box.

```
Private Sub Form_Load()
On Error GoTo ProcError

   OpenConnection
   GetStates

ProcExit:
   Exit Sub

ProcError:
```

```
   MsgBox Err.Number & vbCrLf & Err.Description
   Resume ProcExit

End Sub
```

4. Add the following procedures to handle the click events for the menu controls. These procedures are identical to those developed in How-To 8.3.

```
Private Sub mnuDataDelete_Click()
On Error GoTo ProcError

  DeleteRecord

ProcExit:
  Exit Sub

ProcError:
  MsgBox Err.Number & vbCrLf & Err.Description
  Resume ProcExit

End Sub
Private Sub mnuDataNew_Click()
On Error GoTo ProcError

  AddRecord

ProcExit:
  Exit Sub

ProcError:
  MsgBox Err.Number & vbCrLf & Err.Description
  Resume ProcExit

End Sub

Private Sub mnuDataSave_Click()
On Error GoTo ProcError

  SaveRecord

ProcExit:
  Exit Sub

ProcError:
  MsgBox Err.Number & vbCrLf & Err.Description
  Resume ProcExit

End Sub
Private Sub mnuFileExit_Click()
On Error Resume Next

  Unload Me
  If Err.Number <> 0 Then
    MsgBox Err.Number & vbCrLf & Err.Description
  End If

End Sub
```

5. Create the AddRecord, NewRecord, and SaveRecord procedures. These procedures are also identical to those in How-To 8.3.

```
Private Sub AddRecord()

  rdc.Resultset.AddNew
  txtID.SetFocus

End Sub
Private Sub DeleteRecord()

  ' delete the row
  rdc.Resultset.Delete
  ' back up one row
  rdc.Resultset.MovePrevious
  ' check for beginning of set
  If rdc.Resultset.BOF Then
    rdc.Resultset.MoveFirst
  End If

End Sub
Private Sub SaveRecord()

  Select Case rdc.Resultset.EditMode
    Case rdEditNone
      ' clean record, do nothing
    Case rdEditInProgress
      ' the control handles regular edits
      rdc.UpdateRow
    Case rdEditAdd
      ' use the Update method of the
      ' resultset
      rdc.Resultset.Update
  End Select

End Sub
```

6. Create the OpenConnection procedure. This is based on How-To 8.4 and uses the pubs ODBC DSN to create the connection to the SQL Server.

```
Private Sub OpenConnection()

  Dim sConnect As String

  ' default using a configured DSN
  Set mcon = rdoEnvironments(0).OpenConnection("pubs")

End Sub
```

7. Create the GetStates subroutine. This code uses an **rdoResultset** to populate the **cboState** combo box. It creates a forward-only, read-only cursor based on the States table. Because only one pass through the results is required, a forward-only cursor is sufficient. The `rdExecDirect` option bypasses ODBC's normal step of creating a prepared statement and directly executes the query on the SQL Server.

```
Private Sub GetStates()
' populate the states combo box

  Dim sSQL As String
  Dim rsStates As rdoResultset

  sSQL = "SELECT StateCode FROM States"
  ' we only need one pass through this data,
  ' and will only need to do it once, so we
  ' use a read only, forward only cursor and
  ' the exec direct option
  Set rsStates = mcon.OpenResultset(sSQL, _
    rdOpenForwardOnly, rdConcurReadOnly, rdExecDirect)

  ' populate the combo box
  Do While Not rsStates.EOF
    cboState.AddItem rsStates!StateCode
    rsStates.MoveNext
  Loop

  ' clean up
  rsStates.Close

End Sub
```

How It Works

The primary object you will use in the Remote Data Objects hierarchy is the `rdoResultset` object. The `rdoResultset` object allows you to submit a SQL query (over an `rdoConnection` object) and process the results. Depending on the type of query, you might also be able to add, delete, and update the rows in the resultset.

In this example, the resultset in the `GetStates` procedure is used only to populate the combo box and avoid the use of a data bound combo box control.

Comments

Many of the objects in the Remote Data Objects hierarchy have events in addition to properties and methods. You can use these events by declaring the objects using VB5's new `WithEvents` keyword and write event procedures for these events. For example, the `rdoResultset` object provides the `RowStatusChanged` event that you can use to trigger code that should run if a row is updated or deleted.

8.6 How do I...
Add, update, and delete records in a SQL Server database using Remote Data Objects?

Problem

I would prefer to use unbound controls in my database applications. How can I create an unbound form based on SQL Server data using Remote Data Objects?

Technique

Building unbound applications with Remote Data Objects is no different from building unbound applications using any other data access approach, including Data Access Objects or standard Visual Basic file I/O techniques. Here are the steps:

1. Retrieve the data from the data source; in this example you will use an `rdoResultset` to manage the data.

2. Display the values in the controls on the form.

3. Update the tables in the database when the user moves to a new row, unloads the form, or explicitly requests that the data be saved.

If you've already read Chapter 2, "Accessing a Database with Data Access Objects," you will be familiar with these techniques. The only thing that has changed is the object model used to manage the data. In the previous How-To, you were introduced to using an `rdoResultset` to retrieve data from a SQL Server database. In this How-To, you will extend the use of the `rdoResultset` to inserting, updating, and deleting rows.

How-To 8.5 used a forward-only, read-only cursor—the default for `rdoResultset` objects created using the `OpenResultset` method of an `rdoConnection` object. Because you will now be making changes to the data as well as providing the capability to navigate both forward and backward through the rows, you will need a more flexible type of cursor. Using a keyset-type cursor allows you to add, update, or delete rows with minimal coding complexity and lower resource requirements than a dynamic cursor.

> **NOTE**
>
> If you did not install the States table in How-To 8.5, do so now by running the States.sql SQL script using SQL Enterprise Manager or I-SQL/W. This script creates and populates a table of state names and postal codes for U.S. states.

Steps

Open and run project HT806.vbp. Use the form shown in Figure 8.6 to browse, add, update, or delete rows in the Publishers table. In this example, the RemoteData control has been replaced with Visual Basic code. Toolbar buttons created with a Toolbar control replace the navigation buttons provided by the RemoteData control. With the commands on the Data menu, you can create new rows, save changes to an existing row, or delete the current row.

1. Create a new Standard EXE project, add a reference to Microsoft Remote Data Object 2.0, and save the project as HT806.vbp. Rename **Form1** to **FMain**, save it as FMain.frm, and add the objects and properties shown in Table 8.7.

Table 8.7. Objects and properties for **FMain**.

OBJECT	PROPERTY	VALUE
Form	Caption	Publishers
Toolbar	Name	tb
Label	Name	lbl
	Caption	ID
	Index	0
TextBox	Name	txtID
Label	Name	lbl
	Caption	Name
	Index	1
TextBox	Name	txtName
Label	Name	lbl
	Caption	City
	Index	2
TextBox	Name	txtCity
Label	Name	lbl
	Caption	State
	Index	3
ComboBox	Name	cboState
Label	Name	lbl
	Caption	Country
	Index	4
TextBox	Name	txtCountry

2. Use the menu editor to create the menu controls shown in Table 8.8.

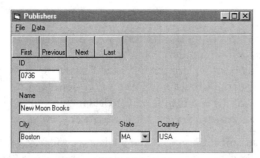

Figure 8.6. The unbound Publishers form.

Table 8.8. Menu controls for `FMain`.

CAPTION	NAME	SHORTCUT KEY
&File	mnuFile	
E&xit	mnuFileExit	
&Data	mnuData	
&Save	mnuDataSave	Ctrl+S
-	mnuDataBar	
&New	mnuDataNew	Ctrl+N
&Delete	mnuDataDelete	

3. Add the following code to the declarations section. The `rdoConnection` and `rdoResultset` objects are used by the form to manage the data in the sample database. The enumeration and the `mlRowState` variable are used to track the current state of the data on the form.

```
Option Explicit

' connection
Private mcon As rdoConnection
' resultset
Private mrsPublishers As rdoResultset
' record state
Private Enum RowState
  RowStateClean = 1
  RowStateDirty = 2
  RowStateNew = 3
End Enum
Private mlRowState As RowState
```

4. Create the `Form_Load` and `Form_Unload` event procedures. In the `Load` event, the form sets up the toolbar, opens the resultset for the Publishers table upon which the form is based, and populates the `cboState` combo box. In the `unload` event, the form saves any changes and closes and releases the object variables created in the declarations section. The `Initialize`, `GetStates`, and `SetupToolbar` procedures are described in steps 9, 11 and 20.

```
Private Sub Form_Load()
On Error GoTo ProcError

  SetupToolbar
  Initialize
  GetStates

ProcExit:
  Exit Sub

ProcError:
  MsgBox Err.Number & vbCrLf & Err.Description
  Resume ProcExit

End Sub
Private Sub Form_Unload(Cancel As Integer)
' save before exiting
On Error GoTo ProcError

  ' save the current row
  SaveRow
  ' close down resultset and connection
  Terminate

ProcExit:
  Exit Sub

ProcError:
  MsgBox Err.Number & vbCrLf & Err.Description
  Resume ProcExit

End Sub
```

5. Create the `tb_ButtonClick` event procedure. This procedure calls procedures to navigate among the rows in the resultset.

```
Private Sub tb_ButtonClick(ByVal Button As ComctlLib.Button)
' toolbar handles navigation

  Select Case Button.Key
    Case "First"
      MoveFirst
    Case "Previous"
      MovePrevious
    Case "Next"
      MoveNext
    Case "Last"
      MoveLast
  End Select

End Sub
```

6. Add the following event procedures to track the edit state of the data on the form. Each procedure changes the module-level **mlRowState** variable to **RowStateDirty** if the current value is **RowStateClean**. This allows later code to determine whether current changes should be sent to the SQL Server as an update or an insert.

```
Private Sub cboState_Click()
' mark row dirty

  If mlRowState = RowStateClean Then
    mlRowState = RowStateDirty
  End If

End Sub
Private Sub cboState_Change()
' mark row dirty

  If mlRowState = RowStateClean Then
    mlRowState = RowStateDirty
  End If

End Sub
Private Sub txtCity_Change()
' mark row dirty

  If mlRowState = RowStateClean Then
    mlRowState = RowStateDirty
  End If

End Sub
Private Sub txtCountry_Change()
' mark row dirty

  If mlRowState = RowStateClean Then
    mlRowState = RowStateDirty
  End If

End Sub
Private Sub txtID_Change()
' mark row dirty

  If mlRowState = RowStateClean Then
    mlRowState = RowStateDirty
  End If

End Sub
Private Sub txtName_Change()
' mark row dirty

  If mlRowState - RowStateClean Then
    mlRowState = RowStateDirty
  End If

End Sub
```

7. Create the `mnuFileExit_Click` event procedure. This procedure unloads the form, ending the application.

```
Private Sub mnuFileExit_Click()
On Error Resume Next

  Unload Me
  If Err.Number <> 0 Then
    MsgBox Err.Number & vbCrLf & Err.Description
  End If

End Sub
```

8. Add the following event procedures for the commands on the Data menu. Each menu command event procedure calls a corresponding subroutine in the form module to perform the requested operation. The `NewRow`, `SaveRow`, and `DeleteRow` procedures are described in steps 12, 13, and 14.

```
Private Sub mnuDataNew_Click()
On Error GoTo ProcError

  NewRow

ProcExit:
  Exit Sub

ProcError:
  MsgBox Err.Number & vbCrLf & Err.Description
  Resume ProcExit

End Sub
Private Sub mnuDataSave_Click()
On Error GoTo ProcError

  SaveRow

ProcExit:
  Exit Sub

ProcError:
  MsgBox Err.Number & vbCrLf & Err.Description
  Resume ProcExit

End Sub
Private Sub mnuDataDelete_Click()
On Error GoTo ProcError

  DeleteRow

ProcExit:
  Exit Sub

ProcError:
  MsgBox Err.Number & vbCrLf & Err.Description
  Resume ProcExit

End Sub
```

9. Create the `Initialize` procedure. This subroutine is called from the `Form_Load` event procedure. It opens a connection to the SQL Server database, creates a resultset using the same query used in the previous RemoteData control examples, and then calls the `ColumnsToControls` procedure to display the first row in the resultset on the form. A keyset cursor with optimistic locking based on row values is used so that the resultset will be updatable.

```
Private Sub Initialize()
' connect and open the publishers resultset
  Dim sConnect As String
  Dim sSQL As String

  ' default using a configured DSN
  Set mcon = rdoEnvironments(0).OpenConnection( _
      "pubs", rdDriverNoPrompt)

  ' initialize the publishers resultset
  ' create the SQL statement
  sSQL = "SELECT pub_id, pub_name, city, state, country " & _
      "FROM publishers"
  ' use a keyset cursor
  Set mrsPublishers = _
      mcon.OpenResultset(sSQL, rdOpenKeyset, rdConcurValues)

  ' display the first row
  ColumnsToControls
  ' mark it clean
  mlRowState = RowStateClean

End Sub
```

10. The `Terminate` procedure, called from the `Form_Unload` event, performs a cleanup operation by closing the module-level `rdoConnection` and `rdoResultset` objects:

```
Private Sub Terminate()
' clean up

  mrsPublishers.Close
  mcon.Close

End Sub
```

11. The `GetStates` procedure is the same code used in How-To 8.5:

```
Private Sub GetStates()
' populate the states combo box

  Dim sSQL As String
  Dim rsStates As rdoResultset

  sSQL = "SELECT StateCode FROM States ORDER BY StateCode"
  ' we only need one pass through this data,
```

```
' and will only need to do it once, so we
' use a read only, forward only cursor and
' the exec direct option
Set rsStates = mcon.OpenResultset(sSQL, _
    rdOpenForwardOnly, rdConcurReadOnly, rdExecDirect)

' populate the combo box
Do While Not rsStates.EOF
  cboState.AddItem rsStates!StateCode
  rsStates.MoveNext
Loop

' clean up
rsStates.Close

End Sub
```

12. Create the `NewRow` procedure. This code saves the current data, clears the controls, and sets the module-level `m1RowState` state variable to `RowStateNew`, in preparation for the creation of a new row in the table.

```
Private Sub NewRow()
' create a new row

' save current data
SaveRow
ClearControls
m1RowState = RowStateNew

End Sub
```

13. Create the `SaveRow` subroutine. The code uses either the `Edit` or `AddNew` method of the `rdoResultset` object to update an existing row or insert a new row, based on the value of the `m1RowState` module-level state flag.

```
Private Sub SaveRow()
' save current data

  Select Case m1RowState
    Case RowStateDirty
      mrsPublishers.Edit
      ControlsToColumns
      mrsPublishers.Update
      m1RowState = RowStateClean
    Case RowStateNew
      mrsPublishers.AddNew
      ControlsToColumns
      mrsPublishers.Update
      m1RowState = RowStateClean
      mrsPublishers.Move 0
    Case Else
      ' nothing to do
  End Select

End Sub
```

14. The `DeleteRow` procedure uses the `Delete` method of the `mrsPublishers` `rdoResultset` object to delete the current row, then calls `MovePrevious` to back up to the previous row:

```
Private Sub DeleteRow()
' delete the current row

  mrsPublishers.Delete
  MovePrevious

End Sub
```

15. Create the `MoveFirst` and `MoveLast` subroutines. Each routine saves the current row, performs the appropriate move operation, displays the new row, and marks it as being clean.

```
Private Sub MoveFirst()
' goto first row

  SaveRow
  mrsPublishers.MoveFirst
  ColumnsToControls
  mlRowState = RowStateClean

End Sub
Private Sub MoveLast()
' goto last row

  SaveRow
  mrsPublishers.MoveLast
  ColumnsToControls
  mlRowState = RowStateClean

End Sub
```

16. Create the `MovePrevious` and `MoveNext` procedures. These are similar to the `MoveFirst` and `MoveLast` routines, but with code added to test for BOF and EOF conditions so that a valid row will always be displayed by the form.

```
Private Sub MovePrevious()
' goto previous row

  SaveRow
  mrsPublishers.MovePrevious
  If mrsPublishers.BOF Then
    mrsPublishers.MoveFirst
  End If
  ColumnsToControls
  mlRowState = RowStateClean

End Sub
Private Sub MoveNext()
' MoveNext w/ EOF handling
```

```
    SaveRow
    mrsPublishers.MoveNext
    If mrsPublishers.EOF Then
      mrsPublishers.MoveLast
    End If
    ColumnsToControls
    mlRowState = RowStateClean

End Sub
```

17. Create the `ColumnsToControls` routine. This procedure copies the values from the current row in the resultset to the controls on the form. In order to eliminate the possibility of writing `Null` values to the `Text` property of the text boxes, a zero-length string is appended to the value of the column.

```
Private Sub ColumnsToControls()
' load the current row in mrsPublishers to the controls

    txtID = mrsPublishers!pub_id & ""
    txtName = mrsPublishers!pub_name & ""
    txtCity = mrsPublishers!city & ""
    cboState = mrsPublishers!state & ""
    txtCountry = mrsPublishers!country & ""

End Sub
```

18. Create the `ControlsToColumns` procedure. This procedure compares the values on the form to the values in the columns and—if they have changed—copies the new values to the columns.

```
Private Sub ControlsToColumns()
' copy controls to current row

    Dim sID As String
    Dim sName As String
    Dim sCity As String
    Dim sState As String
    Dim sCountry As String

    ' get the values
    sID = txtID
    sName = txtName
    sCity = txtCity
    sState = cboState
    sCountry = txtCountry

    ' copy to columns only if changed
    With mrsPublishers
      If !pub_id <> sID Then
        !pub_id = sID
      End If
      If !pub_name <> sName Then
        !pub_name = sName
```

continued on next page

continued from previous page

```
      End If
      If !city <> sCity Then
        !city = sCity
      End If
      If !state <> sState Then
        !state = sState
      End If
      If !country <> sCountry Then
        !country = sCountry
      End If
    End With

End Sub
```

19. The `ClearControls` subroutine writes zero-length strings to each of the controls and is called when creating a new row:

```
Private Sub ClearControls()
' clear existing values from controls

  txtID = ""
  txtName = ""
  txtCity = ""
  cboState = ""
  txtCountry = ""

End Sub
```

20. Enter the following code as the `SetupToolbar` subroutine. This procedure is called at startup and adds the four navigation buttons to the toolbar control.

```
Private Sub SetupToolbar()
' setup toolbar buttons

  With tb.Buttons
    .Add , "First", "First"
    .Add , "Previous", "Previous"
    .Add , "Next", "Next"
    .Add , "Last", "Last"
  End With

End Sub
```

NOTE

In a production application, you should set up more pleasing buttons with appropriate images in an associated `ImageList` control.

How It Works

At startup, the form connects to the SQL Server, submits a query, and captures the results of the query in the `mrsPublishers` `rdoResultset` object. Code attached to the menu controls and toolbar buttons provides the capability for navigation, inserts, updates, and deletes using the methods of the `rdoResultset` object.

NOTE

You can easily implement an `undo` command by reloading the current row from the `rdoResultset` into the controls with a call to the `ColumnsToControls` procedure. A column-level `undo` command could be implemented by restoring only a single column value from the `rdoResultset` object.

Comments

In Chapter 2, "Accessing a Database with Data Access Objects," a more robust approach was implemented using a class module to encapsulate all the data access code. That approach would work equally well with this example. For the sake of simplicity, the more direct approach of placing the data access code directly in the form module was used. Although this code might be somewhat simpler to understand, over the lifetime of an application, it might prove more difficult to maintain due to the tight coupling of the data access code with the user interface code.

QUERYING THE DATABASE

The SQL statement used to provide the source of the data for this form is somewhat simplistic for a server database. Although the pubs sample database contains only a handful of rows, many tables will have hundreds, thousands, or even millions of rows of data. If you issue a SELECT query with no WHERE clause against such a large table in a production application, you will at best produce an application with terrible performance and will quite possibly be summoned to the office of your database administrator and be given a painful lesson in how to submit a proper query. Submitting queries that return only the data you need is always good advice for any database application but is even more critical if you are sending the query to a busy database server.

COMPLEXITY
INTERMEDIATE

8.7 How do I...
Execute a SQL Server stored procedure using Remote Data Objects?

Problem

Many of the queries I need to run are returned as the results of stored procedures on the server. How can I execute a stored procedure and capture the resultset with Remote Data Objects?

Technique

A SQL Server stored procedure is a precompiled set of Transact-SQL statements that are executed using a single statement. Because the statements have been precompiled and the queries have already been optimized, SQL Server can often execute stored procedures much more efficiently than ad hoc SQL statements submitted for processing. Many large database applications are built almost entirely using stored procedures to retrieve and edit rows. Additionally, stored procedures can provide an added measure of security by allowing access to tables and columns that would otherwise be unavailable. A user only needs permission to execute a stored procedure, regardless of the permissions on the underlying tables and columns.

Stored procedures can range from simple **SELECT** queries that return results to complex Transact-SQL procedures taking input and output parameters and returning values and multiple resultsets. Although the details of writing stored procedures on the server is beyond the scope of this chapter, it is not difficult to capture and use the results of stored procedures.

> **NOTE**
>
> Stored procedures always return read-only results.

Depending on the nature of the procedure, you might execute the procedure directly using the **Execute** method of an **rdoConnection** object, or you might capture results of a stored procedure by using an **rdoQuery** or **rdoResultset** object.

THE TROUBLE WITH STORED PROCEDURES

Transact-SQL, from a programming perspective, can be a difficult language to work with. SQL was designed to manage data and database objects, and the commands and system stored procedures are often cryptic. Debugging tools are limited, and in many cases you need to understand the inner workings of a procedure before you can use it. This can make it difficult to create procedures that act as "black boxes" with well-defined interfaces. However, the advantages in data processing efficiency offered by stored procedures often far outweigh these disadvantages, especially for heavily used, large database applications.

Steps

Open and run project HT807.vbp. This example uses a form that is visually identical to the form shown in Figure 8.6 in the preceding How-To. Only two lines of code have been changed, but a minor change of this nature has the potential to provide a significant performance improvement in a production application.

1. Create a new Standard EXE project, add a reference to Microsoft Remote Data Object 2.0, and save the project as HT807.vbp. The single form for the application, FMain is identical to the FMain form used in HT806.vbp with the exception of the change shown below in step 3.

2. Using SQL Enterprise Manager or I-SQL/W, select the pubs database and execute the following SQL Script to create the **spStates** stored procedure:

```
CREATE PROCEDURE spStates AS
  SELECT StateCode FROM States ORDER BY StateCode
Go
GRANT EXECUTE ON spStates TO public
Go
```

NOTE

You will need to have already installed the States table using the States.sql script. The script shown above is in spStates.sql.

3. Replace the **GetStates** procedure with the following code. Two changes were made to the original procedure in HT806.vbp. The **sSQL** string variable and the assignment of the SQL statement were removed, and the **name** parameter of the **OpenResultset** method was replaced with the **spStates** stored procedure. The balance of the project is identical.

```
Private Sub GetStates()
' populate the states combo box

  Dim rsStates As rdoResultset

  ' we only need one pass through this data,
  ' and will only need to do it once, so we
  ' use a read only, forward only cursor and
  ' the exec direct option
  Set rsStates = mcon.OpenResultset("spStates", _
      rdOpenForwardOnly, rdConcurReadOnly, rdExecDirect)

  ' populate the combo box
  Do While Not rsStates.EOF
    cboState.AddItem rsStates!StateCode
    rsStates.MoveNext
  Loop

  ' clean up
  rsStates.Close

End Sub
```

How It Works

The original query was a **SELECT** statement submitted directly to the server for processing:

```
SELECT StateCode FROM States ORDER BY StateCode
```

This was replaced with a stored procedure that executes the same query. Because stored procedures have already been compiled and optimized, a few steps have been saved on the SQL Server each time this query has been submitted. Only a minor change is required to the **GetStates** procedure to take advantage of the stored procedure because the procedure was already designed to use a read-only resultset.

Comments

There might be no difference in the steps the SQL server takes to process the rows for this query. If you execute the original SQL statement directly in SQL Enterprise Manager and then execute the stored procedure (both with the Show Query Plan option turned on), you will see that the plan is identical for both queries. However, you are still saving the SQL Server the time required to compile and optimize the query.

For this type of data, you should design your application to run the query once (either at start time or the first time it is needed) and then cache the data locally for future use. On a table as stable as this one, you could consider permanently retaining a local copy and not querying the server at all. However, most database applications will need to run this type of query routinely. Often many small queries are run to populate lookup tables of coded values and other types of selection lists for combo boxes, list boxes, and so on. This type of data probably does not change often, but might not be stable enough to hardwire the values into the source code.

If you routinely submit a number of these queries in your application, a good solution might be to design a single stored procedure on the server that returns several or possibly all of these queries at once, then cache the results locally after the first execution. When you submit a query or stored procedure that returns multiple resultsets, you use the `MoreResults` method of the `rdoResultset` object to determine whether there are additional resultsets to process. You can also use the `GetRows` method to quickly and easily populate an array with the results of a query for temporary local storage.

COMPLEXITY
INTERMEDIATE

8.8 How do I...
Execute a parameterized SQL Server stored procedure with Remote Data Objects?

Problem

I need to capture the return value of a stored procedure that takes parameters. How can I do this with Remote Data Objects?

Technique

SQL Server stored procedures, like Visual Basic procedures, can take input and output parameters and can return values. To capture these values, you need to use a different technique from that used in How-To 8.7. The `rdoQuery` object provides the `rdoParameters` collection to manage the parameters of a stored procedure.

The question mark character is the placeholder for parameters in a SQL Server query. If a procedure takes parameters, you put question marks in the SQL statement where the parameters would be entered if you were submitting the query interactively. The following SQL statement would create a parameter query based on a `CustLast` column:

```
SELECT CustID, CustFirst, CustLast FROM Customers WHERE CustLast = ?
```

To supply this parameter when you execute the query, you need to create an `rdoQuery` object using the `CreateQuery` method:

```
' cn is a connection object defined elsewhere
' qry is an object variable declared as rdoQuery
' sSQL is a string variable
```

continued on next page

continued from previous page

```
sSQL = "SELECT CustID, CustFirst, CustLast FROM Customers WHERE CustID = ?
Set qry = cn.CreateQuery("",sSQL)
```

This query will now have a single parameter in its `rdoParameters` collection. You can assign a value to the parameter and execute the query:

```
' the parameters collection is zero-based
qry(0) = 12
' rs is an rdoResultset object
Set rs = qry.Execute
```

Stored procedures can also take parameters, but to capture output parameters or return values, you need to use the OBDC call syntax. Here's the beginning of the `sp_addgroup` procedure from the master database:

```
create procedure sp_addgroup
@grpname varchar(30)
```

In addition to the `grpname` input parameter, `sp_addgroup` also returns a value indicating the success or failure of the procedure. With the ODBC call syntax, this query would be created as

```
{? = call sp_addgroup (?) }
```

The question mark at the beginning of the statement acts as a placeholder for the return value, and the question mark at the end acts as a placeholder for the `grpname` parameter. Normally, the ODBC driver can determine whether the parameters are input or output, but you can also supply the direction explicitly by using the `Direction` property of the `rdoParameter` object:

```
qry(0).Direction = rdDirectionInput
```

Along with input and output parameters, you can use `rdParamReturnValue` to specify that a parameter is a stored procedure return value.

Steps

The sample project for this How-To is a SQL Server change password dialog box. Open and run project HT808.vbp to display the form shown in Figure 8.7. The dialog box uses the `sp_password` system stored procedure (in the master database) to change the password for the current user.

NOTE

If you are the sa, you can use `sp_password` to change the password for any user—with or without the existing password. This is a standard security mechanism. Administrators can change, but not read, existing passwords. Windows NT Server domain administrators and Access database administrators have the same capability. This dialog box does not provide that capability. If you have sa authority and need to change the password of another user, execute `sp_password` using SQL Enterprise Manager or I-SQL/w.

Figure 8.7. The Change
Password dialog box.

1. Create a new Standard EXE project and save it as HT808.vbp. Change the name of `Form1` to `FMain` and save it as FMain.frm, and then create the objects and properties shown in Table 8.9.

Table 8.9. Objects and properties for `FMain`.

OBJECT	PROPERTY	VALUE
Form	Caption	Change Password
	Border Style	3 - Fixed Dialog
Label	Name	lbl
	Caption	Old Password
	Index	0
TextBox	Name	txtOld
Label	Name	lbl
	Caption	New Password
	Index	1
TextBox	Name	txtNew
Label	Name	lbl
	Caption	Confirm New Password
	Index	2
TextBox	Name	txtNewConfirm
CommandButton	Name	cmd
	Caption	OK
	Default	True
	Index	0
CommandButton	Name	cmd
	Caption	Cancel
	Cancel	True
	Index	1

2. Add `Option Explicit` to the declarations section of the form module, and then create the `cmd_Click` event procedure. This procedure calls the `ChangePassword` procedure if OK was clicked or unloads the form if Cancel was clicked.

```
Private Sub cmd_Click(Index As Integer)
On Error GoTo ProcError

  Select Case cmd(Index).Caption
    Case "OK"
      ChangePassword
    Case "Cancel"
      Unload Me
  End Select

ProcExit:
  Exit Sub

ProcError:
  MsgBox Err.Number & vbCrLf & Err.Description
  Resume ProcExit

End Sub
```

3. Add the following code as the `ChangePassword` function. This procedure uses the values entered in the text boxes to supply the parameters for the `sp_password` system stored procedure. It first verifies that the user entered the same value in the New Password and Confirm New Password text boxes, then opens a connection to the SQL Server. The pubs DSN is used to open the connection, but any valid connection to the server will work because the procedure name is fully qualified in the master database. After the connection has been established, the procedure creates an `rdoQuery` object, sets the direction of the parameters, and assigns the values of the two input parameters. Finally, the query is executed using the `Execute` method of the `rdoQuery` object, and the return value is captured using the `rdoParameters` collection. The `sp_password` returns `0` if the password was successfully changed, and this value is tested to display an appropriate message based on the return value of the stored procedure.

```
Private Sub ChangePassword()
' change the current user's password
' using the sp_password system stored procedure

  Dim con As rdoConnection
  Dim sSQL As String
  Dim qry As rdoQuery

  Dim sOld As String
  Dim sNew As String
  Dim sNewConfirm As String

  sOld = txtOld
```

```
      sNew = txtNew
      sNewConfirm = txtNewConfirm

      If sNew <> sNewConfirm Then
        ' mismatch, inform, clear values and exit
        MsgBox "New passwords do not match."
        txtNew = ""
        txtNewConfirm = ""
        txtNew.SetFocus
        Exit Sub
      End If

      Set con = _
          rdoEnvironments(0).OpenConnection _
          ("pubs", rdDriverNoPrompt)

      ' use the ODBC call syntax to capture the return value
      ' this is needed to know if the change succeeded
      sSQL = "{? = call master.dbo.sp_password (?,?) }"
      ' create the query object
      Set qry = con.CreateQuery("", sSQL)

      ' set direction for param 0
      qry(0).Direction = rdParamReturnValue
      qry(1).Direction = rdParamInput
      qry(2).Direction = rdParamInput

      ' this is equivalent to using
      ' qry.rdoParameters(1)
      qry(1) = sOld
      qry(2) = sNew

      ' run it
      qry.Execute

      ' sp_password returns 0 if successful
      ' the return parameters is always #0
      If qry(0) = 0 Then
        MsgBox "Password changed."
        Unload Me
      Else
        MsgBox "Unable to change password."
      End If

    End Sub
```

How It Works

Only the ODBC call syntax can be used if you need to capture the output or return parameters from a stored procedure. By using this syntax in the SQL statement, you can create an **rdoQuery** object with an **rdoParameters** collection and use the parameters to supply input values and capture output and return values.

This procedure could also be run by directly providing the old and new password as part of the SQL statement and run using the `Execute` method of an `rdoConnection` object, but you would not be able to determine whether the procedure succeeded or failed because the return value would be unavailable.

Comments

This simple change password dialog box could easily be plugged into any SQL Server database application by changing the code used to open the connection to the server or by supplying a valid connection using a public property of the form.

COMPLEXITY
INTERMEDIATE

8.9   How do I...
Handle Remote Data Objects errors?

Problem

I know that there will be runtime errors generated in my application and that I must trap and handle these errors to make the application robust and reliable. How do I handle errors generated by Remote Data Objects?

Technique

Like any Visual Basic application, you must trap and handle the errors that are generated at runtime, or the Visual Basic runtime DLL will invoke its own default error handler—which simply displays a message and terminates your application. Error-handling techniques for Remote Data Objects applications are similar to the techniques used for handling any other Visual Basic runtime errors, with one subtle but important variation: More than one error can be generated by a single statement in Remote Data Objects.

To allow you to deal with this possibility, Remote Data Objects provides the `rdoErrors` collection. This is a collection of `rdoError` objects you can examine the same way you examine the Visual Basic `Err` object. You can check the `Number`, `Source`, and `Description` properties. An `rdoError` object also provides the `SQLRetCode` and `SQLState` properties for you to examine.

Each of these properties might or might not provide useful information. SQL Server error messages can often be cryptic at best, and although a Visual Basic runtime error is generated, you get only the first error in the `rdoErrors` collection. You will normally need to iterate the `rdoErrors` collection to find the true nature of the problem because the first error is often a generic message such as `Command has been aborted.`—a true but generally useless piece of information for debugging without having the underlying cause of the problem.

The other significant difference between handling errors generated by Remote Data Objects is that you need to be prepared to deal with a much wider array of possible problems, ranging from typical Visual Basic errors like `Invalid Use of Null` (a common error in database applications) to the sudden death of the SQL Server at the other end of the connection. Along with the normal array of possible data manipulation problems (invalid foreign key values, data missing from required columns, and so on), most large SQL Server databases will have a wide variety of often complex business rules that are enforced. If rules are enforced using SQL Server triggers or stored procedures, the error numbers and messages generated will be dependent on the developer that created the Transact-SQL code. If that developer was conscientious in developing the Transact-SQL code, you will receive descriptive and informative messages. If you are developing your own Transact-SQL code, provide as much information as you reasonably can and use a sensible convention for generating error numbers.

NOTE

You can generate errors in Transact-SQL by using the RAISERROR statement.

Although there are standard techniques for trapping and examining errors, the means you use to handle the errors is entirely up to you and dependent on the context of the error. If a rule or some type of constraint is violated, you might be able to provide a message to the user with information about the problem and possible solutions. For more severe errors such as a lost connection to the database server over the network, you might have little choice but to gracefully terminate the application, informing the user of the problem in the process.

There are several avenues available to you to deal with possible problems:

✔ Prevent the errors before they happen. By using combo boxes, lists, and other user interface mechanisms that provide fixed lists of values for the user to select, you can prevent the entry of data that will violate database rules. If a column requires that a value be a member of a particular list of valid values, you should design the application so that only that list is available to the user.

✔ Make explicit tests for known probable errors before submitting data to the server. By handling the problem in advance of the generation of a runtime error, you gain more direct control over the problem and reduce the overhead on the server—which will need to process only validated data.

✔ Iterate the `rdoErrors` collection with a `For...Each` loop to gather as much information as possible about the errors you do encounter.

To whatever degree is possible, do this while debugging the application and take steps to prevent the problems if you can.

✔ As always, set up error handlers in `Sub Main` and all event procedures. Because these procedures are by definition at the top of the Visual Basic call tree, errors in them cannot be raised and will be fatal to your application. If your application must be shut down due to a severe error, close it down gracefully with your own code rather than letting Visual Basic's default runtime error handling terminate the application for you. You might even be able to save edits in progress locally and submit them to the server later when the problem has been cleared up.

YOUR RESPONSIBILITIES AS A DATABASE APPLICATION DEVELOPER

As the developer of a database application, you have two responsibilities that can sometimes be at odds with each other. You need to provide an easy-to-use, high-performance application for the user. Users are mainly concerned with getting their work done and don't care much about the intricacies of SQL Server rules, foreign key constraints, and other problems. At the same time, you need to make sure that only valid data is stored in the database because the data can be worse than useless if it is not reliable.

Most database developers tend to err on the side of caution where data validation is concerned, often at the expense of end user productivity. How strictly you need to enforce your rules will be dependent on the nature of the application. If you are working with a financial application where precision is paramount, you might need to be more severe in your enforcement of business rules. However, it is often the case that developers enforce rules that can potentially be ignored—at least temporarily—for the sake of the productivity of the end user.

Only you can determine how strict you need to be, but you should try to make an effort to sterilize the data only if it's truly necessary. In most cases, it's wishful thinking to believe that you can build an application where no bad data can be entered, so attempts to do so only hurt user productivity. If you are faced with a decision about data validation and rule enforcement, make the decision in the context of the overall goal of the application rather than looking only at the details of table- or column-level rules.

Steps

There is no specific project that demonstrates handling errors from Remote Data Objects. You are probably already well versed with basic Visual Basic error handling techniques, so rather than provide a contrived example, the following steps examine some of the problems you might encounter in the existing examples from How-To 8.3 and How-To 8.8. If you need a review of the essentials of Visual Basic error handling, see How-To 2.8 which covers the basic techniques of runtime error handling.

1. In How-To 8.3, a bound control application was developed that allows you to browse, update, insert, and delete rows in the Publishers table of the pubs sample database. There are two known problems involved in working with the Publishers table that were described in the chapter. First, a rather strange check constraint is enforced on the pub_id column, and, second, there are foreign keys in other tables that reference the pub_id column. Inserts, updates, and deletes can all generate violations of these rules, and the basic error handlers provided in the existing example do not provide any information about the true nature of the problem.

2. Open and run HT803.vbp. The first publisher displayed should be New Moon Books. Change the existing ID value from 0736 to 0737 and attempt to move to the next row using the navigation buttons provided by the RemoteData control. The message shown in Figure 8.8 will be displayed. Following this message will be another, shown in Figure 8.9.

Figure 8.8. The Command has been aborted message.

Figure 8.9. The operation cancelled message.

3. Insert the following code as the **rdc_Error** event procedure. This procedure iterates the **rdoErrors** collection with a **For...Each** loop and builds a message using all the available errors. The message generated reveals the true nature of the problem: The column-level check constraint on the **pub_id** column has been violated.

```
Private Sub rdc_Error( _
  ByVal Number As Long, _
  Description As String, _
  ByVal Scode As Long, _
  ByVal Source As String, _
  ByVal HelpFile As String, _
  ByVal HelpContext As Long, _
  CancelDisplay As Boolean)

Dim sMsg As String
  Dim rerr As rdoError

  For Each rerr In rdoErrors
    sMsg = _
      rerr.Number & ": " & rerr.Description & vbCrLf
  Next
  MsgBox sMsg

End Sub
```

4. In the **mnuDataSave_Click** event, replace the simple **MsgBox** statement in the error handler with the following code. This is the same approach used in the **rdc_Error** event procedure to find out what the real problem is with the error. The original message **Command has been aborted**—although true—is useless without the additional information provided by the **rdoErrors** collection.

```
Dim rerr As rdoError
Dim sMsg As String
For Each rerr In rdoErrors
  sMsg = rerr.Number & ": " & rerr.Description & vbCrLf
Next
MsgBox sMsg
```

5. Run the project again, but this time attempt to delete New Moon Books. The now familiar **Command has been aborted** message appears. Again the message is correct but useless. Replace the **MsgBox** statement in the error handler with the same code used in the two previous steps. If you run the project and again attempt the delete, the **rdoErrors** collection will now reveal that the underlying problem is the violation of a foreign key constraint. With this information available, you can deal with the problem by either cancelling the delete and informing the user or by deleting the associated rows in the foreign table.

6. Sometimes, despite your best efforts, the messages you receive from SQL Server just aren't going to provide any useful information. In How-To 8.8, you created a form that calls the system stored procedure **sp_password**. In SQL Enterprise Manager or I-SQL/w, you can run this stored procedure (which resides in the master database) from any database on the server and change your password. That's how system stored procedures are supposed to work and why they're called system stored procedures—they apply to the entire SQL Server. Based on this information, replace the line of code in the **ChangePassword** subroutine with the following line. At first glance you might expect this to work, but it doesn't. The rather bizarre error message shown in Figure 8.10 is displayed instead of a notification that the password was changed.

```
sSQL = "{? = call sp_password (?,?) }"
```

NOTE

A copy of the application with the incorrect code is available in project HT808R.vbp.

7. The trouble is that a fully qualified name for the procedure in the form database.owner.object is required. Unfortunately, the **rdoErrors** collection does not provide any further information. If you place a breakpoint in the procedure or set the Break on all Errors option in Visual Basic, you can examine the **rdoErrors** collection in the immediate window. The only error available is the one displayed, and it certainly doesn't indicate the true nature of the problem. A search of the Microsoft Technical Support Knowledge Base on the Microsoft Web site using the keywords **rdoquery error** returned (among others) the following article. This article indicates that you need to provide the full path to the stored procedure if you use the technique shown in How-To 8.8 (as well as an alternative method).

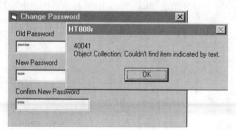

Figure 8.10. A not-so-helpful error message.

HOWTO: Call SQL Server System Stored Procedures from RDO

Last reviewed: April 18, 1997
Article ID: Q166211 The information in this article applies to:

·Microsoft Visual Basic Enterprise Edition for Windows, version 5.0

> **NOTE**
>
> If you aren't already familiar with the Microsoft Knowledge Base,
> you should visit the Web site and learn to use it. The Knowledge
> Base (or just KB) provides a wealth of technical information on all
> Microsoft products and should be your first source of information
> if you encounter a problem. You can query the KB online at
> http://www.microsoft.com/kb/.

How It Works

Standard Visual Basic error handling techniques, in conjunction with the rdoErrors collection, allow you to trap and examine runtime errors returned by Remote Data Objects. Armed with the information provided by the rdoErrors collection, you can build applications that trap and handle runtime errors effectively.

Comments

The information provided by the rdoErrors collection is often helpful, but not always—as demonstrated in the steps above. In order to be productive as a programmer, you'll need to be able to query the resources available in the help files, the Knowledge Base, and other sources to find the solutions to your problems. Finally, don't underestimate the power of your own intuition in solving problems and working out bugs in your application. As you gain experience in programming with Visual Basic and Remote Data Objects, you will eventually learn to anticipate problems and can often solve them with a simple educated guess.

WORKING WITH ODBC RECORDSETS AND THE ODBC API

9

WORKING WITH ODBC RECORDSETS AND THE ODBC API

How Do I...

9.1 Work directly with the ODBC API?

9.2 Pass SQL commands directly to an ODBC server?

9.3 Use transactions with ODBC databases?

9.4 Debug the ODBC interface of my Visual Basic application?

9.5 Navigate ODBC SQL cursors?

9.6 Handle ODBC errors?

The Open Database Connectivity (ODBC) standard has made accessing disparate database formats much easier than in older versions of Visual Basic. But the methods and properties available in Visual Basic don't always provide the specific support you need for a specific ODBC database. The reason is simple: Visual Basic was designed to be as flexible as possible, and that means it has to support as wide a range of database commands as possible.

This chapter assumes that you have basic knowledge of ODBC functions, such as creating data sources and connecting to ODBC databases. If your skills need brushing up, Chapter 6, "External ISAM Database Files," provides information and examples on how to perform most basic ODBC functions, as well as information on how ODBC works.

9.1 Work Directly with the ODBC API

The ODBC API, with its complex functionality, can be daunting. This How-To will help you to understand more fully how the ODBC API is called, what do to with ODBC handles, and the order in which ODBC commands should be handled.

9.2 Pass SQL Commands Directly to an ODBC Server

Sometimes you just need to bypass the protections of Visual Basic and its Jet database engine to take advantage of unique features of the ODBC database. Visual Basic makes it almost as easy to use such specialized SQL commands as it is to use the Visual Basic flavor of SQL statements. This How-To demonstrates a simple change that will make Visual Basic and its Jet database engine send your SQL statement straight through to the database server without checking it under Visual Basic's rules.

9.3 Use Transactions with ODBC Databases

Using transactions with ODBC databases is no different than using transactions with other databases. In this How-To, you'll see how to use transactions in the classic example of making a funds transfer between bank accounts by adding a record to a log file.

9.4 Debug the ODBC Interface of my Visual Basic Application

ODBC comes with a handy tool for debugging a Visual Basic application, or any ODBC application, for that matter. Although using a trace file isn't exactly on a level with using some of today's state-of-the-art debugging tools, it can give you plenty of information to show you where an application is going astray.

9.5 Navigate ODBC SQL Cursors

In ODBC, as in Visual Basic, cursors are important for determining the behavior and performance of your database access. In this How-To, we'll examine the use of various cursor libraries and types with a form that allows you to experiment with various ways of accessing an ODBC recordset.

9.6 Handle ODBC Errors

Although ODBC is a robust system, it is complex and has many opportunities for error conditions. To compensate, it also has a complex and informative error handling system that can help resolve problems, both within the ODBC system and outside (such as when a database is moved without telling ODBC). In this How-To, you'll see how to design a complete error handling system to capture and respond to these errors.

COMPLEXITY
ADVANCED

9.1 How do I...
Work directly with the ODBC API?

Problem

Using the regular Visual Basic data access methods to work with data in ODBC databases is fine as far as it goes. I find that I'm limited by what I can do through Visual Basic, however, even using pass-through SQL statements. How can I use the full ODBC API?

Technique

In this How-To, you'll develop a useful ODBC viewer that gathers in one place much of the information you'll need to evaluate the data sources and drivers that are available to a particular workstation. You can use the same techniques whether the data is located on a single computer with one hard disk or connected to a network with data of widely varying formats on different hardware spread across the network.

All the examples in the How-To use the ODBC API by calling those functions directly. You'll get an idea of how to use the API while developing some useful "wrapper" functions so that continued use of the ODBC API will be easier.

Steps

Load and run the Visual Basic project API.VBP. When the ODBC Database window appears, click the Get ODBC Status button to retrieve a list of the installed data sources and ODBC drivers. Click on one of the Registered ODBC Databases. After a moment, the Data Source window appears, listing all the ODBC API functions the data source and driver support, a count of the number of functions, and a selected list of settings and capabilities of the data source. Click the Quit button to return to the ODBC Database window, then Quit again to exit the program.

1. Create a new project called API.VBP. Then add the form ODBCErrors.FRM and the code module ODBC API **Declarations.BAS** included with the disk that accompanies this book by using Visual Basic's Project | Add File menu command. For now, examine the code module; we'll cover ODBCErrors.FRM more thoroughly in How-To 9.6. The code module contains all the declarations needed for the ODBC API functions and the constants used in many of the functions.

The first section of the module contains the general Declare statements and constants that are needed to use the ODBC API, and some wrapper functions that make using the most common API calls simpler. The name of the code module is modODBCAPI. Review the code in that file as you read the following.

Option Explicit tells Visual Basic to make sure that you declare all variables and objects before using them in order to avoid naming problems. Option Private Module tells Visual Basic that the procedures in this module are not to be used outside of this application. In other words, this procedure does not create objects that other Windows applications can use through OLE.

The miscellaneous Windows API constants are used to change the mouse cursor and to identify a window's state. You will use two Windows API functions, GetFocus and GetParent, so include their Declare statements here. Finally, you should include Public variables for the three handles that you'll use with the ODBC system.

2. The next section of code in the declarations section of the code module includes the Declare statements and constants used by the ODBC API. This section of the module has been adapted for use with Visual Basic from the C language #include file that comes with the ODBC 3.0 SDK. Note that it isn't necessary to include all these Declares and constants in every application. Just use those that your application actually uses or you'll waste a lot of memory.

3. Next, there are a few more Public variables and data types. The ODBCFuncs array holds a list of all the ODBC functions in whichever version of ODBC you are using. This array will be helpful for some of the procedures in this chapter that return information about ODBC. The array is two dimensional, with the function name in the first array and the ODBC conformance level in the second.

Next, a user data-type GetInfo is defined. You'll use this structure in the array ODBCGetInfo when you retrieve ODBC data source information using the ODBC function SQLGetInfo.

```
Public ODBCFuncs(2, SQL_EXT_API_LAST) As String

'User defined type for SQLGetInfo parameters
Type GetInfo
    InfoType As String
    ReturnType As String
End Type

'Array of GetInfo types
Public ODBCGetInfo(SQL_INFO_LAST) As GetInfo
```

4. Now, add the first of the wrapper functions that you'll use to work with ODBC. Add the following code to the ODBCAllocateEnv function procedure in ODBC API Declarations.BAS. You'll use this function to call the SQLAllocEnv function. Before calling any ODBC API function, you must get an environment handle. ODBC will use this handle and a small bit of memory to communicate with your application. As with every ODBC function call, you'll check for success and invoke the error handler if anything goes wrong.

```
Function ODBCAllocateEnv(hEnv As Long)
    Dim intResult As Integer, intPointer As Integer

    ODBCLoadFuncs
    LoadGetInfo
    ODBCAllocateEnv = SQL_SUCCESS

    intPointer = Screen.MousePointer: Screen.MousePointer = vbHourglass
    intResult = SQLAllocEnv(hEnv)
    Screen.MousePointer = vbDefault

    If intResult <> SQL_SUCCESS Then
        ODBCAllocateEnv = intResult
        intResult = frmODBCErrors.ODBCError("Env", hEnv, 0, 0, intResult, _
            "Environment Allocation Error")
        ODBCAllocateEnv = intResult
    End If
    Screen.MousePointer = intPointer
End Function
```

5. Add the following code to the **ODBCConnectDriver** function procedure. When you have allocated memory and received an environment handle, you can set up a connection. This function serves double duty: first to allocate memory and receive a database connection handle (hDbc) and then to make a connection with the data source driver passed to the function in the Server argument. If this function is successful, you can then begin using the connection with the database to manipulate data. This function also allocates an ODBC statement handle for use with SQL statements that are sent to the database.

```
Function ODBCConnectDriver(hDbc As Long, hStmt As Long, Server As String)
    'Establish a connection using SQLDriverConnect
    Dim intResult As Integer, intOut As Integer, intPointer As Integer
    Dim strTemp As String

    intPointer = Screen.MousePointer
    ODBCConnectDriver = SQL_SUCCESS

    Screen.MousePointer = vbHourglass

    intResult = SQLAllocConnect(glng_hEnv, hDbc)
    If intResult <> SQL_SUCCESS Then
        ODBCConnectDriver = intResult
        intResult = frmODBCErrors.ODBCError("Dbc", glng_hEnv, hDbc, _
            0, intResult, "Error allocating hDbc connection handle.")
        Screen.MousePointer = intPointer
        Exit Function
```

continued on next page

continued from previous page

```
        End If

        intResult = SQLDriverConnect(hDbc, GetParent(GetFocus()), strTemp, _
            Len(strTemp), Server, Len(Server), intOut, SQL_DRIVER_COMPLETE)
        If intResult <> SQL_SUCCESS Then
            ODBCConnectDriver = intResult
            intResult = frmODBCErrors.ODBCError("Dbc", glng_hEnv, hDbc, 0, _
                intResult, "Error connecting to driver.")
            Screen.MousePointer = intPointer
            Exit Function
        End If

        intResult = SQLAllocStmt(hDbc, hStmt)
        If intResult <> SQL_SUCCESS Then
            ODBCConnectDriver = intResult
            intResult = frmODBCErrors.ODBCError("Dbc", glng_hEnv, hDbc, 0, _
                intResult, "Error allocating statement handle.")
            Screen.MousePointer = intPointer
            Exit Function
        End If

        Screen.MousePointer = intPointer
    End Function
```

6. The preceding `ODBCConnectDriver` procedure makes a connection through the ODBC function `SQLDriverConnect`, which requires relatively more information to make a connection. When you have the correct connect string, you can use the `SQLConnect` function instead. The `ODBCConnectDS` procedure is built around that function. Add the following code to the `ODBCConnectDS` function procedure. This function also allocates an ODBC statement handle for use with SQL statements that are sent to the database.

```
Function ODBCConnectDS(hEnv As Long, hDbc As Long, hStmt As Long, _
    DataSource As String, UserID As String, Password As String) _
    As Integer

    Dim intResult As Integer, intPointer As Integer

    intPointer = Screen.MousePointer
    ODBCConnectDS = SQL_SUCCESS

    Screen.MousePointer = vbHourglass

    intResult = SQLAllocConnect(hEnv, hDbc)
    If intResult <> SQL_SUCCESS Then
        ODBCConnectDS = intResult
        intResult = frmODBCErrors.ODBCError("Dbc", hEnv, hDbc, 0, _
            intResult, "Error allocating connection handle.")
        Screen.MousePointer = intPointer
        Exit Function
    End If

    intResult = SQLConnect(hDbc, DataSource, Len(DataSource), UserID, _
```

```
        Len(UserID), Password, Len(Password))
    If intResult <> SQL_SUCCESS And _
        intResult <> SQL_SUCCESS_WITH_INFO Then
        ODBCConnectDS = intResult
        intResult = frmODBCErrors.ODBCError("Dbc", hEnv, hDbc, 0, _
            intResult, "Error connecting to data source.")
        Screen.MousePointer = intPointer
        Exit Function
    End If

    intResult = SQLAllocStmt(hDbc, hStmt)
    If intResult <> SQL_SUCCESS Then
        ODBCConnectDS = intResult
        intResult = frmODBCErrors.ODBCError("Dbc", hEnv, hDbc, 0, _
            intResult, "Error allocating statement handle.")
        Screen.MousePointer = intPointer
        Exit Function
    End If

    Screen.MousePointer = intPointer
End Function
```

7. Add the following code to the **ODBCDisconnectDS** function procedure of the ODBC API **Declarations.BAS** code module. Any time you allocate memory and obtain a handle from the ODBC system, you need to release the handle when you are finished with it, certainly no later than when the application ends. Otherwise, that memory may remain allocated and no other Windows application will be able to use it. This function releases any statement handles and both releases and frees connection handles. See the notes in "How It Works" for an explanation of why there are two steps for connection handles. Note that this function doesn't release the ODBC environment handle; this allows you to use these functions as needed within an application while keeping the environment handle available for use.

```
Function ODBCDisconnectDS(hEnv As Long, hDbc As Long, hstmt As Long) _
    As Integer
Dim intResult As Integer, intPointer As Integer

    intPointer = Screen.MousePointer
    ODBCDisconnectDS = SQL_SUCCESS

    Screen.MousePointer = vbHourglass

    If hStmt <> 0 Then
        intResult = SQLFreeStmt(hStmt, SQL_DROP)
        If intResult <> SQL_SUCCESS Then
            ODBCDisconnectDS = intResult
            intResult = frmODBCErrors.ODBCError("Env", hEnv, 0, 0, _
                intResult, "Environment Allocation Error")
        End If
    End If
```

continued on next page

continued from previous page

```
If hDbc <> 0 Then
    intResult = SQLDisconnect(hDbc)
    If intResult <> SQL_SUCCESS Then
        ODBCDisconnectDS = intResult
        intResult = frmODBCErrors.ODBCError("Env", hEnv, 0, 0, _
            intResult, "Environment Allocation Error")
    End If
End If

If hDbc <> 0 Then
    intResult = SQLFreeConnect(hDbc)
    If intResult <> SQL_SUCCESS Then
        ODBCDisconnectDS = intResult
        intResult = frmODBCErrors.ODBCError("Env", hEnv, 0, 0, _
            intResult, "Environment Allocation Error")
    End If
End If

Screen.MousePointer = intPointer
End Function
```

8. Now you need a function to release the environment handle and memory. Add the code for **ODBCFreeEnv** to the ODBC API Declarations.BAS code module. This function simply makes a call to the **SQLFreeEnv** ODBC function.

```
Function ODBCFreeEnv(hEnv As Long) As Integer
If hEnv <> 0 Then
    ODBCFreeEnv = (SQLFreeEnv(hEnv) = SQL_SUCCESS)
    End If
End Function
```

9. Add the following code to the **ODBCLoadFuncs** subprocedure. This function is called from the **ODBCAllocateEnv** procedure to load the function names and conformance levels into the **ODBCFuncs** array.

```
Private Sub ODBCLoadFuncs()
    'load the ODBC API function names into the ODBCFuncs array
    Dim i As Integer

    'Core ODBC API functions
    ODBCFuncs(0, 1) = "SQLAllocConnect"
    ODBCFuncs(0, 2) = "SQLAllocEnv"
    ODBCFuncs(0, 3) = "SQLAllocStmt"
    ODBCFuncs(0, 4) = "SQLBindCol"
    ODBCFuncs(0, 5) = "SQLCancel"
    ODBCFuncs(0, 6) = "SQLColAttributes"
    ODBCFuncs(0, 7) = "SQLConnect"
    ODBCFuncs(0, 8) = "SQLDescribeCol"
    ODBCFuncs(0, 9) = "SQLDisconnect"
    ODBCFuncs(0, 10) = "SQLError"
    ODBCFuncs(0, 11) = "SQLExecDirect"
    ODBCFuncs(0, 12) = "SQLExecute"
    ODBCFuncs(0, 13) = "SQLFetch"
    ODBCFuncs(0, 14) = "SQLFreeConnect"
```

```
    ODBCFuncs(0, 15) = "SQLFreeEnv"
    ODBCFuncs(0, 16) = "SQLFreeStmt"
    ODBCFuncs(0, 17) = "SQLGetCursorName"
    ODBCFuncs(0, 18) = "SQLNumResultCols"
    ODBCFuncs(0, 19) = "SQLPrepare"
    ODBCFuncs(0, 20) = "SQLRowCount"
    ODBCFuncs(0, 21) = "SQLSetCursorName"
    ODBCFuncs(0, 22) = "SQLSetParam"
    ODBCFuncs(0, 23) = "SQLTransact"
    For i = 1 To 23
        ODBCFuncs(1, i) = "Core"
    Next

    'Level 1 ODBC API Functions
    ODBCFuncs(0, 40) = "SQLColumns"
    ODBCFuncs(0, 41) = "SQLDriverConnect"
    ODBCFuncs(0, 42) = "SQLGetConnectOption"
    ODBCFuncs(0, 43) = "SQLGetData"
    ODBCFuncs(0, 44) = "SQLGetFunctions"
    ODBCFuncs(0, 45) = "SQLGetInfo"
    ODBCFuncs(0, 46) = "SQLGetStmtOption"
    ODBCFuncs(0, 47) = "SQLGetTypeInfo"
    ODBCFuncs(0, 48) = "SQLParamData"
    ODBCFuncs(0, 49) = "SQLPutData"
    ODBCFuncs(0, 50) = "SQLSetConnectOption"
    ODBCFuncs(0, 51) = "SQLSetStmtOption"
    ODBCFuncs(0, 52) = "SQLSpecialColumns"
    ODBCFuncs(0, 53) = "SQLStatictics"
    ODBCFuncs(0, 54) = "SQLTables"
    For i = 40 To 54
        ODBCFuncs(1, i) = "Level 1"
    Next

    'Level 2 ODBC API Functions
    ODBCFuncs(0, 55) = "SQLBrowseConnect"
    ODBCFuncs(0, 56) = "SQLColumnPrivileges"
    ODBCFuncs(0, 57) = "SQLDataSources"
    ODBCFuncs(0, 58) = "SQLDescribeParam"
    ODBCFuncs(0, 59) = "SQLExtendedFetch"
    ODBCFuncs(0, 60) = "SQLForeignKeys"
    ODBCFuncs(0, 61) = "SQLMoreResults"
    ODBCFuncs(0, 62) = "SQLNativeSQL"
    ODBCFuncs(0, 63) = "SQLNumParams"
    ODBCFuncs(0, 64) = "SQLParamOptions"
    ODBCFuncs(0, 65) = "SQLPrimaryKeys"
    ODBCFuncs(0, 66) = "SQLProcedureColumns"
    ODBCFuncs(0, 67) = "SQLProcedures"
    ODBCFuncs(0, 68) = "SQLSetPos"
    ODBCFuncs(0, 69) = "SQLSetScrollOptions"
    ODBCFuncs(0, 70) = "SQLTablePrivileges"
    ODBCFuncs(0, 71) = "SQLDrivers"
    ODBCFuncs(0, 72) = "SQLBindParameter"
    For i = 55 To 72
        ODBCFuncs(1, i) = "Level 2"
    Next

End Sub
```

10. Add the following code for `LoadGetInfo`. This subprocedure stores all the `SQLGetInfo` options into the Public array `ODBCGetInfo`. The first dimension contains a string with the ODBC constant used, and the second dimension has a one- or two-character code indicating the type of data returned and the need for any special processing. You'll use that data type and code to present information about the ODBC system in relatively more human terms.

```
Private Sub LoadGetInfo()
    ODBCGetInfo(0).InfoType = "SQL_ACTIVE_CONNECTIONS"
    ODBCGetInfo(0).ReturnType = "I"
    ODBCGetInfo(1).InfoType = "SQL_ACTIVE_STATEMENTS"
    ODBCGetInfo(1).ReturnType = "I"
    ODBCGetInfo(2).InfoType = "SQL_DATA_SOURCE_NAME"
    ODBCGetInfo(2).ReturnType = "S"
    ODBCGetInfo(3).InfoType = "SQL_DRIVER_HDBC"
    ODBCGetInfo(3).ReturnType = "L"
    ODBCGetInfo(4).InfoType = "SQL_DRIVER_HENV"
    ODBCGetInfo(4).ReturnType = "L"
    ODBCGetInfo(5).InfoType = "SQL_DRIVER_HSTMT"
    ODBCGetInfo(5).ReturnType = "L"
    ODBCGetInfo(6).InfoType = "SQL_DRIVER_NAME"
    ODBCGetInfo(6).ReturnType = "S"
    ODBCGetInfo(7).InfoType = "SQL_DRIVER_VER"
    ODBCGetInfo(7).ReturnType = "S"
    ODBCGetInfo(8).InfoType = "SQL_FETCH_DIRECTION"
    ODBCGetInfo(8).ReturnType = "B"
    ODBCGetInfo(9).InfoType = "SQL_ODBC_API_CONFORMANCE"
    ODBCGetInfo(9).ReturnType = "IP"
    ODBCGetInfo(10).InfoType = "SQL_ODBC_VER"
    ODBCGetInfo(10).ReturnType = "S"
    ODBCGetInfo(11).InfoType = "SQL_ROW_UPDATES"
    ODBCGetInfo(11).ReturnType = "SY"
    ODBCGetInfo(12).InfoType = "SQL_ODBC_SAG_CLI_CONFORMANCE"
    ODBCGetInfo(12).ReturnType = "I"
    ODBCGetInfo(13).InfoType = "SQL_SERVER_NAME"
    ODBCGetInfo(13).ReturnType = "S"
    ODBCGetInfo(14).InfoType = "SQL_SEARCH_PATTERN_ESCAPE"
    ODBCGetInfo(14).ReturnType = "S"
    ODBCGetInfo(15).InfoType = "SQL_ODBC_SQL_CONFORMANCE"
    ODBCGetInfo(15).ReturnType = "I"
    ODBCGetInfo(17).InfoType = "SQL_DBMS_NAME"
    ODBCGetInfo(17).ReturnType = "S"
    ODBCGetInfo(18).InfoType = "SQL_DBMS_VER"
    ODBCGetInfo(18).ReturnType = "S"
    ODBCGetInfo(19).InfoType = "SQL_ACCESSIBLE_TABLES"
    ODBCGetInfo(19).ReturnType = "SY"
    ODBCGetInfo(20).InfoType = "SQL_ACCESSIBLE_PROCEDURES"
    ODBCGetInfo(20).ReturnType = "SY"
    ODBCGetInfo(21).InfoType = "SQL_PROCEDURES"
    ODBCGetInfo(21).ReturnType = "SY"
    ODBCGetInfo(22).InfoType = "SQL_CONCAT_NULL_BEHAVIOR"
    ODBCGetInfo(22).ReturnType = "IP"
    ODBCGetInfo(23).InfoType = "SQL_CURSOR_COMMIT_BEHAVIOR"
    ODBCGetInfo(23).ReturnType = "IP"
```

```
ODBCGetInfo(24).InfoType = "SQL_CURSOR_ROLLBACK_BEHAVIOR"
ODBCGetInfo(24).ReturnType = "IP"
ODBCGetInfo(25).InfoType = "SQL_DATA_SOURCE_READ_ONLY"
ODBCGetInfo(25).ReturnType = "SY"
ODBCGetInfo(26).InfoType = "SQL_DEFAULT_TXN_ISOLATION"
ODBCGetInfo(26).ReturnType = "LP"
ODBCGetInfo(27).InfoType = "SQL_EXPRESSIONS_IN_ORDERBY"
ODBCGetInfo(27).ReturnType = "SP"
ODBCGetInfo(28).InfoType = "SQL_IDENTIFIER_CASE"
ODBCGetInfo(28).ReturnType = "IP"
ODBCGetInfo(29).InfoType = "SQL_IDENTIFIER_QUOTE_CHAR"
ODBCGetInfo(29).ReturnType = "S"
ODBCGetInfo(30).InfoType = "SQL_MAX_COLUMN_NAME_LEN"
ODBCGetInfo(30).ReturnType = "I"
ODBCGetInfo(31).InfoType = "SQL_MAX_CURSOR_NAME_LEN"
ODBCGetInfo(31).ReturnType = "I"
ODBCGetInfo(32).InfoType = "SQL_MAX_OWNER_NAME_LEN"
ODBCGetInfo(32).ReturnType = "I"
ODBCGetInfo(33).InfoType = "SQL_MAX_PROCEDURE_NAME_LEN"
ODBCGetInfo(33).ReturnType = "I"
ODBCGetInfo(34).InfoType = "SQL_MAX_QUALIFIER_NAME_LEN"
ODBCGetInfo(34).ReturnType = "I"
ODBCGetInfo(35).InfoType = "SQL_MAX_TABLE_NAME_LEN"
ODBCGetInfo(35).ReturnType = "I"
ODBCGetInfo(36).InfoType = "SQL_MULT_RESULT_SETS"
ODBCGetInfo(36).ReturnType = "SP"
ODBCGetInfo(37).InfoType = "SQL_MULTIPLE_ACTIVE_TXN"
ODBCGetInfo(37).ReturnType = "S"
ODBCGetInfo(38).InfoType = "SQL_OUTER_JOINS"
ODBCGetInfo(38).ReturnType = "SP"
ODBCGetInfo(39).InfoType = "SQL_OWNER_TERM"
ODBCGetInfo(39).ReturnType = "S"
ODBCGetInfo(40).InfoType = "SQL_PROCEDURE_TERM"
ODBCGetInfo(40).ReturnType = "S"
ODBCGetInfo(41).InfoType = "SQL_QUALIFIER_NAME_SEPARATOR"
ODBCGetInfo(41).ReturnType = "S"
ODBCGetInfo(42).InfoType = "SQL_QUALIFIER_TERM"
ODBCGetInfo(42).ReturnType = "S"
ODBCGetInfo(43).InfoType = "SQL_SCROLL_CONCURRENCY"
ODBCGetInfo(43).ReturnType = "B"
ODBCGetInfo(44).InfoType = "SQL_SCROLL_OPTIONS"
ODBCGetInfo(44).ReturnType = "B"
ODBCGetInfo(45).InfoType = "SQL_TABLE_TERM"
ODBCGetInfo(45).ReturnType = "S"
ODBCGetInfo(46).InfoType = "SQL_TXN_CAPABLE"
ODBCGetInfo(46).ReturnType = "IP"
ODBCGetInfo(47).InfoType = "SQL_USER_NAME"
ODBCGetInfo(47).ReturnType = "S"
ODBCGetInfo(48).InfoType = "SQL_CONVERT_FUNCTIONS"
ODBCGetInfo(48).ReturnType = "B"
ODBCGetInfo(49).InfoType = "SQL_NUMERIC_FUNCTIONS"
ODBCGetInfo(49).ReturnType = "B"
ODBCGetInfo(50).InfoType = "SQL_STRING_FUNCTIONS"
ODBCGetInfo(50).ReturnType = "B"
ODBCGetInfo(51).InfoType = "SQL_SYSTEM_FUNCTIONS"
ODBCGetInfo(51).ReturnType = "B"
```

continued on next page

continued from previous page

```
ODBCGetInfo(52).InfoType = "SQL_TIMEDATE_FUNCTIONS"
ODBCGetInfo(52).ReturnType = "B"
ODBCGetInfo(53).InfoType = "SQL_CONVERT_BIGINT"
ODBCGetInfo(53).ReturnType = "B"
ODBCGetInfo(54).InfoType = "SQL_CONVERT_BINARY"
ODBCGetInfo(54).ReturnType = "B"
ODBCGetInfo(55).InfoType = "SQL_CONVERT_BIT"
ODBCGetInfo(55).ReturnType = "B"
ODBCGetInfo(56).InfoType = "SQL_CONVERT_CHAR"
ODBCGetInfo(56).ReturnType = "B"
ODBCGetInfo(57).InfoType = "SQL_CONVERT_DATE"
ODBCGetInfo(57).ReturnType = "B"
ODBCGetInfo(58).InfoType = "SQL_CONVERT_DECIMAL"
ODBCGetInfo(58).ReturnType = "B"
ODBCGetInfo(59).InfoType = "SQL_CONVERT_DOUBLE"
ODBCGetInfo(59).ReturnType = "B"
ODBCGetInfo(60).InfoType = "SQL_CONVERT_FLOAT"
ODBCGetInfo(60).ReturnType = "B"
ODBCGetInfo(61).InfoType = "SQL_CONVERT_INTEGER"
ODBCGetInfo(61).ReturnType = "B"
ODBCGetInfo(62).InfoType = "SQL_CONVERT_LONGVARCHAR"
ODBCGetInfo(62).ReturnType = "B"
ODBCGetInfo(63).InfoType = "SQL_CONVERT_NUMERIC"
ODBCGetInfo(63).ReturnType = "B"
ODBCGetInfo(64).InfoType = "SQL_CONVERT_REAL"
ODBCGetInfo(64).ReturnType = "B"
ODBCGetInfo(65).InfoType = "SQL_CONVERT_SMALLINT"
ODBCGetInfo(65).ReturnType = "B"
ODBCGetInfo(66).InfoType = "SQL_CONVERT_TIME"
ODBCGetInfo(66).ReturnType = "B"
ODBCGetInfo(67).InfoType = "SQL_CONVERT_TIMESTAMP"
ODBCGetInfo(67).ReturnType = "B"
ODBCGetInfo(68).InfoType = "SQL_CONVERT_TINYINT"
ODBCGetInfo(68).ReturnType = "B"
ODBCGetInfo(69).InfoType = "SQL_CONVERT_VARBINARY"
ODBCGetInfo(69).ReturnType = "B"
ODBCGetInfo(70).InfoType = "SQL_CONVERT_VARCHAR"
ODBCGetInfo(70).ReturnType = "B"
ODBCGetInfo(71).InfoType = "SQL_CONVERT_LONGVARBINARY"
ODBCGetInfo(71).ReturnType = "B"
ODBCGetInfo(72).InfoType = "SQL_TXN_ISOLATION_OPTION"
ODBCGetInfo(72).ReturnType = "B"
ODBCGetInfo(73).InfoType = "SQL_ODBC_SQL_OPT_IEF"
ODBCGetInfo(73).ReturnType = "SP"
ODBCGetInfo(74).InfoType = "SQL_CORRELATION_NAME"
ODBCGetInfo(74).ReturnType = "IP"
ODBCGetInfo(75).InfoType = "SQL_NON_NULLABLE_COLUMNS"
ODBCGetInfo(75).ReturnType = "IP"
ODBCGetInfo(76).InfoType = "SQL_DRIVER_HLIB"
ODBCGetInfo(76).ReturnType = "L"
ODBCGetInfo(77).InfoType = "SQL_DRIVER_ODBC_VER"
ODBCGetInfo(77).ReturnType = "S"
ODBCGetInfo(78).InfoType = "SQL_LOCK_TYPES"
ODBCGetInfo(78).ReturnType = "B"
ODBCGetInfo(79).InfoType = "SQL_POS_OPERATIONS"
ODBCGetInfo(79).ReturnType = "B"
```

```
ODBCGetInfo(80).InfoType = "SQL_POSITIONED_STATEMENTS"
ODBCGetInfo(80).ReturnType = "B"
ODBCGetInfo(81).InfoType = "SQL_GETDATA_EXTENSIONS"
ODBCGetInfo(81).ReturnType = "B"
ODBCGetInfo(82).InfoType = "SQL_BOOKMARK_PERSISTENCE"
ODBCGetInfo(82).ReturnType = "B"
ODBCGetInfo(83).InfoType = "SQL_STATIC_SENSITIVITY"
ODBCGetInfo(83).ReturnType = "B"
ODBCGetInfo(84).InfoType = "SQL_FILE_USAGE"
ODBCGetInfo(84).ReturnType = "IP"
ODBCGetInfo(85).InfoType = "SQL_NULL_COLLATION"
ODBCGetInfo(85).ReturnType = "IP"
ODBCGetInfo(86).InfoType = "SQL_ALTER_TABLE"
ODBCGetInfo(86).ReturnType = "B"
ODBCGetInfo(87).InfoType = "SQL_COLUMN_ALIAS"
ODBCGetInfo(87).ReturnType = "SP"
ODBCGetInfo(88).InfoType = "SQL_GROUP_BY"
ODBCGetInfo(88).ReturnType = "IP"
ODBCGetInfo(89).InfoType = "SQL_KEYWORDS"
ODBCGetInfo(89).ReturnType = "SP"
ODBCGetInfo(90).InfoType = "SQL_ORDER_BY_COLUMNS_IN_SELECT"
ODBCGetInfo(90).ReturnType = "SY"
ODBCGetInfo(91).InfoType = "SQL_OWNER_USAGE"
ODBCGetInfo(91).ReturnType = "B"
ODBCGetInfo(92).InfoType = "SQL_QUALIFIER_USAGE"
ODBCGetInfo(92).ReturnType = "B"
ODBCGetInfo(93).InfoType = "SQL_QUOTED_IDENTIFIER_CASE"
ODBCGetInfo(93).ReturnType = "IP"
ODBCGetInfo(94).InfoType = "SQL_SPECIAL_CHARACTERS"
ODBCGetInfo(94).ReturnType = "S"
ODBCGetInfo(95).InfoType = "SQL_SUBQUERIES"
ODBCGetInfo(95).ReturnType = "B"
ODBCGetInfo(96).InfoType = "SQL_UNION"
ODBCGetInfo(96).ReturnType = "B"
ODBCGetInfo(97).InfoType = "SQL_MAX_COLUMNS_IN_GROUP_BY"
ODBCGetInfo(97).ReturnType = "I"
ODBCGetInfo(98).InfoType = "SQL_MAX_COLUMNS_IN_INDEX"
ODBCGetInfo(98).ReturnType = "I"
ODBCGetInfo(99).InfoType = "SQL_MAX_COLUMNS_IN_ORDER_BY"
ODBCGetInfo(99).ReturnType = "I"
ODBCGetInfo(100).InfoType = "SQL_MAX_COLUMNS_IN_SELECT"
ODBCGetInfo(100).ReturnType = "I"
ODBCGetInfo(101).InfoType = "SQL_MAX_COLUMNS_IN_TABLE"
ODBCGetInfo(101).ReturnType = "I"
ODBCGetInfo(102).InfoType = "SQL_MAX_INDEX_SIZE"
ODBCGetInfo(102).ReturnType = "L"
ODBCGetInfo(103).InfoType = "SQL_MAX_ROW_SIZE_INCLUDES_LONG"
ODBCGetInfo(103).ReturnType = "SY"
ODBCGetInfo(104).InfoType = "SQL_MAX_ROW_SIZE"
ODBCGetInfo(104).ReturnType = "L"
ODBCGetInfo(105).InfoType = "SQL_MAX_STATEMENT_LEN"
ODBCGetInfo(105).ReturnType = "L"
ODBCGetInfo(106).InfoType = "SQL_MAX_TABLES_IN_SELECT"
ODBCGetInfo(106).ReturnType = "I"
ODBCGetInfo(107).InfoType = "SQL_MAX_USER_NAME_LEN"
ODBCGetInfo(107).ReturnType = "I"
```

continued on next page

continued from previous page

```
ODBCGetInfo(108).InfoType = "SQL_MAX_CHAR_LITERAL_LEN"
ODBCGetInfo(108).ReturnType = "L"
ODBCGetInfo(109).InfoType = "SQL_TIMEDATE_ADD_INTERVALS"
ODBCGetInfo(109).ReturnType = "B"
ODBCGetInfo(110).InfoType = "SQL_TIMEDATE_DIFF_INTERVALS"
ODBCGetInfo(110).ReturnType = "B"
ODBCGetInfo(111).InfoType = "SQL_NEED_LONG_DATA_LEN"
ODBCGetInfo(111).ReturnType = "SY"
ODBCGetInfo(112).InfoType = "SQL_MAX_BINARY_LITERAL_LEN"
ODBCGetInfo(112).ReturnType = "L"
ODBCGetInfo(113).InfoType = "SQL_LIKE_ESCAPE_CLAUSE"
ODBCGetInfo(113).ReturnType = "SY"
ODBCGetInfo(114).InfoType = "SQL_QUALIFIER_LOCATION"
ODBCGetInfo(114).ReturnType = "IP"
End Sub
```

11. Add the following function to the ODBC API `Declarations.BAS` module. The `ODBCDriverList` function serves as a wrapper for the SQLDrivers API call, retrieving a list of drivers and storing them in a variant array. The `blnIncAttr` flag determines whether to include the driver's attributes string in the array.

```
Public Function ODBCDriverList(lng_hEnv As Long, blnIncAttr As Boolean) _
    As Variant
    Dim strDriverDesc As String * 512, strDriverAttr As String * 2048
    Dim intDriverDescsMax As Integer, lngDriverDesc As Integer
    Dim lngDriverAttr As Integer, intDriverAttrMax As Integer
    Dim intResult As Integer, intErrResult As Integer
    Dim intSaveCursor As Integer
    Dim strDriverList() As String, strTemp As String
    Dim I As Integer

    'Prep our variables
    intDriverDescsMax = 512: intDriverAttrMax = 2048
    intResult = SQL_SUCCESS: I = 0

    intSaveCursor = Screen.MousePointer
    Screen.MousePointer = vbHourglass

    Do Until intResult = SQL_NO_DATA_FOUND
        strDriverDesc = String(512, 0)
        intResult = SQLDrivers(glng_hEnv, SQL_FETCH_NEXT, strDriverDesc, _
            intDriverDescsMax, lngDriverDesc, strDriverAttr, _
            intDriverAttrMax, lngDriverAttr)
        If intResult = SQL_ERROR Then
            intErrResult = frmODBCErrors.ODBCError("Env", glng_hEnv, 0, _
                0, intResult, "Error getting list of registered drivers.")
            Screen.MousePointer = intSaveCursor
            Exit Function
        End If

        If Left(strDriverDesc, 5) <> String(5, 0) Then
            If blnIncAttr Then
                strTemp = Left(strDriverDesc, lngDriverDesc) & _
                    " (" & Left(strDriverAttr, lngDriverAttr) & ")"
```

```
            Else
                strTemp = Left(strDriverDesc, lngDriverDesc)
            End If
            ReDim Preserve strDriverList(I)
            strDriverList(I) = strTemp
            I = I + 1
        End If
    Loop

    Screen.MousePointer = intSaveCursor
    ODBCDriverList = strDriverList
End Function
```

12. Similar to the previous step, add the **ODBCDSNList** function to the module. This function uses the **SQLDataSources** API function to return a variant array of ODBC data sources, optionally with the description string added.

```
Function ODBCDSNList(hEnv As Long, blnIncDesc As Boolean) As Variant
    Dim strDSN As String * 33, strDescription As String * 512
    Dim lngDSN As Long, lngDesc As Long, lngSaveCursor As Long
    Dim intDSNMaxLen As Integer, intDescMaxLen As Integer
    Dim intResult As Integer
    Dim intNameLen As Integer, intErrResult As Integer
    Dim I As Integer
    Dim strDSNList() As String, strTemp As String

    'Prep our variables
    intDSNMaxLen = SQL_MAX_DSN_LENGTH + 1
    intDescMaxLen = 512
    intResult = SQL_SUCCESS


    lngSaveCursor = Screen.MousePointer
    Screen.MousePointer = vbHourglass
    Do Until intResult = SQL_NO_DATA_FOUND
        'Blank out the DSN string with null characters
        strDSN = String(33, 0)
        'Fetch the data sources via the SQLDataSources command
        'Note that the SQL_FETCH_NEXT option will fetch the first
        'data source the first time SQLDataSources() is called.
        intResult = SQLDataSources(glng_hEnv, SQL_FETCH_NEXT, strDSN, _
            intDSNMaxLen, lngDSN, strDescription, intDescMaxLen, lngDesc)
        If intResult = SQL_ERROR Then
            intErrResult = frmODBCErrors.ODBCError("Env", glng_hEnv, _
                0, 0, intResult, "Error getting list of data sources.")
            Screen.MousePointer = lngSaveCursor
            Exit Function
        End If

        'Add the data source data to the global arrays
        If Left(strDSN, 5) <> String(5, 0) Then
            If blnIncDesc Then
                strTemp = Left(strDSN, lngDSN) & " (" & _
                    Left(strDescription, lngDesc) & ")"
            Else
```

continued on next page

continued from previous page

```
                strTemp = Left(strDSN, lngDSN)
            End If
            ReDim Preserve strDSNList(I)
            strDSNList(I) = strTemp
            I = I + 1
        End If
    Loop
    Screen.MousePointer = lngSaveCursor
    ODBCDSNList = strDSNList
End Function
```

13. Put the following code in the **convCh** subroutine. This code converts some of the ODBC properties that return a **Y** or an **N** to a more user-friendly **Yes** or **No**.

```
Private Function convCh(inChar As String, num As Integer)
    inChar = LTrim$(Left$(inChar, num))

    Select Case inChar
        Case "Y"
            convCh = "Yes"
        Case "N"
            convCh = "No"
        Case Else
            convCh = inChar
    End Select

End Function
```

14. That is the last of the code for the wrapper functions. Now, let's add a couple of forms and some code to give the ODBC API a thorough testing. Name the project's default form **frmODBC** and save the file as API.FRM. Add the controls shown in Figure 9.1, setting the properties as shown in Table 9.1.

Table 9.1. Objects and properties for API.FRM.

OBJECT	PROPERTY	SETTING
Form	Name	frmODBC
	Caption	"Chapter 9.1. example"
	StartUpPosition	2 - CenterScreen
ListBox	Name	lstODBCDrivers
	Sorted	True
TextBox	Name	txtODBCStatus
	BackColor	&H00C0C0C0&
ListBox	Name	lstODBCDbs
CommandButton	Name	cmdGetStatus
	Caption	"&Get ODBC Status"

OBJECT	PROPERTY	SETTING
CommandButton	Name	cmdQuit
	Caption	"&Quit"
	Default	True
Label	Name	lblDrivers
	Caption	"Installed ODBC Drivers:"
Label	Name	lblDatabases
	Caption	"&Registered ODBC Databases:"

15. Insert the following code in the declarations section of **frmODBC**. The **Option Explicit** syntax tells Visual Basic to make sure that you declare all variables and objects before using them in order to avoid naming problems. The dynamic arrays will be used to hold various pieces of information about the ODBC system and driver.

```
Option Explicit
```

16. Add the following code to the **Load** event procedure of the form. The txtODBCStatus.Text box gives the user instructions about the next steps to take to gather information about the data sources.

```
Private Sub Form_Load()
    txtODBCStatus.text = "Select Get ODBC Status to begin."
End Sub
```

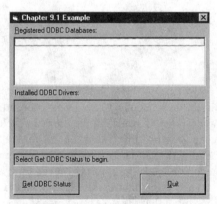

Figure 9.1. The Chapter 9.1 example ODBC Status form.

17. Put the following code in the `GetODBCdbs` subroutine. This code is the first of two procedures that execute after the user clicks the `cmdGetStatus` button. The `GetODBCdbs` subroutine establishes a connection with the ODBC API via the `ODBCDSNList` wrapper function and gets from it a list of all the data sources that are registered with ODBC, placing them in the `lvarTemp` variant array, then loading them into the list box.

```
Dim lvarTemp As Variant, I As Integer

    Screen.MousePointer = vbHourglass
        lvarTemp = ODBCDSNList(glng_hEnv, False)
        If IsArray(lvarTemp) Then
            For I = LBound(lvarTemp) To UBound(lvarTemp)
                lstODBCDbs.AddItem lvarTemp(I)
            Next
        End If
    Screen.MousePointer = vbDefault
End Sub
```

18. Put the following code in the `GetODBCdvrs` subroutine. This code, which is similar to the previous `GetODBCdbs` code, retrieves the list of ODBC drivers that are registered with ODBC by calling the `ODBCDriverList` wrapper function.

```
Private Sub GetODBCdvrs()
Dim lvarTemp As Variant, I As Integer

    Screen.MousePointer = vbHourglass
        lvarTemp = ODBCDriverList(glng_hEnv, True)
        If IsArray(lvarTemp) Then
            For I = LBound(lvarTemp) To UBound(lvarTemp)
                lstODBCDrivers.AddItem lvarTemp(I)
            Next
        End If
    Screen.MousePointer = vbDefault
End Sub
```

19. Put the following code in the `lstODBCDbs_Click` event subroutine. After the list of data sources and drivers is available, the user can click on any of the data source names to get a window listing the ODBC API SQL functions that can be called with that data source and various properties of the data source. This procedure loads the `frmAttributes` form and fills its list box and grid with data about the data source. The `frmAttributes` form is shown modally, meaning that the user must respond to the form by pressing Quit before being able to retrieve data about another data source.

```
Private Sub lstODBCDbs_Click()
Dim DataSource As String
    Dim UserID As String
    Dim Password As String
    Dim intResult As Integer
    Dim ErrResult As Integer
    ReDim FuncList(100) As Integer
    Dim I As Integer, j As Integer

    Screen.MousePointer = vbHourglass
    DataSource = lstODBCDbs.List(lstODBCDbs.ListIndex)

    If ODBCConnectDS(glng_hEnv, glng_hDbc, glng_hStmt, DataSource, _
        UserID, Password) <> SQL_SUCCESS Then
        Screen.MousePointer = vbDefault
    Else
        'Now get the list of functions
        intResult = SQLGetFunctions(glng_hDbc, _
            SQL_API_ALL_FUNCTIONS, FuncList(0))
        If intResult <> SQL_SUCCESS Then
            ErrResult = frmODBCErrors.ODBCError("Dbc", glng_hEnv, _
                glng_hDbc, 0, intResult, _
                "Error getting list of ODBC functions")
            Screen.MousePointer = vbDefault
            Exit Sub
        Else
            Load frmAttributes

            j = 0
            For I = 0 To 99
                If FuncList(I) <> 0 Then
                    frmAttributes.lstFunctions.AddItem ODBCFuncs(0, I)
                    j = j + 1
                End If
            Next

            With frmAttributes
                .txtFuncCount.Text = j
                .Caption = "Data Source: " & DataSource
                .Show vbModal
            End With
            'free the data source connection
            intResult = ODBCDisconnectDS(glng_hEnv, glng_hDbc, _
                SQL_NULL_HSTMT)
            Screen.MousePointer = vbDefault
        End If
    End If
End Sub
```

20. Put the following code in the `cmdQuit_Click` subroutine. This command ends the program.

```
Sub cmdQuit_Click ()
    End
End Sub
```

21. Put the following code in the `Form_Unload` event subroutine. Because this form is the start-up form for the program, any final cleanup should be done when the form is unloaded. The code calls wrapper functions to release memory used by the ODBC API, and it disconnects the program from any open data sources.

```
Private Sub Form_Unload(Cancel As Integer)
    'Clean up the ODBC connections and allocations
    Dim intResult As Integer

    intResult = ODBCDisconnectDS(glng_hEnv, glng_hDbc, glng_hStmt)
    intResult = ODBCFreeEnv(glng_hEnv)
End Sub
```

22. Create a new form with the controls listed in Table 9.2 and save it as ATTR.FRM. This form will be used to display information about the data source. Figure 9.2 shows the form when the program is running.

Table 9.2. Objects and properties for ATTR.FRM.

OBJECT	PROPERTY	SETTING
Form	Name	frmAttributes
	BorderStyle	1 'Fixed Single
	Caption	"Chapter 9.1. example, showing attributes"
	MaxButton	0 'False
CommandButton	Name	cmdQuit
	Caption	"&Quit"
	Default	True
TextBox	Name	txtFuncCount
	BackColor	&H00C0C0C0& (light gray)
ListBox	Name	lstFunctions
	BackColor	&H00C0C0C0& (light gray)
Grid	Name	grdGI
	FixedCols	0
Label	Name	lblFunctions
	Caption	"Functions Available:"
Label	Name	lblFuncCount
	Alignment	1 'Right Justify
	Caption	"Total Functions:"

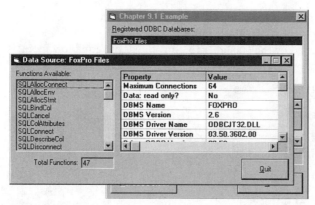

Figure 9.2. The Chapter 9.1 example Data Source Attributes form.

23. Insert the following code in the declarations section of `frmAttributes`. The `Option Explicit` syntax tells Visual Basic to make sure that you declare all variables and objects before using them in order to avoid naming problems.

```
Option Explicit
```

24. Put the following code in the `Form_Load` event subroutine. When the `frmAttributes` form is loaded into memory when the user clicks on an ODBC data source, this procedure sets up some of the properties of the grid control that must be set at runtime and positions the form lower and to the right relative to the `frmODBCStatus` form.

```
Private Sub Form_Load()
'Resize data here
    With grdGI
        .ColWidth(0) = .Width / 2
        .ColWidth(1) = .Width / 2
        .ColAlignment(0) = 1: .ColAlignment(1) = 0
        .Row = 0
        .Col = 0: .Text = "Property"
        .Col = 1: .Text = "Value"
        .FixedAlignment(0) = 2: .FixedAlignment(1) = 2
        .HighLight = False
    End With

    'Load other data source information
    ODBCInfo
End Sub
```

25. Put the following code in the `ODBCInfo` subroutine. This code uses the ODBC API function `SQLGetInfo` to retrieve individual pieces of information about the data source one at a time. The information gathered here is a representative sample of what can be retrieved. As each item is retrieved, a new row in the grid control is added for the data. Some of the data returned by the SQLGetInfo function is converted to a more user-friendly form.

```
Private Sub ODBCInfo()
Dim fInfoType As Integer

    'return values
    Dim intReturn As Integer
    Dim strReturn As String * 255

    Dim lngInfoValue As Long
    Dim intInfoValueMax As Integer
    Dim intInfoValue As Integer
    Dim intResult As Integer
    Dim strTemp As String

    intInfoValueMax = 255

    intResult = SQLGetInfo(glng_hDbc, SQL_ACTIVE_CONNECTIONS, _
        intReturn, intInfoValueMax, intInfoValue)
    If intResult <> SQL_ERROR Then
        grdGI.AddItem "Maximum Connections " & vbTab & _
            IIf(intReturn = 0, "Unknown", LTrim$(Str$(intReturn)))
    End If
    intResult = SQLGetInfo(glng_hDbc, SQL_DATA_SOURCE_READ_ONLY, _
        ByVal strReturn, intInfoValueMax, intInfoValue)
    If intResult <> SQL_ERROR Then
        grdGI.AddItem "Data: read only? " & vbTab & _
            convCh(strReturn, intInfoValue)
    End If
    intResult = SQLGetInfo(glng_hDbc, SQL_DBMS_NAME, ByVal strReturn, _
        intInfoValueMax, intInfoValue)
    If intResult <> SQL_ERROR Then
        grdGI.AddItem "DBMS Name " & vbTab & _
            convCh(strReturn, intInfoValue)
    End If
    intResult = SQLGetInfo(glng_hDbc, SQL_DBMS_VER, ByVal strReturn, _
        intInfoValueMax, intInfoValue)
    If intResult <> SQL_ERROR Then
        grdGI.AddItem "DBMS Version " & vbTab & _
            convCh(strReturn, intInfoValue)
    End If
    intResult = SQLGetInfo(glng_hDbc, SQL_DRIVER_NAME, _
        ByVal strReturn, intInfoValueMax, intInfoValue)
    If intResult <> SQL_ERROR Then
        grdGI.AddItem "DBMS Driver Name " & vbTab & _
            convCh(strReturn, intInfoValue)
    End If
    intResult = SQLGetInfo(glng_hDbc, SQL_DRIVER_VER, _
        ByVal strReturn, intInfoValueMax, intInfoValue)
    If intResult <> SQL_ERROR Then
        grdGI.AddItem "DBMS Driver Version " & vbTab & _
            convCh(strReturn, intInfoValue)
    End If
```

```
        intResult = SQLGetInfo(glng_hDbc, SQL_DRIVER_ODBC_VER, _
            ByVal strReturn, intInfoValueMax, intInfoValue)
        If intResult <> SQL_ERROR Then
            grdGI.AddItem "Driver ODBC Version " & vbTab & _
                convCh(strReturn, intInfoValue)
        End If
        intResult = SQLGetInfo(glng_hDbc, SQL_ODBC_API_CONFORMANCE, _
            intReturn, intInfoValueMax, intInfoValue)
        If intResult <> SQL_ERROR Then
            Select Case intReturn
                Case SQL_OAC_NONE
                    strTemp = "Core Only"
                Case SQL_OAC_LEVEL1
                    strTemp = "Level 1"
                Case SQL_OAC_LEVEL2
                    strTemp = "Level 2"
            End Select
            grdGI.AddItem "ODBC Conformance Level " & vbTab & strTemp
        End If
        intResult = SQLGetInfo(glng_hDbc, SQL_ODBC_SQL_CONFORMANCE, _
            intReturn, intInfoValueMax, intInfoValue)
        If intResult <> SQL_ERROR Then
            Select Case intReturn
                Case SQL_OSC_MINIMUM
                    strTemp = "Minimum Grammar"
                Case SQL_OSC_CORE
                    strTemp = "Core Grammar"
                Case SQL_OSC_EXTENDED
                    strTemp = "Extended Grammar"
            End Select
            grdGI.AddItem "SQL Grammar Level " & vbTab & strTemp
        End If

        If grdGI.Rows > 2 Then grdGI.RemoveItem 1

        Screen.MousePointer = vbDefault
    End Sub
```

26. Put the following code in the **convCh** subroutine. This code converts some of the ODBC properties that return a Y or N to a more user-friendly Yes or No.

```
Private Function convCh(inChar As String, num As Integer)
    inChar = LTrim$(Left$(inChar, num))

    Select Case inChar
        Case "Y"
            convCh = "Yes"
        Case "N"
            convCh = "No"
        Case Else
            convCh = inChar
    End Select

End Function
```

27. Put the following code in the `cmdQuit_Click` event subroutine. This subroutine simply unloads the form when the user clicks the Quit command button.

```
Private Sub cmdQuit_Click()
    Unload frmAttributes
End Sub
```

28. Set the `frmODBC` form as the start-up form for the project. Select Project | Properties from the Visual Basic menu, and click on the General tab from the dialog box that appears. Select `frmODBC` from the Startup Object drop-down list, and then click OK to close the window.

How It Works

This How-To gives a complete example of using several of the most common ODBC API functions from initializing the connection to the data sources and drivers through getting the specific information needed and putting it into a presentable form and then releasing memory. You can adapt many of the techniques easily for obtaining properties to do the real work of connecting to a data source and extracting its data in meaningful forms. Using the ODBC API directly involves more work initially in writing the code, but that work is rewarded by the speed of processing and the easy portability as data are moved and changed into different formats on different machines.

The wrapper functions designed in this How-To make ODBC error handling simpler. When making calls to the `SQLError` ODBC function in `frmODBCErrors`, you need to specify the proper ODBC handle. If you call `SQLError` with the wrong handle for the function that generated an error, you won't get the correct error messages. Using the wrapper functions means you don't have to worry about the correct arguments for the `SQLError` function because they are written into each wrapper function.

This How-To involves two primary steps: getting the list of available data sources and drivers from ODBC, and then making the connection to any individual data sources that are of interest. The `frmODBCStatus` form implements the first step. It calls the functions that initialize and allocate memory for the ODBC environment, then it uses API functions to retrieve the data needed. In this case, you did not retrieve data stored in the data sources but instead received information about the ODBC and data source installation. This is the kind of information necessary to use fully the different data sources with the standard set of ODBC API functions.

After the list of data sources and drivers is compiled, you can retrieve specialized information about any of those sources. Here, you simply displayed the data, but you can use the same techniques to get the data that you can then use immediately to send SQL calls to the drivers.

Two similar subroutines, GetODBCdbs and GetODBCdvrs, are used to retrieve the data source and driver data. By storing the results in global arrays, you can easily manipulate and use the data as needed throughout the application. For sets of data about a particular object, several of the API functions are called repeatedly until all data have been retrieved. As described in How-To 9.6, this is how you would use the API function SQLError to obtain all the sometimes extensive information about an error condition. Visual Basic loop structures are ideal for those ODBC API calls.

In this project, all forms except frmAttributes redraw themselves to size the controls to fill as much of the window as possible. The program does that by keeping forms relatively simple, positioning controls to make logical boundaries for the controls, and then resizing everything to fit. The forms that you can resize are not allowed to go below a size that obscures all information, although you can minimize all forms.

Errors

You can make a number of errors in making a connection to ODBC and a data source, and you must handle them all in the Visual Basic code when using the API. General categories of errors include ODBC not installed on the system, the inability of ODBC to find pieces of itself or data sources that have been moved without updating the ODBC.INI file, and memory allocation problems that prevent a connection from being made. More will be said about ODBC errors in How-To 9.6.

The ODBC wrapper functions (the functions with an "ODBC" prefix) contain their own error handling code, so the calling program doesn't need to check again for errors. The program can still use the primary error code if it needs to change its action based on the success or failure of an API function. Our program, however, must handle errors for API functions that it calls directly. In most cases, that's done by testing the value of the result of the call, then calling the ODBCError wrapper function in frmODBCErrors if necessary.

Making a Connection

Three different ODBC API functions can make a connection to a database: SQLConnect, SQLBrowseConnect, and SQLDriverConnect. Each of them requires different forms of information about the data source to make the connection. The SQLBrowseConnect function is a Level 2 conformance function, so it is less useful in a Visual Basic application because Visual Basic requires Level 1 conformance. See How-To 7.4 for more information about these functions.

Connection Handles

To use a database through ODBC, you must allocate and assign a connection handle. Doing so sets aside a small area of memory, managed by the ODBC Driver Manager and/or the driver, to contain information about the connection.

The ODBC API uses a two-step process for connection handles: allocation and actually making the database connection. Conversely, to completely release the handle, you must both disconnect and free the handle. By using this two-step process, you can customize wrapper functions to fit your application needs—only disconnecting when you reuse the connection handle, and you can customize both disconnecting and releasing the handle when you no longer need it.

Comments

Now you have a basic framework that you can use to make connections to data sources through ODBC and a tool that you can use to complement the ODBC Administrator. As you move further into this chapter, you will build on this How-To, expanding your capabilities.

One point that should be emphasized here is a meticulous need for "cleanliness." Very often, ODBC applications cause problems because the programmer hasn't released connection handles or has somehow referred to incorrect handles due to lack of handling. It is imperative that, if you allocate a handle, you de-allocate it somewhere in code, *explicitly*, before ending your program. Unlike Visual Basic objects, ODBC handles do *not* pass out of scope, even though the variables these handles are assigned to might do so. Consequently, you get a "memory leak": an application that takes memory but doesn't give it back when needed. Eventually, with repeated execution, this application will cause a system to crash.

COMPLEXITY

INTERMEDIATE

9.2 How do I...
Pass SQL commands directly to an ODBC server?

Problem

My database server supports some really cool extensions to SQL, but I can't get them to work with Visual Basic and the data access methods. Visual Basic keeps telling me the SQL syntax is wrong. How do I pass SQL statements directly to the database server so Visual Basic won't protect me from myself?

Technique

Visual Basic 4.0 introduced a slightly different way of executing SQL pass-through queries with ODBC. The technique uses Visual Basic's native data access methods as shown in this How-To, using `CreateQueryDef` and `OpenRecordset`. Using this technique, you can send any SQL syntax supported by the database, including stored procedures in SQL Server and extensions to SQL.

Steps

Open and run the LOGIN.VBP Visual Basic project file. The project automatically connects with the ODBC database and loads the bound data grid with two fields selected in the SQL string, as shown in Figure 9.3. Click Quit to end the program.

1. Create a new project called PASSTHRU.VBP.

2. Name the default form `frmODBC` and save the file as PASSTHRU.FRM. Add the controls shown in Figure 9.3, setting the properties as shown in Table 9.3.

Table 9.3. Objects and properties for PASSTHRU.FRM.

OBJECT	PROPERTY	SETTING
Form	Name	frmPassthru
	Caption	"Chapter 9.2. example"
CommandButton	Name	cmdQuit
	Caption	"Quit"
MSFlexGrid	Name	grdData

3. Insert the following code in the declarations section of the form. The `Option Explicit` syntax tells Visual Basic to make sure that you declare all variables and objects before using them in order to avoid naming problems.

```
Option Explicit
```

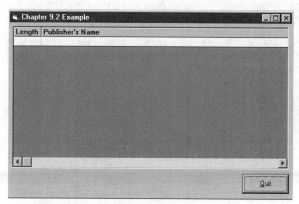

Figure 9.3. The project's main form, showing ODBC data source information.

4. Add the following code in the Load event of the form. Note the large comment in the routine; a limitation in DAO requires that an ODBC data source opened with the DAO library not be a supported database type (in other words, you can't open an Access, dBASE, FoxPro, or Paradox database as an ODBC data source using a DAO object). You'll get a trappable error when attempting to perform such an action. After the data source is loaded, a query is run against it and the **grdData** grid control is populated with the results.

```
Private Sub Form_Load()
Dim dbfTemp As Database, recTemp As Recordset

    With grdData
        .ColWidth(0) = 0.1 * .Width
        .ColWidth(1) = 0.9 * .Width
        .Row = 0
        .Col = 0: .Text = "Length"
        .Col = 1: .Text = "Publisher's Name"
    End With

    On Error Resume Next
    'NOTE:  This example is for syntax only; normally, Visual Basic
    'will not allow you to use DAO with an external Access or ISAM
    '(i.e., DBase IV, Paradox, etc.) database.  To see what happens,
    'create a DSN named Biblio, using the Microsoft Access ODBC driver,
    'pointed toward your copy of BIBLIO.MDB.  You'll get a specific error
    '(3243), indicating the problem, by removing the On Error Resume Next
    'statement (above) and running the project.

    Set dbfTemp = Workspaces(0).OpenDatabase("", dbDriverNoPrompt, _
        False, "ODBC;DSN=Biblio;")

    'Notice the dbSQLPassThrough constant; that tells the ODBC driver
    'to pass the SQL directly to whatever server is providing the data,
    'and not to precompile or check syntax.
    Set recTemp = dbfTemp.OpenRecordset( _
        "SELECT LEN([Publisher's Name]) AS Length, [Publisher's Name]" & _
        " FROM Publishers", dbOpenSnapshot, dbSQLPassThrough)
    If recTemp.RecordCount <> 0 Then
        recTemp.MoveFirst
        Do
            With grdData
                .Row = .Rows - 1
                .Col = 0: .Text = recTemp!Length
                .Col = 1: .Text = recTemp![Publisher's Name]
                .Rows = .Rows + 1
            End With
            recTemp.MoveNext
        Loop Until recTemp.EOF
        grdData.Rows = grdData.Rows - 1
    End If
    On Error GoTo 0
End Sub
```

5. Add the following code to the `Click` event of the `cmdQuit` command button:

```
Private Sub cmdQuit_Click()
    Unload Me
End Sub
```

6. Set the start-up form to `frmODBC`. You can also set an application description, but that is not required for the operation of the application.

How It Works

There are essentially two ways to execute a query in Visual Basic using ODBC: Execute the query using Visual Basic through the Jet database engine or pass the query straight through ODBC to the database system and/or driver.

Visual Basic normally uses the Jet database engine to process queries before they are passed on to the database. When you use a pass-through query, however, the Jet engine is bypassed entirely. Visual Basic still uses its Recordset processor to create and manage the result sets of the query.

The major benefit of a pass-through query is that you can take advantage of any specific capabilities of the database. For example, you can only execute a SQL Server's stored procedures by using a pass-through query. In this case, the grammar of the query is not valid under the SQL grammar used by either Visual Basic or ODBC, so an error would result if Visual Basic processed the query before sending it on.

Pass-through queries are also advantageous for databases in distant locations over the network. Instead of passing a huge amount of data through the network, the database itself does all the processing, returning only a result set (if there is one) back to ODBC and Visual Basic.

Following is a list of other uses for pass-through queries:

✔ To create a new database, table, or index on an external server.

✔ To create or manage Triggers, Defaults, Rules, or stored procedures.

✔ To maintain user accounts or perform other System Administrator tasks.

✔ To run maintenance operations like Microsoft SQL Server's DBCC.

✔ To execute multiple `INSERT` or `UPDATE` statements in a single batch command.

This How-To used the data control to make the connection, but you can also use these techniques with data access objects (DAOs). When using DAOs, all that you need to execute a pass-through SQL statement is to use only a name argument in `CreateQueryDef`. You then assign the SQL command as a string to the SQL property of the `QueryDef`. The following code illustrates the general procedure:

```
Dim dbfTemp as Database, qdfTemp as QueryDef, recTemp as Recordset

'Use the first argument, name, only in CreateQueryDef:
Set qdfTemp = dbfTemp.CreateQueryDef("MYODbCQuery")

qdfTemp.Connect = "ODBC;" "DSN=MyServer;UID=sa;PWD=hithere;DATABASE=pubs"
qdfTemp.SQL = "Exec SELECT * FROM pubs"
qdfTemp.ReturnsRows = True

Set recTemp = qdfTemp.OpenRecordset()
```

Note the use of the `ReturnsRows` property in the preceding code. This property, when set to `True`, tells Visual Basic to use the Jet engine to be ready to receive and manage the `Recordset` (if any) that ODBC and the database returns from the query. The `ReturnsRows` property should be set to `False` for action queries or other commands that do not return records to Visual Basic.

The SQL string assigned to the SQL property of the `QueryDef` object `qdfTemp` uses the syntax of the external database, which may or may not be different from the syntax normally required by Visual Basic. This statement will be passed directly to the external database, as will all other SQL statements that you make using this instance of the `QueryDef` object. This also means your application must be ready to handle any errors that the database returns.

Previous versions of Visual Basic included a `DB_SQLPASSTHROUGH` or `dbSQLPassthrough` (in Visual Basic 4.0) constant for use with `CreateDynaset`, `CreateSnapshot`, or `ExecuteSQL` methods. With the latest version of the Jet database engine, it is now recommended that you use the technique previously demonstrated instead of using these constants.

Comments

Pass-through queries tend to be much faster than their Jet-scrubbed counterparts but often require the programmer to learn a different "flavor" of SQL; many database systems employ their own extensions to ANSI SQL, considered the "standard" SQL. Even Access uses its own version of SQL, with certain commands and translations performed by the DAO's Jet engine. This can make maintenance slightly tougher but, in return, allow access to custom functionality supplied by the database system, as well as provide a boost in performance.

COMPLEXITY
INTERMEDIATE

9.3 How do I...
Use transactions with ODBC databases?

Problem

All my applications are mission-critical, and I need to go to great lengths to make sure that my databases do not get corrupted. Adding to the problem, most of the maintenance procedures done on the ODBC databases aren't simple add-or-update-single-record operations; they involve several steps that must be all completed or not done at all. How do I use Visual Basic with ODBC databases to meet these needs?

Technique

The good news is that you don't need to do anything different with an ODBC database for transactions to work. Visual Basic takes care of all the details of negotiating the transaction with the database, all transparent to your application.

For this How-To, you'll need a data source with two tables, Accounts and LogBook. The structures of these tables are shown in Table 9.4. This particular example uses text files as an ODBC database with the Microsoft Text Files driver, but any data source will do, as long as you can open it in Visual Basic as an ODBC data source. This restriction prohibits the database from being an Access database or any of the ISAM databases supported by Visual Basic. Note that, by using **ODBCDirect**, you can circumvent this—for more information, examine How-To 7.7.

Table 9.4. Tables for use with the Chapter 9.3 example.

TABLE	FIELD	DATA TYPE AND SIZE
Accounts	AccountID	Text(15)
	Balance	Float or Currency
LogBook	Type	Text(10)
	Source	Text(15)
	Destination	Text(15)
	Amount	Float or Currency

Steps

Open and run the TRANS.VBP Visual Basic project file. In the Transfer Bank Funds window, shown in Figure 9.4, select an account from which to transfer money and an account to which to transfer money. Enter an amount to transfer. When you have entered this information, click the Transfer command button to actually transfer the money.

Change one of the To or From accounts to our nonexistent account, D.B. Cooper Savings, and click the Transfer command button again. This time, a message box should appear, indicating that the transaction was not completed and was rolled back.

1. Create a new project, and save it as TRANS.VBP.

2. Name the default form frmODBC, and save the file as TRANS.FRM. Add the controls shown in Figure 9.4, setting the properties as shown in Table 9.5.

Table 9.5. Objects and properties for TRANS.FRM.

OBJECT	PROPERTY	SETTING
Form	Name	frmODBC
	Caption	"Chapter 9.3. example"
TextBox	Name	txtAmount
CommandButton	Name	cmdQuit
	Cancel	True
	Caption	"&Quit"
CommandButton	Name	cmdTransfer
	Caption	"Transfer"
ComboBox	Name	cmbAccounts
	Index	0
ComboBox	Name	cmbAccounts
	Index	1
Label	Name	lblTrans
	Index	2
	Caption	"Amount to Transfer:"
Label	Name	lblTrans
	Index	1
	Caption	"Transfer To:"
Label	Name	lblTrans
	Index	0
	Caption	"Transfer From:"

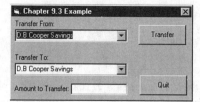

Figure 9.4. Transfer Bank
Funds form.

3. Add the following code to the form's **Load** event procedure and the
Centerform procedure. After centering the form, the **Load** procedure loads
the two list boxes on the form with all the accounts available. The list of
accounts is obtained from an SQL statement to the Accounts Recordset.
Looping through the Recordset puts the same accounts in each list box.

Add a bogus account ID, D.B. Cooper Savings, to test the behavior of the
application when an error condition occurs and the transaction must be
rolled back:

```
Private Sub Form_Load()
Dim wrkBank As Workspace, dbfBank As Database
    Dim recBankRecords As Recordset
    Dim lvarTemp As Variant

    'This example is for syntax only; in order to run it, you'll
    'need to create a Bank Accounts DSN with two tables, as
    'outlined in How-To 9.3

GoTo temp
    Set wrkBank = DBEngine.Workspaces(0)
    Set dbfBank = wrkBank.OpenDatabase("", 0, 0, "ODBC;DSN=Bank Accounts")

    'Get the account names
    Set recBankRecords = dbfBank.OpenRecordset("SELECT " & _
        "AccountID from Accounts")
    If recBankRecords.RecordCount <> 0 Then
        'Populate the list boxes
        recBankRecords.MoveFirst
        Do While Not recBankRecords.EOF
            cmbAccounts(0).AddItem recBankRecords("AccountID")
            cmbAccounts(1).AddItem recBankRecords("AccountID")
            recBankRecords.MoveNext
        Loop
    End If

temp:
    'And now let's add one bogus account that doesn't exist, so that
    'we can test the transaction should it fail to find an account
    cmbAccounts(0).AddItem "D.B Cooper Savings"
    cmbAccounts(1).AddItem "D.B Cooper Savings"
```

continued on next page

continued from previous page

```
'Set the combo lists to the first item
cmbAccounts(0).ListIndex = 0
cmbAccounts(1).ListIndex = 0
End Sub
```

4. Add the following code to the `cmdTransfer_Click` event. This procedure first checks to make sure that a selection has been made in each of the list boxes on the form, that the selected accounts are not the same account, and that a positive amount has been entered in the txtAmount text box. When these conditions are satisfied, the `Transfer` subprocedure is called, using the two account IDs and the transfer amount as arguments:

```
Private Sub cmdTransfer_Click()
If cmbAccounts(0).Text = "" Or cmbAccounts(1).Text = "" Then
        MsgBox "You must select both From and To accounts."
    ElseIf cmbAccounts(0).Text = cmbAccounts(1).Text Then
        MsgBox "Please select two different accounts."
    ElseIf Val(txtAmount.Text) <= 0 Then
        MsgBox "You must specify a positive amount."
    Else
        'Transfer funds. Note that leaving txtAmount as a
        'string eliminates need to reconvert to text in
        'Transfer procedure.
        Transfer cmbAccounts(0).Text, cmbAccounts(0).Text, txtAmount.Text
    End If
End Sub
```

5. Add the following code for the `Transfer` subprocedure to the code section of the form. This is the procedure that actually attempts to transfer the money. First, activate the Visual Basic error handler, telling it to jump to the `TransferFailed` section of code at the bottom of the procedure. Then mark the beginning of the transaction on the `Workspace` object `wrkBank`. Then, create a temporary pass-through query by using the `CreateQueryDef` method on an empty string. (Using an empty string with `CreateQueryDef` and then setting the `Connect` property of the `QueryDef` to an ODBC connect string sets the query up as a pass-through query.) Then execute the three operations that must be performed: subtracting money from one account, adding it to another, and creating a log entry for the transaction.

If everything goes well, the `wrkBank.CommitTrans` statement actually commits all the parts of the transaction to the database. If any error occurred, however, the procedure jumps to the `TransferFailed` error handler, where the transaction is rolled back. In that case, the subprocedure is exited, and the user is returned to the form as though nothing ever happened—and it didn't!

```
Private Sub Transfer(xferFrom As String, xferTo As String, _
    xferAmt As String)
    Dim wrkBank As Workspace, dbfBank As Database
```

```
    Dim qdfBankQuery As QueryDef

    Set wrkBank = DBEngine.Workspaces(0)
    Set dbfBank = wrkBank.Databases(0)

    On Error GoTo TransferFailed
    'Here's the start of the transaction - the BeginTrans command.
    wrkBank.BeginTrans

    'Create temporary pass-through query.
    Set qdfBankQuery = dbfBank.CreateQueryDef("")

    'Perform our transfer transaction; the advantage of wrapping
    'several actions, each dependent upon the previous action's success,
    'is that if any one fails, we can roll back the entire series of
    'changes.
    With qdfBankQuery
        .Connect = "ODBC;DSN=Bank Accounts"
        'Add the transaction into the LogBook table
        .SQL = "INSERT INTO LogBook (Type,Source,Destination,Amount)" & _
            VALUES ('Transfer', xferFrom, xferTo, xferAmount)"
        .Execute
        'Add the amount to the destination balance
        .SQL = "UPDATE Accounts SET Balance = Balance + " & xferAmt & _
            " WHERE AccountID = " & xferTo
        .Execute
        'Subtract the amount from the source balance
        .SQL = "UPDATE Accounts SET Balance = Balance - " & xferAmt & _
            " WHERE AccountID = " & xferFrom
        .Execute
    End With

    'Until this point, none of the actions we've taken above have been
    'committed to the database.  With the CommitTrans method, we will now
    'commit all of the above to the database
    wrkBank.CommitTrans
Exit Sub

TransferFailed:
    MsgBox "Error condition. Transaction rolled back.", vbExclamation
    'If we have a failure at any point, we roll back the transaction
    wrkBank.Rollback
    Exit Sub
End Sub
```

6. Create the Accounts and LogBook tables as detailed in Table 9.4. Enter a few account records in Accounts for use with this How-To. (*Don't* enter a record for D.B. Cooper Savings—that is our test of a failed transaction.) There is no need to enter any records in the LogBook table.

Sample text files, Accounts.txt and LogBook.txt, are included with the sample CD-ROM.

7. Set the start-up form to frmODBC. You can also set an application description, but that is not required for the operation of the application.

How It Works

Using transactions with ODBC databases in Visual Basic is no different than using any other database with Visual Basic, including the native Access `.MDB` files and the supported ISAM databases—as long as the database itself supports transactions. Therein lies one of the true benefits of using ODBC with the Visual Basic data access object: After you have connected to the data source, the Visual Basic programming constructs are used in exactly the same way, regardless of which database is being used and where it is located. Transactions are a Core Level conformance function of ODBC, so all drivers should support them if the underlying database supports transactions. Transactions are always handled by the ODBC driver, not the Driver Manager.

The `BeginTrans`, `CommitTrans`, and `Rollback` methods are methods of both the `Database` and `Workspace` objects in Visual Basic, which gives you a certain amount of control over the scope of the transaction. In Visual Basic, you can have multiple `Database` objects connected to a `Workspace` object while having multiple `Workspace` objects active at one time. (Most applications use only one `Database` object and one `Workspace` object at a time, but Visual Basic does not place this limitation on the application.)

Comments

One limitation that Visual Basic places on transactions in ODBC databases is that you can't use nested transactions. One hopes that this limitation will be removed in future products, because ODBC itself places no limitation of this kind on its data sources. Let us examine the transaction-related features of DAO objects in more detail to better understand the use and limitations of transaction processing.

Transactions **Property**

Not all databases support transactions, but it doesn't hurt to include `BeginTrans`, `CommitTrans`, and `Rollback`. If the database doesn't support transactions, Visual Basic simply ignores these statements so that they have no effect. The `Transactions` property is read only and returns either a `True` or `False` Boolean value. The syntax is simply this:

```
object.Transactions
```

The `Transactions` property applies to `Database`, `Dynaset`, `Recordset`, `Snapshot`, and `Table` objects, defining the scope of the transaction. The `Snapshot` object can only return a `False` value, because you can't make changes to a `Snapshot` object anyway. The `Transactions` property always returns `True` for objects based on a Microsoft Jet database engine object, because you can always use transactions with these objects.

The IsolateODBCTrans Property

You can have multiple isolated transactions involving the same ODBC data source if the underlying database supports this feature. To set up this situation, set the IsolateODBCTrans property of the Workspace object. The IsolateODBCTrans property has the syntax

object.IsolateODBCTrans [= *value*]

in which *object* is a Workspace object and *value* is a Boolean True or False.

Each Workspace can have its own ODBC connection to a database, but this slows system performance. Because transaction isolation isn't normally required, ODBC connections from multiple Workspace objects opened by the same user are shared by default. Some ODBC servers, such as Microsoft SQL Server, don't allow simultaneous transactions on a single connection. If you need to have more than one transaction at a time pending against SQL Server, set the IsolateODBCTrans property to True on each Workspace as soon as you open it so that a separate ODBC connection for each Workspace is established.

To implement this feature in the program in this How-To, add one line of code to the Transfer subprocedure, as shown here:

```
Set wrkBank = DBEngine.Workspaces(0)
Set wrkBank = BankWS.Databases(0)

'Start transaction
wrkBank.IsolateODBCTrans = True      '<<= Add this line
wrkBank.BeginTrans
```

The property can be read as well to determine whether the particular Workspace object supports transaction isolation, returning True or False.

You can find out to what degree the ODBC driver supports transaction isolation with the ODBC API function SQLGetInfo, using the SQL_DEFAULT_TXN_ISOLATION and SQL_DEFAULT_TXN_ISOLATION options. Table 9.6 lists the available values for these items. How-To 6.6 describes a program that allows you to examine the settings for these and many other values.

Table 9.6. Levels of transaction isolation for ODBC databases.

ISOLATION LEVEL	DESCRIPTION
SQL_TXN_READ_UNCOMMITTED	Dirty reads, nonrepeatable reads, and phantoms are possible.
SQL_TXN_READ_COMMITTED	Dirty reads are not possible. Nonrepeatable reads and phantoms are possible.
SQL_TXN_REPEATABLE_READ	Dirty reads and nonrepeatable reads are not possible. Phantoms are possible.
SQL_TXN_SERIALIZABLE	Transactions are serializable. Dirty reads, nonrepeatable reads, and phantoms are not possible.
SQL_TXN_VERSIONING	Transactions are serializable, but a higher level of concurrency is possible.

9.4 How do I...
Debug the ODBC interface of my Visual Basic application?

Problem

My application utilizes ODBC to connect to different databases by using both Visual Basic methods and direct calls to the ODBC API. But something isn't working; I don't get any Visual Basic or ODBC error messages, and I don't always get the right results. How can I figure out what ODBC is doing?

Technique

You can use the ODBC trace file log to record all calls made through the ODBC API, including some of the information about arguments to those functions. In this How-To, a number of ODBC calls are made directly through the API and by using regular Visual Basic data access methods. By turning tracing on before making the calls, you can examine exactly how the selected database is being accessed for data.

Steps

Load and run the DEBUG.VBP Visual Basic project file. The window loads, as shown in Figure 9.5. Select an ODBC data source to use for tracing. If any trace information appears in the ODBC Trace File Contents text box, click the Clear Trace File command button to clear the file. Then click the Open Database command button. After a brief delay, depending on the size of the database file, a list of field data appears in the list box, and the contents list of the trace file is updated. Examine the trace log for the calls made using the Visual Basic OpenDatabase method; note that the number of calls logged depends on the number of records in the database. Then click the Get Functions command button to load the Driver Functions Available list box. Again, updated trace file contents are shown in the Contents text box. You can click the Run All ODBC command button to run both sets of functions at once. During all operations, the status box at the bottom of the form keeps you updated to what is happening, including the use of a gauge control when data is being added to the list boxes. Figure 9.6 shows the results after all trace file data have been gathered.

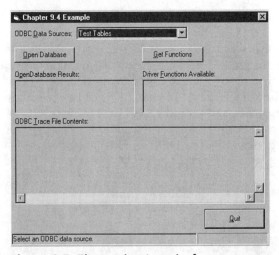

Figure 9.5. The project's main form on startup.

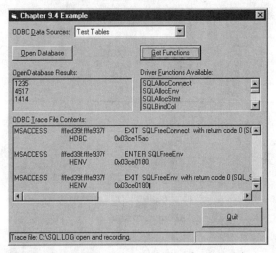

Figure 9.6. The project's main form with
retrieved trace data.

1. Create a new project called DEBUG.VBP. Add the form ODBCErrors.FRM
(see How-To 9.6.) and the code module ODBC API `Declarations.BAS`
(see How-To 9.1.) using Visual Basic's Project | Add File menu command.
The code module contains all the declarations needed for the ODBC API
functions and the constants used in many of the functions.

2. Name the project's default form `frmODBC` and save the file as
DEBUG.FRM. Add the controls as shown in Figure 9.5, setting the
properties as shown in Table 9.7. Make sure that the `lblStatus` label
control and the `gauStatus` control are contained within the `Picture1`
picture box control. The easiest way to do this is to put the control on
the form, then choose Edit | Cut from the Visual Basic menu. Select the
picture box control, and select the Edit | Paste menu item.

Table 9.7. Objects and properties for DEBUG.FRM.

OBJECT	PROPERTY	SETTING
Form	Name	frmODBC
	Caption	"Chapter 9.4. example"
CommandButton	Name	cmdRunODBC
	Cancel	True
	Caption	"&Get Functions"
CommandButton	Name	cmdRunODBC
	Caption	"&Open Database"
CommandButton	Name	cmdQuit
	Caption	"&Quit"
	Default	True
TextBox	Name	txtTraceFile
	BackColor	&H00C0C0C0& (light gray)
	MultiLine	True
	Locked	True
	ScrollBars	3 - Both
ListBox	Name	lstFunctions
	BackColor	&H00C0C0C0& (light gray)
ListBox	Name	lstOpenDatabase
	BackColor	&H00C0C0C0& (light gray)
ProgressBar	Name	pbrStatus
Label	Name	lblStatus
	BackColor	&H00C0C0C0& (light gray)
ComboBox	Name	lstODBCdbs
	Style	2 - Dropdown List
Label	Name	lblDebug
	Index	3
	Caption	"ODBC &Trace File Contents:"
Label	Name	lblDebug
	Index	2
	Caption	"Driver &Functions Available:"

OBJECT	PROPERTY	SETTING
Label	Name	lblDebug
	Index	1
	Caption	"O&penDatabase Results:"
Label	Name	lblDebug
	Index	0
	Caption	"ODBC &Data Sources:"

3. Add the following code to the declarations section of the form. To avoid naming problems, the **Option Explicit** syntax tells Visual Basic to make sure that you declare all variables and objects before using them.

```
Option Explicit

'TraceFile holds the name of the trace file
Dim TraceFile As String
```

4. Add the following code to the **Load** event procedure of the form. After centering the form, environment and connection handles are allocated. Then the installed ODBC data sources are loaded to the **lstODBCdbs** list box. The call to **GetTraceFileName** retrieves the current trace filename from the ODBC API, if one exists. Then any current contents of that trace file are loaded into the **txtTraceFile** text box.

```
Private Sub Form_Load()
    Dim intResult As Integer

    'Allocate the ODBC environment handle
    If ODBCAllocateEnv(glng_hEnv) = SQL_SUCCESS Then
        'Establish an ODBC hDbc handle
        intResult = SQLAllocConnect(glng_hEnv, glng_hDbc)
        If intResult <> SQL_SUCCESS Then
            intResult = frmODBCErrors.ODBCError("Dbc", glng_hEnv, _
                glng_hDbc, 0, intResult, _
                "Error allocating connection handle.")
        End
        End If

        'Load the current list of data sources to list box
        GetODBCdbs
        GetTraceFileName
        LoadTraceFile
        lblStatus = "Select an ODBC data source."
        frmODBC.Show
    Else
        End
    End If
End Sub
```

5. Add the following code to the **GetODBCdbs** subprocedure. This code, called by the **Form_Load** procedure, loads the **lstODBCdbs** list box (actually a combo box masquerading as a list box) with the name of available ODBC data sources. The list of data sources is retrieved through the **ODBCDSNList** function in ODBC API **Declarations.BAS**, using the **SQLDrivers** API function.

```
Private Sub GetODBCdbs()
Dim lvarTemp As Variant, I As Integer

    lvarTemp = ODBCDSNList(glng_hEnv, False)
    If IsArray(lvarTemp) Then
        For I = LBound(lvarTemp) To UBound(lvarTemp)
            lstODBCdbs.AddItem lvarTemp(I)
        Next
    End If

    lstODBCdbs.ListIndex = 0
End Sub
```

6. Add the following code for the **GetTraceFileName** subprocedure. This procedure makes a single call to the ODBC API to retrieve the current name of the trace file, if any. If the call is successful, the existence of a name is verified. If the length of the name string is 0, the file is arbitrarily named \SQL.LOG in the root directory of the application's drive. Finally, a call is made to **SQLSetConnectOption** to turn on tracing. Tracing must be turned off when the form is unloaded so the trace file doesn't continue to grow while running other applications that use ODBC.

```
Function GetTraceFileName()
'Get the name of the trace file ODBC is using
    Dim intResult As Integer
    Dim strFile As String * 128

    GetTraceFileName = True

    lblStatus = "Getting trace file name."
    DoEvents

    'Need strFile to be specified as ByVal because it is listed
    'in the Declare statement as Any
    intResult = SQLGetConnectOption(glng_hDbc, SQL_OPT_TRACEFILE, _
        ByVal strFile)
    If intResult <> SQL_SUCCESS Then
        intResult = frmODBCErrors.ODBCError("Dbc", glng_hEnv, _
            glng_hDbc, 0, intResult, "Error getting trace file name")
        lblStatus = "Error getting trace file from ODBC system."
        GetTraceFileName = False
        Exit Function
    Else
        mstrTraceFile = Left(strFile, InStr(1, strFile, Chr(0)) - 1)
        If Len(mstrTraceFile) = 0 Then
            mstrTraceFile = "C:\SQL.LOG"
```

```
                    intResult = SQLSetConnectOption(glng_hDbc, _
                        SQL_OPT_TRACEFILE, mstrTraceFile)
                    If intResult <> SQL_SUCCESS Then
                        intResult = frmODBCErrors.ODBCError("Dbc", glng_hEnv, _
                            glng_hDbc, 0, intResult, _
                            "Error getting trace file name")
                        GetTraceFileName = False
                        Exit Function
                    End If
                End If

                'Turn tracing on
                lblStatus = "Turning tracing on."
                intResult = SQLSetConnectOption(glng_hDbc, SQL_OPT_TRACE, _
                    SQL_OPT_TRACE_ON)
                If intResult <> SQL_SUCCESS Then
                    intResult = frmODBCErrors.ODBCError("Dbc", glng_hEnv, _
                        glng_hDbc, 0, intResult, "Error setting trace on.")
                    lblStatus = "Error setting trace on."
                    GetTraceFileName = False
                    Exit Function
                End If

                If Left(mstrTraceFile, 1) = "\" Then mstrTraceFile = _
                    "C:" & mstrTraceFile

                lblStatus = "Trace file: " & mstrTraceFile & _
                    " open and recording."
            End If
    End Function
```

7. Add this code to the `LoadTraceFile` subprocedure. This procedure actually loads a fresh copy of the ODBC trace file into the `txtTraceFile` text box. This procedure is run when the form is first loaded and any time you click one of the `cmdRunODBC` command buttons. The procedure first makes sure a trace filename is available and, if the file already exists, checks to make sure that the file isn't too big. (A Visual Basic text box has a limited amount of space, about 64K.) If the file is too big, it is opened with Visual Basic's `Open` command, and only the last `maxRead` characters from the file are read. Otherwise, the whole file is loaded into the text box.

```
Sub LoadTraceFile()
'Load contents of trace file into text box
    Dim intResult As Integer
    Dim intFHandle As Integer
    Dim intMaxChars As Integer
    Dim lngFileSize As Long
    Dim strFileText As String

    'Read in 30K characters at a time
    intMaxChars = 30 * 1024

    If Len(mstrTraceFile) Then
        If GetTraceFileName() Then
```

continued on next page

continued from previous page

```
            If Len(Dir(mstrTraceFile)) Then
                lngFileSize = FileLen(mstrTraceFile)
                intFHandle = FreeFile
                Open mstrTraceFile For Input As #intFHandle

                If lngFileSize > intMaxChars Then
                    If MsgBox("Trace file is too big. Load only most " & _
                        "recent entries?", vbYesNo, _
                        "Trace File Size Problem") = vbYes Then
                        'Position at last intMaxChars characters
                        Seek #intFHandle, lngFileSize - intMaxChars
                        strFileText = Trim(Input(intMaxChars,#intFHandle))
                        'Exclude any partial leading line
                        strFileText = Right(strFileText, _
                            Len(strFileText) - InStr(strFileText, _
                            Chr(13)) - 1)
                        txtTraceFile.Text = ""
                        txtTraceFile.Text = strFileText
                    End If
                Else
                    txtTraceFile.Text = ""
                    txtTraceFile.Text = Input(lngFileSize, #intFHandle)
                End If

                Close intFHandle
            Else
                txtTraceFile.Text = ""
            End If

            'Position the text box at the end of the entries
            txtTraceFile.SelStart = Len(txtTraceFile.Text)
        End If
    End If
End Sub
```

8. Add the following code to the **Click** event procedure of the **cmdRunODBC** command button. Separating the **DoOpenDatabase** and **DoGetFunctions** procedures into two buttons allows you to examine the contents of the trace file for each procedure individually or all together. The trace file can get very large fast, depending on the number of ODBC function calls.

```
Private Sub cmdRunODBC_Click(Index As Integer)
'Run a bunch of ODBC commands to put trace information
    'in the log file

    'Make sure that a data source is selected in the combo box
    If Len(lstODBCdbs.Text) Then
        If Index = 0 Then
            DoOpenDatabase
        Else
            DoGetFunctions
        End If
        LoadTraceFile
    Else
        MsgBox "Please select a data source first."
```

```
        End If
End Sub
```

9. Add the following code to the **DoOpenDatabase** subprocedure. This procedure makes no direct calls to the ODBC API. It opens an ODBC data source and reads in the contents of one field to the list box **lstOpenDatabase**. By entering an empty string for the database name in the **OpenDatabase** method, and including an ODBC connect string in the fourth argument, Visual Basic uses ODBC to open a file and read in the records.

The procedure, as shown in the following code, is set up to read in the contents of a field **Contact** from a database. Change the field name as indicated to try this procedure on one of your data sources. Make sure that there are a fair number of records in the data source (a minimum of about 200 works well) so that you get a good picture of the ODBC calls being made and the way ODBC breaks the result sets down into manageable pieces.

```
Sub DoOpenDatabase()
    Dim dbfTemp As Database, recTemp As Recordset
    Dim I As Integer

    'Start with calls to OpenDatabase
    lblStatus = "Opening database file."
    lstOpenDatabase.Clear
    DoEvents

    On Error GoTo OpenDBError
        Set dbfTemp = OpenDatabase("", False, False, "ODBC;DSN=" _
            & lstODBCdbs.Text)
        'Run an SQL statement - use InputBox to enter SQL statement.
        Set recTemp = dbfTemp.OpenRecordset( _
            InputBox("Enter an SQL statement here.", _
            "Open Database - Test SQL Query"), dbOpenDynaset, _
            dbExecDirect)
    On Error GoTo 0

    If recTemp.RecordCount <> 0 Then
        lblStatus = "Getting the record count for gauge."
        recTemp.MoveLast: recTemp.MoveFirst
        Do Until recTemp.EOF
            pbrStatus.Value = recTemp.PercentPosition
            If Trim(recTemp.Fields(1)) <> "" Then
                lstOpenDatabase.AddItem recTemp.Fields(1)
            End If
            recTemp.MoveNext
            DoEvents
        Loop
    End If

    lblStatus = "OpenDatabase completed."
    pbrStatus.Value = 0
```

continued on next page

continued from previous page

```
Exit Sub

OpenDBError:
    Select Case Err.Number
        Case 3423 'Using Access as ODBC database
            MsgBox "You cannot connect directly to an Access database" & _
                " with the VB data access objects.", vbCritical, _
                "ODBC Error"
        Case 3059 'User cancelled ODBC dialog
        Case 3078 'The DSN can't be opened
            MsgBox "The ODBC data source name isn't connected to a " & _
                "file properly.  Use the ODBC Administrator to fix " & _
                "the problem.", vbCritical, "ODBC Error"
        Case Else
            MsgBox Err.Description, vbExclamation
    End Select
End Sub
```

10. Add the following code to the **DoGetFunctions** subprocedure. Though the **DoOpenDatabase** procedure made no direct calls to the ODBC API, this procedure only makes ODBC calls to connect with a database. The procedure first makes a connection to the data source shown in the **lstODBCdbs** list box, then it makes a call to **SQLGetFunctions** to retrieve the list of functions the ODBC driver supports. This list of functions is put into the **lstFunctions** list box. Note the use of the **ODBCFuncs** array, initialized in the ODBC API **Declarations.BAS** file, to determine the name of each function that is supported.

```
Sub DoGetFunctions()
Dim DataSource As String
    Dim UserID As String
    Dim Password As String
    Dim intResult As Integer
    Dim ErrResult As Integer
    ReDim FuncList(100) As Integer
    Dim I As Integer

    DataSource = lstODBCdbs.List(lstODBCdbs.ListIndex)

    lblStatus = "Making connection and getting list of functions."
    lstFunctions.Clear
    DoEvents

    intResult = ODBCConnectDS(glng_hEnv, glng_hDbc, glng_hStmt, _
        DataSource, UserID, Password)
    If intResult <> SQL_SUCCESS Then
        Screen.MousePointer = vbDefault
        Exit Sub
    End If

    'Now get the list of functions
    intResult = SQLGetFunctions(glng_hDbc, SQL_API_ALL_FUNCTIONS, _
        FuncList(0))
    If intResult <> SQL_SUCCESS Then
```

```
        ErrResult = frmODBCErrors.ODBCError("Dbc", glng_hEnv, glng_hDbc, _
            0, intResult, "Error getting list of ODBC functions")
        Screen.MousePointer = vbDefault
        Exit Sub
    End If

    'Start by clearing the list box
    lstFunctions.Clear

    'Populate the list box with the function names
    For I = 0 To 99
        pbrStatus.Value = I + 1
        If FuncList(I) <> 0 Then
            lstFunctions.AddItem ODBCFuncs(0, I)
            DoEvents
        End If
    Next

    'Close connection (doesn't free glng_hDbc)
    intResult = SQLDisconnect(glng_hDbc)

    lblStatus = "Finished getting function list."
    pbrStatus.Value = 0
End Sub
```

11. Add the following code to the **cmdQuit_Click** event procedure and the **Unload** event procedure. Clicking the Quit command button ends the program. Unloading the form from memory turns tracing off with a call to **SQLSetConnectOption** and releases the ODBC handles that were allocated.

```
Private Sub cmdQuit_Click()
    End
End Sub

Private Sub Form_Unload(Cancel As Integer)
    Dim intResult As Integer

    'Turn tracing off
    intResult = SQLSetConnectOption(glng_hDbc, SQL_OPT_TRACE, _
        SQL_OPT_TRACE_OFF)
    intResult = ODBCDisconnectDS(glng_hEnv, glng_hDbc, glng_hStmt)
    intResult = ODBCFreeEnv(glng_hEnv)
End Sub
```

How It Works

Table 9.8 shows the results of one session using the Get Functions command button designed in this How-To for a Paradox ODBC data source. Each line consists of the ODBC function name followed by the argument name and its value in the call for each of the function's arguments. For the ODBC handles, the value is arbitrarily assigned by the ODBC system, much like the way Windows assigns window handles.

Table 9.8. Sample contents of the ODBC trace file log.

TRACE	FILE	CONTENTS
ODBCDebug	fffed39f:fffe937f	ENTER SQLAllocConnect
	HENV	0x03ce0180
	HDBC *	0x0062c950
ODBCDebug	fffed39f:fffe937f	EXIT SQLAllocConnect with return
		code 0 (SQL_SUCCESS)
	HENV	0x03ce0180
	HDBC *	0x0062c950 (0x03ce15ac)
ODBCDebug	fffed39f:fffe937f	ENTER SQLSetConnectOption
	HDBC	0x03ce15ac
	UWORD	103
	UDWORD	20
ODBCDebug	fffed39f:fffe937f	EXIT SQLSetConnectOption with return
		code 0 (SQL_SUCCESS)
	HDBC	0x03ce15ac
	UWORD	103
	UDWORD	20
ODBCDebug	fffed39f:fffe937f	ENTER SQLDriverConnectW
	HDBC	0x03ce15ac
	HWND	0x00000b74
	WCHAR *	0x03de0600 [-3] ""
	SWORD	-3
	WCHAR *	0x03ce1678
	SWORD	510
	SWORD *	0x0062c9a6
	UWORD	1 <SQL_DRIVER_COMPLETE>
ODBCDebug	fffed39f:fffe937f	EXIT SQLDriverConnectW with return
		code 1 (SQL_SUCCESS_WITH_INFO)
	HDBC	0x03ce15ac
	HWND	0x00000b74
	WCHAR *	0x03de0600 [-3] ""
	SWORD	-3
	WCHAR *	0x03ce1678 [320] "DSN=Test
		Tables;DefaultDir=C:\;
		DriverId=538;FIL=Paradox
		3.X;MaxBufferSize=512;
		PageTimeout=600;"

TRACE	FILE	CONTENTS
	SWORD	510
	SWORD *	0x0062c9a6 (320)
	UWORD	1 <SQL_DRIVER_COMPLETE>
ODBCDebug	fffed39f:fffe937f	ENTER SQLGetInfo
	HDBC	0x03ce15ac
	UWORD	9 <SQL_ODBC_API_CONFORMANCE>
	PTR	51542
	SWORD	2
	SWORD *	0x0062c94e
ODBCDebug	fffed39f:fffe937f	ENTER SQLGetInfoW
	HDBC	0x03ce15ac
	UWORD	9 <SQL_ODBC_API_CONFORMANCE>
	PTR	51542
	SWORD	2
	SWORD *	0x0062c94e
ODBCDebug	fffed39f:fffe937f	EXIT SQLGetInfoW with return code 0
		(SQL_SUCCESS)
	HDBC	0x03ce15ac
	UWORD	9 <SQL_ODBC_API_CONFORMANCE>
	PTR	51542
	SWORD	2
	SWORD *	0x0062c94e (2)
ODBCDebug	fffed39f:fffe937f	EXIT SQLGetInfo with return code 0
		(SQL_SUCCESS)
	HDBC	0x03ce15ac
	UWORD	9 <SQL_ODBC_API_CONFORMANCE>
	PTR	51542
	SWORD	2
	SWORD *	0x0062c94e (2)
ODBCDebug	fffed39f:fffe937f	ENTER SQLGetInfo
	HDBC	0x03ce15ac
	UWORD	6 <SQL_DRIVER_NAME>
	PTR	0x0062c8ec
	SWORD	100
	SWORD *	0x0062c956
ODBCDebug	fffed39f:fffe937f	ENTER SQLGetInfoW
	HDBC	0x03ce15ac

continued on next page

continued from previous page

TRACE	FILE	CONTENTS
	UWORD	6 <SQL_DRIVER_NAME>
	PTR	0x03ce1678
	SWORD	200
	SWORD *	0x0062c956
ODBCDebug	fffed39f:fffe937f	EXIT SQLGetInfoW with return code 0
		(SQL_SUCCESS)
	HDBC	0x03ce15ac
	UWORD	6 <SQL_DRIVER_NAME>
	PTR	0x03ce1678 [24]
		"ODBCJT32.DLL"
	SWORD	200
	SWORD *	0x0062c956 (24)
ODBCDebug	fffed39f:fffe937f	EXIT SQLGetInfo with return code 0
		(SQL_SUCCESS)
	HDBC	0x03ce15ac
	UWORD	6 <SQL_DRIVER_NAME>
	PTR	0x0062c8ec [12]
		"ODBCJT32.DLL"
	SWORD	100
	SWORD *	0x0062c956 (12)
ODBCDebug	fffed39f:fffe937f	ENTER SQLGetInfo
	HDBC	0x03ce15ac
	UWORD	17 <SQL_DBMS_NAME>
	PTR	0x0062c8ec
	SWORD	100
	SWORD *	0x0062c956
ODBCDebug	fffed39f:fffe937f	ENTER SQLGetInfoW
	HDBC	0x03ce15ac
	UWORD	17 <SQL_DBMS_NAME>
	PTR	0x03ce1678
	SWORD	200
	SWORD *	0x0062c956
ODBCDebug	fffed39f:fffe937f	EXIT SQLGetInfoW with return code 0
		(SQL_SUCCESS)
	HDBC	0x03ce15ac
	UWORD	17 <SQL_DBMS_NAME>
	PTR	0x03ce1678 [14] "PARADOX"

TRACE	FILE	CONTENTS
	SWORD	200
	SWORD *	0x0062c956 (14)
ODBCDebug	fffed39f:fffe937f	EXIT SQLGetInfo with return code 0
		(SQL_SUCCESS)
	HDBC	0x03ce15ac
	UWORD	17 <SQL_DBMS_NAME>
	PTR	0x0062c8ec [7] "PARADOX"
	SWORD	100
	SWORD *	0x0062c956 (7)
ODBCDebug	fffed39f:fffe937f	ENTER SQLDisconnect
	HDBC	0x03ce15ac
ODBCDebug	fffed39f:fffe937f	EXIT SQLDisconnect with return code
		0 (SQL_SUCCESS)
	HDBC	0x03ce15ac
ODBCDebug	fffed39f:fffe937f	ENTER SQLFreeConnect
	HDBC	0x03ce15ac
ODBCDebug	fffed39f:fffe937f	EXIT SQLFreeConnect with return code
		0 (SQL_SUCCESS)
	HDBC	0x03ce15ac

Run the program in this How-To, and compare the results using the Visual Basic **OpenDatabase** method and the results of making direct calls to the ODBC API. The method doesn't matter: Visual Basic makes the direct calls to ODBC for you, or you can make the specific calls using the ODBC API.

You can use the contents of the trace file to make sure that the proper calls are made to ODBC and that the function's arguments are what you think they should be.

You can substitute your own code in the **DoGetFunctions** and **DoOpenDatabase** subprocedures to check the calls being made to the ODBC system.

COMPLEXITY
ADVANCED

9.5 How do I...
Navigate ODBC SQL cursors?

Problem

I want to optimize ODBC for the fastest performance I can for my application, and I want to control what type of cursor ODBC employs for my result sets, but

I'm not sure which one to use. How do I determine which one to use and how to use it?

Technique

A cursor is a structure allocated by ODBC to keep track of where you are in a result set. This is the simplistic explanation. What a cursor actually does, however, is determine the behavior of your result set, including where the result set data is kept, how it is managed, and how it is retrieved.

When choosing a cursor, you must consider two major areas. The first is your *cursor library*. ODBC has the capability of employing various types of cursors, which determines how much functionality and performance is available to your application for cursors. The most commonly used is the *ODBC cursor*, included with ODBC. Although not the greatest of performers, it ensures consistency in behavior across multiple databases and is usually the choice for most programmers. But, it is limiting for some databases, which can employ features that may not be directly supported by the "vanilla" support of the ODBC cursor library. Also, in the case of client-server databases in which the database is located on another computer, ODBC needs to bring all the needed data across before it can establish a cursor. This can be time consuming and hard on the client workstation. In the case of many client-server databases, such as SQL Server or Oracle, the server supports another option, *server-side cursors* or *server cursors*. The server manages the temporary data and sends only the data needed for the client's requirements to the client workstation, potentially increasing performance. This option can increase network traffic, however, and the temporary result set must be built on the server, increasing the server's load. In some instances, it can even stop a server database that cannot allocate the needed space for the temporary result set.

If you're not sure which to use, don't worry. For the most part, the ODBC driver for that database can determine which would be most appropriate and provide the support automatically by using the default cursor setting in ODBC.

The second major area of concern is the *cursor type*. The cursor type determines the behavior of the cursor and the resources reserved to ensure that behavior, explained later. The types of cursors commonly in use follow:

✔ *Dynamic keyset*—A dynamic keyset is the most flexible, and the most resource-hungry, of the cursors. The word *dynamic* means that the underlying resultset's membership is changeable; if User B adds a record to a table that User A has a dynamic keyset resultset on, that record appears in User A's resultset. The word *keyset* refers to the set of key values used to identify specific rows in a cursor. Keysets are stored on the server in a server-side keyset cursor and on the workstation on client-side keyset cursors. The benefit to this is simple: fewer data are transferred, because only the key fields are needed to identify a record in the resultset by the cursor, and there is the flexibility of backward and forward scrolling, because the cursor can fetch a specific record by referring to its key fields.

Also, because it can refer to specific records uniquely, the resultset can be *editable*. Think of this as a DAO dynaset-type recordset.

✔ *Keyset*—A keyset is the most commonly used of the cursors. Because it isn't dynamic, its membership is said to be fixed, or *static*. It is capable of scrolling backward and forward, however, just as a dynamic keyset cursor, and is also editable. Think of this as a hybrid DAO snapshot/dynaset-type recordset.

✔ *Static*—A more limited cursor, a static cursor's membership is fixed, like a keyset, but cannot be edited. Think of this as a DAO snapshot-type recordset.

✔ *Forward-only*—The least capable, and usually fastest, cursor available, this cursor's membership is not only static, it can only scroll in one direction—forward. After you read a record and move to the next one, the previous record is no longer accessible. This is VERY useful when reading lookup tables or populating combo or list boxes from a database table or query, but is limited for just about anything else.

In terms of resource, a forward-only cursor requires much less than a dynamic keyset cursor, because the ODBC driver need only fetch one record at a time and not keep track of bookmarks, resultset location, or much else. In terms of flexibility, the dynamic keyset cursor is far more flexible than the forward-only cursor, because not only can you achieve random access in the resultset, you can edit it and view others' edits as well.

Note the defaults for various types of database objects in Visual Basic. If you don't specify a cursor or recordset type in DAO, you usually get a keyset cursor (or dynaset, in DAO terminology). If you don't specify a cursor in ODBCDirect, however, you get a forward-only cursor. Remember to specify a cursor or recordset type, even if you plan on using the default—it makes it easier to debug and maintain later.

This How-To allows you to experiment with the various capabilities and behaviors of cursor with a simple form. Review the instructions below, and pay particular attention to the `cmdOpen_Click` event; this has the good stuff in it.

Steps

Open and run the Cursors.VBP Visual Basic project. After the Cursors form displays, as in Figure 9.7, select a cursor library and cursor type, then click the Open Recordset button. The ODBC Data Sources dialog box will appear, prompting you for a data source and any needed information. Select a data source. After you make a selection, an input box will appear, asking for a SQL query statement to run. Enter a SQL query and click the OK button. The form will then attempt to run the SQL query against the data source specified and populate the `FlexGrid` with data, similar to what's shown in Figure 9.8.

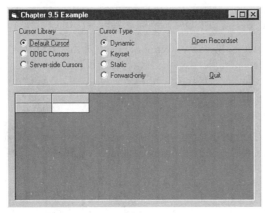

Figure 9.7. Chapter 9.5 example, showing the Cursors form.

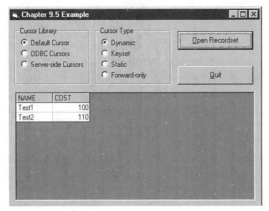

Figure 9.8. Chapter 9.5 example, showing the Cursors form with data.

1. Create a new project, Cursors.VBP.

2. Name the project's default form **frmCursors** and save the file as Cursors.FRM. Add the controls shown in Figure 9.7, setting the properties as shown in Table 9.9.

Table 9.9. Objects and properties for Cursors.FRM.

OBJECT	PROPERTY	SETTING
Form	Name	frmCursors
Frame	Name	fraLibrary
	Caption	"Cursor Library"

OBJECT	PROPERTY	SETTING
OptionButton	Name	optCursorLibrary
	Index	0
	Caption	"Default Cursor"
OptionButton	Name	optCursorLibrary
	Index	1
	Caption	"ODBC Cursor"
OptionButton	Name	optCursorLibrary
	Index	2
	Caption	"Server-side Cursor"
Frame	Name	fraCursorType
	Caption	"Cursor Type"
OptionButton	Name	optCursorType
	Index	0
	Caption	"Dynamic Keyset"
OptionButton	Name	optCursorType
	Index	1
	Caption	"Keyset"
OptionButton	Name	optCursorType
	Index	2
	Caption	"Static"
OptionButton	Name	optCursorType
	Index	3
	Caption	"Forward-only"
CommandButton	Name	cmdSave
	Caption	"&Open Recordset"
CommandButton	Name	cmdQuit
	Caption	"&Quit"
	Cancel	True
MSFlexGrid	Name	grdData

3. Add the following code to the declarations section of **frmCursors**. Note the use of the **ODBCDirect Connection** object; we want to use ODBC for our modus operandi but employ the DAO objects for flexibility.

```
Option Explicit
Private conTemp As Connection, recTemp As Recordset
```

4. Add the following code to the **Load** event of **frmCursors**. The use of **dbUseODBC** ensures that any object we open under the **DBEngine** will use ODBCDirect.

```
'Use ODBCDirect, rather than Jet, for creating our workspaces & databases.
    'See How-To 7.7 for more information on ODBCDirect.
    DBEngine.DefaultType = dbUseODBC
```

5. Add the following code to the **Click** event of **cmdOpen**. This event first determines the cursor library based on the **optCursorLibrary** selection, then creates a connection to a data source specified by the user. After a **Connection** object is created, it then creates a **Recordset** object, based on SQL entered by the user. The type of recordset constructed is based on the cursor type chosen by **optCursorType** selection, and then opened and loaded into the grid. Note the strange **If** statement preceding the **MoveFirst** command. Because a forward-only type cursor can't move backward, it doesn't "know" which record is first. Using the **MoveFirst**, **MoveLast**, or **MovePrevious** commands on a forward-only resultset will cause a trappable error in Visual Basic.

```
Private Sub cmdOpen_Click()
    Dim strSQL As String, lngCursorType As Long, varTemp As Variant
    Dim I As Integer, J As Integer

    On Error Resume Next
        recTemp.Close: conTemp.Close
    On Error GoTo 0

    'Choose the connection's cursor library; this must be done before
    'opening the connection.
    On Error GoTo ErrHandler
        'This, by the way, is a neat trick you can use to check out a
        'group of option buttons with a simple Select Case statement.
        Select Case True
            Case optLibrary(0)
                Workspaces(0).DefaultCursorDriver = dbUseDefaultCursor
            Case optLibrary(1)
                Workspaces(0).DefaultCursorDriver = dbUseODBCCursor
            Case optLibrary(2)
                Workspaces(0).DefaultCursorDriver = dbUseServerCursor
        End Select

    'Get the user to provide the data source with the
    'dbDriverPrompt option.
    Set conTemp = Workspaces(0).OpenConnection("", dbDriverPrompt, _
        False, "ODBC;")

    Select Case True
        Case optCursorType(0)
            'Opens a dynamic-type Recordset object (dynamic cursor).
            lngCursorType = dbOpenDynamic
        Case optCursorType(1)
            'Opens a dynaset-type Recordset object (keyset cursor).
            lngCursorType = dbOpenDynaset
```

```
        Case optCursorType(2)
            'Opens a snapshot-type Recordset object (static cursor).
            lngCursorType = dbOpenSnapshot
        Case optCursorType(3)
            'Opens a forward-only-type Recordset object (no cursor).
            lngCursorType = dbOpenForwardOnly
End Select

strSQL = InputBox("Please enter the SQL query you want to run.", _
    "SQL Query")
If Len(strSQL) Then
    Set recTemp = conTemp.OpenRecordset(strSQL, lngCursorType)
End If

'Load the data into the grid
Screen.MousePointer = vbHourglass
DoEvents
With grdData
    .FixedRows = 1: .FixedCols = 0
    .Rows = 1: .Cols = 0
End With

If recTemp.RecordCount <> 0 Then
    'Retrieve the field names for the column headers
    For Each varTemp In recTemp.Fields
        With grdData
            .Cols = .Cols + 1
            .Row = 0: .Col = .Cols - 1
            .Text = varTemp.Name
        End With
    Next

    'Retrieve the data
    'Note that on a cursorless resultset, only MoveNext is valid.
    'This is the equivalent of the SQL_FETCH_NEXT option for the
    'SQLFetch and SQLExtendedFetch commands, the only option
    'supported on an ODBC cursorless resultset.  That's why
    'we check the cursor type here.
    If lngCursorType <> dbOpenForwardOnly Then recTemp.MoveFirst
    Do Until recTemp.EOF
        J = J + 1
        For I = 0 To grdData.Cols - 1
            varTemp = varTemp & _
                IIf(IsNull(recTemp.Fields(I)), "", _
                    recTemp.Fields(I)) & vbTab
        Next
        If Right(varTemp, 1) = vbTab Then varTemp = _
            Left(varTemp, Len(varTemp) - 1) & vbCr
        recTemp.MoveNext
    Loop
    'We didn't use the RecordCount property because,
    'on certain types of cursors, we will
    'always get back a -1; not useful in this situation.
    With grdData
        .Rows = J + 1
        .Row = 1: .Col = 0
```

continued on next page

continued from previous page

```
                    .RowSel = .Rows - 1: .ColSel = .Cols - 1
                    .Clip = varTemp
                    .Row = 1: .Col = 0
                End With
            End If
            Screen.MousePointer = vbDefault
        On Error GoTo 0
    Exit Sub

    ErrHandler:
        Screen.MousePointer = vbDefault
        MsgBox Err.Description, vbExclamation
    End Sub
```

6. Add the following code to the `Click` event of `cmdQuit`:

```
Private Sub cmdQuit_Click()
    End
End Sub
```

How It Works

The Open Database button, where most of the action takes place, first uses the selected option button in the `optLibrary` control array to determine which cursor library should be used, then executes an `OpenConnection` method to allow the user to choose an ODBC data source.

After the data source is opened in a `Connection` object, the cursor type is chosen based on the selected option button in the `optCursorType` control array, and the user is presented with an input box asking for a SQL statement to be executed. If one is provided, an `OpenRecordset` method is run against our newly created Connection object to create an `ODBCDirect Recordset` object, using our selected cursor type. Then, the grid control is prepared with information from the `Recordset` object's `Fields` collection, and the data is loaded into the grid. At this point, one thing to note is the behavior of the `RecordCount` property. The `RecordCount` property has three "settings," so to speak:

✔ `-1`—For a Recordset to get a count of records, it has to know two things: the first record and the last record. Some cursor types won't supply this—forward-only recordsets, for example, don't "know" where the last record is; they only "know" that they have at least one record, and possibly more. So `-1` is used to inform that at least one record is present, but the total is unknown.

✔ `0`—No records. This is as straightforward as it gets.

✔ `<any positive number>`—The total number of records in the `Recordset` object.

Comments

The use of ODBCDirect allows a demonstration of ODBC cursor handling without having to perform a single ODBC API call. The `Connection` object determines the cursor library, and each `Recordset` object determines its own cursor. This allows for a single connection to manage multiple resultsets, each with a different cursor type, without any problem.

It can be difficult determining which cursor library or type to use. The best advice is to try several on a case-by-case basis until you get a "feel" for how a cursor should perform in certain situations. The cursor performance will vary by type and library, and by database and data amount as well, so feel free to experiment until you find the right combination to give you the performance and flexibility you need for each situation.

COMPLEXITY
ADVANCED

9.6 How do I...
Handle ODBC errors?

Problem

I have been incorporating ODBC into my application, but ODBC just doesn't give me enough information about error conditions. When a function fails, it returns only a -1 or -2. How can I figure out what is wrong?

Technique

Although the ODBC error handling system is fairly complex, it is effective at delivering as much detail about an error condition as is usually needed to identify the source of the error. An error can come from the ODBC Driver Manager, the database driver, or various components in the ODBC connection. A single error event can have several messages coming from different parts of the entire system.

This is the reason `ODBCError` uses the `TreeView` control to display the entire error message hierarchy. The `TreeView` control has, for the purposes of ODBC errors, essentially unlimited capacity to hold information about an error condition, displaying the pieces in an easy to understand outline format.

The main job of the `ODBCError` function presented in this How-To is to loop through repeated calls to `SQLError` until all error messages have been received by the application, while preserving result codes so the application can respond to specific error events.

Steps

Open and run the ErrHandler.VBP Visual Basic project. Click each of the three error command buttons (Driver Connect, Allocate hDbc, and Get Functions, as shown in Figure 9.9) to see how the ODBC system responds to errors and what kind of information is available to help you respond to those errors. If an error occurs, as in Figure 9.10, all the information supplied by the driver will display.

1. Create a new project ErrHandler.VBP. Add the code module ODBC API **Declarations.BAS** (see How-To 9.1), using Visual Basic's Project | Add File menu command. The code module contains all the declarations needed for the ODBC API functions and the constants used in many of the functions, including the error functions in this How-To.

2. Name the project's default form **frmODBC** and save the file as ERRHAND.FRM. Add the controls shown in Figure 9.9, setting the properties as shown in Table 9.10.

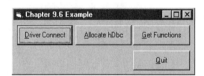

Figure 9.9. The project's main form.

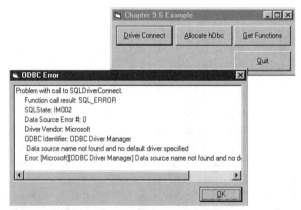

Figure 9.10. The project's ODBC Error form, showing ODBC error information.

Table 9.10. Objects and properties for ERRHAND.FRM.

OBJECT	PROPERTY	SETTING
Form	Name	frmODBC
	Caption	"Chapter 9.6. example"
CommandButton	Name	cmdQuit
	Caption	"&Quit"
CommandButton	Name	cmdAllochDbc
	Caption	"&Allocate hDbc"
CommandButton	Name	cmdGetFunctions
	Caption	"&Get Functions"
CommandButton	Name	cmdDriverConnect
	Caption	"&Driver Connect"

3. Add the following code to the declarations section of the form. The **Option Explicit** syntax tells Visual Basic to make sure that you declare all variables and objects before using them in order to avoid naming problems.

```
Option Explicit
```

4. Include the following code in the **Load** event procedure of the form. This procedure centers the form, then calls **ODBCAllocateEnv** to obtain a valid environmental handle for use with the direct calls to ODBC API functions. This procedure also makes a call to **SQLAllocConnect** for database handles. These valid handles won't always be used to generate ODBC errors, but they are available when needed.

```
Private Sub Form_Load()
    Dim intResult As Integer

    If ODBCAllocateEnv(glng_hEnv) = SQL_SUCCESS Then
        intResult = SQLAllocConnect(glng_hEnv, glng_hDbc)
        If intResult <> SQL_SUCCESS Then
            intResult = frmODBCErrors.ODBCError("Dbc", glng_hEnv, _
            glng_hDbc, 0, intResult, _
            "Error allocating connection handle.")
        End
    End If

    frmODBC.Show
    Else
        End
    End If
End Sub
```

5. Add this code to the `Click` event of the `cmdDriverConnect` command
button. This is the first of the procedures that will be called later with a
deliberate error meant to trigger one or more ODBC errors. The error here
is that the ODBC `SQLDriverConnect` function requires either a complete
connect string or be allowed to prompt the user with its own dialog boxes
for any missing information. In this case, we are passing an empty connect
string while not allowing ODBC to prompt for information by using the
`SQL_DRIVER_NOPROMPT` in the last argument. ODBC will respond with an
error to which we can respond.

```
Private Sub cmdDriverConnect_Click()
Dim intResult As Integer
    Dim connStrIn As String
    Dim connStrOut As String * SQL_MAX_OPTION_STRING_LENGTH
    Dim strOutCount As Integer

    connStrIn = ""

    intResult = SQLDriverConnect(glng_hDbc, Me.hWnd, connStrIn, _
        Len(connStrIn), connStrOut, Len(connStrOut), strOutCount, _
        SQL_DRIVER_NOPROMPT)

    If intResult <> SQL_SUCCESS Then
        intResult = frmODBCErrors.ODBCError("Dbc", glng_hEnv, _
            glng_hDbc, 0, intResult, _
            "Problem with call to SQLDriverConnect.")
        Exit Sub
    End If

    'Free the connection, but not the handle
    intResult = SQLDisconnect(glng_hDbc)
    If intResult <> SQL_SUCCESS Then
        intResult = frmODBCErrors.ODBCError("Dbc", glng_hEnv, _
            glng_hDbc, 0, intResult, _
            "Problem with call to SQLDriverConnect.")
    End If
End Sub
```

6. Add this code to the `Click` event procedure of the `cmdAllochDbc`
command button. This function makes a call to the ODBC function
`SQLAllocConnect` with a null environment handle. This function, which
allocates memory and a handle for a database connection, requires that a
valid environment handle be passed to it so an ODBC error will be
generated.

```
Private Sub cmdAllochDbc_Click()
Dim intResult As Integer

    'Problem: glng_hEnv is passed as a null handle
    intResult = SQLAllocConnect(0, glng_hDbc)
    If intResult <> SQL_SUCCESS Then
        intResult = frmODBCErrors.ODBCError("Dbc", 0, glng_hDbc, _
            0, intResult, "Error allocating connection handle.")
```

```
        frmODBC.Show
        Exit Sub
    End If
End Sub
```

7. Add this code to the cmdGetFunctions_Click event procedure. This third function generates an ODBC error by using an invalid value for the function you want to use in our application, and you are checking whether the driver supports the function. ODBC can't associate the value with any function, so it generates an error.

```
Private Sub cmdGetFunctions_Click()
    Dim intResult As Integer, FuncList(100) As Integer

    'Problem: second argument requests information about a
    'particular function or all functions. The number must
    'be positive.
    intResult = SQLGetFunctions(glng_hDbc, -5, FuncList(0))
    If intResult <> SQL_SUCCESS Then
        intResult = frmODBCErrors.ODBCError("Dbc", glng_hEnv, glng_hDbc, _
            0, intResult, "Error getting list of ODBC functions")
        Screen.MousePointer = vbDefault
        Exit Sub
    End If
End Sub
```

8. Finally, add the following code to the cmdQuit command button's Click event procedure and to the form's Unload event procedure. The Quit command button simply ends the application and the Unload procedure cleans up and releases memory that was allocated in the Load event for connection with ODBC.

```
Private Sub cmdQuit_Click()
    End
End Sub

Private Sub Form_Unload(Cancel As Integer)
    Dim intResult As Integer

    intResult = ODBCDisconnectDS(glng_hEnv, glng_hDbc, glng_hStmt)
    intResult = ODBCFreeEnv(glng_hEnv)
End Sub
```

9. Make sure that the TreeView control is available to this project. Select Project | Components from the Visual Basic menu, and check the Microsoft Windows Common Controls 5.0 component.

10. Add a new form to the Visual Basic project by selecting the Insert Form menu item. Add the controls as shown in Figure 9.10 and set the properties shown in Table 9.11. You can use this form as a general error and display form for any Visual Basic application using the ODBC API directly.

Table 9.11. Objects and properties for ODBCErrors.FRM.

OBJECT	PROPERTY	SETTING
Form	Name	frmODBCErrors
	Caption	"ODBC Error"
	MaxButton	False
CommandButton	Name	cmdQuit
	Caption	"&OK"
	Default	True
TreeView	Name	outErrors
	Style	0 - tvwTextOnly

11. Add this code to the declarations section of the form. Include the comment because this form uses the Visual Basic Outline control to display its results. The `Option Explicit` syntax tells Visual Basic to make sure that you declare all variables and objects before using them in order to avoid naming problems.

```
Option Explicit
```

12. Add the following function to `frmODBCErrors`. The function, `Public`, is called by other routines to display this form.

This ODBC error handler function takes six arguments, as listed in Table 9.12. The call to the `SQLError` function can return information about any of the ODBC handles: environment, connection, or statement. If all three are valid handles, then SQLError uses the statement handle. If that is not valid, it uses the connection handle, otherwise it uses the environment handle. You must include this argument so the correct error information is retrieved. It is quite easy to know which version to use: The first argument of all ODBC functions is the handle of the relevant type. So, for example, when you make the following function call, specify `Env` because the relevant handle is for the environment:

```
intResult = ODBCAllocateEnv(glng_hEnv)
```

Likewise, you would use `Dbc` for the next statement because the first argument is the database connection handle:

```
intResult = SQLDriverConnect(glng_hDbc, Me.hWnd, connStrIn, _
    Len(connStrIn), connStrOut, Len(connStrOut), strOutCount, _
    SQL_DRIVER_NOPROMPT)
```

Table 9.12. Function arguments for ODBCError.

ARGUMENT	DESCRIPTION
strErrType	The handle affected by the error: Env, Dbc, or Stmt
lng_hEnv	The affected ODBC environment handle
lng_hDbc	The affected ODBC connection handle
lng_hStmt	The affected ODBC statement handle
intFuncResult	The return value from the ODBC function that caused the error
strCallingMsg	A custom message that can help to identify the error

The ODBCError function first assigns the intFuncResult code to the return value for the function, so the value remains available to the calling function. Next, it loads the frmODBCErrors form and places the application's custom error message in the first slot on the outline. Next, it converts the calling function's return value into a string representing one of the ODBC function return values, such as SQL_ERROR and SQL_SUCCESS, using a Select Case structure, allowing a more meaningful string to be included on the errors form, adding it to the next location on the outline.

Then the ODBCError function calls SQLError for ODBC's version of events, using a Select Case structure to determine which arguments to use for SQLError. Of the three handles, a null (0) is used as the argument to the right of the relevant handle argument. The Select Case structure is enclosed in a Do...Until loop because ODBC can return multiple errors, and any level of the ODBC hierarchy can generate its own error messages. As long as there are more error messages to return, SQLError does not return SQL_SUCCESS, so the loop tests for that value.

And finally, the function loops through the TreeView to make sure that all levels are visible and displays the form.

```
Public Function ODBCError(strErrType As String, lng_hEnv As Long, _
    lng_hDbc As Long, lng_hStmt As Long, intFuncResult As Integer, _
    strCallingMsg As String) As Integer

    Dim strSQLState As String * 16, strErrMsg As String * 511
    Dim strTemp As String
    Dim lngDSError As Long
    Dim intErrMsgLen As Integer, intResult As Integer, intTemp As Integer
    Dim I As Integer

    ODBCError = intFuncResult
    strSQLState = Space$(16): strErrMsg = _
        Space$(SQL_MAX_MESSAGE_LENGTH - 1)

    outErrors.Nodes.Clear
    outErrors.Nodes.Add , , "CallingMsg", strCallingMsg

    Select Case intFuncResult
```

continued on next page

continued from previous page

```
        Case SQL_ERROR
            strTemp = "SQL_ERROR"
        Case SQL_INVALID_HANDLE
            strTemp = "SQL_INVALID_HANDLE"
        Case SQL_NO_DATA_FOUND
            strTemp = "SQL_NO_DATA_FOUND"
        Case SQL_SUCCESS
            strTemp = "SQL_SUCCESS"
        Case SQL_SUCCESS_WITH_INFO
            strTemp = "SQL_SUCCESS_WITH_INFO"
        Case Else
            strTemp = "Unidentified error code"
    End Select

    outErrors.Nodes.Add "CallingMsg", tvwChild, "FuncResult", _
        "Function call result: " & strTemp

    Do
        Select Case strErrType
            Case "Env"
                intResult = SQLError(lng_hEnv, SQL_NULL_HDBC, _
                    SQL_NULL_HSTMT, strSQLState, _
                    lngDSError, strErrMsg, Len(strErrMsg), intErrMsgLen)
            Case "Dbc"
                intResult = SQLError(lng_hEnv, lng_hDbc, _
                    SQL_NULL_HSTMT, strSQLState, _
                    lngDSError, strErrMsg, Len(strErrMsg), intErrMsgLen)
            Case "Stmt"
                intResult = SQLError(lng_hEnv, lng_hDbc, _
                    lng_hStmt, strSQLState, _
                    lngDSError, strErrMsg, Len(strErrMsg), intErrMsgLen)
        End Select

        If intErrMsgLen > 0 Then
            With outErrors.Nodes
                .Add "FuncResult", tvwChild, "SQLState" & CStr(I), _
                    "SQLState: " & strSQLState
                .Add "FuncResult", tvwChild, "DSNError-" & CStr(I), _
                    "Data Source Error #: " & CStr(lngDSError)
                .Add "FuncResult", tvwChild, "ErrLine1-" & CStr(I), _
                    ParseError(strErrMsg, 1)
                .Add "FuncResult", tvwChild, "ErrLine2-" & CStr(I), _
                    ParseError(strErrMsg, 2)
                .Add "FuncResult", tvwChild, "ErrLine3-" & CStr(I), _
                    ParseError(strErrMsg, 3)
                .Add "FuncResult", tvwChild, "ErrLine4-" & CStr(I), _
                    ParseError(strErrMsg, 4)
            End With
        End If
        I = I + 1
    Loop Until intResult <> SQL_SUCCESS

    outErrors.Nodes("FuncResult").Expanded = True
    outErrors.Nodes("CallingMsg").Expanded = True
    Me.Show vbModal
End Function
```

13. Add the following code to `frmODBCErrors`. The string that is returned from SQLError is of the following general form:

`[identifier][identifier]...supplied text message`

The brackets are actually included in the error message, and the ellipsis indicates that there may be additional bracketed identifiers, depending on the source of the message.

The `ParseError` function breaks out the parts of the message, so `ODBCError` can place each portion on a separate line in the `TreeView` control on `frmODBCErrors`. It allows up to four identifiers as needed, although two is the norm and only rarely are there more than three. Each successive call to `ParseError` with an increasing `Place` argument returns another piece of the error string.

```
Private Function ParseError(ByVal strMessage As String, _
    intPlace As Integer)

    Dim strText As String
    Dim intLPos As Integer, intRPos As Integer
    Dim intCurrentPos As Integer, I As Integer

    Static Brackets(1 To 4, 1 To 2) As Integer
    Static blnMsgType As Boolean

    strMessage = Trim$(strMessage)

    If strMessage <> "" Then
        intCurrentPos = 1
        If intPlace = 1 Then
            For I = 1 To 3
                Brackets(I, 1) = InStr(intCurrentPos, strMessage, "[")
                Brackets(I, 2) = InStr(intCurrentPos, strMessage, "]")
                intCurrentPos = Brackets(I, 2) + 1
            Next
            blnMsgType = (Brackets(3, 1) <> 0)
        End If

        If Brackets(intPlace, 1) > 0 Then
            intLPos = Brackets(intPlace, 1) + 1
            intRPos = Brackets(intPlace, 2) - 1
            strText = Mid(strMessage, intLPos, intRPos - intLPos + 1)
        Else
            strText = Right(strMessage, Len(strMessage) - _
                Brackets(intPlace - 1, 2))
        End If

        Select Case intPlace
            Case 1
                ParseError = "Driver Vendor: " & strText
            Case 2
                ParseError = "ODBC Identifier: " & strText
            Case 3
```

continued on next page

continued from previous page

```
                    ParseError = IIf(blnMsgType, "Data Source: ", "") & strText
                Case 4
                    ParseError = "Error: " & strText
                Case Else
                    ParseError = ""
            End Select
        End If
End Function
```

14. Set the startup form to `frmODBC`. You can also set an application description, but that is not required for the operation of the application.

How It Works

Error conditions are not always a "bad" thing in the ODBC API. ODBC uses errors to transmit information about calls to particular functions, and sometimes the return value simply means the function needs more information to perform. For example, the `SQLBrowseConnect` function is designed to take a starting connect string and return a request for more information. Until the connect string is complete so that a database connection can be made, the function returns `SQL_NEED_DATA`. When the function has everything it needs, possibly after five or more iterations, it returns `SQL_SUCCESS`. Other functions indicate success with information about the result by returning `SQL_SUCCESS_WITH_INFO`. That means a call to `SQLError` will yield more information.

All the valid ODBC function results are listed in Table 9.13. Their numeric values are defined in ODBC API `Declarations.BAS`.

Table 9.13. Valid ODBC function result codes.

RESULT CODE	DESCRIPTION
SQL_SUCCESS	Function completed successfully; no additional information is available.
SQL_SUCCESS_WITH_INFO	Function completed successfully, possibly with a nonfatal error. The application can call SQLError to retrieve additional information.
SQL_NO_DATA_FOUND	All rows from the result set have been fetched.
SQL_ERROR	Function failed. The application can call SQLError to retrieve error information.
SQL_INVALID_HANDLE	Function failed due to an invalid environment handle, connection handle, or statement handle. This indicates a programming error. No additional information is available from SQLError.
SQL_STILL_EXECUTING	A function that was started asynchronously is still executing.
SQL_NEED_DATA	While processing a statement, the driver determined that the application needs to send parameter data values.

Comments

One point mentioned in a previous How-To in this chapter is the need for meticulous "cleanliness" when it comes to allocating and deallocating ODBC resources. An ODBC error, although possibly fatal to your application, should give enough information for your program to handle it appropriately and deal with resource issues. ODBC errors supply a great deal of information about the current "state of affairs," and allow a well-written program to deal with them in a dignified manner. It is quite possible for an ODBC-based program to consider all ODBC errors nonfatal, handling them appropriately based on the error information provided and making intelligent decisions to recover the loss, one way or another.

CHAPTER 10
CRYSTAL REPORTS

10

REPORTS

How do I...

By including Crystal Reports with the Visual Basic programming system, Microsoft provided some very powerful tools for producing reports using data contained in a database. Using the tools that are supplied with Visual Basic, there are three ways to print a report:

✔ *Using the Crystal Reports Designer.* This program must be used to design all reports, and it can print them as well. This means you don't need to run a Visual Basic application to print reports on data maintained by your application. The program, however, can't be distributed to users of your application.

✔ *Using Crystal Reports OLE custom control (OCX).* This OCX is included in the package and can be dropped into a Visual Basic form to control report printing. The control gives your application access to most of the more useful features of the Crystal Reports program.

✔ *Using the Crystal Reports print engine directly.* This method entails direct calls to the Crystal Reports dynamic link library (DLL), and it is certainly the most complex way to print a report. But the DLL gives you access to a lot of information about a particular report that can also be set at runtime. You'll see exactly how to use the print engine and how to handle errors that arise.

All reports must be created using the report designer. Although certain report elements can be changed at runtime through the custom control or print engine, neither has the capability to create a report from scratch.

Most of your applications should use the custom control to print reports. It is easy to use. Properties can easily be set in a Visual Basic control, and any errors that arise are handled through the standard Visual Basic exception-error-handling system. Use the print engine when your application needs to have more detailed information about the report, needs finer control over print options, or demands a very slight increase in speed.

Crystal Reports Toolbar

For many tasks, the Crystal report design program gives you different ways to perform the same task. The program can't be used effectively with only the keyboard; some tasks can't be done at all on the keyboard. One alternative, however, is to use the buttons on the toolbar.

The Crystal Reports toolbar provides mouse-click access to most of the program's main functions. To see what a button does, hold the mouse cursor over the button and read the button's function in the status bar at the bottom of the screen.

Running and Configuring Crystal Reports Designer

The Crystal Reports Designer works as a separate process from Visual Basic and keeps the report definition in a report definition file with an .rpt file extension.

You should try to save your report definition files in your Visual Basic project directory to make project management and program distribution easier.

If you installed Visual Basic with the defaults, you'll find a Crystal Reports icon in the Microsoft Visual Basic 5.0 program group. You can also start Crystal Reports by selecting Add-Ins | Report Designer from the Visual Basic main menu.

All the How-To's in this chapter assume that your Crystal Reports Designer program is set up the way ours is. Select File | Options from the Crystal Reports main menu. On the Layout tab, check the Show Field Names option. On the New Report tab (see Figure 10.1), check the Use Report Gallery for new reports option. You can also enter a report directory as the default location for report definition files.

Sample Databases in the How-To's

The How-To's in this chapter use the Microsoft Access .MDB file BIBLIO.MDB that was shipped with Visual Basic. If you selected the default program locations when you installed Visual Basic, the Visual Basic files are located in the \Program Files\Visual Basic directory. If these files are not located in the default directories, you'll need to tell Crystal where to find them.

Table 10.1 lists the tables in the BIBLIO.MDB database. You might want to add one index (duplicates are OK) on the Au_ID field in the Title Author table to speed reporting. Use either Microsoft Access or the VisData sample application that is included with Visual Basic to add the index.

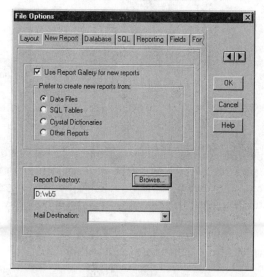

Figure 10.1. The Crystal Reports Designer File Options dialog box.

Table 10.1. Tables from BIBLIO.MDB.

TABLE NAME	DESCRIPTION
Authors	Book author names
Publishers	Names, phones, and other information about each publisher
Title Author	Records linking the Author and Titles tables
Titles	Books published by each company

You can find the next set of tables, shown in Table 10.2, in the file CRYSTAL.MDB, which is included on the CD-ROM. These files make up a basic order-entry system.

Table 10.2. Tables from CRYSTAL.MDB.

TABLE NAME	DESCRIPTION
Company	Company name and information
Header	Order invoice header
Detail	Order detail records

The last database is Mailing List, in the file MAIL.MDB. Create this new table using the fields shown in Table 10.3. It is easiest if you place the file in the same directory as the .RPT file that uses it.

Table 10.3. Mailing List table in MAIL.MDB.

FIELD NAME	DATA TYPE	SIZE
Contact	Text	30
Addr1	Text	40
City	Text	30
State	Text	20
Zip	Text	10
Week Day	Text	10

Enter some sample data in the Mailing List table. Table 10.4 lists a few sample lines of the table in MAIL.MDB on the disk enclosed with this book. Enter various Contact names and Week Days. Include a number of records from each City, State, and Zip. There are more than 600 records in MAIL.MDB on the disk.

Table 10.4. Sample data in Mailing List table in MAIL.MDB.

CONTACT	ADDR1	CITY	STATE	ZIP	WEEK DAY
Resident	4 Goodyear Street	Boulder	Colorado	80302-0302	Monday
Occupant	2291 Arapahoe	Irvine	California	92711-2002	Monday

CONTACT	ADDR1	CITY	STATE	ZIP	WEEK DAY
Resident	8 Hazelnut	Irvine	California	92711-3810	Monday
Occupant	2 Orion	Aliso Viejo	California	92656-4200	Sunday
Medical Practitioner	1 Jenner	Tacoma	Washington	98402-8402	Thursday
Medical Practitioner	Civic Center	Anaheim	California	92805-2805	Tuesday
Occupant	2 Park Plaza	Irvine	California	92714-2714	Thursday

10.1 Determine Which Records Will Be Printed

Using the Crystal Reports custom control, you can specify at runtime the records to be printed by sending a Crystal Reports formula to the print engine. In this How-To, you'll create a report using three tables linked together and a simple Visual Basic program to show how you can control the records printed at runtime.

10.2 Create Subtotals and Other Calculated Fields

Crystal Reports has a rich variety of built-in capabilities for creating very complex reports. This How-To describes how to create a bulk mail report based on an address file, sorting, grouping, and performing calculations needed for completion of a mailing's paperwork. You certainly can't get too much more complex than a system created over 200 years by the federal bureaucracy!

10.3 Control the Order in Which Records Will Be Printed

Although the Crystal Reports design program provides a very flexible report design and creation environment, you can change the record sort order from a Visual Basic application, giving you essentially unlimited flexibility to print different reports, as you'll see in this How-To. You'll also see how to change the group sort order, giving you another level of flexibility using database reports.

10.4 Print Labels Using Crystal Reports

Crystal Reports makes it easy to produce almost any type of label using a database. In this How-To, you'll create mailing labels complete with attractive graphics and a return address.

10.5 Create and Print Form Letters

By using formulas and the flexible formatting in Crystal Reports, you can use your data to produce form letters. But how do you print different page headers and footers? And how do you customize the text for each recipient in your mailing list? This How-To gives you all the information you need to use Crystal Reports for form letters.

10.6 Print Field Data Without Extra Spaces Between the Fields

Although not as complete a set of tools as Visual Basic, Crystal Reports does have a number of useful string manipulation and conversion functions and operators. In this How-To, you'll design a customer directory showing names, addresses, and the page number as a single formula field, giving the report a more natural and finished look.

10.7 Use the Crystal Reports Custom Control to Print Reports

Giving your application the capability to produce complex database reports is as simple as dropping the Crystal Reports custom control into a form in your application and setting a few properties. In this How-To, you'll create a handy utility to print any report by setting connection and destination options.

10.8 Prevent Blank Lines from Being Printed When a Field Contains No Data

Crystal Reports provides two options that conserve space when reports are printed: the Suppress Blank Lines property for report sections and Print on Multiple Lines property for text boxes. Both options are put to good use in this How-To, creating a report from frequently incomplete data.

10.9 Create Cross-Tab Reports

Using Crystal Reports to produce cross-tab reports is very easy when using the Cross-Tab layout window. In fact, the hardest part of creating the report is developing a clear picture of how to analyze the data, but Crystal Reports makes it easy to try different options until the report gives the information needed. This How-To demonstrates how to create a summary of customers by city and day of the week that they receive service.

10.10 Handle Errors Generated by Crystal DLL

One of the three ways of interacting with Crystal Reports through Visual Basic is through direct function calls to the print engine dynamic link library (DLL). The functions allow an application to get or set various pieces of information about Crystal Reports and a report file, and to invoke the printing of a report. But the errors generated by the print engine must be handled properly, and you'll see how in this How-To.

10.11 Control the Position of the Crystal Print Preview Window

Your application needs to set only a few properties of the Crystal Reports control to change the appearance of the Crystal Reports print preview window. In this How-To, you'll create a handy utility to print any report after customizing the appearance properties of the control.

10.12 Generate Reports Using User-Entered Variables

Many of the design elements of a Crystal report can be changed on-the-fly in a Visual Basic application. Although there aren't enough control properties to completely change an existing report or create a new report, there are enough changeable properties available that a Visual Basic application can create entirely different reports using the same data. This How-To creates a Crystal report that allows records to be printed in different orders while filtering the records and customizing the report heading and page numbering.

COMPLEXITY

BEGINNING

10.1 How do I...
Determine which records will be printed?

Problem

The recordset that I need to print changes every time a report is run. How can I let the application user specify at runtime which records to print?

Technique

Many of the parameters used to print a Crystal report through a Visual Basic application can be set using the Crystal Reports custom control. In this How-To, you'll create a simple report of authors and the computer books they've written. Because our BIBLIO.MDB file contains several of the authors' birth years, you can write a Visual Basic program that allows users to set a range of birth years to be printed, set a minimum or maximum birth year, or set no limits at all, printing all the authors.

Steps

Load and run the Visual Basic application Authors.vbp. The form shown in Figure 10.2 appears. Enter a starting or an ending year, or both, and click the Run Report button to print the report to a preview window. The Visual Basic 5 BIBLIO.MDB contains more than 16,000 authors, so this job might take a little while.

Start by creating a simple report that can be modified through Visual Basic during printing. Start the Crystal Reports program.

1. Click the New Report toolbar button or select File | New from the main menu. The New Report Gallery appears, as shown in Figure 10.3. Click the Standard option button.

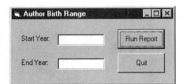

Figure 10.2. The Author
Birth Range selection form.

Figure 10.3. The New Report Gallery.

2. When the Create Report Expert dialog appears, click the Data File button, and use the common dialog to select the location of your Biblio.MDB file.

3. Click the Next button to proceed to tab 2: Links. Notice that Crystal has automatically created a set of table Smart Links based on fields with the same names in different tables (see Figure 10.4).

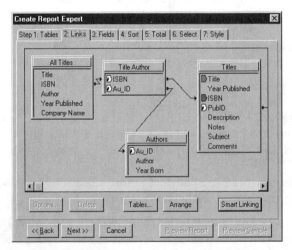

Figure 10.4. Automatic table links defined by
Crystal Reports.

4. Click the Next button to proceed to tab 3: Fields. Add the fields listed in Table 10.5 to your report by double-clicking on the field name or selecting the field name and clicking Add.

Table 10.5. Computer author report tables and fields.

TABLE	FIELD
Authors	Author
Authors	Year Born
Titles	Title
Titles	Year Published

5. On tab 4: Sort, add the `Authors.Author` field as a grouping field, and specify ascending order.

6. On tab 5: Total, remove `Authors.Year Born` and `Titles.Year Published` from the Total Fields box. Add the `Titles.Title` field and specify `count` as the function in the pull-down list, as shown in Figure 10.5. Remove the checkmark next to Add Grand Totals.

7. Ignore tab 6: Select, and proceed to tab 7: Style. Enter the text `A Time for Computer Authors` as the report title.

8. Click Preview Sample to view the results. Enter `First 500` for the number of records to view. Experiment with the Report Zoom button (three different-size squares), page navigation (upper-right), and scrollbars. *Hint:* Crystal's button hints float in the status bar on the *bottom right* of the screen.

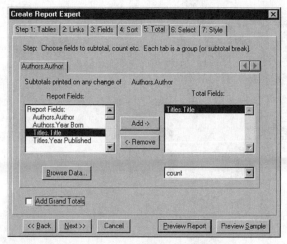

Figure 10.5. Author report total fields.

9. Click on the Design tab to return to design mode. Your report design should look as shown in Figure 10.6. Move the `Year Born` data field from the Details band to the Group #1 Header band. Delete the `Author` field from the Details band.

10. Modify the number formats for `Year Born` and `Year Published` by right-clicking each field and choosing Change Formats. The dialog box shown in Figure 10.7 appears. Uncheck the Thousands Separator box.

11. Save the report as Authors.rpt for use from the Author Birth Range form.

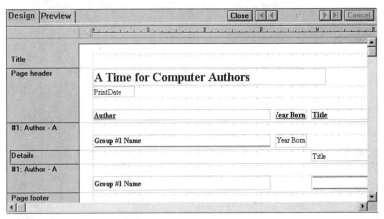

Figure 10.6. Author report design view.

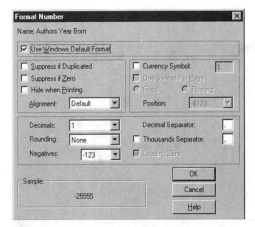

Figure 10.7. The Crystal Format Number dialog box.

12. Create a new Standard EXE Visual Basic project in your work area. Save the default form as Authors.frm and the project as Authors.vbp.

13. From the Project Components menu, select Crystal Reports Control and Microsoft Common Dialog Control 5.0, and click OK.

14. Place controls on the form as shown in Figure 10.2, setting the properties as shown in Table 10.6. Note that the common dialog and Crystal Reports controls are invisible at runtime, so place them anywhere that is convenient.

Table 10.6. Objects and properties for Authors.frm.

OBJECT	PROPERTY	SETTING
Form	Name	frmAuthors
	Caption	"Author Birth Range"
TextBox	Name	txtEnd
TextBox	Name	txtStart
CommandButton	Name	cmdQuit
	Caption	"Quit"
CommandButton	Name	cmdReport
	Caption	"Run Report"
CommonDialog	Name	cdOpenReport
CrystalReport	Name	crptAuthors
Label	Name	Label2
	Caption	"End Year:"
Label	Name	Label1
	Caption	"Start Year:"

15. Select the Crystal Reports control. Invoke the custom property pages for the control by clicking the Custom property in the property box and then the ellipsis button (…). The Property Pages dialog box shown in Figure 10.8 appears.

16. Be sure that the Crystal Reports Custom properties are set as shown in Table 10.7. The `ReportFileName` text box is left blank because that value will be set using the common dialog control.

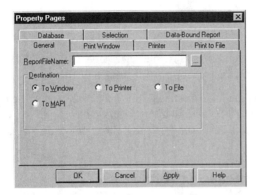

Figure 10.8. Crystal Reports control
property pages.

Table 10.7. Custom properties for the Crystal Reports control.

PROPERTY	SETTING
ReportFileName	" "
Destination	To Window

17. Add the following code to the form's **Load** event procedure. This code
simply moves the form to the lower-right portion of the screen, out of the
way of the report window when it appears.

```
Private Sub Form_Load()
    'Move the form to the lower-right of screen
    Me.Move Screen.Width - 1.1 * Me.Width, _
        Screen.Height - 1.25 * Me.Height
End Sub
```

18. Insert the following code in the **Click** event procedure of the **cmdReport**
command button. This code performs two main functions: validating the
data that has been entered in the two text boxes and setting the properties
of the Crystal Reports control.

Validation is performed for simple errors in the start and end years—
checking that the start year is before or equal to the end year and that the
years are in a reasonable range for computer book authors (being
conservative: 1850 to the present!).

```
Private Sub cmdReport_Click()
    Dim strSelectCritera As String
    Dim strDbName As String
    Static strSaveDir As String

    'Check for errors in the input year boxes
    If (Val(txtStart.Text) > Val(txtEnd.Text)) And Val(txtEnd.Text) Then
```

```
            MsgBox "Start year must be before End year."
            Exit Sub
        End If
        If Val(txtStart.Text) And Val(txtStart.Text) < 1850 And _
            Val(txtStart.Text) > Year(Now) Then
            MsgBox "Please enter a start year in the range 1850 to " & Year(Now)
            Exit Sub
        End If
        If Val(txtEnd.Text) And Val(txtEnd.Text) < 1850 And _
            Val(txtEnd.Text) > Year(Now) Then
            MsgBox "Please enter an ending year in the range 1850 to " & Year(Now)
            Exit Sub
        End If

        'Get the file to print using Common Dialog
        cdOpenReport.InitDir = strSaveDir
        cdOpenReport.ShowOpen

        'Let's be nice and "remember" the directory for the next use
        strSaveDir = cdOpenReport.filename

        If Len(cdOpenReport.filename) Then
            'Adding the data to the control
            crptAuthors.Destination = 0 'To Window
            crptAuthors.ReportFileName = cdOpenReport.filename
            If Len(txtStart.Text) And Len(txtEnd.Text) Then
                'Year range entered
                strSelectCritera = "{Authors.Year Born} in " & _
                    txtStart.Text & " to " & txtEnd.Text
            ElseIf Len(txtStart.Text) And Len(txtEnd.Text) = 0 Then
                'Only starting year selected
                strSelectCritera = "{Authors.Year Born} >= " & _
                    txtStart.Text
            ElseIf Len(txtStart.Text) = 0 And Len(txtEnd.Text) Then
                strSelectCritera = "{Authors.Year Born} <= " & _
                    txtEnd.Text
            Else
                'Both boxes are emtpy; don't limit range
                strSelectCritera = ""
            End If
            crptAuthors.SelectionFormula = strSelectCritera

            ' Get the Biblio.mdb database location
            strDbName = strBiblioDb()
            ' Assign the data file location for the report
            crptAuthors.DataFiles(0) = strDbName

            'Run the report
            crptAuthors.Action = 1
        Else
            'User pressed Cancel in Common Dialog
            MsgBox "No report file selected."
        End If
    End Sub
```

After activating a common dialog Open File window to get the name of the report to use (select AUTHORS.RPT), the program sets several properties of the Crystal Reports control: `Destination`, `ReportFileName`, and `SelectionFormula`. Remember that we set a few properties in the control as well. The program checks to see that a combination of start and end was selected (all records will print if nothing was entered) and creates the selection string used to set the `SelectionFormula` property. Finally, the report is printed by setting the Crystal Reports control's `Action` property to 1.

19. Add the following code to the `Click` event of the `cmdQuit` command button, to provide an exit point from the program:

```
Private Sub cmdQuit_Click()
    Unload Me
End Sub
```

How It Works

All the actions of the Crystal Reports control are controlled by setting its various properties. A number of properties can specify exactly how the report is printed, as listed in Table 10.17 at the end of this chapter. There are additional properties, but those listed in the table are the most useful in controlling the print behavior of the report.

Setting the `Action` property of the control to 1 causes the report to print. The Crystal Reports control uses this property as a pseudo-control method. It is very important to note that printing the report does not tie up the program at the point where the `Action` property is set to 1. In most cases, after the report writer has begun, the Visual Basic program continues executing, so you can't perform any actions that are dependent on the completion of the report. On the other hand, your program can continue executing and performing other tasks while the report prints.

Crystal Reports Formula Formats

For the control properties that require formulas, such as `SelectionFormula` and `GroupSelectionFormula`, the formulas specified must be in the Crystal Reports format, which is quite different from the format of a Visual Basic statement. The formula itself is used to set the property as a Visual Basic string, so any string literals needed in the formula must be enclosed in single quotation marks. In the case of the `Sub` procedure `cmdReport_Click` in this How-To, this formula is used when both a starting year and an ending year are specified:

```
"{Authors.Year Born} in " & txtStart.Text & " to " & txtEnd.Text
```

If the start year is 1940 and the end year is 1950, the actual formula sent to Crystal Reports is this:

```
"{Authors.Year Born} in 1940 to 1950"
```

The following example shows how a string in the Visual Basic variable `stateName` would be coded:

```
"{Market.State} = '" & stateName & "'"
```

Note the inclusion of the single quotation marks, because the string literal must be enclosed by single quotation marks. If `California` is the content of the `stateName` variable, Crystal Reports receives this statement as this:

```
"{Market.State} = 'California'"
```

It is very important to avoid extraneous spaces in the string sent to the report. If the preceding Visual Basic string were instead set to

```
"{Market.State} = ' " & stateName & " '"
```

the following formula would be sent to the report:

```
"{Market.State} = ' California '"
```

As a result, only records with a leading space before "California" would print in the report, because of the extra space at the beginning of the criteria string.

More information about Crystal Reports formula formats can be found in the documentation for Crystal Reports.

COMPLEXITY
ADVANCED

10.2 How do I...
Create subtotals and other calculated fields?

Problem

How do I make Crystal Reports calculate subtotals and make other calculations that I need? All my data is in an Access .MDB file, but several of the fields I need aren't data fields at all but are calculated from the fields in the file.

Technique

Crystal Reports supports a rich set of calculation tools and functions that allows you to make almost any type of calculation on database field data. It usually takes some work to get everything working properly, but when you are finished, you will have a powerful tool that can be used repeatedly.

In this How-To, you'll use those tools to create a bulk mail report, which can be used as the basis for completing the post office paperwork for bulk mailings. Getting the figures needed for the postage calculation involves sorting the zip codes, counting them in various groups, and checking to see which groups meet the minimum quantity requirements for the lowest postage rates.

Bulk Mailing Basics

This chapter won't be a primer on bulk mailing (the rules change constantly anyway), but here are a few basics so that the report created in this How-To will be clearer. The premise of the bulk mailing system is that if you are willing to do some of the work for the post office, you should get a break on postage. The breaks are attractive enough that a whole mailing industry has arisen around preparing mailings to qualify for those breaks.

This How-To uses a subset of all the different bulk mail categories. The categories you'll design into the report are five-digit presort, three-digit presort, state presort, and first class (the "catch-all" category). When you sort bulk mail, follow these steps:

1. Sort all the mailing pieces into groups that have 10 or more pieces going to the same first five digits of the zip code. Bundle those by the five-digit zip code, count them, and multiply the total by .191, the lowest postage cost of the categories used here. This gives you the total cost of that category of mail.

2. From the remaining pieces of mail (those that don't have at least 10 pieces per five-digit zip code), sort and extract the pieces that have at least 10 pieces going to the same first three digits of the zip code. Bundle those groups, multiply the postage by .191, and set them aside.

3. Again from the remaining pieces, select and sort all the pieces that have at least 10 pieces going to the same state. Bundle, calculate the postage using .238 per piece, and set the pieces aside.

4. Finally, gather all the remaining pieces and place first-class stamps on them. They can go with the mailing, but you aren't saving any money on them.

Before you start planning to pay your bills using bulk mail, you must have several hundred pieces mailed at the same time, and the same item must be mailed to every address. You can't even include a note in that letter, unless you include the same note to all the other people.

There is actually another category after the state level for multistate pieces, but each additional layer complicates things at an increasing rate. So to avoid having an entire book about a single Crystal report for bulk mailing, this How-To is limited to these categories.

Steps

The steps in this How-To show in detail how to create a bulk mail report that calculates postage and sorting order. On completion, the report, which will look as shown in Figure 10.9, will show two windows: one showing the report header and the other showing the report footer. To open and run a report in Crystal Reports, select File | Open from the Crystal main menu, and select the

BULKMAIL.RPT report. To print the report, click the Print button on the toolbar, or select File | Print from the main menu. To preview the report on-screen, click the Print Preview button on the toolbar, or select File | Print Preview from the Crystal Reports main menu. The general design details are shown in the various tables throughout this How-To. You'll go through the individual steps needed to create the bulk mail report. Figure 10.10 shows the main report elements in the Crystal Reports design window.

1. This How-To uses the MAIL.MDB database described in the introduction to this chapter. Start Crystal Reports, and start a new report by clicking the New Report toolbar button or selecting File | New from the main menu. Click on Standard when the Create New Report Gallery appears.

2. Click on Data File when the Create Report Expert screen appears. Use the dialog box to find the MAIL.MDB Access database file installed in the How-To.102 directory. Click Done to close the dialog box.

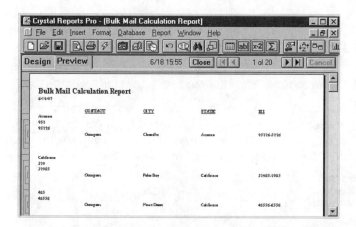

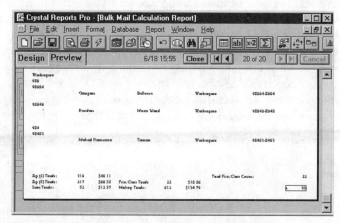

Figure 10.9. Print preview of bulk mail report.

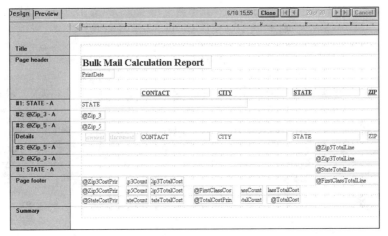

Figure 10.10. Crystal Reports design window for bulk mail report.

3. From the Fields tab, add the `Contact`, `City`, `State`, and `Zip` fields from the MailingList table.

4. On the Style tab, enter `Bulk Mail Calculation Report` as the title.

5. Insert a formula field by either clicking the Insert Formula toolbar button or selecting Insert Formula Field from the main menu. Name the formula `@Zip5Increment`. Be sure to leave off the @ when typing the name. Enter the following code in the Edit Formula window:

```
WhilePrintingRecords;
NumberVar Zip5Count;
Zip5Count := Zip5Count + 1;
```

The Edit Formula window should look like what's shown in Figure 10.11 when you have entered the `@Zip5Increment` formula text. Click the Check button to have Crystal Reports evaluate the formula and check for errors. Click Accept when you're finished. After the Edit Formula window closes, your cursor is dragging a dotted box around the design window. Move your cursor to the Page Footer section of the screen, and click your left mouse button. This click drops the new field onto the report page. Don't worry about the exact location because we will hide the field later.

6. In the same way, enter the `@TotalCountIncrement` formula:

```
WhilePrintingRecords;
NumberVar Zip5Count;
Zip5Count := Zip5Count + 1;
```

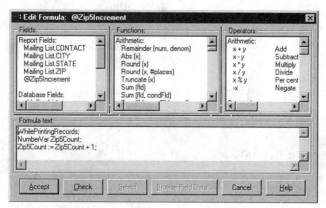

Figure 10.11. The `Zip5Increment` formula entry.

7. Format the newly added fields by right-clicking each one and choosing Change Format from the popup menu. Check the Hide when printing box. (Notice the other format choices available, and try to keep the formatting options in mind when you develop your reports.)

8. Shorten each of the fields and headers by approximately one-half inch, and move all the fields to the right side of the page. Click on the Contact header, and then Ctrl-click on the `Contact` field. Click over one of the black "ears" on the one Contact header, and shorten the field. You can also select multiple fields by choosing Edit | Select Fields from the main menu or by clicking the Select Fields toolbar button. After you make all the detail fields smaller, place them toward the right side of the detail line to leave room for section headers on the left side of the page.

9. Add a section to the report to group information by state. Select Insert | Group Section from the Crystal Reports main menu. From the first list box, select `Mailing List.STATE`. Note that the outermost group sections must be entered first, because subsequent sections will be inserted within the preceding innermost section. Make sure that the sorting field is set to ascending order, which is the default. Click OK to create the report section.

10. Insert the `STATE` field in the #1 State group by using Insert | Database Field from the main menu or the Insert Database Field toolbar button.

11. Insert the formula `@StatePrint`, which prints the total number of state addresses if they number at least 10. Place the field to the far right in the #1 State group footer band.

```
WhilePrintingRecords;
NumberVar StateCount;
NumberVar StateTotalCount;
```

continued on next page

continued from previous page

```
NumberVar StateCost;
NumberVar StateUnitCost;
NumberVar FirstClassCount;
NumberVar FirstClassCost;

if StateCount >= 10 then
    StateCost := StateCost + (StateCount * StateUnitCost)
else
    FirstClassCount := FirstClassCount + StateCount;

if StateCount >= 10 then
    StateTotalCount := StateTotalCount + StateCount;


if StateCount >= 10 then
    StateCount;
```

12. Insert @StateTotalLine, which prints a text prompt for the total number of state addresses. Place the field just to the left of the StatePrint formula field.

```
WhilePrintingRecords;
NumberVar StateCount;

if StateCount >= 10 then
    "Total Count for " + {Mailing List.STATE} + ": "
else
    " "
```

13. Insert the formula @StateReset, which resets the State count to 0. The field will be hidden, so place the field anywhere in the #1 State group header band, make it a small width, and hide it by changing its format. It is usually convenient to place hidden fields to the far right. This formula is placed in the header area to ensure that the StateCount variable is reset to 0 at the beginning of every state. The WhilePrintingRecords statement ensures that the Crystal Reports will calculate this formula during printing and not before reading records.

```
WhilePrintingRecords;
NumberVar StateCount;
StateCount := 0;
```

14. Format the @StateReset field to hide it while printing. Format the @StatePrint field to have zero decimal places. Check the Suppress if Zero box. The Format Number dialog box should look as shown in Figure 10.12.

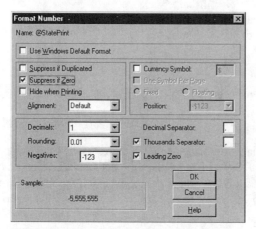

Figure 10.12. Formatting for zero decimal places.

15. Insert the formula field @Zip_3, which takes the first three digits of the zip code. For the moment, place the field on the report somewhere that is convenient. You'll move it in a moment, after creating the next group section.

```
{Mailing List.ZIP}[1 to 3]
```

16. Add the three-digit Zip group section. Select Insert | Group Section from the Crystal Reports main menu. From the first list box, select the formula @Zip_3. Make sure that the sorting field is set to ascending order, which is the default.

17. Move the @Zip_3 formula field to the far left of the #2 @Zip_3 group header band.

18. Insert the formula @Zip3Print, which prints the total number of three-digit zip code addresses if there are at least 10. Place the field to the far right of the #2 @Zip_3 group footer band.

```
WhilePrintingRecords;
NumberVar Zip3Count;
NumberVar Zip3TotalCount;
NumberVar Zip3Cost;
NumberVar Zip3UnitCost;
NumberVar StateCount;
if Zip3Count >= 10 then
    Zip3Cost := Zip3Cost + (Zip3Count * Zip3UnitCost)
else
    StateCount := StateCount + Zip3Count;
if Zip3Count >= 10 then
    Zip3TotalCount := Zip3TotalCount + Zip3Count;
if Zip3Count >= 10 then
    Zip3Count;
```

19. Insert the formula `@Zip3TotalLine`, which prints the text for the total number of three-digit zip addresses.

```
WhilePrintingRecords;
NumberVar Zip3Count;
if Zip3Count >= 10 then
    "Total Count for " + {Mailing LIst.ZIP}[1 to 3] + ": "
else
    ""
```

20. Insert the formula field `@Zip3Reset`, which resets the three-digit `Zip` count to `0`. The field will be hidden, so place the field anywhere in the #2 @Zip_3 group section header band, and make it a minimum width. Placing hidden fields out of the way to the far right is usually most convenient.

```
WhilePrintingRecords;
NumberVar Zip3Count;
Zip3Count := 0;
```

21. Format the `@Zip3Reset` field to hide it while printing. Format the `@Zip3Print` field to have zero decimal places and to suppress if zero.

22. Insert the formula field `@Zip_5`, which takes the first five digits of the zip code. For the moment, place the field somewhere that is convenient on the report. You'll move it in a moment, after creating the next group section.

```
{Mailing List.ZIP}[1 to 5]
```

23. Now add the five-digit Zip group section. Select Insert | Group Section from the Crystal Reports main menu. From the first list box, select the formula `@Zip_5`. Make sure that the sorting field is set to ascending order, which is the default.

24. Move the `@Zip_5` formula field to the far left of the #3 @Zip_5 group section header band.

25. Insert the formula `@Zip5Print`, which prints the total number of five-digit zip code addresses if there are at least 10. Place the field to the far right of the #3 @Zip_5 group section footer band.

```
WhilePrintingRecords;
NumberVar Zip5Count;
NumberVar Zip5TotalCount;
NumberVar Zip3Count;
NumberVar Zip5Cost;
NumberVar Zip5UnitCost;
if Zip5Count >= 10 then
    Zip5Cost := Zip5Cost + (Zip5Count * Zip5UnitCost)
else
    Zip3Count := Zip3Count + Zip5Count;
```

```
if Zip5Count >= 10 then
    Zip5TotalCount := Zip5TotalCount + Zip5Count;
if Zip5Count >= 10 then
    Zip5Count;
```

26. Insert the formula @Zip5TotalLine, which prints the text for the total number of five-digit zip addresses.

```
WhilePrintingRecords;
NumberVar Zip5Count;
if Zip5Count >= 10 then
    "Total Zip (5) Count for " + {Mailing LIst.ZIP}[1 to 5] + ": "
else
    ""
```

27. Insert the formula field @Zip5Reset, which resets the five-digit Zip count to 0. The field will be hidden, so place the field anywhere in the #3 @Zip_5 group section header band, and make it a minimum width. Placing hidden fields to the far right is usually convenient.

```
WhilePrintingRecords;
NumberVar Zip5Count;
Zip5Count := 0;
```

28. Format the @Zip5Reset field to hide it while printing. Format the @Zip5Print field to have zero decimal places and to suppress printing if zero.

29. Set the sorting order of the fields in the report by selecting Report Sort Records from the Crystal Reports main menu. The three group sections should already appear in the Sort Fields list, because by default the group sections in the report are sorted by the group field. Add the zip code field by selecting that field in the Report Fields list on the left, and either double-click on that field or click the Add button. Make sure that the order setting is set to ascending, which is the default. The Record Sort Order window should now appear as shown in Figure 10.13.

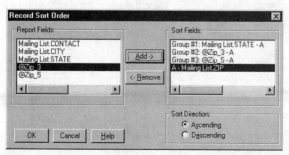

Figure 10.13. Setting the record sort order.

30. Insert the formula field @TotalCountReset, which sets the total count to 0 at the beginning of the report. The field will be hidden, so place the field anywhere in the page header band, and make it a small width. Placing hidden fields to the far right is usually convenient. For convenience, this field also sets the postage amounts for the different classes of mail.

```
WhilePrintingRecords;
NumberVar Zip5UnitCost;
NumberVar Zip3UnitCost;
NumberVar StateUnitCost;
NumberVar FirstClassUnitCost;
Zip5UnitCost := .191;
Zip3UnitCost := .191;
StateUnitCost := .256;
FirstClassUnitCost := .320;
```

31. Next, add the fields to the page footer. This is where you'll place the various counts and total postage for the different classes of mail. Start by adding the @FirstClassPrint formula field, which is the total count of the "miscellaneous" category of mail. Place the field in the top line of the page footer section, as far right as possible.

```
WhilePrintingRecords;
NumberVar FirstClassCount;
NumberVar FirstClassCost;
NumberVar FirstClassUnitCost;
FirstClassCost := FirstClassCount * FirstClassUnitCost;
FirstClassCount;
```

32. Add the @FirstClassTotalLine, which is the heading for the total count of the miscellaneous category of mail. Place the field in the top line of the page footer section, just to the left of the @FirstClassPrint field.

```
WhilePrintingRecords;
NumberVar FirstClassCount;
"Total First Class Count: ";
```

33. Now add the various running and final total formula fields. Add the @Zip3CostPrint formula field, which is the total count label of the three-digit zip category of mail. Place the field in the top line of the page footer section, at the far left.

```
WhilePrintingRecords;
"Zip (3) Totals:"
```

34. Add the @Zip3Count formula field. This is the running count of the number of pieces of mail that qualify for three-digit zip bulk rates. Add the field just to the right of the @Zip3CostPrint field. Format the field to have zero decimal places.

```
WhilePrintingRecords;
NumberVar Zip3TotalCount;
Zip3TotalCount;
```

35. Add the @Zip3TotalCost formula field. This field prints the running cost of the three-digit zip mail. Add the field just to the right of the @Zip3Count field. The cost of each category is calculated as we go, so all we need to do here is print the total. Format the field to have a currency symbol by checking the Currency Symbol checkbox in the Format Number dialog box, shown previously in Figure 10.12.

```
WhilePrintingRecords;
NumberVar Zip3Cost;
Zip3Cost;
```

36. Add the @Zip5CostPrint formula field, which is the total count label of the five-digit zip category of mail. Place the field in the second line of the page footer section, to the far left.

```
WhilePrintingRecords;
NumberVar Zip5Cost;
"Zip (5) Totals:";
```

37. Add the @Zip5Count formula field. This is the running count of the number of pieces of mail that qualify for five-digit zip bulk rates. Add the field just to the right of the @Zip5CostPrint field. Format the field to have zero decimal places.

```
WhilePrintingRecords;
NumberVar Zip5TotalCount;
Zip5TotalCount;
```

38. Add the @Zip5TotalCost formula field. This field prints the running cost of the five-digit zip mail. Add the field just to the right of the @Zip5Count field. The cost of each category is calculated as the mail is processed, so only the total is printed here. Format the field to have a currency symbol by checking the Currency Symbol checkbox in the Format Number dialog box.

```
WhilePrintingRecords;
NumberVar Zip5Cost;
Zip5Cost;
```

39. Add the @StateCostPrint formula field, which is the total count label of the state category of mail. Place the field in the third line of the page footer section, to the far left.

```
WhilePrintingRecords;
"State Totals:";
```

40. Add the @StateCount formula field. This is the running count of the number of pieces of mail that qualify for state bulk rates. Add the field just to the right of the @StateCostPrint field. Format the field to have zero decimal places.

```
WhilePrintingRecords;
NumberVar StateTotalCount;
StateTotalCount;
```

41. Add the @StateTotalCost formula field. This field prints the running cost of the state mail. Add the field just to the right of the @StateCount field. The cost of each category is calculated as the mail is processed, so only the total is printed here. Format the field to have a currency symbol by checking the Currency Symbol checkbox in the Format Number dialog box.

```
WhilePrintingRecords;
NumberVar StateCost;
StateCost;
```

42. Add the @FirstClassCostPrint formula field, which is the total count label of the miscellaneous category of mail that is charged full fare. Place the field in the second line of the page footer section, to the right of the five-digit zip information.

```
WhilePrintingRecords;
"First Class Totals:";
```

43. Add the @FirstClassCount formula field. This is the running count of the number of pieces of mail that don't qualify for bulk rates. Add the field just to the right of the @FirstClassCostPrint field.

```
WhilePrintingRecords;
NumberVar FirstClassCount;
FirstClassCount;
```

44. Add the @FirstClassTotalCost formula field. This field prints the running cost of the first-class mail. Add the field just to the right of the @FirstClassCount field. The cost of each category is calculated as the mail is processed, so only the total is printed here.

```
WhilePrintingRecords;
NumberVar FirstClassCost;
FirstClassCost;
```

45. Add the @TotalCostPrint formula field, which is the total count label of all the categories of mail. Place the field in the third line of the page footer section, below the first-class mail information.

```
WhilePrintingRecords;
"Mailing Totals:";
```

46. Add the @TotalCount formula field. This is the running count of the number of pieces of all the mail. Add the field just to the right of the @TotalCostPrint field.

```
WhilePrintingRecords;
NumberVar TotalCount;
TotalCount;
```

47. Add the @TotalCost formula field. This field prints the running cost of all the mail. Add the field just to the right of the @TotalCount field. The cost of each category is calculated as the mail is processed, so only the total is printed here.

```
WhilePrintingRecords;
NumberVar Zip5Cost;
NumberVar Zip3Cost;
NumberVar StateCost;
NumberVar FirstClassCost;
NumberVar TotalCost;
TotalCost := Zip5Cost + Zip3Cost + StateCost + FirstClassCost;
TotalCost;
```

48. When you are finished inserting the various fields and group sections, the design should look something like what's shown in Figure 10.14. This screen shows the design window with the main menu File | Options | Show Field Names option checked and all the hidden fields unhidden so that they appear more clearly.

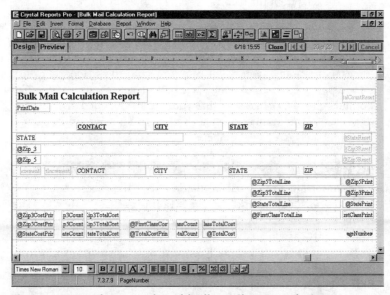

Figure 10.14. The completed bulk mail report design.

49. Select File | Print Preview to preview the report, or click on the Print Preview button in the toolbar. To print the report, select File | Print Printer in the main menu, or click on the Print toolbar button.

How It Works

Crystal Reports gives you all the tools you need to create complex reports. The bulk mail report created in this How-To approaches the upper limit of complexity of a typical database report.

By using formulas in Crystal Reports, you can create customized fields to present data in almost any form you want, including a wide variety of database formats to which you can connect with the Open Database Connectivity (ODBC) standard. See Chapter 7, "Connecting to an ODBC Server," for a discussion of ODBC.

Many formulas start with the `WhilePrintingRecords` function. Although probably overkill in some cases, this function forces the formula to be evaluated while records are being printed. This is the normal order of evaluation:

✔ If no database or group field is included in the formula, the formula is evaluated before the program reads database records.

✔ If a database is included in the formula, the formula is evaluated while the program reads database records.

✔ If a group field, page # field, subtotal, and so on is included in the formula, the formula is evaluated after database records are read and while the data from the records is being printed in the report.

Including `WhilePrintingRecords` ensures that formulas are evaluated as the report is being printed. Other functions, `BeforeReadingRecords` and `WhileReadingRecords`, can be used to perform formula evaluations at different times. For example, you might want to record the system time at the beginning of a report for use throughout. `WhileReadingRecords` lets the Crystal Reports formula check to make sure that you haven't included elements in the formula that need to be evaluated while printing, such as group calculations or report elements such as a page number.

NOTE

One important note must be made about the placement of the `@FirstClassCount` and `@FirstClassTotalCost` fields. The `@FirstClassTotalCost` field must be placed on a lower line than the `@FirstClassCount` field; otherwise, the total cost will be incorrect. Crystal Reports generally performs its calculations in a row order, so placing `@FirstClassTotalCost` on the same line to the left of `@FirstClassCount` calculates the cost before the final count is updated.

Subtotals and Other Group Calculations

Crystal Reports provides the capability to "band" the report, which means to group similar records for grouping, sorting, and calculating. Virtually any field or portion of a field can be used to group data at various levels. In this How-To, you grouped by state, five-digit zip code, and three-digit zip code. In the latter two groups, you used the first five or three digits of the zip code, using the following Crystal Reports substring array notation:

```
{database.field}[1 to 5]
```

Crystal Reports sorts records at various levels, providing options for sorting the different groups you designate, the groups themselves, and the records within the groups. This capability made it simple to put the records in the right sort order for the bulk mail groupings and to put them into the right groups. Formulas then determined whether the post office's requirement for a minimum number of mail pieces was met.

Crystal Reports provides a set of grand total functions that makes it easy to provide subtotals and counts of data, as well as statistical analysis, at any group level. That way, complex formulas aren't needed in many cases. Everything in this How-To was done without any outside database processing.

Comments

Crystal formulas provide tremendous flexibility to meet your reporting needs, but they can become cumbersome, as they did in this How-To. It might make more sense to write complex reports through the use of intermediate database tables. Create the table with complex formulas in code and SQL, and then write a Crystal report to display the summarized information. The use of a private class module to build the reporting table helps make code maintenance easier.

COMPLEXITY
BEGINNING

10.3 How do I...
Control the order in which records will be printed?

Problem

I want to be able to print the same Crystal report in different sort orders, but this task is a pain—and it is time-consuming to leave my Visual Basic application to make a change to the report in the Crystal Reports Designer program. How can I set a report's sort order from my application?

Technique

As you first saw in How-To 10.1, many of the parameters used to print a Crystal report through a Visual Basic application can be easily set using the Crystal Reports custom control. In this How-To, you'll create a list of computer book publishers. Through a Visual Basic program, you'll change the sort order of the report at runtime.

Steps

Load and run the Visual Basic application PUBLISH.VBP. Click one of the Report buttons to view the report in a preview window in zip, name, or city sort order. See Figure 10.15.

Start by creating a simple report that can be modified through Visual Basic during printing. Start the Crystal Reports program.

1. Click on the New Report toolbar button, or select File | New from the main menu. The New Report Gallery appears. Click the Listing option button.

2. When the Create Report Expert appears, click the Data File button, and use the common dialog to select the location of your Biblio.MDB file.

3. On the Fields tab, add the fields listed in Table 10.8 to your report by either double-clicking on the field name or selecting the field name and clicking Add.

Table 10.8. Computer publisher report tables and fields.

TABLE	FIELD
Publishers	State
Publishers	Zip
Publishers	Telephone
Publishers	City
Publishers	Name

4. On the Style tab, enter the text `Computer Book Publishers` as the report title.

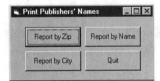

Figure 10.15. The Print Publishers' Names selection window.

5. Preview the report.

6. Now add the State group section. Inserting this section keeps the records grouped by state, so the individual records are sorted by zip, name, or city within each state. Select Insert | Group Section from the Crystal Reports main menu. From the first list box, select `Publishers.State`. Make sure that the sorting option is set to ascending order, which is the default. You won't enter any other fields in this group section.

7. This is the report you'll use. Remember to save the file, calling it PUBLISH.RPT.

8. Start Visual Basic and create a new Standard EXE project in your work area. Save the default form as PUBLISH.FRM, and save the project as PUBLISH.VBP. Select Project Components from the Visual Basic main menu, and make sure that the Crystal Reports control is selected. Add the READINI.BAS file to the project to find your copy of the BIBLIO.MDB file.

9. Place controls on the form as shown in Figure 10.15, and set the properties as shown in Table 10.9. Note that the Crystal Reports control is invisible at runtime, so place it anywhere on the form that is convenient. Note also that the three report command buttons make up a control array.

Table 10.9. Objects and properties for PUBLISH.FRM.

OBJECT	PROPERTY	SETTING
Form	Name	frmPublishers
	Caption	"Print Publishers' Names"
CommandButton	Name	cmdQuit
	Caption	"Quit"
CommandButton	Name	cmdReport
	Caption	"Report by Zip"
	Index	0
CommandButton	Name	cmdReport
	Caption	"Report by City"
	Index	1
CommandButton	Name	cmdReport
	Caption	"Report by Name"
	Index	2
CrystalReport	Name	crptPublishers
	ReportFileName	"D:\Waite\Chapter.10\
		How-to.103\Publish.rpt"
	Destination	0 'To Window

10. Add the following code to the **Click** event of the **cmdReport** command-button control array. This procedure sets **ReportFileName** to "PUBLISH.RPT" in the application's path, sets the **SortFields** property of the Crystal Reports custom control to the sort order desired, and assigns the Crystal Reports print preview window title. Then it sets the **Action** property to 1 to print the report.

```
Private Sub cmdReport_Click(Index As Integer)

    Dim strDbName As String

    ' Get the Biblio.mdb database location
    strDbName = strBiblioDb()
    ' Assign the data file location for the report
    crptPublishers.DataFiles(0) = strDbName
    ' Assign the report file name
    crptPublishers.ReportFileName = App.Path & "\Publish.rpt"
    'Set up the Report control
    Select Case Index
        Case 0    'Print by Zip
            crptPublishers.SortFields(0) = "+{Publishers.Zip}"
            crptPublishers.WindowTitle = "Publishers by Zip Code"
        Case 1    'Print by City
            crptPublishers.SortFields(0) = "+{Publishers.City}"
            crptPublishers.WindowTitle = "Publishers by City"
        Case 2    'Print by Name
            crptPublishers.SortFields(0) = "+{Publishers.Name}"
            crptPublishers.WindowTitle = "Publishers by Company Name"
    End Select
    crptPublishers.Action = 1
End Sub
```

11. Add the following code to the **Click** event of the **cmdQuit** command button, to provide an exit point from the program:

```
Private Sub cmdQuit_Click()
    Unload Me
End Sub
```

12. Add the following code to the form's **Load** event procedure. This code simply moves the form to the lower-right portion of the screen, out of the way of the report window when it appears.

```
Private Sub Form_Load()
    'Move the form to the lower right of screen
    Me.Move Screen.Width - 1.1 * Me.Width, _
        Screen.Height - 1.25 * Me.Height
End Sub
```

How It Works

This is all it takes to create a report in Crystal Reports and an application in Visual Basic that controls the sort order of the report. Entering a State group section causes the overall sort order of the report always to be by state. Then the individual publisher records are sorted within each state. Leaving out the group section would cause all records to be sorted by zip, city, or name, without regard to state.

This How-To uses the properties of the Crystal Reports custom control. You have to change only a single property, `SortFields`, to set the sort order. `SortFields` is an array, so you can enter as many sort fields as you want. In fact, the following groups of Visual Basic code would also keep all the records sorted by state and then by the secondary sort order:

```
CrystalReport1.SortFields(0) = "+{Publishers.State}"
CrystalReport1.SortFields(1) = "+{Publishers.Zip}"

CrystalReport1.SortFields(0) = "+{Publishers.State}"
CrystalReport1.SortFields(1) = "+{Publishers.City}"

CrystalReport1.SortFields(0) = "+{Publishers.State}"
CrystalReport1.SortFields(1) = "+{Publishers.Name}"
```

The plus sign at the beginning of each field name means to sort the records in ascending order. Use a minus sign to sort in descending order. The use of ascending and descending sort orders for different fields can be mixed and matched in a single report as much as you like.

Crystal Reports also has the capability to sort the group sections in any order you like. This can be set either in the report itself or again through the Crystal Reports custom control, using the `GroupSortFields` property in the same way as the `SortFields` property is used. So, for example, in this report you could have specified sorting the state groups in descending order, starting with Washington and progressing to Alaska at the end of the report.

Comments

This How-To illustrates one of the most frequent changes required for a report, changing the sort order. Consider using this feature carefully on very large, frequently used reports if the underlying database does not provide a convenient index. The Crystal Reports engine is pretty good at using database indices to retrieve data in the order it is needed, but a poorly sorted report can take forever to run.

10.4 How do I...
Print labels using Crystal Reports?

Problem

I need to produce mailing labels for our marketing program. How can I use Visual Basic to print the labels we need automatically so that they are ready for use in our mailings?

Technique

This How-To uses Crystal Reports' Mailing Labels design window. Crystal Reports ships with various standard Avery label formats, so there is a pretty good chance that the exact label you need is one of the Avery formats. Even if it isn't, it is quite easy and straightforward to modify one of the formats or create your own label.

This How-To can be combined with How-To 10.2, which creates a bulk mailing report, to print labels already sorted for bulk mailing, with the postage already calculated.

Steps

The steps in this How-To show in detail how to create a shipping label. To open and run a report in Crystal Reports, select File | Open from the Crystal main menu, and select the SHIPLBL.RPT report file, as shown in Figure 10.16. To print the report, click the Print button on the toolbar, or select File | Print from the main menu. To preview the report on-screen, click the Print Preview button on the toolbar, or select File | Print Preview from the Crystal Reports main menu.

1. This How-To uses the MAIL.MDB database described in the introduction to this chapter. Start Crystal Reports, and start a new report by clicking the New Report toolbar button or selecting File | New from the main menu. Click on Mail Label when the Create New Report Gallery appears.

2. Click on Data File when the Create Report Expert appears. Use the dialog box to find the MAIL.MDB Access database file installed in the How-To.104 directory. Click Done to close the dialog box.

3. From the Fields tab, add the **Contact** and **ADDR1** fields to the report.

Figure 10.16. Crystal Reports
design view for SHIPLBL.RPT.

4. Now, instead of placing the `City`, `State`, and `Zip` fields separately, you'll use a Crystal Reports formula so that all three fields appear on the same line without extra spaces. Start by clicking the Formula button on the Fields tab. Name the formula `CityStateZip`, click OK, and enter this formula:

```
TrimRight({Mailing LIst.CITY}) + ", " + TrimRight({Mailing LIst.STATE}) _
    + " " + {Mailing LIst.ZIP}
```

The Crystal Reports `TrimRight` function removes extra spaces from text fields. Click Check to make sure that the formula is correct, and then click Accept to define the formula. Click the Add button to include `@CityStateZip` with the printed fields in the righthand window.

5. On the Label tab, select an Avery shipping/address label (Avery 5164). This label is 4 inches wide by 3.33 inches high, so there are two columns of three labels. That leaves room for both a snazzy return address and the addressee information.

Select the Avery 5164 label by scrolling down through the Choose Mailing Label Type list box. Click on that entry, and you are finished designing the label layout. The Label tab of the Create Report Expert dialog box should then look like the one shown in Figure 10.17. You can also select the print sequence, either across or down first, by making a selection in the Printing Direction box. Leave the default set at Across then Down. Click OK to insert this format into the report.

6. Click Preview Report to see the basic report. After reviewing the labels, switch to design view by clicking the Design tab.

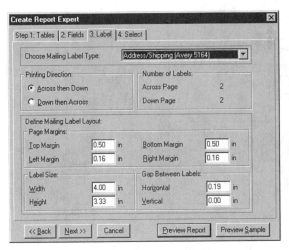

Figure 10.17. The Create Report Expert
dialog box.

7. Select the three fields on the report by Ctrl-clicking on each field in turn. Right-click and use the Change Font dialog box to increase the font size to 12 points. You can also change font attributes by using the font toolbar at the bottom of the Crystal Reports Designer window. Drag the three fields down the label to just below the middle on the left side.

8. Add a graphic element in the upper-left corner. Select Insert | Picture from the main menu, or click the Insert Picture button on the toolbar. When the Choose Graphic File box appears, select a graphics file from any of the supported formats: Windows bitmap (BMP), CompuServe (GIF), PC Paintbrush (PCX), TIFF (TIF), or TARGA (TGA). EARTH.GIF, courtesy of NASA and the Galileo spacecraft program, is included on the disk that accompanies this book.

After you select the file, click OK and the image appears on the Crystal Reports design screen. Position it so that the upper-left corner of the image is at or near the upper-left corner of the label, inside the left vertical and top horizontal gray lines. Choose Format | Picture from the main menu, and format the picture 2 inches wide and 1.5 inches tall, as shown in Figure 10.18. You'll need to play with the aspect ratio (the ratio of height to width) to get it to look right. Because of different screen and printer aspect ratios, what looks right on the screen might not look right on your printer.

9. Enter three text fields, and enter the text `Global Research Network`, `One Uranus Place`, and `Houston, Texas 04107`. Place these text fields in the upper-right quarter of the label next to the picture. Format the fields for a 12-point bold italic font.

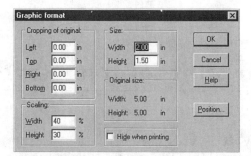

Figure 10.18. The Graphic format dialog box.

10. Insert a horizontal dividing line to split the two address areas of the label, by either selecting Insert Line from the main menu or clicking on the Insert Line button on the toolbar. Place the point of the line drawing tool directly on the label's left border, with the gray vertical line near the left edge of the label. Click and hold down the left mouse button as you drag the tool to the right edge of the label. Release the mouse button. If you need to, adjust the position or length of the line just as you would with any other field. Format the line to your preferred thickness.

11. Some versions of Crystal Reports enlarge the label size on the design window when you increase the font size on a line of the report. This causes you to end up with only one or two rows of labels on the page, rather than three rows. To restore the proper label size, scroll down to the bottom of the label. Notice that the bottom section border (the line that extends into the gray area to the left of the design area) is one-half to one-fourth inch below the rectangle of the label. Drag the bottom section edge as far up as it will go, adjacent to the dashed gray line. In other words, the bottom edge of the label, the bottom edge of the section, and the dashed line should all be very close to one another.

12. Remember to save the file, calling it SHIPLBL.RPT.

How It Works

When you run this report, Crystal uses the label format specifications to repeat different records across and down the page. The selected graphic is automatically included on each label.

Comments

Designing labels with Crystal Reports is essentially the same as designing any other report. Crystal Reports has support for most of the labels you'll need. If none of the formats is exactly right, pick something close and change the sizes and format to fit your needs.

COMPLEXITY
BEGINNING

10.5 How do I...
Create and print form letters?

Problem

Now that I can print my mailing labels, how can I print the form letters that will go into the mailing envelopes? How can I use my database with text to prepare form letter reports?

Technique

By using a couple of formatting tricks with Crystal Reports, you can use the report writer to generate almost any type of database report you need. This How-To shows how you can use Crystal Reports to replace your word processor's mail merge, and how to use formulas and field formatting to present your data in the most attractive format.

Steps

The steps in this How-To show in detail how to create a multipage form letter. To open and run a report in Crystal Reports, select File | Open from the Crystal main menu, and select the FORMLTR.RPT report file, as shown in Figure 10.19. To print the report, click the Print button on the toolbar, or select File | Print from the main menu. To preview the report on-screen, click the Print Preview button on the toolbar, or select File | Print Preview from the Crystal Reports main menu.

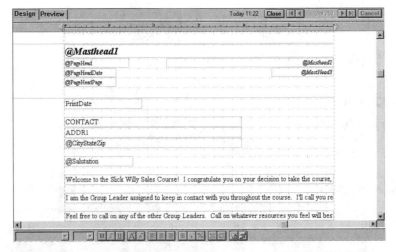

Figure 10.19. Crystal Reports design view for FORMLTR.RPT.

1. This How-To uses the MAIL.MDB database described in the introduction to this chapter. Start Crystal Reports, and begin a new report by clicking the New Report toolbar button or selecting File | New from the main menu. Click the Custom button when the Create New Report Gallery appears.

2. Click on Data File in the lower-right corner after the Create Report Expert expands. Use the dialog box to find the MAIL.MDB Access database file installed in the How-To.105 directory. Click Done to close the dialog box. A screen similar to that shown in Figure 10.20 appears.

3. As you design the report, be sure to save your work periodically by selecting File | Save (or File | Save As, the first time) from the Crystal Reports main menu.

4. Because we don't want extra column headings for a form letter, Select File | Options from the main menu. On the Layout tab, uncheck the Insert Detail Field Titles option.

5. Start by inserting the date for the letter. Select Insert | Special Field | Print Date Field. Locate the field in the detail section, to the far left.

6. Expand the size of the detail section by dragging the bottom gray line of the section down as far as it will go. Alternatively, place the text cursor on the last line of the detail section and press Enter as many times as needed to expand the section.

7. In the Insert Database Field window, double-click on the `Contact` field; then enter it in the detail line, or drag it from the Insert Database Field window. Place the field on the second line after the `Date` field.

8. Repeat the last step for the `Addr1` field, placing it on the line after the `Contact` field.

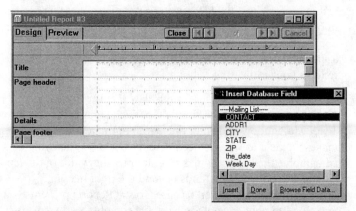

Figure 10.20. Crystal Reports blank report design view.

9. Now, instead of placing the `City`, `State`, and `Zip` fields separately, you'll use a Crystal Reports formula so that all three fields appear on the same line without extraneous spaces. Start by clicking the Done button on the Insert Database Field window to get it out of the way. Select Insert | Formula Field from the Crystal Reports main menu, and enter the name `CityStateZip` in the Formula name text box. Click OK, and enter this formula:

```
TrimRight({Mailing LIst.CITY}) + ", " + TrimRight({Mailing LIst.STATE})
    + " " + {Mailing LIst.ZIP}
```

The Crystal Reports `TrimRight` function removes extra spaces from text fields. Click Check to make sure that the formula is correct; then click Accept to place the formula field on the report, on the line under the `Addr1` field.

10. You'll use another formula field for the salutation. Select Insert | Formula Field from the Crystal Reports main menu, and enter the name `Salutation` in the Formula name text box. Click OK, and enter this formula:

```
"Dear " + TrimRight({Mailing LIst.CONTACT}) + ","
```

The `Contact` field in the Mailing List table has generic names, such as `Medical Practitioner` and `Occupant`. You can easily modify this formula to accommodate a `Salutation` field, an actual name, or the ever-so-personal "Dear Sir or Madam."

11. Set the margins for the letter. Select File | Page Margins from the main menu, and enter `1.00` inch for the top and bottom margins and `1.25` inches for the side margins. Click OK to return to the report and set the margins.

12. Now you'll enter the body of the letter. In this How-To, you'll enter the text in separate text fields for each paragraph so that you can enter fields in certain paragraphs to customize each letter. You can also enter all the text in a single text field if you don't need to customize the text, or even in a single formula field. The latter method tends to get a bit unwieldy and reduces your formatting options.

Crystal Reports has a rather serious flaw that turns what should be a single step into two steps. If you simply type each paragraph's text into the Edit Text Field window and enter the field into the report, Crystal Reports makes the field as wide as needed to fit the text. When you're using entire paragraphs, the field becomes several times the width of the report. When a Crystal Reports field extends beyond the right margin, there is no way to make the field narrower because Crystal Reports prevents you from grabbing the right edge of the field. On top of that, there is no field formatting option for field width, so you'll need to enter a text field with a single space in it and place that field on the report. You should then edit the text of the field, entering the text you actually want. Then you can size the field to the full width of the report.

Start by expanding the detail section, if necessary. Select Insert | Text Field from the main menu, or click the Insert Text button on the toolbar. Enter one or two spaces, and click OK to place the field on the report. Place the field on the second line after the salutation, at the left margin. Format the field's font for 12-point type.

13. Go back into the field to edit the text by right-clicking on the field and then selecting Edit Text Field from the popup menu, or by selecting Edit | Text Field from the main menu. Enter the following text in the Edit Text Field window. When you're finished typing, click the Accept button to insert the field on the report, and stretch the field to the full width of the report.

```
Welcome to the Slick Willy Sales Course!  I congratulate you on your
decision to take the course, because with hard work and study the
experience should greatly increase your sales skills.  I can speak from
experience—after I took the course five years ago, my sales success
went up dramatically.
```

The field remains one line long in the report design window. When you format the following fields, you'll set an option that tells Crystal Reports to expand the field vertically to show all the text.

14. Repeating the procedure in the preceding two steps, enter each of the following paragraphs in a separate text field. You'll need to enter a lot of text so that the letter is two pages long, to illustrate how to format different page headers.

```
I am the Group Leader assigned to keep in contact with you throughout
the course.  I'll call you regularly to find out how you are doing,
whether you need any help, answer any questions you might have, and
help you get the most out of the course.  I'd be happy to meet with
you to discuss the course, too—sometimes face to face is the only way
to work out issues.  This applies not only to the class material but
also to particular sales calls or prospects you might like to discuss.

Feel free to call on any of the other Group Leaders.  Call on whatever
resources you feel will best help you become a better salesperson.

Please come to class with the homework prepared, for two reasons.
First, doing the work is the only way to learn the material.  The class
will be a waste of your time if you don't learn anything!  Second, we
will use the assignments in class the following week.
```

continued on next page

continued from previous page

The reading assignments are important too, not just for the lessons
they contain, but because you'll occasionally be called upon to give
summaries of the readings.

And finally, read through the next week's lesson in the workbook, so
you'll have an idea of what to expect in class and can be prepared to
discuss the lessons.

The single most important way to learn the material and use it
successfully is to use it during the following week. Plan ahead and
incorporate it into your sales calls. Think about how to make it work
for you. In fact, not everything will work for you directly, but you
can almost always adapt a concept to your advantage.

Charley and all of the Group Leaders arrive at the classroom by 5:30
P.M. the night of each class, so come early if you'd like to discuss any
of the material in person. Also, as I previously mentioned, any of us
can meet with you during the week.

15. Now, enter a customized paragraph. Select Insert | Formula Field from the
main menu, or click the Insert Formula Field button on the toolbar. Name
the field **CustomParagraph**, and enter this formula:

```
WhilePrintingRecords;
StringVar para;
if {Mailing LIst.CONTACT} = "Medical Practioner" then
    para := "Since you live in the city of " +
    TrimRight({Mailing LIst.CITY}) +
    ", you can take advantage of our convenient MedShuttle. "
else
    if {Mailing LIst.CONTACT} = "Occupant" then
        para := "In the city of " + TrimRight({Mailing LIst.CITY}) +
        ", there is an excellent rail system, " +
        "with a stop within walking distance of the meeting room. "
    else
        para := "Please arrange your own transportation from "
        + TrimRight({Mailing List.CITY}) + ". ";

para := para +
"Please call us at 800-555-1212 if you need more information about getting here."
```

16. Enter the final two text fields. The Sincerely yours…Group Leader lines
can be in a single text field, using carriage returns at the end of each line.

We want you to be successful in the class and in your selling future.
Let us know if there is any way we can help you achieve that success.

Sincerely yours,

Bill Morehours
Group Leader

17. Format these detail section fields as shown in Table 10.10. The most important setting is Print on Multiple Lines for all the paragraph fields so that the text fields will expand vertically to accommodate all the text in the paragraph.

Table 10.10. The detail section fields and formatting.

REPORT ELEMENT	VALUES
Detail Section	New Page After
PrintDate	Date, Default Alignment, 1 March, 1999
Mailing List.CONTACT	String, Default Alignment
Mailing List.ADDR1	String, Default Alignment
@CityStateZip	String, Default Alignment
@Salutation	String, Default Alignment
Paragraph text fields	String, Default Alignment, MultipleLines, 12 pt Font
@CustomParagraph	String, Default Alignment, MultipleLines, 12 pt Font

18. Now, enter the fields for the page header. You have two sets of fields: one for the first page of the letter with your company name and address, and another for the second page header showing the addressee, date, and page. Use a Boolean variable `FirstPage` to keep track of whether this is the first page of the letter.

Select Insert | Formula Field from the main menu, or click the Insert Formula Field button on the toolbar. Name the formula `Masthead1`, and enter the following formula. Place the field on the top line of the page header, at the left margin.

```
WhilePrintingRecords;
BooleanVar FirstPage;
if FirstPage then
    FirstPage := False
else
    FirstPage := True;
if FirstPage then
    "Slick Willy Sales and Aerobics Training";
```

19. Select Insert | Formula Field from the main menu, or click the Insert Formula Field button on the toolbar. Name the formula `Masthead2`, and enter the following formula. Place the field against the right margin on the second line of the page header.

```
WhilePrintingRecords;
BooleanVar FirstPage;
if FirstPage = True then
    "One Pennsylvania Avenue, Nashville, Tennessee 80104";
```

20. Select Insert | Formula Field from the main menu, or click the Insert Formula Field button on the toolbar. Name the formula `Masthead3`, and enter the following formula. Place the field against the right margin on the third line of the page header.

```
WhilePrintingRecords;
BooleanVar FirstPage;
if FirstPage = True then
    "(800) 555-9875";
```

21. Now, enter the second set of page header fields, for the second page of the letter. Select Insert | Formula Field from the main menu, or click the Insert Formula Field button on the toolbar. Name the formula `PageHead`, and enter the following formula. Place the field against the left margin on the second line of the page header, under `@Masthead1`.

```
WhilePrintingRecords;
BooleanVar FirstPage;
if FirstPage = False then
    {Mailing LIst.CONTACT};
```

22. Select Insert | Formula Field from the main menu, or click the Insert Formula Field button on the toolbar. Name the formula `PageHeadDate`, and enter the following formula. Place the field against the left margin on the third line of the page header.

```
WhilePrintingRecords;
BooleanVar FirstPage;
if FirstPage = False then
    Today;
```

23. Select Insert | Formula Field from the main menu, or click the Insert Formula Field button on the toolbar. Name the formula `PageHeadPage`, and enter the following formula. Place the field against the left margin on the third line of the page header.

```
WhilePrintingRecords;
BooleanVar FirstPage;
if FirstPage = False then
    "Page 2";
```

24. Expand the size of the page header section to be one line longer than the bottom-most field so that both pages will have a blank line between the page header and the start of the text (detail section).

25. Format the page header section fields as shown in Table 10.11.

Table 10.11. The page header section fields and formatting.

REPORT ELEMENT	VALUES
Header Section	Visible, New Page Before, Keep Together
@Masthead1	String, Default Alignment, 16pt Font, Bold Italic
@PageHead	String, Default Alignment
@Masthead2	String, Right Alignment, 10pt Font, Italic
@PageHeadDate	Date, Default Alignment, 1 March, 1999
@Masthead3	String, Right Alignment, 10pt Font, Italic
@PageHeadPage	String, Default Alignment

26. Run the report, making sure that the different page headers print on the correct page.

How It Works

This How-To used a Crystal Reports Boolean variable to keep track of which page was printing. Although Crystal Reports can print different headers and footers on the first page of the report, it treats *all* subsequent pages as "nonfirst pages." In situations such as this form letter, in which each record prints one or more full pages, keep track of where you are by using formulas.

As mentioned in the preceding set of steps, the text for the letter can be put into fields, it can come from the database in memo fields, or it can all be put into one large text field. It really depends on a few factors:

✔ If every letter will be the same, with only one or two small customizations, use the technique in this How-To, in which a text field is used for each paragraph. This technique gives you the best combination of formatting flexibility and customization.

✔ If all the text of the letters is the same, you could use one large text field to hold it all. This means all the text must be formatted the same, and you must use trial and error to get the page headers and footers to work right. Also, Crystal Reports has a problem with General Protection Faults and some video drivers, particularly when editing text fields that have some trailing space configurations.

✔ If the text in each letter changes substantially, and if much of the text is in the table you use for the report, you can use database fields in combination with text fields and formulas to control to a low level of detail how each letter is formatted and what information it contains.

Other than keeping track of which header to print, this form letter report is created in the same way as the other reports in this chapter. Crystal Reports formulas provide you with a great deal of flexibility in presenting database records in the most useful format.

Comments

Using Crystal Reports to print form letters probably isn't the best way to perform the task. Today's word processors make the job easy. Generally, they can use data in a wide variety of formats and provide far more formatting flexibility. But as this How-To shows, Crystal Reports has its own wide variety of flexible tools to perform many printing jobs on its own. Who was it who said, "If the only tool you have is a screwdriver, the whole world looks like a screw"?

COMPLEXITY
BEGINNING

10.6 How do I...
Print field data without extra spaces between the fields?

Problem

When I create a report, I always need to put individual fields on the report for each database field. My database splits a client's name into "Mr.," "John," and "Jones," and I'd like that name to appear as "Mr. John Jones." How can I do this in Crystal Reports?

Technique

This How-To creates a customer directory list using Crystal Reports's string functions and operators to make the report fields appear as one field, even though the information is in several different fields. After the report is created, the functions and operators that Crystal Reports provides to manipulate strings in your database will be discussed.

Steps

The steps in this How-To show in detail how to create a customer directory. To open and run a report in Crystal Reports, select File | Open from the Crystal main menu, and select the CUSTDIR.RPT report file, as shown in Figure 10.21. To print the report, click the Print button on the toolbar, or select File | Print

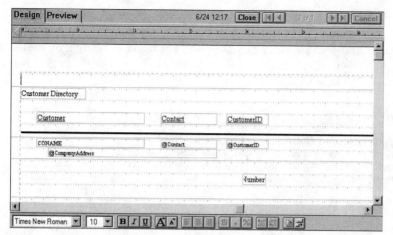

Figure 10.21. Crystal Reports design view for CUSTDIR.RPT.

from the main menu. To preview the report on-screen, click the Print Preview button on the toolbar, or select File | Print Preview from the Crystal Reports main menu.

1. This How-To uses the CRYSTAL.MDB database described in the introduction to this chapter. Start Crystal Reports, and begin a new report by clicking the New Report toolbar button or selecting File | New from the main menu. Click the Custom button when the Create New Report Gallery appears.

2. Make sure that Detail field names are automatically inserted into the page header. Select File | Options from the main menu. On the Layout tab, check the Insert Detail Field Titles option.

3. Click on Data File in the lower-right corner after the Create Report Expert expands. Use the dialog box to find the CRYSTAL.MDB Access database file installed in the How-To.106 directory. Click Done to close the dialog box.

4. Start by adjusting the margins for the report. Select File | Page Margins from the Crystal Reports main menu. Set the top margin to 0.5 inch and the other three margins to 1.0 inch.

5. Double-click on the CoName field and enter it in the detail line, or drag it from the Insert Database Field window. Place the field about one-fourth inch from the left margin in the detail section.

6. Now, create an @Contact field, using the FormAddress, ContactFN, and ContactLN fields. Select Insert | Formula Field from the Crystal Reports main menu, or click the Insert Formula Field button on the toolbar. Name the field Contact, and enter this formula. Place the field to the right of the CoName field.

```
WhilePrintingRecords;
StringVar BuiltStr;

if Length({COMPANY.FORMADDRES}) > 0 then
    BuiltStr := TrimRight({COMPANY.FORMADDRES}) + " ";
BuiltStr := BuiltStr + TrimRight({COMPANY.CONTACTFN}) + " "
+ TrimRight({COMPANY.CONTACTLN});
```

7. Select Insert | Formula Field from the Crystal Reports main menu, or click the Insert Formula Field button on the toolbar. Name the field CustomerID, and enter this formula. Place the field to the right of the @Contact formula field.

```
TrimRight({COMPANY.CUSTNUM})
```

8. Enlarge the height of the detail section by one line by dragging the lower-section line down with the mouse. To expand the section using the keyboard, place the text cursor at the beginning of the last line of the section and press Enter once.

9. Select Insert | Formula Field from the Crystal Reports main menu, or click the Insert Formula Field button on the toolbar. Name the field CompanyAddress, and enter this formula. Place the field on the second line of the detail section, about a half inch to the right of the left margin. Delete the field title Crystal Reports automatically generated from the page header section.

```
WhilePrintingRecords;
TrimRight({COMPANY.ADDRESS}) + ", " +
TrimRight({COMPANY.CITY}) + ", " +
TrimRight({COMPANY.STATE}) + " " +
{COMPANY.ZIP_POSTAL}
```

10. Format these detail section fields as shown in Table 10.12.

Table 10.12. The detail section fields and formatting.

REPORT ELEMENT	VALUES
Detail Section	Visible
@CustomerID	String, Centered Alignment
COMPANY.CONAME	String, Default Alignment
@Contact	String, Default Alignment
@CompanyAddress	String, Default Alignment, Multiple Lines

11. Insert a report heading in the page header. Select Insert | Text Field from the Crystal Reports main menu, and enter `Customer Directory`. Place the field at the upper-left corner of the report area. Wait to adjust the width of the field until you change the font size.

12. As you entered fields in the detail section, Crystal Reports should have inserted corresponding column titles in the page header section. Adjust those text fields so that they are more or less above the appropriate field. You'll need to adjust them later when everything else is finished so that they are aesthetically pleasing.

13. Expand the size of the page header by dragging the lower edge down one line of text. Select Insert | Line from the Crystal Reports main menu, or click the Insert Line button on the toolbar. Place the tip of the drawing tool at the left margin, just a bit lower than the bottom edge of the line of column headings. Drag the tool across the width of the report, and release the mouse button at the right margin. Click the line with the right mouse button, and select Change Format from the popup menu, or select Format | Line from the main menu. On the Width line, select the third box from the right, for a line width of 2.50 points. Click OK to close the Line Format window.

14. Add a page number in the page footer section. Select Insert | Special Field | Page Number.

15. Format the page header and footer section fields, as shown in Table 10.13.

Table 10.13. The page header and footer section fields and formatting.

REPORT ELEMENT	VALUES
Header Section	Visible, New Page Before, Keep Together
Text Field	Customer Directory
	String, Centered Alignment, 14pt Font, Bold Italic
Text Field	Contact
	String, Left Alignment
Text Field	Customer
	String, Left Alignment
Text Field	Customer ID
	String, Centered Alignment
Line	2.50pt Width
Footer Section	Visible, New Page After, Keep Together, Print at Page,
	Bottom
@PageNo	String, Right Alignment

16. This finishes the Customer Directory report. Remember to save the file, calling it CUSTDIR.RPT.

How It Works

Crystal Reports has several functions and operators for converting other data types to strings and manipulating strings to appear the way you want. Table 10.14 lists the primary functions that Crystal Reports provides for this purpose, and Table 10.15 lists the operators that are most useful.

Table 10.14. Useful Crystal Reports functions for manipulating strings.

FUNCTION	DESCRIPTION
Length(*x*)	Indicates the number of characters in the string, including leading and trailing spaces.
LowerCase (*x*)	Converts all alphabetical characters in the string to lowercase.
NumericText(*fieldname*)	Indicates whether all characters are numeric.
ReplicateString(*x*, *n*)	Prints string *x*, *n* times.
ToNumber (*x*)	Converts the string to a number.
ToText (*x*)	Converts a number to a text string, with two decimal places.
ToText (*x*, #*places*)	Converts a number to a text string, with # decimal places.
TrimLeft (*x*)	Removes leading spaces from the string.
TrimRight (*x*)	Removes trailing spaces from the string.
UpperCase (*x*)	Converts all alphabetical characters in the string to uppercase.

Table 10.15. Useful Crystal Reports operators for manipulating strings.

FUNCTION	DESCRIPTION
+	Concatenation
[]	Subscript
In	In string

Crystal Reports treats a string like an array of characters, so you can use array notation to extract characters from a string, as shown in the following examples. Using a field called **Address**:

```
{Company.Address} = "1245 East Elm Lane"
```

Use the substring operator in the following lines to show different extractions:

```
{Company.Address}[1 to 5] equals "1245 "
{Company.Address}[6 to 200] equals "East Elm Lane"
{Company.Address}[3 to Len(TrimRight({Company.Address}))]
    equals "45 East Elm Lane"
```

Here are a couple of final notes about strings in Crystal Reports:

✔ When you trim and concatenate strings, remember to add spaces where you need them. For example, you needed to include a space within the quotation marks when you concatenated the `FormAddress`, `ContactFN`, and `ContactLN` fields. Otherwise, there would have been no space between the names.

✔ In some databases, such as Paradox, it isn't necessary to use the `TrimRight` function to eliminate trailing spaces. Paradox includes a null character at the end of the string, effectively making the length of the string the number of characters without trailing spaces. It doesn't hurt to include the `TrimRight` function, because the format could change in the future or you might need to adapt the report to be used with another database.

Comments

Although Crystal provides a great many options for manipulating strings, consider carefully the best way to accomplish your goal, especially if the database server is able to perform your task. The use of SQL allows you to perform many string operations in the database and simplifies Crystal operations. In some cases, printing directly from Visual Basic might be the best solution.

COMPLEXITY
BEGINNING

10.7   How do I...
Use the Crystal Reports custom control to print reports?

Problem

My application needs to print different reports from different databases. Sometimes the reports should be sent to a printer, sometimes to a file, and still other times just to the screen. How can I give that control to the user and make sure that the choices made are valid?

Technique

Allowing your application to make several choices at runtime is simple with the Crystal Reports custom control. It is a matter of making sure that the right options are set and giving that information to the control at runtime. In this How-To, you will create a Visual Basic application that can print any Crystal report, allowing the user to have control over the printed report and its destination.

Because Crystal Reports provides its own print preview window and interface routines for printing to files and a printer, all you need to do is start the report. How-To 10.11 illustrates how the appearance of the Crystal Reports print preview window can be controlled through an application.

Steps

Load and run the Visual Basic application CONTROL.VBP. On the Set Report Printing Options window, shown in Figure 10.22, enter or change any of the properties: the Crystal report to print, the connection string elements needed to connect to the database used in the report, and the destination of the report and associated properties. After a report has been selected and valid groups of properties set, the Print Report button is enabled. Click the button to print the report to the destination you selected.

1. Start Visual Basic and create a new project in your work area. Save the default form as CONTROL.FRM, and save the project as CONTROL.VBP. Select Tools | Custom Controls from the Visual Basic main menu, and make sure that the Microsoft Common Dialog, 3D, and Crystal Reports controls are selected.

2. Place controls on the form as shown in Figure 10.22, setting properties as listed in Table 10.16. Note that the common dialog, timer, and Crystal Reports controls are invisible at runtime, so place them anywhere that is convenient. Note also that the txtConnect text boxes form a control array.

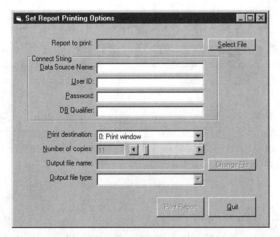

Figure 10.22. The Set Report Printing Options window (frmControl).

Table 10.16. Objects and properties for CONTROL.FRM.

OBJECT	PROPERTY	SETTING
Form	Name	frmControl
	BackColor	&H00C0C0C0&
	Caption	"Set Report Printing Options"
Timer	Name	tmrReady
	Interval	500
CommandButton	Name	cmdPrint
	Caption	"Print &Report"
	Enabled	0 'False
CommandButton	Name	cmdQuit
	Caption	"&Quit"
HScrollBar	Name	hsbCopies
	LargeChange	10
	Max	100
	Min	1
	Value	1
ComboBox	Name	lstFileType
	Style	2 'Dropdown List
TextBox	Name	txtReportToPrint
CommandButton	Name	cmdNewReport
	Caption	"&Select File"
CommandButton	Name	cmdFileName
	Caption	"Change &File"
TextBox	Name	txtFileName
ComboBox	Name	lstDestination
	Style	2 'Dropdown List
TextBox	Name	txtCopies
	ReadOnly	-1 'True
	TabStop	0 'False
	Text	"1"
SSFrame	Name	frmConnect
	caption	"Connect String"
TextBox	Name	txtConnect(0)
TextBox	Name	txtConnect(1)
TextBox	Name	txtConnect(2)
TextBox	Name	txtConnect(3)

continued on next page

continued from previous page

OBJECT	PROPERTY	SETTING
Label	Name	Label1
	Alignment	1 'Right Justify
	Caption	"&Data Source Name:"
Label	Name	Label2
	Alignment	1 'Right Justify
	Caption	"&User ID:"
Label	Name	Label4
	Alignment	1 'Right Justify
	Caption	"&Password:"
Label	Name	Label5
	Alignment	1 'Right Justify
	Caption	"D&B Qualifier:"
Label	Name	lblFileType
	Alignment	1 'Right Justify
	Caption	"&Output file type:"
Label	Name	Label10
	Alignment	1 'Right Justify
	Caption	"Report to print:"
CommonDialog	Name	cdFileName
	Dialogtitle	"Report File Destination Name"
	Filter	"Text File (*.txt)¦*.txt¦Document (*.doc)¦*.doc¦All Files (*.*)¦*.*"
Label	Name	lblFileName
	Alignment	1 'Right Justify
	Caption	"Output file name:"
CrystalReport	Name	CrystalReport1
	Reportfilename	""
	Destination	0
	Copiestoprinter	1
	Printfilename	""
	Printfiletype	0
	Selectionformula	""
	Groupselectionformula	""
	Connect	""
	Username	""

OBJECT	PROPERTY	SETTING
Label	Name	Label9
	Alignment	1 'Right Justify
	Caption	"&Print destination:"
Label	Name	lblCopies
	Alignment	1 'Right Justify
	Caption	"&Number of copies:"

3. Add the following code to the form's **Load** event procedure. This code starts by loading the options in the two list boxes for the print destination and file type, for reports that will be printed to a file. The code then calls the procedure for **lstDestination_Click** to set the starting condition of the controls related to printing to a file. Then, it centers the form.

```
Private Sub Form_Load()
    'Build the list control lists
    lstDestination.AddItem "0: Print window"
    lstDestination.AddItem "1: Printer"
    lstDestination.AddItem "2: File"
    lstDestination.ListIndex = 0

    lstFileType.AddItem "0: Fixed field width"
    lstFileType.AddItem "1: Tab delimited, with quotes"
    lstFileType.AddItem "2: Space delimited"
    lstFileType.AddItem "3: Data interchange format (DIF)"
    lstFileType.AddItem "4: Comma delimited"
    lstFileType.AddItem "5: Reserved"
    lstFileType.AddItem "6: Tab delimited, no quotes"

    'Set the visibility of the appropriate controls
    lstDestination_Click

    'Center the form
    frmControl.Move (Screen.Width - frmControl.Width) / 2, _
        (Screen.Height - frmControl.Height) / 2
End Sub
```

4. Add the following two procedures to the respective **Click** events of the **cmdFileName** and **cmdNewReport** command buttons. Each of these procedures first sets the default extension, dialog box title, and filter for the common dialog control, then opens the File Open dialog box. Then the selected filename is inserted in the related text box. The **cmdFileName** procedure gets the file to which the report is printed if that option is selected. The **cmdNewReport** gets the filename of the Crystal report file that will be printed.

```
Private Sub cmdFileName_Click()
    cdFileName.DefaultExt = "txt"
    cdFileName.DialogTitle = "Report File Destination Name"
    cdFileName.Filter = _
        "Text File (*.txt)¦*.txt¦Document (*.doc)¦*.doc¦All Files (*.*)¦*.*"
    cdFileName.ShowOpen
    txtFileName.Text = cdFileName.FileName
End Sub

Private Sub cmdNewReport_Click()
    cdFileName.DefaultExt = "rpt"
    cdFileName.DialogTitle = "Select Report File"
    cdFileName.Filter = "Report File (*.rpt)¦*.rpt¦All Files (*.*)¦*.*"
    cdFileName.ShowOpen
    txtReporttoPrint.Text = cdFileName.FileName
End Sub
```

5. Insert the following code into the **Change** event procedure of the **hsbCopies** horizontal scrollbar. When the user clicks on the scrollbar, the new value of the control is copied into the **txtCopies** text box so that the correct amount is shown. The new value is also used to set the Crystal Reports control property **CopiesToPrinter** so that it is all ready to go when the report is printed. Note that this property applies only to reports sent to a printer.

```
Private Sub hsbCopies_Change()
    txtCopies.Text = hsbCopies.Value
    CrystalReport1.CopiesToPrinter = hsbCopies.Value
End Sub
```

6. Add the following code to the **Click** event procedure of the **lstDestination** list box. This procedure maintains the controls that are enabled and disabled so that the user is presented only with options that apply to the current selection in the Print Destination list box. If the report is to be printed to a Crystal Reports print preview window, the copies, file type, and name options do not apply, so they are disabled. If the report will be printed to the printer, the number of copies is relevant, and that option is enabled. When the report will be printed to a file, the filename and type options are enabled. The procedure also clears any options that are disabled so that the old option does not appear when disabled.

Note that instead of being disabled, the labels are set to dark gray so that they don't disappear against the light-gray form background color. This is the same color that is used when command buttons are disabled. When a label is enabled, the forecolor is set to black as a default.

Note that this procedure only enables and disables controls; it does not actually set any of the Crystal Reports control properties.

```
Private Sub lstDestination_Click()
    'Enable appropriate options, based on ListIndex
    Select Case lstDestination.ListIndex
        Case 0 'Print to window
            lblFileName.ForeColor = &H404040
            txtFileName.Enabled = False
            txtFileName.Text = ""
            cmdFileName.Enabled = False

            lblFileType.ForeColor = &H404040
            lstFileType.Enabled = False
            lstFileType.Text = ""

            lblCopies.ForeColor = &H404040
            txtCopies.Enabled = False
            txtCopies.Text = 1
            hsbCopies.Value = 1

        Case 1 'Print to printer
            lblFileName.ForeColor = &H404040
            txtFileName.Enabled = False
            txtFileName.Text = ""
            cmdFileName.Enabled = False

            lblFileType.ForeColor = &H404040
            lstFileType.Enabled = False
            lstFileType.Text = ""

            lblCopies.ForeColor = &H0&
            txtCopies.Enabled = True
            txtCopies.Text = 1
            hsbCopies.Value = 1

        Case 2 'Print to file
            lblFileName.ForeColor = &H0&
            txtFileName.Enabled = True
            txtFileName.Text = ""
            cmdFileName.Enabled = True

            lblFileType.ForeColor = &H0&
            lstFileType.Enabled = True
            lstFileType.Text = ""

            lblCopies.ForeColor = &H404040
            txtCopies.Enabled = False
            txtCopies.Text = 1
            hsbCopies.Value = 1
    End Select
End Sub
```

7. Enter the following code in the **lstFileType** list box **Click** event procedure. The full range of file type options that Crystal Reports provides for the **PrintFileType** property is included. You can also leave it out and compensate for the missing sequence number. If the selected number is otherwise valid, the **PrintFileType** property of the control is set.

```
Private Sub lstFileType_Click()
    'Can't use the Crystal Reports reserved value
    If lstFileType.ListIndex = 5 Then
        MsgBox "Reserved value not available. Please select another."
        lstFileType.ListIndex = 0
        lstFileType.Text = ""
    Else
        CrystalReport1.PrintFileType = lstFileType.ListIndex
    End If
End Sub
```

8. Add the following code to the **LostFocus** event procedure of the **txtConnect** text box. The **txtConnect** text boxes make up a four-element control array. When a member of this array loses the focus, the **Connect** string is rebuilt and assigned to the **Connect** property of the Crystal Reports control. The **Connect** string is made up of a data source name, user ID, password, and database qualifier name. The **Connect** string can consist of any, some, or none of these items. These items are needed only if the report being printed connects to a database that requires this information. After the string is rebuilt, it is assigned to the **Connect** property of the control.

You also could have used the **Change** event for this code, but then the string would be rebuilt every time the user typed a single character in one of the text boxes. Using **LostFocus**, the string is rebuilt only when the focus is moved, as it must be if the report is printed immediately after a change is made in one of these text boxes.

```
Private Sub txtConnect_LostFocus(Index As Integer)
    'Something in one of the control array boxes changed,
    'so rebuild the connect string
    Dim Connect As String

    If Len(txtConnect(0).Text) Then
        Connect = "DSN=" & txtConnect(0).Text & ";"
    End If
    If Len(txtConnect(1).Text) Then
        Connect = Connect & "UID=" & txtConnect(1).Text & ";"
    End If
    If Len(txtConnect(2).Text) Then
        Connect = Connect & "PWD=" & txtConnect(2).Text & ";"
    End If
    If Len(txtConnect(3).Text) Then
        Connect = Connect & "DSQ=" & txtConnect(3).Text & ";"
    End If

    CrystalReport1.Connect = Connect
End Sub
```

9. Insert the following code in the Change event procedure of the
txtReportToPrint text box. To keep things user-friendly, change the
caption of the cmdNewReport command button, depending on the
contents of the txtReportToPrint text box. Because the contents have
changed, set the ReportFileName property of the Crystal Reports control.

```
Private Sub txtReportToPrint_Change()
    'Contents have changed, so reset cmdNewReport caption
    If Len(txtReporttoPrint.Text) Then
        cmdNewReport.Caption = "&Change File"
        CrystalReport1.ReportFileName = txtReporttoPrint.Text
    Else
        cmdNewReport.Caption = "&Select File"
        CrystalReport1.ReportFileName = ""
    End If
End Sub
```

10. Insert this code in the Change event procedure of the txtFileName text
box. The code changes the caption of the cmdFileName command button,
depending on the contents of the txtFileName text box. Because the
contents have changed, set the PrintFileName property of the Crystal
Reports control.

```
Private Sub txtFileName_Change()
    'Contents have changed, so reset cmdFileName caption
    'and set the PrintFileName property
    If Len(txtFileName.Text) Then
        cmdFileName.Caption = "Change &File"
        CrystalReport1.PrintFileName = txtFileName.Text
    Else
        cmdFileName.Caption = "Select &File"
        CrystalReport1.PrintFileName = ""
    End If
End Sub
```

11. Enter the following code in the Timer event of the tmrReady timer control.
So that the Print Report command button is not always enabled, a timer
control polls the current contents of the controls that must be in a certain
state to be able to print. Because the Interval property of the control is
set to 500, this procedure checks every half second (slow by computer
standards but adequate for use here) to see whether the report can be
printed. If so, it enables the cmdPrint command button. If not, it disables
the button.

The only condition that must always be met is for a Crystal report
filename to be entered in the txtReportToPrint text box. If the user has
elected to print the report to a file, both a file type and a filename must be
available for printing.

Note that no error checks are performed in this procedure. Part of the reason is to keep the example simple, but it's also because errors from the Crystal Reports control are trappable using Visual Basic's error-handling procedures. You'll see more about Crystal Reports errors in How-To 10.10.

```
Private Sub tmrReady_Timer()
    'Check every half second to see if report is ready to print
    'If it is, enable the Print Report command button
    Dim Ready As Boolean

    Ready = True
    If Len(txtReporttoPrint.Text) < 5 Then
        Ready = False
    End If
    If lstDestination.ListIndex = 2 And (txtFileName.Text = "" _
        Or lstFileType.Text = "") Then
        Ready = False
    End If

    cmdPrint.Enabled = IIf(Ready, True, False)
End Sub
```

12. Enter this short procedure in the **Click** event procedure of the **cmdPrint** command button. Because we have updated the properties of the Crystal Reports control as they have changed, all this procedure needs to do is set the **Action** property of the Crystal Reports control to **1**, which prints the report.

```
Private Sub cmdPrint_Click()
    'Since the button is enabled, we're OK to print
    CrystalReport1.Action = 1
End Sub
```

13. Add the following code to the **Click** event procedure of the **cmdQuit** command button, providing an exit point for the program:

```
Private Sub cmdQuit_Click()
    End
End Sub
```

How It Works

Using the Crystal Reports control is the same as using any other Visual Basic custom control—except for a few different properties. Most of the properties can be set at design time, some at runtime, and some at either time. Table 10.17 lists the control properties that are the most useful with Visual Basic applications.

Table 10.17. Properties of the Crystal Reports custom control.

PROPERTY	DESCRIPTION
Action	Prints the specified report.
Connect	Logs on to an external database.
CopiesToPrinter	Sets the number of copies to print.
DataFiles	Sets a new location of the database to be used.
Destination	Sets the output location: preview window, file, or printer.
Formulas	Sets the value of an existing formula in the report.
GroupSelectionFormula	Sets the condition for selecting groups of records.
GroupSortFields	Specifies the sort order of the group sections (not the records in the groups).
LastErrorNumber	Retrieves the error number from the last print request.
LastErrorString	Returns a description of the error with the last print request.
Password	Sets the password used to access the database.
PrintFileName	If Destination is file, sets the name of the file.
PrintFileType	If Destination is file, specifies the type of file to create.
ReportFileName	Specifies the report to print, including full pathname.
SelectionFormula	Specifies the formula used to select records.
SortFields	Specifies the fields used to sort records, and ascending or descending.
UserName	Specifies the user name, if required to access the database.

How-To 10.11 examines how the appearance of the print preview window can be modified at runtime.

Comments

The Crystal Reports ActiveX control provides tremendous flexibility for report control. As you design your applications, consider where and how you will integrate reports from the start. Dynamic selection of report filenames and databases, combined with 32-bit Windows long filenames, lets you build a flexible reporting mechanism you can add to by simply distributing new report definition (.rpt) files.

COMPLEXITY
INTERMEDIATE

10.8 How do I...
Prevent blank lines from being printed when a field contains no data?

Problem

We use some tables that have many fields that only occasionally have any data in them. How can I set up a report so that a line prints only when it has data, and still allow memo fields with lots of data to print in their entirety?

Technique

This How-To uses two of Crystal Reports's space-saving features, the Suppress Blank Lines option and Print on Multiple Lines option for text boxes. The Suppress Blank Lines option applies to an entire section, setting the report to print only lines that contain data. That means you can conserve paper and save trees that would otherwise be needed to print much longer reports containing many blank fields.

The Print on Multiple Lines option lets you place a text box on the report as a single line so that the box doesn't need to be made large enough to show the longest possible string, wasting space on the report. This option tells Crystal Reports to go ahead and expand the field vertically to fit the text if the text requires two or more lines. Otherwise, only the portion of the string that fits in the first line of the field will print on the report.

Even when using these two options, you still need to design reports intelligently. It would be easy to have a line with several fields, any of which could be blank or contain data. The line would print if *any* of the fields has data, so you need to try to put only a single field on each line or group fields together that are likely to be blank at the same time.

This How-To uses the Publishers, Publishers Comments, and Titles tables in the BIBLIO.MDB file. Each table has several fields that are often blank, mixed in with long memo fields.

Steps

The steps in this How-To show in detail how to create a fairly complex report from multiple tables while allowing for missing information. To open and run a report in Crystal Reports, select File | Open from the Crystal main menu, and select the TITLES.RPT report file, as shown in Figure 10.23. To print the report, click the Print button on the toolbar, or select File | Print from the main menu. To preview the report on-screen, click the Print Preview button on the toolbar, or select File | Print Preview from the Crystal Reports main menu.

1. This How-To uses the BIBLIO.MDB database described in the introduction to this chapter. Start Crystal Reports, and begin a new report by clicking the New Report toolbar button or selecting File | New from the main menu. Click the Custom button when the Create New Report Gallery appears.

2. Make sure that `Detail` field names are not automatically inserted into the page header section. Select File | Options from the main menu. On the Layout tab, uncheck the Insert Detail Field Titles option.

3. Click on Data File in the lower-right corner after the Create Report Expert expands. Use the dialog box to locate the BIBLIO.MDB Access database file installed with Visual Basic.

4. Start by adjusting the margins for the report. Select File | Page Margins from the Crystal Reports main menu. Set the top margin to `0.5` inch and the other three margins to `1.0` inch.

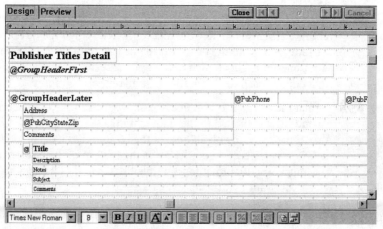

Figure 10.23. Crystal Reports design view for the Publisher Titles report.

5. Add an asterisk at the beginning of the detail line to make the individual titles (detail section) stand out more clearly to the reader of the report. Enter this as a formula field, because it is conceivable that a record in the table would not have a title but would still have other relevant information. Select Insert | Formula Field from the main menu, or click the Insert Formula Field button on the toolbar. Enter the formula name `Bullet`, and insert the following formula. Place the field about one-fourth of an inch from the left margin, and make its width just wide enough for the asterisk.

```
if Not IsNull({Titles.Title}) then
    "*"
```

6. Double-click on the `Titles.Title` field and enter it in the detail line, or drag it from the Insert Database Field window. Place the field just to the right of the `Bullet` field. Don't adjust the width until after the font size is set.

7. Expand the size of the detail section by dragging the lower boundary down as far as it will go. Because Crystal Reports limits the amount by which you can expand a section's size, you might need to expand the section again as you add fields.

8. Double-click on the `Description` field and enter it in the detail line, or drag it from the Insert Database Field window. Place the field on the line below the `Title` field, about one-fourth of an inch to the right of the title. Drag the right border to the right margin so that the field takes up the remaining width of the report.

9. In the same way, add the `Notes`, `Subject`, and `Comments` fields to the report, adding each below the preceding field. Align the `Notes` and `Subject` fields with the `Description` field, and place the `Comments` field about one-fourth of an inch to the right. Expand all the fields so that the right edge of each field is at the right margin of the report.

10. Format these detail section fields as shown in Table 10.18. Remember to expand the `Title` field to the right margin after changing the font to bold. Also, if there are any blank lines at the bottom of the detail section, drag the lower detail section border up to the bottom of the `Comments` field. A very quick way to format for multiple lines is to double-click the field for which you want to format a string.

Table 10.18. The detail section fields and formatting.

REPORT ELEMENT	VALUES
Detail Section	Visible, Suppress Blank Lines
@Bullet	String, Default Alignment
Titles.Title	String, Default Alignment, Font 10pt Bold, Multiple Lines

REPORT ELEMENT	VALUES
Titles.Description	String, Default Alignment, Multiple Lines
Titles.Notes	String, Default Alignment, Multiple Lines
Titles.Subject	String, Default Alignment, Multiple Lines
Titles.Comments	Memo, Default Alignment, Multiple Lines

11. Now add the Company Name group section. Select Insert | Group Section from the Crystal Reports main menu. From the first list box, select `Publishers.Company Name`. Leave the sorting option set to ascending order, which is the default, and click OK to proceed.

12. The first field you'll enter in this group section is the publisher's company name. There is a problem, however, with simply adding the field to the report. Some of the publishers have a long list of books that will span more than one page, whereas others have none. It would be nice to be able to reprint the company name at the beginning of the next page if that company's list of books continues from one page to the next. So you'll enter the company name as a formula, testing to see whether this is a continuation. Select Insert | Formula Field from the Crystal Reports main menu, or click the Insert Formula Field button on the toolbar. Name the formula `GroupHeaderLater`, and enter the following formula. The formula first checks to see whether the preceding company name was null, in which case the name is printed. Otherwise, the new company name is checked to see whether it is the same as the preceding name. If it isn't, you'll start a list for a new company and print the name. If this is a continuation list, you'll print the name in a formula field that can be put in the page header.

```
If PreviousIsNull({Publishers.Company Name}) then
    {Publishers.Company Name}
else
    if Previous ({Publishers.Company Name})  {Publishers.Company Name} then
        {Publishers.Company Name}
    else
        " "
```

13. Next, enter the publisher's phone number. There might not be a phone number in the file, and we want to label the number as the phone (and later the fax number as the fax); therefore, you should enter a formula field. That way, you won't have the word `Phone:` sitting in the report with nothing else there. Select Insert | Formula Field from the Crystal Reports main menu, or click the Insert Formula Field button on the toolbar. Name the formula `PubPhone`, and enter the following formula. Place the field to the right of the `@GroupHeadLater` field.

```
WhilePrintingRecords;
if Length({Publishers.Telephone}) > 0 then
    "Phone: " + {Publishers.Telephone}
```

14. Do the same thing for the fax number. Select Insert | Formula Field from the Crystal Reports main menu, or click the Insert Formula Field button on the toolbar. Name the formula **PubFax**, and enter the following formula. Place the field to the right of the @PubPhone field.

```
WhilePrintingRecords;
if Length({Publishers.Fax}) > 0 then
    "Fax: " + {Publishers.Fax}
```

15. Double-click on the **Address** field in the Insert Database Field window and enter it in the group section, or drag it from the Insert Database Field window. Place the field on the line below the @GroupHeaderLater field, about one-fourth of an inch to the right of that field. Drag the right border to make the width of the field the same as the @GroupHeaderLater field.

16. The city, state, and zip code should appear together on one line, so enter them as a formula field. Select Insert | Formula Field from the Crystal Reports main menu, or click the Insert Formula Field button on the toolbar. Name the formula **PubCityStateZip**, and enter the following formula. Place the field on the line after the **Address** field in the group section header.

```
WhilePrintingRecords;
TrimRight({Publishers.City}) + ", " + TrimRight({Publishers.State}) +
" " + {Publishers.Zip}
```

17. Double-click on the **Publisher.Comments** field in the Insert Database Field window and enter it in the group section, or drag it from the Insert Database Field window. Place the field on the line below the @PubAddress field, and align the left edge with that field. Drag the right edge of the field to the report's right margin.

18. Now, enter the fields in the group footer that show the number of titles the publisher has on the list. Select Insert | Text Field from the main menu, or click the Insert Text Field button on the toolbar. Enter **Title(s)** in the field, and place the field in the first group section footer line, at the far right margin. Adjust the size of the field so that it is only wide enough to show the text.

19. To insert a summary field, you must first highlight the field you want to count. Click on the **Title** field in the detail section, and then select Insert | Summary from the main menu so that the Insert Summary window appears. Select **Count** from the first list box, and leave the second list box at the default group section #1 sorting and grouping. The window should look like the one shown in Figure 10.24 just before you click OK to enter the field. Place this field so that it reaches from the left margin to the left edge of the Title(s) text box.

20. Format these group section fields as shown in Table 10.19.

Table 10.19. The detail section fields and formatting.

REPORT ELEMENT	VALUES
Group header #1:	Suppress Blank Lines, Keep Section Together
@PubFax	String, Default Alignment
@PubPhone	String, Default Alignment
@GroupHeaderLater	String, Default Alignment, 12pt Font, Bold Italic, Multiple Lines
Publishers.Address	String, Default Alignment
@PubCityStateZip	String, Default Alignment
Comments	Default Alignment, Multiple Lines
Title(s)	String, Default Alignment
Group footer #1:	Suppress Blank Lines
Count of Titles.Title	Numeric, Default Alignment, Leading Minus, 0 Decimal Places, Rounding: None, Thousands Symbol: ',', Decimal Symbol: '.'

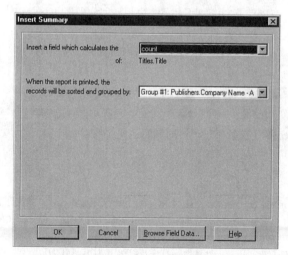

Figure 10.24. The Insert Summary window.

21. Now move to the page header and footer. Select Insert | Text Field from the main menu, or click the Insert Text Field button on the toolbar. Enter the text `Publisher Titles Detail`, and place the field at the upper-left corner of the page header section. Wait to widen the field until you change the font so that Crystal Reports doesn't make the field so wide that you can't adjust the right edge.

22. Now, enter a group header to print the publisher's company name if the list of titles continues from the preceding page. Select Insert | Formula Field from the main menu, or click the Insert Formula Field button on the toolbar. Name the formula `@GroupHeaderFirst`, and enter the following formula. Place the field on the third line of the page header, but don't adjust its width yet.

```
if Previous({Publishers.Company Name}) = {Publishers.Company Name} then
    {Publishers.Company Name} + " continued"
else
    " "
```

23. Now, enter a page number field in the page footer section. Select Insert | Formula Field from the main menu, or click the Insert Formula Field button on the toolbar. Name the formula `@PageNo`, and enter the following formula. Place the field on the third line of the page footer at the far-right edge of the line.

```
"Page " + ToText(PageNumber, 0)
```

24. Format these page header and footer fields as shown in Table 10.20.

Table 10.20. The page header and footer fields and formatting.

REPORT ELEMENT	VALUES
Text Field	Publisher Titles Detail, 14 pt Font, Bold
@GroupHeaderFirst	String, Default Alignment, 12pt Font, Bold Italic
@PageNo	String, Right Alignment

How It Works

When you run this report, you should see blank lines only where they were intentionally left in the report. Leave margins at the top and bottom because some white space makes a report more easily read and understood.

Two interesting features were used to create this report. The first is the `Suppress Blank Lines` section formatting option. Using this option means that all you have to do is make sure that no extraneous text appears on a line that otherwise would be blank so that the line is not printed at all. The **phone** and fax fields were put into formulas rather than separate text fields to make some of the text fields the full (or nearly full) width of the report. This way, if any field is blank, the entire line won't print. If two or more fields could be blank on the same line, all the fields would have to be blank for the line not to print, resulting in a checkerboard effect if some fields contain data and others do not.

The other interesting feature used in this report was a summary field. Crystal Reports automatically calculates the maximum, minimum, count, and distinct count on any fields indicated. This How-To used a summary field to keep count of how many titles each publisher had on the list.

Comments

Most of this How-To has focused on making a report "pretty." Although programming style is tremendously important to how well a system works, good appearances will be remembered by anyone who sees your creations.

COMPLEXITY
INTERMEDIATE

10.9 How do I...
Create cross-tab reports?

Problem

I use a table that needs to be summarized weekly in a cross-tab style report. It is almost impossible to produce the report in Visual Basic before printing it. Can I use Crystal Reports to produce a cross-tab report from my tables?

Technique

Crystal Reports can analyze data as well as print it. One method is a cross-tab report, which summarizes two or more dimensions of data in tables. In this How-To you will create a marketing analysis report that produces a breakdown of customers by city and the day of the week they were serviced, giving totals by weekday and by city.

Steps

The steps in this How-To show in detail how to create a cross-tab report. To open and run a report in Crystal Reports, select File | Open from the Crystal main menu, and select the MAILANAL.RPT report file, shown in Figure 10.25. To print the report, click the Print button on the toolbar, or select File | Print from the main menu. To preview the report on-screen, click the Print Preview button on the toolbar, or select File | Print Preview from the Crystal Reports main menu.

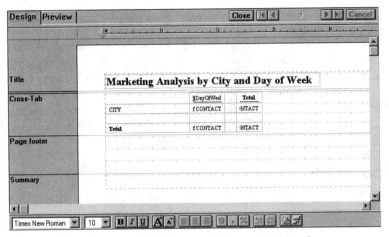

Figure 10.25. The Crystal Reports design window for marketing analysis report.

1. This How-To uses the MAIL.MDB database described in the introduction to this chapter. Start Crystal Reports, and start a new report by clicking the New Report toolbar button or selecting File | New from the main menu. Click on Cross-Tab when the Create New Report Gallery appears.

2. Click on Data File when the Create Report Expert appears. Use the dialog box to find the MAIL.MDB Access database file installed in the How-To.109 directory. Click Done to close the dialog box.

3. From the Fields tab, add the `Contact`, `City`, `State`, and `Zip` fields from the MailingList table.

4. On the Style tab, enter `Bulk Mail Calculation Report` as the title.

5. After you select the database file to use for the report, the CrossTab window appears, as shown in Figure 10.26. The layout of this window makes it easy to visualize the final report. You will need to enter the field or formula used for the rows and columns, and then enter a field or formula for the data that is contained in the body of the report. Crystal Reports will then handle all the calculations to produce the report.

6. Start by double-clicking on the Mailing List table name in the Fields list box so that the fields in the table appear. Drag the `Mailing List.CITY` field to the Rows cross-tab list. This tells Crystal Reports that a list of cities contained in the file will compose the rows of the report.

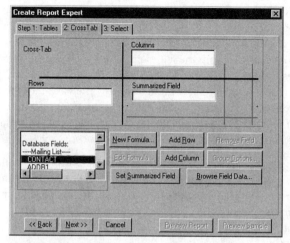

Figure 10.26. The Crystal Reports Create
Report Expert.

7. You will want to use the days of the week for the report columns. But first consider the space you have. There will be a column for each day of the week, plus one for the list of city names and another for the total for each city, so there will be nine columns altogether. If you don't abbreviate the days of the week, the data won't fit on a report, or part of the names will get cut off. Unfortunately, Crystal Reports can't print text vertically, so you should use a formula field to print only the first three characters of each day's name.

Click the New Formula button, and enter DayOfWeek as the formula name. Enter the following formula, which tells Crystal Reports to use a substring consisting of the first three characters of the name. Drag the new formula to the Columns cross-tab list.

```
{Mailing List.Week Day}[1 to 3]
```

8. The last step is to tell Crystal Reports what information will make up the body of the table. You just want to count contacts, so drag the Contact field to the Summarized field. (The default function for the summarized field is Count, so you won't need to make a change. You'll see in a moment how to change that.) That's all there is to designing the cross-tab layout, so click Preview Report to see the results so far.

9. All that is left to do is to reposition and resize the cross-tab fields so that the font can be read, and to enter a report title and page number. Start by setting the four margins of the report to 0.5 inch by selecting File | Page Margins from the main menu.

10. Next, move the cross-tab grid to the left so that there will be enough room on the page for all nine columns in the report. Use the mouse to drag the vertical line on the left side of the `DayOfWeek` column to the left until it is about 1 to 1.5 inches from the left margin, leaving enough room for the city names to print. The space to the right of the `Total` column will contain the day-of-the-week columns. Narrow the `Week Day` column to about three-fourths of an inch and the `Total` column to about one-half of an inch. You'll need to set the spacings by trial and error when all the report elements have been entered into the report.

11. To enter a report heading, select Insert | Text Field from the main menu, or click the Insert Text Field button on the toolbar. Enter `Marketing Analysis by City and Day of Week`, and place the field in the upper-left position in the page header. Change the font size to 14 point by using the list of font sizes in the font toolbar, and click the B in the toolbar to make the font bold.

12. Enter a page number field on the page footer. First, show the Page Footer section by right-clicking in the gray left margin of the design window and selecting Show/Hide Sections from the menu. Show the Page Footer section. Then, select Insert | Formula Field from the main menu, or click the Insert Formula Field button on the toolbar. Name the formula `PageNo`, and enter the following formula. Place the field in the lower-left portion of the page footer, against the left margin.

```
"Page " + ToText(PageNumber, 0)
```

13. If you want to make changes to the cross-tab design of the report, use the right mouse button to click in the gray area to the left of the page edge in the Cross-Tab detail section, and select Cross-Tab Layout from the popup menu. Then make any changes you want in the same Cross-Tab layout window you used to create the report. To use a summarization function other than `Count`, highlight the grid cell at the intersection of the `City` row and `Week Day` column, and select Edit | Summary Field from the main menu. Figure 10.27 shows the options available. The options for any given report depend on the type of field data selected for the `Summarization` field in the Cross-Tab layout window.

How It Works

Creating a cross-tab report in Crystal Reports is an almost trivial task when you understand how to present data using this type of report. The table used in this How-To consists of names, addresses, dates, and weekdays. By using a cross-tab report, you transform this data into a breakdown of clients by week, day, and geographic location. In fact, the hardest part of producing the report is to size and position the report elements so that all the fields show their data and everything fits on the page.

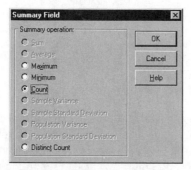

Figure 10.27. Cross-tab summarization function selections.

Creating the report is easy, partially because the same record selection, sorting, and formatting options are available with cross-tab reports as with other report formats used in this chapter.

Comments

One rather serious flaw of Crystal Reports is that any fields or columns that are off the right side of the report page do not print and cannot be reached in the report design window. You can change the page orientation to landscape by using File | Printer Setup, but even that orientation is not wide enough for some reports.

COMPLEXITY
ADVANCED

10.10 How do I...
Handle errors generated by Crystal DLL?

Problem

I am using the Crystal Reports print engine to make direct calls to the engine DLL, but the function returns a zero and does not extract the information I need. How can I get error information from Crystal Reports?

Technique

The Crystal Reports print engine provides two functions for getting error information after a call to a print engine function has been made: `PEGetErrorCode` and `PEGetErrorText`. This How-To extracts interesting information about a report file while making calls to these functions after function calls. You'll see how to create a handy utility that can be used on any Crystal report file.

Steps

Load and run the Visual Basic application CRWERROR.VBP. When the Crystal Reports Error window appears, as shown in Figure 10.28, click the Get New Report File button, and select the report about which you want information. After selecting a report, click the Get Specifications button. In a few moments, the program extracts the list of sort and group-sort fields used in the report, the record selection formula, the group selection formula, and the list of tables available for use by the report.

1. Start Visual Basic and create a new project in your work area. Save the default form as CRWERROR.FRM and the project as CRWERROR.VBP. Select Tools | Custom Controls from the Visual Basic main menu, and make sure that the Microsoft Common Dialog and Microsoft Grid controls are selected. Because you are using direct calls to the print engine, you won't need the Crystal Reports control for this project.

2. Place controls on the form as shown in Figure 10.28, setting properties as given in Table 10.21. Note that the common dialog and timer controls are invisible at runtime, so place them anywhere that is convenient.

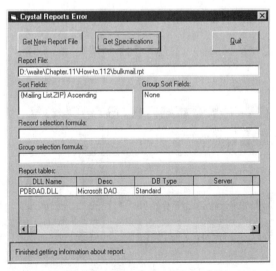

Figure 10.28. Layout of the Crystal Reports Error window (frmCrystalError).

Table 10.21. Objects and properties for CRWERROR.FRM.

OBJECT	PROPERTY	SETTING
Form	Name	frmCrystalError
	BorderStyle	3 'Fixed Double
	Caption	"Crystal Reports Error"
	MaxButton	0 'False
	MinButton	0 'False
TextBox	Name	txtGroupSelection
TextBox	Name	txtRecordSelection
ListBox	Name	lstGroupSortFields
	Sorted	-1 'True
Timer	Name	tmrTicker
	Enabled	0 'False
	Interval	100
PictureBox	Name	Picture1
	Align	2 'Align Bottom
Label	Name	lblTicker
	Weight	700 (bold)
Label	Name	lblStatus
ListBox	Name	lstSortFields
	Sorted	-1 'True
CommandButton	Name	cmdQuit
	Cancel	-1 'True
	Caption	"&Quit"
CommandButton	Name	cmdGetSpecs
	Caption	"Get &Specifications"
	Enabled	0 'False
CommandButton	Name	cmdNewReport
	Caption	"Get &New Report File"
TextBox	Name	txtReportFile
Label	Name	lblTableCount
	Alignment	1 'Right Justify
Label	Name	Label6
Grid	Name	grdTables
	FixedCols	0
	Highlight	0 'False
Label	Name	Label5
	Caption	"Group selection formula:"

continued on next page

continued from previous page

OBJECT	PROPERTY	SETTING
Label	Name	Label4
	Caption	"Record selection formula:"
Label	Name	Label3
	Caption	"Group Sort Fields:"
Label	Name	Label2
	Caption	"Sort Fields:"
Label	Name	Label1
	Caption	"Report File:"
CommonDialog	Name	cdOpenReport
	DefaultExt	"RPT"
	DialogTitle	"Open Crystal Reports .rpt File"
	Filter	"Report File (*.rpt)¦*.rpt¦All Files (*.*)¦*.*"

3. Enter the following code into the declarations section of the form. To avoid naming problems, **Option Explicit** tells Visual Basic to make sure that you declare all variables and objects before using them. Then the constant **gridCols** is set to the number of columns; using a module global value makes it easy to add columns if you want to add more information about a table. The **colHeads** array holds the names of the columns for quick and easy presentation of information about the contents of a particular cell in the grid. **gJobno** is a handle that Crystal Reports returns from an initialization function for a print job that is used in subsequent function calls.

```
Option Explicit
'Special controls used: Microsoft Grid and Crystal Reports
'custom control

'Constant and array for use with grid control
Private Const gridCols As Integer = 8
Dim colHeads() As String

'Keep the Crystal print job number in a Public variable
'This is value returned by PEOpenPrintJob function
Public gJobno As Integer
```

4. Add the following code to the form's **Load** event procedure. This code starts by centering the form, then calls the **GridSetup** initialization procedure for **grdTables**. It then calls the Crystal Reports **PEOpenEngine** function to open and initialize the print engine for use by this application.

```
Private Sub Form_Load()
    Dim result As Integer
```

```
    'Start by centering form
    frmCrystalError.Move (Screen.Width - Me.Width) / 2, _
        (Screen.Height - Me.Height) / 2

    'Initialize the grid for table data
    GridSetup
    Me.Show

    'Open the Crystal print engine
    Ticker "Opening print engine.", True
    DoEvents
    frmCrystalError.Refresh

    result = PEOpenEngine()
    If result = False Then
        result = PError()
        Exit Sub
    End If

End Sub
```

5. Enter the following code in the **GridSetup** Sub procedure. It contains the initialization procedures for setting the grid control, the number of columns, the column widths, and the column headings. The column headings are stored in a **colHeads** array to make it easier to label the actual value of a grid cell when it is double-clicked.

```
Sub GridSetup()
    'Collect together all of the grid initialization
    'We don't yet know the number of rows
    Dim i As Integer
    ReDim colHeads(gridCols)

    grdTables.Cols = gridCols
    For i = 0 To 7
        grdTables.ColWidth(i) = 1500
        grdTables.FixedAlignment(i) = 2    'Centered
    Next

    'Put in titles for the columns
    grdTables.Row = 0
    grdTables.Col = 0
    colHeads(0) = "DLL Name"
    grdTables.Text = colHeads(grdTables.Col)
    grdTables.Col = 1
    colHeads(1) = "Desc"
    grdTables.Text = colHeads(grdTables.Col)
    grdTables.Col = 2
    colHeads(2) = "DB Type"
    grdTables.Text = colHeads(grdTables.Col)
    grdTables.Col = 3
    colHeads(3) = "Server"
    grdTables.Text = colHeads(grdTables.Col)
    grdTables.Col = 4
    colHeads(4) = "DB Name"
```

continued on next page

continued from previous page

```
    grdTables.Text = colHeads(grdTables.Col)
    grdTables.Col = 5
    colHeads(5) = "User ID"
    grdTables.Text = colHeads(grdTables.Col)
    grdTables.Col = 6
    colHeads(6) = "Password"
    grdTables.Text = colHeads(grdTables.Col)
    grdTables.Col = 7
    colHeads(7) = "Location"
    grdTables.Text = colHeads(grdTables.Col)

End Sub
```

6. Enter the following code to the `ClearGrid` **Sub** procedure. When a new
report file is selected, the grid is cleared of all existing values so that there
is no confusion about which report the values shown apply to.

```
Sub ClearGrid()
    Dim i As Integer

    'Setting fewer than 2 rows gets rid of vertical borders
    'in top row in many cases
    grdTables.Rows = 2

    'Clear out the remaining top row
    grdTables.Row = 1
    For i = 0 To gridCols - 1
        grdTables.Col = i
        grdTables.Text = ""
    Next
    grdTables.Col = 0
End Sub
```

7. Enter the following code into the `cmdNewReport`'s **Click** procedure. The
procedure activates the common dialog File Open window so that the user
can specify a report file to use. After the window is closed and a file has
been selected, the procedure puts the filename into the `txtReportFile`
text box and then clears the data from the other controls on the form. If no
filename was selected in the File Open window, then the information in
the form, whether blank or not, is left unchanged.

```
Private Sub cmdNewReport_Click()
    'Get a report file name
    cdOpenReport.ShowOpen

    If Len(cdOpenReport.FileName) Then
        txtReportFile.Text = cdOpenReport.FileName
        cmdGetSpecs.Enabled = True

        'Clear the data from previous report
        lstSortFields.Clear
        lstGroupSortFields.Clear
        txtGroupSelection.Text = ""
        txtRecordSelection.Text = ""
        ClearGrid
```

```
        End If

    End Sub
```

8. Add the following code to the **cmdGetSpecs Click** event procedure. This is the parent function that calls several other functions to actually extract the information from the report file. The **Ticker Sub** procedure puts a status message on the status bar (a label control), and it starts or stops the rotating timer so that the user doesn't think the computer has frozen during the sometimes long delays in obtaining information. This procedure opens and then closes a report job by calls to **PEOpenPrintJob** and **PEClosePrintJob**, getting and freeing the **gJobno** print handle.

```
Private Sub cmdGetSpecs_Click()
    Dim result As Integer

    'Clear the list boxes
    lstSortFields.Clear
    lstGroupSortFields.Clear

    Ticker "Opening print report file and getting job number.", True
    gJobno = PEOpenPrintJob(txtReportFile)

    If GetSortFields = False Then
        Ticker "Problem getting sort field data.", False
        Exit Sub
    End If
    If GetGroupSortFields = False Then
        Ticker "Problem getting group sort field data.", False
        Exit Sub
    End If
    If GetRecordSelection = False Then
        Ticker "Problem getting record selection data.", False
        Exit Sub
    End If
    If GetGroupSelection = False Then
        Ticker "Problem getting group selection data.", False
        Exit Sub
    End If
    If GetTables = False Then
        Ticker "Problem getting table data.", False
        Exit Sub
    End If

    'Close the report engine
    PEClosePrintJob (gJobno)
    Ticker "Finished getting information about report.", False
End Sub
```

9. Add the following code to the **GetSortFields** function procedure. With a call to **PEGetNSortFields** to get the number of sort fields in the report, and then repeated calls to **PEGetNthSortField**, all the sort fields are revealed.

Fields are returned from PEGetNthSortField in the order determined by
the report's sorting priority. Note that this is the *record* sort order, not the
group section sort order. As the fields are retrieved, the field name and the
sort direction are added to the lstSortFields list box. If the report
contains no sort fields (PEGetNSortFields returns 0), "None" is entered
into the list box.

Note that two print-engine function calls are required for each sort field.
The PEGetNthSortField function returns a handle to the field name, so
PEGetHandleString is called to get the actual string containing the name.

The GetSortFields function returns True if everything went OK and
False if there were errors in any calls to a print engine function.

```
Function GetSortFields()
    'Get the specs on the sort fields, if any
    Dim result As Integer
    Dim i As Integer
    Dim hName As Long
    Dim nameLen As Integer
    Dim Direction As Integer
    Dim fieldName As String * 255

    Ticker "Getting number and names of sort fields.", True
    DoEvents

    result = PEGetNSortFields(gJobno)
    GetSortFields = True
    If result Then
        For i = 0 To result - 1
            result = PEGetNthSortField(gJobno, i, hName, nameLen, Direction)
            If result = False Then
                result = PError()
                GetSortFields = False
                Exit Function
            End If
            result = PEGetHandleString(hName, fieldName, nameLen)
            If result = False Then
                result = PError()
                GetSortFields = False
                Exit Function
            End If
            fieldName = Left(fieldName, nameLen - 1)
            lstSortFields.AddItem Trim(fieldName) & IIf(Direction, _
                " Ascending", " Descending")
        Next
    Else
        lstSortFields.AddItem "None"
    End If
End Function
```

10. Enter the following code to the `GetGroupSortFields` function procedure. With a call to `PEGetNGroupSortFields` to get the number of group sort fields in the report, and then repeated calls to `PEGetNthGroupSortField`, all the group sort fields are revealed.

```
Function GetGroupSortFields()
    'Get the specs on the group sort fields, if any
    Dim result As Integer
    Dim i As Integer
    Dim hName As Long
    Dim nameLen As Integer
    Dim Direction As Integer
    Dim fieldName As String * 255

    Ticker "Getting number and names of group sort fields.", True
    DoEvents

    result = PEGetNGroupSortFields(gJobno)
    GetGroupSortFields = True
    If result Then
        For i = 0 To result - 1
            result = PEGetNthGroupSortField(gJobno, i, hName, nameLen, Direction)
            If result = False Then
                result = PError()
                GetGroupSortFields = False
                Exit Function
            End If
            result = PEGetHandleString(hName, fieldName, nameLen)
            If result = False Then
                result = PError()
                GetGroupSortFields = False
                Exit Function
            End If
            lstGroupSortFields.AddItem fieldName & Str(Direction)
        Next
    Else
        lstGroupSortFields.AddItem "None"
    End If
End Function
```

The order in which the fields are returned from `PEGetNthGroupSortField` is determined by the sorting priority in the report. Note that this is the *group* sort order, not the record section sort order. As the fields are retrieved, the field name and the sort direction are added to the `lstGroupSortFields` list box. If the report contains no group sort fields (`PEGetNGroupSortFields` returns `0`), `"None"` is entered into the list box. `PEGetHandleString` is again called to get the actual string containing the name.

The `GetGroupSortFields` function returns `True` if everything went OK and `False` if there were any errors in any calls to a print engine function.

11. Enter the following code in the `GetRecordSelection` function procedure. The `PEGetSelectionFormula` function call retrieves a handle to the string with the formula, and `PEGetHandleString` is called to get the actual string containing the name. The string that is returned has a null at the end of it, so copy only the left portion of the string that actually has characters.

```
Function GetRecordSelection()
    'Get the formula for selecting records in the report
    Dim result As Integer
    Dim hName As Long
    Dim formulaLen As Integer
    Dim formula As String * 255

    Ticker "Getting record selection formula.", True
    DoEvents

    GetRecordSelection = True

    result = PEGetSelectionFormula(gJobno, hName, formulaLen)
    If result = False Then
        result = PError()
        GetRecordSelection = False
        Exit Function
    End If
    result = PEGetHandleString(hName, formula, formulaLen)
    If result = False Then
        result = PError()
        GetRecordSelection = False
        Exit Function
    End If

    'String has a null at the end
    If Len(Trim(formula)) - 1 Then
        txtRecordSelection.Text = formula
    Else
        txtRecordSelection.Text = "None"
    End If
End Function
```

12. Insert this code into the `GetGroupSelection` function procedure. Using the same method as used in `GetRecordSelection`, extract the group selection formula from the report file by using the `PEGetGroupSelectionFormula`.

```
Function GetGroupSelection()
    'Get the formula for selecting groups in the report
    Dim result As Integer
    Dim hName As Long
    Dim formulaLen As Integer
    Dim formula As String * 255

    Ticker "Getting group selection formula.", True
    DoEvents
```

```
    GetGroupSelection = True

    result = PEGetGroupSelectionFormula(gJobno, hName, formulaLen)
    If result = False Then
        result = PError()
        GetGroupSelection = False
        Exit Function
    End If
    result = PEGetHandleString(hName, formula, formulaLen)
    If result = False Then
        result = PError()
        GetGroupSelection = False
        Exit Function
    End If

    'String has a null at the end
    If Len(Trim(formula)) - 1 Then
        txtGroupSelection.Text = formula
    Else
        txtGroupSelection.Text = "None"
    End If

End Function
```

13. Enter the following code in the `GetTables` function procedure. This procedure extracts information about each of the tables included in the report. This procedure uses three `Type` variables defined in GLOBAL.BAS: `PETableType`, `PELogonInfo`, and `PETableLocation`. Each of these variables contains one or more pieces of information about each table, so list all meaningful information in the grid, which consists of eight columns.

The first step is to initialize the size and string members of the `Type` variables. Then, with a call to `PEGetNTables` to get the number of tables in the report, a loop retrieves all the information for each table. The last part of the procedure puts each piece of information in a column of the grid. If there are no tables in the report (a very rare occurrence), `"None"` is entered into the first column of the first row.

```
Function GetTables()
    'Get the data on tables used in report
    Dim result As Integer
    Dim i As Integer
    Dim hName As Long
    Dim nameLen As Integer
    Dim Direction As Integer
    Dim fieldName As String * 255
    Dim tableInfo As PETableType        'PETableType defined in global.bas
    Dim tableLogOn As PELogonInfo       'PELogOnInfo defined in global.bas
                                        'PETableLocation defined in global.bas
    Dim tableLocation As PETableLocation
```

continued on next page

continued from previous page

```
'Initialize the table structures
tableInfo.StructSize = Len(tableInfo)
tableInfo.DLLName = Chr$(0)
tableInfo.DescriptiveName = Chr$(0)
tableLogOn.StructSize = Len(tableLogOn)
tableLogOn.ServerName = Chr$(0)
tableLogOn.DatabaseName = Chr$(0)
tableLogOn.UserID = Chr$(0)
tableLogOn.Password = Chr$(0)
tableLocation.StructSize = Len(tableLogOn)
tableLocation.Location = Chr$(0)

Ticker "Getting number of tables in report.", True
DoEvents

result = PEGetNTables(gJobno)
lblTableCount.Caption = "Table Count: " & Trim(Str(result))

GetTables = True
grdTables.Rows = result + 1

If result Then
    For i = 0 To result - 1
        result = PEGetNthTableType(gJobno, i, tableInfo)
        If result = False Then
            result = PError()
            GetTables = False
            Exit Function
        End If
        result = PEGetNthTableLogonInfo(gJobno, i, tableLogOn)
        If result = False Then
            result = PError()
            GetTables = False
            Exit Function
        End If
        result = PEGetNthTableLocation(gJobno, i, tableLocation)
        If result = False Then
            result = PError()
            GetTables = False
            Exit Function
        End If

        'Add the data to grid
        grdTables.Row = i + 1
        grdTables.Col = 0
        grdTables.Text = tableInfo.DLLName
        grdTables.Col = 1
        grdTables.Text = tableInfo.DescriptiveName
        grdTables.Col = 2
        Select Case tableInfo.DBType
            Case PE_DT_STANDARD
                grdTables.Text = "Standard"
            Case PE_DT_SQL
                grdTables.Text = "SQL"
        End Select
        grdTables.Col = 3
```

```
                    grdTables.Text = tableLogOn.ServerName
                    grdTables.Col = 4
                    grdTables.Text = tableLogOn.DatabaseName
                    grdTables.Col = 5
                    grdTables.Text = tableLogOn.UserID
                    grdTables.Col = 6
                    grdTables.Text = tableLogOn.Password
                    grdTables.Col = 7
                    grdTables.Text = tableLocation.Location

            Next
        Else
            grdTables.Col = 0
            grdTables.Row = 1
            grdTables.Text = "None"
        End If

    End Function
```

14. Enter the following code in the **DblClick** event procedure of the
grdTables grid. Because some of the information about the report's tables
can be long strings (particularly path and filenames), the user can double-
click on any cell and have the full string appear in the status label at the
bottom of the form. The **colHeads** array is used to preface the string with
the name of the column. By using the array, you won't need to move the
cell selection to the top of the column to read the column name.

```
Private Sub grdTables_DblClick()

    'Check first to see if clicked on fixed row - ignore if so
    If grdTables.SelStartRow Then
        Ticker colHeads(grdTables.SelStartCol) & ": " & grdTables.Text, False
    End If
End Sub
```

15. Enter the following **PError** function procedure. Because the print engine
provides two functions for retrieving error information about a function
call, this function makes the necessary calls and presents a dialog box with
the error data.

```
Function PError()
    'Error occurred in a call to the Crystal DLL
    Dim PErrCode As Integer
    Dim PErrDesc As String * 255
    Dim errLen As Integer
    Dim result As Integer
    Dim hError As Long

    PErrCode = PEGetErrorCode(gJobno)
    result = PEGetErrorText(gJobno, hError, errLen)
    result = PEGetHandleString(hError, PErrDesc, errLen)
    MsgBox "Print engine error no. " & Trim(Str(PErrCode)) _
        & ": " & Trim(PErrDesc)
End Function
```

16. Enter the following two procedures in the `Timer` event procedure of the `tmrTicker` timer control and in the `Ticker Sub` procedure. Because some calls to print engine functions can take a bit of time, a spinning line character lets the user know that the computer has not frozen. This is particularly useful if the database used in the report is located somewhere out on a network.

The first procedure simply changes the character to simulate motion. The second procedure puts a status message into the status bar and enables or disables the timer control as appropriate.

```
Private Sub tmrTicker_Timer()
    Static Ticker As Integer

    Select Case Ticker
        Case 0
            lblTicker.Caption = "/"
            Ticker = 1
        Case 1
            lblTicker.Caption = "-"
            Ticker = 2
        Case 2
            lblTicker.Caption = "\"
            Ticker = 3
        Case 3
            lblTicker.Caption = "¦"
            Ticker = 0
    End Select

End Sub

Sub Ticker(captionMsg As String, tickerOn As Boolean)
    lblStatus.Caption = captionMsg
    If tickerOn Then
        tmrTicker.Enabled = True
    Else
        tmrTicker.Enabled = False
        lblTicker.Caption = ""
    End If
End Sub
```

17. Enter the following code in the `Click` event procedure of the `cmdQuit` command button, to provide an exit path for the program:

```
Private Sub cmdQuit_Click()
    End
End Sub
```

18. Enter the following code in the `Unload` event procedure of the form. Because each open print job is closed in the same procedure in which it is opened, all you need to do here is close the print engine, with a call to `PECloseEngine`.

```
Private Sub Form_Unload(Cancel As Integer)
    'Shut down the print engine
    PECloseEngine
End Sub
```

How It Works

There are two print engine functions that retrieve information about errors: `PEGetErrorCode` and `PEGetErrorText`. Most of the print engine functions return either `True` or `False` to indicate success or failure. The two error functions can then be called for more specific error information. Table 10.22 shows the different errors that the print engine can return through these two error functions.

Table 10.22. Crystal Reports print engine error messages.

CODE	DESCRIPTION
500	Not enough memory is available to complete the call.
501	You have specified a job number that does not exist.
502	You have specified a handle that does not exist.
503	The string you are calling with `PEGetHandleString` is too long for the buffer.
504	You have specified a report that does not exist in the path.
505	You have made the `PEStartPrintJob` call without specifying a destination.
506	You have tried to set an Nth filename that is out of range.
507	There is an error in the filename you specified.
508	The field number you specified is out of the existing range.
509	The program can't add the field name you specified.
510	The program can't add the formula name you specified.
511	You have specified a sort direction other than those allowed.
512	The print engine must be open for the call to be successful.
513	The printer driver for the printer you specified is missing.
514	The name you have specified for the export file already exists.
515	There is a formula error in the replacement formula text.
516	The group section you specified is now invalid in the report.
517	Only one application can access the print engine at a time.
519	No print window is available to make your call successful.
520	You are trying to start a print job that has already been started.
521	The summary field specified as a group sort field is invalid or nonexistent.
522	There are not enough Windows system resources to process the function.
523	You have specified an invalid group condition.
524	You tried to initiate printing while Crystal Reports was already printing a job.

continued on next page

continued from previous page

CODE	DESCRIPTION
525	There is something wrong with the report you are trying to open.
526	You haven't specified a default printer.
528	You have specified an invalid line number.
529	The program requires more room than is available on the disk.
530	The program is encountering another file problem besides disk full.
531	You have specified an incorrect password.
532	The database DLL is corrupt.
533	Something is wrong with the database you have specified.
534	The database DLL is corrupt.
535	You have attempted to log on using incomplete or incorrect session parameters.
536	You have attempted to log on using incomplete or incorrect logon parameters.
537	The table you have specified cannot be found.
538	There is an internal error.
539	You have specified an invalid date using the `PESetPrintDate` command.
540	The DLL required by your export call is either missing or out of date.
542	The previous page control cannot be used when you're already at the first page.
543	The next page control cannot be used when you're already at the last page of the report.
544	Access to the report file is denied.
546	The program can't open the report because OLE 2.0 cannot be loaded.
547	You have specified an invalid row or column field in your cross-tab report.
548	You are trying to run a cross-tab report without specifying a summarized field.
999	There is an internal error.

In this How-To, the return value is saved in a result variable; then a separate call is made to the `PError` procedure in the form:

```
result = PEGetNthSortField(...)
If result = False Then
    result = PError()
    Exit Function
End If
```

Another way to make the call is to use code of the following form:

```
If PEGetNthSortField(...) = False Then
    'Error-handling code
End If
```

Although the second form has the advantage of simplicity, the preceding form retains the result of the print engine function call for later reuse or review. Use whichever form makes sense in the context of your application.

Not all the print engine functions return success or failure through the return value of a function call. For some functions, the information sought is returned from the function. These functions return the count of something, such as tables or fields. You can still make a call to the print engine error functions, although more often than not, a **0** return value means failure of the particular print engine function. It could also mean that the report has **0** items of that type.

Comments

One glaring and unfortunate shortcoming of the library of print engine functions is its lack of a function that can retrieve the names of the tables used in a report. You were able to garner a great deal of information about the tables, but not their names nor whether a particular table was actually used in the report.

This last point is an interesting symptom of a quirk in the Crystal report files. All the tables available in a database specified in the report are included in the list of report tables, whether or not they are used in the report. You can go in and manually delete extraneous tables one by one (although there probably isn't a need to), but otherwise you don't know which tables are in use. This is the most robust of systems, but at least you can get at some of the information in a report file.

COMPLEXITY
BEGINNING

10.11 How do I...
Control the position of the Crystal print preview window?

Problem

My application needs to allow the user to customize the appearance of the Crystal Reports print preview window, including the location, size, and window elements. How can I give that control to the user and make sure that the choices made are valid?

Technique

Allowing your application or its user to make several choices at runtime is simple with the Crystal Reports control. It is a matter of making sure that the right options are set and setting the properties of the control at runtime. In this How-To, you will create a Visual Basic application that can print any Crystal report, allowing the user to have control over the appearance of the Crystal Reports print preview window.

Steps

Load and run the Visual Basic application WINDOW.VBP. When the Set Report Printing Options window appears, as shown in Figure 10.29, click the Select File button and select a report to print. Then change any of the other control settings to modify the print preview window location and size and the title of the window. You can also choose whether the window has a control box or Min or Max buttons. Click the Print Report button to preview the report in the customized window.

1. Start Visual Basic and create a new project in your work area. Save the default form as WINDOW.FRM and the project as WINDOW.VBP. Select Tools | Custom Controls from the Visual Basic main menu, and make sure that the Microsoft Common Dialog and Crystal Reports custom controls are selected.

2. Place the controls on the form as shown in Figure 10.29, and set the properties as listed in Table 10.23. Note that the common dialog is invisible at runtime, so place it anywhere that is convenient.

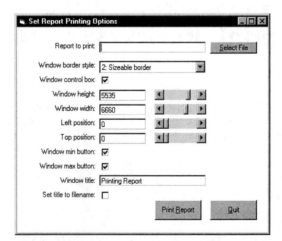

Figure 10.29. The Set Report Printing Options window (frmWindow).

Table 10.23. Objects and properties for WINDOW.FRM.

OBJECT	PROPERTY	SETTING
Form	Name	frmWindow
	Caption	"Set Report Printing Options"
CheckBox	Name	chkSetToFileName
	Alignment	1 'Right Justify
TextBox	Name	txtTitle
	Text	"Printing Report"
CheckBox	Name	chkMaxButton
	Alignment	1 'Right Justify
	Value	1 'Checked
CheckBox	Name	chkMinButton
	Alignment	1 'Right Justify
	Value	1 'Checked
HScrollBar	Name	hsbTop
HScrollBar	Name	hsbLeft
HScrollBar	Name	hsbWidth
HScrollBar	Name	hsbHeight
TextBox	Name	txtTop
TextBox	Name	txtLeft
TextBox	Name	txtWidth
TextBox	Name	txtHeight
CheckBox	Name	chkControlBox
	Alignment	1 'Right Justify
	Value	1 'Checked
ComboBox	Name	lstBorder
	Style	2 'Dropdown List
CommandButton	Name	cmdPrint
	Caption	"Print &Report"
CommandButton	Name	cmdQuit
	Caption	"&Quit"
TextBox	Name	txtReportToPrint
CommandButton	Name	cmdNewReport
	Caption	"&Select File"
Label	Name	Label11
	Alignment	1 'Right Justify
	Caption	"Set title to filename:"

continued on next page

continued from previous page

OBJECT	PROPERTY	SETTING
Label	Name	Label9
	Alignment	1 'Right Justify
	Caption	"Window title:"
Label	Name	Label8
	Alignment	1 'Right Justify
	Caption	"Window max button:"
Label	Name	Label7
	Alignment	1 'Right Justify
	Caption	"Window min button:"
Label	Name	Label6
	Alignment	1 'Right Justify
	Caption	"Top position:"
Label	Name	Label5
	Alignment	1 'Right Justify
	Caption	"Left position:"
Label	Name	Label4
	Alignment	1 'Right Justify
	Caption	"Window width:"
Label	Name	Label3
	Alignment	1 'Right Justify
	Caption	"Window height:"
Label	Name	Label2
	Alignment	1 'Right Justify
	Caption	"Window control box:"
Label	Name	Label1
	Alignment	1 'Right Justify
	Caption	"Window border style:"
Label	Name	Label10
	Alignment	1 'Right Justify
	Caption	"Report to print:"
CommonDialog	Name	cdFileName
	DialogTitle	""
	Filter	""
CrystalReport	Name	CrystalReport1
	ReportFileName	""
	Destination	0
	SelectionFormula	""

OBJECT	PROPERTY	SETTING
	GroupSelectionFormula	""
	Connect	""
	UserName	""

3. Enter the following code into the declarations section of the form. To avoid problems, **Option Explicit** tells Visual Basic to make sure that you declare all variables and objects before using them.

```
Option Explicit
```

4. Enter the following code in the **Load** event procedure of the form. This procedure initializes the controls on the form. It begins by loading the **lstBorder** list box with the range of settings for the **WindowBorderStyle** control, initializing both the list box and the Crystal Reports control to the sizable border option.

Next, defaults are set for the window size properties. To start, set the default Crystal Reports print preview window to the same size as the **frmWindow** form. Default to show the window at the upper-left corner of the screen, and set the ranges of values for the horizontal scrollbars as detailed here:

✔ Set each of the minimums to **0**.

✔ Set the range of each scrollbar to the full height or width of the screen, as appropriate.

✔ Set the **LargeChange** property to 1/100th of the range.

✔ Set the **SmallChange** property to 1/1000th of the range.

Visual Basic uses twips as the screen unit of measurement, and the Crystal Reports custom control uses pixels, which causes difficulties. Fortunately, Visual Basic has two **Screen** object properties that give the conversion between the two measurements: **TwipsPerPixelX** (horizontal) and **TwipsPerPixelY** (vertical).

Finally, the procedure centers the form.

```
Private Sub Form_Load()
    'Build the list control contents
    lstBorder.AddItem "0: No border"
    lstBorder.AddItem "1: Fixed single line border"
    lstBorder.AddItem "2: Sizeable border"
    lstBorder.AddItem "3: Fixed double border"
    lstBorder.ListIndex = 2
    CrystalReport1.WindowBorderStyle = lstBorder.ListIndex

    'Set the window height and width equal to Me
```

continued on next page

continued from previous page

```
    'and the maximums to the screen size
    hsbHeight.Value = Me.Height
    hsbHeight.Max = Screen.Height
    hsbHeight.LargeChange = hsbHeight.Max / 100
    hsbHeight.SmallChange = hsbHeight.Max / 1000
    txtHeight.Text = hsbHeight.Value
    CrystalReport1.WindowHeight = txtHeight.Text / Screen.TwipsPerPixelY

    hsbWidth.Value = Me.Width
    hsbWidth.Max = Screen.Width
    hsbWidth.LargeChange = hsbWidth.Max / 100
    hsbWidth.SmallChange = hsbWidth.Max / 1000
    txtWidth.Text = hsbWidth.Value
    CrystalReport1.WindowWidth = txtWidth.Text / Screen.TwipsPerPixelX

    'Set the initial window position to the left side of screen
    hsbLeft.Value = 0
    hsbLeft.Max = 0.9 * Screen.Width
    hsbLeft.LargeChange = hsbLeft.Max / 100
    hsbLeft.SmallChange = hsbLeft.Max / 1000
    txtLeft.Text = hsbLeft.Value
    CrystalReport1.WindowLeft = txtLeft.Text

    hsbTop.Value = 0
    txtTop.Text = hsbTop.Value
    hsbTop.LargeChange = hsbTop.Max / 100
    hsbTop.SmallChange = hsbTop.Max / 1000
    CrystalReport1.WindowTop = txtTop.Text

    CrystalReport1.WindowControlBox = chkControlBox.Value
    CrystalReport1.WindowMinButton = chkMinButton.Value
    CrystalReport1.WindowMaxButton = chkMaxButton.Value
    CrystalReport1.WindowTitle = txtTitle.Text


    'Center the form
    frmWindow.Move (Screen.Width - frmWindow.Width) / 2, _
        (Screen.Height - frmWindow.Height) / 2
End Sub
```

5. Enter the following code in the **cmdNewReport**'s **Click** procedure. The procedure activates the common dialog File Open window so that the user can specify a report file to use. After the window is closed and a file has been selected, the procedure puts the filename into the **txtReportToPrint** text box and updates the **ReportFileName** property of the Crystal Reports control.

```
Private Sub cmdNewReport_Click()
    cdFileName.DefaultExt = "rpt"
    cdFileName.DialogTitle = "Select Report File"
    cdFileName.Filter = "Report File (*.rpt)¦*.rpt¦All Files (*.*)¦*.*"
    cdFileName.ShowOpen
    txtReportToPrint.Text = Lcase$(cdFileName.FileName)
    CrystalReport1.ReportFileName = txtReportToPrint.Text
End Sub
```

6. Put this code into the Change event procedure of the `txtReportToPrint` text box. Any time the selected report filename changes, the caption of the command button changes to reflect whether there is a file in the text box. At the same time, the `ReportFileName` property of the Crystal Reports control is updated.

```
Private Sub txtReportToPrint_Change()
    'Contents have changed, so reset cmdNewReport caption
    If Len(txtReportToPrint.Text) Then
        cmdNewReport.Caption = "&Change File"
        CrystalReport1.ReportFileName = txtReportToPrint.Text
    Else
        cmdNewReport.Caption = "&Select File"
        CrystalReport1.ReportFileName = ""
    End If
End Sub
```

7. Enter the following code in the Click event of the `lstBorder` list box. Any time the selection in the list box changes, the `WindowBorderStyle` property is updated so that it is ready to print a report.

```
Private Sub lstBorder_Click()
    CrystalReport1.WindowBorderStyle = lstBorder.ListIndex
End Sub
```

8. Enter the following three Click event procedures. When any of the check boxes changes, the new value is immediately entered into the applicable Crystal Reports control property.

```
Private Sub chkControlBox_Click()
    CrystalReport1.WindowControlBox = chkControlBox.Value
End Sub

Private Sub chkMaxButton_Click()
    CrystalReport1.WindowMaxButton = chkMaxButton.Value
End Sub

Private Sub chkMinButton_Click()
    CrystalReport1.WindowMinButton = chkMinButton.Value
End Sub
```

9. Enter the following procedures in the Change event procedure of the different horizontal scrollbars. Any time the value of one of the scrollbars changes, the related text box changes and the new value is used to reset the related property of the Crystal Reports control. It might be more efficient to use the **LostFocus** event to update the Crystal Reports control, but because you need to use the **Change** event to update the text box anyway, you should do the update here.

```
Private Sub hsbHeight_Change()
    txtHeight.Text = hsbHeight.Value
    CrystalReport1.WindowHeight = hsbHeight.Value / Screen.TwipsPerPixelY
End Sub

Private Sub hsbLeft_Change()
    txtLeft.Text = hsbLeft.Value
    CrystalReport1.WindowLeft = hsbLeft.Value / Screen.TwipsPerPixelX
End Sub

Private Sub hsbTop_Change()
    txtTop.Text = hsbTop.Value
    CrystalReport1.WindowTop = hsbTop.Value / Screen.TwipsPerPixelY
End Sub

Private Sub hsbWidth_Change()
    txtWidth.Text = hsbWidth.Value
    CrystalReport1.WindowWidth = hsbWidth.Value / Screen.TwipsPerPixelX
End Sub
```

10. In this case, it makes things simpler to use the **LostFocus** event of a Visual Basic control. Enter this code into the **LostFocus** event procedure of the **txtTitle** text box. Any time the focus leaves this text box, the **WindowTitle** property of the Crystal Reports control is updated.

```
Private Sub txtTitle_LostFocus()
    CrystalReport1.WindowTitle = txtTitle.Text
End Sub
```

11. Enter the following code into the **Click** event of the **chkSetToFileName** check box control. This option provides a handy way for the user to change the title on the report window to the filename of the selected report. Because the text box changes, update the **WindowTitle** property immediately.

```
Private Sub chkSetToFileName_Click()
    txtTitle.Text = txtReportToPrint.Text
    CrystalReport1.WindowTitle = txtTitle.Text
End Sub
```

12. Enter the following code into the **Click** event of the **cmdPrint** command button. This procedure actually starts printing the report to the Crystal Reports print preview window. If no report filename is selected, a message box says so and ends the procedure. Otherwise, after error handling is turned on, the report is printed.

Error handling while using the Crystal Reports custom control is done by the standard Visual Basic error-handling routines. In this procedure, the Crystal Reports error is displayed and the procedure is ended:

```
Private Sub cmdPrint_Click()
    'A report must be selected
    If Len(txtReportToPrint.Text) Then
        On Error GoTo CrystalError
        CrystalReport1.Action = 1
    Else
        MsgBox "Please select a report to run first."
    End If
OuttaHere:
    Exit Sub

CrystalError:
    MsgBox "Error " & Err & ": " & Err.Description, vbCritical, "Crystal Error"
    Resume OuttaHere
End Sub
```

13. Add the following code to the `Click` event of the `cmdQuit` command button to provide an exit point from the program:

```
Private Sub cmdQuit_Click()
    End
End Sub
```

How It Works

This program just sets up controls to contain the properties of the control window's appearance and resets the properties when the contents of the controls change. That's all there is to running a Crystal report from a Visual Basic application using the Crystal Reports control!

Comments

When you include a Crystal reporting subsystem in your application, the window positioning functions can be quite valuable in improving system appearance. Few things are more aggravating than losing sight of your work while a potentially less-important part of the system insists on dominating the screen.

COMPLEXITY
INTERMEDIATE

10.12 How do I...
Generate reports using user-entered variables?

Problem

Each time I print a report, I need to change elements of the report, such as the record sort order, the heading, and the name of the person running the report. How can I run a report through a Visual Basic application and change selected elements of the report?

Technique

This How-To takes advantage of three properties that the Crystal Reports custom control provides to modify the conditions under which a report is printed at runtime in a Visual Basic application. It is simply a matter of setting the properties of the control.

Steps

Load and run the Visual Basic application MAILLIST.VBP. From the Print Sorted Mailing List window (see Figure 10.30), select a report type to print (City, State, or Zip) and either enter a particular value to use in selecting records or leave the field blank to include all records. Select a page number format to be used, and then click the Print Report button to preview the report.

1. You'll start by creating a simple report that you can modify when printing through Visual Basic (see Figure 10.31). Start Crystal Reports, and start a new report by clicking the New Report toolbar button or selecting File | New from the main menu. Click on Standard when the Create New Report Gallery appears.

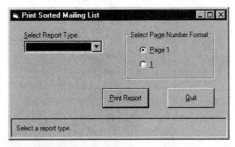

Figure 10.30. The Print Sorted Mailing List window (frmMailList).

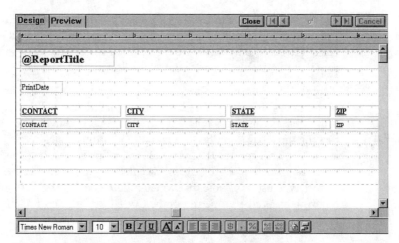

Figure 10.31. The Crystal Reports design window for a mailing list report.

2. Click on Data File when the Create Report Expert appears. Use the dialog box to find the MAIL.MDB Access database file installed in the How-To.A12 directory. Click Done to close the dialog box.

3. From the Fields tab, add the `Contact`, `City`, `State`, `Zip`, and `Week Day` fields from the Mailing List table.

4. Preview the report and save the report file, calling it MAILLIST.RPT.

5. Because you want to be able to change the report heading from the Visual Basic application, enter the heading as a formula with a default value. That way, if the application doesn't change the title, something relatively meaningful will print. Select Insert | Text Field from the Crystal Reports main menu, or click the Insert Text Field button on the toolbar. Name the formula field `ReportTitle`, and enter this formula:

```
'Mailing List'
```

Format the title to be 14-point font, bold by using the font toolbar at the bottom of the Crystal Reports design window.

6. Insert the page number formula field `@PageFooter` by selecting Insert | Formula Field from the main menu or clicking the Insert Formula Field button on the toolbar. Enter this formula:

```
"Page " + ToText(PageNumber,0)
```

7. That's all there is to the report. Note that you didn't set up any sorting at all, nor any group sections. Next, you'll see how to make changes through a Visual Basic application. Remember to save the report file, calling it MAILLIST.RPT.

8. Start Visual Basic and create a new project in your work area. Save the default form as MAILLIST.FRM, and save the project as MAILLIST.VBP. Select Project | Components from the Visual Basic main menu, and make sure that the Crystal Reports control is selected.

9. Place the controls on the form as shown in Figure 10.30, and set the properties as shown in Table 10.24. Note that the Crystal Reports control is invisible at runtime, so place it anywhere that is convenient. Note also that the three page-number-format option buttons make up a control array. The label control lblInstruction and text box txtValue have their Visible properties set to False; place them in the open area below the Report Type list box. Note that you are "hard coding" the name of the report to use in the properties of the Crystal Reports control; change its location to wherever the report is located on your drive.

Table 10.24. Objects and properties for MAILLIST.FRM.

OBJECT	PROPERTY	SETTING
Form	Name	frmMailList
	Caption	"Print Sorted Mailing List"
CommandButton	Name	cmdQuit
	Caption	"&Quit"
CommandButton	Name	cmdReport
	Caption	"&Print Report"
	Default	-1 'True
TextBox	Name	txtValue
	Visible	0 'False
Frame	Name	Frame1
	Caption	"Select Page Number Format"
OptionButton	Name	optPageNoType
	Caption	"page &one"
OptionButton	Name	optPageNoType
	Caption	"&1"
OptionButton	Name	optPageNoType
	Caption	"&Page 1"
	Value	-1 'True
PictureBox	Name	Picture1
	Align	2 'Align Bottom
Label	Name	lblStatus
ComboBox	Name	lstReportType
	Style	2 'Dropdown List

OBJECT	PROPERTY	SETTING
Label	Name	Label1
	Caption	"&Select Report Type:"
Label	Name	lblInstruction
	AutoSize	-1 'True
	Visible	0 'False
CrystalReport	Name	CrystalReport1
	ReportFileName	"C:\VB\REPORT\MAILLIST.RPT"
	Destination	0 'To Print Preview Window
	SelectionFormula	""
	GroupSelectionFormula	""
	Connect	""
	UserName	""

10. Enter the following code in the **Load** event procedure of the form. This procedure initializes the **lstReportType** list box to the types of reports available and sets the default page format as "Page 1."

```
Private Sub Form_Load()
    'Load the lstReportType list box
    lstReportType.Clear
    lstReportType.AddItem "City"
    lstReportType.AddItem "State"
    lstReportType.AddItem "Zip"

    lblStatus.Caption = "Select a report type."

    'Set the report file name
    CrystalReport1.ReportFileName = App.Path & "\MAILLIST.RPT"
    'Set the initial value of the page format
    optPageNoType_Click (0)
End Sub
```

11. Add the following code to the **lstReportType Click** event procedure. When a particular report type is selected, the text of the **lblInstruction** label is set to prompt for the appropriate value, and it and the **txtValue** text box are made visible. If the text of the **lstReportType** field is empty, the **Visible** property of the two controls is set to **False**.

```
Private Sub lstReportType_Click()
    If Len(lstReportType.Text) Then
        Select Case lstReportType.Text
            Case "City"
                lblInstruction.Caption = "&Enter the City name:"
                lblStatus.Caption = "Enter a city name or blank for all."
            Case "State"
                lblInstruction.Caption = "&Enter the State name:"
```

continued on next page

continued from previous page

```
                        lblStatus.Caption = "Enter a state name or blank for all."
                Case "Zip"
                        lblInstruction.Caption = "&Enter the Zip Code:"
                        lblStatus.Caption = "Enter a zip code or blank for all."
        End Select

        txtValue.Text = ""

        lblInstruction.Visible = True
        txtValue.Visible = True

        txtValue.SetFocus

    Else
        lblInstruction.Visible = False
        txtValue.Text = ""
        txtValue.Visible = False
    End If

End Sub
```

12. Add the following code to the **Click** event procedure of the
optPageNoType option button control array. Recall that you entered the
page number in the report footer as a formula field **@PageFooter**. You also
set the default formula to print a page number in the form "page one." Any
time the report is printed through the Crystal Reports program, the page
number appears in the same form. This Visual Basic program simply sets
the **@PageFooter** formula to whatever formula you want, in this case, one
of the three formats shown in the option button group, "Page 1," "1," or
"page one."

```
Private Sub optPageNoType_Click(Index As Integer)
    'Set the page number format
    Select Case Index
        Case 0
            CrystalReport1.Formulas(1) = "PageFooter= 'Page ' + _
                ToText(PageNumber, 0)"
        Case 1
            CrystalReport1.Formulas(1) = "PageFooter= ToText(PageNumber, 0)"
    End Select

End Sub
```

13. Add the following code to the **Click** event procedure of the **cmdReport**
command button. Now that the relevant properties of the report have
been set, it is time to actually print it. In contrast to previous How-To's, a
different technique for setting the properties is demonstrated here. They
are all set at once at print time, instead of as they are changed on the form
(with the exception of the page number format). Use whichever technique
works best in the context of your application.

Three different types of reports can be printed using this program:

✔ For one city or all cities, sorted by city and zip.

✔ For one state or all states, sorted by state, city, and zip.

✔ For one zip code or all zip codes, sorted by zip.

Any of the initial digits of a zip code can be entered to obtain a zip code list; the program selects all the zip codes that begin with those starting characters.

For each selected report type, this procedure first sets the SelectionFormula, which filters the records for the particular city, state, or zip code. If no value was entered, the records for all of that particular group are filtered. Then the formulas you built into the report are reset as appropriate. In the case of a city report, for example, the report title formula @ReportTitle is set to "Mailing List for City of *<city name>*" or "Full City Mailing List" if no city name was entered. Finally, the SortFields array of fields for sorting is set. In each case, three elements of the array are set, clearing any elements that are not used for the particular report. If you didn't clear unused array elements, they would remain set for the next report unless explicitly overwritten.

```vb
Private Sub cmdReport_Click()
    Dim ZipDigits As String

    lblStatus.Caption = "Setting report options. Please wait..."
    DoEvents

    Select Case lstReportType.Text
      Case "City"
          'Set the filter and title for the report
          If Len(txtValue) Then
              CrystalReport1.SelectionFormula = "{Mailing LIst.CITY}= '" _
                  & txtValue & "'"
              CrystalReport1.Formulas(0) = _
                  "ReportTitle= 'Mailing List for City of " & txtValue & "'"
          Else
              CrystalReport1.SelectionFormula = ""
              CrystalReport1.Formulas(0) = _
                  "ReportTitle= 'Full City Mailing List'"
          End If

          'Set the sort order and clear second element
          CrystalReport1.SortFields(0) = "+{Mailing LIst.CITY}"
          CrystalReport1.SortFields(1) = "+{Mailing LIst.ZIP}"
          CrystalReport1.SortFields(2) = ""

      Case "State"
          'Set the filter and title for the report
          If Len(txtValue) Then
```

continued on next page

continued from previous page

```
            CrystalReport1.SelectionFormula = _
                "{Mailing LIst.STATE}= '" & txtValue & "'"
            CrystalReport1.Formulas(0) = _
                "ReportTitle= 'Mailing List for State of " & txtValue & "'"
        Else
            CrystalReport1.SelectionFormula = _
                "{Mailing LIst.STATE}= {Mailing LIst.STATE}"
            CrystalReport1.Formulas(0) = _
                "ReportTitle= 'Full State Mailing List'"
        End If

        'Set the sort order
        CrystalReport1.SortFields(0) = "+{Mailing LIst.STATE}"
        CrystalReport1.SortFields(1) = "+{Mailing LIst.CITY}"
        CrystalReport1.SortFields(2) = "+{Mailing LIst.ZIP}"

    Case "Zip"
        'Set the filter and title for the report
        If Len(txtValue) Then
            ZipDigits = Trim(Str(Len(txtValue)))
            CrystalReport1.SelectionFormula = _
                "{Mailing LIst.ZIP}[1 to " _
                & ZipDigits & "]= '" & txtValue & "'"
            CrystalReport1.Formulas(0) = _
                "ReportTitle= 'Mailing List for Zip Code " & txtValue & "'"
        Else
            CrystalReport1.SelectionFormula = _
                "{Mailing LIst.ZIP}= {Mailing LIst.ZIP}"
            CrystalReport1.Formulas(0) = _
                "ReportTitle= 'Full Zip Code Mailing List'"
        End If

        'Set the sort order
        CrystalReport1.SortFields(0) = "+{Mailing LIst.ZIP}"
        CrystalReport1.SortFields(1) = ""
        CrystalReport1.SortFields(2) = ""
    End Select

    'Print the report
    lblStatus.Caption = "Printing the report. Please wait..."
    DoEvents
    CrystalReport1.Action = 1

    lblStatus.Caption = "Enter new selections and print or quit."
    DoEvents

End Sub
```

14. Add the following code to the Click event of the cmdQuit command button to provide an exit point from the program:

```
Private Sub cmdQuit_Click()
    End
End Sub
```

How It Works

This How-To takes advantage of properties of the Crystal Reports custom control to modify the design of the report at runtime. These changes stay in effect only for the lifetime of the Crystal Reports custom control in the form, and they are not saved in the report file itself. This means that if the form with the control is unloaded, the options revert to the settings in the report until you explicitly set them again. This "stickiness" trait of the control makes it critical to set any unused formulas or fields to a null string if they aren't required for the current operation.

If you specified any particular sorting order in the report design, setting the particular formula or field through your application would replace that formula for this report. So if a report has five formula fields and you change only two, the other three fields remain as they were set in the report.

Three formula and field properties of the custom control were used in this How-To:

✔ `SelectionFormula`: There is one selection formula in each report. But because it is a Crystal Reports formula, it can be as complex as you care to make it. In this How-To, the `City`, `State`, and `Zip` fields of the report are set to the particular values entered; if no values are entered, they are set to empty strings so that all records print.

✔ `Formulas`: Any formula contained in the report file can be changed at runtime through the Crystal Reports control. In this How-To, the `@ReportTitle` and `@PageFooter` formulas were changed.

✔ `SortFields`: This property resets the record sort order of the report. A similar `GroupSortFields` property wasn't used in this program, but it can be used to reset the sorting order of any groups in the report. Both of these properties are implemented as arrays so that fields entered into the array are sorted in the order of the 0th element, 1st element, and so on.

It is important to remember that the format of any formulas set in Visual Basic must be in the Crystal Reports format of formulas, not Visual Basic's statement format. This requires placing the entire formula in double quotation marks and placing any literals used in the formula in single quotation marks. This is the reason for the convoluted form of this setting for the `Formulas(0)` property:

```
"ReportTitle= 'Mailing List for City of " & txtValue & "'"
```

Comments

This How-To has shown the power of Crystal Reports to improve your development by setting different OCX control properties. The creative combination of multiple control properties can help you deliver high-quality results to your customers.

CHAPTER 11
SECURITY AND
MULTIUSER ACCESS

11

SECURITY AND MULTIUSER ACCESS

How do I...

When multiple users have access to a database, two issues become overwhelmingly important:

✔ Ensuring that users accessing the database simultaneously do not inadvertently interfere with each other's operations.

✔ Ensuring that only authorized users have access to the data.

This chapter presents techniques for handling both of these issues. The first 3 How-To's deal with the issue of simultaneous multiuser access, and the remaining 10 How-To's show you how to use Visual Basic to implement security with the Jet database engine.

11.1 Open a Database So That Others Cannot Access It While the User Is Working with It

When your application will run in a multiuser environment, the application and the Jet database engine need to work together to control access to common data. This How-To shows how to implement the most exclusive method of access to multiuser resources, locking an entire database.

11.2 Open a Table So That Others Cannot Access It While the User Is Working with It

Most of the time, locking an entire database results in limited functionality of the client software that needs to access that database. In this How-To, you will learn how to gain exclusive read and write access to individual tables.

11.3 Work with Locked Records

If you decide not to lock an entire database or table for exclusive use, the Jet engine takes over and locks clusters of records at a time as users access them. This How-To shows how to work with the Jet engine to implement record locking in your application.

11.4 Work with Secured Microsoft Access Database Files

Microsoft Access database files have a sophisticated set of security features that can be turned on simply by password-protecting the Admin account. The security features are implemented at two levels: the individual database file, and the workgroup. The workgroup is defined by a system database. This How-To shows you how to work with secured Microsoft Access databases.

11.5 Assign Permissions for Database Objects

Each table and query in a Microsoft Access database file has associated with it a set of permissions for each user in the workgroup. This How-To shows you how to read and change permissions for users.

11.6 Change Ownership of Database Objects

The user who creates a table or query in a Microsoft Access database becomes its owner. With the appropriate permissions, you can change the owner of a table or query. This How-To shows you the technique to accomplish this task.

11.7 Change or Delete Database Passwords

The system administrator occasionally needs the ability to changes a user's password, and sometimes remove it all together. This How-To shows how to accomplish this job through Visual Basic.

11.8 Use a Single Password for Data Access for All Users

You know that you can set individual passwords for each user in a workgroup, but what if you simply want to put a password on the database itself? This How-To shows you exactly how to do just that.

11.9 Add New Users to a System Database

A system database includes an entry for each user in the workgroup. This How-To shows you how to create new users and add them to that workgroup.

11.10 Define New Groups in a System Database

As the need to add new users comes about, the need to add new groups to a system database also arises. This How-To shows you how to add new groups to a system database using Visual Basic.

11.11 Add Users to Groups and Delete Users from Groups

This How-To shows you how to add and remove any user in the system database to and from any group.

11.12 Track User Activity in a Database

It is nice to know which users did what to your database. Sometimes we wish there was a way they had to sign what they did. The How-To will show you how to create an audit trail with any particular recordset to keep track of user activity in an Access database.

11.13 Create and Use an Encrypted Database

This How-To will show you how to create and convert encrypted databases so that others cannot access them with a product other than Access or Visual Basic.

11.1 How do I...

Open a database so that others cannot access it while the user is working with it?

Problem

I have a database that I need to access from my application. It is important that no other user can access the database if my application is running, even if they are using the same project I am. How can I ensure that only one instance of my program can access the database at a time?

Technique

Using the Microsoft Jet engine, shared data access is the default data mode. In this mode, the Jet engine takes care of page locking of the database. To open the database exclusively, you must explicitly state that this is your intention by passing a true value as the second parameter of the `OpenDatabase` method.

Steps

The Exclusive project is designed to illustrate the two distinct data modes used when opening a database, exclusive and shared. Open the Exclusive.vbp project and compile it to an EXE file. Invoke this executable twice to create two instances of the application. You should see the USER form opened twice, as shown in Figure 11.1. To open the database exclusively, click the Open Exclusive command button, or to open the database using the shared data mode, click the Open Shared command button. Notice the combinations permitted when opening the database with the two instances of the Exclusive project. You can open the database exclusively only if no other user has the database open at all, and you can open the database shared only if no other user has the database opened exclusively. To close the database, click the Close Database command button.

1. Create a new project and call it Exclusive.vbp. Change the properties of the default form, `Form1`, to those listed in Table 11.1, and save it as frmExclusive.frm.

Figure 11.1. Two instances of the Exclusive project.

Table 11.1. Objects and properties for the Exclusive project.

OBJECT	PROPERTY	SETTING
Form	Name	frmExclusive
	Caption	"USER"
Command button	Name	cmdOpenExclusive
	Caption	"Open &Exclusive"
Command button	Name	cmdOpenShared
	Caption	"Open &Shared"
Command button	Name	cmdCloseDatabase
	Caption	"&Close Database"
Command button	Name	cmdExit
	Caption	"E&xit"
	Cancel	-1 'True
	Default	-1 'True
Label	Name	lblDBStatusLabel
	Caption	"Database Status"
Label	Name	lblDBStatus
	Caption	" "

2. Enter the following form-level variable and constant declarations to be used throughout the project:

```
Option Explicit

' this is the database object variable used throughout this project
Private db As Database

' these are private constants used to indicate the desired state
' of the database when opened
Private Const OPEN_EXCLUSIVE = True
Private Const OPEN_SHARED = False
```

3. Now enter the code to initialize the `frmExclusive` form to display the database as closed by calling the `cmdCloseDatabase_Click` event.

```
Private Sub Form_Initialize()

    ' when the form is initialized, ensure that the proper states of
    ' the command buttons and labels are set by calling the Close
    ' Database command button's click event
    cmdCloseDatabase_Click

End Sub
```

4. Code both the `cmdOpenExclusive_Click` and the `cmdOpenShared_Click` events with a call to the `OpenDB` procedure, passing the appropriate form-level constant to indicate the data mode desired by the user.

```
Private Sub cmdOpenExclusive_Click()

    ' call the OpenDB procedure of this project, passing the
    ' OPEN_EXCLUSIVE constant (this constant holds the value of TRUE)
    OpenDB OPEN_EXCLUSIVE

End Sub

Private Sub cmdOpenShared_Click()

    ' call the OpenDB procedure of this project, passing the
    ' OPEN_SHARED constant (this constant holds the value of FALSE)
    OpenDB OPEN_SHARED

End Sub
```

5. When closing the database, set the **db** object variable to nothing, and set the command button **Enabled** properties to the correct state, allowing the user only to open the database, because it is now closed. The code for the Close Database command button appears here:

```
Private Sub cmdCloseDatabase_Click()

    ' set the database object variable to nothing, which is
    ' the equivalent of closing the database
    Set db = Nothing

    ' change the label that displays the database status to closed
    lblDBStatus = "CLOSED"

    ' only allow the user to open the database and not close it
    cmdOpenExclusive.Enabled = True
    cmdOpenShared.Enabled = True
    cmdCloseDatabase.Enabled = False

End Sub
```

6. Enter the code for the Exit command button. This first calls the Close Database click event of the command button to set the database object to nothing, unloading the project afterward to terminate the project.

```
Private Sub cmdExit_Click()

    ' call the close database command button click event to ensure
    ' that the database is closed before we terminate the project
    cmdCloseDatabase_Click

    ' end the application by calling Unload
    Unload Me

End Sub
```

7. Next, enter the code for the OpenDB procedure used to open the database for either exclusive or shared mode. If the user decides to open the database exclusively, the OPEN_EXCLUSIVE constant is passed to this procedure and onto the OpenDatabase method of the database object. This constant holds the value of True and opens the database exclusively. The other choice, OPEN_SHARED, passes a value of False to the OpenDatabase method.

```
Private Sub OpenDB(bDataMode As Boolean)

' if any error is encountered, call the code specified by the
' ERR_OpenDB label
On Error GoTo ERR_OpenDB:

    Dim sDBName As String

    ' on slower machines, this may take a moment; therefore,
    ' we will change the mousepointer to an hourglass to indicate
    ' that the project is still working
    Screen.MousePointer = vbHourglass

    ' retrieve the database name and path from the ReadINI module
    sDBName = DBPath

    ' open the database using the desired data mode specified by the user
    ' if bDataMode = OPEN_EXCLUSIVE then the value of bDataMode is TRUE,
    ' telling the OpenDatabase method to open the database exclusively;
    ' otherwise, OPEN_SHARED = FALSE, opening the database in a shared mode
    Set db = dbengine.Workspaces(0).OpenDatabase(sDBName, bDataMode)

    ' if we are at this point, then the database was opened succesfully,
    ' now display the appropriate label depending on the data mode selected
    Select Case bDataMode

        Case OPEN_EXCLUSIVE:
            lblDBStatus = "OPEN: EXCLUSIVE"

        Case OPEN_SHARED:
            lblDBStatus = "OPEN: SHARED"
```

continued on next page

continued from previous page

```
    End Select

    ' only allow the user to close that database, and do not allow
    ' opening of the database again
    cmdOpenExclusive.Enabled = False
    cmdOpenShared.Enabled = False
    cmdCloseDatabase.Enabled = True

    ' set the mousepointer to the default icon
    Screen.MousePointer = vbDefault

Exit Sub

ERR_OpenDB:

    ' set the mousepointer to the default icon
    Screen.MousePointer = vbDefault

    ' call the DatabaseError procedure, passing the Err object, which
    ' describes the error that has just occurred
    DatabaseError Err

End Sub
```

8. To finish this project, enter the code that is used to respond to errors opening the database. This code is as follows:

```
Private Sub DatabaseError(oErr As ErrObject)

    Dim sMessage As String

    ' these are the constant values used to represent the two errors
    ' that we are going to trap in this code
    Const DB_OPEN = 3356    ' database already open in shared mode
    Const DB_IN_USE = 3045  ' database already open exclusively

    With oErr

        ' select the appropriate code depending upon the error number
        Select Case .Number

            ' attempted to open the database exclusively, but it is
            ' already open in shared mode
            Case DB_OPEN:
                sMessage = "You cannot open the database exclusively " _
                        & "because it is already opened by another user."

            ' attempted to open the database either exclusively or
            ' shared, but it is opened exclusively by another user
            Case DB_IN_USE:
                sMessage = "You cannot open the database because it is " _
                        & "opened exclusively by another user."

            ' unexpected error: display the error number and description
            ' for the user
            Case Else
```

```
                sMessage = "Error #" & .Number & ": " & .Description

        End Select

    End With

    ' display the message for the user
    MsgBox sMessage, vbExclamation, "DATABASE ERROR"

    ' ensure that the database is closed because of the error, and
    ' properly set all the command button enabled properties as well as
    ' the status label
    cmdCloseDatabase_Click

End Sub
```

How It Works

When you open an Access database exclusively in one instance of the Exclusive project, assuming that the database is not opened by any other project, the Jet engine indicates that no other application can open the database by putting codes in the LDB file named after your database. In the case of this project, we use the ORDERS.MDB database. The file named ORDERS.LDB indicates how the database is opened and by whom.

Comments

This project uses an all-or-nothing concept when locking the data from other users. Either the data can be accessed by others or it cannot. Sometimes this is too general of a technique to use when developing a multiuser application. In How-To 11.2, we will use table locking to allow more flexible manageability of our database.

COMPLEXITY
BEGINNING

11.2 How do I...

Open a table so that others cannot access it while the user is working with it?

Problem

My application accesses shared data through the Jet engine. The default record-locking scheme that Jet uses works great for many instances. I need advanced record locking on particular tables so that others cannot access the entire table when my application does. How do I open a table with exclusive access?

Technique

By default, the recordset that you add will have shared rights to other users unless you explicitly request otherwise. You can indicate what kind of permissions you will grant other users when accessing that table.

The syntax for the `OpenRecordset` method is

```
Set rs = db.OpenRecordset(TableName, dbOpenTable, Options)
```

where `rs` is your recordset object variable, `db` is your database object variable, and `TableName` is the name of a valid table in the `db` object. The second parameter, `dbOpenTable`, is the type of recordset to be used. This parameter can be replaced with `dbOpenDynaset`, `dbOpenSnapshot`, `dbOpenDynamic`, or `dbOpenForwardOnly`. The valid options are listed in Table 11.2.

Table 11.2. Options for the `OpenRecordset` method.

OPTION	DESCRIPTION
dbDenyRead	Deny read permissions to other users
dbDenyWrite	Deny write permissions to other users

By using the `dbDenyRead` and `dbDenyWrite` options, we can open a table exclusively or with partial sharing rights to other users.

Steps

Open and compile the TableLocker.vbp project. Create two instances of the TableLocker project by double-clicking its icon twice from Windows Explorer. Move one form down to reveal the other (they start up in the same position). You should see the forms shown in Figure 11.2.

Figure 11.2. Two instances of the TableLocker project.

You can set the permissions assigned to opening the table by using the two check boxes on the form, and then pressing the Open Table command button. You can add records and then close the table by pressing the appropriate command buttons.

Experiment with opening the table with the two instances of the project. If you open the table with exclusive rights (deny read access) with one instance and then attempt to open it with the other in any way, you will be unsuccessful. When this happens, the application asks whether you want to open the table with Read Only access. If this is possible, the table will open but deny you the right to add records.

1. Create a new project and save it as TableLocker.vbp. Edit Form1 to include the objects and properties listed in Table 11.3, and save it as frmTableLocker.vbp.

Table 11.3. Objects and properties for the Exclusive project.

OBJECT	PROPERTY	SETTING
Form	Name	frmTableLocker
	Caption	"USER"
Frame	Name	fraTableSharing
Check box	Name	chkDenyRead
	Caption	"Deny others Read Access to Table"
Check box	Name	chkDenyWrite
	Caption	"Deny others Write Access to Table"
Command button	Name	cmdOpenTable
	Caption	"&Open Table"
Command button	Name	cmdAddRecord
	Caption	"&Add Record"
Command button	Name	cmdCloseTable
	Caption	"&Close Table"
Command button	Name	cmdExit
	Caption	"E&xit"

2. Enter the following declarations for the form-level database and recordset object variables:

```
Option Explicit

' form-level object variables used to access the database and
' recordset objects used throughout this project
Private db As Database
Private rs As Recordset
```

3. Now enter the code to initialize the form to indicate that the table is closed:

```
Private Sub Form_Initialize()

    ' initialize the form controls to show that the table is closed
    ' upon startup of project
    cmdCloseTable_Click

End Sub
```

4. Open the database in the **Form_Load** event as shown next. The **DBPath** function is from the ReadINI module included with the distribution CD-ROM to indicate where the **ORDERS** database is located on your machine.

```
Private Sub Form_Load()

    Dim sDBName As String

    ' obtain the name and path of the table to be used in this
    ' project from the ReadINI module
    sDBName = DBPath

    ' open the database
    ' by not specifying an exclusive mode, the database is opened in
    ' shared mode
    Set db = DBEngine.Workspaces(0).OpenDatabase(sDBName)

End Sub
```

5. By placing the following code in the **Form_Unload** event, you are ensured that it is run even if the user does not terminate the application by using the Exit command button:

```
Private Sub Form_Unload(Cancel As Integer)

    ' close the database and recordset objects by setting them to nothing
    Set db = Nothing
    Set rs = Nothing

End Sub
```

6. Now enter the **cmdOpenTable_Click** event code as show next. This event opens the table using the check box values of the **frmTableLocker** form to determine the permissions assigned to the opening of the table. If an error occurs, the application calls the **TableError** routine to gracefully handle it and perhaps tries opening the table again.

```
Private Sub cmdOpenTable_Click()

    ' if an error occurs, call the ERR_cmdOpenTable_Click code located
    ' at the end of this procedure
    On Error GoTo ERR_cmdOpenTable_Click:
```

```
    ' local variable used to store permissions
    Dim nAccessValue As Integer

    ' set the mouse pointer to an hourglass because on some machines,
    ' this could take a few seconds
    Screen.MousePointer = vbHourglass

    ' default the permissions to nothing (all access okay)
    nAccessValue = 0

    ' apply the proper permissions that were restricted by the user
    If (chkDenyRead) Then nAccessValue = nAccessValue + dbDenyRead
    If (chkDenyWrite) Then nAccessValue = nAccessValue + dbDenyWrite

    ' open the table using the permission variable
    Set rs = db.OpenRecordset("Customers", dbOpenTable, nAccessValue)

    ' set the index to the PrimaryKey used later in GetPrimaryKey
    rs.Index = "PrimaryKey"

    ' release any locks that may be on the table, and process any
    ' data that is waiting to be completed
    DBEngine.Idle dbRefreshCache

    ' allow the correct status of the enabled property of the
    ' frmTableLocker controls
    cmdOpenTable.Enabled = False
    chkDenyRead.Enabled = False
    chkDenyWrite.Enabled = False
    cmdAddRecord.Enabled = True
    cmdCloseTable.Enabled = True

    ' set the mousepointer back to its default because we are now finished
    Screen.MousePointer = vbDefault

Exit Sub

ERR_cmdOpenTable_Click:

    ' an error has occurred; therefore, change the mousepointer back
    ' to an hourglass
    Screen.MousePointer = vbDefault

    ' call the TableError function, passing the error object describing
    ' the error that has occurred
    ' if a value of True is returned, we are going to try opening the
    ' table again with read-only access
    If (TableError(Err)) Then
        chkDenyRead = False
        chkDenyWrite = False
        nAccessValue = dbReadOnly
        Resume
    End If

End Sub
```

7. When the user clicks the Add Record command button, a dummy record is added to the table using a unique primary key that is obtained by calling the GetUniqueKey function. Again, if there is an error, the TableError routine is called to handle it. The code for the cmdAddRecord_Click event is as follows:

```
Private Sub cmdAddRecord_Click()

' if an error occurs, call the ERR_cmdAddRecord code located at the
' end of this procedure
On Error GoTo ERR_cmdAddRecord:

    Dim lPrimaryKey As Long
    Dim sMessage As String

    ' used to populate fields in Customer table
    ' this is necessary because most of the fields belong to indexes,
    ' making them required fields
    Const DUMMY_INFO = "<>"

    ' retrieve a unique key from the GetPrimaryKey routine
    lPrimaryKey = GetPrimaryKey

    With rs

        ' add a new record
        .AddNew

        ' fill in the required fields
        .Fields("Customer Number") = lPrimaryKey
        .Fields("Customer Name") = DUMMY_INFO
        .Fields("Street Address") = DUMMY_INFO
        .Fields("City") = DUMMY_INFO
        .Fields("State") = DUMMY_INFO
        .Fields("Zip Code") = DUMMY_INFO

        ' make saves (if an error will occur, it will be here)
        .Update

    End With

    ' if we got this far, add new record was successfull
    sMessage = "Record added successfully!"
    MsgBox sMessage, vbInformation, "ADD RECORD"

Exit Sub

ERR_cmdAddRecord:

    ' an error has occurred; call the TableError function and pass
    ' the Err object describing the error
    TableError Err

End Sub
```

8. Enter the `cmdCloseTable_Click` event code. This code sets the recordset object variable to nothing (the equivalent of closing the recordset) and sets the `Enabled` property of the controls on the form to their appropriate state.

```
Private Sub cmdCloseTable_Click()

    ' set the rs object variable to nothing, closing the recordset
    Set rs = Nothing

    ' properly display the controls on the frmTableLocker form
    chkDenyRead.Enabled = True
    chkDenyWrite.Enabled = True
    cmdOpenTable.Enabled = True
    cmdAddRecord.Enabled = False
    cmdCloseTable.Enabled = False

End Sub
```

9. Enter the `cmdExit_Click` code shown next to end the project. The `Unload Me` code will invoke the `Form_Unload` event where the database and recordset object variables will be set to nothing.

```
Private Sub cmdExit_Click()

    ' using Unload Me will call Form_Unload where the form-level
    ' database and recordset object variables will be set to nothing
    Unload Me

End Sub
```

10. The `GetPrimaryKey` function returns a unique key based on the `Customer Name` field of the Customers table that we are accessing:

```
Private Function GetPrimaryKey()

    ' return a unique primary key based on the Customer Number field
    With rs

        ' if there are records in the table already, find the last one
        ' and add one to the Customer Number as a unique Primary Key;
        ' otherwise, there are no records in the table so return 1 for
        ' the first new record to be added
        If (Not (.EOF And .BOF)) Then

            .MoveLast

            GetPrimaryKey = .Fields("Customer Number") + 1

        Else

            GetPrimaryKey = 1

        End If
```

continued on next page

continued from previous page

```
        End With

End Function
```

11. The `TableError` function contains the code that handles all the input and output errors that occur within this application. If the user cannot open the table with the permissions that were requested, they are asked whether they want to try again with read-only access. Enter the code for the `TableError` function:

```
Private Function TableError(oErr As ErrObject) As Boolean

    Dim sMessage As String
    Dim nResponse As Integer

    ' these are the constant values used to represent the four errors
    ' that we are going to trap in this code

    Const TB_OPEN = 3262         ' database already open in shared mode
    Const TB_IN_USE = 3261       ' database already open exclusively
    Const TB_READ_ONLY = 3027    ' can't save, read only
    Const TB_LOCKED = 3186       ' table is locked, cannot update

    ' default the return value of the function to false, which will
    ' indicate that we do not want to try again
    TableError = False

    With oErr

        ' select the appropriate code depending upon the error number
        Select Case .Number

            ' the table couldn't be opened using the permissions requested;
            ' ask the user if they would like to open it in read-only mode
            Case TB_OPEN, TB_IN_USE:

                sMessage = "There was an error opening the table. " _
                        & "Would you like to try read only mode?"

                nResponse = MsgBox(sMessage, vbYesNo + vbQuestion, "ERROR")

                If (nResponse = vbYes) Then TableError = True

                Exit Function

            ' the table is read only and you cannot add a new record
            Case TB_READ_ONLY:

                sMessage = "You cannot add a record because the " _
                        & "database is currently opened with read " _
                        & "only status."

            ' the table is locked and you cannot add a new record
```

```
        Case TB_LOCKED:

            sMessage = "You cannot add a record because the " _
                     & "database is currently locked by another " _
                     & "user."

        ' unexpected error: display the error number and
        ' description for the user
        Case Else

            sMessage = "Error #" & .Number & ": " & .Description

    End Select

End With

' display the message for the user
MsgBox sMessage, vbExclamation, "TABLE ERROR"

' ensure that the database is closed because of the error, and
' properly set all the command button enabled properties, as well
' as the status label
cmdCloseTable_Click

End Function
```

How It Works

This project uses the **dbDenyRead** and **dbDenyWrite** options when opening the Customer table to deny rights to other users when they attempt to open the table. If another user attempts to open the table that is already opened with **dbDenyRead**, it is considered opened exclusively. If the table is already opened with the **dbDenyWrite** option, the user can only open the table with a **dbReadOnly** option, not allowing new records or editing of ones that already exist.

Comments

There is another parameter that can be specified when a table is being opened, referred to as the **LockEdits** parameter. Table 11.4 describes the options that can be used for the **LockEdits** parameter.

Table 11.4. The LockEdits parameter.

OPTION	DESCRIPTION
dbPessimistic	Page is locked at Edit method
dbOptimistic	Page is locked at Update method

dbPessimistic is the default value for this fourth parameter of the OpenRecordset method and indicates that the page is to be locked as soon as the Edit method is encountered. The dbOptimistic option works a little differently—it waits until the Update method is called to lock the page. The main reason for using the dbOptimistic option is to allow less time for the page to be locked. These options are used in How-To 11.3.

COMPLEXITY
INTERMEDIATE

11.3 How do I...
Work with locked records?

Problem

My application is being designed to allow multiple users to access the same data. It is inevitable that sooner or later two users will attempt to edit the same data. How do I write proper record-locking code to guard my application from situations like this and to ensure database integrity?

Technique

As touched on in How-To 11.2, we can set the way in which a record is locked by accessing the LockEdits property of the recordset. In doing this, we can set the value of this property to either pessimistic or optimistic. The default value for LockEdits is True, which corresponds to pessimistic. By setting this property to False, we obtain optimistic record locking.

Pessimistic record locking locks the record during the time indicated by the call to the Edit method and the call to the Update method of a recordset. Optimistic record locking locks the record during the call to the Update method.

Due to the potential dangers of database corruption with multiuser access, we can expect to encounter numerous trappable runtime errors with record locking. The errors are listed here:

✔ Error 3167: Record is deleted.

✔ Error 3197: Record has changed; operation halted.

✔ Error 3260: Record currently locked by another user, cannot update.

It has become an acceptable programming technique to trap these errors and respond to them at such times. It is common to expect some or all of these errors when running a multiuser application as we will in this project.

Steps

Open the RecordLocker project and compile it. Open two instances of the project and run them simultaneously. You should see the forms shown in Figure 11.3. With one instance, open a record for editing. With the other instance, select pessimistic record locking and edit the record. You will receive an error because the application is attempting to lock the record from the time the `Edit` method is called. Try changing the record locking to optimistic and editing the record. You will be able to get to this point; however, if you now click the Update button, you will receive an error. This is because optimistic record locking attempts to lock the record when the `Update` method is called.

The user can navigate the recordset by using the four buttons below the option buttons. The user can also refresh the current record by clicking the Refresh button. This step is useful to ensure that you have the most up-to-date information for the current record in case another user has already changed it.

1. Create a new project and call it RecordLocker.vbp. Create the objects and change the properties as listed in Table 11.5. Save the form as frmRecordlocker.frm. Note that the `cmdMove` command buttons are a control array.

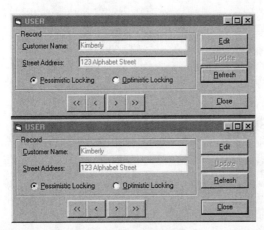

Figure 11.3. Two instances of the RecordLocker project.

Table 11.5. Objects and properties for the Exclusive project.

OBJECT	PROPERTY	SETTING
Form	Name	frmRecordLocker
	Caption	"USER"
Frame	Name	fraRecord
Text box	Name	txtCustomerName
Text box	Name	txtStreetAddress
Option button	Name	optPessimisticLocking
	Caption	"Pessimistic Record Locking"
Option button	Name	optOptimisticLocking
	Caption	"Optimistic Record Locking"
Command button	Name	cmdEdit
	Caption	"&Edit"
Command button	Name	cmdUpdate
	Caption	"&Update"
Command button	Name	cmdRefresh
	Caption	"&Refresh"
Command button	Name	cmdClose
	Caption	"&Close"
Command button	Name	cmdMove
	Caption	"<<"
	Index	0
Command button	Name	cmdMove
	Caption	"<"
	Index	1
Command button	Name	cmdMove
	Caption	">"
	Index	2
Command button	Name	cmdMove
	Caption	">>"
	Index	3
Label	Name	lblCustomerName
	Caption	"&Customer Name"
Label	Name	lblStreetAddress
	Caption	"&Street Address"

2. Enter the following form-level variables in the declarations section of your project. The first two variables are used to hold the database and recordset objects. The m_bEditMode variable is used to indicate whether the project is in edit mode. The last two declarations are constant values used to determine whether the LockEdits property of the recordset is set to PESSIMISTIC or OPTIMISTIC.

```
Option Explicit

' form-level object variables that hold the database and recordset
' objects used throughout this project
Private db As Database
Private rs As Recordset

' form-level boolean variable used to indicate when the current
' record is in edit mode
Private m_bEditMode As Boolean

' form-level constant declarations used to indicate pessimistic or
' optimistic record locking
Private Const PESSIMISTIC = True
Private Const OPTIMISTIC = False
```

3. Now enter the code to open the database and recordset in the Form_Load event. This code also determines whether the recordset is empty (ending the application if so), and if not, it displays the first record.

```
Private Sub Form_Load()

    Dim sDBName As String

    ' get the path and name of the database used in this project
    ' from the ReadINI module
    sDBName = DBPath

    ' open the database and recordset
    Set db = DBEngine.Workspaces(0).OpenDatabase(sDBName)
    Set rs = db.OpenRecordset("Customers", dbOpenDynaset)

    With rs

        ' if the recordset is empty, then inform the user and end
        If (.EOF And .BOF) Then

            MsgBox "Table Empty!", vbExclamation, "ERROR"
            Unload Me

        Else

            ' move to the first record and display it
            .MoveFirst
            DisplayRecord

        End If
```

continued on next page

continued from previous page

```
    End With

    ' set the optPessimisticLocking value to true (this will
    ' automatically call the optPessimisticLocking_Click event
    optPessimisticLocking = True

End Sub
```

4. The `Form_Unload` event is called when the application is terminated. By setting the form-level object variables **db** and **rs** to nothing, we achieve the same status as if closing them with the **Close** method.

```
Private Sub Form_Unload(Cancel As Integer)

    ' set the form-level object variables for the database and
    ' recordset to nothing (this is the same as closing each object)
    Set db = Nothing
    Set rs = Nothing

End Sub
```

5. Enter the `cmdEdit_Click` code shown next. This event first checks to see whether the record is in edit mode and updates the record if it is. After this, the recordset is placed in edit mode via the **Edit** method. If an error is going to occur, it will be here. If the user has selected pessimistic locking and the record is currently open, an error will occur. If no error was encountered, the text boxes are enabled to allow editing, and the form-level Boolean flag, **m_bEditMode**, is set to **True** to indicate that edit mode is on.

```
Private Sub cmdEdit_Click()

' if there is an error, goto the code labeled by ERR_cmdEdit_Click
On Error GoTo ERR_cmdEdit_Click:

    ' if the current record is in edit mode, call UpdateRecord
    If (m_bEditMode) Then UpdateRecord

    ' set the record to edit mode
    rs.Edit

    ' indicate that the record is in edit mode through the
    ' m_m_bEditMode form-level boolean variable
    m_bEditMode = True

    ' disable the edit command button and enable the update command
    ' button and text box controls
    cmdEdit.Enabled = False
    cmdUpdate.Enabled = True
    txtCustomerName.Enabled = True
    txtStreetAddress.Enabled = True

Exit Sub
```

```
ERR_cmdEdit_Click:

    ' an error has occurred, call the RecordError routine with the
    ' error object that describes the error and a string indicating
    ' the method attempted at the time of the error
    RecordError Err, "edit"

End Sub
```

6. The code for the `cmdUpdate_Click` event is easy. Simply call the `UpdateRecord` routine as shown here:

```
Private Sub cmdUpdate_Click()

    ' update the current record in the database
    UpdateRecord

End Sub
```

7. Now enter the code for the `cmdRefresh_Click` event as shown next. This code again updates the record if it was in edit mode, then performs a requery of the recordset and displays the current record.

```
Private Sub cmdRefresh_Click()

    ' if the current record is in edit mode, call UpdateRecord
    If (m_bEditMode) Then UpdateRecord

    ' requery dynaset and move the record pointer
    With rs
        .Requery
        .MoveNext
        .MovePrevious
    End With

    ' redisplay the current record
    DisplayRecord

End Sub
```

8. Enter the code for the `cmdClose_Click` event as shown here. This ends the application, and the `Form_Unload` event is automatically called.

```
Private Sub cmdClose_Click()

    ' end the application, this will call the Form_Unload event
    Unload Me

End Sub
```

9. Now enter the code for both option buttons on the `frmRecordLocker` form as shown next. Each event checks to see whether the record is in edit mode and performs an update if it is. Next, the `LockEdits` property of the recordset is set to the locking method of choice.

```
Private Sub optPessimisticLocking_Click()

    ' if the current record is in edit mode, call UpdateRecord
    If (m_bEditMode) Then UpdateRecord

    ' set the LockEdits property of the recordset to Pessimistic
    ' record locking
    rs.LockEdits = PESSIMISTIC

End Sub

Private Sub optOptimisticLocking_Click()

    ' if the current record is in edit mode, call UpdateRecord
    If (m_bEditMode) Then UpdateRecord

    ' set the LockEdits property of the recordset to Optimistic record
    ' locking
    rs.LockEdits = OPTIMISTIC

End Sub
```

10. Now enter the code for the `cmdMove_Click` event. This event occurs when any of the four command buttons belonging to the control array `cmdMove` has been pressed. By comparing the `Index` variable that is passed as an argument to this event with the constants defined, the correct recordset navigation is applied and the new record is displayed.

```
Private Sub cmdMove_Click(Index As Integer)

    ' local constant values used to indicate which command button
    ' was pressed
    ' each constant corresponds to the index of each command button
    Const MOVE_FIRST = 0
    Const MOVE_PREVIOUS = 1
    Const MOVE_NEXT = 2
    Const MOVE_LAST = 3

    ' if the current record is in edit mode, call UpdateRecord
    If (m_bEditMode) Then UpdateRecord

    With rs

        Select Case Index

            ' move to the first record
            Case MOVE_FIRST:
                .MoveFirst
```

```
' move to the previous record; if the record pointer is
' before the first record, then move to the first record
Case MOVE_PREVIOUS:
    .MovePrevious
    If (.BOF) Then .MoveFirst

' move to the next record; if the record pointer is
' beyond the last record, then move to the last record
Case MOVE_NEXT:
    .MoveNext
    If (.EOF) Then .MoveLast

' move to the last record
Case MOVE_LAST:
    .MoveLast

        End Select

    End With

    ' display the current record after moving to a new one
    DisplayRecord

End Sub
```

11. The following code displays the record. Enter this in the General section of your project. If a new record is displayed, it cannot be in edit mode; therefore, we set the **m_bEditMode** variable to **False** and disable the Update command button while enabling the Edit command button.

```
Private Sub DisplayRecord()

    ' disable the customer name and fill it with the current
    ' record's corresponding field value
    With txtCustomerName
        .Text = rs.Fields("Customer Name")
        .Enabled = False
    End With

    ' disable the street address and fill it with the current
    ' record's corresponding field value
    With txtStreetAddress
        .Text = rs.Fields("Street Address")
        .Enabled = False
    End With

    ' enable the edit and disable the update command buttons
    cmdEdit.Enabled = True
    cmdUpdate.Enabled = False

    ' currently not in edit mode
    m_bEditMode = False

End Sub
```

12. Enter the **UpdateRecord** code now. This procedure updates the recordset with the values that are shown on the form. If the recordset **LockEdits** property was set to optimistic and the record is currently opened by another user at this time, the **Update** method causes an error. We trap the error and call the **RecordError** procedure as shown toward the end of this procedure.

```
Private Sub UpdateRecord()

' if there is an error, goto the code labeled by ERR_UpdateRecord
On Error GoTo ERR_UpdateRecord:

    ' set the new values of the record fields to those displayed on the
    ' form and update the record (this is where an error can occur)
    With rs
        .Fields("Customer Name") = txtCustomerName
        .Fields("Street Address") = txtStreetAddress
        .Update
    End With

    ' display the updated record
    DisplayRecord

Exit Sub

ERR_UpdateRecord:

    ' an error has occurred, call the RecordError routine with the error
    ' object that describes the error and a string indicating the method
    ' attempted at the time of the error
    RecordError Err, "update"

End Sub
```

13. Finally, enter the **RecordError** code, which displays the proper error message for the user based on the error object that was passed to it as a parameter:

```
Private Sub RecordError(oErr As ErrObject, sAction As String)

    Dim sMessage As String

    ' error constant used to indicate that the current record is
    ' locked and cannot be updated or edited
    Const RECORD_LOCKED = 3260

    With Err

        Select Case .Number

            ' the record cannot be edited
            Case RECORD_LOCKED:
                sMessage = "Cannot " & sAction & " at this time because " _
                        & "the record is currently locked by another " _
                        & "user."
```

```
        ' an unexpected error has occurred
        Case Else:
            sMessage = "ERROR #" & .Number & ": " & .Description

    End Select

End With

' display the error message created above
MsgBox sMessage, vbExclamation, "ERROR"

End Sub
```

How It Works

This How-To uses the `LockEdits` property of the recordset object to determine how a particular record is locked. If the user selects pessimistic locking, the default setting for the Jet engine, then the record becomes locked immediately upon calling the `Edit` method of the recordset. This lock remains on until the `Update` method of the recordset is called.

On the other hand, if the user has selected optimistic record locking for the `LockEdits` property, the record is locked only when the `Update` method is called. The advantage to this alternative is that the record is not locked for a potentially long period as with pessimistic locking; however, the data in the record can change during the time between the calls to the `Edit` and `Update` methods. If this is the case, a trappable runtime error occurs.

This project allows navigation of the recordset with four command buttons that emulate the data control VCR navigation buttons. When the user clicks a navigation button, the record pointer is repositioned to the first, previous, next, or last record. If the record pointer goes before the first record or after the last, the application traps the potential error and repositions the record pointer to the first or last record.

Comments

In the preceding three How-To projects, we have dealt with constantly checking error codes to determine the state of a database, table, or record. It is very important to always be a courteous programmer. By this, I mean properly coding your applications so that they will prevent error messages from occurring not only in your own project, but also in other developers' applications.

Table 11.6 lists the most commonly occurring error messages you might encounter when dealing with locking databases.

Table 11.6. Common database-locking error messages.

ERROR NUMBER	IS GENERATED WHEN...
3167	You use `Edit`, and the record has been deleted since the last time you read it.
3186	You use `Update` on a new or edited record, and the record's page is locked by another user.
3197	You use `Edit` or `Update`, and the record has changed since the last time you read it.
3027	You try to write to a table you have opened as read only.
3260	You use `Addnew`, `Edit`, or `Update`, and the record's page is locked by another user.
3261	You try to open a table that another user has opened with `dbDenyRead` or `dbDenyWrite`.
3262	You try to open a table with `dbDenyRead` or `dbDenyWrite`, and another user has the table open.
3356	You try to open a database already opened exclusively by another, or you try to open exclusively a database that another user already has opened.

These error messages can be detected at various points in a project and should be trapped whenever possible.

COMPLEXITY
INTERMEDIATE

11.4 How do I...
Work with secured Microsoft Access database files?

Problem

I need to create a secure Microsoft Access database file and have my Visual Basic program manipulate it. How can I do this?

Technique

Microsoft Access databases support a wide variety of security features. The Jet engine can control which users and applications can access databases, tables, or fields. Security features are managed through the use of a system database. By convention, the database is usually named SYSTEM.MDW.

Every Microsoft Access user is assigned to a workgroup, and a copy of SYSTEM.MDW is established for each workgroup. An entry for each user in the Windows Registry points to the correct copy of SYSTEM.MDW for the user's assigned workgroup. This file is specified with the key `HKEY_LOCAL_MACHINE\ SOFTWARE\Microsoft\Office\8.0\Access\Jet\3.5\Engines`. In this How-To, you'll see the techniques for accessing the objects in a secured Microsoft Access database.

Permissions

Each Microsoft Access database file includes a set of permissions that give users certain specified rights to the database and to the objects within the database. For the database itself, two permissions can be granted: the right to open the database (`Open Database`) and the right to open the database exclusively (`Open Exclusive`).

Although Microsoft Access security covers all database object types, the only data objects that can be accessed from Visual Basic are tables and queries. Table 11.7 lists the seven permissions that can be granted for table and query objects. Granting any of these permissions except Read Design implies the granting of others as well, and these implied permissions are also shown in the table.

Table 11.7. Permissions for Microsoft Access tables and queries.

PERMISSION	IMPLIES THESE ADDITIONAL PERMISSIONS
Read Design	(none)
Modify Design	Read Design, Read Data, Update Data, Delete Data
Administer	All other permissions
Read Data	Read Design
Update Data	Read Data, Read Design
Insert Data	Read Data, Read Design
Delete Data	Read Data, Read Design

Groups and Users

Everyone who accesses a Microsoft Access database is a user and is identified by a user name. Users can also be assigned to groups. Every group has a group name. Users and groups for a specified workgroup are stored in the system database file (usually SYSTEM.MDW). You can use Microsoft Access (or Visual Basic) to create users and groups and to assign users to groups.

You grant permissions by users or by groups. Users inherit the rights of their group, unless you specify otherwise. Assume, for example, that you have a group named Payroll Department. You assign the entire group only Read Data permission to the Pay Rates table (and Read Design permission, which is implied by Read Data). For two users within the group, Tom and Betty, you also assign Update Data, Insert Data, and Delete Data permissions. For one user in the group, Pat, you revoke Read Data permission. The specific permission assignments you have made for users Tom, Betty, and Pat override the group permissions for those users.

Secured and Unsecured Systems

All the foregoing is transparent—and relatively unimportant—as long as you are working with an unsecured system. When the Workgroup Administrator application creates a new system database—and thereby creates a new workgroup—the system is by default an unsecured system. All users are assigned empty strings ("") as passwords. Users do not log in when they start Access, and your Visual Basic program does not need to provide a user name or password, because all users are logged in automatically with the default name Admin and the password "".

This all changes as soon as the Admin user's password changes, because a password-protected Admin account makes the system into a secured system. Each time a user starts Microsoft Access in a secured system, he or she must provide a user name, and that name must be registered in the workgroup's copy of the system database. If the system database contains a password other than "" for the user, it must be provided at login. In like manner, before your Visual Basic program can access a database in a secured system, it must provide a valid user name and a password (if the user is assigned a password).

Security ID Numbers

Every user and group has a Security ID (SID)—a binary string that is created by the Jet engine and stored in the system database where the user or group is defined. With several important exceptions, a user or group SID is built by the Jet database engine based on two pieces of information:

✔ The user's name.

✔ The user's personal identifier (PID), an alphanumeric string between 4 and 20 characters that must be provided when a new user is added to the system database. (See How-To 11.9 for information on how to add users to the system database.)

The Security ID (SID), therefore, uniquely identifies a user or group.

Security IDs and Object Permissions

Object permissions are defined by assignment to an SID. You can think of a permission as a keyhole through which access to an object can be obtained, and the SID as a unique key that can open the keyhole. (See Figure 11.4.) Each object has a set of keyholes, one matching the SID "key" for each user or group that has a specific permission. When you assign a permission for an object (a process covered in How-To 11.5), you in effect "drill another keyhole" into the object and encode it with the SID of a specific user or group.

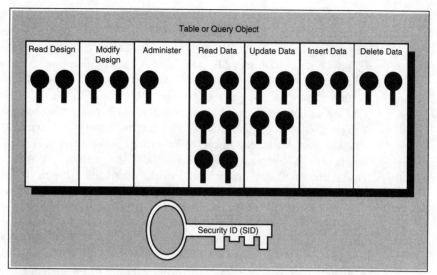

Figure 11.4. Security IDs and permissions.

Ensuring a Secure Database

It is altogether too easy to think you have "secured" a Microsoft Access database yet actually have a security system with gaping holes. The holes can exist because of the fact that the predefined default users and groups are exceptions to the way SIDs are built. Default users' and groups' SIDs are built as shown in Table 11.8.

Table 11.8. Security ID sources for default users and groups.

USER OR GROUP	SECURITY ID (SID) SOURCE
Admin user	Hard-coded and identical in every system database
Guest user	Hard-coded and identical in every system database
Users group	Hard-coded and identical in every system database
Guests group	Hard-coded and identical in every system database
Admins group	Built by the Jet engine from three pieces of data: a user name, a company name, and an ID number

The information in Table 11.8 has extremely important implications for database security. The Admin user's SID is hard-coded and identical in every system database; that means that objects created by the Admin user can be accessed by the Admin user in any system database. All someone needs to do to gain access to an object created by an Admin user from any system database is to create a new system database and log in as Admin. Admin is the default user; in an unsecured system, all users are Admin. Therefore, if you create an object in an unsecured system, that object belongs to Admin and cannot be secured.

One solution (recommended by Microsoft in the Microsoft Access documentation) is to delete the Admin user from the system database. This is permissible as long as the Admins group contains at least one other user.

Unlike the Admin user SID, the Admins group SID is unique to each system database. Note in Table 11.8 that the Admins group SID requires an ID number. If the system database was created by the Microsoft Access setup program, the ID number component of the Admins group SID is taken from the setup disks, and each set of setup disks is uniquely encoded. If the system database is created through the Microsoft Access Workgroup Administrator, the ID number component is computed based on an identifier entered by the person who creates the system database with the Workgroup Administrator.

This scheme prevents someone who is a member of an Admins group in one system database from automatically getting Admins group permissions when accessing database files through other system databases; because the Admins group SIDs are different, the permissions are different (recall the concept of unique keyholes and keys from Figure 11.4). But it also means that all users who are currently members of the Admins group of the system database in use when the database was originally created will always have the ability to change permissions on all objects in the database—and this ability cannot be removed by anyone. Therefore, when you create a database you intend to secure, you should be cognizant of who is defined to the system database as part of the Admins group.

Another implication of Table 11.8 is that permissions assigned to the Guests or Users group through one system database will be available to members of the Guests or Users group in any system database. Therefore, assign the Guests or Users groups only the permissions you are willing to give to anyone. If you need to assign permissions to a group of users and you want to restrict who can access those permissions, create a new group (see How-To 11.10 for details on how to create a group and assign users to it).

Accessing a Secured System Through Visual Basic

Before your application can access a secured Microsoft Access system, it needs to provide the Jet engine with several pieces of information:

✔ The application must specify which system database file the application wants to use. This is normally a file named SYSTEM.MDW.

✔ The application must provide a user name that is listed in that system database file.

✔ If that user name has a password, the application must provide the password.

After the Jet engine knows where to look for user names and passwords, you provide a user name and password. This is done by straightforward assignment to **DBEngine** properties:

```
DBEngine.DefaultUser = "Annette"
DBEngine.DefaultPassword = "mouseketeer"
```

The user name is not case sensitive. The password *is* case sensitive. If the password is recorded in the system database as **Mouseketeer** and you supply **mouseketeer**, the login attempt will fail.

Workspaces and Sessions

The Jet engine implements most database security features through the **Workspace** object and its **Groups** and **Users** collection. A **Workspace** object is a member of the **Workspaces** collection of the **Database** object.

When you set the **IniPath**, **DefaultUser**, and **DefaultPassword** properties of the **DBEngine** object, you are actually setting the user name and password for the default workspace. The default workspace can be accessed by its name, **DBEngine.Workspaces("#Default Workspace#")**, in which the # symbols are part of the name, or as **DBEngine.Workspaces(0)**.

A **Workspace** object defines a session for a user. *Session* and *workspace* are close to being synonyms. Within a session, you can open multiple databases. Transactions occur within sessions.

For the default workspace, a session begins when you set the **DefaultUser** and **DefaultPassword** properties for the **DBEngine** object. After you have successfully initialized the default session, your program can create additional password-protected sessions.

To open a new session, you create a new **Workspace** object by using the **CreateWorkspace** method of the **DBEngine** object. The **CreateWorkspace** method takes three required arguments: **Name** (the name of the workspace), **UserName**, and **Password**. You can append the **Workspace** object to the **DBEngine** object's **Workspaces** collection—although you do not need to add the **Workspace** object to the collection to use the object. This code fragment initializes the default workspace, then creates a new **Workspace** object named **My Space** for the user **Lucy**, whose password is **diamonds**. It then opens a database within the new workspace.

```
Dim wkSpace as Workspace
Dim db as Database

DBEngine.IniPath = "D:\MYAPP\THEINI.INI"
DBEngine.DefaultUser = "Mary"
DBEngine.DefaultPassword = "contrary"
Set wkSpace = DBEngine.CreateWorkspace("My Space", "Lucy", "diamonds")
Set db = wkSpace.OpenDatabase("BIBLIO.MDB")
```

Note that you must get logged into the **DBEngine** object via the **DefaultUser** and **DefaultPassword** objects before you can create additional workspaces.

Steps

Open the Secure project (Secure.vbp) and run it. You will first see a dialog box indicating the system database name that is to be used in the application. The next dialog box is that of a typical logon screen, as shown in Figure 11.5. Here you can enter different user names and passwords to access the database.

1. Create a new project and name it Secure.vbp. Add the objects and edit the properties as shown in Table 11.9; then save the form as frmSecure.frm.

Table 11.9. Objects and properties for the Exclusive project.

OBJECT	PROPERTY	SETTING
Form	Name	frmSecure
	Caption	"Secure"
Text box	Name	txtUserName
Text box	Name	txtPassword
Command button	Name	cmdOK
	Caption	"&OK"
	Default	True
Command button	Name	cmdCancel
	Caption	"&Cancel"
	Cancel	True
Label	Name	lblUserName
	Caption	"&User Name"
Label	Name	lblPassword
	Caption	"&Password"

Figure 11.5. The Secure project.

2. There are no form-level variables to declare in this project, so go directly to entering the **Form_Load** code as shown next. This code sets the **DBEngine** properties with the default user and password to access the SYSTEM.MDW file.

```
Private Sub Form_Load()

' if there is an error, goto the code labeled by ERR_Form_Load
On Error GoTo ERR_Form_Load:

    ' local variables used to hold the user name and password
    Dim sUser As String
    Dim sPassword As String

    With DBEngine

        ' set the system database INI path (registry key)
        DBEngine.IniPath = GetINIPath

        ' set system database file
        .SystemDB = GetWorkgroupDatabase

        ' set default user information
        sUser = "Admin"
        sPassword = "myturn"

        ' assign default user information
        .DefaultUser = sUser
        .DefaultPassword = sPassword

        ' display current system database
        MsgBox "The system database is " & .SystemDB, vbInformation

    End With

Exit Sub


ERR_Form_Load:

    ' display the error information and then end the application
    With Err
        MsgBox "ERROR #" & .Number & ": " & .Description, vbExclamation, _
            "ERROR"
    End With

    Unload Me

End Sub
```

3. Now enter the code for **cmdOK_Click**. This event creates a new **Workspace** object with the supplied information from the **frmSecure** form and if it is successful, it opens a recordset obtaining some information.

```
Private Sub cmdOK_Click()

' if an error occurs, then goto the code labeled by ERR_cmdOK_Click
On Error GoTo ERR_cmdOK_Click:

    ' local object variables used to hold the database, recordset,
    ' and workspace
    Dim db As Database
    Dim rs As Recordset
    Dim ws As Workspace

    ' local variable used to store database path and name
    Dim sDBName As String

    ' local variables used to store the user name and password
    Dim sUserName As String
    Dim sPassword As String

    ' if there is no user name, inform the user and exit the procedure
    ' if there is a user name, assign the name and password
    If (txtUserName = "") Then

        MsgBox "You must enter a user name.", vbExclamation, "ERROR"

        txtUserName.SetFocus
        Exit Sub

    Else

        sUserName = txtUserName
        sPassword = txtPassword

    End If

    ' create a new workspace for the user
    Set ws = DBEngine.CreateWorkspace _
                ("NewWorkspace", sUserName, sPassword)

    ' obtain the database name and path from ReadINI and then open
    ' the database
    sDBName = DBPath
    Set db = ws.OpenDatabase(sDBName)

    ' ensure that we have connected by creating a recordset of some data
    Set rs = db.OpenRecordset("SELECT * FROM Customers")

    ' inform the user that we are successful
    MsgBox "User " & txtUserName & " connected successfully!", _
            vbInformation, "SUCCESS"

Exit Sub

ERR_cmdOK_Click:

    ' display the error information and then end the application
    With Err
```

```
        MsgBox "ERROR #" & .Number & ": " & .Description, vbExclamation, _
            "ERROR"
    End With

End Sub
```

4. Now add the trivial code to end the project in the `cmdCancel_Click` event:

```
Private Sub cmdCancel_Click()

    ' end the application
    Unload Me

End Sub
```

How It Works

When the application starts, `frmSecure` is loaded. The `Load` event connects to the system database designated in the Windows Registry and, if it is successful, displays a message showing the name of that database. When the user clicks the OK button, the click event creates a new `Workspace` object, opens ORDERS.MDB, and opens a recordset based on a table in ORDERS.MDB. If these steps are successful, the user name and password are valid and the user has Read Data privileges to the table.

Comments

In previous versions of Visual Basic, the Jet engine looked in INI files for the name of the system database file. With Visual Basic 5.0 and the Jet 3.5 engine, the system database file is located in the Windows Registry. Probably the most likely spot to find this file would be in your Windows system directory.

COMPLEXITY
ADVANCED

11.5 How do I...
Assign permissions for database objects?

Problem

I need to write an application for the system administrators where I work to allow them to change the permissions of users for Access databases. These administrators don't necessarily have Access available to them. How do I provide this capability through my own Visual Basic application?

Technique

Permissions for a database are stored in a system table in the database. If you have Administer access to the database, you can change these permissions through Access or Visual Basic.

Each Microsoft Access database object owns a `Containers` collection. Each `Container` object in the collection collects information about a specific type of object. The `Container` object named `Tables` contains information about all the `Table` and `Query` objects in the database. Each `Container` object owns a `Documents` collection. Each `Document` object in a collection holds information about one instance of the object type represented by the container. Each `Document` object in the `Tables` container represents one `Table` or `Query` object. Each `Document` has a `UserName` property and a `Permissions` property. At any given time, the `Permissions` property value is a long integer that represents the permissions that the user named by the `UserName` property has to the table or query represented by the `Document` object.

The values of the `Permissions` object for each combination of permissions for users other than the Admin user are shown in Table 11.10. (The values for the Admin user, Administer, and Modify Design permissions vary, depending on whether the object represented by the document is a `Table` or a `Query`.) Each permission named in the "Permission or Permissions" column includes not only the named permission but also all its implied permissions. For example, the value of the `Permissions` property is `20` when Read Data and its implied permission Read Design are `True`; the value is `116` when Update Data and Delete Data and all the implied properties of both are `True`.

Table 11.10. Permissions property values for users other than Admin.

PERMISSION OR PERMISSIONS	VALUE OF PERMISSIONS PROPERTY
No permissions	0
Read Design	4
Read Data	20
Insert Data	52
Update Data	84
Update Data and Insert Data	116
Delete Data	148
Insert Data and Delete Data	180
Update Data and Delete Data	212

PERMISSION OR PERMISSIONS	VALUE OF PERMISSIONS PROPERTY
Update Data, Insert Data, and Delete Data	244
Modify Design	65756
Modify Design and Insert Data	65788
Administer	852478

You can determine the permissions a user has for a table or a query by setting the `UserName` property of the `Document` object to the user's name and then reading the `Permissions` property. If you have Administer permission for the table or query, you can set permissions for other users by setting the `UserName` property and then assigning a value to the `Permissions` property.

Steps

Open and run the Permitter project. You should see the form shown in Figure 11.6. Select a combination of a single user and a table or query from the two list boxes on the Permitter form. You can change various properties set for each combination and save them by clicking the Save button. Notice the permission code above the check boxes. It changes according to the combinations of permissions granted to the user for the given table or query.

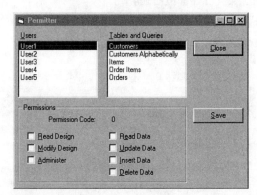

Figure 11.6. The Permitter project.

1. Create a new project and name it Permitter.vbp. Add and edit the objects and properties as listed in Table 11.11, and save the form as frmPermitter.frm. Note that all the checkboxes are part of a control array.

Table 11.11. Objects and properties for the Permitter project.

OBJECT	PROPERTY	SETTING
Form	Name	frmPermitter
	Caption	"Permitter"
List box	Name	lstUsers
List box	Name	lstTablesAndQueries
Command button	Name	cmdSave
	Caption	"&Save"
Command button	Name	cmdClose
	Caption	"&Close"
	Cancel	-1 'True
	Default	-1 'True
Frame	Name	fraPermissions
	Caption	"Permissions"
Check box	Name	chkPermission
	Caption	"&Read Design"
	Index	0
Check box	Name	chkPermission
	Caption	"&Modify Design"
	Index	1
Check box	Name	chkPermission
	Caption	"&Administer"
	Index	2
Check box	Name	chkPermission
	Caption	"R&ead Data"
	Index	3
Check box	Name	chkPermission
	Caption	"&Update Data"
	Index	4
Check box	Name	chkPermission
	Caption	"&Insert Data"
	Index	5
Check box	Name	chkPermission
	Caption	"&Delete Data"
	Index	6

OBJECT	PROPERTY	SETTING
Label	Name	lblPermissionCode
	Caption	"Permission Code:"
Label	Name	lblPermissions
	Caption	"0"
Label	Name	lblUsers
	Caption	"&Users"
Label	Name	lblTablesAndQueries
	Caption	"&Tables and Queries"

2. First enter the form-level declarations in the declarations section of the project. The database object variable will serve as the home of the database object referred to throughout the project. The constant declarations with the PER_ prefix correspond to the seven check boxes on the frmPermitter form. The last set of declarations, those preceded by the DB_ characters, is used to indicate the different values associated with the permissions.

```
Option Explicit

' form-level object variable used to store database object
Private db As Database

' form-level constant declarations which correspond to check boxes
' on the frmPermitter form
Const PER_READ_DESIGN = 0
Const PER_MODIFY_DESIGN = 1
Const PER_ADMINISTER = 2
Const PER_READ_DATA = 3
Const PER_UPDATE_DATA = 4
Const PER_INSERT_DATA = 5
Const PER_DELETE_DATA = 6

' form-level constant declarations which indicate various permissions
Const DB_NOPERMISSIONS = 0
Const DB_READDESIGN = 4
Const DB_READDATA = 20
Const DB_INSERTDATA = 52
Const DB_UPDATEDATA = 84
Const DB_UPDATEINSERTDATA = 116
Const DB_DELETEDATA = 148
Const DB_INSERTDELETEDATA = 180
Const DB_UPDATEDELETEDATA = 212
Const DB_UPDATEINSERTDELETEDATA = 244
Const DB_MODIFYDESIGN = 65756
Const DB_MODIFYDESIGN_INSERTDATA = 65788
Const DB_READSEC = 131072
Const DB_ADMINISTER = 852478
```

3. Enter the Form_Load event as shown next. This code sets the default user and password of the **DBEngine** object. You might have to change the values of these two variables to your system administrator's name and password. The database is then open, and the two list boxes on the form are populated. If there are no current users for the database, the application is terminated.

```
Private Sub Form_Load()

' if there is an error, then goto the code section labeled by ERR_Form_Load
On Error GoTo ERR_Form_Load:

    Dim sUserName As String
    Dim sPassword As String
    Dim sDBName As String

    ' assign default user name and password
    sUserName = "Admin"
    sPassword = ""

    With DBEngine

        ' set system database path and name
        .SystemDB = GetWorkgroupDatabase

        ' set default user name and password
        .DefaultUser = sUserName
        .DefaultPassword = sPassword

        ' get path and name of database from ReadINI module
        sDBName = DBPath

        ' open database
        Set db = .Workspaces(0).OpenDatabase(sDBName)

    End With

    ' populate the two list boxes with the available users, tables,
    ' and queries from database
    FillUserList
    FillTableAndQueriesList

    ' if there are no valid users, inform the user and exit the application
    If (lstUsers.ListCount < 1) Then

        MsgBox "There are no users!", vbExclamation, "USERS"
        cmdClose_Click

    End If

    ' initialize the list boxes to point to the first item in each list box
    lstUsers.ListIndex = 0
    lstTablesAndQueries.ListIndex = 0

Exit Sub
```

```
ERR_Form_Load:

    ' display error for the user
    With Err
        MsgBox "ERROR #" & .Number & ": " & .Description, vbExclamation, _
               "ERROR"
    End With

End Sub
```

4. Enter the `Form_Unload` code now. This code ensures that the database object is released by setting it to nothing when the application is terminated.

```
Private Sub Form_Unload(Cancel As Integer)

    ' close the database
    Set db = Nothing

End Sub
```

5. Now enter both the `lstUsers` and the `lstTablesAndQueries Click` event code. Each event relies on the other's list box having a selected item. If there is a selected item in the corresponding list box, the `ReadPermissions` procedure is called to gather the permission information for the user and table/query combination, checking off the appropriate check boxes on the form.

```
Private Sub lstUsers_Click()

    ' if the TablesAndQueries list box is set to one of the items, call the
    ' ReadPermissions procedure, and if there was an error, unselect all
    ' check boxes
    If (lstTablesAndQueries.ListIndex >= 0) Then
        If (Not ReadPermissions()) Then

            lstUsers.ListIndex = -1
            UnCheckAll

        End If
    End If

End Sub

Private Sub lstTablesAndQueries_Click()

    ' if the Users list box is set to one of the items, call the
    ' ReadPermissions procedure, and if there was an error, unselect all
    ' check boxes
    If (lstUsers.ListIndex >= 0) Then
        If (Not ReadPermissions()) Then

            lstTablesAndQueries.ListIndex = -1
            UnCheckAll
```

continued on next page

continued from previous page

```
        End If
    End If

End Sub
```

6. The `chkPermission_Click` event handles all the seven checkboxes found on the `frmPermitter` form. This code ensures that the correct combinations of checkboxes are set. Enter the following code:

```
Private Sub chkPermission_Click(Index As Integer)

    Dim nCount As Integer


    With chkPermission(Index)

        ' set the appropriate check box values dependent upon the others
        Select Case Index

            Case PER_READ_DESIGN:
                If (.Value = vbUnchecked) Then
                    For nCount = 0 To 6
                        chkPermission(nCount).Value = vbUnchecked
                    Next nCount
                End If

            Case PER_MODIFY_DESIGN:
                If (.Value = vbChecked) Then
                    chkPermission(PER_READ_DESIGN).Value = vbChecked
                    chkPermission(PER_READ_DATA).Value = vbChecked
                    chkPermission(PER_UPDATE_DATA).Value = vbChecked
                    chkPermission(PER_INSERT_DATA).Value = vbChecked
                Else
                    chkPermission(PER_ADMINISTER).Value = vbUnchecked
                End If

            Case PER_ADMINISTER:
                If (.Value = vbChecked) Then
                    For nCount = 0 To 6
                        chkPermission(nCount).Value = vbChecked
                    Next nCount
                End If

            Case PER_READ_DATA:
                If (.Value = vbChecked) Then
                    chkPermission(PER_READ_DESIGN).Value = vbChecked
                Else
                    chkPermission(PER_MODIFY_DESIGN).Value = vbUnchecked
                    chkPermission(PER_UPDATE_DATA).Value = vbUnchecked
                    chkPermission(PER_DELETE_DATA).Value = vbUnchecked
                    chkPermission(PER_INSERT_DATA).Value = vbUnchecked
                    chkPermission(PER_ADMINISTER).Value = vbUnchecked
                End If

            Case PER_UPDATE_DATA:
                If (.Value = vbChecked) Then
```

```
                chkPermission(PER_READ_DESIGN).Value = vbChecked
                chkPermission(PER_READ_DATA).Value = vbChecked
            Else
                chkPermission(PER_ADMINISTER).Value = vbUnchecked
                chkPermission(PER_MODIFY_DESIGN).Value = vbUnchecked
            End If

        Case PER_INSERT_DATA:
            If (.Value = vbChecked) Then
                chkPermission(PER_READ_DESIGN).Value = vbChecked
                chkPermission(PER_READ_DATA).Value = vbChecked
            Else
                chkPermission(PER_ADMINISTER).Value = vbUnchecked
            End If

        Case PER_DELETE_DATA:
            If (.Value = vbChecked) Then
                chkPermission(PER_READ_DESIGN).Value = vbChecked
                chkPermission(PER_READ_DATA).Value = vbChecked
            Else
                chkPermission(PER_ADMINISTER).Value = vbUnchecked
                chkPermission(PER_MODIFY_DESIGN).Value = vbUnchecked
            End If

    End Select

  End With

End Sub
```

7. Enter the cmdSave_Click event code now. This code calculates the PermissionCode value from the checkboxes on the form and saves it to the Permissions property of the appropriate Document object.

```
Private Sub cmdSave_Click()

' if there is an error, goto the code labeled by ERR_cmdSave_Click
On Error GoTo ERR_cmdSave_Click:

    Dim oDocument As Document
    Dim lPermissionCode As Long

    ' set the document object variable to the proper selected table or
    ' query from the list box
    Set oDocument = _
            db.Containers("Tables").Documents(lstTablesAndQueries.Text)

    ' create the proper permission code dependent upon the selected check
    ' boxes of frmPermitter

    If chkPermission(PER_ADMINISTER) = vbChecked Then

        lPermissionCode = DB_ADMINISTER

    ElseIf chkPermission(PER_MODIFY_DESIGN) = vbChecked Then
        If chkPermission(PER_INSERT_DATA) = vbChecked Then
```

continued on next page

continued from previous page

```
                lPermissionCode = DB_MODIFYDESIGN_INSERTDATA

        Else

                lPermissionCode = DB_MODIFYDESIGN

        End If
    ElseIf chkPermission(PER_UPDATE_DATA) = vbChecked Then
        If chkPermission(PER_INSERT_DATA) = vbChecked Then
            If chkPermission(PER_DELETE_DATA) = vbChecked Then

                lPermissionCode = DB_UPDATEINSERTDELETEDATA

            Else

                lPermissionCode = DB_UPDATEINSERTDATA

            End If
        Else

                lPermissionCode = DB_UPDATEDATA

        End If
    ElseIf chkPermission(PER_INSERT_DATA) = vbChecked Then
        If chkPermission(PER_DELETE_DATA) = vbChecked Then

                lPermissionCode = DB_INSERTDELETEDATA

        Else

                lPermissionCode = DB_INSERTDATA

        End If
    ElseIf chkPermission(PER_DELETE_DATA) = vbChecked Then

            lPermissionCode = DB_DELETEDATA

    ElseIf chkPermission(PER_READ_DATA) = vbChecked Then

            lPermissionCode = DB_READDATA

    ElseIf chkPermission(PER_READ_DESIGN) = vbChecked Then

            lPermissionCode = DB_READDESIGN

    Else

            lPermissionCode = DB_NOPERMISSIONS

    End If

    With oDocument

        ' save the permission code to the document object for the proper
        ' user
        .UserName = lstUsers.Text
```

```
        If (UCase$(.UserName) = "ADMIN") Then _
                lPermissionCode = lPermissionCode + DB_READSEC

        .Permissions = lPermissionCode
        lblPermissions.Caption = .Permissions

    End With

Exit Sub

ERR_cmdSave_Click:

    ' display the error for the user
    With Err
        MsgBox "ERROR #" & .Number & ": " & .Description, vbExclamation, _
                "ERROR"
    End With

End Sub
```

8. Enter the `cmdClose_Click` event code given next. This simply ends the application.

```
Private Sub cmdClose_Click()

    ' close the application
    Unload Me

End Sub
```

9. The `UnCheckAll` procedure, as shown here, is called from throughout the application to clear all the checkboxes on the form:

```
Private Sub UnCheckAll()

    Dim nCount As Integer

    ' set all the permission checkboxes to unchecked
    For nCount = 0 To 6
        chkPermission(nCount).Value = vbUnchecked
    Next nCount

End Sub
```

10. Now enter both the `FillUserList` and the `FillTableAndQueriesList` procedures as shown next. The `FillUserList` procedure populates the `lstUsers` list box with the information found in the `Users` collection of the new workspace, and the `FillTableAndQueriesList` procedure populates the `lstTablesAndQueries` list box with the tables and queries found in the `Documents` collection of the `Tables` container.

```
Private Sub FillUserList()

    Dim oUser As User
```

continued on next page

continued from previous page

```
        ' populate the user list boxes with all users except CREATOR, ENGINE,
        ' and ADMIN (these shouldn't be changed)
        For Each oUser In DBEngine.Workspaces(0).Users

            With oUser

                If (UCase$(.Name) <> "CREATOR") _
                And (UCase$(.Name) <> "ENGINE") _
                And (UCase$(.Name) <> "ADMIN") Then

                    lstUsers.AddItem .Name

                End If

            End With

        Next

End Sub

Private Sub FillTableAndQueriesList()

    Dim oDocument As Document

    ' populate the TableAndQueries list boxes with all the available tables
    ' and queries except the system ones
    For Each oDocument In db.Containers("Tables").Documents

        With oDocument
            If (Left$(.Name, 4) <> "MSys") Then _
                    lstTablesAndQueries.AddItem .Name
        End With

    Next

End Sub
```

11. The `ReadPermissions` function returns a Boolean value: `True` for success and `False` for failure. This code breaks down the `Permissions` property of the appropriate `Document` object and checks off the corresponding check boxes of the `frmPermitter` form.

```
Function ReadPermissions() As Boolean

' if there is an error, then goto the code labeled by ERR_ReadPermissions
On Error GoTo ERR_ReadPermissions:

    Dim nCount As Integer
    Dim lPermissionCode As Long
    Dim oDocument As Document

    ' set the document object to the appropriately selected table or query
    Set oDocument = _
            db.Containers("Tables").Documents(lstTablesAndQueries.Text)
```

```
' set the user name and get the current permissions for that user
With oDocument
    .UserName = lstUsers.Text
    lblPermissions.Caption = .Permissions
    lPermissionCode = .Permissions
End With

' set all check boxes to unchecked
UnCheckAll

' set the appropriate check boxes for the current permission for the
' user selected
Select Case lPermissionCode

    Case DB_READDESIGN
        chkPermission(PER_READ_DESIGN).Value = vbChecked

    Case DB_READDATA
        chkPermission(PER_READ_DATA).Value = vbChecked
        chkPermission(PER_READ_DESIGN).Value = vbChecked

    Case DB_INSERTDATA
        chkPermission(PER_INSERT_DATA).Value = vbChecked
        chkPermission(PER_READ_DESIGN).Value = vbChecked
        chkPermission(PER_READ_DATA).Value = vbChecked

    Case DB_UPDATEDATA
        chkPermission(PER_UPDATE_DATA).Value = vbChecked
        chkPermission(PER_READ_DESIGN).Value = vbChecked
        chkPermission(PER_READ_DATA).Value = vbChecked

    Case DB_UPDATEINSERTDATA
        chkPermission(PER_UPDATE_DATA).Value = vbChecked
        chkPermission(PER_INSERT_DATA).Value = vbChecked
        chkPermission(PER_READ_DESIGN).Value = vbChecked
        chkPermission(PER_READ_DATA).Value = vbChecked

    Case DB_DELETEDATA
        chkPermission(PER_DELETE_DATA).Value = vbChecked
        chkPermission(PER_READ_DESIGN).Value = vbChecked
        chkPermission(PER_READ_DATA).Value = vbChecked

    Case DB_INSERTDELETEDATA
        chkPermission(PER_DELETE_DATA).Value = vbChecked
        chkPermission(PER_READ_DESIGN).Value = vbChecked
        chkPermission(PER_READ_DATA).Value = vbChecked
        chkPermission(PER_INSERT_DATA).Value = vbChecked

    Case DB_UPDATEDELETEDATA
        chkPermission(PER_UPDATE_DATA).Value = vbChecked
        chkPermission(PER_READ_DESIGN).Value = vbChecked
        chkPermission(PER_READ_DATA).Value = vbChecked
        chkPermission(PER_DELETE_DATA).Value = vbChecked

    Case DB_UPDATEINSERTDELETEDATA
        chkPermission(PER_UPDATE_DATA).Value = vbChecked
        chkPermission(PER_READ_DESIGN).Value = vbChecked
```

continued on next page

continued from previous page

```
            chkPermission(PER_READ_DATA).Value = vbChecked
            chkPermission(PER_DELETE_DATA).Value = vbChecked
            chkPermission(PER_INSERT_DATA).Value = vbChecked

    Case DB_MODIFYDESIGN
            chkPermission(PER_MODIFY_DESIGN).Value = vbChecked
            chkPermission(PER_READ_DESIGN).Value = vbChecked
            chkPermission(PER_READ_DATA).Value = vbChecked
            chkPermission(PER_UPDATE_DATA).Value = vbChecked
            chkPermission(PER_DELETE_DATA).Value = vbChecked

    Case DB_MODIFYDESIGN_INSERTDATA
            chkPermission(PER_MODIFY_DESIGN).Value = vbChecked
            chkPermission(PER_READ_DESIGN).Value = vbChecked
            chkPermission(PER_READ_DATA).Value = vbChecked
            chkPermission(PER_UPDATE_DATA).Value = vbChecked
            chkPermission(PER_INSERT_DATA).Value = vbChecked
            chkPermission(PER_DELETE_DATA).Value = vbChecked

    Case DB_ADMINISTER
            For nCount = 0 To 6
                chkPermission(nCount).Value = vbChecked
            Next nCount

    End Select

    ' indicate success
    ReadPermissions = True

Exit Function

ERR_ReadPermissions:

    ' display the error for the user
    With Err
        MsgBox "ERROR #" & .Number& & ": " & .Description, vbExclamation, _
                "ERROR"
    End With

    ' indicate failure
    ReadPermissions = False

End Function
```

How It Works

When the form loads, the program connects to the system database, opens the ORDERS database, and populates the two list boxes according to the available information from these two databases. When the user selects both a valid user and a table or query from the list boxes, the **ReadPermissions** function is called to display the options available for the combination through seven checkboxes on the form. The user can change these permissions and then save them by clicking the Save button. The application then calculates a new value for the

`Permissions` property of the appropriate user/document combination and saves it to the system database.

Comments

The Permissions help screen identifies built-in constants for representing values of the `Permissions` property. If you look up these constants in the Object Browser, you can see their values. Using these built-in variables is tricky, however, because it is not always clear which implied properties each is including. The values in Table 11.10 were obtained experimentally, by changing the permissions in Microsoft Access and reading the resulting value of the `Permissions` property through Visual Basic.

COMPLEXITY
INTERMEDIATE

11.6 How do I...
Change ownership of database objects?

Problem

How can I give system administrators the ability to change the owner of various tables and queries through my Visual Basic application?

Technique

Every data object in Microsoft Access has an owner. The default owner is the creator of that object. The owner has specific permissions that others do not necessarily have. These permissions include the right to grant full privileges to himself or others.

The name of the owner of a table or query resides in the `Owner` property of the appropriate `Document` object that represents the data object. A user with Administer permission can change the owner of any data object by changing the name of the `Owner` property.

Steps

Open and run the project OWNERSHIP.VBP. If the user name and password variables, located in the `Form_Load` event, are correct, you should see the form shown in Figure 11.7. When a user clicks on a table or query in the list box, the owner of that data object is selected from the other list box. By selecting a different user from the list and clicking the Save button, you can change ownership of the data object.

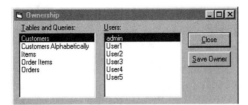

Figure 11.7. The Ownership project.

1. Create a new project and call it OWNERSHIP.VBP. Use **Form1** to create the objects and edit the properties as listed in Table 11.12. Save the form as frmOwnership.frm.

Table 11.12. Objects and properties for the Ownership project.

OBJECT	PROPERTY	SETTING
Form	Name	frmOwnership
	Caption	"Ownership"
List box	Name	lstUsers
List box	Name	lstTablesAndQueries
Command button	Name	cmdSave
	Caption	"&Save"
Command button	Name	cmdClose
	Caption	"&Close"
	Cancel	-1 'True
	Default	-1 'True
Label	Name	lblUsers
	Caption	"&Users:"
Label	Name	lblTablesAndQueries
	Caption	"&Tables And Queries"

2. Begin by entering the following code into the declarations section of the project:

```
Option Explicit

' form-level object variable used to hold the database object
Private db As Database
```

3. Now enter the **Form_Load** event code as listed next. Change the **sUserName** and **sPassword** variables to hold the values of your Administrator's user name and password.

```
Private Sub Form_Load()

' if there is an error, then goto the code section labeled by ERR_Form_Load
On Error GoTo ERR_Form_Load:

    Dim sUserName As String
    Dim sPassword As String
    Dim sDBName As String

    ' assign default user name and password
    sUserName = "Admin"
    sPassword = ""

    With DBEngine

        ' set system database path and name
        .SystemDB = GetWorkgroupDatabase

        ' set default user name and password
        .DefaultUser = sUserName
        .DefaultPassword = sPassword

        ' get path and name of database from ReadINI module
        sDBName = DBPath

        ' open database
        Set db = .Workspaces(0).OpenDatabase(sDBName)

    End With

    ' populate the two list boxes with the available users, tables, and
    ' queries from database
    FillUserList
    FillTableAndQueriesList

    ' if there are no valid users, inform the user and exit the application
    If (lstUsers.ListCount < 1) Then

        MsgBox "There are no users!", vbExclamation, "USERS"
        cmdClose_Click

    End If

    ' initialize the list boxes to point to the first item in each list box
    lstUsers.ListIndex = 0
    lstTablesAndQueries.ListIndex = 0

Exit Sub

ERR_Form_Load:

    ' display error for the user
    With Err
        MsgBox "ERROR #" & .Number & ": " & .Description, vbExclamation, _
            "ERROR"
```

continued on next page

continued from previous page
```
        End With

End Sub
```

4. Enter the `Form_Unload` code to ensure that the database object variable is closed and released before the application finishes termination:

```
Private Sub Form_Unload(Cancel As Integer)

    ' close the database
    Set db = Nothing

End Sub
```

5. Now enter the code for both the `FillTableAndQueriesList` and the `FillUserList` procedures. These two routines are very similar to those found in the preceding How-To. The `FillTableAndQueriesList` procedure populates the `lstTablesAndQueries` list box with the names of the data objects in the `Tables` container. The `FillUserList` routine populates the `lstUsers` list box with the users found in the `Users` collection of the current `Workspace` object.

```
Private Sub FillTableAndQueriesList()

    Dim oDocument As Document

    ' populate the TableAndQueries list boxes with all the available tables
    ' and queries except the system ones
    For Each oDocument In db.Containers("Tables").Documents

        With oDocument
            If (Left$(.Name, 4) <> "MSys") Then _
                    lstTablesAndQueries.AddItem .Name
        End With

    Next

End Sub

Private Sub FillUserList()

    Dim oUser As User

    ' populate the user list boxes with all users except CREATOR and ENGINE
    ' (these shouldn't be changed)
    For Each oUser In DBEngine.Workspaces(0).Users

        With oUser

            If (UCase$(.Name) <> "CREATOR") _
            And (UCase$(.Name) <> "ENGINE") Then

                lstUsers.AddItem .Name

            End If
```

```
        End With

    Next

End Sub
```

6. Now enter the `lstTablesAndQueries_Click` event code as listed here. This code finds the owner of the selected data object from the Users list by comparing it to the `Owner` property of the selected `Document` object.

```
Private Sub lstTablesAndQueries_Click()

    Dim nCount As Integer
    Dim sCurOwner As String

    With lstUsers

        ' loop through each user until the owner of the selected table or
        ' query is found
        For nCount = 0 To .ListCount - 1

            sCurOwner = _
                db.Containers("Tables").Documents(lstTablesAndQueries.Text).Owner

                If (.List(nCount) = sCurOwner) Then .ListIndex = nCount

        Next nCount
    End With

End Sub
```

7. The `cmdSave_Click` event code simply changes the value of the `Owner` property of the `Documents` object to that of the selected user from the `lstUsers` list box:

```
Private Sub cmdSave_Click()

' if there is an error, goto the code labeled by ERR_cmdSave_Click
On Error GoTo ERR_cmdSave_Click:

    ' assign the new owner to the select table or query
    db.Containers("Tables").Documents(lstTablesAndQueries.Text).Owner = _
            lstUsers.Text

Exit Sub

ERR_cmdSave_Click:

    ' display error for the user
    With Err
        MsgBox "ERROR #" & .Number & ": " & .Description, vbExclamation, _
                "ERROR"
    End With

End Sub
```

8. Finally, enter the code for the `cmdClose_Click` event to terminate the application:

```
Private Sub cmdClose_Click()

    ' end the application
    Unload Me

End Sub
```

How It Works

When the program is started, the system database is accessed using the default user and password properties. With this database, the `lstTablesAndQueries` list box is populated with the available data objects. The Users list box is populated with all the users available in the given workgroup. When the user selects a data object from the list, the `Owner` property of that data object is used to find the user who is the owner of it. With a click of the Save button on the `frmOwnership` form, the `Owner` property is changed to the currently selected user in the `lstUsers` list box.

Comments

We have added extensive error-handling code to the preceding few How-To's. This is because of the complexity involved, and the precision necessary, when accessing the system database. A lot of the code will vary from machine to machine and user to user, depending on user names and passwords.

If you are working on a single PC that is not part of a network, there is a very good chance that you will have only one or two users listed in the `lstUsers` list box. To add more users to your system, jump to How-To 11.9 to see a project that enables you to add more users.

COMPLEXITY
BEGINNING

11.7 How do I...
Change or delete database passwords?

Problem

How do I give the system administrators at my site the ability to change users' passwords for Access databases from my Visual Basic applications?

Technique

Each user's password is stored in the **Password** property of the corresponding **User** object. The current user's password is stored in the **Password** property of the current **Workspace** object.

The **Password** property cannot be read through Visual Basic, and it cannot be directly set. To change the password, you must use the **NewPassword** method for a given user. The **NewPassword** method has two arguments, the first being the current password and the second being the new password. Ordinary users cannot change their passwords without knowing the current ones.

Users with Administer power can change other users' passwords as well as their own without the need to know the current password. Instead, an empty string is passed to the **NewPassword** method in place of the current password.

Steps

Open and run the PASSWORDS.VBP project. A list of available users appears on the form, as shown in Figure 11.8. You can change the password of a given user by clicking the Change Password button, or you can delete the password for a user by clicking the Delete Password button.

1. Create a new project and save it as PASSWORDS.VBP. Use **Form1** to add the objects and edit the properties as listed in Table 11.3. Save the form as frmPasswords.frm.

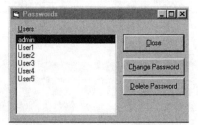

Figure 11.8. The Passwords project.

Table 11.13. Objects and properties for the Passwords project.

OBJECT	PROPERTY	SETTING
Form	Name	frmPasswords
	Caption	"Passwords"
List box	Name	lstUsers
Command button	Name	cmdChangePassword
	Caption	"C&hange Password"
Command button	Name	cmdDeletePassword
	Caption	"&Delete Password"
Command button	Name	cmdClose
	Caption	"&Close"
	Cancel	-1 'True
	Default	-1 'True
Label	Name	lblUsers
	Caption	"&Users"

2. Begin by entering the `Form_Load` event code to access the system database and the call to `FillUserList`, which populates the `lstUsers` list box. If there are no users in the list, the application terminates.

```
Private Sub Form_Load()

' if there is an error, then goto the code section labeled by ERR_Form_Load
On Error GoTo ERR_Form_Load:

    Dim sUserName As String
    Dim sPassword As String

    ' assign default user name and password
    sUserName = "Admin"
    sPassword = ""

With DBEngine

    ' set system database path and name
    .SystemDB = GetWorkgroupDatabase

    ' set default user name and password
    .DefaultUser = sUserName
    .DefaultPassword = sPassword

End With

    ' populate the users list box with the available users
    FillUserList

    ' if there are no valid users, inform the user and exit the application
    If (lstUsers.ListCount < 1) Then
```

```
            MsgBox "There are no users!", vbExclamation, "USERS"
            cmdClose_Click

     End If

     ' initialize the list boxes to point to the first item in users list
     lstUsers.ListIndex = 0

Exit Sub

ERR_Form_Load:

     ' display error for the user
     With Err
         MsgBox "ERROR #" & .Number & ": " & .Description, vbExclamation, _
             "ERROR"
     End With

     ' end the application
     cmdClose_Click

End Sub
```

3. Enter the code for the **Click** event of the **cmdChangePassword** command button as shown next. This code asks for the old password, the new password, and a confirmation of the new password; then it calls the **ChangePassword** routine to change the password. Users logged in as Admin do not have to specify anything for the old password because they have the power to change the current password without any knowledge of it.

```
Private Sub cmdChangePassword_Click()

     ' local variables used to store passwords
     Dim sOldPassword As String
     Dim sNewPassword As String
     Dim sConPassword As String

     ' ask for old password
     sOldPassword = InputBox("Please enter the old password for user '" _
                             & lstUsers.Text & "'.", "CHANGE PASSWORD")

     ' ask for new password
     sNewPassword = InputBox("Please enter the new password for user '" _
                             & lstUsers.Text & "'.", "CHANGE PASSWORD")

     ' confirm new password
     sConPassword = InputBox("Please confirm new password for user '" _
                             & lstUsers.Text & "'.", "CHANGE PASSWORD")

     ' if new password is not equivalent to the confirmed password,
     ' notify the user and end the task; otherwise, change the password
     If (sNewPassword <> sConPassword) Then
```

continued on next page

continued from previous page

```
            MsgBox "New password does not match confirmed password.", _
                    vbExclamation, "ERROR"

        Else

            ChangePassword sOldPassword, sNewPassword

        End If

End Sub
```

4. Now enter the code to delete a password located in the `Click` event of the `cmdDeletePassword` command button. This event asks for the old password and calls the `ChangePassword` routine with an empty string as a new password to delete the current password. Again, if the user is logged on as Admin, as in this example, it is unnecessary to enter an old password.

```
Private Sub cmdDeletePassword_Click()

    ' local variable used to store old password
    Dim sOldPassword As String

    ' ask for old password
    sOldPassword = InputBox("Please enter the old password for user '" _
                        & lstUsers.Text & "'.", "DELETE PASSWORD")

    ' change the password
    ChangePassword sOldPassword, ""

End Sub
```

5. Enter the code for the `cmdClose_Click` event to terminate the application:

```
Private Sub cmdClose_Click()

    ' end the application
    Unload Me

End Sub
```

6. The `FillUserList` routine is listed next. This procedure adds all the current users of the workgroup to the `lstUsers` list box except for `CREATOR` and `ENGINE`. These should not be changed; therefore, they are not available for access by the user.

```
Private Sub FillUserList()

    Dim oUser As User

    ' populate the user list boxes with all users except CREATOR and ENGINE
    ' (these shouldn't be changed)
    For Each oUser In DBEngine.Workspaces(0).Users
```

```
            With oUser

                If (UCase$(.Name) <> "CREATOR") _
                And (UCase$(.Name) <> "ENGINE") Then

                    lstUsers.AddItem .Name

                End If

            End With

        Next

    End Sub
```

7. Finally, enter the `ChangePassword` routine that is listed here. This procedure takes two arguments. The first is the old password, and the second is the new password. If there are no errors, the password is changed using the `NewPassword` method.

```
Private Sub ChangePassword(sOldPassword As String, _
                    sNewPassword As String)

' if there is an error, then goto the code labeled by ERR_ChangePassword
On Error GoTo ERR_ChangePassword:

    ' constant used to define application-defined error
    Const ERR_PASSWORD_TOO_LONG = 32000

    ' if the new password is too long, raise application-defined error
    If (Len(sNewPassword) > 14) Then Error ERR_PASSWORD_TOO_LONG

    ' change password, given the old and new passwords
    DBEngine.Workspaces(0).Users(lstUsers.Text).NewPassword sOldPassword, _
                                                    sNewPassword

    ' if we got this far, we must be successful; notify the user
    MsgBox "Password successfully changed for user '" _
            & lstUsers.Text & "'", vbInformation, "SUCCESS"

Exit Sub

ERR_ChangePassword:

    ' local variable used to hold error message
    Dim sMessage As String

    With Err

        Select Case .Number

            ' application-defined error, password too long
            Case ERR_PASSWORD_TOO_LONG:
                sMessage = "The password must be 14 characters or less."
```

continued on next page

continued from previous page

```
           ' unexpected error, create error message with number and
           ' description
           Case Else:
               sMessage = "ERROR #" & .Number & ": " & .Description

       End Select

   End With


   ' display error for the user
   MsgBox sMessage, vbExclamation, "ERROR"

End Sub
```

How It Works

After the program accesses the system database in the `Form_Load` event, the list box on the form is populated with the available users in the workgroup. When a user selects a user from the list and clicks the Change Password button, old and new passwords are sent to the `ChangePassword` procedure, where a call to the `NewPassword` method changes the password. When the user clicks the Delete Password button, an empty string is passed to the `ChangePassword` procedure to set the new password to nothing, therefore deleting it.

COMPLEXITY

BEGINNING

11.8   How do I...
Use a single password for data access for all users?

Problem

I want to secure my Access database, but I do not think it is necessary for each user to have his or her own password. Instead, I want to create a password that I could change for the entire database, regardless of the user. How do I create a single password for an entire Access database with Visual Basic?

Technique

The same concept as shown in How-To 11.7 is applied here. The `NewPassword` method is used to change the password for a given Access database.

The `NewPassword` not only applies to the `User` object, but it also is available with the `Database` object. When you specify a password for a database, you must connect to that database in the future with a string indicating the valid password.

This string is passed as an argument to the `OpenDatabase` method as shown in this example:

```
Set db = _
    DBEngine.Workspaces(0).OpenDatabase(DBName, True, False, ";pwd=PASSWORD")
```

Here, `db` is a database object, `DBName` is a valid path and name of an Access database, and `PASSWORD` is the password for the given database.

Steps

Open and run the DatabasePassword.vbp project. You should see the form as shown in Figure 11.9. When a user clicks the Open Database button, she is prompted with an input box asking for the password for the database. If there is no password, the user simply presses Enter. After the database is open, the user can change the password by clicking the Change Password button. Just as with changing a user's password, the project prompts for the old password as well as the new and a confirmation of the new password. If all is successful, the password is changed.

1. Create a new project and save it as DatabasePassword.vbp. Add the objects and edit the properties of **Form1** as shown in Table 11.14. Afterward, save the form as frmDatabasePassword.frm.

Figure 11.9. The DatabasePassword project.

Table 11.14. Objects and properties for the DatabasePassword project.

OBJECT	PROPERTY	SETTING
Form	Name	frmDatabasePassword
	Caption	"Database Password"
Command button	Name	cmdOpenDatabase
	Caption	"&Open Database"
Command button	Name	cmdChangePassword
	Caption	"Change &Password"
Command button	Name	cmdCloseDatabase
	Caption	"&Close Database"
Command button	Name	cmdExit
	Caption	"&Exit"
	Cancel	-1 'True
	Default	-1 'True

2. Enter the following code in the declarations section of your project. The db object variable is used to store the database object, and the NO_ERROR constant declaration is used throughout the project to indicate success.

```
Option Explicit

' form-level object variable declaration used to hold database object
Private db As Database

' form-level constant declaration used to indicate success
Private Const NO_ERROR = 0
```

3. Now enter the familiar Form_Load event as shown next. This event, as the others of the previous How-To sections, establishes a link with the system database using a default user and password. These variables might need to be altered by the user to her own Administer values.

```
Private Sub Form_Load()

' if there is an error, then goto the code section labeled by ERR_Form_Load
On Error GoTo ERR_Form_Load:

    Dim sUserName As String
    Dim sPassword As String

    ' assign default user name and password
    sUserName = "Admin"
    sPassword = ""

    With DBEngine
```

```
                    ' set system database path and name
                    .SystemDB = GetWorkgroupDatabase

                    ' set default user name and password
                    .DefaultUser = sUserName
                    .DefaultPassword = sPassword

            End With

            ' initialize database to closed state to disable various buttons
            cmdCloseDatabase_Click

    Exit Sub

    ERR_Form_Load:

            ' display error for the user
            With Err
                MsgBox "ERROR #" & .Number & ": " & .Description, vbExclamation, _
                        "ERROR"
            End With

            ' end the application
            cmdExit_Click

    End Sub
```

4. Add the code that ensures that the database is closed in the `Form_Unload` event as shown here:

```
    Private Sub Form_Unload(Cancel As Integer)

            ' ensure that the database is closed upon shutdown of application
            cmdCloseDatabase_Click

    End Sub
```

5. Now enter the code for the `cmdOpenDatabase_Click` event of the Open Database command button. This code prompts the user for the current database password, creates a password string, and passes it to the `OpenDatabase` method. If all is successful, the user is notified that the database is open, and the Change Password and Close Database buttons are enabled.

```
    Private Sub cmdOpenDatabase_Click()

    ' if there is an error, goto the code labeled by ERR_cmdOpenDatabase_Click
    On Error GoTo ERR_cmdOpenDatabase_Click:

        Dim sPassword As String
        Dim sDBName As String

        ' local constant declaration of application-defined error
        Const ERR_NOT_VALID_PASSWORD = 3031
```

continued on next page

continued from previous page

```
' ask user for the password of the database
sPassword = InputBox("Please enter database password.", _
                     "OPEN DATABASE")

' create connection string
sPassword = ";pwd=" & sPassword

' retrieve database name and path from the ReadINI module
sDBName = DBPath

' attempt to open the database
Set db = DBEngine.Workspaces(0).OpenDatabase _
             (sDBName, True, False, sPassword)

ERR_cmdOpenDatabase_Click:

    Dim sMessage As String

    With Err

        ' determine error
        Select Case .Number

            ' there is no error, inform the user of success and enable the
            ' use of the change password and close database command buttons
            Case NO_ERROR:
                sMessage = "Database opened successfully."

                cmdOpenDatabase.Enabled = False
                cmdChangePassword.Enabled = True
                cmdCloseDatabase.Enabled = True

            ' password is incorrect
            Case ERR_NOT_VALID_PASSWORD:
                sMessage = "Invalid password."

            ' unexpected error, inform the user
            Case Else:
                sMessage = "ERROR #" & .Number & ": " & .Description

        End Select

        ' display the error for the user
        MsgBox sMessage, _
               IIf(.Number = NO_ERROR, vbInformation, vbExclamation), _
               IIf(.Number = NO_ERROR, "SUCCESS", "ERROR")

    End With

End Sub
```

6. The `cmdChangePassword_Click` event prompts the user for the old password, the new, and a confirmation to successfully change the password by calling the `NewPassword` method of the `Database` object. Enter the following code:

```
Private Sub cmdChangePassword_Click()

' if there is an error,
' goto the code labeled by ERR_cmdChangePassword_Click
On Error GoTo ERR_cmdChangePassword_Click:

    ' local variables used to store passwords
    Dim sOldPassword As String
    Dim sNewPassword As String
    Dim sConPassword As String

    ' private constant declarations for application-defined errors
    Const ERR_PASSWORDS_DIFFER = 32000
    Const ERR_PASSWORD_TOO_LONG = 32001

    ' ask for old password
    sOldPassword = InputBox("Please enter the old password for the " _
                        & "database.", "CHANGE PASSWORD")

    ' ask for new password
    sNewPassword = InputBox("Please enter the new password for the " _
                        & "database.", "CHANGE PASSWORD")

    If (Len(sNewPassword) > 14) Then Error ERR_PASSWORD_TOO_LONG

    ' confirm new password
    sConPassword = InputBox("Please confirm new password for the " _
                        & "database.", "CHANGE PASSWORD")

    ' if new password is not equivalent to the confirmed password,
    ' notify the user and end the task; otherwise, change the password
    If (sNewPassword <> sConPassword) Then Error ERR_PASSWORDS_DIFFER

    ' change the password
    db.NewPassword sOldPassword, sNewPassword

ERR_cmdChangePassword_Click:

    Dim sMessage As String

    With Err

        ' select appropriate error
        Select Case .Number

            ' no error has occurred, inform the user of success
            Case NO_ERROR:
                sMessage = "Password changed successfully."

            ' new and confirmed passwords are different
            Case ERR_PASSWORDS_DIFFER:
                sMessage = "The confirmed password does not match the " _
                        & "new password."
```

continued on next page

continued from previous page

```
                    ' password is longer than 14 characters
                    Case ERR_PASSWORD_TOO_LONG:
                        sMessage = "The password must be 14 characters or less."

                    ' unexpected error, inform the user
                    Case Else:
                        sMessage = "ERROR #" & .Number & ": " & .Description

            End Select

            ' display the error for the user
            MsgBox sMessage, _
                    IIf(.Number = NO_ERROR, vbInformation, vbExclamation), _
                    IIf(.Number = NO_ERROR, "SUCCESS", "ERROR")

    End With

End Sub
```

7. The `Click` event of the Close Database command button is listed next. This procedure simply releases the database object by setting it equal to nothing and disables the Change Password and Close Database buttons, as well as enabling the Open Database button. The final event, `cmdExit_Click`, ends the application. Enter these procedures now:

```
Private Sub cmdCloseDatabase_Click()

    ' close the database
    Set db = Nothing

    ' only allow the user to open the database
    cmdOpenDatabase.Enabled = True
    cmdChangePassword.Enabled = False
    cmdCloseDatabase.Enabled = False

End Sub

Private Sub cmdExit_Click()

    ' end the application
    Unload Me

End Sub
```

How It Works

When the DatabasePassword project is initialized, the system database is addressed with the default user name and password. When the user opens the database, he is prompted for the current password. This password is used to create a string that is passed to the `OpenDatabase` method to open the database object.

When the user selects to change the current database password, he is asked to supply the old and a new password, as well as a confirmation of the new password. With a call to the `NewDatabase` method of the database object, the password is changed.

It should be noted that the password cannot be changed when a database is opened in shared mode. As in this How-To, you must open the database exclusively (by specifying `True` as the second argument to the `OpenDatabase` method) to change the password.

Comments

Every How-To in this chapter uses the same database, the ORDERS.MDB database file. When you are through with this How-To, be sure to change the database password back to a null string so that the other How-To projects can successfully access the database!

COMPLEXITY
BEGINNING

11.9 How do I...
Add new users to a system database?

Problem

I need to give system administrators at my user sites the ability to add new users to the system database. How do I accomplish this task through Visual Basic?

Technique

The `Workspace` object has a collection called `Users`. Each user defined in the system database has a corresponding `User` object within the `Users` collection. To add a new user, you must first create a new `User` object. The new `User` object must be supplied a name, a PID, and, optionally, a password.

The PID is a case-sensitive alphanumeric string between 4 and 20 characters in length. This PID is used by the Jet engine in combination with the user name to build a security ID for a user.

After the `User` object is created, it is appended to the `Users` collection of the current `Workspace` object via the `Append` method.

Steps

Open and run the AddUser.vbp project. You should see the form shown in Figure 11.10. To add a user, click the Add User button and supply a user name and password; the PID string is calculated from the user name. If the user is successfully added, you will see a message box indicating so, and the list box on the form will be updated to include the new user.

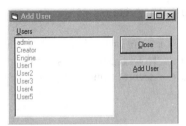

Figure 11.10. The AddUser
project.

1. Create a new project and call it AddUser.vbp. Using **Form1**, add the objects
and edit the properties as shown in Table 11.15, saving the form as
frmAddUser.frm.

Table 11.15. Objects and properties for the AddUser project.

OBJECT	PROPERTY	SETTING
Form	Name	frmAddUser
	Caption	"Add User"
List box	Name	lstUsers
Command button	Name	cmdAddUser
	Caption	"&Add User"
Command button	Name	cmdClose
	Caption	"&Close"
	Cancel	-1 'True
	Default	-1 'True
Label	Name	lblUsers
	Caption	"&Users"

2. There are no form-level declarations in this project, so go ahead and enter
the **Form_Load** event code as shown next. This code accesses the system
database using the default user name, Admin, and an empty string
password. After this is done, the **FillUserList** procedure is called to
show all the available users in the system database.

```
Private Sub Form_Load()

' if there is an error, then goto the code section labeled by ERR_Form_Load
On Error GoTo ERR_Form_Load:

    Dim sUserName As String
    Dim sPassword As String

    ' assign default user name and password
```

```
    sUserName = "Admin"
    sPassword = ""

    With DBEngine

        ' set system database path and name
        .SystemDB = GetWorkgroupDatabase

        ' set default user name and password
        .DefaultUser = sUserName
        .DefaultPassword = sPassword

    End With

    ' populate the users list box with the available users
    FillUserList

Exit Sub

ERR_Form_Load:

    ' display error for the user
    With Err
        MsgBox "ERROR #" & .Number & ": " & .Description, vbExclamation, _
               "ERROR"
    End With

    ' end the application
    cmdClose_Click

End Sub
```

3. Now enter the code for the `Click` event of the `cmdAddUser` command button. This event asks the user for both a user name and a password. After error-checking the input values, the procedure calls the `GetNewPID` procedure to receive a personal identifier. This event then creates a new `User` object with this information and appends it to the `Users` collection of the current `Workspace` object.

```
Private Sub cmdAddUser_Click()

' if there is an error, then goto code labeled by ERR_cmdAddUser_Click
On Error GoTo ERR_cmdAddUser_Click:

    ' local variables used to store passwords
    Dim sNewUserName As String
    Dim sNewPassword As String
    Dim sConPassword As String

    ' local variables used for the new user
    Dim sPID As String
    Dim oNewUser As User

    ' constant declarations for application-defined error messages
    Const ERR_NO_USER_NAME = 32000
```

continued on next page

continued from previous page

```
      Const ERR_PASSWORD_TOO_LONG = 32001
      Const ERR_PASSWORDS_NOT_EQUAL = 32002


      ' enter a new user name
      sNewUserName = InputBox("Please enter a new user name.", "ADD USER")


      ' trim excess white spaces from the user name
      sNewUserName = Trim$(sNewUserName)


      ' if no user name is entered, notify the user and abandon task
      If (sNewUserName = "") Then Error ERR_NO_USER_NAME


      ' ask for new password
      sNewPassword = InputBox("Please enter the new password for user '" _
                         & sNewUserName & "'.", "ADD USER")


      ' if the password is too long, notify the user and end the task
      If (Len(sNewPassword) > 14) Then Error ERR_PASSWORD_TOO_LONG


      ' confirm new password
      sConPassword = InputBox("Please confirm new password for user '" _
                         & sNewUserName & "'.", "ADD USER")


      ' if new password is not equivalent to the confirmed password,
      ' notify the user and end the task
      If (sNewPassword <> sConPassword) Then Error ERR_PASSWORDS_NOT_EQUAL


      'get a PID for the new user
      sPID = GetNewPID(sNewUserName)


      With DBEngine

          ' create a new user object from user name, pid, and password
          Set oNewUser = .Workspaces(0).CreateUser(sNewUserName, _
                                                   sPID, _
                                                   sNewPassword)


          ' append the new users to the workspace
          .Workspaces(0).Users.Append oNewUser

      End With


      ' repopulate list box with new users
      FillUserList


      ' notify the user of success
      MsgBox "User '" & sNewUserName & "' added successfully.", _
             vbInformation, "ADD USER"

  Exit Sub

  ERR_cmdAddUser_Click:

      ' variable used for error message
      Dim sMessage As String


      With Err
```

```
            ' create an error message for given error code
            Select Case .Number

                Case ERR_NO_USER_NAME:
                    sMessage = "You did not enter a user name."

                Case ERR_PASSWORD_TOO_LONG:
                    sMessage = "The password must be 14 characters or less"

                Case ERR_PASSWORDS_NOT_EQUAL:
                    sMessage = "The confirmed password is not equivalent to " _
                            & "the new password."

                ' unexpected error, create an error message from the error
                ' number and description
                Case Else:
                    sMessage = "ERROR #" & .Number & ": " & .Description

            End Select

        End With

        ' display the error message for the user
        MsgBox sMessage, vbExclamation, "ERROR"

    End Sub
```

4. Enter the following code to terminate the application:

```
Private Sub cmdClose_Click()

    ' end the application
    Unload Me

End Sub
```

5. Now enter the **FillUserList** procedure, which populates the **lstUsers** list box with all the users listed in the system database:

```
Private Sub FillUserList()

    Dim oUser As User

    With lstUsers

        ' clear current list of users
        .Clear

        ' populate the user list boxes with all users
        For Each oUser In DBEngine.Workspaces(0).Users
            .AddItem oUser.Name
        Next

    End With

End Sub
```

6. Finally, enter the `GetNewPID` function, which creates a new PID string for the specified user name, ensuring that it is at least 4 but no more than 20 characters:

```
Private Function GetNewPID(sUserName As String) As String

    Dim sPID As String

    ' create new PID
    sPID = sUserName

    If (Len(sPID) > 20) Then

        ' if the PID is greater than 20 characters, shorten it
        sPID = Left$(sPID, 20)

    Else

        ' if the PID is less than 4 characters, add some underscores
        While (Len(sPID) < 4)
            sPID = sPID & "_"
        Wend

    End If

    ' return newly created PID value
    GetNewPID = sPID

End Function
```

How It Works

When the `AddUser` project is started, the code reads the system database to populate the list box on the form with the available users. When the user decides to add a new user by clicking the Add User button, he must enter both a new user name and a password. The user name is used to create a PID string. The name, PID, and password are then used to create a new `User` object, which is then appended to the existing `Users` collection.

Comments

To remove a user from the system database, simply use the `Delete` method of the `Workspace` object's `Users` collection to delete the desired user, as shown here:

```
DBEngine.Workspaces(0).Users("USERNAME").Delete
```

Here, *USERNAME* is a name of a user who is currently in the `Users` collection of the current workspace.

COMPLEXITY
BEGINNING

11.10 How do I...
Define new groups in a system database?

Problem

How do I give system administrators the ability to define new groups in the system database through Visual Basic?

Technique

The techniques used in this How-To directly correspond to those used in How-To 11.9. To add a new group to the **Groups** collection of the current **Workspace** object, you must first create a new **Group** object from a group name and a PID.

In previous versions of Microsoft Jet, the identifier used for a group was called a GID (group identifier). Now, to make things uniform, it is called a PID (personal identifier) as it is for a user.

The PID is used in the same manner that it is for a user. It is used in conjunction with the group name to build a Security ID for the group. After the group is created with its name and PID, it is then appended to the **Groups** collection of the current **Workspace** object.

Steps

Open and run the AddGroup.vbp project. You should see the form shown in Figure 11.11. To add a group, click the Add Group button and supply the application with a name for the new group. If all is successful, you will see a verification message box and the new group in the list of groups on the form.

1. Create a new project and save it as AddGroup.vbp. Use **Form1** to create the objects and edit the properties as listed in Table 11.16. Save this form as frmAddGroup.frm.

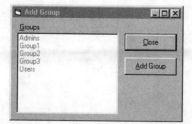

Figure 11.11. The AddGroup project.

Table 11.16. Objects and properties for the AddGroup project.

OBJECT	PROPERTY	SETTING
Form	Name	frmAddGroup
	Caption	"Add Group"
List box	Name	lstGroups
Command button	Name	cmdAddGroup
	Caption	"&Add Group"
Command button	Name	cmdClose
	Caption	"&Close"
	Cancel	-1 'True
	Default	-1 'True
Label	Name	lblGroups
	Caption	"&Groups"

2. Enter the Form_Load event code shown next. This code accesses the system database with the default user name and password assigned to the sUserName and sPassword variables, respectively. After this is done, a call to FillGroupList populates the list box on the frmAddGroup form.

```
Private Sub Form_Load()

' if there is an error, then goto the code section labeled by ERR_Form_Load
On Error GoTo ERR_Form_Load:

    Dim sUserName As String
    Dim sPassword As String

    ' assign default user name and password
    sUserName = "Admin"
    sPassword = ""

    With DBEngine

        ' set system database path and name
        .SystemDB = GetWorkgroupDatabase

        ' set default user name and password
        .DefaultUser = sUserName
        .DefaultPassword = sPassword

    End With

    ' populate the group list box with the available groups
    FillGroupList

Exit Sub

ERR_Form_Load:
```

```
' display error for the user
With Err
    MsgBox "ERROR #" & .Number & ": " & .Description, vbExclamation, _
           "ERROR"
End With

' end the application
cmdClose_Click

End Sub
```

3. Now enter the code for the **Click** event of the **cmdAddGroup** command button. This code asks the user for a new group name and calls **GetNewPID** to create a personal identifier for the new group. With this information, a new **Group** object is created and appended to the **Groups** collection of the current workspace.

```
Private Sub cmdAddGroup_Click()

' if there is an error, then goto code labeled by ERR_cmdAddGroup_Click
On Error GoTo ERR_cmdAddGroup_Click:

    ' local variables used to store new group name
    Dim sNewGroupName As String

    ' local variables used for the new group
    Dim sPID As String
    Dim oNewGroup As Group

    ' constant declaration for application-defined error message
    Const ERR_NO_GROUP_NAME = 32000

    ' enter a new group name
    sNewGroupName = InputBox("Please enter a new group name.", "ADD GROUP")

    ' trim excess white spaces from the group name
    sNewGroupName = Trim$(sNewGroupName)

    ' if no group name is entered, notify the user and abandon task
    If (sNewGroupName = "") Then Error ERR_NO_GROUP_NAME

    'get a PID for the new group
    sPID = GetNewPID(sNewGroupName)

    With DBEngine

        ' create a new group object from group name, PID, and password
        Set oNewGroup = .Workspaces(0).CreateGroup(sNewGroupName, sPID)

        ' append the new groups to the workspace
        .Workspaces(0).Groups.Append oNewGroup

    End With
```

continued on next page

continued from previous page

```
    ' repopulate list box with new groups
    FillGroupList

    ' notify the user of success
    MsgBox "Group '" & sNewGroupName & "' added successfully.", _
           vbInformation, "ADD GROUP"

Exit Sub

ERR_cmdAddGroup_Click:

    ' variable used for error message
    Dim sMessage As String

    With Err

        ' create an error message for given error code
        Select Case .Number

            Case ERR_NO_GROUP_NAME:
                sMessage = "You did not enter a group name."

            ' unexpected error, create an error message from the error
            ' number and description
            Case Else:
                sMessage = "ERROR #" & .Number & ": " & .Description

        End Select

    End With

    ' display the error message for the user
    MsgBox sMessage, vbExclamation, "ERROR"
    Stop
    Resume
End Sub
```

4. Enter the code for the **cmdClose_Click** event, which terminates the application:

```
Private Sub cmdClose_Click()

    ' end the application
    Unload Me

End Sub
```

5. Now enter the **FillGroupList** procedure, which populates the **lstGroups** list box with the groups found in the system database:

```
Private Sub FillGroupList()

    Dim oGroup As Group

    With lstGroups
```

```
        ' clear current list of groups
        .Clear

        ' populate the group list boxes with all groups
        For Each oGroup In DBEngine.Workspaces(0).Groups
            .AddItem oGroup.Name
        Next

    End With

End Sub
```

6. To complete the project, enter the `GetNewPID` function, which accepts the new `GroupName` as an argument used to create the PID that is returned. The PID is ensured to be between 4 and 20 characters in length.

```
Private Function GetNewPID(sGroupName As String) As String

    Dim sPID As String

    ' create new PID
    sPID = sGroupName

    If (Len(sPID) > 20) Then

        ' if the PID is greater than 20 characters, shorten it
        sPID = Left$(sPID, 20)

    Else

        ' if the PID is less than 4 characters, add some underscores
        While (Len(sPID) < 4)
            sPID = sPID & "_"
        Wend

    End If

    ' return newly created PID value
    GetNewPID = sPID

End Function
```

How It Works

This application begins by accessing the system database and populating the list box with the groups that are listed within it. When a user decides to add a new group by clicking the Add Group button, the user is asked to supply a new group name. A PID is then created from this group name, and with both of these variables, a new **Group** object is created. This object is then appended to the **Groups** collection of the current workspace using the **Append** method. Finally, the list box is repopulated with the inclusion of the new group.

Comments

To remove a group from a system database, simply use the `Delete` method of the `Workspace` object's `Groups` collection to delete the desired group, as shown here:

```
DBEngine.Workspaces(0).Groups("GROUPNAME").Delete
```

Here, *GROUPNAME* is a valid name of a group that belongs to the `Groups` collection of the current `Workspace` object.

COMPLEXITY
BEGINNING

11.11 How do I...
Add users to groups and delete users from groups?

Problem

How do I give system administrators at my user sites the ability to add and remove users from different groups, using Visual Basic?

Technique

The `Group` object owns a collection called `Users`. Each user who belongs to the group is represented by a `User` object within the `Users` collection. If a `User` object exists in a system database, you can add that user to a group by first using the `CreateUser` method of the `Group` object to create a temporary `User` object, supplying the user name of a user who is defined within the current system database.

After this job is done, you append the temporary `User` object to the `Users` collection of an existing `Group` object.

Steps

Open and run the AddUsersToGroups.vbp project. You should see the form shown in Figure 11.12. You can select the group you want to work with from the combo box at the top of the form. A list box on the left lists all the available users in the system database, and the list box on the right shows the users who are currently part of the selected group.

To move a user into the currently selected group, select a user from the list of available users and click the > button to move that user to the list of included users. To remove a user from a group, select the user from the list of included users and click the < button. To add all users to a group, click the >> button, and to remove all users from a group, click the << button. Changes are immediate, so be careful!

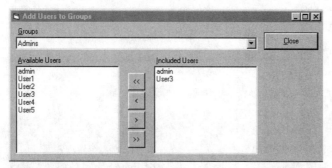

Figure 11.12. The AddUsersToGroups project.

To delete a user from a group, you use the **Delete** method of the **Group** object's **Users** collection.

1. Create a new project and name it AddUsersToGroups.vbp. Add and edit the objects and properties as shown in Table 11.17, and then save the form as frmAddUsersToGroups.frm. Notice that the four **cmdMove** command buttons are part of a control array.

Table 11.17. Objects and properties for the AddUsersToGroups project.

OBJECT	PROPERTY	SETTING
Form	Name	frmAddUsersToGroups
	caption	"Add Users to Groups"
Combo box	Name	cboGroups
	Style	2 'Dropdown List
List box	Name	lstAvailableUsers
	Sorted	-1 'True
List box	Name	lstIncludedUsers
	Sorted	-1 'True
Command button	Name	cmdMove
	Caption	"<<"
	Index	0
Command button	Name	cmdMove
	Caption	"<"
	Index	1
Command button	Name	cmdMove
	Caption	">"
	Index	2

continued on next page

continued from previous page

OBJECT	PROPERTY	SETTING
Command button	Name	cmdMove
	Caption	">>"
	Index	3
Command button	Name	cmdClose
	Caption	"&Close"
	Cancel	-1 'True
	Default	-1 'True
Label	Name	lblGroups
	Caption	"&Groups"
Label	Name	lblAvailableUsers
	Caption	"&Available Users"
Label	Name	lblIncludedUsers
	Caption	"&Included Users"

2. Enter the code for the Form_Load event as shown here. This code initializes the DBEngine with the default user name and passwords defined in the sUserName and sPassword variables. The event then calls the FillAvailableUserList and FillGroupCombo procedures to populate the form with the available users and groups from the system database.

```
Private Sub Form_Load()

' if there is an error, then goto the code section labeled by ERR_Form_Load
On Error GoTo ERR_Form_Load:

    Dim sUserName As String
    Dim sPassword As String

    ' assign default user name and password
    sUserName = "Admin"
    sPassword = ""

    With DBEngine

        ' set system database path and name
        .SystemDB = GetWorkgroupDatabase

        ' set default user name and password
        .DefaultUser = sUserName
        .DefaultPassword = sPassword

    End With

    ' populate the users list box with the available users
    FillAvailableUserList
```

```
' if there are no valid users, inform the user and exit the application
If (lstAvailableUsers.ListCount < 1) Then

    MsgBox "There are no users!", vbExclamation, "USERS"
    cmdClose_Click

End If

' populate the group combo box and select the first group automatically
FillGroupCombo
cboGroups.ListIndex = 0

Exit Sub

ERR_Form_Load:

    ' display error for the user
    With Err
        MsgBox "ERROR #" & .Number & ": " & .Description, vbExclamation, _
            "ERROR"
    End With

    ' end the application
    cmdClose_Click

End Sub
```

3. Now enter the code that repopulates the **lstIncludedUsers** list box when the user selects a new group from the **cboGroups** combo box:

```
Private Sub cboGroups_Click()

    ' fill the included users text boxes for the selected group
    FillIncludedUsers

End Sub
```

4. Enter the code for the **Click** event of the **cmdMove** command buttons now. This event handles all four of the move buttons between the two list boxes on **frmAddUsersToGroups**. Using the locally declared constants to indicate the different buttons, users are either removed or added to the current group by a call to either **RemoveUserFromGroup** or **AddUserToGroup**.

```
Private Sub cmdMove_Click(Index As Integer)

    Dim nCount As Integer

    ' constant declarations that correspond to the four move buttons on
    ' the frmAddUsersToGroups form
    Const MOVE_REMOVE_ALL = 0
    Const MOVE_REMOVE = 1
    Const MOVE_ADD = 2
    Const MOVE_ALL = 3

    Select Case Index
```

continued on next page

continued from previous page

```
              ' remove all included users from list
              Case MOVE_REMOVE_ALL:
                  With lstIncludedUsers
                      For nCount = 0 To .ListCount - 1
                          RemoveUserFromGroup .List(nCount)
                      Next nCount
                  End With

              ' if a user is selected, remove it
              Case MOVE_REMOVE:
                  With lstIncludedUsers
                      If (.ListIndex < 0) Then Exit Sub
                      RemoveUserFromGroup .Text
                  End With

              ' if a user is selected, add it
              Case MOVE_ADD:
                  With lstAvailableUsers
                      If (.ListIndex < 0) Then Exit Sub
                      AddUserToGroup .Text
                  End With

              ' add all users from available users list box
              Case MOVE_ALL:
                  With lstAvailableUsers
                      For nCount = 0 To .ListCount - 1
                          AddUserToGroup .List(nCount)
                      Next nCount
                  End With

          End Select

          ' repopulated the included user list box
          FillIncludedUsers

    End Sub
```

5. Enter the code to terminate the application in the `cmdClose_Click` event:

```
Private Sub cmdClose_Click()

    ' end the application
    Unload Me

End Sub
```

6. Now enter the `FillGroupCombo`, `FillAvailableUserList`, and `FillIncludedUsers` procedures, which all use the system database to populate their corresponding controls with groups available, users available, or users in the selected group:

```
Private Sub FillGroupCombo()

    Dim oGroup As Group
```

```
        ' populate the group combo box with all available groups
        For Each oGroup In DBEngine.Workspaces(0).Groups
            cboGroups.AddItem oGroup.Name
        Next

    End Sub

    Private Sub FillAvailableUserList()

        Dim oUser As User

        ' populate the user list boxes with all users except CREATOR and ENGINE
        For Each oUser In DBEngine.Workspaces(0).Users
            With oUser
                If (UCase$(.Name) <> "CREATOR") _
                And (UCase$(.Name) <> "ENGINE") Then

                    lstAvailableUsers.AddItem .Name

                End If
            End With
        Next

    End Sub

    Private Sub FillIncludedUsers()

        Dim oUser As User

        With lstIncludedUsers

            ' clear the included users list box
            .Clear

            ' add all the included users for the given group
            For Each oUser In _
                    DBEngine.Workspaces(0).Groups(cboGroups.Text).Users

                .AddItem oUser.Name

            Next

        End With

    End Sub
```

7. Next enter the code to add a new user to a group. This procedure creates a new **User** object with the name of the selected user and then appends the object to the **Users** collection of the selected group.

```
Private Sub AddUserToGroup(sUserName As String)

' if there is an error, goto code labeled by ERR_AddUserToGroup
On Error GoTo ERR_AddUserToGroup:
```

continued on next page

continued from previous page

```
    Dim oUser As User

    ' constant declaration for error when user is already in group
    Const ERR_USER_IN_GROUP = 3032


    With DBEngine.Workspaces(0).Groups(cboGroups.Text)

        ' create a user and add him to the group
        Set oUser = .CreateUser(sUserName)
        .Users.Append oUser

    End With

Exit Sub

ERR_AddUserToGroup:

    With Err
        Select Case .Number

            ' if user is in group already, continue execution
            Case ERR_USER_IN_GROUP:
                Resume Next

            ' unexpected error, notify user
            Case Else
                MsgBox "ERROR #" & .Number & ": " & .Description, _
                       vbExclamation, "ERROR"

        End Select
    End With

End Sub
```

8. Finally, enter the code to remove a user from a group. The procedure
`RemoveUserFromGroup`, shown next, uses the `Delete` method of the `Users`
collection to remove the specified user from the `Group` object.

```
Private Sub RemoveUserFromGroup(sUserName As String)

    ' remove user from group
    DBEngine.Workspaces(0).Groups(cboGroups.Text).Users.Delete sUserName

End Sub
```

How It Works

When the application begins, it accesses the system database with default values
for user name and password. This database is used to populate the combo box
of `frmAddUsersToGroups` with all the available groups and the Available Users
list box with all the users listed in the database.

When a user selects a group, the Users collection of that Group object is used to populate the Included Users list box. To move users in to the specified group, a new User object is created and appended to the Users collection. To remove users from the group, the Remove method of the Users collection is used with the specified user.

COMPLEXITY
BEGINNING

11.12 How do I...
Track user activity in a database?

Problem

I want to somehow keep a log to track which users created or edited records in my Access database. How do I track user activity in a database using Visual Basic?

Technique

By creating two fields in a recordset, you can track both the user who modified a record and the date and time a record was modified. The first field, used to track the user, is populated with the current user name taken from the UserName property of the current Workspace object.

The second field, the date and time a user modified a record, is populated with the function Now, which returns the current date and time.

Steps

Open and run the project Tracker.vbp. After entering a valid user name and password, you should see the form shown in Figure 11.13. A list view control shows the records of the Customers table in the ORDERS.MDB database. The Order Number, User Name, and Last Modified information is displayed.

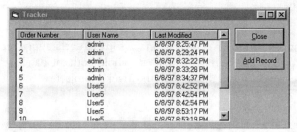

Figure 11.13. The Tracker project.

By clicking the Add Record button, you can add a dummy record to the recordset that gets populated in the list view control. The user name specified at the start of the application is used to populate the User Name field of the recordset, and the current date and time is entered into the Last Modified field.

1. Create a new project and name it Tracker.vbp. Go to the Project | Components menu selection, and choose Microsoft Windows Common Controls 5.0 from the list to include the list view control in your project.

2. Use Form1 in your project to add and edit the objects and properties as shown in Table 11.18. Use the (Custom) property in the property window of the list view control to add the three ColumnHeaders listed in Table 11.18. Save the form as frmTracker.frm.

Table 11.18. Objects and properties for the Tracker project.

OBJECT	PROPERTY	SETTING
Form	Name	frmTracker
	Caption	"Tracker"
ListView	Name	lstCustomers
	View	3 'Report View
	HideColumnHeaders	0 'False
ColumnHeader	Text	"Order Number"
ColumnHeader	Text	"User Name"
	SubItemIndex	1
ColumnHeader	Text	"Last Modified"
	SubItemIndex	2
Command button	Name	cmdAddRecord
	Caption	"&Add Record"
Command button	Name	cmdClose
	Caption	"&Close"
	Cancel	-1 'True
	Default	-1 'True

3. Now enter the form-level object variables in the declarations section of your project. These variables are used to hold both the database and the recordset objects used throughout the Tracker project.

```
Option Explicit

' form-level object variables used to store database and recordset objects
Private db As Database
Private rs As Recordset
```

4. Enter the `Form_Load` event code as shown next. This code asks the user to enter both a valid user name and a password from those in the system database to open the Orders database and call the `PopulateListView` procedure.

```
Private Sub Form_Load()

' if there is an error, goto the code labeled by ERR_Form_Load
On Error GoTo ERR_Form_Load:

    ' local constant declaration for invalid user name or password error
    Const ERR_INVALID_INFORMATION = 3029

    Dim sUserName As String
    Dim sPassword As String
    Dim sDBName As String

    ' get user name
    sUserName = InputBox("Enter user name.", "LOGON")

    ' get user password
    sPassword = InputBox("Enter password.", "LOGON")

    With DBEngine

        ' set system database path and name
        .SystemDB = GetWorkgroupDatabase

        ' set default passwords
        .DefaultUser = sUserName
        .DefaultPassword = sPassword

        ' retrieve database path and name from ReadINI module
        sDBName = DBPath

        ' open database with given user and password
        Set db = .Workspaces(0).OpenDatabase(sDBName)

    End With

    ' populate the list view control
    PopulateListView

Exit Sub

ERR_Form_Load:

    Dim sMessage As String

    With Err

        Select Case .Number

            ' invalid user or password
            Case ERR_INVALID_INFORMATION:
                sMessage = "Invalid user name or password."
```

continued on next page

continued from previous page

```
                    ' unexpected error, notify the user
                    Case Else
                        sMessage = "ERROR #" & .Number & ": " & .Description

                End Select

            End With

            ' display the message for the user
            MsgBox sMessage, vbExclamation, "ERROR"

            ' end the application
            cmdClose_Click

    End Sub
```

5. Enter the code to close and release the database and recordset object variables in the **Form_Unload** event:

```
Private Sub Form_Unload(Cancel As Integer)

    ' close the recordset and database
    Set rs = Nothing
    Set db = Nothing

End Sub
```

6. Now enter the **cmdAddRecord_Click** event code to add a new record. Notice the two fields, **User Last Modified** and **DateTime Last Modified**. These are populated with the **UserName** property of the current workspace and the **Now** method to successfully create an auditing trail that we will use to track which user created a given record.

```
Private Sub cmdAddRecord_Click()

' if an error occurs, call the ERR_cmdAddRecord code located at the end of
' this procedure
On Error GoTo ERR_cmdAddRecord:

    Dim sMessage As String
    Dim lPrimaryKey As Long

    ' used to populate fields in Customer table
    ' this is necessary because most of the fields belong to indexes making
    ' them required fields
    Const DUMMY_INFO = "<>"

    ' retrieve a unique key from the GetPrimaryKey routine
    lPrimaryKey = GetPrimaryKey

    With rs

        ' add a new record
        .AddNew
```

```
                  ' fill in the required fields
                  .Fields("Customer Number") = lPrimaryKey
                  .Fields("Customer Name") = DUMMY_INFO
                  .Fields("Street Address") = DUMMY_INFO
                  .Fields("City") = DUMMY_INFO
                  .Fields("State") = DUMMY_INFO
                  .Fields("Zip Code") = DUMMY_INFO

                  ' set the user name, date, and time of new record to track users
                  .Fields("User Last Modified") = DBEngine.Workspaces(0).UserName
                  .Fields("DateTime Last Modified") = Now

                  ' make saves (if an error will occur, it will be here)
                  .Update

              End With

              PopulateListView

              ' if we got this far, add new record was successfull
              sMessage = "Record added successfully!"
              MsgBox sMessage, vbInformation, "ADD RECORD"

      Exit Sub

      ERR_cmdAddRecord:

          ' display error for user
          With Err
              MsgBox "ERROR #" & .Number & ": " & .Description, vbExclamation, _
                      "ERROR"
          End With

      End Sub
```

7. Enter the code to terminate the application on the pressing of the **cmdClose** command button:

```
Private Sub cmdClose_Click()

    ' end the application
    Unload Me

End Sub
```

8. Now enter the **GetPrimaryKey** function, which uses the **Customer Number** field of the last record in the ORDERS.MDB database to create a new unique key:

```
Private Function GetPrimaryKey()

    ' return a unique primary key based on the Customer Number field
    With rs
```

continued on next page

continued from previous page

```
    ' if there are records in the table already, find the last one and
    ' add one to the Customer Number as a unique Primary Key; otherwise
    ' there are no records in the table, so return 1 for the first new
    ' record to be added
    If (Not (.EOF And .BOF)) Then

        .MoveLast

        GetPrimaryKey = .Fields("Customer Number") + 1

    Else

        GetPrimaryKey = 1

    End If

End With

End Function
```

9. Finally, enter the code for the **PopulateListView** procedure, which repopulates the list view control with the entire Customer table, showing which user added which order number, along with the date and time the record was added:

```
Private Sub PopulateListView()

    Dim oItem As ListItem

    ' show headers of list view and clear the contents of the ListItems
    ' collection
    With lstCustomers
        .HideColumnHeaders = False
        .ListItems.Clear
    End With

    ' repopulate the recordset
    Set rs = db.OpenRecordset("Customers", dbOpenTable)

    With rs

        ' order the records by the primary key
        .Index = "PrimaryKey"

        ' add all records to the list view
        While (Not rs.EOF)

            Set oItem = lstCustomers.ListItems.Add(, , _
                            .Fields("Customer Number"))

            oItem.SubItems(1) = .Fields("User Last Modified")
            oItem.SubItems(2) = .Fields("DateTime Last Modified")

            .MoveNext
```

```
        Wend

      End With

  End Sub
```

How It Works

When the application begins, it asks the user to enter a user name and password, which are checked against the system database when the `OpenDatabase` method is used to access ORDERS.MDB. If the user correctly entered a valid user name and corresponding password, the list view control of the Tracker project is populated with the contents of the Customer table showing the `Order Number`, `User Last Modified`, and `DateTime Last Modified` fields to form an auditing trail of the modification to the recordset.

When the user chooses to add a record by clicking the Add Record button, a new record is created using a newly created primary key. In addition, the current date and time as well as the current user name (taken from the `UserName` property of the current `Workspace` object) are used.

Comments

When you set the `DefaultUser` and `DefaultPassword` properties of the DBEngine object, you are logging in to the system database with that user. It should be noted that after these properties are set, you cannot change them during the life of your application. You must terminate the program and restart it to log on as a new user.

COMPLEXITY
BEGINNING

11.13 How do I...
Create and use an encrypted database?

Problem

I want to prohibit other users from viewing my Access database files from various word processors and spy applications. How can I encrypt my database using Visual Basic?

Technique

To encrypt an Access database, you must either specify encryption upon creation of the database or compact the database into a newly encrypted file. To decrypt an Access database, you must decrypt it to a newly created file using `CompactDatabase` as well.

Steps

Open and run the Encryptor.vbp project. You should see the form shown in Figure 11.14. To create a newly encrypted database, click the Create a New Encrypted Database button. You then are asked to specify a database path and name through a common dialog form.

To encrypt an existing database, click the Encrypt an Existing Database button, and specify the database to encrypt and a database path and name of the file to encrypt to. Conversely, to decrypt a database, click the Decrypt an Existing Database button, and enter the database to decrypt along with the database to decrypt to.

Do not enter a current database name to encrypt or decrypt to; rather, enter a name of a database that does not exist.

1. Create a new project and call it Encryptor.vbp. Go to the Project | Components menu selection and choose Microsoft Common Dialog Control 5.0 from the list to include the File Open Common Dialog control in your project.

2. Add the objects and edit the properties as shown in Table 11.19. Save the form as frmEncryptor.frm.

Table 11.19. Objects and properties for the Encryptor project.

OBJECT	PROPERTY	SETTING
Form	Name	frmEncryptor
	Caption	"Encryptor"
Common Dialog	Name	cdlFile
	Filter	"MS Access Databases (*.mdb)"
Command button	Name	cmdCreateDatabase
	Caption	"Create a &New Encrypted Database"
Command button	Name	cmdEncryptDatabase
	Caption	"&Encrypt an Existing Database"
Command button	Name	cmdDecryptDatabase
	Caption	"&Decrypt an Existing Database"
Command button	Name	cmdClose
	Caption	"&Close"
	Cancel	-1 'True
	Default	-1 'True

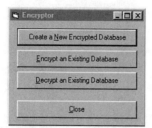

Figure 11.14. The
Encryptor project.

3. Now enter the following constant declarations in the declarations section
of your project. These are used to indicate application-defined errors later
in the project.

```
Option Explicit

' form-level constant declarations of application-defined errors
Private Const NO_ERROR = 0
Private Const ERR_DATABASE_EXISTS = 3204
```

4. Enter the code for the **Form_Load** event as shown here. Not only does this
code log on to the system database as the other How-To projects did, but
it also initializes the common dialog control used in this project.

```
Private Sub Form_Load()

' if there is an error, goto the code labeled by ERR_Form_Load
On Error GoTo ERR_Form_Load:

    Dim sUserName As String
    Dim sPassword As String

    sUserName = "admin"
    sPassword = ""

    With DBEngine

        ' set system database path and name
        .SystemDB = GetWorkgroupDatabase

        ' set default passwords
        .DefaultUser = sUserName
        .DefaultPassword = sPassword

    End With

    With cdlFile
```

continued on next page

continued from previous page

```
                    ' set various properties of the common dialog control
                    .Flags = cdlOFNExplorer
                    .DefaultExt = "mdb"

            End With

    Exit Sub

    ERR_Form_Load:

        ' display the error message for the user
        With Err
            MsgBox "ERROR #" & .Number & ": " & .Description, vbExclamation, _
                    "ERROR"
        End With

        ' end the application
        cmdClose_Click

    End Sub
```

5. Now enter the code for the **Click** event of the **cmdCreateDatabase** command button. This code uses the common dialog control to ask the user the name of the database to create. When given this name, the event creates an empty encrypted database.

```
Private Sub cmdCreateDatabase_Click()

' if there is an error, goto the code labeled by ERR_cmdCreateDatabase_Click
On Error GoTo ERR_cmdCreateDatabase_Click:

    Dim db As Database
    Dim sNewDatabase As String

    With cdlFile

            ' get the name of the database to encrypt or decrypt to
            .filename = ""
            .DialogTitle = "DATABASE TO CREATE"
            .Action = 1
            sNewDatabase = .filename

            ' if the name was not given, abandon task
            If (sNewDatabase = "") Then Exit Sub

    End With

    ' create the encrypted database
    Set db = DBEngine(0).CreateDatabase(sNewDatabase, _
                dbLangGeneral, dbEncrypt)

    ' close the database
    Set db = Nothing

ERR_cmdCreateDatabase_Click:

    Dim sMessage As String
```

```
    With Err

        ' determine error
        Select Case .Number

            ' there is no error, inform the user of success
            Case NO_ERROR:
                sMessage = "Database created successfully. "

            ' the database already exists
            Case ERR_DATABASE_EXISTS:
                sMessage = "You must choose a database that does not " _
                        & "already exist."

            ' unexpected error, inform the user
            Case Else:
                sMessage = "ERROR #" & .Number & ": " & .Description

        End Select

        ' display the error for the user
        MsgBox sMessage, _
                IIf(.Number = NO_ERROR, vbInformation, vbExclamation), _
                IIf(.Number = NO_ERROR, "SUCCESS", "ERROR")

    End With

End Sub
```

6. Enter the code for the `cmdEncryptDatabase_Click` and the
`cmdDecryptDatabase_Click` events as shown next. These procedures both
call the `Encryptor` routine to either encrypt or decrypt a database,
depending on the argument passed to the routine.

```
Private Sub cmdEncryptDatabase_Click()

    ' call procedure to encrypt database
    Encryptor dbEncrypt

End Sub

Private Sub cmdDecryptDatabase_Click()

    ' call procedure to decrypt database
    Encryptor dbDecrypt

End Sub
```

7. Enter the `cmdClose_Click` event code to terminate the application:

```
Private Sub cmdClose_Click()

    ' terminate the application
    Unload Me

End Sub
```

8. Finally, enter the following `Encryptor` procedure, which takes an `Integer` argument that will be passed to the `CompactDatabase` method. This argument will be either `dbEncrypt` or `dbDecrypt`, depending on which button the user pressed.

```
Private Sub Encryptor(nAction As Integer)

' if there is an error, goto the code labeled by ERR_Encryptor
On Error GoTo ERR_Encryptor:

    Dim sCurDatabase As String
    Dim sNewDatabase As String

    Dim sActionString As String

    ' create string depending upon action decided by user
    If (nAction = dbEncrypt) Then
        sActionString = "ENCRYPT"
    Else
        sActionString = "DECRYPT"
    End If

    With cdlFile

        ' get the name of the database to encrypt or decrypt
        .filename = ""
        .DialogTitle = "DATABASE TO " & sActionString
        .Action = 1
        sCurDatabase = .filename

        ' if the name was not given, abandon task
        If (sCurDatabase = "") Then Exit Sub

        ' get the name of the database to encrypt or decrypt to
        .filename = ""
        .DialogTitle = "DATABASE TO " & sActionString & " TO"
        .Action = 1
        sNewDatabase = .filename

        ' if the name was not given, abandon task
        If (sNewDatabase = "") Then Exit Sub

    End With

    ' encrypt the database
    DBEngine.CompactDatabase sCurDatabase, sNewDatabase, , nAction

ERR_Encryptor:

    Dim sMessage As String

    With Err

        ' determine error
        Select Case .Number
```

```
        ' there is no error, inform the user of success
        Case NO_ERROR:
            sMessage = "Database successfully " _
                    & LCase$(sActionString) & "ed to file '" _
                    & sNewDatabase & "'."

        ' the database already exists
        Case ERR_DATABASE_EXISTS:
            sMessage = "You must choose a database that does not " _
                    & "already exist."

        ' unexpected error, inform the user
        Case Else:
            sMessage = "ERROR #" & .Number & ": " & .Description

    End Select

    ' display the error for the user
    MsgBox sMessage, _
            IIf(.Number = NO_ERROR, vbInformation, vbExclamation), _
            IIf(.Number = NO_ERROR, "SUCCESS", "ERROR")

    End With

End Sub
```

How It Works

At the start of this application, the user is logged on to the system database using the default values for both the user name and the password. When the user decides to create a new database, the dbEncrypt option is included in the CreateDatabase method to indicate that encryption is to be used on the database.

If the user decides to either encrypt or decrypt an existing database, he must actually create a new database from the existing one by using the CompactDatabase method with an option of dbEncrypt or dbDecrypt. The database to be created from the CompactDatabase method cannot already exist.

Comments

In this How-To, we started off accessing the system database in the Form_Load event given the default Admin user name and password, although the project did not necessarily need to access the system database.

Encryption is not really going to help you much unless you also add a password, which we did not do in this application. Encryption stops others from viewing an Access database with anything but Access itself and Visual Basic. Because both of these tools are readily available, do not count on encryption for being your only source of security. The framework is here for system database security, and this is why we included its access in the Form_Load event.

CHAPTER 12
THE WINDOWS REGISTRY AND STATE INFORMATION

12.

THE WINDOWS REGISTRY AND STATE INFORMATION

How do I...

The Windows Registry is a remarkable component of Windows 95. It is used to store information about every application installed on your machine and replaces the original INI files of Windows 3.x. The information that is held in the Registry ranges from file paths to encrypted registration keys for ActiveX controls.

You can view the contents of the Windows Registry by locating the RegEdit application in your Windows directory. After launching this application, you can view the contents of any key stored in the Registry. You can also edit, create, or delete folders and keys within these folders; however, you should take extreme caution in doing so, because these values are of great importance. Make sure you know and realize what you are doing with the information in the Windows Registry before you decide to change anything.

In this chapter, we will dive into the Windows Registry and see how we can get it to work for us. We will accomplish this by using it to save state information for our application and our data access. We will also look into changing specific information that is inherent on every user's machine to tune and maximize performance in our applications.

12.1 Enter and Retrieve Windows Registry Entries from Visual Basic

When you exit most applications and then restart them later, you will notice that the screens appear to be just as you left them earlier. This technique of storing an application's state information is discussed in this How-To.

12.2 Put Data Access-Related Information into an Application's Section of the Registry

Sometimes it is important to use data access specifications that most other applications do not use. It is important, however, to maintain the reliability of the original specifications in the Window Registry. This How-To presents a project used to store state information for data access in the Windows Registry and to temporarily change the settings for data access.

12.3 Determine Which Database and Report-Related Files Need to Be Distributed with My Applications

Many times when creating a set of distribution disks for your application, you forget to include specific files relating to databases or reports. This How-To explains which files are necessary for each of these components.

12.4 Tune the Jet Database Engine Through Windows Registry Entries

If you are the down-and-dirty type when it comes to tweaking your machine for optimum performance, this How-To is for you. Here we show you how to make each of the keys relating to the Jet database engine tick.

12.5 Tune the ODBC Engine Using Windows Registry Entries

As well as fine-tuning the Jet database engine through the Windows Registry, you also can tune the ODBC engine. In this How-To, we will explain just how to do this.

12.1 How do I...
Enter and retrieve Windows Registry entries from Visual Basic?

Problem

My applications need to store specific state information. For example, I would like to store the position and size of the windows used in my projects so that the next time a user loads the program, it appears to continue where he left off. How do I store state information for my applications using Visual Basic?

Technique

Back in the days of Windows 3.*x*, applications used INI files to store state information for their programs. Apparently, this led to having numerous INI files spread throughout users' drives. With the introduction of Windows 95, we now have what is called the Windows Registry.

The Windows Registry acts as a Grand Central Station for INI files. Not only is application state information stored in the Registry, but registrations for OCXs also reside here. By using the same statements that we used to access INI files for Windows 3.*x* applications, we can work with the Windows Registry. There are four in all:

✔ GetSetting—Used to retrieve a single key's setting.

✔ GetAllSettings—Used to retrieve all keys and their corresponding settings for a given section in the Registry.

✔ SaveSetting—Used to save a setting for a particular key.

✔ DeleteSetting—Used to delete a key for a given section.

Visual Basic has a special section set aside for state information of users' applications. This section is labeled by the key HKEY_CURRENT_USER\ Software\VB and VBA Program Settings. By using the four statements previously listed, we can create, read, and alter settings in the VB and VBA Program Settings area of the Windows Registry to effectively record our application's state information.

Steps

Load and run RegistryEditor.vbp. You will see the form shown in Figure 12.1. The Application Name and Section text boxes are set to the default values used for this application. Change these values to see different section keys. After you select a key, you can edit it and click the Save Setting command button to save the setting. End the application by clicking the Close button.

1. Create a new project and name it RegistryEditor.vbp. Add the objects listed in Table 12.1 and edit their properties as shown. Save the form as frmRegistryEditor.frm.

Table 12.1. Objects and properties for the Registry Editor project.

OBJECT	PROPERTY	SETTING
Form	Name	frmRegistryEditor
	Caption	"Registry Editor"
Text box	Name	txtApplicationName
	Caption	"VB5DBHT Chapter 12"
Text box	Name	txtSection
	Caption	"Settings"
Text box	Name	txtSetting
	Caption	" "
List box	Name	lstKeys
Command button	Name	cmdClose
	Caption	"&Close"
	Cancel	-1 'True
	Default	-1 'True
Command button	Name	cmdSave
	Caption	"&Save Setting"
Label	Name	lblApplicationName
	Caption	"&Application Name:"
Label	Name	lblSection
	Caption	"Se&ction:"
Label	Name	lblKeys
	Caption	"&Key(s):"
Label	Name	lblSetting
	Caption	"Se&tting:"

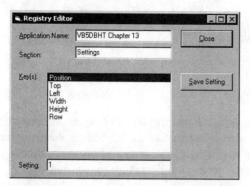

Figure 12.1. The Registry Editor project.

2. Enter the declaration for the form-level variant variable used to store keys and settings from the Windows Registry:

```
Option Explicit

' form-level variable used to store keys and settings for desired
' application and section
Private m_vSettings As Variant
```

3. When the application begins, automatically populate the screen with the default information by calling the `RepopulateKeys` routine that we will enter later:

```
Private Sub Form_Load()

    ' initialize the application by populating the key list box
    RepopulateKeys

End Sub
```

4. Now enter the code for the `lstKeys_Click` event as shown here. When the user changes the key to be displayed, the application will load the new corresponding setting and display it in the Setting text box.

```
Private Sub lstKeys_Click()

    ' error message of choice when error has occurred obtaining setting
    Const ERRMSG_INVALID_SETTING = "<ERROR>"

    ' set the txtSetting text box to the value of the key in the Registry
    txtSetting = GetSetting(txtApplicationName, _
                    txtSection, _
                    lstKeys.Text, _
                    ERRMSG_INVALID_SETTING)

    ' if there was an error in the retrieval process, disable editing of
    ' the key's setting
```

continued on next page

continued from previous page

```
    If (txtSetting <> ERRMSG_INVALID_SETTING) Then
        lstKeys.Enabled = True
        txtSetting.Enabled = True
        cmdSave.Enabled = True
    End If

End Sub
```

5. When the user changes the name of the application or the section to find keys for, we want to repopulate the list box displaying them. This task is carried out with a call to the **RepopulateKeys** routine in the **txtApplicationName_Change** and **txtSection_Change** events, as shown here:

```
Private Sub txtApplicationName_Change()

    ' repopulate the key list box when the application name has changed
    RepopulateKeys

End Sub

Private Sub txtSection_Change()

    ' repopulate the key list box when the section name has changed
    RepopulateKeys

End Sub
```

6. Enter the following code to end the application:

```
Private Sub cmdClose_Click()

    ' end the application
    Unload Me

End Sub
```

7. Now enter the code for the **cmdSave_Click** event, which uses the **SaveSetting** statement to save the information on the form to the Windows Registry:

```
Private Sub cmdSave_Click()

    ' save the selected key information from the desired information on
    ' the form
    SaveSetting txtApplicationName, _
                txtSection, _
                lstKeys.Text, _
                txtSetting

End Sub
```

8. Finally, enter the following code for the **RepopulateKeys** routine. When this code is called, the application attempts to populate the list box with all the available keys for the given application and section name. If this information does not correspond to a section in the Registry, an error occurs. The **RepopulateKeys** routine traps this error and gracefully exits the procedure, leaving the Key list box empty and disabling any controls used to edit Key settings.

```
Private Sub RepopulateKeys()

' if there is an error, goto the code labeled by ERR_RepopulateKeys
On Error GoTo ERR_RepopulateKeys:

    Dim nCount As Integer

    ' errors that are expected to be encountered
    Const ERR_INVALID_PROC_CALL = 5
    Const ERR_TYPE_MISMATCH = 13


    With lstKeys

        ' clear the listbox and setting text box
        .Clear
        txtSetting = ""

        ' disable editing functions
        lstKeys.Enabled = False
        txtSetting.Enabled = False
        cmdSave.Enabled = False

        ' retrieve available keys for given application name and section
        ' this will cause an ERR_INVALID_PROC_CALL error if one of the text
        ' box controls are empty
        m_vSettings = GetAllSettings(txtApplicationName, txtSection)

        ' add each setting to the key list box
        ' this will case an ERR_TYPE_MISMATCH error if there are no keys
        ' for the selected application and section names
        For nCount = 0 To UBound(m_vSettings, 1)
            .AddItem m_vSettings(nCount, 0)
        Next nCount

        ' select the first item in the list box
        .ListIndex = 0

    End With

Exit Sub

ERR_RepopulateKeys:
```

continued on next page

continued from previous page

```
    With Err

        Select Case .Number

            ' if the error is expected, do nothing but end the procedure
            Case ERR_INVALID_PROC_CALL, ERR_TYPE_MISMATCH:

            ' unexpected error, display for the user
            Case Else:
                MsgBox "ERROR #" * .Number & ": " & .Description, _
                        vbExclamation, "ERROR"

        End Select

    End With

End Sub
```

How It Works

When this project is run, the list box control of the form is populated with the keys available for the given application and section names using the `GetAllSettings` statement. If the section does not exist in the Windows Registry, an error occurs, and the application is ended gracefully. If there are keys, the list box is populated, and the controls that are related to editing the key's setting are enabled.

After you decide to change the setting for a given key selected from the list box, you click the Save Setting button. The code that is in the `cmdSave_Click` event uses the `SaveSetting` statement to save the current key's value.

Choosing a new key from the list box control causes the code to execute the `GetSetting` statement, which retrieves an individual setting for a specified application name, section, and key.

Comments

In this project, we saved all the key's settings as strings in the Windows Registry. This is because the `txtSetting` text box's `Text` property returns a string value. If you were to use this project to save the information for your application's position and size, you would have to change the string value returned to a `Long` value.

This problem can be avoided by using a variable with a Long data type in the `SaveSetting` statement. Visual Basic creates a new key with the data type of the specified setting.

COMPLEXITY
BEGINNING

12.2 How do I...
Put data access-related information into an application's section of the Registry?

Problem

My application calls for DAO settings that are not considered standard. I can manually edit the Registry key settings to the values that my application requires; however, other programs will be affected by my changes. How do I temporarily change the DAO settings every time a user runs my projects?

Technique

By using the techniques discussed in How-To 12.1, we know that we can save state information for our application. Visual Basic does not care what kind of information this is; therefore, we can just as easily store DAO setting information as we can the application's position and height.

To temporarily change the DAO settings for the Jet engine, we can use the `SetOption` method of the `DBEngine` object. Using this command, we can change the values of parameters that Jet uses to access data. These changes are made until we change them again or the DBEngine is actually closed.

In all, there are 11 parameters we can use to alter the Jet and DAO's behavior. These parameters and their associated keys—in the `Jet\3.5\Engines\Jet 3.5\` section of the Windows Registry—are listed in Table 12.2.

Table 12.2. Objects and properties for the Set Options project.

KEY	PARAMETER ENUMERATION CONSTANT
PageTimeout	dbPageTimeout
SharedAsyncDelay	dbSharedAsyncDelay
ExclusiveAsyncDelay	dbExclusiveAsyncDelay
LockRetry	dbLockRetry
UserCommitSync	dbUserCommitSync
ImplicitCommitSync	dbImplicitCommitSync
MaxBufferSize	dbMaxBufferSize
MaxLocksPerFile	dbMaxLocksPerFile
LockDelay	dbLockDelay
RecycleLVs	dbRecycleLVs
FlushTransactionTimeout	dbFlushTransactionTimeout

Steps

Open and run SetOptions.vbp. You will see the form shown in Figure 12.2. By selecting the key from the combo box, you will see the associated setting for the key in the Setting text box. Changing the key's setting and clicking the Save Setting button will not only save the value of the setting, but also temporarily change the parameter for the DBEngine object. If you delete the key by clicking the Delete Key button, you will remove the key from the section for our state information in the Registry. The next time you go to view the key, you will see the default setting of the key.

1. Create a new project and name it SetOptions.vbp. Add the controls and edit their properties as shown in Table 12.3 for the default form, Form1. Save the form as frmSetOptions.frm.

Table 12.3. Objects and properties for the Set Options project.

OBJECT	PROPERTY	SETTING
Form	Name	frmSetOptions
	Caption	"Set Options"
Combo box	Name	cboKeys
	Style	2 'Dropdown List
Text box	Name	txtSetting
	Caption	" "
Command button	Name	cmdClose
	Caption	"&Close"
	Cancel	-1 'True
	Default	-1 'True
Command button	Name	cmdSave
	Caption	"&Save Setting"
Command button	Name	cmdDelete
	Caption	"&Delete Key"
Label	Name	lblKey
	Caption	"&Key:"
Label	Name	lblSetting
	Caption	"Se&tting:"

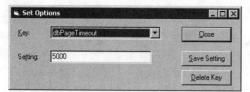

Figure 12.2. The Set Options project.

2. Now enter the following code in the declarations section of the project. The form-level Long variable is used to store the currently selected key from the combo box on the form. The other two declarations are constants and are used to represent the default application and section names used for this project.

```
Option Explicit

' form-level variable used to store the selected parameter from the list
' in the keys combo box
Private m_lSelectedParameter As Long

' form-level constant declarations used throughout the application to name
' the application and section when using the Get and Save settings methods
Private Const APPLICATION_TITLE = "VB5DBHT Chapter 12"
Private Const SECTION_NAME = "Jet 3.5"
```

3. Now enter the `Form_Load` event code as shown next. This code calls the `LoadJetRegistryInformation` routine, which we will code in a separate module later, to retrieve all the keys for the specified application and section of the Windows Registry. The event then adds all the available parameters to the combo box control and selects the first one.

```
Private Sub Form_Load()

    ' load all Jet Registry settings from application section of the
    ' Windows Registry
    LoadJetRegistryInformation APPLICATION_TITLE, SECTION_NAME

    With cboKeys

        ' add all the available parameters for the SetOption method

        .AddItem "dbPageTimeout"
        .AddItem "dbSharedAsyncDelay"
        .AddItem "dbExclusiveAsyncDelay"
        .AddItem "dbLockRetry"
        .AddItem "dbUserCommitSync"
        .AddItem "dbImplicitCommitSync"
        .AddItem "dbMaxBufferSize"
        .AddItem "dbMaxLocksPerFile"
        .AddItem "dbLockDelay"
        .AddItem "dbRecycleLVs"
```

continued on next page

continued from previous page

```
        .AddItem "dbFlushTransactionTimeout"

        ' select the first item in the combo box control
        .ListIndex = 0

    End With

End Sub
```

4. Now enter the code for the **cboKeys_Click** event, which is called every time the user selects a new key from the combo box. This event retrieves the current setting for the chosen key from the application's section of the Windows Registry. If there is no specified entry for the key in this section, the **lDefaultSetting** is used instead.

```
Private Sub cboKeys_Click()

    Dim lDefaultSetting As Variant

    With cboKeys

        ' get a long value from the text version of the key
        m_lSelectedParameter = GetParameterFromKey(.Text)

        ' obtain the default setting for the key
        lDefaultSetting = GetDefaultKeySetting(.Text)

        ' display the current setting from the applications Registry
        ' settings if there is one, otherwise, display the default
        txtSetting = GetSetting(APPLICATION_TITLE, _
                                SECTION_NAME, _
                                .Text, _
                                lDefaultSetting)

    End With

End Sub
```

5. Enter the following code to end the application:

```
Private Sub cmdClose_Click()

    ' end the application
    Unload Me

End Sub
```

6. The following code is used to save the current key and setting combination to the application's section of the Registry. This is done with the **SaveSetting** statement. In addition to the Registry entry, the **SetOption** method of the **DBEngine** object is called to temporarily change the setting of the desired parameter to the new value. If the user entered

an incorrect data type for the key, an error is generated and the user is
notified.

```
Private Sub cmdSave_Click()

' if there is an error, goto the code labeled by ERR_cmdSave_Click
On Error GoTo ERR_cmdSave_Click:

    ' constant declarations for expected errors
    Const ERR_TYPE_MISMATCH = 13
    Const ERR_RESERVED_ERROR = 3000

    ' attempt to set the DBEngine option for the given key
    ' an error will occur here if an incorrect setting data type is
    ' entered by the user
    DBEngine.SetOption m_lSelectedParameter, GetValueFromSetting(txtSetting)
        IIf(IsNumeric(txtSetting), CLng(txtSetting), txtSetting)

    ' if the SetOption method was successful, then save the new setting
    ' value in the application Registry section
    SaveSetting APPLICATION_TITLE, SECTION_NAME, cboKeys.Text, txtSetting

    ' inform the user of the success
    MsgBox "Change has been made.", vbInformation, "Set Option"

Exit Sub
```

```
ve_Click:

Message As String

Err

elect Case .Number

        ' wrong data type entered for key setting
        Case ERR_TYPE_MISMATCH, ERR_RESERVED_ERROR:
            sMessage = "Value is of incorrect format."

        ' unexpected error, create a message from the error
        Case Else:
            sMessage = "ERROR #" & .Number & ": " & .Description

    End Select

End With

    ' inform the user of the error
    MsgBox sMessage, vbExclamation, "ERROR"

    ' repopulate the setting text box with the current or default key
    ' setting and set focus to the text box

    cboKeys_Click
    txtSetting.SetFocus

End Sub
```

7. The following code simply deletes the key from the application's section in the Windows Registry and notifies the user of the success:

```
Private Sub cmdDelete_Click()

    ' remove the setting from the application section of the Windows
    ' Registry
    DeleteSetting APPLICATION_TITLE, SECTION_NAME, cboKeys.Text

    ' refresh the setting text box with the default value
    cboKeys_Click

    ' inform the user of the success
    MsgBox "Key has been deleted.", vbInformation, "Delete Key"

End Sub
```

8. The second half of this project begins with adding a new module. You can do this by choosing Project | Add Module from the Visual Basic menu. Rename the module **RegistryInformation** and save it as RegistryInformation.bas. The remaining code for this project should be entered in this module.

9. In the **RegistryInformation** module, enter the first routine to be used, which is the **LoadJetRegistryInformation**, as shown here. This routine loads all the settings and keys for the given application and section names. For each key specified in the corresponding section of the Registry, the **SetOption** method of the **DBEngine** object is called to temporarily change the value of the given parameter for the life of this application. If there are no settings for the given application and section names, an error is trapped and the routine exits gracefully.

```
Public Sub LoadJetRegistryInformation(sApplicationName As String, _
                                      sSectionName As String)

' if there is an error, goto the code labeled by
' ERR_LoadJetRegistryInformation
On Error GoTo ERR_LoadJetRegistryInformation:

    Dim vSettings As Variant
    Dim nCount As Integer

    ' constant declaration for expected error
    Const ERR_TYPE_MISMATCH = 13

    ' obtain all the settings from the Registry section for the given
    ' application
    vSettings = GetAllSettings(sApplicationName, sSectionName)

    ' set all the options that were specified in the Jet 3.5 section for
    ' the current application
    For nCount = 0 To UBound(vSettings, 1)
```

```
            DBEngine.SetOption GetParameterFromKey _
                            (vSettings(nCount, 0)), _
                            GetValueFromSetting(vSettings(nCount, 1))

        Next nCount

    Exit Sub

    ERR_LoadJetRegistryInformation:

        With Err

            Select Case .Number

                ' there was no settings specified in the Registry for the
                ' given application, just continue without displaying an
                ' error message
                Case ERR_TYPE_MISMATCH:

                ' unexpected error, create a message from the error
                Case Else:
                    MsgBox "ERROR #" & .Number & ": " & .Description, _
                            vbExclamation, "ERROR"

            End Select

        End With

    End Sub
```

10. Now enter the public function `GetValueFromSetting`, which accepts a variant as an argument and returns either a `Long` or a `String`, depending on the data type of the argument:

```
Public Function GetValueFromSetting(vSetting As Variant) As Variant

    ' if the setting is a number, return a long, otherwise return a string

    If (IsNumeric(vSetting)) Then
        GetValueFromSetting = CLng(vSetting)
    Else
        GetValueFromSetting = CStr(vSetting)
    End If

End Function
```

11. The following function returns the default setting for the specified key name. These defaults were obtained from Visual Basic Books Online and can be changed to your desired settings.

```
Public Function GetDefaultKeySetting(sKey As String) As Variant

    ' return the default key setting for the key specified

    Select Case sKey
```

continued on next page

continued from previous page

```
        Case "dbPageTimeout":
            GetDefaultKeySetting = 5000

        Case "dbSharedAsyncDelay":
            GetDefaultKeySetting = 0

        Case "dbExclusiveAsyncDelay":
            GetDefaultKeySetting = 2000

        Case "dbLockEntry":
            GetDefaultKeySetting = 20

        Case "dbUserCommitSync":
            GetDefaultKeySetting = "Yes"

        Case "dbImplicitCommitSync":
            GetDefaultKeySetting = "No"

        Case "dbMaxBufferSize":
            GetDefaultKeySetting = 0

        Case "dbMaxLocksPerFile":
            GetDefaultKeySetting = 9500

        Case "dbLockDelay":
            GetDefaultKeySetting = 100

        Case "dbRecycleLVs":
            GetDefaultKeySetting = 0

        Case "dbFlushTransactionTimeout":
            GetDefaultKeySetting = 500

    End Select

End Function
```

12. Finally, enter the code for the public function `GetParameterFromKey` as shown here. This function returns the corresponding parameter enumeration value for a specified key.

```
Public Function GetParameterFromKey(ByVal sKey As String) As Long

    ' return the correct constant for the given key

    Select Case sKey

        Case "dbPageTimeout":
            GetParameterFromKey = dbPageTimeout

        Case "dbSharedAsyncDelay":
            GetParameterFromKey = dbSharedAsyncDelay

        Case "dbExclusiveAsyncDelay":
            GetParameterFromKey = dbExclusiveAsyncDelay
```

```
        Case "dbLockRetry":
            GetParameterFromKey = dbLockRetry

        Case "dbUserCommitSync":
            GetParameterFromKey = dbUserCommitSync

        Case "dbImplicitCommitSync":
            GetParameterFromKey = dbImplicitCommitSync

        Case "dbMaxBufferSize":
            GetParameterFromKey = dbMaxBufferSize

        Case "dbMaxLocksPerFile":
            GetParameterFromKey = dbMaxLocksPerFile

        Case "dbLockDelay":
            GetParameterFromKey = dbLockDelay

        Case "dbRecycleLVs":
            GetParameterFromKey = dbRecycleLVs

        Case "dbFlushTransactionTimeout":
            GetParameterFromKey = dbFlushTransactionTimeout

    End Select

End Function
```

How It Works

This project uses two files for code. The first file, the frmSetOptions form, holds the information for displaying and altering the application's Jet engine state information.

The second file used in this project, the RegistryInformation module, is designed to be portable and to be added to your own project. By calling LoadJetRegistryInformation and passing the application's name and section, the procedure loads all the state information stored for the Jet in the specified section of the Windows Registry. It then uses the SetOption method to temporarily change the parameter values of Jet engine access for the life of your application.

Comments

It is important not to change the values of the actual settings for the Jet in the key Jet\3.5\Engines\Jet 3.5\, because it is very likely this is where the rest of your applications are finding the parameter values for Jet DAO access. If for some reason you decide to change these values and need to set them back to their original values, you can find the default settings in Microsoft Visual Basic Books Online, in the "Initializing the Microsoft Jet 3.5 Database Engine" section.

For more information on the meaning of the parameters used in this section, see How-To 12.4, "Tune the Jet database engine through Windows Registry entries."

COMPLEXITY
INTERMEDIATE

12.3 How do I...
Determine which database and report-related files need to be distributed with my applications?

Problem

I am creating an application that uses the Jet database engine and Crystal Reports. How do I determine the files I need to distribute with my application?

Technique

Before Visual Basic 5.0, life was rough. Actually, life is still rough, but we are getting there. Creating distribution disks for your application was a headache up until now. Things got a little better. It is still usually suggested, however, to use a setup application to create distribution disks. Microsoft offers us the Application Setup Wizard to do just that.

Steps

Run the Application Setup Wizard that came with Visual Basic 5.0. You will see the wizard as shown in Figure 12.3.

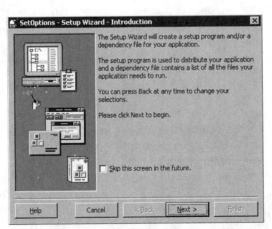

Figure 12.3. The Application Setup Wizard—Introduction.

1. Click the Next button and you will see the panel shown in Figure 12.4. In this panel, you select the project that you want to create an installation setup for and the type of setup.

2. Click the Next button and you will see the panel shown in Figure 12.5. This panel asks you what kind of setup distribution you want. Choose Floppy disk, Single Directory, or Disk Directories.

3. If you choose a Single Directory installation, choose the directory in which you want the installation to be placed, as shown in Figure 12.6.

4. If your application uses installable ISAMs, as do the How-To's in Chapter 6, select the desired components next. You would use the panel shown in Figure 12.7.

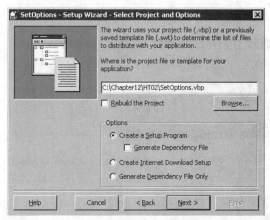

Figure 12.4. Select Project and Options.

Figure 12.5. Distribution method.

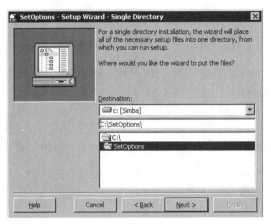

Figure 12.6. Single Directory installation.

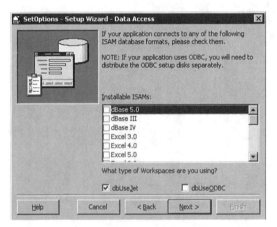

Figure 12.7. Data access.

5. Next, if your application uses any ActiveX server components, add them to the panel shown in Figure 12.8.

6. After adding your ActiveX server components, add any additional dependency files as shown in Figure 12.9.

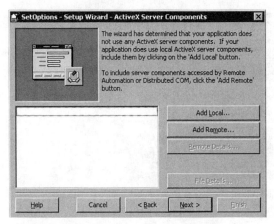

Figure 12.8. Adding ActiveX server components.

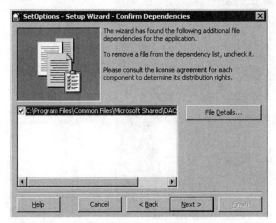

Figure 12.9. Confirming dependencies.

7. Click the Next button and the wizard will begin determining which files are necessary for your installation. When the wizard is done, you will see the panel shown in Figure 12.10, where you can add or remove files to the list.

8. After you have finished choosing the files necessary for your installation, you will see the Finish panel, shown in Figure 12.11. Click Finish to complete the installation setup process.

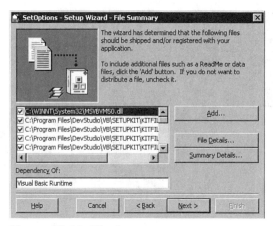

Figure 12.10. File Summary.

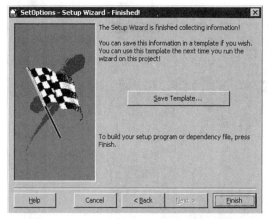

Figure 12.11. Setup Wizard complete.

How It Works

Problems arise sometimes when files become lost or when the Setup Wizard does not find all the files necessary to be included in our distribution disks. All the files that actually have meaning to us to run our application are considered runtime files.

Runtime Files

There is a checklist of standard runtime files that you should work through when creating a set of distribution disks. This checklist is as follows:

✔ The program's main executable.

✔ Any database (MDB files for Access) or report files (RPT files for Crystal Reports).

✔ Any other data files (DAT), text files (TXT), or Registry files (REG). These files are those that will not be found by a wizard, but accessed from within your application.

✔ Any ActiveX components (OCX files).

✔ The Visual Basic runtime DLL (MSVBVM50.DLL).

✔ Any other dependency files (DLL or EXE).

You should be able to know immediately what database, report, data, and ActiveX files you are to add to your setup disks, because these are files that you explicitly added to your project. The Visual Basic runtime DLL (MSVBVM50.DLL) is necessary for every Visual Basic application. The trickiest files to find are component dependency files.

Component Dependencies

Component dependencies are files that are necessary in order to use specific ActiveX controls and particular components that are added as references from your application. There are a number of resources, however, to locate the proper dependency files that are important to you.

First off, it is important to always consult the documentation on all third-party components to see which DLLs are necessary in order to use the product. In most cases, REG files are also necessary. These files have registration information that is entered into the Windows Registry and that is used to determine the licensing usage available to the user for the particular component.

The second source for finding the appropriate dependency files for your distribution disks is the Visual Basic documentation. All the included components are covered by documentation that explains which files are necessary in order for them to work properly. All ActiveX controls will come with DEP files, if they don't already. Crystal Reports comes with a file named CRYSTL32.DEP. These files are used by the Setup Wizard to determine which files are necessary for installation.

The third and most important source of information is the VB5DEP.INI file. This file replaces the original SWDEPEND.INI file of earlier times and describes the dependencies used by Visual Basic.

The VB5DEP.INI file can be found in the Visual Basic \SetupKit\Kitfil32 directory. This file lists necessary dependencies for all available Visual Basic components. This file is used by the Setup Wizard to determine the appropriate files necessary to successfully run your application.

Comments

The following code is a portion of the CRYSTL32.DEP file. It lists the information necessary to successfully incorporate the CRYSTL32.OCX ActiveX control.

```
[CRYSTL32.ocx]
Dest=$(WinSysPath)
```

continued on next page

continued from previous page

```
Register=$(DLLSelfRegister)
Version=4.6.37.14
Uses1=CRPE32.DLL
Uses2=ComCat.dll
Uses3=
CABFileName=CRYSTL32.cab
CABDefaultURL=http://activex.microsoft.com/controls/vb5
CABINFFile=CRYSTL32.inf
```

The header of this portion of code, [CRYSTL32.ocx], indicates the file in question. The first key, Dest, indicates where the file should be stored on the installation machine (in this case, the Windows System path).

The second parameter, Register, indicates that the file will self-register in the Windows Registry. The Version parameter clearly holds the file's version number to compare with older files during the installation process.

After this, a list of additional dependencies is given with the parameter form of UsesX, where X is the number of the dependency. These are files that the actual file being installed (CRYSTL32.OCX) uses to reference; therefore, they in turn must also be installed. The CABFileName parameter is the name of the installation file for the particular installed file, and CABINFFile is the file that contains the installation information for the installed file.

I skipped the CABDefaultURL parameter, which indicates the default Web site that is used in reference to the installed file for upgrades or more information.

COMPLEXITY
ADVANCED

12.4 How do I...
Tune the Jet database engine through Windows Registry entries?

Problem

My application needs to alter the way the Jet engine is initiated in the Windows Registry in order to obtain better performance. I know I can edit the Windows Registry using RegEdit, but I do not know what to actually do. How do I tune the Jet engine through the Windows Registry?

Technique

When you install the Microsoft Jet engine for the very first time, two DLL files are registered in the Windows Registry. These files are MSJET35.DLL and MSRD2X35.DLL. When these files are registered, two entries are created in the HKEY_LOCAL_MACHINES\Software\Microsoft\Jet\3.5\Engines folder. This is done automatically when you install Access 97.

The first of these keys represents the path to the system database file. The typical path for this key would be the system directory of Windows; therefore, no path is necessary, because the system directory is usually part of the default path. The following is an example of this SystemDB key:

```
SystemDB = "C:\WINDOWS\SYSTEM\SYSTEM.MDB"
```

The second key that is created is called CompactBYPkey. When this key is set to anything but 0, databases will be compacted in the order of the primary key. If no primary key exists, the database is compacted in base-table order. A value of 0 for the CompactBYPkey key will instruct the Jet engine to compact databases in base-table order. The default value for this key is nonzero, as in the following example:

```
CompactBYPkey = 1
```

It should be noted that this setting is good only for databases created with the Microsoft Jet database engine, version 3.0 or later. Any database of an earlier version will compact by base-table order automatically.

The Microsoft Jet is controlled by keys set in the \HKEY_LOCAL_MACHINES \Software\Microsoft\Jet\3.5\Engines\Jet 3.5 folder of the Windows Registry. The default settings for these keys are shown in Table 12.4.

Table 12.4. The Jet\3.5\Engines\Jet 3.5 keys and default values.

KEY	DEFAULT
PageTimeout	5000
SharedAsyncDelay	0
ExclusiveAsyncDelay	2000
LockRetry	20
UserCommitSync	Yes
ImplicitCommitSync	No
MaxBufferSize	0
MaxLocksPerFile	9500
LockDelay	100
FlushTransactionTimeout	500
Threads	3

By adjusting these settings, you can manipulate how the Jet engine operates in every program that uses these settings. The keys listed in Table 12.4 are briefly described in the text that follows.

Steps

Run the RegEdit application that is in the Windows directory on your machine. Locate the \HKEY_LOCAL_MACHINES\Software\Microsoft\Jet\3.5\Engines\ Jet 3.5 section of the Registry and you should see something similar to what's shown in Figure 12.12.

1. Choose a key in the section that you are now in. Choose Edit | Modify from the RegEdit menu.

2. Edit the value of the key that you have selected. For a complete list of the available keys for this section, see the "How It Works" section of this How-To.

3. Click the OK button to save your changes or Cancel to abort.

How It Works

The following is a list of the keys that make up the \HKEY_LOCAL_MACHINES \Software\Microsoft\Jet\3.5\Engines\Jet 3.5 section of the Windows Registry and a description of each.

PageTimeout

The `PageTimeout` key is used to indicate the time interval between when data that is not read-locked is placed in an internal cache and when that data is invalidated. This key is measured in milliseconds, with a default value of `5000`, or 5 seconds.

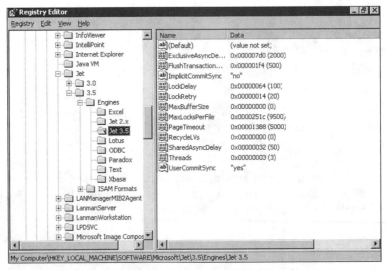

Figure 12.12. The \HKEY_LOCAL_MACHINES\Software\ Microsoft\Jet\3.5\Engines\Jet 3.5 of the Windows Registry.

FlushTransactionTimeout

The FlushTransactionTimeout key disables the ExclusiveAsyncDelay and SharedAsyncDelay keys with a value of 1. A value of 0 enables these keys. The FlushTransactionTimeout is the value that will start asynchronous writes only after the amount of time specified has expired and no pages have been added to the cache. An exception to this statement is that if the cache exceeds the MaxBufferSize, the cache will start asynchronous writing even if the time has expired. For instance, the Microsoft Jet 3.5 database engine will wait 500 milliseconds during non-activity or until the cache size is exceeded before starting asynchronous writes.

LockDelay

The LockDelay key holds a value in milliseconds used to determine the time between lock requests indicated by the LockRetry key. This key was added to prevent "bursting" (overloading of the network) that would occur with certain network operating systems.

MaxLocksPerFile

The MaxLocksPerFile key holds a value indicating the maximum number of Microsoft Jet transactions. If the locks in a transaction attempt to exceed the MaxLocksPerFile key value, the transaction is split into multiple parts and partially committed. This concept was conceived in order to prevent NetWare 3.1 server crashes when the specified NetWare lock limit is exceeded, as well as to improve performance with both NetWare and Windows NT.

LockRetry

The LockRetry key indicates the number of times to repeat attempts to access a locked page before returning a lock conflict message. The default value for the LockRetry key is 20.

RecycleLVs

The RecycleLVs key is used to indicate whether Microsoft Jet is to recycle Long value pages. These include the Memo, Long Binary (OLE object), and Binary data types. With Microsoft Jet 3.0, if the RecycleLVs key was not set, these Long value pages would be recycled when the last user closed the database. Microsoft Jet 3.5 will start to recycle most Long value pages when the database is expanded—in other words, when groups of pages are added. When this feature is enabled, you will notice a performance drop when using Long value data types. With Microsoft Access 97, this feature is automatically enabled and disabled.

MaxBufferSize

The MaxBufferSize key represents the size of the database engine internal cache. This value is represented in kilobytes. The MaxBufferSize key must be an integer greater than or equal to 512. The default value for the MaxBufferSize varies, depending on the amount of RAM installed on the user's system. The formula for calculating the default is as follows:

```
((RAM - 12MB) / 4) + 512KB
```

Here, *RAM* is the amount of memory on the current system, measured in megabytes (MB). To set the value of the `MaxBufferSize` to the default, simply set the key to `0`.

Threads

The `Threads` key represents the number of background threads available to the Microsoft Jet database engine. The default value for the `Threads` key is `3`.

UserCommitSync

The `UserCommitSync` key indicates whether the system should wait for a commit to finish. If the value is `Yes`, which is the default, the system will wait for a commit to finish. If the value is `No`, the system will perform the commit asynchronously.

ImplicitCommitSync

The `ImplicitCommitSync` key represents whether the system will wait for a commit to finish. A default value of `No` will instruct the system to continue without waiting for the commit to finish, whereas a value of `Yes` will cause the system to wait.

ExclusiveAsyncDelay

The `ExclusiveAsyncDelay` key specifies the amount of time (in milliseconds) an asynchronous flush of an exclusive database is to be deferred. The default value for this key is `2000` milliseconds (2 seconds).

SharedAsyncDelay

The `SharedAsyncDelay` key represents the amount of time (in milliseconds) to defer an asynchronous flush of a shared database. The default for the `SharedAsyncDelay` is `0`.

COMPLEXITY
ADVANCED

12.5 How do I...
Tune the ODBC engine using Windows Registry entries?

Problem

My application needs to alter the way in which the ODBC engine is initiated in the Windows Registry in order to obtain better performance. I know I can edit the Windows Registry using `RegEdit`, but I do not know what to actually do. How do I tune the ODBC engine through the Windows Registry?

Technique

The ODBC engine keys are stored in the Windows Registry in the \HKEY_LOCAL_MACHINE\Software\Microsoft\Jet\3.5\Engines\ODBC section. Table 12.5 lists the available keys and their respective default values.

Table 12.5. The Jet\3.5\Engines\ODBC keys and default values.

KEY	DEFAULT
LoginTimeout	20
QueryTimeout	60
ConnectionTimeout	600
AsyncRetryInterval	500
AttachCaseSensitive	0
AttachableObjects	'TABLE', 'VIEW', 'SYSTEM TABLE', 'ALIAS', 'SYNONYM'
SnapshotOnly	0
TraceSQLMode	0
TraceODBCAPI	0
DisableAsync	1
JetTryAuth	1
PreparedInsert	0
PreparedUpdate	0
FastRequery	0

By adjusting the values of any of these keys, you can affect the way any application that uses the ODBC Jet engine accesses data. The following is a brief description of each of the keys represented in Table 12.5.

Steps

Run the `RegEdit` application that is in the Windows directory on your machine. Locate the \HKEY_LOCAL_MACHINE\Software\Microsoft\Jet\3.5\Engines\ODBC section of the Registry and you should see something similar to Figure 12.13.

1. Choose a key in the section that you are now in. Choose Edit | Modify from the RegEdit menu.

2. Edit the value of the key that you have selected. For a complete list of the available keys for this section, see the "How It Works" section of this How-To.

3. Click OK to save your changes or Cancel to abort.

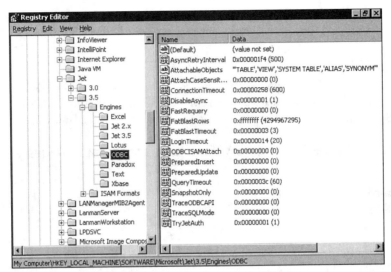

Figure 12.13. The \HKEY_LOCAL_MACHINE\Software\
Microsoft\Jet\3.5\Engines\ODBC section of the Windows Registry.

How It Works

Following is a list of the keys that make up the \HKEY_LOCAL_MACHINE\
Software\Microsoft\Jet\3.5\Engines\ODBC section of the Windows Registry and a
description of each.

LoginTimeout

The LoginTimout key is used to store the maximum number of seconds a login
attempt can take. After the specified time, timing out occurs with an error. The
default for LoginTimout is 20 seconds.

QueryTimeout

The QueryTimeout key is used to store the maximum number of seconds the
entire processing time can take to run a query before actually timing out. The
default value for this key is 60 seconds. If the DisableAsync key is set to its
default of 0, the QueryTimeout key is used to indicate the time in seconds
waited for a response from the server between polls for the completion of a
query.

ConnectionTimeout

The ConnectionTimeout key is used to store the maximum amount of seconds a
cached connection may remain idle before timing out. The default value for the
ConnectionTimeout key is 600 seconds (10 minutes).

AsyncRetryInterval

The `AsyncRetryInverval` is used to measure the time allotted between polls to figure if the server has completed processing a query. The `AsyncRetryInterval` key is measured in milliseconds, with a default of **500**. This key is available only for asynchronous processing.

AttachCaseSensitive

The `AttachCaseSensitive` key is used to determine what type of matching is enabled for linking tables. A default value of **0** indicates that the linking process is not case sensitive, whereas a value of **1** indicates that the tables must match according to case.

AttachableObjects

The `AttachableObjects` key holds a list of server object types that are allowed to be linked. The default value for this key is `'TABLE'`, `'VIEW'`, `'SYSTEM TABLE'`, `'ALIAS'`, `'SYNONYM'`.

SnapshotOnly

The `SnapshotOnly` key indicates whether `Recordsets` objects must be snapshots (default value of **0**) or can be dynasets (value of **1**).

TraceSQLMode

The `TraceSQLMode` key is equivalent to the `SQLTraceMode` key. It indicates whether a trace of SQL statements that are sent to an ODBC data source will be recorded in SQLOUT.TXT. The default value for the `TraceSQLMode` key is **0**, or no. A value of **1** indicates yes.

TraceODBCAPI

The `TraceODBCAPI` key indicates whether ODBC API calls are traced in the ODBCAPI.TXT file. A value of **0** indicates no, and **1** indicates yes. The default for this key is no.

DisableAsync

The `DisableAsync` key is an indicator of whether to force synchronous query execution. This key can be set to either its default of **1** for a force of synchronous query execution or **0** for using asynchronous query execution if possible.

JetTryAuth

The `JetTryAuth` key indicates whether the Microsoft Access user name and password are to be used to log in to the server before prompting. The default value is yes (**1**). A value of **0** indicates no.

PreparedInsert

The `PreparedInsert` key is used to determine whether to use a prepared `INSERT` statement that inserts data in all columns. The default value for this key is 1, which indicates to use a prepared INSERT statement. A value of 0 would indicate to use a custom INSERT statement that inserts only non-null values. By using prepared INSERT statements, nulls can overwrite server defaults. In addition, triggers can execute on columns that were not inserted explicitly.

PreparedUpdate

The PreparedUpdate key is used to determine whether to use a prepared UPDATE statement that updates data in all the available columns. A value of 0 is the default. This indicates that a custom UPDATE statement is to be used and sets only columns that have changed. A value of 1 specifies to use a prepared UPDATE statement.

FastRequery

The FastRequery key is used to indicate whether to use a prepared SELECT statement for parameterized queries. The default value is no, or 0. A value of 1 indicates yes.

ACTIVEX AND AUTOMATION

13

ACTIVEX AND AUTOMATION

How do I...

847

13.8 Include an editable report writer in a Visual Basic application?

13.9 Work with the Windows Registry for my ActiveX classes?

13.10 Create my own custom data control?

13.11 Create my own data bound control?

ActiveX Overview

ActiveX is the umbrella name Microsoft applies to developer technology that implements the *Component Object Model* (COM). At its heart, COM allows applications to communicate with each other and use each other's features without regard to the original development language, date of development, or version compatibility. The component object model started from the concepts of *object-oriented programming* (OOP) and extended that model into the operating system to allow any COM program object to communicate successfully with any other COM object supporting the desired interfaces.

OBJECT-ORIENTED PROGRAMMING

Object-oriented programming provides disciplines and methods for source code re-use and recycling. OOP engineering concepts define an environment in which program objects model "real-world" objects. Each object is responsible for its own data, program logic, lifetime, and interfaces to the outside world. Formally, the academic experts tell us that "true" objects must support *encapsulation*, *inheritance*, and *polymorphism*.

Encapsulation means that each object provides a safe container (or capsule) for its *properties* (data) and *methods* (code). The object defines which properties and methods it will allow other objects to see (*public*) and which ones remain only inside the object (*private*). Inheritance means that a new object can be defined as a "kind of" another object and gain all the "parent" object's properties and methods without doing any work. Polymorphism is the capability of a derived object to change or override the inherited methods of its parents. You can have a dog object with a method to bark, and you can then have a big dog and a little dog inherited from the parent dog, each with a bark—but those two barks can be different (woof, and WOOF WOOF, for example) if that method is overridden in the new object.

COM Has Its Roots in OOP

The component object model (COM) and the distributed component object model (DCOM) extend the object-oriented programming (see sidebar) paradigm to allow preexisting software applications and objects to interact through a published, stable specification. Microsoft's first widely published implementation of the component object model was *Object Linking and Embedding* (OLE). This technology allowed previously compiled programs to embed or link their objects (Word documents or Excel spreadsheets) into new documents or forms.

Unfortunately, VB5 does not fully implement object-oriented programming. In particular, polymorphism is given short shrift. In traditional OOP, an object can inherit methods from a parent and then change or override only selected methods without having to re-implement all the parent's methods. With VB5, the programmer must implement all inherited methods of a parent object even if only one method is to be changed. By using the `Implements` keyword, a programmer tells the VB5 compiler that the class is implementing an interface derived from another class. The "bird" object "flies on" feathered wings. The "airliner" object "flies on" metal wings. In VB5, both the bird and the airliner classes would be declared to *implement* the `FlyingThing` class in order to encapsulate the `FlyingThing`'s properties and methods. Both birds and airliners are flying objects, and both implement a "flies on" property, but they appear to share similar properties and behaviors even though they are different objects.

ActiveX and Visual Basic 5

Visual Basic 5 provides several ways to incorporate ActiveX technologies in applications, determined primarily by how the calling application fits into the ActiveX component's environment:

✔ Code components serve as a library of objects available to calling applications. Built as Visual Basic class modules, the services can be built as *dynamic link libraries* (DLLs), can be separate EXE files, or can be statically bound into the calling application. The remainder of this chapter focuses on ActiveX code components.

✔ ActiveX controls are functionally equivalent to the visual controls you put on your forms. They differ from other ActiveX components in that they talk back to the calling application by raising events whose responses can modify the behavior of the control. ActiveX controls run in the caller's process space and communicate directly through memory.

✔ ActiveX documents are forms designed to appear within Internet browser windows. They are very similar to ActiveX controls because they must be used within a browser container. They are similar to code components in that they can be implemented as DLL or EXE files and run either within the calling process environment (DLL) or as a separate process (EXE).

The three ActiveX methods share the use of the Component Object Model as the operating-environment glue that allows successful communication between components.

Building and Using Code Components

As developers, we build all our ActiveX code components as *class modules*. At the simple, practical level, Visual Basic 5 treats class modules as objects implementing properties and methods in just the same manner in which we can use the Visual Basic label control from our code. We can set the `Caption` property and then invoke the `Refresh` method to ensure that the caption is displayed immediately. Visual Basic will help us write the code with its code completion features and will show us as we type the defined properties and methods for each object in the application. As a result, programmers will reuse existing code more often, develop systems faster, and produce more reliable systems. The use of classes to develop our features and functions helps keep other programmers from using our code in ways we did not intend.

ActiveX code components publish properties and methods that are available for use in your application. An ActiveX code component can be included in an application by referencing a component from the Project menu in the development environment. When included, component properties and methods can be invoked from the calling application as though the calling application had all the component application's functionality. For example, an application referencing a Microsoft Office EXE component can use the Visual Basic for Applications (VBA) methods to manipulate the Office component's properties to create powerful business solutions.

Visual Basic 4 called code components *object linking and embedding*, which is used to embed or link another application's object within the calling application. The calling application is called the container. A Visual Basic application acting as the container can use the `OLE Container` control to display linked or embedded objects belonging to server applications. The type of object depends on the server. A spreadsheet program typically provides worksheet objects and graph objects. A word processing program provides document objects. A graphics program provides picture objects.

13.1 Use OLE to Allow Users to Edit Pictures, Documents, and Spreadsheets Embedded in an Application's Database

You can use the `OLE Object` field type in a Microsoft Access database file to store linked or embedded objects, then display those objects on a Visual Basic form. Users can view or edit the object from within the Visual Basic application. This How-To shows you how to use an `OLE Container` control linked to a data control to accomplish this task.

13.2 Provide Access to Database Files Through a Private Class Module

The first step to creating an ActiveX code component is to create and debug a private class module that implements all the desired properties and methods. This How-To shows you a simple class-based replacement for the data control that implements core functions.

13.3 Publish My ActiveX Private Class So That Others Can Use It

After you build a useful class module for simple data access, other members of your workgroup or corporation might find it useful. Company policy, however, requires that your class module's functions only be distributed as object code—you can't share your source. This How-To shows how to convert your class module into an ActiveX DLL that can be used by other applications.

13.4 Provide Controlled Access to an Encrypted, Password-Protected Database

Visual Basic 5 has given the language a much stronger and more useful set of object-oriented features with ActiveX. This How-To demonstrates a method of creating an ActiveX EXE component in Visual Basic that can be used from other applications, or even from other machines, while hiding the details of its operation and encapsulating its data.

13.5 Use Microsoft Access as an ActiveX Server to Print Reports from Visual Basic

The application design requires that all reports be centrally administered, and the Access database has been selected as the report repository. This How-To demonstrates using Microsoft Access from Visual Basic to print reports defined within the database.

13.6 Use Microsoft Access Queries Containing User-Defined Functions from Visual Basic

Sometimes, an application needs to take advantage of Access database functions that are not available directly to Visual Basic 5. This How-To demonstrates using Microsoft Access as a component to use a query containing a user-defined function.

13.7 Convert Database Data to a Spreadsheet Form That Can Be Used to Edit and Analyze Data

Although Visual Basic is an extremely powerful and flexible tool and environment, it lacks many specialized functions for financial, statistical, and scientific analyses of data in a database. This How-To shows how you can use the specialized statistical functions from Microsoft Excel to make statistical calculations on any database accessible to Visual Basic.

13.8 Include an Editable Report Writer in a Visual Basic Application

One of the biggest advantages of using ActiveX code components with Visual Basic applications is that you can use the functionality of other applications in Visual Basic. In this How-To, you will see how you can use all the power of Microsoft Word in Visual Basic, eliminating the need to duplicate the programming in your own code.

13.9 Work with the Windows Registry for My ActiveX Classes

ActiveX code components bring lots of power and flexibility to your applications, but they rely on correct registration in order for other programs to find them. This How-To shows the use of the registration server to register and "unregister" your controls.

13.10 Create My Own Custom Data Control

The data control provided with Visual Basic 5 is a powerful tool for building many applications, but it can add tremendous amounts of processing overhead because it is a general-purpose tool with methods and events that no one needs for most projects. This How-To shows you how to build a custom data control purpose-built for a single table using data access objects.

13.11 Create My Own Data Bound Control

The data bound list box provided with Visual Basic is quite powerful, but using a data control to populate can add a lot of unnecessary overhead to an application. This How-To shows you a data bound combo box control that loads a specific code value type such as HAIRCOLOR from a specified database.

COMPLEXITY
INTERMEDIATE

13.1 How do I...

Use OLE to allow users to edit pictures, documents, and spreadsheets embedded in my application's database?

Problem

I'm creating a customer service database with a table that documents contacts with customers. When the customer is sent a letter, I'd like to put a copy of the actual word processing document into the table. How can I do this with Visual Basic?

Technique

Microsoft Access provides the OLE Object field type into which you can place either a linked or an embedded OLE object. An embedded object is actually stored in the database. Linked objects are not stored in the database; rather, the database stores a reference to the file containing the object.

The Visual Basic OLE Container control is a control used to place an OLE object onto a form. The OLE Container control is then bound to an OLE Object field in a Microsoft Access database through a data control. The data control and OLE Container control together manage the retrieval and updating of the OLE Object field and the display of the field's contents on the form.

Visual Basic can insert a new object into a Microsoft Access database OLE Object field in two ways. The OLE Container control's InsertObjectDlg box displays the Insert Object dialog box. The dialog box enables the user to choose to create a new object from any application on the system that can act as an OLE Server. This creates an embedded object. The dialog box also gives the user the means to select a file containing an OLE object and to designate that the object be stored as an embedded or a linked object.

If the Clipboard contains an object created by an OLE Server application, and if the current control is an OLE Container, Visual Basic can paste the contents of the Clipboard into the control. The OLE Container's Paste method pastes the object into the control in the default format (which depends on the type of object). The PasteSpecial method displays a dialog box that lets the user select the format for those object types that support more than one format.

Steps

Open the project Embedded.VBP. If necessary, edit the DatabaseName property of the datObjects control to point to a copy of Chapter13.MDB. Then run the project. The form shown in Figure 13.1 appears. Use the record navigation buttons of the data control to page through the records. As you display a record, the application shows you the contents of the OLE Object field, the type of object, and the name of the object. Double-click on the object, and Paintbrush opens with the object displayed. Edit the object in Paintbrush, and then choose File | Exit from the Paintbrush menu. When the dialog box appears asking whether you want to update the link to the Visual Basic application, click Yes.

On the form, click the Add button. Click on the OLE Container control, and then choose Edit | Insert Object. The Insert Object dialog box appears, as shown in Figure 13.2. To create a new embedded object from one of the listed applications, choose the object from the list and click OK. To create an object from a file, choose the Create from File option. When the Insert Object dialog box changes in appearance (see Figure 13.3), either enter a filename or click Browse and select a file from the File Open dialog box that appears. If you want to select a linked object, click the Link check box. To create an embedded object, leave the Link check box blank.

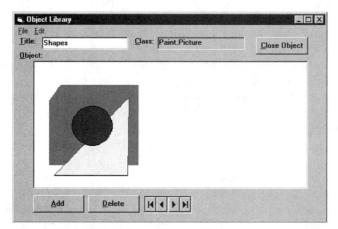

Figure 13.1. The Object Library form.

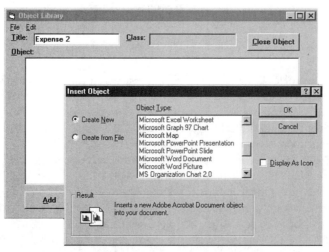

Figure 13.2. The Insert Object dialog box.

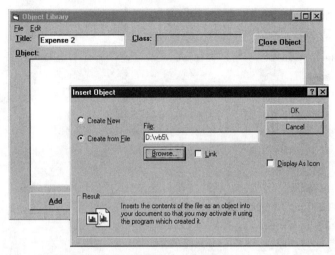

Figure 13.3. The Insert Object dialog box with the
Create from File option selected.

1. Create a new project called Embedded.VBP. Use **Form1** to create the
objects and properties listed in Table 13.1, and save the form as
OBJLIB.FRM. If you have moved the files installed by the distribution
disk, edit the **DatabaseName** property of the data control on **Form1** to point
to the current location of Chapter13.MDB.

Table 13.1. Objects and properties for the Object Library form.

OBJECT	PROPERTY	SETTING
Form	Name	Form1
	Caption	"Object Library"
Name	CommandButton	cmdClick
	Caption	"&Close Object"
Name	CommandButton	cmdDelete
	Caption	"&Delete"
Name	CommandButton	cmdAdd
	Caption	"&Add"
Name	TextBox	txtTitle
	DataField	"Title"
	DataSource	"datObjects"
Name	Data	datObjects
	Connect	"Access"
	DatabaseName	"D:\Waite\Chapter10\Chapter13.mdb"

continued on next page

continued from previous page

OBJECT	PROPERTY	SETTING
	RecordsetType	1 'Dynaset
	RecordSource	"ObjectLibrary"
Name	Label	lblClass
	DataField	"Object Type"
	DataSource	"datObjects"
Name	OLE	oleObject
	DataField	"Object"
	DataSource	"datObjects"
	SizeMode	3 'Zoom
Name	Label	Label1
	AutoSize	-1 'True
Name	Label	Label2
	AutoSize	-1 'True

2. Use the Visual Basic menu editor to create the menu shown in Table 13.2.

Table 13.2. Menu specifications for the Object Library form.

CAPTION	NAME	SHORTCUT KEY
&File	mnuFile	
----E&xit	mnuFileExit	
&Edit	mnuEdit	
----&Paste	mnuEditPaste	Ctrl+V
----Past&e Special	mnuEditPasteSpecial	
---- ----	mnuEditSep	
----&Insert Object	mnuEditInsertObject	

3. Add the following code to the declarations section of **Form1**. This variable tracks deletions in progress when the data control fires a reposition event in response to the **MoveNext** issued during **cmdDelete_Click** processing.

```
Private mblnDeleting As Boolean
```

4. Enter the following code as the **Click** event for **cmdAdd**:

```
Private Sub cmdAdd_Click()
    Data1.Recordset.AddNew
End Sub
```

5. Enter the following code as the **Click** event for **cmdDelete**:

```
Private Sub cmdDelete_Click()

    On Error GoTo DeleteError
    mblnDeleting = True
    datObjects.Recordset.Delete
    'oleObject.Class = ""
    datObjects.Recordset.MoveNext
    ' Handle the "no current record" case.
    If datObjects.Recordset.EOF Then
        ' Handle the special case of deleting the
        ' last record
        datObjects.Recordset.MoveLast
    End If
    mblnDeleting = False

    ' Reset the error handler
    On Error GoTo 0
    Exit Sub

DeleteError:
    If Err.Number = 3021 Then               ' No current record
        Resume Next
    End If

End Sub
```

6. Enter the following code as the **Click** event for **mnuEdit**. If the Edit menu is opened when the **OLE Container** control is the active control, the Edit menu's Insert Object item is enabled. The procedure looks at the **PasteOK** property of the **OLE Container** control. If **PasteOK** is **True**, the object currently on the Windows Clipboard supports OLE, so the Paste and PasteSpecial items are enabled. If **PasteOK** is **False**, the item on the Clipboard cannot be an OLE object, so Paste and PasteOK are disabled. If the active control is anything other than the **OLE Container** control, all the Edit menu choices are disabled.

```
Private Sub mnuEdit_Click()
    If Me.ActiveControl.Name = "oleObject" Then
        mnuEditPaste.Enabled = oleObject.PasteOK
        mnuEditPasteSpecial.Enabled = oleObject.PasteOK
        mnuEditInsertObject.Enabled = True
    Else
        mnuEditPaste.Enabled = False
        mnuEditPasteSpecial.Enabled = False
        mnuEditInsertObject.Enabled = False
    End If
End Sub
```

7. Enter the following code as the **Click** event of the Edit menu's Insert Object item. This code calls the **InsertObjDlg** method of the OLE object. That method displays the Insert Object dialog box and manages the actual insertion of the object designated by the user. If the user inserts a new object, the procedure then gets the `Class` property of the `OLE Container` control and displays it in the Class label on the form.

```
Private Sub mnuEditInsertObject_Click()
    OLE1.InsertObjDlg
    If OLE1.DataChanged Then
        lblClass.Caption = OLE1.Class
    End If
End Sub
```

8. Enter the following code as the `Click` event for `mnuPaste`. When the user chooses this menu item, the code pastes the object currently on the Clipboard into the `OLE Container` control and updates the Class label on the form.

```
Private Sub mnuEditInsertObject_Click()
    oleObject.InsertObjDlg
    If oleObject.DataChanged Then
        lblClass.Caption = oleObject.Class
    End If
End Sub
```

9. Enter the following code as the `Click` event for `mnuPasteSpecial`. When the user chooses this menu item, the code invokes the `PasteSpecialDlg` method of the `OLE Container` control. This method displays the Paste Special dialog box, which allows the user to choose the format and linkage type to be used for the object.

```
Private Sub mnuEditPasteSpecial_Click()
    oleObject.PasteSpecialDlg
    lblClass.Caption = oleObject.Class
End Sub
```

10. Enter the following code as the `Click` event for `cmdCloseObject` to update the Access database OLE Object database field:

```
Private Sub cmdCloseObject_Click()

    ' Save the updated object
    If oleObject.DataChanged Or txtTitle.DataChanged Then
        datObjects.UpdateRecord
    End If

End Sub
```

11. Enter the following code as the `Click` event for `mnuFileExit`:

```
Private Sub mnuFileExit_Click()

    If oleObject.DataChanged Or txtTitle.DataChanged Then
        datObjects.UpdateRecord
    End If
```

```
      Unload Me

End Sub
```

12. Enter the following code as the **Reposition** event for **datObject**. This procedure checks to see whether we are in the middle of a delete operation before referencing a potentially non-existent data-bound **oleObject**. The **mblnDeleting** variable controls accidentally reentering the validation event when the data control is positioned at "No current record" after deletion of the last record.

```
Private Sub datObjects_Reposition()

    If Not mblnDeleting Then
        ' Update the label for the oleObject class if the reposition is
        ' not a MoveNext after deletion of the last record. The change
        ' to the lblClass value forces another validation and
        ' record update attempt. The update attempt after the deletion
        ' of the last record causes a "no current record" error
        If lblClass.Caption = "" Then
            lblClass.Caption = oleObject.Class
        End If
    End If

End Sub
```

13. Enter the following code for the **Form_Load** event. This procedure sets the database name for the data control to be the database in the application directory.

```
Dim strDbName As String
    Dim strResponse As String

    On Error GoTo LoadError

    ' Set the database of the data control
    strDbName = App.Path
    strDbName = strDbName & "\Chapter13.mdb"
    datObjects.DatabaseName = strDbName

    ' Indicate that we are not currently deleting a
    ' record
    mblnDeleting = False

    Exit Sub

LoadError:
    MsgBox Err.Description & Chr(13) & "from " & Err.Source _
            & " — Number: " & CStr(Err.Number)
    Unload Me

End Sub
```

How It Works

The OLE Container control contains the image of the data you are storing, the name of the application used to manipulate the data, and the actual object data (embedded) or a reference to the actual object data (linked). For example, when you embed a spreadsheet in the OLE Container control, the display image of the spreadsheet, the application name (usually Excel), and the spreadsheet data itself are stored in the OLE Container control.

The data control is responsible for storing the embedded object in the Access OLE object database field. You might notice the "extra" work required to deal with the case of record movement after deleting the last record. The form uses a control variable (mblnDeleting) to determine whether a delete operation is in progress. The variable is checked in the Reposition event to prevent use of the oleObject.Class field when the last record has been deleted from the recordset and the unfortunate No current record error. There are 12 data validation constants for the data control to meet every programmer's potential needs, but they can cause unfortunate extra work if a reference to control data is required during a different event's firing. In this case, the Reposition event needs to check a field value, forcing a validation event before the Reposition event is complete.

The OLE Container control does almost all the work for this application for us by managing the properties and methods exposed by the ActiveX Automation components registered on the application's computer. Simply double-click on the OLE Container control, and people using the application have almost all the capabilities of the embedded or linked component. The only limitation is that embedded or linked document saving is through the OLE container rather than through the application.

Comments

The properties of the OLE Container control give you a great deal of control over how the control works in your application. Two of the most useful properties are the edit-in-place property—actually a setting of the MiscFlags property—and the SizeMode property. More details on other OLE Container control properties can be found in the Visual Basic 5 documentation.

Editing in Place

If an ActiveX Automation application implements in-place editing, the user can edit an object right from your Visual Basic form. When the user double-clicks on the OLE Container control, the menu bar changes to the one used by the server application that created the object, and any toolbars associated with the server application appear. The full facilities of the server application are available to the containing application. When the user moves the focus off the OLE Container control, the menus are restored to those of the client (Visual Basic) application.

Unless you specify otherwise, editing in-place is active for those server applications that support it. To disable editing in-place, set the MiscFlags property to the built-in constant value of 2 (or use the constant `vbOLEMiscFlagDisableInPlace`).

Controlling the Size

Windows gives the user the ability to resize forms. You might not always know in advance the size of the object that will be stored in a database; therefore, Visual Basic enables you to control how the OLE `Container` or the object it contains is sized. This is implemented through the settings of the `SizeMode` property, which are shown in Table 13.3. The default for the `SizeMode` property is 2 (Autosize).

Table 13.3. Settings for the `SizeMode` property of the OLE Container control.

SETTING	MEANING
0--vbOLESizeClip	The object is displayed actual size. If the object is larger than the control, the image is clipped by the control.
1--vbOLESizeStretch	The object's image is sized to fill the control. May not maintain the original proportions.
2--vbOLESizeAutoSize	The control is resized to display the entire object. Maintains proportions, but requires that the OLE Container control resize event be handled to change the size of the form or the container.
3--vbOLESizeZoom	The object is resized to fill as much as possible of the control while maintaining the original proportions.

COMPLEXITY
INTERMEDIATE

13.2 How do I...
Provide access to database files through a private class module?

Problem

I'm writing a company-wide expense reporting system and need to control the data access to the expense detail table to ensure that all data is correctly edited before insertion. How do I create a private class module with properties and methods to manage and protect the contents of the expense detail table?

Technique

For this How-To, consider an expense detail table (contained in Expense.MDB). The fields of this table are listed in Table 13.4.

Table 13.4. Expense detail table definition.

FIELD	TYPE
ExpenseID	Long—Auto increment
EmployeeId	Text
ExpenseType	Text
AmountSpent	Currency
Description	Text
DatePurchased	Date/Time
DateSubmitted	Date/Time

The people in the accounting department are very concerned that any entries made to this table always pass certain edit checks. They are most concerned that the submission date always be set to the current date. They want no back-dated submissions to make it look as though they're working slowly. We have decided to manage the expense detail table with a Visual Basic class module to encapsulate the table properties and enforce the critical submission-date requirement.

Class Modules Form the Object Core

Visual Basic class modules implement program objects and are the core building blocks of all ActiveX code components. Each class implements public or private properties and methods. Properties are data items such as an expense amount. Methods are code procedures that act on the properties. Public items are exposed outside the class to the calling application. Private items are restricted to access by members of the class unless you choose to expose selected methods as *friends* to be invoked directly by code contained within the same project.

The expense detail class will be constructed to have properties (data items) corresponding to each table field, plus an additional property to contain the Access database filename. The class assumes that the table is named Expenses. All properties are implemented with the **Private** keyword to ensure that callers cannot access the data directly. A private declaration limits access to a variable or function to code contained within the same module. Access to properties is through the **Property Let** and **Property Get** methods. These special-purpose, public method procedures assign values to and retrieve values from their properties. As values are set and retrieved, the **Let** and **Get** procedures can perform simple edits or complex calculations.

Linking Forms and Classes

The easiest way to link a simple form and its maintenance class is through two subroutines, one for setting the object's values and the other for getting changed object values. These subroutines transfer values between the form's controls and the object's properties by means of the **Property Let** and **Property Set** methods. The subroutines are called before any of the object's data movement methods are called.

Building Class Modules

In Visual Basic 5, you can build class modules by typing the entire program module or by using the Class Builder utility. This add-in speeds initial class module construction by automating property variable naming and construction of all required skeleton methods. Unfortunately, the Class Builder cannot delete classes after they are created. The most efficient way to use the Class Builder is to use it for initial definition of most of the class and then to use manual editing for the remainder of the code maintenance.

The principal benefit of using the Class Builder utility is that it automatically makes all properties private and creates public **Property Let** and **Property Get** methods to allow calling applications to manipulate the object's properties. Although this approach incurs some additional processing overhead, especially in a private class module used only in your application, it automatically provides placeholders where you can later add code to manipulate properties as they are set.

Steps

Open the project ActiveXExpense.VBP and run the project. The form shown in Figure 13.4 appears. Experiment with the form to understand its simple behavior. The class module implements the most common data control methods.

1. Create a new project in your work area named ActiveXExpense.VBP, and use **frmExpClient** to create the objects and properties listed in Table 13.5.

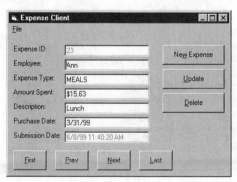

Figure 13.4. The Expense Client form.

Table 13.5. Objects and properties for the Expense Client form.

OBJECT	PROPERTY	SETTING
Form	Name	frmExpClient
	Caption	"Expense Client"
CommandButton	Name	cmdLast
	Caption	"&Last"
CommandButton	Name	cmdNext
	Caption	"&Next"
CommandButton	Name	cmdPrev
	Caption	"&Prev"
CommandButton	Name	cmdFirst
	Caption	"&First"
CommandButton	Name	cmdDelete
	Caption	"&Delete"
CommandButton	Name	cmdUpdate
	Caption	"&Update"
CommandButton	Name	cmdNewExpense
	Caption	"Ne&w Expense"
MaskEdBox	Name	mskAmountSpent
	Format	"$#,##0.00;($#,##0.00)"
TextBox	Name	txtSubmitDate
TextBox	Name	txtPurchaseDate
TextBox	Name	txtDescription
TextBox	Name	txtExpenseType
TextBox	Name	txtEmployeeId
TextBox	Name	txtExpenseId
Label	Name	Label1
	Caption	"Expense ID:"
Label	Name	Label2
	Caption	"Employee:"
Label	Name	Label3
	Caption	"Expense Type:"
Label	Name	Label4
	Caption	"Amount Spent:"
Label	Name	Label5
	Caption	"Description:"
Label	Name	Label6
	Caption	"Purchase Date:"

OBJECT	PROPERTY	SETTING
Label	Name	Label7
	Caption	"Submission Date:"

2. Use the Visual Basic menu editor to create the menu shown in Table 13.6.

Table 13.6. Menu specifications for the Expense Client form.

CAPTION	NAME	SHORTCUT KEY
&File	mnuFile	
----E&xit	mnuFileExit	

3. Enter the following code into the declarations section of `frmExpClient`. This line declares a private `ExpenseDetail` class variable to manage the expense details.

```
Private expDetailClass As New ExpenseDetail
```

4. Enter the following code as the `Click` event of the `cmdNewExpense` button. The `ExpenseDetail` class does error trapping for us, so the command button handlers can manage the object as a modal function modifying the database. The `strResponse` variable provides any required feedback for immediate display.

```
Private Sub cmdNewExpense_Click()

    Dim strResponse As String
    strResponse = SetObjectValues

    If "OK" = strResponse Then
        strResponse = expDetailClass.Insert
        If "OK" <> strResponse Then
            MsgBox strResponse
            Exit Sub
        End If
        Call ReadObjectValues
    Else
        MsgBox strResponse
    End If

End Sub
```

5. Enter the following code as the `Click` event of the `cmdUpdate` button:

```
Private Sub cmdUpdate_Click()
' Updates current record with form values

    Dim strResponse As String
    strResponse = SetObjectValues
```

continued on next page

continued from previous page

```
        If "OK" = strResponse Then
            strResponse = expDetailClass.Update
            If "OK" <> strResponse Then
                MsgBox strResponse
                Exit Sub
            End If
            Call ReadObjectValues
        Else
            MsgBox strResponse
        End If

End Sub
```

6. Enter the following code as the **Click** event of the **cmdDelete** button:

```
Private Sub cmdDelete_Click()
' Deletes current record from database

    Dim strResponse As String

    strResponse = expDetailClass.Delete
    If "OK" <> strResponse Then
        MsgBox strResponse
    Else
        Call ReadObjectValues
    End If

End Sub
```

7. Enter the following code for the **Click** events of the movement buttons. With the exception of the invoked class methods, these event procedures are virtually identical—they invoke a class method, check the result, and display an error message or data.

```
Private Sub cmdFirst_Click()
' Positions to first record in recordset and displays values

    Dim strResponse As String

    strResponse = expDetailClass.MoveFirst
    If "OK" <> strResponse Then
        MsgBox strResponse
    Else
        Call ReadObjectValues
    End If

End Sub

Private Sub cmdLast_Click()
' Positions to last record in recordset and displays values

    Dim strResponse As String

    strResponse = expDetailClass.MoveLast
    If "OK" <> strResponse Then
        MsgBox strResponse
```

```
        Else
            Call ReadObjectValues
        End If

    End Sub

    Private Sub cmdNext_Click()
    ' Positions to Next record in recordset and displays values

        Dim strResponse As String

        strResponse = expDetailClass.MoveNext
        If "OK" <> strResponse Then
            MsgBox strResponse
        Else
            Call ReadObjectValues
        End If

    End Sub

    Private Sub cmdPrev_Click()
    ' Positions to Previous record in recordset and displays values

        Dim strResponse As String

        strResponse = expDetailClass.MovePrev
        If "OK" <> strResponse Then
            MsgBox strResponse
        Else
            Call ReadObjectValues
        End If

    End Sub
```

8. Enter the following code for the procedure **SetObjectValues**. This
function invokes the Expense Detail class's public methods to set the
object's property values. The expense type is limited by the object
to values of TRAVEL, MEALS, OFFICE, AUTO, or TOLL/PARK. The
strSetExpenseType method converts the input to uppercase characters
and checks for a valid value. Invalid input results in the method returning
an informative display message.

```
Private Function SetObjectValues() As String
' Sets related object values from form fields

    Dim strResponse As String

    strResponse = expDetailClass.strSetExpenseType(txtExpenseType.Text)

    On Error GoTo TypeError

    If "OK" = strResponse Then
        expDetailClass.strEmployeeId = txtEmployeeId.Text
        expDetailClass.strDescription = txtDescription.Text
        expDetailClass.dtmDatePurchased = txtPurchaseDate.Text
```

continued on next page

continued from previous page

```
            expDetailClass.curAmountSpent = CCur(mskAmountSpent.Text)
    End If

    SetObjectValues = strResponse
    Exit Function

TypeError:
    If Err.Number = 13 Then
        expDetailClass.curAmountSpent = 0
        Resume Next
    End If

End Function
```

9. Enter the following code for the procedure `ReadObjectValues`. Note that the form code doesn't have to deal with any potential null values from the database; it just displays the results.

```
Private Sub ReadObjectValues()
' Read the object values into the form fields

    txtExpenseId.Text = CStr(expDetailClass.lngExpenseId)
    txtEmployeeId.Text = expDetailClass.strEmployeeId
    txtExpenseType.Text = expDetailClass.strExpenseType
    txtDescription.Text = expDetailClass.strDescription
    mskAmountSpent.Text = CStr(expDetailClass.curAmountSpent)
    txtPurchaseDate.Text = CStr(expDetailClass.dtmDatePurchased)
    txtSubmitDate.Text = CStr(expDetailClass.dtmDateSubmitted)

End Sub
```

10. Enter the following code for the **Form_Load** event. The invocation of the class's **strDbName Property Let** method causes the object to open the specified database and position its hidden recordset to the first record. An error handler is required in this procedure because **Property Let** procedures cannot return a signal value but can raise errors.

```
Private Sub Form_Load()
' Get the ActiveX object to open its database and position
' to the first record
    Dim strDbName As String
    Dim strResponse As String

    On Error GoTo LoadError

    strDbName = App.Path
    strDbName = strDbName & "\Expense.mdb"
    expDetailClass.strDbName = strDbName
    strResponse = expDetailClass.MoveFirst
    If "OK" <> strResponse Then
        MsgBox strResponse
    Else
        Call ReadObjectValues
    End If

    Exit Sub
```

```
LoadError:
    MsgBox Err.Description & Chr(13) & "from " & Err.Source _
           & " — Number: " & CStr(Err.Number)
    Unload Me

End Sub
```

11. Enter the following code for the **Form_Unload** event. Although this client is using the expense detail class as a private module whose memory will be released when the form is unloaded, EXE and DLL objects will usually not release resources until no caller is making references. Setting an object to the value **Nothing** is the caller's way to tear down the object connection gracefully.

```
Private Sub Form_Unload(Cancel As Integer)

    Set expDetailClass = Nothing

End Sub
```

12. Enter the following code for the **Click** event of **mnuFileExit**:

```
Private Sub mnuFileExit_Click()

    Unload Me

End Sub
```

13. Use the VB Class Builder to create the skeleton of the Expense Detail class. Select Project | Add Class Module. Double-click on VB Class Builder to start the Class Builder add-in. As shown in Figure 13.5, select File | New | Class, and then name the new class **ExpenseDetail**.

14. Select the newly created **ExpenseDetail** class. Select File | New | Property, and create a property named **lngExpenseId** with Long data type, as shown in Figure 13.6. Continue adding properties until you have defined everything listed in Table 13.7.

Table 13.7. Properties and data types for the ExpenseDetail class.

PROPERTY	DATA TYPE
lngExpenseID	Long
strEmployeeId	String
strExpenseType	String
curAmmountSpent	Currency
strDescription	String
dtmDatePurchased	Date
dtmDateSubmitted	Date
strDbName	String

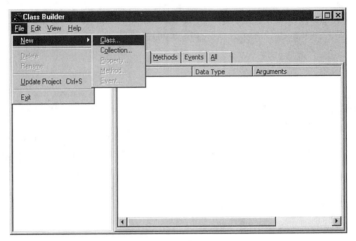

Figure 13.5. The VB Class Builder.

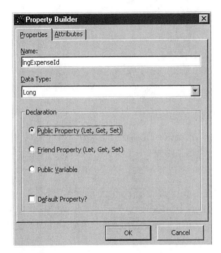

Figure 13.6. The VB Property
Builder.

15. Click on the Methods tab of the Class Builder utility to define the methods
and return types listed in Table 13.8. Be sure to define a return data type.
Update the project and exit the Class Builder.

Table 13.8. Methods and data types for the `ExpenseDetail` class.

METHOD	RETURN DATA TYPE
Delete	String
Insert	String

METHOD	RETURN DATA TYPE
Update	String
MoveFirst	String
MoveNext	String
MovePrev	String
MoveLast	String

16. Add the variables in bold type to the declarations section of your class module. The other variables were created by the Property Builder. The class needs database and recordset variables to perform its work, and it uses the **RecSetOpen** Boolean variable to force closing the recordset and database if a running version of the class is passed a new database name.

```
Option Explicit

'local variable(s) to hold property value(s)
Private mvarlngExpenseId As Long 'local copy
Private mvarstrEmployeeId As String 'local copy
Private mvarstrExpenseType As String 'local copy
Private mvarcurAmountSpent As Currency 'local copy
Private mvarstrDescription As String 'local copy
Private mvardtmDatePurchased As Date 'local copy
Private mvardtmDateSubmitted As Date 'local copy
Private mvarstrDbName As String 'local copy
' Database variables needed to keep track of current
' database condition
Private mdbExpense As Database
Private mrecExpense As Recordset
Private mblnRecSetOpen As Boolean
```

17. Remove the **Property Let** procedures for **lngExpenseId** and **dtmDateSubmitted** from the class module. The Access database engine automatically assigns the **ExpenseId**, and the **Insert** method assigns the date submitted. A class module designed to protect the database can't allow these changes.

18. Modify the **Property Let** procedure for the **strDbName** property as shown next. Whenever the database name property is changed, we need to close an open recordset and database and then open the desired database and recordset.

```
Public Property Let strDbName(ByVal vData As String)
'used when assigning a value to the property, on the left
'side of an assignment.
'Syntax: X.strDbName = 5

    On Error GoTo OpenError

    If mblnRecSetOpen Then
        mrecExpense.Close
```

continued on next page

continued from previous page

```
        mdbExpense.Close
    End If
    mvarstrDbName = vData
    Set mdbExpense = DBEngine.Workspaces(0).OpenDatabase(mvarstrDbName)
    Set mrecExpense = mdbExpense.OpenRecordset("Expenses")
    mblnRecSetOpen = True

    Exit Property

OpenError:
    ' Since we are designing this class for potential unattended
    ' operation, we'll have to raise an error on our own
    Err.Raise Number:=Err.Number
    Err.Clear
    Exit Property

End Property
```

19. Prepare the **Class Initialize** and **Class Terminate** procedures as shown next. The **Initialize** procedure ensures that all critical variables have their *initial values* set correctly even if we programmers think that they are already set. The **Terminate** procedure cleans up any messes we might have made along the way.

```
Private Sub Class_Initialize()

    ' Indicate that the database is not yet open
    mblnRecSetOpen = False
    ' Clear all object variables
    Call ClearObject

End Sub

Private Sub Class_Terminate()

    ' We don't really care about errors when cleaning up.
    On Error Resume Next
    ' Close the recordset
    mrecExpense.Close
    ' Close the expense database
    mdbExpense.Close
    ' Reset the error handler
    On Error GoTo 0
    Exit Sub

End Sub
```

20. Define the private **ClearObject** procedure to clear the object's properties to known safe values that won't cause database errors and that will look "empty" to anyone reading the values from a caller's form:

```
Private Sub ClearObject()
' Clears all object variables

    mvarlngExpenseId = 0
```

```
    mvarstrEmployeeId = ""
    mvarstrExpenseType = ""
    mvarcurAmountSpent = 0
    mvarstrDescription = ""
    mvardtmDatePurchased = CDate("1/1/1980")
    mvardtmDateSubmitted = CDate("1/1/1980")

End Sub
```

21. Define the procedures to map the recordset field values to the object's variables. Note the use of the `With` construct to improve runtime performance code readability. The `With` construct tells Visual Basic to add the `With` reference to the front of any ambiguous variable references. The source code is easier to read because it is more succinct. Performance is improved because the runtime library doesn't have to search all possible reference values for each assignment statement. In effect, the `With` shorthand works equally well for the programmer and the runtime application.

```
Private Sub SetRecordset(recExp As Recordset)
' Copies current values to Recordset

    With recExp
        !EmployeeId = mvarstrEmployeeId
        !ExpenseType = mvarstrExpenseType
        !AmountSpent = mvarcurAmountSpent
        !Description = mvarstrDescription
        !DatePurchased = mvardtmDatePurchased
        !DateSubmitted = mvardtmDateSubmitted
    End With

End Sub

Private Sub GetRecordset(recExp As Recordset)
' Copies current values to Recordset

    With recExp
        mvarlngExpenseId = 0 + !ExpenseID
        mvarstrEmployeeId = "" & !EmployeeId
        mvarstrExpenseType = "" & !ExpenseType
        mvarcurAmountSpent = 0 + !AmountSpent
        mvarstrDescription = "" & !Description
        mvardtmDatePurchased = !DatePurchased
        mvardtmDateSubmitted = !DateSubmitted
    End With

End Sub
```

22. Create the special expense-type assignment method to provide editing and message response capabilities. This code checks that the assigned value is one of the defined values and responds with an error message if the value is not acceptable. The object supports no other method to set the expense type, so the table is protected.

```
Public Function strSetExpenseType(ByVal vData As String) As String
' Sets the expense type to an allowed value
    Dim strTemp As String
    strTemp = UCase$(vData)

    If strTemp = "TRAVEL" _
    Or strTemp = "MEALS" _
    Or strTemp = "OFFICE" _
    Or strTemp = "AUTO" _
    Or strTemp = "TOLL/PARK" Then
        mvarstrExpenseType = strTemp
        strSetExpenseType = "OK"
    Else
        strSetExpenseType = "Expense type must be TRAVEL, MEALS, " _
                        & "OFFICE, AUTO, or TOLL/PARK"

    End If

End Function
```

23. Create the **Insert**, **Update**, and **Delete** methods. These methods closely mimic the interaction of the data control and its recordset, but they do not suffer from the intervening events that make direct programming with the data control problematic.

```
Public Function Insert() As String
' Inserts a brand-new record into the database and leaves the
' newly inserted values as the current object values.

    On Error GoTo InsertError
    With mrecExpense

        .AddNew
        mvardtmDateSubmitted = Now
        Call SetRecordset(mrecExpense)
        .Update
        'Move to the most recently modified record
        .Bookmark = .LastModified
        Call GetRecordset(mrecExpense)
    End With

    Insert = "OK"

    Exit Function

InsertError:
    ' Return the error description
    Insert = Err.Description
    Err.Clear
    Exit Function

End Function

Public Function Update() As String
' Updates Expenses table from current object values
Dim strSql As String
```

```
        On Error GoTo UpdateError
        With mrecExpense
            .Edit
            Call SetRecordset(mrecExpense)
            .Update
            .Bookmark = .LastModified
            Call GetRecordset(mrecExpense)
        End With
        Update = "OK"

        Exit Function

UpdateError:
    ' Return the error description
    Update = Err.Description
    Err.Clear
    Exit Function
End Function

Public Function Delete() As String
' Deletes the expense detail record whose value is current
' from the database

    On Error GoTo DeleteError

    With mrecExpense
        .Delete
        If 0 = .RecordCount Then
            Call ClearObject
        Else
            .MoveNext
            If .EOF Then
                Call ClearObject
            Else
                Call GetRecordset(mrecExpense)
            End If
        End If
    End With

    Delete = "OK"

    Exit Function

DeleteError:
    ' Return the error description
    Delete = Err.Description
    Err.Clear
    Exit Function

End Function
```

24. Create the Move methods to mimic the data control's movement methods. Note that these four procedures are nearly identical.

```
Public Function MoveFirst() As String
' Retrieve the first record
```

continued on next page

continued from previous page

```vb
      On Error GoTo MoveError
      With mrecExpense
          If True = .BOF _
          And True = .EOF Then
              ' Empty recordset
              MoveFirst = "BOF"
          Else
              ' Move to the first record
              .MoveFirst
              Call GetRecordset(mrecExpense)
              MoveFirst = "OK"
          End If
      End With

      Exit Function

MoveError:
      ' Return the error description
      MoveFirst = Err.Description
      Err.Clear
      Exit Function
End Function

Public Function MoveNext() As String
' Moves to next Expenses table record and sets current object values

      On Error GoTo MoveError

      With mrecExpense
          If True = .BOF _
          And True = .EOF Then
              ' Empty recordset
              MoveNext = "EOF"
          Else
              ' Move to the next record
              .MoveNext
              If mrecExpense.EOF Then
                  MoveNext = "EOF"
              Else
                  Call GetRecordset(mrecExpense)
                  MoveNext = "OK"
              End If
          End If
      End With

      Exit Function

MoveError:
      ' Return the error description
      MoveNext = Err.Description
      Err.Clear
      Exit Function
End Function

Public Function MovePrev() As String
' Retrieve the record prior to the current one
```

```vb
    On Error GoTo MoveError

    With mrecExpense

        If True = .BOF _
        And True = .EOF Then
            ' Empty recordset
            MovePrev = "BOF"
        Else
            ' Move to the previous record
            .MovePrevious
            If .BOF Then
                MovePrev = "BOF"
            Else
                Call GetRecordset(mrecExpense)
                MovePrev = "OK"
            End If
        End If


    End With

    Exit Function

MoveError:
    ' Return the error description
    MovePrev = Err.Description
    Err.Clear
    Exit Function
End Function

Public Function MoveLast() As String
' Retrieve the last record

    On Error GoTo MoveError

    With mrecExpense
        If True = .BOF _
        And True = .EOF Then
            ' Empty recordset
            MoveLast = "EOF"
        Else
            ' Move to the last record
            .MoveLast
            Call GetRecordset(mrecExpense)
            MoveLast = "OK"
        End If
    End With

    Exit Function

MoveError:
    ' Return the error description
    MoveLast = Err.Description
    Err.Clear
    Exit Function
End Function
```

How It Works

On Form_Load (step 10), the client application sets the database name for the class, causing the database and recordset to open in the class module. The MoveFirst method positions the class's recordset at the first record and populates the object's properties. The ReadObjectValues procedure copies the object values to the display fields. Each command button on the form invokes a method very similar to a data control method without the data control's performance overhead or frequently annoying events.

Comments

The use of a private class to manage your objects or tables is the starting of the *n-tier* architecture for your applications. In n-tier architectures, presentation (or input/output) is managed by one set of components, business rules by a second tier (class modules), and data by another tier (rules and triggers contained in the database management system). The advantage of objects in this environment is that underlying technology can be changed without affecting the callers as long as the interfaces remain stable.

Finally, you can easily convert class modules to ActiveX DLLs or ActiveX EXEs by including them in a different project and recompiling. You can test and debug a new class as a private module and then convert it to an EXE or a DLL. How-To 13.2 converts the ExpenseDetail class to an ActiveX DLL.

COMPLEXITY
BEGINNING

13.3 How do I...
Publish my ActiveX private class so that others can use it?

Problem

The staff in the accounting department love the new ExpenseDetail class and the concept of "black box" interfaces, but they are very worried that employees using the private class in source-code form might compromise the class's security by modifying the code to inflate their own expense reimbursements. How can I prevent access to my class's source code while letting other projects take advantage of the ExpenseDetail class?

Technique

There are several ways to publish your class's properties and methods without revealing the source code. After all, major software publishers do it every day. The technique is to convert the class module into an ActiveX DLL or EXE. This How-To demonstrates using the ExpenseDetail class module in an ActiveX DLL.

Steps

To preview the `ExpenseDetail` DLL on your system, you first need to register the code component in your system Registry. Visual Basic will register the component for you automatically if you compile once. Open the ActiveXDll.VBP project. Select File | Make ActiveX.DLL to compile the component. Open the ActiveXExpense.vbp project and run it. You should see the form shown in Figure 13.4 because the form file is identical; only the project composition was changed for the main application program.

1. Create a new project in Visual Basic, and specify an ActiveX DLL project when prompted. In the project window, right-click the highest-level project item, and edit the project properties as shown in Figure 13.7. The **Project Name** field is used within Visual Basic and must contain no spaces or hyphens. The project description is stored in your system Registry and provides the reference to your code component.

2. Select Project | Add File and add ExpenseDetail.cls to your project. This file is identical to the ExpenseDetail.cls file you wrote in How-To 13.2.

3. Select ExpenseDetail.cls in the project window. Ensure that the **Instancing** property is set to **5-Multi-use**. A *Public, Multiuse* class can be created by an external reference, such as the Expense Client form, and can be used by multiple programs simultaneously.

4. Select File | Make ActiveX.DLL to compile your ActiveX DLL.

5. Open the ActiveXExpense.vbp project. Select Project | References to display the form shown in Figure 13.8. Be sure to check the reference for the ActiveX DLL you just created.

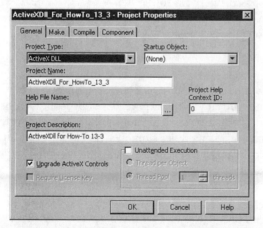

Figure 13.7. Setting the ActiveX DLL project properties.

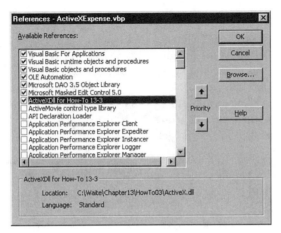

Figure 13.8. Adding a reference to the ActiveX DLL.

6. Run the Expense Client project to observe the same behavior as in How-To 13.2.

How It Works

The Expense Client with an ActiveX DLL class works the same way as the bound class because the programs are identical. The power of the Component Object Model is letting the various pieces work together without the Expense Client form needing to know how the class code works. It needs only the names and calling parameters for the public methods and properties exposed by the ActiveX DLL. The exposed interfaces to the ActiveX DLL are made available on your computer when you compile the ActiveX DLL by virtue of Visual Basic 5's automatically registering the DLL in your system Registry.

Comments

As you work more with building your own code components, plan to develop a test-and-debug strategy. In How-To 13.2, we developed (and probably tested and debugged) a test client form and a class module linked directly into the project. This approach to class modules simplifies development by allowing you to use the Visual Basic debugger. After the ActiveX DLL is compiled, you can use only the Visual C++ debugger.

Be aware that the use of ActiveX components on your system can eventually lead to excessive Registry entries, especially if you periodically delete and move your development DLL files. How-To 13.9 discusses two Registry utilities from Microsoft that can help keep your Registry under control.

COMPLEXITY
BEGINNING

13.4 How do I...
Provide controlled access to an encrypted, password-protected database?

Problem

I have a highly sensitive, protected database for which I must strictly control access—hiding even the details of its format, source, and location, and giving controlled access to sections of the data. How can I create a Visual Basic object that can be used in other applications while protecting the database?

Technique

By creating an ActiveX EXE with a public class object, you can control everything about the database—hiding the details about the database itself, and giving the container application (the application creating and using the object) only limited access to the contents of any or all tables. Because the class methods that access the data are defined by your class module, you can limit access to only one or a few tables, only certain records or a limited number of records, or whatever constraints you choose to place on the database. As far as the container application is concerned, the data could be coming from a network, another program, or anywhere.

Steps

Open the Visual Basic SECURED.VBP project. Start the application by selecting Run | Start from the Visual Basic main menu, pressing F5, or clicking the Run icon on the Visual Basic toolbar. Minimize that instance of Visual Basic. Start Microsoft Excel from the Windows Program Manager, and open the SECURED.XLS workbook. Run the `Main` macro application by selecting Tools | Macro, selecting the `Main` macro, and clicking Run. `Main` creates a spreadsheet with the contents of the database table and then releases the database object. Exit Excel and stop the Visual Basic SECURED application.

1. Start Visual Basic and create a new project in your work area. Select ActiveX EXE as the project type from the new project window, as shown in Figure 13.9. Save the project as SECURED.VBP.

2. This How-To uses Visual Basic's data access objects, so they must be available to the project. Select Project | References from the Visual Basic main menu, and make sure that the Microsoft DAO 3.5 Object Library is checked.

Figure 13.9. The New Project window.

3. Copy the ExpenseDetail.cls file from How-To 13.3 to your work area, and rename it to ExeExpenseDetail.cls. Remove the default Class1.cls file. Add the ExeExpenseDetail.cls file to your project. Set the properties of the class as shown in Table 13.9.

Table 13.9. Objects and properties for class module ExeExpenseDetail.cls.

PROPERTY	SETTING
Instancing	3—Single Use
Name	ExeExpenseDetail

4. Enter the following code in the **Initialize** event procedure for the class. The **Initialize** event is the rough equivalent to a form's **Load** event procedure, doing all the work needed when a new instance of a class is created by the calling application. In this case, all that is done is to set the location of the hidden database. This code assumes that Chapter13.MDB is in the application path; set this location to whatever drive, path, and file you want to use.

```
Private Sub Class_Initialize()

    On Error GoTo OpenError

    ' Put all the required security code here where it is
    ' protected by compilation.
    mvarstrDbName = App.Path & "\Expense.mdb"
    Set mdbExpense = DBEngine.Workspaces(0).OpenDatabase(mvarstrDbName)
    Set mrecExpense = mdbExpense.OpenRecordset("Expenses")
    mblnRecSetOpen = True

    Exit Sub
```

```
OpenError:
    ' Since we are designing this class for potential unattended
    ' operation, we'll have to raise an error on our own
    Err.Raise Number:=Err.Number
    Err.Clear
    Exit Sub

End Sub
```

5. Enter the following code in the **Class Terminate** procedure. We suppress errors because we're trying to shut down anyway.

```
Private Sub Class_Terminate()

    ' We don't really care about errors when cleaning up.
    On Error Resume Next
    ' Close the recordset
    mrecExpense.Close
    ' Close the expense database
    mdbExpense.Close
    ' Reset the error handler
    On Error GoTo 0
    Exit Sub

End Sub
```

6. Enter the following code in the **FieldCount** and **GetField** procedures. These procedures define the public methods of the class.

```
Public Function FieldCount() As Integer
    FieldCount = 7
End Function

Public Function GetField(intColumn As Integer) As Variant
' Return the requested field
    Select Case intColumn
        Case 0
            GetField = mvarlngExpenseId
        Case 1
            GetField = mvarstrEmployeeId
        Case 2
            GetField = mvarstrExpenseType
        Case 3
            GetField = mvarcurAmountSpent
        Case 4
            GetField = mvarstrDescription
        Case 5
            GetField = mvardtmDatePurchased
        Case 6
            GetField = mvardtmDateSubmitted

    End Select

End Function

Public Property Get BOF() As Boolean
```

continued on next page

continued from previous page

```
        BOF = rs.BOF
End Property

Public Property Get EOF() As Boolean
        EOF = rs.EOF
End Property

Property Get FieldCount() As Long
        FieldCount = rs.Fields.Count
End Property

Property Get RecordCount() As Long
        Dim bm As String

        'Save our location in the recordset
        bm = rs.Bookmark
        rs.MoveLast
        RecordCount = rs.RecordCount

        'Return to the starting position in the recordset
        rs.Bookmark = bm
End Property
```

7. Change all the **Public Property** procedures to **Private Property** procedures to prevent inadvertent access to the class properties. Change the **Public** functions for insert, update, and delete to **Private** functions. Remove the **Property Let** procedure for **strDbName**.

8. Insert a new code module into the project by selecting Insert | Module from the Visual Basic main menu. Set the name of the module to **modSecuredAccess**, and save the file as SECURED.BAS.

9. Enter the following code in the **Sub Main** procedure. No specific initialization code is required here, but there needs to be at least an empty **Sub Main** to provide an entry point for OLE when another application uses this class.

```
Sub Main()
End Sub
```

10. Set the project options to make the application act as an ActiveX EXE component. Select Project | Properties from the menu. The project properties are shown in Table 13.10.

The **Project Name** is particularly important; this is the application name used in the Windows Registry entry for the application. The object created by this application will then be referred to as

```
VBHTOpenSecuredDB.SecuredDatabase
```

in programs that use the object.

Table 13.10. Project properties for SECURED.VBP.

PROPERTY	SETTING
Startup Object	Sub Main
Project Name	VBHTOpenSecuredDB
Project Description	Open Secured and Encrypted Chapter13.MDB

11. Because the operating system needs an executable file to extract information about the class, select File | Make EXE from the Visual Basic main menu. Name the program SECURED.EXE, and compile the application. Correct any errors that the compiler flags.

12. Execute the application by selecting Run | Start from the main menu, pressing F5, or clicking the Run icon on the Visual Basic toolbar. The program loads and then waits for another application to create an object. This approach allows us to debug the standalone EXE file from the Visual Basic environment while a different application invokes our program's services.

13. Start Microsoft Excel. Create a new workbook by selecting File | New from the main menu or by clicking the New Workbook icon on the toolbar. Save the file by selecting File | Save As from the main menu or by clicking the Save icon on the toolbar, and save the file as SECURED.XLS.

14. Insert a new macro module in the workbook by selecting Insert | Macro Module from the Excel main menu. Insert the following Visual Basic code into the module. This procedure starts by creating an instance of the **SecuredDatabase** object, then uses the object's properties and methods to move through the database and enter the records into a new worksheet. Note that the Excel application is unaware of where the information is coming from or even how the database is being accessed. All of those details are hidden in the SECURED.EXE file.

```
Option Explicit

Sub main()
    Dim numFields As Long
    Dim strResponse As String

    Dim objExpenseDetail As Object
    Set objExpenseDetail = _
        CreateObject("VBHTOpenSecuredDB.ExeExpenseDetail")

    Dim i As Long
    Dim j As Integer

    numFields = objExpenseDetail.FieldCount
    Sheets.Add

    'Format the column headings
```

continued on next page

continued from previous page

```
    ActiveSheet.Cells(1, 1).Select
    Selection.ColumnWidth = 5
    ActiveCell.FormulaR1C1 = "ID"
    Selection.Font.FontStyle = "Bold"
    Selection.HorizontalAlignment = xlCenter

    ActiveSheet.Cells(1, 2).Select
    Selection.ColumnWidth = 10
    ActiveCell.FormulaR1C1 = "Employee"
    Selection.Font.FontStyle = "Bold"
    Selection.HorizontalAlignment = xlCenter

    ActiveSheet.Cells(1, 3).Select
    Selection.ColumnWidth = 8
    ActiveCell.FormulaR1C1 = "Type"
    Selection.Font.FontStyle = "Bold"
    Selection.HorizontalAlignment = xlCenter

    ActiveSheet.Cells(1, 4).Select
    Selection.ColumnWidth = 10
    ActiveCell.FormulaR1C1 = "Amount"
    Selection.Font.FontStyle = "Bold"
    Selection.HorizontalAlignment = xlCenter

    ActiveSheet.Cells(1, 5).Select
    Selection.ColumnWidth = 15
    ActiveCell.FormulaR1C1 = "Description"
    Selection.Font.FontStyle = "Bold"
    Selection.HorizontalAlignment = xlCenter

    ActiveSheet.Cells(1, 6).Select
    Selection.ColumnWidth = 10
    ActiveCell.FormulaR1C1 = "Purchased"
    Selection.Font.FontStyle = "Bold"
    Selection.HorizontalAlignment = xlCenter

    ActiveSheet.Cells(1, 7).Select
    Selection.ColumnWidth = 15
    ActiveCell.FormulaR1C1 = "Submitted"
    Selection.Font.FontStyle = "Bold"
    Selection.HorizontalAlignment = xlCenter


    'Put the records into the worksheet
    i = 0
    strResponse = objExpenseDetail.MoveFirst
    Do While "OK" = strResponse
        i = i + 1
        For j = 0 To numFields - 1
            ActiveSheet.Cells(i + 1, j + 1).Select
            ActiveCell.FormulaR1C1 = objExpenseDetail.GetField(j)
        Next
        strResponse = objExpenseDetail.MoveNext
    Loop

    ActiveSheet.Cells(1, 1).Select
```

```
'Clean up by releasing the memory used for objExpenseDetail
Set objExpenseDetail = Nothing
End Sub
```

15. Run the **Main** Excel procedure by selecting Tools | Macro from the main menu, selecting the **Main** macro from the list, and clicking the Run button, or by clicking the Run button from the Macro toolbar while the cursor is within the Main procedure.

How It Works

Visual Basic uses class modules to create objects that can be exposed to other applications. This is essentially the same process used by the Jet engine to expose data access objects or by Microsoft Excel to expose **Worksheet** or **Chart** objects.

This How-To has focused on the details of the ActiveX interface between Visual Basic and Excel. Note the comments in the code where you might include parameters for opening secured databases. That information is completely hidden from Excel. For more information about using secured databases, see Chapter 11, "Security and Multiuser Access."

By defining **Property Get**, **Property Let**, and **Public Sub** and **Function** procedures, you can define exactly the information that the class reveals to the outside world and the actions that it takes in response to demands placed on it by the outside applications.

The most important part of setting up the class so that it is visible to outside applications is setting the project's properties. The fact that this is a separate EXE code component makes debugging somewhat tricky. The easiest way to debug an ActiveX EXE under development is to start by doing most of the work with the class module bound into an application EXE. After the class module has been debugged, add it into an Active EXE project. You can still debug the class within an ActiveX EXE by running a copy of Visual Basic dedicated to the class.

Comments

This class was defined to be what is called "Single Use" in ActiveX terminology in order to ensure that different callers would not affect other callers' data stored within the class. In this ActiveX EXE, the database name, recordset position, and property values contain state, or context, information that is related to the calling program. For example, the correct invocation of the **MoveNext** method assumes that the class properties are correctly set for the caller. If we allowed two different programs to access the ActiveX EXE, Caller A's **MoveNext** would cause Caller B's **MovePrev** to return an erroneous result. A multiuse ActiveX EXE class requires that all the information required for a successful method invocation is contained in the method's parameters and return values. If more than one invocation is required to retrieve the required data, the class should be defined to be single-use.

COMPLEXITY
BEGINNING

13.5 How do I...
Use Microsoft Access as an ActiveX server to print reports from Visual Basic?

Problem

The database provided for my Visual Basic project has already been developed, and the prototyping phase developed several Access reports that we want to use again in the final application. Because all workstations will have Access installed, we want to use this technique. How do I invoke and Access report from within a Visual Basic 5 application?

Technique

Microsoft Access is an ActiveX EXE code component. It exposes its Visual Basic for Applications properties and methods just as any other ActiveX EXE does. The most powerful command for use in automating Access as a code component is the **DoCmd** method of the Access Application object. **DoCmd** allows your program to issue most commands within Access that a person sitting at the keyboard can do with a mouse and keyboard.

Steps

Open the project AccessReport.vbp. The form shown in Figure 13.10 appears. Click on the command button. Switch to the Access application to view, and print the prepared report. (See Figure 13.11.)

1. Create a new project named AccessReport.vbp in your work area. Create the objects and properties listed in Table 13.11.

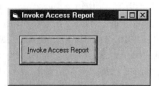

Figure 13.10. The Invoke Access Report form.

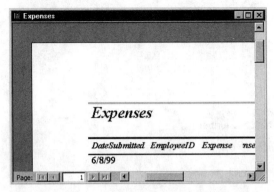

Figure 13.11. The Access Expense report.

Table 13.11. Objects and properties for the Access Expense form.

OBJECT	PROPERTY	SETTING
Name	Form	frmInvokeAccessReport
	Caption	"Invoke Access Report"
Name	CommandButton	cmdInvokeReport
	Caption	"&Invoke Access Report"

2. Be sure to select OLE Automation and the Microsoft Access Object Library in the Project References menu. OLE Automation supports the program's capability to create and communicate with Access. The Access Object Library allows you to use symbolic constant names for Access-defined constants.

3. Insert the following code for the Click event of cmdInvokeReport:

```
Private Sub cmdInvokeReport_Click()
' Invokes an Access report in print preview mode
' Get the ActiveX object to open its database and position
' to the first record
    Dim strDbName As String
    Dim objAccess As Object

    On Error GoTo LoadError

    strDbName = App.Path
    strDbName = strDbName & "\Expense.mdb"
    Set objAccess = CreateObject("Access.Application")
    With objAccess
        .OpenCurrentDatabase FilePath:=strDbName
        .DoCmd.OpenReport ReportName:="ExpenseReport", _
            View:=Access.acPreview
    End With
```

continued on next page

continued from previous page

```
    ' Give up CPU control
    DoEvents

    Set objAccess = Nothing

    Exit Sub

LoadError:
    MsgBox Err.Description & Chr(13) & "from " & Err.Source & _
        " — Number: " & CStr(Err.Number)
Unload Me

End Sub
```

How It Works

When you click the command button, the Visual Basic `CreateObject` method starts Access. The reference to `"Access.Application"` is resolved by the Windows operating system through the system registry. The two commands given to the Access application object open the database and prepare the report in print preview mode. People can then print the report from within Access.

Inspection of this code shows that using another application to do your bidding is straightforward; the difficult part is discovering which methods and properties are exposed by the object. For Access and the other Microsoft Office applications, the easiest way to discover the available properties and methods is to use that application's Help files. Use the Help contents to find a reference to Visual Basic, switch to the linked Help file, and then search the Help index for the application object. The various methods and properties of the application object should lead you to the commands you need in order to get your job done.

Comments

Although requiring a person to print the report to the printer might seem like an extra step, it takes advantage of the print preview capabilities of Access and provides quite a bit of program polish with very little development work. Before deploying an automated application such as this one, you probably want to enforce some degree of security on the database as discussed in Chapter 11, "Security and Multiuser Access."

COMPLEXITY
MODERATE

13.6 How do I...
Use Microsoft Access queries containing user-defined functions from Visual Basic?

Problem

Sometimes you will need to use Access user-defined functions within your Visual Basic programs. Unfortunately, Access user-defined functions can be run only by Access. How can I use Access to return data from a query containing a user-defined function?

Technique

To use an Access query containing a user-defined function, you first need an Access-based recordset. Because Access exposes its object methods and properties, we can directly manipulate Access recordsets from Visual Basic by using the Visual Basic for Applications methods exposed by Access. The VBA syntax for working with recordsets is identical to Visual Basic 5 syntax, so no learning curve is required. It is important to remember, however, that the Access recordset is running in a different process, and the performance is likely to be much slower than a native recordset. Both Visual Basic and Access recordsets can be included in the same application. In this way, the slower ActiveX Automation recordset is used only when required for the user-defined function query.

This application uses two Access queries to provide required data. The first provides a list of employees who have submitted expense reports:

```
SELECT DISTINCT EmployeeID
FROM Expenses;
```

The second query is parameter-driven and invokes the user-defined function MyUpper to force the employee name to all uppercase letters:

```
PARAMETERS EmpToFind Text;
SELECT Expenses.ExpenseID, MyUpper([EmployeeID]) AS Expr1,
    Expenses.ExpenseType, Expenses.AmountSpent, Expenses.Description,
    Expenses.DatePurchased, Expenses.DateSubmitted
FROM Expenses
WHERE (((MyUpper([EmployeeID]))=[EmpToFind]))
ORDER BY Expenses.ExpenseID;
```

The EmpToFind parameter limits the query records to only one employee.

Steps

Open the AccessParams.vbp project. If necessary, modify the database location for the database grid's data control to point to your installation directory. Run the application by pressing the F5 key. The form shown in Figure 13.12 appears. Select an employee and click the Set Employee button to limit the view of expense details to only one employee. Use the data movement buttons to view the selected employee's expenses.

1. Create a new project named AccessParams.vbp in your work area. Copy the ExpenseDetail.cls file from How-To 13.2 to this new project as ExpDetailParam.cls.

2. Select Project | References from the main Visual Basic menu, and select the references shown here:

Ole Automation
Microsoft DAO 3.5 Object Library
Microsoft Masked Edit Control 5.0
Microsoft Data Bound Grid Library
Microsoft Access 8.0 Object Library

3. Modify the declarations section of ExpDetailParam.cls to look as shown next. The new object variables allow direct control of the Access recordset. Declaring `mobjAccess` as an Access.Application object enables Visual Basic's code-completion features in the editor for lazy typists.

```
Option Explicit

'local variable(s) to hold property value(s)
Private mvarlngExpenseId As Long 'local copy
Private mvarstrEmployeeId As String 'local copy
Private mvarstrExpenseType As String 'local copy
Private mvarcurAmountSpent As Currency 'local copy
Private mvarstrDescription As String 'local copy
Private mvardtmDatePurchased As Date 'local copy
Private mvardtmDateSubmitted As Date 'local copy
Private mvarstrDbName As String 'local copy
Private mvarstrEmpToQuery As String 'local copy

Private mblnQueryOpen As Boolean

Private mobjAccess As New Access.Application
Private mobjRecSetExpense As Object
```

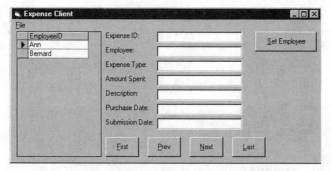

Figure 13.12. The Access User-Defined Function form.

4. Modify the `strDbName Property Let` procedure to open the Access query rather than a Visual Basic recordset:

```
Public Property Let strDbName(ByVal vData As String)
'used when assigning a value to the property, on the left side
'of an assignment.
'Syntax: X.strDbName = 5

    On Error GoTo OpenError

    If mblnQueryOpen Then
        mobjAccess.CloseCurrentDatabase
    End If
    mvarstrDbName = vData
    mobjAccess.OpenCurrentDatabase mvarstrDbName
    mobjAccess.Application.Visible = False
    mobjAccess.DBEngine.Workspaces(0).Databases(0). _
            QueryDefs("ExpForOneEmployee").Parameters("EmpToFind"). _
            Value = mvarstrEmpToQuery
    Set mobjRecSetExpense = mobjAccess.DBEngine.Workspaces(0). _
            Databases(0).QueryDefs("ExpForOneEmployee"). _
            OpenRecordset()

    mblnQueryOpen = True

    Exit Property

OpenError:
    ' Since we are designing this class for potential unattended
    ' operation, we'll have to raise an error on our own
    Err.Raise Number:=Err.Number
    Err.Clear
    Exit Property

End Property
```

5. Add a new **Property Let** procedure for the name of the employee to query. This procedure closes an open recordset, changes the employee name, and issues a new query.

```
Public Property Let strEmpToQuery(ByVal vData As String)
'used when assigning a value to the property, on the left side
'of an assignment.
'Syntax: X.strEmpToQuery = 5
    mvarstrEmpToQuery = vData
    On Error GoTo OpenError

    If mblnQueryOpen Then
        mobjRecSetExpense.Close
    End If
    mobjAccess.DBEngine.Workspaces(0).Databases(0). _
            QueryDefs("ExpForOneEmployee").Parameters("EmpToFind"). _
            Value = mvarstrEmpToQuery
    Set mobjRecSetExpense = mobjAccess.DBEngine.Workspaces(0). _
            Databases(0).QueryDefs("ExpForOneEmployee"). _
            OpenRecordset()
    mblnQueryOpen = True

    Exit Property

OpenError:
    ' Since we are designing this class for potential unattended
    ' operation, we'll have to raise an error on our own
    Err.Raise Number:=Err.Number
    Err.Clear
    Exit Property

End Property
```

6. Remove the **Delete**, **Update**, and **Insert** methods from the class. Remove the **SetRecordSet** subroutine from the class.

7. Change all code references to **mrecExpense** to **mobjRecSetExpense** throughout the class module.

8. Add the new class property to the **ClearObject** procedure:

```
Private Sub ClearObject()
' Clears all object variables

    mvarlngExpenseId = 0
    mvarstrEmployeeId = ""
    mvarstrExpenseType = ""
    mvarcurAmountSpent = 0
    mvarstrDescription = ""
    mvardtmDatePurchased = CDate("1/1/1980")
    mvardtmDateSubmitted = CDate("1/1/1980")
    mvarstrEmpToQuery = ""

End Sub
```

9. Replace the `Class Initialize` and `Terminate` procedures. We force termination of the Access code component in the `Terminate` procedure.

```
Private Sub Class_Initialize()

    ' Indicate that the database is not yet open
    mblnQueryOpen = False
    ' Clear all object variables
    Call ClearObject

End Sub

Private Sub Class_Terminate()

    ' Close the recordset
    mobjRecSetExpense.Close
    mobjAccess.CloseCurrentDatabase
    mobjAccess.Quit

End Sub
```

10. Create a form to test the `ExpDetailParam` class with the objects properties shown in Table 13.12. Show only the `Employee ID` column for the database grid. Inspection of the Access database used in this project will show that the `ExpEmployeeNames` is an Access query, not a table. Visual Basic can use queries for recordsets and will display queries in the data control's `RecordSource` pull-down list.

Table 13.12. Objects and properties for the Access Params form.

OBJECT	PROPERTY	SETTING
Form	Name	frmExpClient
	Caption	"Expense Client"
Data	Name	datExpEmployees
	Caption	"Exp Employees"
	DatabaseName	"D:\Waite\Chapter13\[sr]
		HowTo06\Expense.mdb"
	RecordsetType	2 'Snapshot
	RecordSource	"ExpEmployeeNames"
DBGrid	Name	dbgExpEmployee
	DataSource	datExpEmployees
	AllowDelete	False
	AllowUpdate	False
CommandButton	Name	cmdSetEmployee
	Caption	"&Set Employee"

continued on next page

continued from previous page

OBJECT	PROPERTY	SETTING
CommandButton	Name	cmdLast
	Caption	"&Last"
CommandButton	Name	cmdNext
	Caption	"&Next"
CommandButton	Name	cmdPrev
	Caption	"&Prev"
CommandButton	Name	cmdFirst
	Caption	"&First"
MaskEdBox	Name	mskAmountSpent
	Format	"$#,##0.00;($#,##0.00)"
	PromptChar	"_"
TextBox	Name	txtSubmitDate
TextBox	Name	txtPurchaseDate
TextBox	Name	txtDescription
TextBox	Name	txtExpenseType
TextBox	Name	txtEmployeeId
TextBox	Name	txtExpenseId
Label	Name	Label1
	Caption	"Expense ID:"
Label	Name	Label2
	Caption	"Employee:"
Label	Name	Label3
	Caption	"Expense Type:"
Label	Name	Label4
	Caption	"Amount Spent:"
Label	Name	Label5
	Caption	"Description:"
Label	Name	Label6
	Caption	"Purchase Date:"
Label	Name	Label7
	Caption	"Submission Date:"

11. Use the Visual Basic menu editor to create the menu shown in
Table 13.13.

Table 13.13. Menu specifications for the Access Params form.

CAPTION	NAME	SHORTCUT KEY
&File	mnuFile	
----E&xit	mnuFileExit	

12. Add the following code to the **Click** event of **cmdSetEmployee**. This procedure obtains the employee name from the selected database grid row, sets the class module's **strEmpToQuery** value, and moves to the first expense for the selected employee.

```
Private Sub cmdSetEmployee_Click()
' Sets Employee ID textbox and initiates new query for expenses
' for the selected employee
    Dim strResponse As String

    On Error GoTo QueryError

    txtEmployeeId.Text = dbgExpEmployee.Columns(0).Text
    expDetailParam.strEmpToQuery = dbgExpEmployee.Columns(0).Text
    strResponse = expDetailParam.MoveFirst
    If "OK" <> strResponse Then
        MsgBox strResponse
    Else
        Call ReadObjectValues
    End If

    Exit Sub

QueryError:
    MsgBox Err.Description & Chr(13) & "from " & Err.Source & _
        " — Number: " & CStr(Err.Number)
    Exit Sub

End Sub
```

13. Add the following code to the **Click** event for the movement buttons:

```
Private Sub cmdFirst_Click()
' Positions to first record in recordset and displays values

    Dim strResponse As String

    strResponse = expDetailParam.MoveFirst
    If "OK" <> strResponse Then
        MsgBox strResponse
    Else
        Call ReadObjectValues
    End If

End Sub

Private Sub cmdLast_Click()
```

continued on next page

continued from previous page

```
' Positions to last record in recordset and displays values

    Dim strResponse As String

    strResponse = expDetailParam.MoveLast
    If "OK" <> strResponse Then
        MsgBox strResponse
    Else
        Call ReadObjectValues
    End If

End Sub

Private Sub cmdNext_Click()
' Positions to Next record in recordset and displays values

    Dim strResponse As String

    strResponse = expDetailParam.MoveNext
    If "OK" <> strResponse Then
        MsgBox strResponse
    Else
        Call ReadObjectValues
    End If


End Sub

Private Sub cmdPrev_Click()
' Positions to Previous record in recordset and displays values

    Dim strResponse As String

    strResponse = expDetailParam.MovePrev
    If "OK" <> strResponse Then
        MsgBox strResponse
    Else
        Call ReadObjectValues
    End If

End Sub
```

14. Define a `ReadObjectValues` procedure to transfer data from the class properties:

```
Private Sub ReadObjectValues()
' Read the object values into the form fields

    txtExpenseId.Text = CStr(expDetailParam.lngExpenseId)
    txtEmployeeId.Text = expDetailParam.strEmployeeId
    txtExpenseType.Text = expDetailParam.strExpenseType
    txtDescription.Text = expDetailParam.strDescription
    mskAmountSpent.Text = CStr(expDetailParam.curAmountSpent)
    txtPurchaseDate.Text = CStr(expDetailParam.dtmDatePurchased)
    txtSubmitDate.Text = CStr(expDetailParam.dtmDateSubmitted)

End Sub
```

15. Create Form Load and Unload procedures to initialize and tear down the application:

```
Private Sub Form_Load()
' Get the ActiveX object to open its database and position
' to the first record
    Dim strDbName As String
    Dim strResponse As String

    On Error GoTo LoadError

    strDbName = App.Path
    strDbName = strDbName & "\Expense.mdb"
    expDetailParam.strDbName = strDbName
    strResponse = expDetailParam.MoveFirst
    If "OK" <> strResponse Then
        MsgBox strResponse
    Else
        Call ReadObjectValues
    End If

    Exit Sub
LoadError:
    MsgBox Err.Description & Chr(13) & "from " & _
        Err.Source & " — Number: " & CStr(Err.Number)
    Unload Me
End Sub

Private Sub Form_Unload(Cancel As Integer)

    Set expDetailParam = Nothing

End Sub
```

16. Add the following code to the Click event of mnuFileExit:

```
Private Sub mnuFileExit_Click()

    Unload Me

End Sub
```

How It Works

When the form loads, the application sets the database name of the class using the Property Let strDBName procedure (step 4). This first reference to an Access.Application object causes a new Access process to start for our work on behalf of the class. The Access application is made invisible to minimize confusion on the application screen. The query parameter is set to retrieve an employee, and the recordset is created within the class. The class's navigation methods are, in turn, connected to the navigation buttons on the form.

When the `cmdSetEmployee` button is clicked, the class's employee name property is set from the current record on the grid. The class is notified of the employee name change through the `strEmpToQuery Property Let` procedure. The query parameter is changed, and the recordset is reopened to display expenses for a different employee.

This How-To illustrates a generic programming technique frequently used to logically "partition" data displays on forms. For example, you might want to display payment histories for multiple customers in a service bureau application. The use of a grid to display possible customer choices with a detail form for the payments is an example of a partitioning form.

Comments

More and more complex Visual Basic applications are being designed with n-tier architectures relying on different tiers to perform different functions. In this How-To, we are using a classic three-tier architecture consisting of the form, the class, and the Access queries. This approach helps make program code maintenance easier over the long term because interfaces are clear. The use of the Access `ExpEmployee` query to show only one row per employee uses the power inherent in the database engine to preprocess data before using precious bandwidth sending multiple rows and forcing the client to eliminate duplicates.

COMPLEXITY
MODERATE

13.7 How do I...
Convert database data to a spreadsheet form that can be used to edit and analyze data?

Problem

I have a table with numeric results on which I need to perform some statistical analyses to make the data meaningful. Visual Basic doesn't have an easy way to analyze complex data, nor does it have many statistical analysis functions. How can I do the analyses that I need using a spreadsheet so that I can massage the data?

Technique

Although Visual Basic is missing many of the standard statistical and financial functions that many business and scientific applications need, Microsoft Excel has a rich source of such functions. Using ActiveX Automation, it is relatively easy to create an Excel spreadsheet, populating it with the data from a database, and entering whatever Excel formulas are needed for analysis.

You will need Excel for this How-To, although this same technique can be used with most of the popular spreadsheet applications available for Windows. All that any such spreadsheet needs is support for object linking or embedding 2 or greater, as well as some way of discovering the objects that the application makes visible to OLE Automation. Microsoft provides a program with many of its other products, including the OLE SDK and some of its programming languages, called OLE2VIEW, which examines an application and presents a list of the objects available and their properties and methods.

Steps

Open the Visual Basic DataAnal.VBP project. Start the application by selecting Run | Start from the Visual Basic main menu, by pressing F5, or by clicking the Run icon on the Visual Basic toolbar. Click on the Select Database button, and select any Access .MDB file. Select a table from the Table combo box, and then click on Load Spreadsheet to select the numeric fields from the table and enter them into an Excel spreadsheet. When the spreadsheet is finished loading (see Figure 13.13), click the down arrow on the Results combo box to examine the average, median, and standard deviation for each of the fields in the table. Double-click on the spreadsheet to edit it or examine a cell's contents.

1. Start Visual Basic and create a new project. Save the default form as DATAANAL.FRM, and save the project as DATAANAL.VBP. This project uses the Microsoft Common Dialog control, so select Project | Components from the main Visual Basic menu, and make sure that the control is selected in the list.

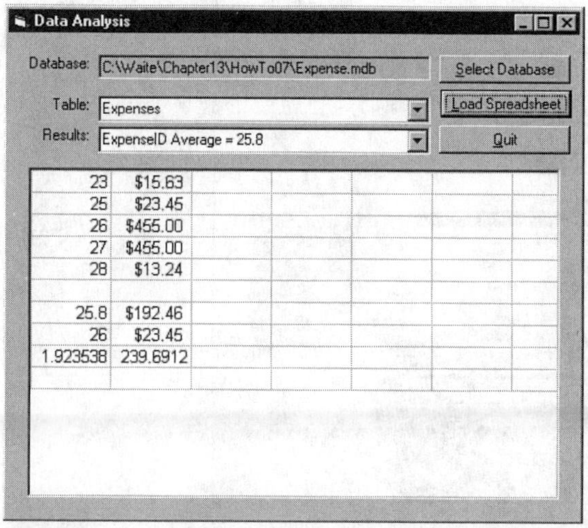

Figure 13.13. The Data Analysis result screen for project DataAnal.vbp.

2. This How-To uses Visual Basic's data access objects, so they must be available to the project. Select Project | References from the Visual Basic main menu, and make sure that the Microsoft DAO 3.5 Object Library is checked.

3. Because this application uses the Microsoft Excel 5.0 Object Library, you need to make sure that Visual Basic has access to that library. Select Tools | References from the Visual Basic main menu, and make sure that the box in front of the Excel object library is checked, as shown in Figure 13.14. If it doesn't appear in the list, click the Browse button and add the file XL5EN32.OLB in the Excel program directory, probably C:\Program Files\Office. Normally, however, the Excel installation program activates the object library in the Windows Registry.

If you attempt to run this program without Excel installed, the `cmdLoadSS_Click` event procedure traps the error and shows a message box about the error.

4. Start Microsoft Excel and minimize the application. Having Excel running during development speeds programming because you don't have to wait for Excel to load every time you start the project.

5. Place controls on the form as shown in Figure 13.13, setting properties as shown in Table 13.14. Note that the common dialog control is invisible at runtime, so you can place it anywhere on the form that is convenient. Also note that the menu `Raisan` can be called anything you like; it is necessary only to allow the Excel menu to appear on the form when the OLE object is activated.

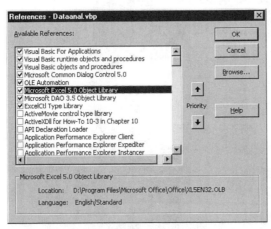

Figure 13.14. Setting object references for Dataanal.vbp.

Table 13.14. Objects and properties for DATAANAL.FRM.

OBJECT	PROPERTY	SETTING
Form	Name	frmDataAnal
	Caption	"Data Analysis"
	NegotiateMenus	True
ComboBox	Name	lstResults
CommandButton	Name	cmdLoadSS
	Caption	"&Load Spreadsheet"
	Enabled	0 'False
ComboBox	Name	lstTables
CommandButton	Name	cmdQuit
	Caption	"&Quit"
	Default	-1 'True
CommandButton	Name	cmdSelectDB
	Caption	"&Select Database"
TextBox	Name	txtFileName
	BackColor	&H00C0C0C0& (Light gray)
Label	Name	Label3
	Alignment	1 'Right Justify
	Caption	"Results:"
OLE	Name	oleExcel
	OLETypeAllowed	1 'Embedded
Label	Name	Label2
	Alignment	1 'Right Justify
	Caption	"Table:"
CommonDialog	Name	cdSelectFile
	DefaultExt	"MDB"
	DialogTitle	"Open Database File"
	Filter	"Access Db (*.mdb)¦*.mdb¦All Files (*.*)¦*.*"
Label	Name	Label1
	Alignment	1 'Right Justify
	Caption	"Database:"
Menu	Name	mnuRaisan
	Caption	"Raisan"
	Visible	0 'False

6. Enter the following code into the declarations section of the form. **dbSS** is used as a global database object, and the two constants control the actions of the OLE custom control.

```
'This project makes use of an Excel 5.0 worksheet,
'so the Excel 5.0 Object Library must be specified
'in the VB Tools Reference menu.

Dim dbSS As Database

Const OLE_CreateEmbed As Integer = 0
Const OLE_Activate As Integer = 7
```

7. Enter the following code in the **cmdSelectDB Click** event procedure. This procedure sets up and shows the file open common dialog box for a database to analyze. If a database is selected, it extracts the names of all the tables, and populates the **lstTables** combo box.

```
Private Sub cmdSelectDB_Click()
    'Select a new database file to analyze
    Dim strFileName As String
    Dim X As TableDef
    Dim saveCursor

    'Open the file open common dialog
    cdSelectFile.InitDir = App.Path
    cdSelectFile.ShowOpen
    If Len(cdSelectFile.filename) Then
        saveCursor = Me.MousePointer
        Me.MousePointer = vbHourglass

        txtFileName = cdSelectFile.filename

        'Open the database
        Set dbSS = OpenDatabase(txtFileName)

        'Load the lstTables combo box
        lstTables.Clear
        If dbSS.TableDefs.Count Then
            For Each X In dbSS.TableDefs
                'Exclude system tables
                If Not X.Name Like "MSys*" Then
                    lstTables.AddItem X.Name
                End If
            Next
            lstTables.ListIndex = 0
        End If
        Me.MousePointer = saveCursor
    Else
        MsgBox "No file selected."
    End If
End Sub
```

8. Add this code to the `cmdLoadSS` Click event procedure. When the user clicks the Load Spreadsheet button, the selected table is examined for all the numeric fields, and the names of those fields are put in the `fieldTypes` array. At the end of the `For Each...Next` loop, the variable `i` will contain the number of numeric fields. If there are no numeric fields, the user is shown a message and the procedure exits. (For simplicity, the number of fields is limited to 26 so that you don't have to deal with double-lettered column names such as "AA," "AB," and "BB.") Then the table is opened, and the data from each record for each numeric field is placed in the spreadsheet. After that process is complete, formulas to calculate the average, median, and standard deviation are inserted at the bottom of each column. The columns are assigned unique names so that you can read the values and put them in the `lstResults` combo box.

```
Private Sub cmdLoadSS_Click()
    'If button is enabled, we can start
    Dim rsTable As Recordset
    Dim fld As Field
    Dim fieldTypes() As String
    Dim i As Integer, j As Integer
    Dim rowNo As Integer
    Dim cellRange As String
    Dim cellValue As Variant
    Dim cellPlace As String
    Dim cellName As String
    Dim totalRows As Integer
    Dim nameExcel As String
    Dim temp As String
    Dim ssName As String
    Dim saveCursor

    saveCursor = Me.MousePointer
    Me.MousePointer = vbHourglass

    'Create an array of all numerical fields to include in
    'the spreadsheet
    i = 0
    For Each fld In dbSS.TableDefs(lstTables.Text).Fields
        If fld.Type = dbInteger Or _
                fld.Type = dbLong Or _
                fld.Type = dbCurrency Or _
                fld.Type = dbSingle Or _
                fld.Type = dbDouble Then
            i = i + 1
            ReDim Preserve fieldTypes(i)
            fieldTypes(i) = fld.Name
        End If
    Next

    If i = 0 Then
        MsgBox "There are no numeric columns in the table. Exiting⇐
            procedure."
Me.MousePointer = saveCursor
```

continued on next page

continued from previous page

```
        Exit Sub
    End If

    'For convenience, limit the number of columns to 26 so
    'we don't have to do anything fancy to columns AA, AB,
    'and so on
    i = IIf(i > 26, 26, i)

    'Open the recordset of the table
    Set rsTable = dbSS.OpenRecordset(lstTables.Text)

    On Error GoTo OLError
    oleExcel.CreateEmbed "", "Excel.Sheet.8"
    On Error GoTo 0
    ssName = oleExcel.object.Name

    Do While Not rsTable.EOF
        rowNo = rowNo + 1
        For j = 1 To i
            cellValue = rsTable(fieldTypes(j))
            oleExcel.object.Worksheets(1).Cells(rowNo, j).Value = cellValue
        Next
        rsTable.MoveNext
    Loop

    'Insert the formulas to calculate the average, median, and
    'standard deviation, and name the cells
    totalRows = rowNo
    rowNo = totalRows + 2
    For j = 1 To i
        cellRange = ColName(j) & "1:" & ColName(j) & Trim(Str(totalRows))
        cellValue = "=AVERAGE(" & cellRange & ")"
        cellPlace = "=Sheet1!$" & ColName(j) & "$" & Trim(Str(rowNo)) _
                    & ":$" & ColName(j) & "$" & Trim(Str(rowNo))
        oleExcel.object.Worksheets(1).Cells(rowNo, j).Value = cellValue
        cellName = "average" & Trim(Str(j))
        oleExcel.object.Parent.Names.Add Name:=cellName, _
            RefersTo:=cellPlace
    Next
    rowNo = rowNo + 1
    For j = 1 To i
        cellRange = ColName(j) & "1:" & ColName(j) & Trim(Str(totalRows))
        cellValue = "=MEDIAN(" & cellRange & ")"
        cellPlace = "=Sheet1!$" & ColName(j) & "$" & Trim(Str(rowNo)) _
                    & ":$" & ColName(j) & "$" & Trim(Str(rowNo))
        oleExcel.object.Worksheets(1).Cells(rowNo, j).Value = cellValue
        cellName = "median" & Trim(Str(j))
        oleExcel.object.Parent.Names.Add Name:=cellName, _
            RefersTo:=cellPlace
    Next
    rowNo = rowNo + 1
    For j = 1 To i
        cellRange = ColName(j) & "1:" & ColName(j) & Trim(Str(totalRows))
        cellValue = "=STDEV(" & cellRange & ")"
        cellPlace = "=Sheet1!$" & ColName(j) & "$" & Trim(Str(rowNo)) _
                    & ":$" & ColName(j) & "$" & Trim(Str(rowNo))
        oleExcel.object.Worksheets(1).Cells(rowNo, j).Value = cellValue
```

```
            cellName = "stdev" & Trim(Str(j))
            oleExcel.object.Parent.Names.Add Name:=cellName, _
                RefersTo:=cellPlace
        Next

        'Lastly, put the results in the lstResults control
        lstResults.Clear
        For j = 1 To i
            nameExcel = "average" & Trim(Str(j))
            lstResults.AddItem fieldTypes(j) & " Average = " _
                    & oleExcel.object.Worksheets(1).Range(nameExcel).Value
        Next
        For j = 1 To i
            nameExcel = "median" & Trim(Str(j))
            lstResults.AddItem fieldTypes(j) & " Median = " _
                    & oleExcel.object.Worksheets(1).Range(nameExcel).Value
        Next
        For j = 1 To i
            nameExcel = "stdev" & Trim(Str(j))
            lstResults.AddItem fieldTypes(j) & " Standard Deviation = " _
                    & oleExcel.object.Worksheets(1).Range(nameExcel).Value
        Next
        lstResults.ListIndex = 0

        Me.MousePointer = saveCursor
        Exit Sub

OLError:
    MsgBox "An OLE error occurred, probably because Excel is not installed⇐
        on this computer."
    Unload Me
End Sub
```

9. Add the following code to the **ColName** procedure. This function provides an easy way to convert a column number to its equivalent letter value.

```
Private Function ColName(colNo As Integer)
    Dim alpha As String

    alpha = "ABCDEFGHIJKLMNOPQRSTUVWXYZ"
    ColName = Mid$(alpha, colNo, 1)
End Function
```

10. Add this code to the **lstTables Click** event procedure. When the form first loads, the **cmdLoadSS** command button is disabled, because there is no database table selected from which to load data. After the user has selected a database and a table, it is possible to load the spreadsheet.

```
Private Sub lstTables_Click()
    If Len(lstTables.Text) Then
        cmdLoadSS.Enabled = True
    Else
        cmdLoadSS.Enabled = False
    End If
End Sub
```

11. Enter this code for the **cmdQuit Click** event procedure. The **Set** statement releases the **dbSS** database object, and then the program ends.

```
Private Sub cmdQuit_Click()
    Set dbSS = Nothing
    End
End Sub
```

How It Works

An ActiveX Automation object can be either linked or embedded in an OLE control. If all you want to do is see the object, linking is the way to go, because the object isn't stored in the application. If you want to visually edit your Visual Basic application, however, you must embed the object. Then you can "activate" the object for editing by double-clicking it at runtime. Double-clicking is the default for activation, but the default can be changed by setting the **AutoActivate** property of the control.

The key to using the OLE control with visual editing is to make sure that it is properly configured for the object, in this case an Excel spreadsheet. For embedded objects, the control's **OLETypeAllowed** must be either **1** (embedded) or **2** (either). The object is then created using this line in **cmdLoadSS_Click()**:

```
oleExcel.CreateEmbed "", "Excel.Sheet.8"
```

If you want the embedded object's application menus to appear when you activate the object, you need to have a menu as part of the form. If your application doesn't otherwise need a menu, create a dummy menu as you did here, name it anything you like, and set the **Visible** property of the single menu item to **False**. That way, the object's menu will appear. If your application does use a menu, create it as you normally would, but set the **NegotiatePosition** property of each menu item to **None**, **Left**, **Middle**, or **Right**, to indicate to Visual Basic how you want to sort the various menu items between the two menus.

Comments

ActiveX Automation is a powerful tool for your programming arsenal, but it might not always be the appropriate tool given the power of the macro languages such as Visual Basic for Applications that are now embedded in many applications. For use by an analyst who uses Excel for much of the day, this task might have been better programmed in VBA from Excel. If the analyst later wants to change something, the VBA macro is right there in the spreadsheet. For use as part of an Executive Information System (EIS), where several spreadsheets and Access reports might be required for the complete solution, driving the spreadsheet from Visual Basic might make more sense. Keeping all the custom code for an EIS in one place can simplify application maintenance.

COMPLEXITY
MODERATE

13.8 How do I...
Include an editable report writer in a Visual Basic application?

Problem

I want to give the users of my application the ability to edit the appearance of the reports generated by my application. Crystal Reports doesn't allow that. The report can be previewed or printed only if the user happens to own Crystal. How can I produce a report based on a database and let the users edit it?

Technique

Using Visual Basic with Microsoft Word and the other Microsoft Office applications gives enormous flexibility to your applications. Instead of taking all the time and effort needed to program a mini word processor or other application, you can use all the power of Microsoft Word. Even using one of the many custom controls available for Visual Basic works only if you can find one that has the particular features you need at a reasonable cost. Why not use the tools you already have?

Unlike the other Office applications, Microsoft Word makes a single object available to other applications like WordBasic. But creating a single WordBasic object gives you access to virtually all the features of Word. When you create a WordBasic object, Word itself starts, allowing you to create new documents, load and save documents, and even do spell-checking.

This How-To uses a WordBasic object to create a database report, which is then embedded in an OLE custom control on a form. The user can make any changes needed, using Word's own menus and toolbars.

Steps

Open the Visual Basic RPTWRITE.VBP project. Start the application by selecting Run | Start from the Visual Basic main menu, by pressing F5, or by clicking the Run icon on the Visual Basic toolbar. Click the Create Report button, and select any Access .MDB file. After the data is processed and the report is created, the file is presented in the OLE control, as shown in Figure 13.15. The report is saved to a temporary file, TEMPRPT.DOC, in the application directory. Double-click on the report window to activate visual editing and make any changes required. Because a toolbar is not provided with this application, any active Word toolbars appear as floating toolbars. When you are finished editing, click the Save File button to save the report as a Word document of your choice.

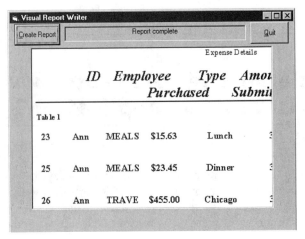

Figure 13.15. The Visual Report Writer form.

1. Start Visual Basic and create a new project. Save the default form as RPTWRITE.FRM, and save the project as RPTWRITE.VBP. This project uses the Microsoft Common Dialog control, so select Tools | Custom Controls from the main Visual Basic menu, and make sure that the control is selected in the list.

2. Start Microsoft Word and minimize the application. Having Word running during development speeds programming because you don't have to wait for Word to load every time you start the project.

3. Place controls on the form as shown in Figure 13.15, setting the properties as shown in Table 13.15. Note that the common dialog control is invisible at runtime, so you can place it anywhere on the form that is convenient. Note too that the menu `mnuFratsaBlatz` can be called anything you like; it is necessary to allow the Word menu to appear on the form only when the OLE object is activated.

Table 13.15. Objects and properties for RPTWRITE.FRM.

OBJECT	PROPERTY	SETTING
Form	Name	frmReportWriter
	Caption	"Visual Report Writer"
	NegotiateMenus	True
PictureBox	Name	picHead
	Align	1 'Align Top
	Appearance	0 'Flat
	BackColor	&H00C0C0C0&
	BorderStyle	0 'None

OBJECT	PROPERTY	SETTING
CommandButton	Name	cmdSave
	Caption	"&Save File"
CommandButton	Name	cmdQuit
	Caption	"&Quit"
CommandButton	Name	cmdReport
	Caption	"&Create Report"
	Default	-1 'True
Label	Name	lblStatus
	Alignment	2 'Center
	BorderStyle	1 'Fixed Single
CommonDialog	Name	cdBiblio
	CancelError	-1 'True
	DefaultExt	"MDB"
	DialogTitle	"BIBLIO.MDB Location"
	FileName	"biblio.mdb"
	Filter	"BIBLIO Database (biblio.mdb)¦biblio.mdb¦All Files (*.*)¦*.*¦"
OLE	Name	oleWord
	OLETypeAllowed	1 'Embedded
Menu	Name	mnuFratsaBlatz
	Caption	"&FratsaBlatz"
	NegotiatePosition	1 'Left
	Visible	0 'False

4. Enter the following code into the declarations section of the form. The `ColumnTabs`, `ColumnHeaders`, and `ColumnWidths` arrays are used to store report formatting information so that any modifications can be made in one place rather than in several different procedures. The OLE constants are activation and deactivation methods for the OLE control.

```
Option Explicit

Dim mobjWord As Object

Dim strColumnTabs(6) As String
Dim strColumnHeaders(7) As String
Dim strColumnWidths(7) As String

'OLE Control Constants
Const OLE_Activate As Integer = 7
Const OLE_Deactivate As Integer = 9
```

5. Enter the following code in the form's **Load** event procedure. After a status message is put on the form, the Word object used throughout this application is created. The creation of that object starts Word running, so minimize it to get it out of the way. (Unfortunately, the **AppMinimize** command doesn't always work. You can manually minimize it, although it is interesting to watch the report being generated!) Finally, the column names and tabs arrays are initialized and the column widths calculated.

```
Status "Creating a Word object"
    Me.Show
    Me.Refresh

    'Create a Microsoft Word object
    Set mobjWord = GetObject("", "Word.Basic")
    mobjWord.AppMinimize ("Microsoft Word")

    cmdReport.Enabled = True
    cmdQuit.Enabled = True

    'Set up standard layout information
    Call SetColumns

    Status "Click on Create Report to create the report."
End Sub
```

6. Enter the following code into the form's **Resize** event procedure. When you use an OLE control containing an object that presents text to the user, you should allow the user to resize the form to see as much or as little of the data as wanted. In this case, the report can go on for many pages, so allowing resizing enables the user to examine and edit the report even in full screen if desired. In this case, resizing is keyed to a couple of static values, the lefthand location of the Create Report button and the height of the picture box at the top. This helps to keep the form in aesthetically pleasing proportion. Note that enough of a border must be kept around the OLE control to allow for Word's rulers at the top and left side of the control; these rulers extend outside the bounds of the control itself.

```
Private Sub Form_Resize()
    Dim intBorder As Integer
    Dim intWindowWidth As Integer

    intBorder = picHead.Height
    intWindowWidth = Me.ScaleWidth

    cmdReport.Height = intBorder
    cmdQuit.Height = intBorder

    cmdQuit.Left = intWindowWidth - cmdQuit.Width - cmdReport.Left
    lblStatus.Width = cmdQuit.Left - lblStatus.Left - cmdReport.Left
    lblStatus.Top = (picHead.Height - lblStatus.Height) / 2

    oleWord.Left = intBorder
```

```
    oleWord.Width = Me.ScaleWidth - 2 * intBorder
    oleWord.Height = Me.ScaleHeight - oleWord.Top - intBorder

End Sub
```

7. Enter the cmdReport `Click` event procedure in the code section of the form. When the user clicks the Create Report button, this procedure opens the database and prepares it for producing the report. Then, after the database is opened, the procedure calls the `Print` procedures to insert headers, footers, titles, and column headers into the report. A table is inserted into the report and formatted, and then the data is entered into the table using a `Do While` loop. On completion, the report is saved to a temporary file in the application directory and is shown in the OLE control as an embedded object.

```
Private Sub cmdReport_Click()
    Dim strTitle As String
    Dim intIdx As Integer
    Dim strInsertText As String
    Dim strFileName As String
    Dim uexpExpDetail As New ExpenseDetail
    Dim strResponse As String

    Status "Opening database table"

    On Error GoTo ExpDetailError

    ' Use the common dialog to open a database.
    cdExpenseFile.InitDir = App.Path
    cdExpenseFile.ShowOpen

    uexpExpDetail.strDbName = cdExpenseFile.filename

    Status "Creating a new Word document"

    mobjWord.FileNew
    strTitle = "Expense Details"

    Status "Inserting header and footer information"
    PrintHeader strTitle, strColumnTabs(), strColumnHeaders()
    PrintFooter "Enlighthened Software, Inc."
    PrintReportTitle strTitle
    PrintColHeaders strColumnTabs(), strColumnHeaders()

    'Start printing the report
    Status "Adding data to report"
    mobjWord.TableInsertTable NumColumns:=7, _
        NumRows:=2, _
        InitialColWidth:="2 in"
    For intIdx = 0 To 7
        With mobjWord
            .TableSelectColumn
            .TableColumnWidth ColumnWidth:=strColumnWidths(intIdx)
            .NextCell
```

continued on next page

continued from previous page

```
                .NextCell
        End With
    Next

    'Format the paragraph height
    mobjWord.TableSelectTable
    mobjWord.FormatParagraph Before:="6 pt"

    'Select the first cell in the table
    'mobjWord.TableSelectColumn
    mobjWord.NextCell

    strResponse = uexpExpDetail.MoveFirst

    Do While "EOF" <> strResponse
        With mobjWord
            strInsertText = CStr(uexpExpDetail.lngExpenseId)
            .Insert strInsertText
            .NextCell
            strInsertText = uexpExpDetail.strEmployeeId
            .Insert strInsertText
            .NextCell
            strInsertText = uexpExpDetail.strExpenseType
            .Insert strInsertText
            .NextCell
            strInsertText = _
                Format$(uexpExpDetail.curAmountSpent, "Currency")
            .Insert strInsertText
            .NextCell
            strInsertText = uexpExpDetail.strDescription
            .Insert strInsertText
            .NextCell
            strInsertText = _
                Format$(uexpExpDetail.dtmDatePurchased, "General Date")
            .Insert strInsertText
            .NextCell
            strInsertText = _
                Format$(uexpExpDetail.dtmDateSubmitted, "General Date")
            .Insert strInsertText
            .NextCell
            .TableInsertRow
        End With
        strResponse = uexpExpDetail.MoveNext
    Loop

    'Save the Word document
    mobjWord.ToolsOptionsSave SummaryPrompt:=0

    strFileName = App.Path & "\TempRpt.doc"
    'Word won't let us save a file over an existing document
    If Len(Dir(strFileName)) Then
        Kill strFileName
    End If
    mobjWord.FileSaveAs Name:=strFileName

    oleWord.CreateEmbed strFileName
```

```
        oleWord.Refresh

        Status "Report complete"

        Exit Sub

ExpDetailError:
        If Err.Number = 70 Then
            Resume Next
        Else
            MsgBox Err.Description & Chr(13) & "from " & Err.Source _
                & " — Number: " & CStr(Err.Number)
            Exit Sub
        End If

End Sub
```

8. Enter this code in the `SetColumns Sub` procedure. Using the tab settings in the `ColumnTabs` array, this procedure calculates the distance between tab settings. These widths will be used to size the Word table's column widths so that the data appears below the corresponding column header. The `If...Else...End If` structure is used because the first column width will be the actual setting for the first tab. This procedure counts on the tabs being in ascending order, or from left to right on the page.

```
Sub SetColumns()
    Dim intIdx As Integer

    strColumnHeaders(0) = "ID"
    strColumnTabs(0) = "0.5"
    strColumnHeaders(1) = "Employee"
    strColumnTabs(1) = "1.25"
    strColumnHeaders(2) = "Type"
    strColumnTabs(2) = "2.0"
    strColumnHeaders(3) = "Amount"
    strColumnTabs(3) = "2.75"
    strColumnHeaders(4) = "Description"
    strColumnTabs(4) = "4.0"
    strColumnHeaders(5) = "Purchased"
    strColumnTabs(5) = "5.0"
    strColumnHeaders(6) = "Submitted"
    strColumnTabs(6) = "6.5"

    For intIdx = LBound(strColumnTabs) To UBound(strColumnTabs)
        If intIdx Then
            strColumnWidths(intIdx) = _
                Str$(Val(strColumnTabs(intIdx)) - _
                Val(strColumnTabs(intIdx - 1)))
        Else
            strColumnWidths(intIdx) = strColumnTabs(intIdx)
        End If
    Next
End Sub
```

9. Enter the following code in the **PrintColHeaders Sub** procedure of the form. This procedure inserts the column headings into the report. Note that this procedure is used twice: once for the first page of the report under the report title, and again in the Word Header so that the headings appear on all subsequent pages. Note that the WordBasic command **ViewHeader** is used twice, acting as a toggle between showing and closing the header.

```
Sub PrintColHeaders(Tabs() As String, ColHeaders() As String)
    Dim intIdx As Integer

    'Assumes cursor is at the beginning of the proper location
    mobjWord.InsertPara
    mobjWord.LineUp
    mobjWord.FormatParagraph Before:="12 pt", _
        After:="6 pt"
    For intIdx = 0 To UBound(Tabs)
        mobjWord.FormatTabs Position:=Tabs(intIdx) + Chr$(34), _
            Align:=0
    Next
    For intIdx = 0 To UBound(ColHeaders) - 1
        mobjWord.Insert ColHeaders(intIdx) + Chr$(9)
    Next

    With mobjWord
        .StartOfLine
        .SelectCurSentence
        .CharRight 1, 1
        .FormatFont Points:="12", _
            Font:="Times New Roman", _
            Bold:=1
        .FormatBordersAndShading ApplyTo:=0, _
            BottomBorder:=2
        .LineDown
    End With
End Sub
```

10. Enter the following code in the **PrintFooter Sub** procedure to insert page footers into the report. Note that the WordBasic command **ViewFooter** is used twice, acting as a toggle between showing and closing the footer.

```
'Insert the report footer
mobjWord.ViewFooter
mobjWord.FormatTabs ClearAll:=1
mobjWord.FormatTabs Position:="7.0" + Chr$(34), _
    DefTabs:="0.5" + Chr$(34), _
    Align:=2, _
    Leader:=0
mobjWord.StartOfLine
mobjWord.Insert Company + Chr$(9) + "Page "
mobjWord.InsertPageField
mobjWord.SelectCurSentence
mobjWord.FormatFont Points:="12", _
    Font:="Times New Roman", _
```

```
        Bold:=1

    mobjWord.ViewFooter
End Sub
```

11. Add the following code to the **PrintReport Sub** procedure. Continuing the use of WordBasic commands through OLE, a title is passed to this procedure, entered on the report, and formatted with a larger font and a drop-shadow box. The box does not appear on the report shown in the OLE control, but it will appear when the report is printed.

```
Sub PrintReportTitle(Title As String)
    With mobjWord
        .StartOfDocument
        .InsertPara
        .StartOfDocument
        .Insert Title
        .StartOfLine
        .SelectCurSentence
        .FormatFont Points:="18", _
            Font:="Times New Roman", _
            Bold:=1, _
            Italic:=1
        .CenterPara

        .FormatBordersAndShading ApplyTo:=0, _
            Shadow:=0

        'Leave the cursor on the following line
        .LineDown
    End With
End Sub
```

12. Enter the following code into the **PrintHeader Sub** procedure. The calling procedure passes a report title to this procedure, along with the **Tabs** and **ColHeaders** arrays. The first page of the report will be different from the rest of the report. It will have the page title, but the subsequent pages will have the report title at the top of the page and will be left justified. The column headings are added to the header so that they show on all pages. Recall that the column headings were placed on the first page of the report, under the report title, as well.

```
Sub PrintHeader(Title As String, Tabs() As String, ColHeaders() As String)
    Dim intIdx As Integer

    With mobjWord
        'For now, set DifferentFirstPage to no
        .FilePageSetup TopMargin:="0.8" + Chr$(34), _
            BottomMargin:="0.8" + Chr$(34), _
            LeftMargin:="0.75" + Chr$(34), _
            RightMargin:="0.75" + Chr$(34), _
            ApplyPropsTo:=4, _
            DifferentFirstPage:=0
```

continued on next page

continued from previous page

```
    End With

    'Insert the report header
    With mobjWord
        .ViewHeader
        .FormatTabs ClearAll:=1
        .FormatTabs Position:="7.0" + Chr$(34), _
            DefTabs:="0.5" + Chr$(34), _
            Align:=2
        .StartOfLine
        .SelectCurSentence
        .CharRight 1, 1
        .FormatFont Points:="12", _
            Font:="Times New Roman", _
            Bold:=1
        .StartOfLine
        .Insert Title + Chr$(9)
        .InsertDateTime DateTimePic:="d' 'MMMM', 'yyyy", _
            InsertAsField:=0
        .InsertPara
        .InsertPara
    End With

    PrintColHeaders Tabs(), ColHeaders()

    mobjWord.ViewHeader    'Closes if it is open

    'Now set DifferentFirstPage
    mobjWord.FilePageSetup DifferentFirstPage:=1

End Sub
```

13. Enter the following code in the **Status Sub** procedure in the form. By passing a string to this procedure, you can keep the user up-to-date on the progress of the report, because it can take some time to generate the report if the data source is large. A useful enhancement of this might be to add a progress gauge or an accumulated record count to show actual progress through the table.

```
Sub Status(txtCaption)
    lblStatus.Caption = txtCaption
    lblStatus.Refresh
End Sub
```

14. Enter the following code in the **cmdQuit Click** and **Unload** event procedures. When the Quit button is clicked, a final status message is shown and the application is ended. When the form is unloaded, the **objWord** object is released by being set to **Nothing**.

```
Private Sub cmdQuit_Click()
    Status "Ending application"
    Unload Me
End Sub
```

```
Private Sub Form_Unload(Cancel As Integer)
    'Shut down Word
    Set objWord = Nothing
End Sub
```

How It Works

This How-To uses many of the formatting and inserting commands available in WordBasic. If you are going to modify the code in this How-To, you should have a copy of the Word Developer's Kit, which has lots of detailed information about WordBasic and, of course, Word itself.

The easiest way to become familiar with WordBasic is to use the macro recorder in Word. Before creating a document or formatting it, turn the recorder on by selecting Tools | Macro, enter a unique name for the macro, and then click Record. Word then records all of your steps, not as individual keystrokes but as fully formed commands using WordBasic. When you are finished making changes, simply click the button with the blue square in the floating Macro Recorder toolbar. You can then open the macro using Tools | Macro | Edit, and you can examine or even cut and paste it into your application. You'll need to reformat the code to conform to Visual Basic's named arguments syntax, and you'll need to enclose the code with With *<object name>*...End With so that Visual Basic knows which object to apply the commands to. Alternatively, you can append the object name to the front of the WordBasic command for individual lines. Both methods are demonstrated throughout the code in this How-To.

A Word table was used to contain the data in the report. Not only does this make it easy to line up the different fields in the report, but it also simplifies the problem of having fields too long to fit in the width allocated on a single line of the report. By changing the paragraph formatting in the table's cells, you can achieve virtually any appearance you want. Alternatively, you could use the ColumnTabs array to put data on the report the same way the column headers were. This approach might be easier if a record's fields will be on multiple lines on the report, but you can also use Word's Merge Cells and other table formatting to achieve different effects on the different lines of a record.

Remember that it is easiest to design the report in Word first and then translate the design into a Visual Basic program, with or without the macro recorder.

If you want the embedded object's application menus to appear when you activate the object, you need to have a menu as part of the form. If your application doesn't otherwise need a menu, create a dummy menu, name it anything you like, and set the Visible property of the single menu item to False. That way, the object's menu will appear. If your application does use a menu, create it as you normally would, but set the NegotiatePosition property of each menu item to None, Left, Middle, or Right, to give Visual Basic an indication of how you want to sort the various menu items between the two menus.

How-To 13.7 used the Microsoft Excel Object Library, and a reference to it had to be explicitly included in the Tools | References menu selection in Visual Basic. Microsoft Word, however, embeds its single object in its program files. As a result, you don't have to explicitly include a reference to it, because OLE starts the Word program anyway, making the object available to your application.

COMPLEXITY
INTERMEDIATE

13.9 How do I...
Work with the Windows Registry for my ActiveX classes?

Problem

All this work you are doing with ActiveX components means that your development computer is going to require some maintenance. How do I keep my Windows Registry neat and tidy?

Technique

All ActiveX components must be registered in order to work correctly. The Windows Registry contains information about each ActiveX component available on your system and the location of the required files to use the component. ActiveX EXE files created by Visual Basic 5 automatically include the code to register themselves in the system Registry. Visual Basic will also register ActiveX DLL files on your development machine. You will need to register your DLLs on machines to which you distribute your programs. The RegSvr32.EXE program is designed to add and remove Registry entries for your components.

Steps

1. Start a DOS command box, and change to your Windows System32 directory, usually C:\WINDOWS\SYSTEM32 on Windows 95 and C:\WINNT\SYSTEM32 on Windows NT.

2. Invoke REGSVR32, passing the name of the ActiveX.DLL file from How-To 13.3:

```
C:\WINDOWS\SYSTEM32> REGSVR32 D:\WAITE\CHAPTER.13\HOW-TO.103\ACTIVEX.DLL
```

Figure 13.16 shows the results.

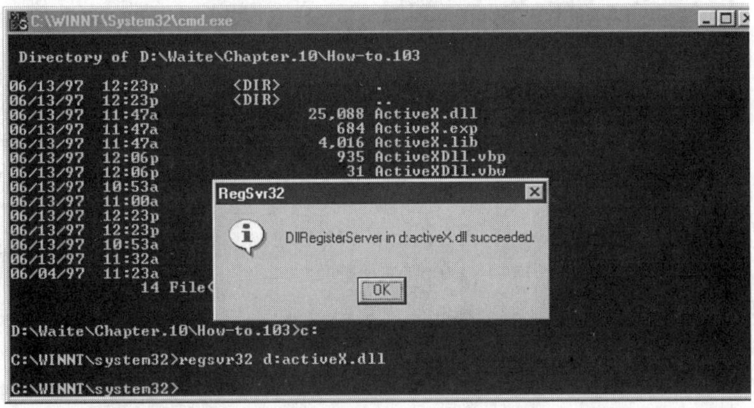

Figure 13.16. RegSvr32 run results.

How It Works

Every Windows system has a Registry containing information about nearly everything on the system. The Registry is divided into HKEY classes for the current configuration, current user, users, machine, and root. For the purposes of keeping our ActiveX components running, we are concerned with the HKEY_CLASSES_ROOT section of the Registry. The component object model uses the Registry in two ways to resolve ActiveX component references—by name and CLSID. The name for a component is assigned by you in the Project properties dialog box. ActiveXDll_For_HowTo_13_3.ExpenseDetail was assigned as the full name for How-To 13.3. Component names are in the form <Application>.<Object> in the event that a single DLL or EXE file contains more than one public object. The CLSID is generated by Windows as a GUID (globally unique identifier). The GUID is a 16-byte unique key presented on the screen by Windows as a formatted hexadecimal string. A typical CLSID might look like {3CF0F563-0DC0-11D1-9AF0-004033373A8F}.

Windows uses the name of a component as a key into the Registry to find the associated CLSID. The CLSID can then be used to find all the required information about the component so that Windows can run it. The information for the ActiveX.DLL from How-To 13.3 includes

✔ The InProcServer32 filename to load to run the component.

✔ The ProgID set as the project name on the project properties page (the same as the registered name).

✔ The TypeLib identifying the interface defined by the component (so that incompatible client programs will not be allowed to invoke the component).

✔ The version number identifying the version of the component program installed (relative to the version number requested by the calling program).

You can manually inspect and modify the Windows Registry by invoking the RegEdt32.EXE program from your Windows system directory.

In this How-To, RegSvr32 loads the specified DLL and invokes `DllRegisterServer` to cause the DLL to be registered on the system. Whenever you use Visual Basic to create an object, the runtime library looks in the Registry for the logical name you supplied, and then loads the associated implementing file. For example, when you request an `Access.Application` object, the Registry is accessed to determine which program on which drive should be started to provide the required services.

Comments

RegSvr32 can also be used to unload DLL files from the Registry with the following syntax:

```
REGSVR32 /U <FileName>.DLL
```

Sometimes, manually unregistering and then reregistering a component can help convince an otherwise balky application to run. Frequently, the cause of application run failure is a missing DLL file called by one of your components. Running RegSvr32 for each of your components can sometimes help isolate missing DLL files.

In addition to RegSvr32, Microsoft has a program called RegClean available from its Internet Web site. RegClean audits the Registry on a machine and removes entries for which the enabling component is missing. Suppose, for example, that you manually purged all the files for Excel from your system without running the uninstall program. All your registered DLLs would be gone, but the Registry entries would still be there, pointing to non-existent files. ActiveX components for Excel will then fail to run correctly. RegClean cleans up the Registry entries to remove these "dangling" entries pointing to non-existent files. The program also leaves behind an "undo" file when you are finished to help restore mistaken removals.

COMPLEXITY
INTERMEDIATE

13.10 How do I...
Create my own custom data control?

Problem

I like the power of the Visual Basic 5 data control, but I want something with more speed and a different user interface. How can I mimic the data control's functions but make it run faster?

Technique

Building a data control is simpler than it sounds, but the debug and test environment is more complex than a form-based project because an ActiveX control must run in both the design-time and the runtime environments. Design-time code runs when controls are dropped onto the form, when objects are resized, and when control properties are changed.

In outline, ActiveX controls are developed in the following general sequence:

✔ Plan the control's properties, methods, events, and visual interface.

✔ Create the development and test environment.

✔ Design and develop the visual and design-time interfaces.

✔ Add the code for the data control's functions.

Most of the time spent developing an ActiveX control is spent on the visual interface and the design-time requirements of a visual control.

Plan the control

Control planning is the easiest and hardest part of development—easiest because everyone knows what a data control needs to do, and hardest because we also have to handle "nasty" things that might be thrown up in our development or support paths. Nobody wants to support a control that crashes every time somebody does something unexpected. Fortunately, Visual Basic's object-oriented features help us expect and prevent errors.

The goal of the simple data control is to provide many of the conveniences of the Visual Basic data control with fast performance and complete source code availability. This data control will support four movement operations (first, previous, next, and last) and three data change operations (add new, update, and delete). The visual implementation of all operations will be *constituent control* buttons placed on the control. A constituent control is one we will place on top of our control to deliver a desired function. Any existing ActiveX control that has been designed to be placed on another control can be a constituent control for another project. All the common controls that shipped with Visual Basic 5 can be used as constituent controls, including text boxes, buttons, frames, list boxes, pictures, labels, and shapes. The OLE Automation control cannot be used as a constituent control. If you plan to distribute your control to others, even at no charge, be sure to check your license agreements and the Visual Basic 5 Books Online carefully.

Build the Development and Test Environment

The development and test environment for an ActiveX control is different from that of standard EXE projects because ActiveX controls have both design-time and runtime code attributes which can be different. The most important distinction is the way in which the control stores design-time property values.

Properties such as the captions, data sources, and database names must be stored at design time if they are specified.

The development and test environment is implemented as a project group in order to have the ActiveX control project and the test form project available simultaneously. Whenever the control's object (visual design) window is closed, the control is placed into design-time run mode, and the design-time code can be debugged within a single Visual Basic programming session.

Develop the Visual and Design-Time Interfaces

Your control's visual interface is the most obvious part of your work because the visual behavior is what everyone will notice. At design time, we deal with the resize event for managing constituent control sizes and control properties that need to be saved with the form. In the case of our private data control, we worry about saving the database location.

Develop the Core Functions

Finally, we can develop the core functions and events for the data control. The core operations displayed by the buttons are directly implemented with the underlying data access object (DAO) methods. The public events notify the form of changes in the underlying data and of validation required prior to new, updated, or delete records. The validation event is not fired when the data changes through control movement.

Steps

Open the project ExpDataControl.vbg. The form shown in Figure 13.17 appears. Experiment with the form and its buttons to get a feel for how this data control works.

1. Create a new ActiveX control project in your work area. Name the default User Control object ctlExpenseDetail. Select Project | References from the main menu, and include a reference to the Microsoft DAO 3.5 Object Library. Make sure that the OLE Automation library is not selected.

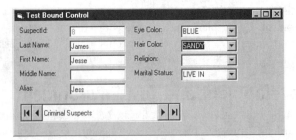

Figure 13.17. The DataControl Test form.

2. Select Project | Project1 properties from the Visual Basic 5 main menu, or right-click Project1 in the Project Explorer window and select properties from the object menu. Name the project `ExpDetailControl`. Set the project description to `Expense Detail ActiveX Control`, as shown in Figure 13.18. The description will be saved to your Windows system registry when you compile your project. Save the control and project files.

3. Add a new project to your work area by selecting File | Add Project from the main menu. The Add Project window appears, as shown in Figure 13.19. Select Standard EXE from the New tab.

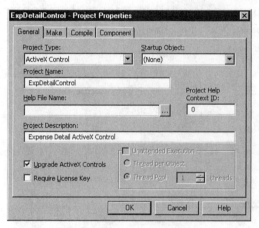

Figure 13.18. The Project Properties window.

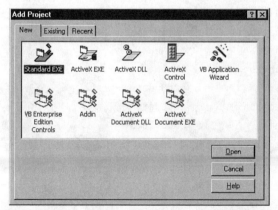

Figure 13.19. The Add Project window to add Standard EXE to the test environment.

4. Name the default form `TestDataControl` and the default project `prjTestDataControl`. Save the project and project group. When prompted, name the project group `ExpDataControl.vbg`. Project groups help you debug related projects from a single Visual Basic 5 session.

5. Add seven command buttons and two frames to the control as shown in Figure 13.20. Don't worry about exact placement because the resize event will manage final placement and sizing. (These visual elements are almost the same as those in How-To 13.2.)

6. Set the properties of the control elements as shown in Table 13.16.

Table 13.16. Objects and properties for the expense data control.

OBJECT	PROPERTY	SETTING
UserControl	Name	ExpDataControl
Frame	Name	fraBorder
	Caption	"Expense Data Control"
Frame	Name	fraNavigate
	Caption	"Navigate"
CommandButton	Name	cmdFirst
	Caption	"&First"
CommandButton	Name	cmdPrev
	Caption	"&Prev"
CommandButton	Name	cmdNext
	Caption	"&Next"
CommandButton	Name	cmdLast
	Caption	"&Last"
Frame	Name	fraMaintain
	Caption	"Maintain"
CommandButton	Name	cmdNew
	Caption	"Ne&w"
CommandButton	Name	cmdUpdate
	Caption	"&Update"
CommandButton	Name	cmdDelete
	Caption	"&Delete"

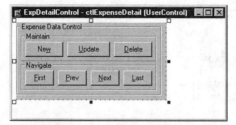

Figure 13.20. Expense data control visual elements.

One of the most challenging parts of developing an ActiveX control is determining which events will fire and their order. This How-To employs Debug.Print statements to trace control behavior, especially during design time. The first statement in most of the control's event procedure is usually this:

```
Debug.Print "Event Name" & Extender.Name
```

At both design time and runtime, this statement causes a debug trace in the immediate window of all control behaviors. The Extender object reflects the control's container into your code in order to access important information about the control's environment. Standard Extender properties for a control include Name, Visible, Enabled, Top, Left, Height, and Width. These properties exist in your container's object but can be of value to your code for resizing and property initialization. You can use the trace information to learn more about design-time events and their effect on your control.

7. Add the following code to the UserControl_Resize event of your control:

```
Private Sub UserControl_Resize()
' Resize constituent controls to look "nice"
Dim intMargin As Integer
Dim intHeight As Integer
Dim intWidth As Integer

    ' Trace our behavior
    Static intCountResized As Integer
    intCountResized = intCountResized + 1
    Debug.Print Extender.Name & " Resized " _
        & Str$(intCountResized) & " times"

    ' Adjust the placement of the border frame
    fraBorder.Move 0, 0, ScaleWidth, ScaleHeight
```

continued on next page

continued from previous page

```
        ' Calculate the standard margin as a proportion of
        ' the total control width.
        intMargin = ScaleWidth / 36

        ' Calculate and adjust the sizes of the internal frames.
        intHeight = (ScaleHeight - (1.5 * intMargin) - intMargin) / 2
        intWidth = ScaleWidth - (2 * intMargin)
        fraMaintain.Move intMargin, (intMargin * 2), _
            intWidth, intHeight
        fraNavigate.Move intMargin, _
            (fraMaintain.Top + fraMaintain.Height), _
            intWidth, intHeight

        ' Adjust the maintenance button sizes and locations
        ' based on the number of buttons and margins required.
        ' We need an extra margin in the height because the frame
        ' caption takes about one margin.
        intHeight = fraMaintain.Height - (3 * intMargin)
        intWidth = (fraMaintain.Width - (4 * intMargin)) / 3
        cmdNew.Move intMargin, _
            2 * intMargin, _
            intWidth, intHeight
        cmdUpdate.Move cmdNew.Left + intWidth + intMargin, _
            2 * intMargin, _
            intWidth, intHeight
        cmdDelete.Move cmdUpdate.Left + cmdUpdate.Width + intMargin, _
            2 * intMargin, _
            intWidth, intHeight

        ' Adjust the movement button sizes and locations based on
        ' the number of buttons and margins required.
        intHeight = fraNavigate.Height - (3 * intMargin)
        intWidth = (fraNavigate.Width - (5 * intMargin)) / 4
        cmdFirst.Move intMargin, _
            2 * intMargin, _
            intWidth, intHeight
        cmdPrev.Move cmdFirst.Left + intWidth + intMargin, _
            2 * intMargin, _
            intWidth, intHeight
        cmdNext.Move cmdPrev.Left + intWidth + intMargin, _
            2 * intMargin, _
            intWidth, intHeight
        cmdLast.Move cmdNext.Left + intWidth + intMargin, _
            2 * intMargin, _
            intWidth, intHeight

End Sub
```

Although lengthy, the `Resize` event code just works from the outside of the control inward, making sure that everything fits on the control with pleasant margins.

8. Set a breakpoint at the beginning of the `Resize` event procedure. Run the design-time environment of your control by closing the control's object design window (where you add buttons and frames). Notice that the toolbox icon for your UserControl has changed from gray to color. (See Figure 13.21.)

9. Get ready to test your `Resize` event procedure. Select View | Immediate Window from the main menu. Open the `TestDataControl` form design window. Select your new UserControl icon from the Visual Basic 5 Toolbox, and draw a control on the form. Don't be surprised when your `Resize` event breakpoint is fired, because every time the control is dropped onto a form or resized, this event occurs. Take a moment to walk through the resize code and get a feel for its behavior. Don't forget to clear the breakpoint when you are done.

10. Close the form's design window and stop the design-time instance of the UserControl by opening the UserControl design window.

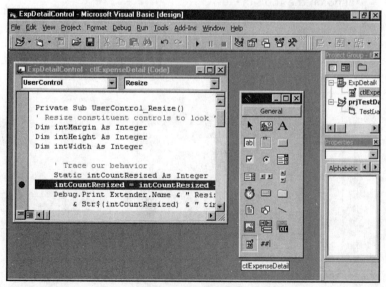

Figure 13.21. The Visual Basic Toolbox with the user control active.

DEBUGGING AND TESTING USERCONTROL OBJECTS

Debugging UserControl objects is straightforward when all the rules are clear. The Visual Basic development environment automatically runs the control's design-time instance whenever the UserControl's object design window is closed. The UserControl's icon is then activated on the toolbox palette. Any breakpoints or Debug object statements in the UserControl code are then activated, and you can debug design-time code as you manipulate the UserControl on forms or set properties.

However, you might find the instance of your control on the form hatched over (not running in design mode) when you want to test with no apparent way to get the design-time code running. This turn of events is usually caused by a runtime compile-on-demand error, forcing a project reset and premature (in the programmer's mind) return to the design environment. Try manually compiling all the projects in the group to correct this error. Select File | Make Project Group from the Visual Basic main menu. Usually, recompiling the UserControl's .OCX file clears up design-time environment. Alternatively, you can turn off the Compile On Demand check box on the General tab of the Options dialog box found on the Tools menu.

11. From the UserControl code window, add a Caption property by selecting Tools | Add Procedure from the main menu. Name the procedure Caption, and declare it as a public property. (See Figure 13.22.) Click OK.

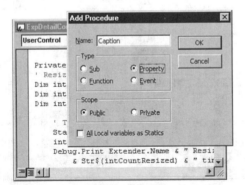

Figure 13.22. The Visual Basic Add Procedure window to declare the Caption property.

12. Modify the `Caption` Property Let and `Property Get` procedures as shown next. Be sure to change the variant declarations to string declarations.

```
Public Property Get Caption() As String

    Caption = fraBorder.Caption

End Property

Public Property Let Caption(ByVal strNewValue As String)

    ' Place the caption in the border frame.
    fraBorder.Caption = strNewValue
    ' Notify the container so that the property
    ' window may be updated
    PropertyChanged "Caption"

End Property
```

13. Add the following code to the `UserControl_InitProperties` event. Every time the control is placed onto a form, the caption will be set to the control's name. (Remember that referencing a property from within a class causes the `Property Let` function to be called.)

```
Private Sub UserControl_InitProperties()
    ' Trace behavior.
    Debug.Print Extender.Name & ": InitProperties"
    ' Set the Caption property
    Caption = Extender.Name

End Sub
```

14. Add the following code to the `UserControl WriteProperties` procedure. The `WriteProperties` event is called whenever the form is saved.

```
Private Sub UserControl_WriteProperties(PropBag As PropertyBag)

    ' Trace behavior.
    Debug.Print Extender.Name & ": WriteProperties"
    'Save the caption property to the property bag.
    PropBag.WriteProperty "Caption", Caption, _
        Extender.Name

End Sub
```

15. Add the following code to the `UserControl ReadProperties` event to retrieve the saved properties:

```
Private Sub UserControl_ReadProperties(PropBag As PropertyBag)

    ' Trace behavior.
    Debug.Print Extender.Name & ": ReadProperties"
    'Retrieve the caption
```

continued on next page

continued from previous page

```
        Caption = PropBag.ReadProperty("Caption", _
                Extender.Name)

End Sub
```

16. Compile the entire project by selecting File | Make Project Group from the main menu. Close the UserControl design window and open the test form design window. Place a `UserControl` object on the test form. Experiment with the `Caption` property from the Visual Basic properties window in design mode. Try saving, closing, and reopening the form, and observe what happens in the immediate window.

17. Add the following declarations to the UserControl to define our recordset and the fields to be managed:

```
' Variables to define and control the recordset
Private mblnRecSetOpen As Boolean
Private mdbExpense As Database
Private mrecExpense As Recordset
Private mstrDbName As String

' Module variables to hold property value(s)
Private mlngExpenseId As Long
Private mstrEmployeeId As String
Private mstrExpenseType As String
Private mcurAmountSpent As Currency
Private mstrDescription As String
Private mdtmDatePurchased As Date
Private mdtmDateSubmitted As Date
```

18. Define property procedures for the expense detail table by selecting Tools | Add Procedure from the main menu when the UserControl code is active on-screen. Name the property `strDatabaseName` and declare it to be a public property. Modify the generated `Property Get` and `Let` procedures as shown next. This property can be set only at runtime because we don't want to bother with opening and closing recordsets during form design. The `Let` procedure checks to see whether the recordset is already open and closes it before opening it again.

```
Public Property Get strDatabaseName() As String
' Returns the database name to the container
    strDatabaseName = mstrDbName

End Property

Public Property Let strDatabaseName(ByVal strNewValue As String)
' Assigns database name to control and closes and opens the
' control's recordset

    ' Trace behavior.
    Debug.Print Extender.Name & ": Let strDatabaseName"

    ' Don't allow database to be set at design time
    If Ambient.UserMode = False Then
```

```
        Err.Raise Number:=31013, _
            Description:= _
            "Property is read-only at design time."
        Exit Property
    End If

    On Error GoTo OpenError

    If mblnRecSetOpen Then
        mrecExpense.Close
        mdbExpense.Close
    End If
    mstrDbName = strNewValue
    Set mdbExpense = DBEngine.Workspaces(0).OpenDatabase(mstrDbName)
    Set mrecExpense = mdbExpense.OpenRecordset("Expenses")
    mblnRecSetOpen = True

    Exit Property

OpenError:
    ' Since we are designing this class for potential unattended
    ' operation, we'll have to raise an error on our own
    Err.Raise Number:=Err.Number
    Err.Clear
    Exit Property

End Property
```

19. Add some code to initialize the state control variables of the control so that the recordset open and close logic works correctly:

```
Private Sub UserControl_Initialize()
' Initialize control's core variables

    ' Trace behavior, but we can't use the name because
    ' the extender object is not available
    Debug.Print "Initialize"

    mblnRecSetOpen = False

End Sub
```

20. Add a **Terminate** event procedure to close the database and recordset. Note that the Visual Basic documentation states very clearly that control terminate event handlers *must* manage their own errors because there is usually nothing in the container application on the call stack to handle an error. For the same reason, never raise an error from a terminate event. For tracing purposes, the **Extender** object is no longer available for retrieving the control's name.

```
Private Sub UserControl_Terminate()

    ' Trace behavior.
    Debug.Print "UserControl_Terminate"
```

continued on next page

continued from previous page

```
' We don't really care about errors when cleaning up.
On Error Resume Next
' Close the recordset
mrecExpense.Close
' Close the expense database
mdbExpense.Close
' Reset the error handler
On Error GoTo 0
Exit Sub

End Sub
```

21. The control will expose two events to its container—one for data changes and the other for validation. Add the following code to the declarations section of the UserControl:

```
' Data changed event for data control movement
    ' or internally generated change tells the container
    ' that the control's view of the data has changed
    Public Event DataChanged()

    ' Action enum for validate event eases container
    ' code development
    Public Enum EXP_CHANGE_TYPE
        expAddNewValidate
        expUpdateValidate
        expDeleteValidate
    End Enum

    ' Validate response enum tells the control whether to
    ' proceed with the data change
    Public Enum EXP_RESPONSE_TYPE
        expOK
        expCancel
    End Enum

    ' Validate event for data control
    Public Event Validate(ByRef Response As EXP_RESPONSE_TYPE, _
            ByVal Change As EXP_CHANGE_TYPE)
```

The DataChanged event will tell the containing form that the underlying data has changed and that the container should refresh its view of the data. The public Enum declarations assist the developer of the containing form in understanding the event parameters. The Validate event will tell the containing form that a data change is about to take place and provide an opportunity for cancellation by the container.

22. Implement three helper subroutines to move data between record fields and the control data variables and to clear the object variables:

```
Private Sub SetRecordset(recExp As Recordset)
' Copies current values to Recordset

    With recExp
```

```
            !EmployeeId = mvarstrEmployeeId
            !ExpenseType = mvarstrExpenseType
            !AmountSpent = mvarcurAmountSpent
            !Description = mvarstrDescription
            !DatePurchased = mvardtmDatePurchased
            !DateSubmitted = mvardtmDateSubmitted
        End With

End Sub

Private Sub GetRecordset(recExp As Recordset)
' Copies current values to Recordset

    With recExp
        mvarlngExpenseId = 0 + !ExpenseID
        mvarstrEmployeeId = "" & !EmployeeId
        mvarstrExpenseType = "" & !ExpenseType
        mvarcurAmountSpent = 0 + !AmountSpent
        mvarstrDescription = "" & !Description
        mvardtmDatePurchased = !DatePurchased
        mvardtmDateSubmitted = !DateSubmitted
    End With

End Sub

Private Sub ClearObject()
' Clears all object variables

    mlngExpenseId = 0
    mstrEmployeeId = ""
    mstrExpenseType = ""
    mcurAmountSpent = 0
    mstrDescription = ""
    mdtmDatePurchased = CDate("1/1/1980")
    mdtmDateSubmitted = CDate("1/1/1980")

End Sub
```

23. Implement the core data movement operations by providing code to work for the movement button clicks:

```
Private Sub cmdFirst_Click()
' Move to the first record

    On Error GoTo MoveError
    If mblnRecSetOpen Then
        With mrecExpense
            If Not (True = .BOF _
            And True = .EOF) Then
                ' Dataset is not empty.
                ' Move to the first record.
                .MoveFirst
                Call GetRecordset(mrecExpense)
                RaiseEvent DataChanged
            End If
        End With
```

continued on next page

continued from previous page

```
        End If

        Exit Sub

MoveError:
        ' Return the error description
        Err.Raise Number:=Err.Number, Source:=Err.Source, _
            Description:=Err.Description
        Err.Clear
        Exit Sub

End Sub

Private Sub cmdLast_Click()
' Move to the last record

    On Error GoTo MoveError
    If mblnRecSetOpen Then
        With mrecExpense
            If Not (True = .BOF _
            And True = .EOF) Then
                ' Dataset is not empty.
                ' Move to the last record.
                .MoveLast
                Call GetRecordset(mrecExpense)
                RaiseEvent DataChanged
            End If
        End With
    End If

        Exit Sub

MoveError:
        ' Return the error description
        Err.Raise Number:=Err.Number, Source:=Err.Source, _
            Description:=Err.Description
        Err.Clear
        Exit Sub

End Sub

Private Sub cmdNext_Click()
' Move to the next record

    On Error GoTo MoveError
    If mblnRecSetOpen Then
        With mrecExpense
            If True = .BOF _
            And True = .EOF Then
                .MoveLast
            Else
                ' Dataset is not empty.
                ' Move to the previous record.
                .MoveNext
```

```
                        If .EOF Then
                            .MoveLast
                        End If
                    End If
                End If
                Call GetRecordset(mrecExpense)
                RaiseEvent DataChanged
            End With
        End If

        Exit Sub

MoveError:
        ' Return the error description
        Err.Raise Number:=Err.Number, Source:=Err.Source, _
            Description:=Err.Description
        Err.Clear
        Exit Sub

End Sub

Private Sub cmdPrev_Click()
' Move to the previous record

    On Error GoTo MoveError

    If mblnRecSetOpen Then
        With mrecExpense
            If True = .BOF _
            And True = .EOF Then
                .MoveFirst
            Else
                ' Dataset is not empty.
                ' Move to the previous record.
                .MovePrevious
                If .BOF Then
                    .MoveFirst
                End If
            End If
            Call GetRecordset(mrecExpense)
            RaiseEvent DataChanged
        End With
    End If

    Exit Sub

MoveError:
    ' Return the error description
    Err.Raise Number:=Err.Number, Source:=Err.Source, _
        Description:=Err.Description
    Err.Clear
    Exit Sub

End Sub
```

24. Implement the data maintenance operations by adding `Click` event procedures for the New, Update, and Delete buttons:

```
Private Sub cmdNew_Click()
' Inserts a brand-new record into the database and leaves the newly
' inserted values as the current object values.

Dim uexpResponse As EXP_RESPONSE_TYPE

    On Error GoTo InsertError
    RaiseEvent Validate(uexpResponse, expAddNewValidate)
    If expOk = uexpResponse Then
        With mrecExpense
            .AddNew
            mdtmDateSubmitted = Now
            Call SetRecordset(mrecExpense)
            .Update
            'Move to the most recently modified record
            .Bookmark = .LastModified
            Call GetRecordset(mrecExpense)
            RaiseEvent DataChanged
        End With
    End If

    Exit Sub

InsertError:
    ' Return the error description
    Err.Raise Number:=Err.Number, Source:=Err.Source, _
        Description:=Err.Description
    Err.Clear
    Exit Sub

End Sub

Private Sub cmdUpdate_Click()
' Updates Expenses table from current object values
Dim uexpResponse As EXP_RESPONSE_TYPE

    On Error GoTo UpdateError
    RaiseEvent Validate(uexpResponse, expAddNewValidate)
    If expOk = uexpResponse Then
        With mrecExpense
            .Edit
            Call SetRecordset(mrecExpense)
            .Update
            'Move to the most recently modified record
            .Bookmark = .LastModified
            Call GetRecordset(mrecExpense)
            RaiseEvent DataChanged
        End With
    End If

    Exit Sub

UpdateError:
```

```
        ' Return the error description
        Err.Raise Number:=Err.Number, Source:=Err.Source, _
            Description:=Err.Description
        Err.Clear
        Exit Sub

End Sub

Private Sub cmdDelete_Click()
' Deletes the expense detail record whose value is
' current from the database

Dim uexpResponse As EXP_RESPONSE_TYPE

    On Error GoTo DeleteError

    RaiseEvent Validate(uexpResponse, expAddNewValidate)
    If expOk = uexpResponse Then
        With mrecExpense
            .Delete
            If 0 = .RecordCount Then
                Call ClearObject
            Else
                .MoveNext
                If .EOF Then
                    Call ClearObject
                Else
                    Call GetRecordset(mrecExpense)
                End If
            End If
        End With
    End If
    RaiseEvent DataChanged

    Exit Sub

DeleteError:
    ' Return the error description
    Err.Raise Number:=Err.Number, Source:=Err.Source, _
        Description:=Err.Description
    Err.Clear
    Exit Sub

End Sub
```

25. Provide **Property Get** and **Let** procedures for the core data variables
implemented by the control. Note that cutting and pasting the property
procedures one pair at a time is much easier than using the Add Procedure
dialog box from step 18.

```
Public Property Get curAmountSpent() As Currency
    ' Return the control's current amount
    curAmountSpent = mcurAmountSpent

End Property
```

continued on next page

continued from previous page

```
Public Property Let curAmountSpent(ByVal curNewValue As Currency)
    ' Set the amount spent
    mcurAmountSpent = curNewValue

End Property

Public Property Get dtmDatePurchased() As Date
    ' Return the control's current purchase date
    dtmDatePurchased = mdtmDatePurchased

End Property

Public Property Let dtmDatePurchased(ByVal dtmNewValue As Date)
    ' Set the purchase date
    mdtmDatePurchased = dtmNewValue

End Property

Public Property Get dtmDateSubmitted() As Date
    ' Return the control's current submitted date.
    ' There is no property Let procedure because the
    ' value is set only when the record is created.
    dtmDateSubmitted = mdtmDateSubmitted

End Property

Public Property Get lngExpenseId() As Long
    ' Return the database-assigned ExpenseID.
    ' Note that there is no Property Let procedure
    ' because the database makes the key assignment.

    lngExpenseId = mlngExpenseId

End Property

Public Property Get strDescription() As String
    ' Return the control's current description
    strDescription = mstrDescription

End Property

Public Property Let strDescription(ByVal strNewValue As String)
    ' Set the expense description
    mstrDescription = strNewValue

End Property

Public Property Get strEmployeeId() As String
    ' Return the control's current employee ID
    strEmployeeId = mstrEmployeeId

End Property
```

```
Public Property Let strEmployeeId(ByVal strNewValue As String)
    ' Set the employee ID
    mstrEmployeeId = strNewValue

End Property

Public Property Get strExpenseType() As String
    ' Return the control's current expense type
    strExpenseType = mstrExpenseType

End Property

Public Property Let strExpenseType(ByVal strNewValue As String)
' Sets the expense type to an allowed value
    Dim strTemp As String

    strTemp = UCase$(strNewValue)
    If strTemp = "TRAVEL" _
    Or strTemp = "MEALS" _
    Or strTemp = "OFFICE" _
    Or strTemp = "AUTO" _
    Or strTemp = "TOLL/PARK" Then
        mstrExpenseType = strTemp
    Else
        Err.Raise Number:=31013, _
            Description:="Expense type must be TRAVEL, MEALS, " _
                        & "OFFICE, AUTO, or TOLL/PARK"
        'Err.Clear
        Exit Property
    End If

End Property
```

The `strExpenseType Property Let` procedure illustrates raising a field-level validation error from a User Control. The `lngExpenseId` and `dtmDateSubmitted` properties do not have `Let` procedures because these properties are set by the database and insert code.

26. The actual data properties should be available only at runtime and should not appear on the control's property page. Select Tools | Procedure Attributes from the main menu. Click Advanced. Select each data property in turn from the Name list box, check Don't show in Property Browser, and click the Apply button. Figure 13.23 shows the advanced Procedure Attributes dialog box.

27. Complete the Test Data Control form so that it looks as shown in Figure 13.17, and set the form's control attributes as shown in Table 13.17. Note that the `Amount` field is stored in a masked edit control.

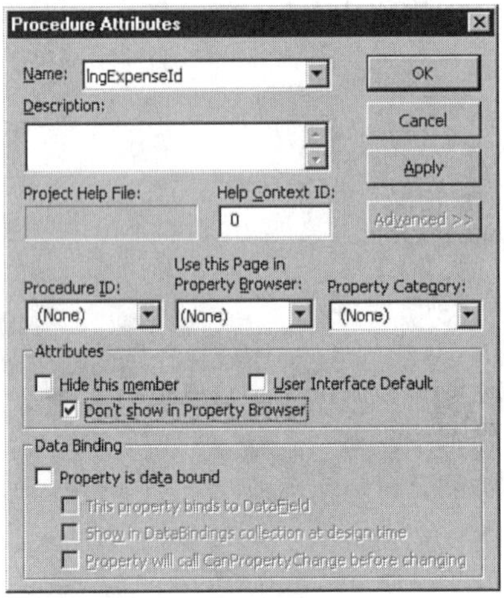

Figure 13.23. The advanced
Procedure Attributes dialog box.

Table 13.17. Objects and properties for the Test Data Control form.

OBJECT	PROPERTY	SETTING
Form	Name	TestDataControl
	Caption	"Test Data Control"
ExpDetailControl	Name	expControl
	Caption	"Expense Control"
MaskEdBox	Name	mskAmountSpent
	Format	"$#,##0.00;($#,##0.00)"
	PromptChar	"_"
TextBox	Name	txtSubmitDate
TextBox	Name	txtPurchaseDate
TextBox	Name	txtDescription
TextBox	Name	txtExpenseType
TextBox	Name	txtEmployeeId
TextBox	Name	txtExpenseId
Label	Name	Label1
	Caption	"Expense ID:"
Label	Name	Label2
	Caption	"Employee:"
Label	Name	Label3
	Caption	"Expense Type:"

OBJECT	PROPERTY	SETTING
Label	Name	Label4
	Caption	"Amount Spent:"
Label	Name	Label5
	Caption	"Description:"
Label	Name	Label6
	Caption	"Purchase Date:"
Label	Name	Label7
	Caption	"Submission Date:"

28. Use the Visual Basic menu editor to create the menu shown in Table 13.18.

Table 13.18. Menu specifications for the Object Library form.

CAPTION	NAME	SHORTCUT KEY
&File	mnuFile	
----E&xit	mnuFileExit	

29. Add the following code to the **DataChanged** event for the expense user control. Whenever the control notifies the form that a change has been made, the helper routine updates the displayed values.

```
Private Sub expControl_DataChanged()

    ' The data has changed in the control, so update the form
    Call ReadObjectValues

End Sub
```

30. Add the **ReadObjectValues** helper routine to display the control's values:

```
Private Sub ReadObjectValues()
' Read the object values into the form fields

    txtExpenseId.Text = CStr(expControl.lngExpenseId)
    txtEmployeeId.Text = expControl.strEmployeeId
    txtExpenseType.Text = expControl.strExpenseType
    txtDescription.Text = expControl.strDescription
    mskAmountSpent.Text = CStr(expControl.curAmountSpent)
    txtPurchaseDate.Text = CStr(expControl.dtmDatePurchased)
    txtSubmitDate.Text = CStr(expControl.dtmDateSubmitted)

End Sub
```

31. Add the following code to the **Validate** event of the user expense control. The control raises this event when one of the data maintenance buttons is pressed. The error handler is needed to capture errors raised by the control's **Property Let** routines. The **Property Let** routines are called by **SetObjectValues**.

```
Private Sub expControl_Validate _
    (Response As ExpDetailControl.EXP_RESPONSE_TYPE, _
    ByVal Change As ExpDetailControl.EXP_CHANGE_TYPE)
' A command button has been pushed; update the control's
' data if needed

    On Error GoTo ValidateError

    Select Case Change
        Case expAddNewValidate, expUpdateValidate
            Call SetObjectValues
            Response = expOk
        Case expDeleteValidate
            Response = expOk
        Case Else
            Response = expCancel
    End Select

    Exit Sub
ValidateError:
        MsgBox Err.Description & " from " _
            & Err.Source & " — " _
            & CStr(Err.Number)
        Response = expCancel
        Exit Sub

End Sub
```

32. Add the following helper routine to update the control's data values from the form fields:

```
Private Sub SetObjectValues()
' Sets related object values from form fields

    expControl.strExpenseType = txtExpenseType.Text
    expControl.strEmployeeId = txtEmployeeId.Text
    expControl.strDescription = txtDescription.Text
    expControl.dtmDatePurchased = txtPurchaseDate.Text
    expControl.curAmountSpent = CCur(mskAmountSpent.Text)

    Exit Sub

End Sub
```

33. Add the following **Form_Load** procedure to initialize the control's recordset:

```
Private Sub Form_Load()
' Get the ActiveX object to open its database
```

```
    Dim strDbName As String
    Dim strResponse As String

    On Error GoTo LoadError

    strDbName = App.Path
    strDbName = strDbName & "\Expense.mdb"
    expControl.strDatabaseName = strDbName

    Exit Sub

LoadError:
    MsgBox Err.Description & Chr(13) & "from " & Err.Source _
        & " — Number: " & CStr(Err.Number)
    Unload Me

End Sub
```

34. Add the following procedure to the mnuFileExit Click event to exit the program:

```
Private Sub mnuFileExit_Click()

    Unload Me

End Sub
```

How It Works

The handcrafted data control works by encapsulating recordset movement commands and visual controls in a simple wrapper exposing the database name, two events, and the data value properties (fields). The control itself manages all recordset navigation and the screen interface buttons.

The control begins useful functions when the strDatabaseName property is set and the recordset is opened. The strDatabaseName property is created to be read-only at design time. Changing it at design-time results in a error message being displayed in the development environment.

The control's constituent buttons provide the heart of the user control. Whenever a movement button is clicked, the recordset is moved to a valid record, and the DataChanged event is raised to cause the containing application to retrieve current field values from the control's property values. When a database maintenance button is clicked, the control raises the Validate event to allow the containing form to update the control's copy of the data and to perform any display operations before the database is changed.

The data values of the control are implemented in runtime only and are hidden from the design-time properties window of the container. The strExpenseType control raises a private error event to indicate an invalid type together with an explanatory message. The Property Let procedure was not implemented for the lngExpenseId property because it is assigned by the database when a new record is inserted in the database.

Constituent Controls

Constituent controls are preexisting ActiveX controls placed onto ActiveX controls being developed. In this How-To, frame and button constituent controls were placed onto the simple data control. The caption of the data control was visually displayed as the caption of the surrounding frame. Although we didn't use the technique here, it is possible to expose individual constituent control events as events of the control. For example, if we wanted to raise a `CommandFirstClick` event from the control when the constituent `cmdFirst` button click event occurred, we would declare a new event in the declarations section and add a `RaiseEvents` call in the button click event.

```
Option Explicit

Public Event CommandFirstClick()

Private Sub cmdFirst_Click()
' Move to the first record

' … Useful, productive code

    ' Tell the container about the click
    RaiseEvent CommandFirstClick

End Sub
```

Debugging ActiveX Controls

Most of the debugging for an ActiveX control project can be accomplished with the simple project group approach shown in this How-To. Unfortunately, errors raised from `Property Let` procedures cannot be debugged in this way. Visual Basic seems to assume that all errors raised by the `Property Let` procedure must be handled by the Visual Basic "End or Debug" dialog box before the calling container gets a chance to handle the error. The workaround for this problem is to compile the control to its .OCX file and open just the test form's project from Visual Basic. Then the error will be trapped in the containing test form.

Comments

This control was built entirely by hand to illustrate the nuts and bolts of making a data control work within the ActiveX control environment. An ActiveX control skeleton can also be built quickly using the ActiveX Control Interface Wizard available as a Microsoft-supplied add-in to the Visual Basic 5 environment. The Wizard generates all the code required for managing most "standard" ActiveX properties and events, which were ignored in this How-To in the interest of keeping the core data control code more readable. You should use this add-in to develop robust controls that might receive wider distribution through your programming team or corporation.

You can also implement a specialized ActiveX data control function by placing a standard data control on an ActiveX control as a constituent control. This approach would certainly provide more rapid development than starting from button pasting, but at a potential cost in performance and complexity.

COMPLEXITY
INTERMEDIATE

13.11 How do I...
Create my own data bound control?

Problem

I've created a database table for providing code values for list boxes. How can I write a data-bound ActiveX list box control to quickly populate itself from the code value table and be data bound to a control on my form?

Technique

This How-To shows the creation of an enhanced combo box control that fills itself with allowed choices from a code value table contained in the application's database. The CodeValue.mdb database is located in the How-To.E02 directory on the CD-ROM. The main Subject data table contains information on criminal suspects, and the Code10 table contains possible values for suspect attributes such as hair color and eye color. The table is called Code10 because it returns 10-character fields based on 10-character code types. Table 13.19 describes the suspect table, and Table 13.20 describes the Code10 table.

Table 13.19. The Suspect table.

FIELD
SuspectId
LastName
FirstName
MiddleName
Alias
EyeColor
HairClr
Religion
MaritalStatus

Table 13.20. The Code10 table.

FIELD	DESCRIPTION
CodeType10	Type of code values to return—for example, HAIRCOLOR.
CodeValue10	Data value to populate in combo boxes for the code type—for example, Blond.
CodeDesc	Description of this particular type-value pair.

The new control will function almost the same as a standard combo box with the addition of a *code type* to load and an open database object to use for creating the recordset. The ActiveX Control Interface Wizard will write most of the code for this control based on its dialog inputs.

Steps

1. Open the project group TestBoundGroup.vbg and run the application. The form in Figure 13.24 appears. Become familiar with the application, especially the combo box behavior.

2. Create a new ActiveX control project in your work area. Place a single combo box on the control and name it **cmbCodeValue**. Name the project **BoundComboControl** and the control **ctlBoundCombo**. Save the project.

3. Select Add-Ins | Add-In Manager from the main menu, and check the VB ActiveX Control Interface Wizard. Click OK to close the dialog box.

4. Select Add-Ins | ActiveX Control Interface Wizard from the main menu. Click Next to begin defining the **BoundComboControl** interface.

5. Declare the standard properties, events, and methods in the control's interface. Add the **Change** event from the Available names list to the Selected Names list by selecting Change on the left and clicking the > button. Similarly, add the **ListCount**, **ListIndex**, **Style**, and **Text** properties to the interface. Figure 13.25 shows the Select Interface Members dialog box. Click Next to proceed.

Figure 13.24. The Test Bound Control form.

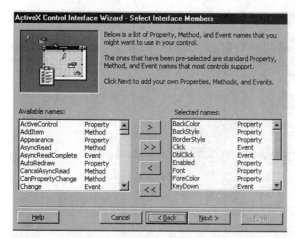

Figure 13.25. The ActiveX Control Interface
Wizard - Select Interface Members dialog box.

6. Click New to add the properties, methods, and events listed in
Table 13.21. Click Next to proceed.

Table 13.21. The properties and method for the Bound Combo control.

TYPE	NAME	DESCRIPTION
Property	objDatabase	Object variable to contain the open database object from which the combo box should be loaded.
Property	strCodeType	Value for code type to select—for example, HAIRCOLOR.
Method	Reload	Reloads the list box from the database.

7. Use the Set Mapping dialog box (see Figure 13.26) to map most of the
public interface properties, methods, and events to the constituent combo
box control by selecting most of the public names from the lefthand list
box and then selecting cmbCodeValue from the Control pull-down list. *Do
not map* the objDatabase and strSqlWhere properties nor the Refresh
method. Click Next to proceed.

8. Set the attributes of the unmapped interface members using the Set
Attributes dialog box shown in Figure 13.27. The attribute values are
shown in Table 13.22.

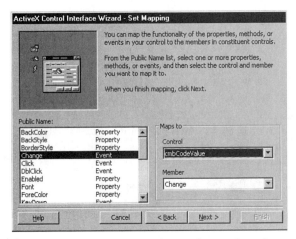

Figure 13.26. The Control Interface Wizard - Set Mapping dialog box.

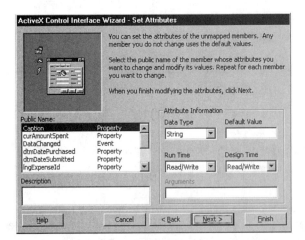

Figure 13.27. The Control Interface Wizard - Set Attributes dialog box.

Table 13.22. Members and properties for the Bound Combo control.

MEMBER	DATA TYPE	RUNTIME	DESIGN-TIME	DESCRIPTION
objDatabase	Object	Write Only	Not Available	Open database object supplied at runtime by container.
strCodeType	String	Read/Write	Read/Write	Code value type to retrieve.

9. Add the following code as for the UserControl Resize event:

```
Private Sub UserControl_Resize()
' Resize the combo box to the size of the control

' The height can't be changed for certain styles, so
    ' we won't support any height changes.
    Height = cmbCodeValue.Height
    ' Resize the combo box without using the Move method.
    cmbCodeValue.Top = 0
    cmbCodeValue.Left = 0
    cmbCodeValue.Width = ScaleWidth

End Sub
```

10. Make the UserControl project by selecting File | Make BoundComboControl.ocx from the main menu. Correct any compilation errors you find before proceeding.

11. Select File | Add Project from the main menu. Select Standard EXE from the Add Project dialog box. Name the default form **frmTestBoundCombo** and the project **prjTestBoundCombo**. Save the project group and name the group **TestBoundGroup** when prompted.

12. Close the **cmbBoundControl** design window to activate the control in design mode. Test the resize event code by resizing the control on the form.

13. Define the **Text** property to be a data-bound field on the form. Make the control's code the active window in Visual Basic by opening and clicking in the window. Select Tools | Procedure Attributes from the main menu, and select **Text** as the name. Click Advanced to show more options. Check all four options in the Data Binding frame. (See Figure 13.28.)

14. Modify the **Text Property Let** procedure to look like the following code. The **CanPropertyChange** function asks the container whether the specified value can be changed and the return value should be observed, even though Visual Basic currently always returns **True**.

```
Public Property Let Text(ByVal New_Text As String)
    If CanPropertyChange("Text") Then
        cmbCodeValue.Text() = New_Text
        PropertyChanged "Text"
    End If
End Property
```

15. Add the following code to the **Change** event of **cmbDataBound** to make sure that the container knows that something changed:

```
Private Sub cmbCodeValue_Change()

    ' Notify the container of data change
    PropertyChanged "Text"

End Sub
```

Figure 13.28. The Procedure
Attributes for a data-bound
property.

16. Add a `PropertyChanged` call to the `Click` event of `cmbDataBound`:

```
Private Sub cmbCodeValue_Click()
    RaiseEvent Click
    PropertyChanged "Text"
End Sub
```

17. Modify the wizard-generated `Reload` method to be a procedure (`Sub`)
rather than a function, and add the following code to fill the combo box:

```
Public Sub Reload()
' Reload the combo box
Dim strSql As String
Dim rsCodes As Recordset

    cmbCodeValue.Clear
    ' If the code type has been set
    If "" <> strCodeType Then
        ' Build an SQL statement.
        strSql = "SELECT CodeValue10 FROM Code10 WHERE " _
                 & "CodeType10 = '" & strCodeType _
                 & "' ORDER BY CodeValue10"
        'Get a recordset.
        Set rsCodes = objDatabase.OpenRecordset(strSql, _
                    vbRSTypeSnapShot, dbForwardOnly)
        Do While Not rsCodes.EOF
            ' Add the items.
            cmbCodeValue.AddItem "" & rsCodes("CodeValue10")
            rsCodes.MoveNext
        Loop
    End If
```

```
'Close the recordset
rsCodes.Close

Exit Sub

End Sub
```

18. Modify the objDatabase Property Set routine to invoke the Reload method:

```
Public Property Set objDatabase(ByVal New_objDatabase As Object)

    Set m_objDatabase = New_objDatabase
    PropertyChanged "objDatabase"

    ' Set the object database and invoke the Reload method to
    ' put data into the combo box
    If "" <> strCodeType Then
        Call Reload
    End If

End Property
```

19. Complete building the TestBoundControl form by adding fields, labels, and a data control until it looks as shown in Figure 13.20. Table 13.23 lists the form's objects and properties.

Table 13.23. Objects and properties for the Test Bound Control form.

OBJECT	PROPERTY	SETTING
Form	Name	frmTestBoundCombo
	Caption	"Test Bound Control"
Data	Name	dtaSuspects
	Caption	"Criminal Suspects"
	Connect	"Access"
	DatabaseName	"D:\Waite\Chapter.13\How-to.E02\CodeValues.mdb"
	RecordSource	"Subject"
ctlBoundCombo	Name	usrEyeBound
	DataField	"EyeColor"
	DataSource	"dtaSuspects"
	strCodeType	"EYECOLOR"
ctlBoundCombo	Name	usrHairBound
	DataField	"HairClr"
	DataSource	"dtaSuspects"
	strCodeType	"HAIRCOLOR"

continued on next page

continued from previous page

OBJECT	PROPERTY	SETTING
ctlBoundCombo	Name	usrReligionBound
	DataField	"Religion"
	DataSource	"dtaSuspects"
	strCodeType	"RELIGION"
ctlBoundCombo	Name	usrMarStatBound
	DataField	"MaritalStatus"
	DataSource	"dtaSuspects"
	strCodeType	"MAR STAT"
TextBox	Name	txtSuspectId
	DataField	"SuspectId"
	DataSource	"dtaSuspects"
	Enabled	0 'False
TextBox	Name	txtLastName
	DataField	"LastName"
	DataSource	"dtaSuspects"
TextBox	Name	txtFirstName
	DataField	"FirstName"
	DataSource	"dtaSuspects"
TextBox	Name	txtMiddleName
	DataField	"MiddleName"
	DataSource	"dtaSuspects"
TextBox	Name	txtAlias
	DataField	"Alias"
	DataSource	"dtaSuspects"
Label	Name	Label1
	AutoSize	-1 'True
	Caption	"SuspectId:"
Label	Name	Label2
	AutoSize	-1 'True
	Caption	"Last Name:"
Label	Name	Label3
	AutoSize	-1 'True
	Caption	"First Name:"
Label	Name	Label4
	AutoSize	-1 'True
	Caption	"Middle Name:"

OBJECT	PROPERTY	SETTING
Label	Name	Label5
	AutoSize	-1 'True
	Caption	"Alias:"
Label	Name	Label6
	AutoSize	-1 'True
	Caption	"Eye Color:"
Label	Name	Label7
	AutoSize	-1 'True
	Caption	"Hair Color:"
Label	Name	Label8
	AutoSize	-1 'True
	Caption	"Religion:"
Label	Name	Label9
	AutoSize	-1 'True
	Caption	"Marital Status:"

20. Add the following code to the Form_Load event:

```
Private Sub Form_Load()

    dtaSuspects.DatabaseName = App.Path & "\CodeValues.mdb"
    dtaSuspects.Refresh
    ' Initialize the bound combo controls
    Set usrEyeBound.objDatabase = dtaSuspects.Database
    Set usrHairBound.objDatabase = dtaSuspects.Database
    Set usrReligionBound.objDatabase = dtaSuspects.Database
    Set usrMarStatBound.objDatabase = dtaSuspects.Database

End Sub
```

How It Works

When the form loads, the **Set** statements for the bound combo boxes cause the combo boxes to be filled. Any time the combo box contents are changed by a click or change event, **PropertyChanged** is called to inform the containing form that a bound control has changed. The container, in turn, notifies the **dtaSuspects** data control. Most of the control code was generated by the ActiveX Control Interface Wizard to propagate constituent control properties to the bound control.

The ActiveX Interface Control Wizard provides a capable tool for building and extending your own component library. This bound combo box control for displaying code values runs faster than a **DBCombo** control and reduces the visual clutter of its containing form at design time. With a little more work, it could be extended to include a single property page to browse for the Code Types through design-time SQL statements, as well as setting the underlying combo box style.

Comments

The advantage of working with The ActiveX Interface Control Wizard is in the robustness and automated checklist it gives you in the creation of your control. The wizard reminds the developer about *all* the properties and methods of constituent controls in order to ensure that the properties and methods expected by a developer are seamlessly implemented into the control's behavior.

CHAPTER 14

ADVANCED DATABASE TECHNIQUES

14.

ADVANCED DATABASE TECHNIQUES

How do I...

Many times, there's just one more thing that needs to be done for everything to work correctly. The How-To's in this chapter cover various advanced features of database programming that help polish your applications. The database backup and replication features are particularly valuable because they can help you reduce support time and costs for your applications. A simple automated backup program in the Windows startup group can save hours of headaches after your application or customer has made a serious mistake.

14.1 Search for Database Records Using a Soundex Algorithm

The Soundex feature available in many database management systems (DBMSs) allows searching for names of people, places, or streets without knowing the exact spelling. This How-To demonstrates using the Soundex function and points out some common problems with its use.

14.2 Back Up Selected Database Objects at a Set Schedule

The `SQL SELECT...INTO` statement provides a smooth way to perform a very selective online backup. This How-To uses an enhanced ActiveX timer control to periodically back-up selected database objects.

14.3 Replicate a Database Using the Jet Engine

Access and the Jet engine allow you to copy databases and keep their contents synchronized in different locations. This How-To demonstrates creating and synchronizing a replicated database.

14.4 Omit Specified Objects from Replicas

By default, replication makes copies of everything in your database. This How-To demonstrates keeping some objects local when making a replica set.

14.5 Create a Nonreplicated Version of a Replicated Database

Strictly speaking, you cannot make a nonreplicated version of a replicated database, but you can remove a replica from the replica set and change the replica so that its structure can be modified. This How-To changes a replica database into a standalone database.

COMPLEXITY
BEGINNING

14.1 How do I...

Search for database records using a Soundex algorithm?

Problem

The people answering the telephones in the order entry department sometimes have a difficult time understanding people's names when they call in. How can I write more forgiving SQL queries to look up names?

Technique

This How-To uses the Soundex function of Microsoft SQL Server. The sample SQL statements should also work with Sybase databases. Soundex is an encoding method for converting character strings into four digit codes. The goal is to provide a fuzzier search pattern for people trying find name-based data.

Steps

1. Connect to a SQL database from your workstation using a SQL command processor such as ISQL/W.

2. Issue the following commands to set up a test environment and open the file SOUNDEX.SQL from the How-To directory:

```
if exists (select * from sysobjects
    where id = object_id('dbo.SoundexText') and sysstat & 0xf = 3)
    drop table dbo.SoundexTest
GO

CREATE TABLE dbo.SoundexTest (
    LastName char (20) NULL ,
    FirstName char (20) NULL
)
GO

INSERT INTO SoundexTest VALUES ('Brown', 'Laura')
INSERT INTO SoundexTest VALUES ('Browne', 'Laura')
INSERT INTO SoundexTest VALUES ('Brun', 'Laura')
INSERT INTO SoundexTest VALUES ('Braun', 'Laura')
INSERT INTO SoundexTest VALUES ('Broom', 'Laura')

INSERT INTO SoundexTest VALUES ('Harper', 'Bill');
INSERT INTO SoundexTest VALUES ('Harpster', 'Bill');
INSERT INTO SoundexTest VALUES ('Hahpah', 'Bill');
INSERT INTO SoundexTest VALUES ('Hobber', 'Bill');
INSERT INTO SoundexTest VALUES ('Hopper', 'Bill');
INSERT INTO SoundexTest VALUES ('Hooper', 'Bill');

INSERT INTO SoundexTest VALUES ('Kennedy', 'Dennis');
INSERT INTO SoundexTest VALUES ('Kenney', 'Dennis');
INSERT INTO SoundexTest VALUES ('Kennealy', 'Dennis');
INSERT INTO SoundexTest VALUES ('Kenney', 'Dennis');
```

3. Issue the following SELECT statement to verify that all rows were inserted into the database. All rows should be retrieved and displayed as in Table 14.1.

```
SELECT * FROM SoundexTest ORDER BY LastName, FirstName
```

Table 14.1. SELECT all rows results.

LAST NAME	FIRST NAME
Braun	Laura
Broom	Laura
Brown	Laura
Browne	Laura
Brun	Laura
Hahpah	Bill
Harper	Bill
Harpster	Bill
Hobber	Bill
Hooper	Bill
Hopper	Bill
Kennealy	Dennis
Kennedy	Dennis
Kenney	Dennis
Kenney	Dennis

4. Issue a Soundex SELECT to find "Brown." Table 14.2 shows all five Lauras.

```
SELECT * FROM SoundexTest
WHERE SOUNDEX (LastName) = SOUNDEX ('Brown')
ORDER BY LastName, FirstName
```

Table 14.2. SELECT SOUNDEX ('Brown') results.

LAST NAME	FIRST NAME
Braun	Laura
Broom	Laura
Brown	Laura
Browne	Laura
Brun	Laura

5. Use Soundex to find the various "Harper" records. Table 14.3 shows the results for various search targets.

```
SELECT * FROM SoundexTest
WHERE SOUNDEX (LastName) = SOUNDEX ('Harper')
ORDER BY LastName, FirstName

SELECT * FROM SoundexTest
WHERE SOUNDEX (LastName) = SOUNDEX ('Harp')
ORDER BY LastName, FirstName
```

```
SELECT * FROM SoundexTest
WHERE SOUNDEX (LastName) = SOUNDEX ('Hopper')
ORDER BY LastName, FirstName
```

Table 14.3. SELECT SOUNDEX results with different keys.

TARGET	LAST NAME	FIRST NAME
"Harper"	Harper	Bill
	Hahpah	Bill
	Harper	Bill
	Harpster	Bill
	Hooper	Bill
	Hopper	Bill
"Harp"	No records returned	
	Hahpah	Bill
	Harper	Bill
	Harpster	Bill
	Hooper	Bill
	Hopper	Bill
"Hopper"	Hooper	Bill
	Hopper	Bill

How It Works

The Soundex algorithm was established by the United States government to provide name searching for the Social Security Administration and the National Archives. The Soundex code is created by taking the first letter of the string and then adding values according to Table 14.4.

Table 14.4. Soundex coding guide.

CODE DIGIT	LETTER
0	All others or word too short
1	B, P, F, V
2	C, S, G, J, K, Q, X, Z
3	D, T
4	L
5	M, N
6	R

Table 14.5 shows the generated Soundex code and the last name for our sample data. Usually, Soundex will give a reasonable result, but it can make some interesting mistakes if the "R" is missed in a query. Notice in particular that the Soundex for "Harper" and "Hopper" don't match. Soundex can also be problematic if too few letters are provided for coding. Because all vowels and the silent letters H, Y, and W are dropped from the coding digits, a Soundex search for "BR" will not return any of our "B" names.

Table 14.5. Soundex coding results.

SOUNDEX CODE	LAST NAME
B650	Brown
B650	Browne
B650	Brun
B650	Braun
B650	Broom
H616	Harper
H612	Harpster
H100	Hahpah
H160	Hopper
H160	Hobber
H160	Hooper
K530	Kennedy
K500	Kenney
K540	Kennealy

Comments

This sample showed a way to use the SOUNDEX function in queries. Unfortunately, these SELECT statements are very inefficient because they force the database manager to examine each row of the table. If SOUNDEX makes sense for your application, try to create a column whose value is the SOUNDEX of the target column, and then create an index on the SOUNDEX column.

COMPLEXITY
INTERMEDIATE

14.2 How do I...
Back up selected database objects at a set schedule?

Problem

There are several tables in my database that need to be automatically backed up periodically. How can I force an automatic backup on a periodic basis?

Technique

The solution to this problem requires two core components: an enhanced timer and a database backup routine. The enhanced timer will be implemented as an ActiveX control that supports a "time to trigger" property and notification event. The database backup routine will create a new database and use a `SELECT...INTO` statement to implement the selective backup. The remainder of the project is a test form.

The extended timer control is required because the standard Visual Basic control only supports timers of approximately one minute in length. The extended timer control is driven by the `TimeToTrigger` property and will raise its `ExtendedTimerPop` event once per day at the specified time. The standard Visual Basic timer is repeatedly enabled until the time to trigger is within one minute of the current time. Then, the Visual Basic timer is set to the precise number of seconds required to meet the `TimeToTrigger` property exactly.

Steps

Open the Backup.vbg project group to preview this project. Compile the enhanced timer control and then the Backup Test project. Run the Backup Test project (see Figure 14.1). Enter a near future time in the Trigger Time field, and click the Start Timer button. Wait patiently until your system clock is one minute past the trigger time. Close the form and check in the application directory for a newly created backup copy of the Expense.MDB file whose name begins with the letters "BU" (for backup).

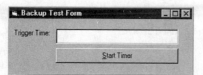

Figure 14.1. The Backup Test Form dialog box.

1. Create a new ActiveX Control project. Name the control
`ctlEnhancedTimer` and the project `prjEnhancedTimer`.

2. Select the `ctlEnhancedTimer` control and set its `InvisibleAtRunTime`
property to `True`.

3. Draw a single timer control on the object and name it `tmrCheckIt`. Save
the project.

4. Select Add-Ins | Add-In Manager from the main menu, and make sure that
the VB ActiveX Control Interface Wizard is available in your environment
by clicking its checkbox. Select Add-Ins | ActiveX Control Interface
Wizard from the main menu.

5. Click the Next button to proceed to the Select Interface Members dialog
box (see Figure 14.2). Remove all names except the enabled property from
the Selected names window on the right.

6. Click Next to proceed to Create Custom Interface Members. Add the
single property and event listed in Table 14.6 to the control.

Table 14.6. Property and event for the extended timer control.

TYPE	NAME	DESCRIPTION
Property	TimeToTrigger	Date/Time variable to contain the desired trigger time for timer.
Event	ExtendedTimerPop	Notifies the container that the TimeToTrigger has arrived.

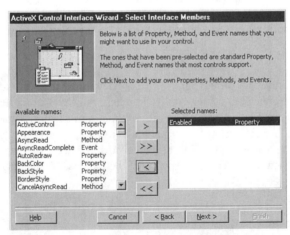

Figure 14.2. The Select Interface Members
dialog box.

7. Click Next to proceed to the Wizard's Set Mapping dialog box. Select the public name `Enabled` and map it to the timer control's `Enabled` member, as shown in Figure 14.3.

8. Click Next to set attributes for the extended timer control. Use the Wizard's dialog box to set the `TimeToTrigger` property to be a Date variable with read/write capabilities at both runtime and design time.

9. Click Finish to have the Wizard complete the skeleton code.

10. Add a Boolean control variable to the Declarations section of the user control. This variable determines whether the last internal timer has been set for final event notification to the container.

```
Option Explicit
'Default Property Values:
Const m_def_TimeToTrigger = 0
'Property Variables:
Dim m_TimeToTrigger As Date
'Event Declarations:
Event ExtendedTimerPop()

' Private control variable
Private m_bLastInternalTimer As Boolean
```

11. Add the `SetTimer` helper procedure to set the internal timer control's interval property:

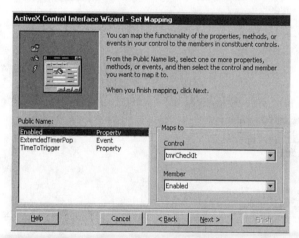

Figure 14.3. Mapping the timer control member.

```
Private Function SetTimer() As Integer
' Determine if this should be the last internal
' timer call
    Dim lDifference As Long

    lDifference = DateDiff("s", TimeValue(Now()), _
                  TimeValue(TimeToTrigger))
    If lDifference < 30 And lDifference > 0 Then
        ' This is the last timer to use
        m_bLastInternalTimer = True
        SetTimer = CInt(lDifference) * 1000
    Else
        ' Set timer for 30 more seconds
        m_bLastInternalTimer = False
        SetTimer = 30000
    End If

End Function
```

12. Add the following code to the timer event of the contained timer to implement a continuous, event-fired loop to achieve the desired long timer:

```
Private Sub tmrCheckIt_Timer()
' Handle the internal timer pop

    If m_bLastInternalTimer Then
        ' Notify the container
        tmrCheckIt.Enabled = False
        RaiseEvent ExtendedTimerPop
    Else
        ' Wait a while longer
        tmrCheckIt.Interval = SetTimer()
        tmrCheckIt.Enabled = True
    End If

End Sub
```

13. Add the following code to the `UserControl_InitProperties` procedure to set the initial timer value:

```
Private Sub UserControl_InitProperties()
' Set up the timer variables

    ' Set the timer
    If Ambient.UserMode = True Then
        tmrCheckIt.Interval = SetTimer()
    End If

    m_TimeToTrigger = m_def_TimeToTrigger

End Sub
```

14. Add the following boldface code to the `Property Let Enabled` procedure. The interval must be set correctly if the container enables the extended timer control at runtime.

```
Public Property Let Enabled(ByVal New_Enabled As Boolean)
    If Ambient.UserMode = True Then
        tmrCheckIt.Interval = SetTimer()
    End If
    tmrCheckIt.Enabled() = New_Enabled
    PropertyChanged "Enabled"
End Property
```

15. Add the following code to the `Property Let TimeToTrigger` procedure. The check for a valid date is required to prevent invalid calculations.

```
Public Property Let TimeToTrigger(ByVal New_TimeToTrigger As Date)

    ' Check that the new value is a valid date.
    If Not IsDate(New_TimeToTrigger) Then
        Err.Raise 380
        Err.Clear
        Exit Property
    End If

    m_TimeToTrigger = New_TimeToTrigger
    PropertyChanged "TimeToTrigger"
End Property
```

16. Add the following code to the `UserControl_Resize` procedure to keep the control approximately the same size as the timer control:

```
Private Sub UserControl_Resize()
' Resize the user control to a fixed size

    Size 420, 420

End Sub
```

17. Select File | Make EnhancedTimer.ocx from the Visual Basic main menu to compile the control. Correct any compilation errors.

18. Select File | Add Project from the main menu, and add a new Standard EXE project to your Visual Basic environment. Name the default form `frmBackupTest`. Name the new project `prjBackupTest`. Save the project group and all its components. Name the project group `Backup` when prompted.

19. Test the design-time behavior of the control by drawing the control on the form and experimenting with resizing the control.

20. Add a textbox, label, and command button to the test form and set the properties as listed in Table 14.7.

Table 14.7. Objects and properties for the Backup Test form.

OBJECT	PROPERTY	SETTING
Form	Name	frmBackupTest
	Caption	"Backup Test Form"
CommandButton	Name	cmdStartTimer
	Caption	"&Start Timer"
TextBox	Name	txtTriggerTime
ctlEnhancedTimer	Name	ctlEnhancedTimer1
Label	Name	Label1
	AutoSize	-1 'True
	Caption	"Trigger Time:"

21. Add the following code to the `cmdStartTimer_Click` procedure to set the time to trigger and to enable the control:

```
Private Sub cmdStartTimer_Click()
' Start the timer

    If Not IsDate(txtTriggerTime.Text) Then
        MsgBox "Invalid time format"
    Else
        ctlEnhancedTimer1.TimeToTrigger = txtTriggerTime.Text
        ctlEnhancedTimer1.Enabled = True
    End If

End Sub
```

22. Add the following code to the `ctlEnhancedTimer1_ExtendedTimerPop` procedure to allow for control testing before beginning on the database backup code:

```
Private Sub ctlEnhancedTimer1_ExtendedTimerPop()

    Debug.Print "Extended timer pop"

End Sub
```

23. Compile and test the form. Be sure to save the project group.

24. In the project group window, make the `prjBackupTest` project active by highlighting it with the mouse. Select Project | Add Class Module from the Visual Basic main menu. When the Add Class Module dialog box appears, as in Figure 14.4, select VB Class Builder.

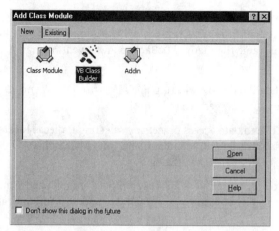

Figure 14.4. The Add Class Module dialog box.

25. Select File | New Class from the Class Builder menu. Name the class `clsBackupTable` and click OK.

26. Highlight `clsBackupTable` in the Class Builder Classes window. Add the properties listed in Table 14.8 to the class by selecting File | New Property from the Class Builder menu or by right-clicking in the Properties tab. Figure 14.5 shows the completed Properties tab.

Table 14.8. Properties for the `clsBackupTable` module.

NAME	DATA TYPE	DECLARATION
TableName	String	Public Property
Database	Object	Public Property

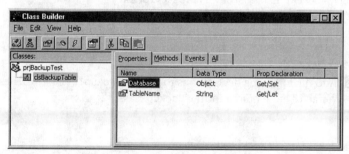

Figure 14.5. The completed Properties tab for `clsBackupTable`.

27. Click on the Class Builder Methods tab. Add a new method by selecting File | New method from the Class Builder menu or by right-clicking on the Methods tab. Name the method **DoBackup** and give it no arguments and no return data type.

28. Exit from Class Builder by selecting File | Exit from the menu. Update the project with your changes. Save the project group.

29. Add a reference to data access objects by selecting Project | References from the Visual Basic main menu and checking Microsoft DAO 3.5 Object Library. Click OK to close the dialog box.

30. Add the following code to the **DoBackup** procedure to actually implement the table backup by creating a new .MDB file and copying the data:

```
Public Sub DoBackup()
Dim strDbName As String, strSql As String
Dim dbNew As Database

    On Error GoTo DbError
    ' Format a database name from the current time
    strDbName = Format(Now, "Buyyyymmmddhhnnss") & ".mdb"
    strDbName = App.Path & "\" & strDbName
    ' Make sure there isn't already a file with the name of
    ' the new database.
    If Dir(strDbName) <> "" Then Kill strDbName

    ' Create the new database
    Set dbNew = Workspaces(0).CreateDatabase(strDbName, dbLangGeneral)
    ' Create a SQL command string to create the backup
    strSql = "SELECT " & TableName & ".* INTO " _
             & TableName & " IN '" & strDbName _
             & "' FROM " & TableName
    mvarDatabase.Execute strSql

    Exit Sub

DbError:
    Err.Raise Err.Number, Err.Source, Err.Description
    Err.Clear
    Exit Sub

End Sub
```

31. Add the following declarations to the **frmBackupTest** form. These variables are required for the **Backup** class.

```
Option Explicit

Private usrBackupTable As New clsBackupTable
Private dbOpenDb As Database
```

32. Add a `Form_Load` procedure to initialize the `Backup` class:

```
Private Sub Form_Load()
Dim strDbName As String

    On Error GoTo DbError
    strDbName = App.Path & "\Expense.mdb"
    ' Open a database for the Backup class to use
    Set dbOpenDb = Workspaces(0).OpenDatabase(strDbName)
    Set usrBackupTable.Database = dbOpenDb
    usrBackupTable.TableName = "Expenses"
    Exit Sub

DbError:
    MsgBox Err.Description & " from " & Err.Source _
        & " Number = " & CStr(Err.Number)
    End

End Sub
```

33. Complete the `ctlEnhancedTimer1_ExtendedTimerPop` procedure by adding an invocation of the `DoBackup` procedure. Don't forget the error handler.

```
Private Sub ctlEnhancedTimer1_ExtendedTimerPop()

    On Error GoTo BackupError

    Debug.Print "Extended timer pop"
    usrBackupTable.DoBackup
    ' Restart the timer
    ctlEnhancedTimer1.Enabled = True
    Exit Sub

BackupError:
    MsgBox Err.Description & " from " & Err.Source _
        & " Number = " & CStr(Err.Number)
    Exit Sub

End Sub
```

How It Works

Examine the `ctlEnhancedTimer1_ExtendedTimerPop` procedure (step 33) to see the core of the automatic backup logic. When the timer pops, the `DoBackup` procedure is invoked and the timer is restarted. The `Form_Load` procedure initializes the `Backup` class, and the button click initially sets the timer.

Comments

In addition to solving a particular problem, this How-To demonstrated the use of component programming to promote code reuse. The `BackupTable` class can have many uses outside of this project, especially if it was modified to allow multiple table names instead of just one. A variation on the `BackupTable` class could also be used in a program placed in the Windows Startup program group to provide an automatic backup every time Windows is restarted.

The enhanced timer control can simplify many aspects of your current timer programs because it works reliably for more than a minute. You might want to consider adding a schedule table to the enhanced timer control to allow for multiple events or a schedule such as daily, weekly, or monthly.

COMPLEXITY
INTERMEDIATE

14.3 How do I...
Replicate a database using the Jet engine?

Problem

The sales representatives in our company like to enter their expense reports on their laptop computers. How can I capture the expenses they enter in the field into the main expense database file?

Technique

Jet database replication allows you to create database copies and keep them synchronized. Both database design and contents are copied whenever the databases are synchronized. Replication creation requires that you make one database your design master and then invoke the `MakeReplica` method to create additional database copies. Use the `Synchronize` method to make the data consistent between two databases.

Steps

Open the project Replicate.vbp (see Figure 14.6). Use the browse buttons and select a source and replica database name. Do not choose a database you care for a great deal because it will be changed. Click Create Replica to create a replica database. Use the VisData data maintenance utility (in the VB5 directory) to change a record in one of the databases. Click Synchronize. Use VisData to verify the change was propagated to the other database.

1. Create a new Standard EXE project in your workspace. Name the default form `frmReplicate` and the project `prjReplicate`. Save the form and project to disk.

2. Select Project | Components from the main menu, and check Microsoft Common Dialog Control 5.0 (see Figure 14.7). Select Project | References from the Visual Basic main menu and activate the Microsoft DAO 3.5 Object Library by checking its box in the selection list.

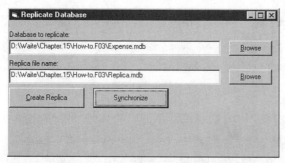

Figure 14.6. The Replicate Database form.

Figure 14.7. Selecting the Microsoft
Common Dialog Control 5.0.

3. Draw textboxes, labels, command buttons, and a common dialog control
on the form as shown in Figure 14.6. Set the form's objects and properties
as listed in Table 14.9.

Table 14.9. Objects and properties for the Replicate Database form.

OBJECT	PROPERTY	SETTING
Form	Name	frmReplicate
	Caption	"Replicate Database"
CommandButton	Name	cmdOpenTo
	Caption	"&Browse"

continued on next page

continued from previous page

OBJECT	PROPERTY	SETTING
CommandButton	Name	cmdSynchronize
	Caption	"S&ynchronize"
CommandButton	Name	cmdCreateReplica
	Caption	"&Create Replica"
CommandButton	Name	cmdOpenFrom
	Caption	"&Browse"
TextBox	Name	txtReplicaDbName
TextBox	Name	txtDbNameFrom
CommonDialog	Name	cdOpenFile
	Filter	"Access Files (*.mdb)¦*.mdb"
Label	Name	Label1
	AutoSize	-1 'True
	Caption	"Database to replicate:"
Label	Name	Label2
	AutoSize	-1 'True
	Caption	"Replica file name:"

4. Add the following code to the Browse button procedures:

```
Private Sub cmdOpenFrom_Click()
' Open the Replicate from database file
    cdOpenFile.InitDir = App.Path
    cdOpenFile.ShowOpen
    txtDbNameFrom.Text = cdOpenFile.filename

End Sub

Private Sub cmdOpenTo_Click()
' Open the Replicate to database file
    cdOpenFile.InitDir = App.Path
    cdOpenFile.filename = "Replica.mdb"
    cdOpenFile.ShowOpen
    txtReplicaDbName.Text = cdOpenFile.filename

End Sub
```

5. Add the `MakeReplicable` procedure to the form's code. This procedure checks for the existence of the `Replicable` property, adds it if needed, and sets the value to "T" to make the "from" database a Design Master.

```
Function MakeReplicable(ByRef dbMaster As Database) As Boolean
' Makes the passed database replicable
Dim prpReplicable As Property
Dim intIdx As Integer
Dim bFound As Boolean

    On Error GoTo DbError
```

```
    ' Check for existence of the replicable property
    For intIdx = 0 To (dbMaster.Properties.Count - 1)
        If dbMaster.Properties(intIdx).Name = "Replicable" Then
            bFound = True
            Exit For
        End If
    Next

    If Not bFound Then
        ' Create the property
        Set prpReplicable = dbMaster.CreateProperty("Replicable", _
                        dbText, "T")
        ' Append it to the collection
        dbMaster.Properties.Append prpReplicable
    End If

    ' Set the value of Replicable to true.
    dbMaster.Properties("Replicable").Value = "T"

    MakeReplicable = True

    Exit Function

DbError:
    MsgBox Err.Description & " From: " & Err.Source _
            & "Number: " & Err.Number
    MakeReplicable = False
    Exit Function

End Function
```

6. Add the `CopyReplica` helper function. This function actually creates a replica database using the "from" database as a source.

```
Function CopyReplica(ByRef dbMaster As Database, strRepName As String) _
    As Boolean
' Makes a replica database from the passed master

    On Error GoTo DbError

    ' If the target file exists, purge it
    If Dir(strRepName) <> "" Then Kill strRepName

    dbMaster.MakeReplica strRepName, "Replica of " & dbMaster.Name

    CopyReplica = True

    Exit Function

DbError:
    MsgBox Err.Description & " From: " & Err.Source _
            & "Number: " & Err.Number
    CopyReplica = False
    Exit Function

End Function
```

7. Add the following code to the `cmdCreateReplica_Click` procedure. This procedure gains exclusive control of the database, makes it a Design Master, and creates the specified replica. The `bContinue` Boolean prevents proceeding past an error.

```
Private Sub cmdCreateReplica_Click()
' Create a replica from the named database
Dim dbMaster As Database
Dim bContinue As Boolean

    On Error GoTo DbError

    ' Open the database in exclusive mode
    Set dbMaster = Workspaces(0).OpenDatabase(txtDbNameFrom.Text, True)

    ' Make the database the Design Master
    bContinue = MakeReplicable(dbMaster)

    ' Make the replica
    bContinue = CopyReplica(dbMaster, txtReplicaDbName.Text)

    dbMaster.Close

    Exit Sub

DbError:
    MsgBox Err.Description & " From: " & Err.Source _
            & "Number: " & Err.Number
    Exit Sub

End Sub
```

8. Add the code for the `cmdSynchronize_Click` procedure. This procedure synchronizes the contents of two databases in the same replica set with each other.

```
Private Sub cmdSynchronize_Click()

Dim dbMaster As Database

    On Error GoTo DbError

    ' Open the database in non-exclusive mode
    Set dbMaster = Workspaces(0).OpenDatabase(txtDbNameFrom.Text, False)

    ' Synchronize the databases
    dbMaster.Synchronize txtReplicaDbName.Text, _
                dbRepImpExpChanges

    dbMaster.Close

    Exit Sub

DbError:
    MsgBox Err.Description & " From: " & Err.Source _
```

```
                    & "Number: " & Err.Number
        Exit Sub

End Sub
```

How It Works

When you replicate databases, Jet modifies the database properties and the structure of your tables substantially in order to track record and design changes. The `Synchronize` method uses these additional structures to track database design and data changes and apply the changes consistently over many databases.

The core concept of replication is the *replica set* governed by a single *Design Master* database. The Design Master is the place where all design changes must occur for all replicas. A database is a member of a replica set if it was created as a replica of the Design Master or as a replica of an existing replica. Any member of the replica set can synchronize data with any other member of the replica set. Figure 14.8 shows the basic relationships.

Database Modifications

Jet makes several database modifications when you make a database replicable. Once these changes are made, most of them are permanent.

The new database properties are `Replicable`, `ReplicaID`, and `DesignMasterID`. The `Replicable` property indicates that the database can be replicated and that the table structures have been modified. Once a database has been made replicable with the addition of the `Replicable` property, the `ReplicaID` is a unique identifier for this database file.

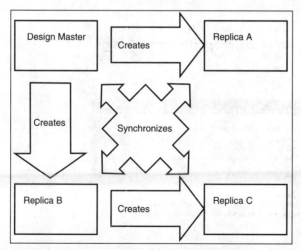

Figure 14.8. Replica set showing creation and synchronization.

The `DesignMasterID` is a unique identifier specifying the database that can initiate all design changes for the replica set. Jet replication uses *GUIDs* (globally unique identifiers) wherever it needs a unique key for a database or field value. A GUID is a 16-byte generated value that is designed to be unique no matter where or when it is assigned. GUID values are usually displayed in hexadecimal notation with added hyphens for visual clarity. The database that is the Design Master has the same values for `ReplicaID` and `DesignMasterID`. Figure 14.9 shows the important database properties for a Design Master database as viewed by the VisData application that ships with Visual Basic. Figure 14.10 shows the same properties for a replica. Note that the `DesignMasterID` GUID is the same as the `ReplicaID` GUID for the Design Master database. The replica database in Figure 14.10 has the `ReplicaID` of the Design Master database as its `DesignMasterID`. Equal values for `ReplicaID` and `DesignMasterID` are what define a database as a Design Master.

In addition to database property changes, making a database replicable adds about a dozen system tables to the database to track the Design Master, other

Figure 14.9. Database properties for a Design Master.

Figure 14.10. Database properties for a replica.

replicas, table aliases, schema design problems, synchronization system errors, local replica-to-replica exchange logs, data conflicts, schedules, deleted records, and generation history. Because of all the property and system table changes, making a database replicable is a permanent operation. Once the `Replicable` database property is set to `"T"`, it cannot be changed.

Table Modifications

In addition to database modifications, replication changes the table structures by adding three columns: a unique identifier, a generation identifier, and a lineage indicator. The unique identifier is stored in the `s_GUID` column and contains a globally unique identifier for this record in any replica.

The generation identifier is used to speed up incremental synchronization so that only changed records need to be sent to other replicas. Each time a record is changed, the generation number is set to 0. At synchronization time, all records with generation number 0 are sent. The generation number is then set at both databases to one higher than the last generation number assigned. In addition, records with higher generation numbers are sent because they reflect more recent changes. Record additions and deletions are also reconciled between the two databases.

The lineage indicator is used to help resolve conflicts between simultaneous updates to data in different databases. When the same record is updated in two different replicas, a conflict may result. The `Synchronize` method resolves this conflict by using the `s_Lineage` field to determine which record will be placed into both databases. The losing database will have a copy of the losing record in a table named *table_name*_Conflict, where *table_name* is the original table name. For example, a conflict-losing record from the Expenses table would be saved at the losing location only into the Expenses_Conflict table.

Comments

Replication is a powerful tool in your database programming kit, but will require careful planning to implement successfully. Design considerations for replicated databases can become problematic because of our friend Murphy of the famous law ("If anything can go wrong, it will go wrong, and at the worst possible time"). I believe that Murphy might have been an optimist when it comes to complex replication schemes. Microsoft's core replication technology does a marvelous job of managing *one-way* replication. "One-way" implies that the data will be changed in only one location. With central administration, one-way data is the contents of list boxes, zip code tables, and product definitions that you want to push out to field laptops. For data collection, one-way means that a central site is collecting from multiple remote sites.

Two-way replication increases programming requirements because of the need to design and develop conflict-resolution programs and procedures. The placement of conflict-losing records into only one database might make it difficult to implement conflict-resolution programs in the desired location. For example, a sales automation application might want all conflict resolutions managed at the home office, but the Synchronize method might place a conflict notification into a sales rep's laptop in East Podunk. Handcrafted code may then be required to find the remote conflicts and transport them back to the home office. One way to avoid conflicts is to use one-way replication only and separate tables into databases according to their direction of data movement.

In addition to the synchronization itself, you should consider carefully your approach to how and when you plan to compact databases and run the RepairDatabase method. Compaction removes all deleted records physically from the database and assists with compaction of the generations of tables whose designs have changed. The RepairDatabase method inspects all system areas and tables for correctness and discards any incorrect data. A database that was open for write operations during a power failure or system crash can be left in a possibly corrupt state that should be repaired by the RepairDatabase method.

COMPLEXITY
INTERMEDIATE

14.4 How do I...
Omit specified objects from replicas?

Problem

Replication is working great for my data-collection application, but the experimental tables in the Design Master database keep getting replicated to the field. How can I omit undesired objects from the replicas?

Technique

The Jet KeepLocal property was designed to prevent database objects from being propagated during replication. Just set value KeepLocal to "T" in the database's Properties collection and the object won't be replicated.

Steps

Open the project Replicate.vbp in the How-To.F04 directory (Figure 14.6). Use the browse buttons and select Expenses.mdb as the master database name and Replica.mdb as the replica database name. Click Create Replica to create a replica database. Use the VisData data maintenance utility (in the VB5 directory) to inspect the structures of the original and replica databases to verify that the replica contains only the Expenses table.

1. Start with the completed form from How-To 14.3.

2. Add the SetKeepLocal helper function to the form's code:

```
Function SetKeepLocal(dbTarget As Database, strCollName _
    As String, strObjectName As String) As Boolean
' Sets KeepLocal to "T" for the passed object.

    Dim intIdx As Integer
    Dim blnFound As Boolean
    Dim tdfTableDef As TableDef
    Dim prpProperty As Property
    Dim docDocument As Document
    Dim qdfQueryDef As QueryDef

    On Error GoTo ErrorHandler

    Select Case strCollName

        Case "Forms", "Reports", "Modules", "Scripts"
            Set docDocument = _
                dbTarget.Containers(strCollName).Documents(strObjectName)
            blnFound = False
            For intIdx = 0 To docDocument.Properties.Count - 1
                If docDocument.Properties(intIdx).Name _
                = "KeepLocal" Then
                    blnFound = True
                    Exit For
                End If
            Next intIdx
            If Not blnFound Then
                Set prpProperty = docDocument.CreateProperty _
                    ("KeepLocal", dbText, "T")
                docDocument.Properties.Append prpProperty
            Else
                docDocument.Properties("KeepLocal").Value = "T"
            End If

        Case "TableDefs"
            Set tdfTableDef = dbTarget.TableDefs(strObjectName)
            blnFound = False
            For intIdx = 0 To tdfTableDef.Properties.Count - 1
                If tdfTableDef.Properties(intIdx).Name _
                = "KeepLocal" Then
                    blnFound = True
                    Exit For
                End If
            Next intIdx
            If Not blnFound Then
                Set prpProperty = tdfTableDef.CreateProperty _
                    ("KeepLocal", dbText, "T")
                tdfTableDef.Properties.Append prpProperty
            Else
                tdfTableDef.Properties("KeepLocal").Value = "T"
            End If

        Case "QueryDefs"
            Set qdfQueryDef = dbTarget.QueryDefs(strObjectName)
            blnFound = False
            For intIdx = 0 To qdfQueryDef.Properties.Count - 1
```

continued on next page

continued from previous page

```
                If qdfQueryDef.Properties(intIdx).Name _
                = "KeepLocal" Then
                    blnFound = True
                    Exit For
                End If
            Next intIdx
            If Not blnFound Then
                Set prpProperty = qdfQueryDef.CreateProperty _
                    ("KeepLocal", dbText, "T")
                qdfQueryDef.Properties.Append prpProperty
            Else
                qdfQueryDef.Properties("KeepLocal").Value = "T"
            End If

    End Select

    SetKeepLocal = True
    Exit Function


ErrorHandler:
    MsgBox Err.Description & " From: " & Err.Source _
            & "Number: " & Err.Number
    SetKeepLocal = False
    Exit Function

End Function
```

3. Update the `cmdCreateReplica_Click` procedure to read like this:

```
Private Sub cmdCreateReplica_Click()
' Create a replica from the named database
Dim dbMaster As Database
Dim bContinue As Boolean

    On Error GoTo DbError

    ' Open the database in exclusive mode
    Set dbMaster = Workspaces(0).OpenDatabase(txtDbNameFrom.Text, True)

    ' Keep everything but the expenses table local
    bContinue = SetKeepLocal(dbMaster, "QueryDefs", _
                "ExpEmployeeNames")
    If bContinue Then _
        bContinue = SetKeepLocal(dbMaster, "QueryDefs", _
                    "ExpForOneEmployee")
    If bContinue Then _
        bContinue = SetKeepLocal(dbMaster, "TableDefs", _
                    "ObjectLibrary")

    ' Make the database the Design Master
    If bContinue Then _
        bContinue = MakeReplicable(dbMaster)
```

```
    ' Make the replica
    If bContinue Then _
        bContinue = CopyReplica(dbMaster, txtReplicaDbName.Text)

    dbMaster.Close

    Exit Sub

DbError:
    MsgBox Err.Description & " From: " & Err.Source _
            & "Number: " & Err.Number
    Exit Sub

End Sub
```

How It Works

When the `KeepLocal` property is set to `"T"`, the `CreateReplica` method doesn't create a replica of the database object. If you later want to replicate an object that was originally kept local, change its `Replicable` property to `"T"` in the Design Master and synchronize the replicas to propagate the additions. The VisData utility that ships with Visual Basic can be used to make many of these changes.

Comments

In addition to the `KeepLocal` property, partial replication allows replicas to contain only part of the Design Master's data. To make a partial replica:

✔ Specify the `dbRepMakePartial` option on the `MakeReplica` method.

✔ Use the `TableDefs ReplicaFilter` property and the `Relations PartialReplica` property to specified the desired records.

✔ Invoke the `Database PopulatePartial` method to move the desired data into the replica.

COMPLEXITY
INTERMEDIATE

14.5 How do I...
Create a nonreplicated version of a replicated database?

Problem

I've created a set of replica databases, but I want to allow one copy to be modified by another developer in her test environment. How can I cut a replica out of the replica set so that it can be changed independently of the others?

Technique

Within a set of replicas, only one database is allowed to have design changes such as table creation or field size changes. All other replicas must have their design changes made at the Design Master database and synchronized through the replica set. This strict requirement ensures that the Data Access Objects **Synchronize** method can adequately track and implement changes. After all, "too many cooks spoils the broth." But there are times when a replica needs to be cut out of the replica set. The reasons might include testing a new replication schema without affecting the existing replica set, quality assurance testing of the replication methods, or a major application design change. The core technique for returning design independence to a replica database for structure changes is to make the replica into a new Design Master.

Steps

Open the project BreakReplica.vbp (see Figure 14.11). Select Replica.mdb as your database. Click Break Replica. Verify that you can modify table definitions using the VisData utility.

1. Create a new Standard EXE project in your workspace. Name the default form **frmBreakReplica** and the project **prjBreakReplica**. Save the form and project to disk.

2. Select Project | Components from the main menu, and check Microsoft Common Dialog Control 5.0. Select Project | References from the Visual Basic main menu and activate the Microsoft DAO 3.5 Object Library by checking its box in the selection list.

3. Draw controls on the form so that it looks like Figure 14.11. Don't forget to add a common dialog control. Set the form's objects and properties as listed in Table 14.10.

Figure 14.11. The Break Replica Set form.

Table 14.10. Objects and properties for the Break Replica Set form.

OBJECT	PROPERTY	SETTING
Form	Name	frmBreakReplica
	Caption	"Break Replica Set"
CommandButton	Name	cmdBreakReplica
	Caption	"&Break Replica"
CommandButton	Name	cmdOpenFrom
	Caption	"&Browse"
CommonDialog	Name	cdOpenFile
	Filter	"Access Files (*.mdb)¦*.mdb"
TextBox	Name	txtDbNameFrom
Label	Name	Label1
	AutoSize	-1 'True
	Caption	"Database to remove from set:"

4. Add the following code to the `cmdOpenFrom_Click` procedure to select a filename:

```
Private Sub cmdOpenFrom_Click()
' Open the Replicate from database file
    cdOpenFile.InitDir = App.Path
    cdOpenFile.ShowOpen
    txtDbNameFrom.Text = cdOpenFile.filename

End Sub
```

5. Add the following code to the `cmdBreakReplica_Click` procedure to set the selected database's `DesignMasterID` to itself:

```
Private Sub cmdBreakReplica_Click()
Dim dbReplica As Database

    On Error GoTo DbError

    ' Open the database in exclusive mode
    Set dbReplica = Workspaces(0).OpenDatabase(txtDbNameFrom.Text, True)

    dbReplica.DesignMasterID = dbReplica.ReplicaID

    dbReplica.Close

    Exit Sub

DbError:
    MsgBox Err.Description & " From: " & Err.Source _
            & "Number: " & Err.Number
    Exit Sub

End Sub
```

How It Works

To remove a database from the restrictions placed on replicas, you need to make the database replica its own design master by setting the `DesignMasterID` to the `ReplicaID` as shown in step 5. The database will be immediately cut out of the replica set and will no longer be easily able to synchronize data structure or content changes with its previous replica siblings. In other words, breaking a database out of a replica set should be considered permanent. In a production environment, the breakup could be very inconvenient if done incorrectly.

Replicated databases remain replicated with all the extra properties and system tables once the database's `Replicable` property is set to `"T"`. In How-To 14.3, we discussed the changes made to the database when it is converted to a replica. Breaking a database out of a replica set will not make the database nonreplicable; it will only allow the database to have its own design changes. All the extra data will still be in the database.

Comments

Replication is a fairly permanent decision, but it can be a powerful tool, especially with the use of the partial replication methods to propagate design changes with very little coding effort. A package being distributed to many locations can use replication to propagate design changes while never transmitting any data. Field database design changes can be managed by distributing a new, empty member of the replica set with the required design changes, and synchronizing with a replica filters set to pass no records.

A

SQL REFERENCE

With the use of commands, predicates, clauses, operators, aggregate functions, and joins, the Structured Query Language (SQL) can successfully compose a query that returns a specified range of fields.

SQL is a language that ties in closely with the Microsoft Jet Engine and DAO. By indicating relations between tables and other queries of a database, through SQL, records are temporarily created and are passed back to the recordset object of the database object in Visual Basic.

This appendix serves as a quick reference and introduction to SQL. Using this reference, you should be able to create your own SQL statements in Visual Basic to better exploit the power of the Microsoft Jet Engine and its components.

SQL Statement Classifications

SQL statements are broken into two distinct classifications, both of which are discussed in detail in this appendix. The first classification, the Data Definition Language (DDL), is used to create, modify, or remove the actual definitions in a particular database. The second classification, the Data Manipulation Language (DML), is used to create, modify, remove, or gather information that resides in the structure of the database. In other words, you would use DDL to create tables, fields, and indexes, and you would use DML to populate, alter, and retrieve the information that resides in the tables and fields.

Table A.1 lists the seven available SQL commands that are the basis of any SQL statement. These commands indicate what kind of query the SQL statement actually is. Table A.1 also indicates the classification of each command listed, either definition (DDL) or manipulation (DML). A SQL command is used with other components of a SQL statement to create either an action query or a selection query. Action queries are those that begin with a SQL command other than SELECT. As you might guess, a query beginning with SELECT is a selection query.

Table A.1. SQL commands.

COMMAND	CLASSIFICATION	DESCRIPTION
CREATE	Definition	Create a table, a field, or an index.
ALTER	Definition	Modify a table by adding a field or changing a field definition.
DROP	Definition	Drop a table or an index.
SELECT	Manipulation	Query a database with given parameters.
INSERT	Manipulation	Insert multiple records with one operation.
UPDATE	Manipulation	Change information throughout a range with given parameters.
DELETE	Manipulation	Remove records from the table.

When using queries, you will use various clauses that are implemented in the SQL statement. The available clauses for SQL used by the Microsoft Jet engine are listed in Table A.2 with a short description of each.

Table A.2. SQL clauses.

CLAUSE	DESCRIPTION
FROM	Specifies the table from which data is queried.
WHERE	Specifies the condition(s) for the query.
GROUP BY	Specifies the group(s) for the selected information.
HAVING	Specifies the condition(s) for each group in the query.
ORDER BY	Specifies the order of the query.

The first of these clauses, FROM, is used to indicate the table or query used to gather the information for the SQL statement. More than one table or query can be listed in the statement, using the FROM clause. When doing so, you are creating at least one join in your query. Joins are discussed later in this appendix.

The second clause, WHERE, lists the condition or conditions that must be met for a record to be included in the query results. Each condition is evaluated using conditional operators. Multiple conditions are listed using logical operators. A list of available conditional and logical operators is shown in Table A.3.

Table A.3. SQL operators.

OPERATOR	TYPE	CONDITION IS MET WHEN
AND	Logical	Both expressions are true.
OR	Logical	Either expression is true.
NOT	Logical	The expression is false.
<	Comparison	The first expression is *less than* the second expression.
<=	Comparison	The first expression is *less than or equal to* the second expression.
>	Comparison	The first expression is *greater than* the second expression.
>=	Comparison	The first expression is *greater than or equal to* the second expression.

OPERATOR	TYPE	CONDITION IS MET WHEN
=	Comparison	The first expression is *equal to* the second expression.
<>	Comparison	The first expression is *not equal to* the second expression.
BETWEEN	Comparison	The value belongs to a specified set of values.
LIKE	Comparison	The value matches the pattern specified.
IN	Comparison	The record belongs to a particular group in a database.

The third SQL clause, GROUP BY, is used to group the query's result set. GROUP BY uses at least one field name from a table or query listed in the statement's FROM clause to evaluate the records and group similar values. You can also use an aggregate function in a SQL statement to create summaries of the groups in the recordset. The list of available aggregate functions is shown in Table A.4.

Table A.4. SQL aggregate functions.

FUNCTION	DESCRIPTION
AVG	Returns the average value of a specified field.
COUNT	Returns the number of records in a query.
SUM	Returns the sum of the values in a specified field.
MAX	Returns the largest value in a specified field.
MIN	Returns the smallest value in a specified field.

The fourth SQL clause, HAVING, specifies conditions (of the same syntax used for the WHERE clause) the groups must meet to be included in the resulting recordset.

The last SQL clause, ORDER BY, uses field names to order the result set in a specified manner. More information on all the SQL commands and clauses is given in detail throughout this appendix.

Data Definition Language

Data Definition Language statements are used to create, alter, or remove tables, fields, and indexes from a database. The three SQL commands used to do so are CREATE, DROP, and ALTER. All three are action queries.

Action queries, in Visual Basic, can be initiated in one of two ways. The first method of invoking an action query is by using a QueryDef object. The second is by using the Execute method of the database object, as shown here:

```
db.Execute sSQLStatement
```

This assumes that db is a database object variable successfully set to a valid database and sSQLStatement is a valid string variable containing a valid action SQL statement.

The CREATE Command

The CREATE command is used to create tables and indexes in a specified database. To create a table in a given database, use the CREATE TABLE statement with the syntax shown here:

```
CREATE TABLE table (fld1 type [(sz)] [NOT NULL] [idx1] [, fld2 type [(sz)]
         [NOT NULL] [idx2] [, ...]] [, CONSTRAINT MFidx [, ...]])
```

In the preceding syntax, the table name succeeds the actual **CREATE TABLE** statement and is followed by a comma-delimited list of field definitions that are used to create the specified table. At least one field must be listed in parentheses as shown. Any valid database type can be used to indicate the type of field to be created, and a size (*sz*) can be specified for text and binary fields.

The following example creates a new table in the **db** database with three fields:

```
db.Execute "CREATE TABLE Customers (CustNum INTEGER, " _
        & "CustName TEXT (25), Address TEXT (30))"
```

The new table created is called Customers. It contains an integer field named **CustNum** and two text fields named **CustName** and **Address**.

Using the **NOT NULL** optional parameter, you can specify that the field can never have a **NULL** value. If a **NULL** value is assigned to a field created with this option, a runtime error will occur. The following example is a more bulletproof table definition:

```
db.Execute "CREATE TABLE Customers (CustNum INTEGER NOT NULL, " _
        & "CustName TEXT NOT NULL (25), Address TEXT (30))"
```

This version of the **CREATE TABLE** action query specifies that the **Number** and **CustName** field values cannot consist of any **NULL** values. The **Address** field, however, can.

You can also use the **CONSTRAINT** clause in a **CREATE TABLE** statement to create an index either on an individual field or on multiple fields. The following example creates an index in a new table:

```
db.Execute "CREATE TABLE Customers (" _
        & "CustNum INTEGER CONSTRAINT CustNumIndex PRIMARY, " _
        & "CustName TEXT (25), Address TEXT (30))"
```

This example creates a table with three fields as shown before, but it also adds an index named **CustNumIndex** for the **CustNum** field.

To create an index on multiple fields, you can also use the **CONSTRAINT** clause as shown in this example:

```
db.Execute "CREATE TABLE Customers (CustNum INTEGER, " _
        & "CustName TEXT (25), Address TEXT (30), " _
        & "CONSTRAINT CustIndex UNIQUE (CustNum, CustName))"
```

Notice that the new index created by the **CONSTRAINT** clause, named **CustIndex**, is composed of both the **CustNum** and the **CustName** fields described in the SQL statement. The difference between creating an individual field index and creating a multiple field index with the **CREATE TABLE** statement is that with the individual fields, you indicate the **CONSTRAINT** clause after the given field, without a comma. Creating indexes of multiple fields with the **CONSTRAINT** clause, you specify the index after the fields in the index are created, separated by a comma, listing the individual fields, as shown in the last example. More information on the **CONSTRAINT** clause can be found in the "Using the **CONSTRAINT** Clause" section, later in this appendix.

You do not necessarily have to create indexes in the **CREATE TABLE** statement—you can also explicitly create indexes using the **CREATE INDEX** statement, as shown in this example:

```
db.Execute "CREATE UNIQUE INDEX CustIndex ON Customers (CustNum, CustName)"
```

This statement leads to the same result as is derived by the last **CREATE TABLE** statement.

The syntax for the **CREATE INDEX** statement is as follows:

```
CREATE [UNIQUE] INDEX idx ON table (fld1 [ASC¦DESC]
     [, fld2 [ASC¦DESC], ...])
     [WITH {PRIMARY ¦ DISALLOW NULL ¦ IGNORE NULL}]
```

When using the **CREATE INDEX** statement, specifying the **UNIQUE** option, as shown in the preceding example, you are telling the Jet engine that no two combinations, for the values of the fields listed, are to be allowed, thus creating a unique index on the fields. By default, indexes are created in ascending order (**ASC** keyword), but you can specify to list the order of the values of an index in descending order by using the **DESC** keyword after the corresponding field name.

The last portion of the **CREATE INDEX** statement allows you to specify, in more detail, how an index is to be handled. You do this with the **WITH** clause of the **CREATE INDEX** statement. To create a primary key on the table indicated, use the **WITH PRIMARY** statement. This statement creates a unique index that is now the primary key. Only one primary key can exist per table—attempting to create an additional one will result in a runtime error.

You can also prohibit the use of **NULL** values in an index with the **WITH DISAL-LOW NULL** statement, or you can allow **NULL** values with the **WITH IGNORE NULL** statement.

The **ALTER** Command

The second command belonging to the SQL Data Definition Language is **ALTER**. You can use the **ALTER TABLE** statement to complete four distinct tasks:

✔ Add a new field to a table.

✔ Delete a field from a table.

✔ Add a new index to a table.

✔ Delete an index from a table.

Only one field or index can be added or deleted with each **ALTER TABLE** statement. The syntax for **ALTER TABLE** is shown here:

```
ALTER TABLE table {ADD {COLUMN fld type[(size)] [NOT NULL] [CONSTRAINT idx]
     ¦ CONSTRAINT MFidx} ¦ DROP {COLUMN fld ¦ CONSTRAINT indexname}}
```

The following example creates a new field in an existing table named Customers:

```
db.Execute "ALTER TABLE Customers ADD COLUMN PhoneNum TEXT (12)"
```

Just as you can add a field to a table, you can delete one, as shown in the following example:

```
db.Execute "ALTER TABLE Customers DROP PhoneNum"
```

You can also specify new indexes just as you did with **CREATE TABLE**, except that you can add the index after the table is already created, as shown here:

```
db.Execute "ALTER TABLE Customers " _
        & "ADD CONSTRAINT NameAndPhoneIndex (CustName, PhoneNum)"
```

Now you can delete that index with this final example:

```
db.Execute "ALTER TABLE Customers DROP CONTRAINT NameAndPhoneIndex"
```

Using the CONSTRAINT Clause

So far we have seen the **CONSTRAINT** clause in both the **CREATE** and the **ALTER** SQL commands. Now we will take a closer look at this clause and discover how powerful it really is.

In its simplest form, a constraint is an index. Not only does the **CONSTRAINT** clause allow you to create or remove indexes, as shown in the **CREATE** and **ALTER** command sections, but you can also create primary and foreign keys to define relations and enforce referential integrity.

As shown earlier, by example, there are two versions of the **CONSTRAINT** statement, one for individual field indexes and one for multiple field indexes. The syntax for a single field index is shown here:

```
CONSTRAINT name {PRIMARY KEY ¦ UNIQUE ¦ NOT NULL ¦
        REFERENCES foreigntable
        [(foreignfield1, foreignfield2)]}
```

The syntax for a multiple field index **CONSTRAINT** is this:

```
CONSTRAINT name
        {PRIMARY KEY (primary1[, primary2 [, ...]]) ¦
        UNIQUE (unique1[, unique2 [, ...]]) ¦
        NOT NULL (notnull1[, notnull2 [, ...]]) ¦
        FOREIGN KEY (ref1[, ref2 [, ...]])
            REFERENCES foreigntable
                [(foreignfield1 [, foreignfield2 [, ...]])]}
```

The name of the index to be created is specified directly after the **CONSTRAINT** keyword. In either versions, you can create three types of indexes:

✔ A **UNIQUE** index. A **UNIQUE** index has no two fields, as indicated in the **CONSTRAINT** clause, with the same values.

✔ A **PRIMARY KEY** index. A **PRIMARY KEY** is, by definition, unique. This means that all the fields included in the primary key definition must also be unique.

✔ A **FOREIGN KEY** index. A **FOREIGN KEY** is an index that uses another table to create an index on the current one.

You can create a foreign key to create a relation between multiple fields, as in the following example:

```
db.Execute "ALTER TABLE Customers " _
        & "ADD CONSTRAINT NewIndex " _
        & "FOREIGN KEY (CustNum) REFERENCES Orders (CustNum)"
```

This example creates a relation between the Customers table and the Orders table of the **db** database object. A new index is created, **NewIndex**, that is linking the two tables based on the **CustNum** field name.

The DROP **Command**

The **DROP** command comes in two flavors, **DROP TABLE** and **DROP INDEX**. As you might easily guess, the **DROP TABLE** statement removes an existing table from a database, as shown here:

```
db.Execute "DROP TABLE Customers"
```

The **DROP INDEX** statement works similarly to the **DROP TABLE** statement, except that it removes an index from a given table, as shown in this example:

```
db.Execute "DROP INDEX CustNumIndex ON Customers"
```

For reference, the syntax of the **DROP** command is as follows:

```
DROP {TABLE table ¦ INDEX idx ON table}
```

Data Manipulation Language

Data Manipulation Language commands create a mix of action and selection queries. The commands **SELECT**, **INSERT**, **UPDATE**, and **DELETE** are used to quickly and efficiently, through the use of the Jet engine performance, manipulate the data residing in specified tables.

The SELECT **Command**

The **SELECT** command differs from all other SQL commands in that it is a part of a selection query rather than an action query. When we're using a selection query in a Visual Basic application, it is most commonly set in a recordset object of a given database. Assuming that **rs** is a valid recordset object and **db** is a database object already set to a valid database file, we can use the following statement to gather all the records in the Customers table of the **db** object:

```
Set rs = db.OpenRecordset("SELECT * FROM Customers")
```

This example uses the most generic and basic form of a **SELECT** statement. This section explains the various components of the **SELECT** statement and describes how each component can be used to effectively sort and filter records according to the need of the programmer.

The syntax for the **SELECT** statement is as follows:

```
SELECT [predicate]
        { * ¦ table.* ¦
        [table.]field1 [AS alias1] [, [table.]field2 [AS alias2] [, ...]]}
FROM    tableexpression [, ...] [IN externaldatabase]
[WHERE... ]
[GROUP BY... ]
[HAVING... ]
[ORDER BY... ]
```

It is quite understandable to be overwhelmed by this declaration, but not all the clauses included in this syntax are necessarily used together—although they could be.

Take the following SELECT statement, for example:

```
SELECT DISTINCT CustNum, CustName
FROM Customers
WHERE (CustNum >= 100) AND (CustNum <= 120)
ORDER BY CustName;
```

This statement retrieves only the fields CustNum and CustName from the Customers table. The WHERE clause in this statement shows two conditions. The first condition says that the CustNum field values must be greater than or equal to 100. The second condition states that the CustNum field values must be less than or equal to 120. So far, we see that the SELECT statement shown previously will return the CustNum and CustName for all records with a customer number between 100 and 120. The last part of this statement says to order the records returned by the query by the CustName field—in other words, in alphabetical order. We can also request the records to be returned in reverse alphabetical order by placing the DESC keyword after the ORDER BY CustName clause.

Multiple conditions can be used in a SELECT statement, as shown in this statement. For a complete list of operators for conditions, both logical and comparison, see Table A.4 at the beginning of this section.

It should be noted that the DISTINCT keyword following the SELECT command is called a predicate. This keyword indicates that only distinct (unique) combinations of fields will be returned. In this example, if we had three records in the Customers table with the same customer number and name but with different addresses, only one record would be returned. If we were to add the Address field to the list of fields in the SELECT statement, we would receive three records for the same customer number and name because the combination (number, name, and address) is unique for each record returned.

The DISTINCT keyword is not the only predicate available in a SELECT statement. Table A.5 lists the four available predicates for a SELECT statement.

Table A.5. SELECT predicates.

PREDICATE	DESCRIPTION
ALL	Returns all records, even duplicates.
DISTINCT	Returns only unique records, based on fields specified in the statement.
DISTINCTROW	Returns only unique records, based on all fields in the specified table(s), even those not listed in the SELECT statement.
TOP	Returns the first n records or the top p percentage of records of the selected recordset.

The default predicate used in SELECT statements not indicating a predicate is ALL. ALL returns all records that are met by the conditions of the selection query.

The TOP predicate is used in conjunction with the ORDER BY clause of a SELECT statement. It can be used in one of two ways:

✔ TOP *n* returns the first *n* records.

✔ TOP *p* PERCENT returns the top *p* percentage of the entire recordset.

Following is an example of the TOP predicate:

```
SELECT TOP 10 PERCENT OrderNum, OrderPrice
FROM Orders
ORDER BY OrderPrice;
```

This statement would return the top 10 percent of records in the Orders table, based on the OrderPrice field. If we were to order the recordset returned by this statement by the OrderNum field, we would get the top 10 percent of records based on the OrderNum, which would probably not make a whole lot of sense.

It is worth pointing out that if there are identical values for the ORDER BY field that is specified, there is a chance that more than the desired number of records will be returned. Assume, for instance, that I wanted to get the top 10 parts, based on quantity ordered. If there were 9 distinct quantity amounts that topped the list and 2 others that followed, with the same value, I would have 11 records in all when I only wanted 10. The same is true for the TOP *p* PERCENT format. If I wanted to retrieve the top 2 percent of part prices with my selection query, I would use the following statement:

```
SELECT TOP 2 PERCENT PartName
FROM Orders
ORDER BY PartPrice;
```

This example returns the names of the items priced in the top 2 percent. If I have numerous items all with the same price, they are considered one item, so I can very easily retrieve more records than I expected. It is also important to understand what you are asking for when using the TOP predicate. For instance, it might be easy to think that you are getting the top 10 customers based on money spent, but you must specifically state that you want the selection to be made on a field such as TotalMoneySpent as compared to TotalOrderPrice.

You can also group records that are returned from a query by using the GROUP BY clause in a SELECT statement, as in the following example:

```
SELECT PartName, Count(PartName)
FROM Orders
WHERE (PartPrice > 10)
GROUP BY PartName;
```

This SELECT statement gathers and groups all the records from the Orders table whose PartPrice field values are greater than 10. These records are then grouped by the PartNum field and only the PartNum field, and a count of the number of each type of part sold is returned. In other words, the resulting recordset contains the distinct names of parts that cost over $10 and a count of the number of orders for each part.

The function COUNT, in this example, is called an aggregate function. Other aggregate functions include AVG, SUM, MAX, and MIN. A list of aggregate functions and their descriptions is given in Table A.4.

Another example of using an aggregate function is shown here:

```
SELECT PartName, SUM(PartPrice)
FROM Orders
WHERE (PartPrice > 10)
GROUP BY PartName
HAVING (SUM(PartPrice) > 1000) AND (PartName LIKE "WIDGET*");
```

In this example, we introduce the HAVING clause. This clause acts very similarly to the WHERE clause, except that the condition specified is tested after the grouping has occurred, unlike the WHERE clause, which tests conditions of records to be included in the groups. The preceding SELECT statement gathers distinct part names and a sum of the total prices sold from the Orders table. The only condition for records to be included in this grouping is that the price of each part be greater than 10.

After the groups have been created by the Jet engine, only the groups with a total PartPrice summary of more than 1000 are included. In addition to this condition, we see the use of the LIKE keyword. The LIKE keyword can be used anywhere a condition can be specified. LIKE uses pattern matching to check whether a field should be included in a resulting recordset. In this example, only groups with a PartName field value beginning with the characters WIDGET will be included in the recordset.

Joins

Joins are a very commonly used function of a SELECT statement. Joins are used to create temporary relations between tables when evaluating a selection query. Following is the syntax for using joins in a SELECT statement:

```
SELECT ...
FROM table1 [LEFT ¦ RIGHT] JOIN table2 ON (table1.fld1 CompOp table2.fld2)
```

The CompOp is a comparison operator (refer to Table A.3). A join affects the FROM clause of a SELECT statement, as shown in the preceding syntax declaration.

Left and right joins mirror each other in definition. A left join (called a left outer join) includes all records from table1, even if no related records are found in table2. A right join (called a right outer join) includes all records from table2, even if no related records are found in table1. Take the following statement, for example:

```
SELECT Customers.*, Orders.*
FROM Customers LEFT JOIN Orders ON (Customers.CustNum = Orders.CustNum);
```

This example returns all fields from the Customers table and only the fields from the Orders table that have matching CustNum fields. In other words, the resulting recordset from this statement would include all the customers and information on orders for those customers that did order.

To create a join that returns only records that are included in both tables (inner join), you do not have to use the JOIN clause at all, as shown in this example:

```
SELECT Customers.*, Orders.*
FROM Customers, Orders
WHERE (Customers.CustNum = Orders.CustNum);
```

This statement would return a shorter recordset than the earlier statement, given that there are customers who did not place orders. In this **SELECT** statement, only the customers who placed orders qualify to be returned in the recordset.

Although it is unnecessary to do so, there is a SQL clause to specify inner joins, as shown in this example:

```
SELECT Customers.*, Orders.*
FROM Customers INNER JOIN Orders ON (Customers.CustNum = Orders.CustNum);
```

This statement is the equivalent to the preceding one, and in many cases it is actually easier to read and comprehend at a glance.

You might also care to specify more than one condition in any of your joins, as shown in this example:

```
SELECT Customers.*, Orders.*
FROM Customers INNER JOIN Orders
ON ((Customers.CustNum = Orders.CustNum)
AND (Customers.Flag = Orders.Flag));
```

If you really want to go overboard, and many times you might find that you need to, you can nest joins within each other, as shown in the following example:

```
SELECT Customers.*, Orders.*, Tax.*
FROM Customers INNER JOIN
  (Orders INNER JOIN Tax ON (Orders.State = Tax.State))
    ON (Customers.CustNum = Orders.CustNum));
```

This **SELECT** statement returns all the records in which there is a customer number from the Customers table and Orders table and a state in the Orders table and the Tax table.

You can nest either a left join or a right join inside an inner join; however, you cannot nest an inner join inside either a left join or a right join.

The INSERT Command

The **INSERT** command is used in the **INSERT INTO** statement to create an append query, a type of action query. You can use this command to add single or multiple rows to a table. This is the syntax for adding a single row, using the **INSERT INTO** statement:

```
INSERT INTO table [(fld1[, fld2[, ...]])]
VALUES (val1[, val2[, ...])
```

Using this syntax, you can add single rows to a table. You must specify each field and its value that you want to add. If you leave out a field and its corresponding value, a **Null** value is automatically inserted into the field. The new records are appended to the end of the table. Following is an example of how to add a row to a specific table:

```
INSERT INTO Customers (CustNum, CustName)
VALUES (1, "Kimberly");
```

If other fields are in the Customers table, they are assigned a **Null** value.

The syntax for adding multiple rows differs slightly:

```
INSERT INTO table2 [(fld1[, fld2[, ...]])]
SELECT [table1.]fld1[, fld2[, ...]
FROM ...
```

This syntax takes a specified selection of records from *table1* and inserts them into *table2*. The number of fields for both tables must be the same and in the correct order. The following example demonstrates the INSERT INTO statement:

```
INSERT INTO Delivered (CustNum, DelPart, PriceCharged)
SELECT CustNum, PartName, PartPrice
FROM Orders
WHERE (Delivered = True);
```

This example inserts all the delivered orders from the Orders table into the corresponding fields of the Delivered table.

The INSERT INTO statement appends records at the end of an existing table, but you can also use a similar statement and selection of records to create a new table, as in this example:

```
SELECT CustNum, PartName, PartPrice
INTO DeliveredBackup
FROM Orders
WHERE (Delivered = True);
```

This example creates a new table called DeliveredBackup, with the identical fields and properties of the fields listed in the SELECT clause from the Orders table. The new table would include all the records with the Delivered field value of True.

The UPDATE Command

The UPDATE command is used to set information in a current table to a new value. The syntax for the UPDATE command is as follows:

```
UPDATE table
SET value
WHERE criteria
```

The value of the SET clause in the UPDATE statement is an assignment expression that will alter the current value of the selected records of the table specified. Here is an example of the UPDATE statement:

```
UPDATE Orders
SET OrderTotal = (PartPrice * Quantity);
```

If no WHERE clause is specified, as in this example, the UPDATE query makes the necessary changes to all the records in the specified table. In this example, the OrderTotal field is calculated based on the PartPrice and Quantity field values for the corresponding record.

It is possible to update multiple fields for each record with a single SQL UPDATE query, as shown in this next example:

```
UPDATE Orders
SET OrderTotal = (PartPrice * Quantity),
```

```
     Discount = (PartPrice * .05) * Quantity
WHERE (OrderDate < #1/1/1998#);
```

This example gives a new value to both the `OrderTotal` field and the `Discount` field for all records whose `OrderDate` field value is before January 1, 1998. Notice the use of the number signs (#) before and after the date criteria in the `WHERE` clause. This is the correct notation for specifying dates in a condition.

It should be noted that `UPDATE` queries cannot be reversed, and care should be taken to ensure that the correct records are selected for the update. To check and see which fields are going to be updated before the execution of the `UPDATE` statement, create a selection query with the same criteria as the `UPDATE` query.

The DELETE **Command**

The `DELETE` command is used to perform bulk deletions of records within a specified table in one operation. You can specify conditions to select the records from a table to delete. When you use the `DELETE` command, entire records are deleted, not individual fields. The syntax for the `DELETE` command is shown here:

```
DELETE table.*
FROM table
WHERE ...
```

Following is an example of a `DELETE` statement:

```
DELETE *
FROM Customers
WHERE (LastOrderDate <= #6/20/73#);
```

This example deletes all the records in the Customers table in which the last order date was June 20, 1973, or earlier (we don't need their business anyway!).

The `DELETE` command can be used to delete all the data in a particular table while maintaining the actual structure and definition of that table, as shown in this example:

```
DELETE * FROM Orders;
```

This command could obviously be very dangerous; therefore, it is advised that you use this form of the `DELETE` command with extreme caution.

Comments

SQL is a convenient, effective, and easy way to organize data for your applications. By using the commands described in this appendix, you can select, filter, order, and group records in any way you need. The Structured Query Language is much more involved than is described in this brief reference, but by knowing just these basic commands and functions, you can create just about any desired recordset from your raw data.

B

DATA ACCESS OBJECT REFERENCE

The data access object model provides you with an object-oriented interface to all the data manipulation techniques inherent in Microsoft Jet Database files. Figure B.1 shows the entire DAO object model in its hierarchical form.

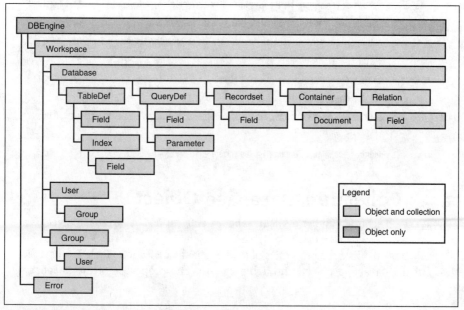

Figure B.1. The data access object model.

This appendix is designed as a reference to all the objects that are included in the DAO object model. The collections and objects are listed in alphabetical order with tables indicating and describing all the available methods and properties available to each.

Containers **Collection,** Container **Object**

The Containers collection contains all the Container objects that are part of a database. A container name can be Database, Tables, or Relations. Table B.1 lists the methods of the Containers collection; Table B.2 lists the properties of the Containers collection. Table B.3 lists the properties of the Container object.

Table B.1. Containers collection methods.

METHOD	DESCRIPTION
Refresh	Updates the contents of the collection to reflect the current status of the database.

Table B.2. Containers collection properties.

PROPERTY	DESCRIPTION
Count	The number of objects in the collection.

Table B.3. Container object properties.

PROPERTY	DESCRIPTION
AllPermissions	Returns all permissions for the user named by UserName, including those that are inherited from the user's group as well as the user's specific permissions.
Inherit	Sets or returns a value that indicates whether the document will receive a default Permissions property setting.
Name	Sets a user-defined name for the DAO object.
Owner	Sets the owner of the current Container object.
Permissions	Sets the permissions available for the user, of the current Container object, named by UserName.
UserName	Indicates the name of the user for the current Container object.

Databases **Collection,** Database **Object**

The Database object is a member of the Databases collection. The Database object is a means of access to an open database file. Table B.4 lists the methods of the Databases collection, and Table B.5 lists the properties of the Databases collection. Table B.6 lists the methods of the Database object, and Table B.7 lists the properties of the Database object.

Table B.4. Databases collection methods.

METHOD	DESCRIPTION
Refresh	Updates the contents of the collection to reflect the current status of the database.

Table B.5. Databases collection properties.

PROPERTY	DESCRIPTION
Count	Returns the number of objects in the collection.

Table B.6. Database object methods.

METHOD	DESCRIPTION
Close	Closes the current Database object.
CreateProperty	Creates a new Property object.
CreateQueryDef	Creates a new QueryDef object and adds it to the QueryDefs collection.
CreateRelation	Creates a new Relation object and adds it to the Relations collection.
CreateTableDef	Creates a new TableDef object and adds it to the TableDefs collection.
Execute	Executes the specified SQL action query.
MakeReplica	Makes a new replica from another database replica.
NewPassword	Assigns a new password to the Database object.
OpenRecordset	Creates a new Recordset object and adds it to the Recordsets collection.
PopulatePartial	Synchronizes changes in a partial replica with the full replica and repopulates the partial replica based on the current replica filters.
Synchronize	Synchronizes two replicas.

Table B.7. Database object properties.

PROPERTY	DESCRIPTION
CollatingOrder	Returns the sequence of the sort order in text and string comparison.
Connect	Returns information about the source of an open connection.
Connection	Returns a connection object corresponding to the current Database object.
Name	Sets a user-defined name for the DAO object.
QueryTimeout	Indicates the number of seconds to wait until an error is reported when executing a query.
RecordsAffected	Indicates the number of records that were affected by the last call of the Execute method.
Replicable	Indicates whether the current Database object can be replicated.
ReplicaID	Returns a 16-byte value that uniquely identifies a database replica.
Transactions	Indicates whether an object supports transactions.
Updatable	Indicates whether an object is updatable.

continued on next page

continued from previous page

PROPERTY	DESCRIPTION
V1xNullBehavior	Indicates whether zero-length strings in Text or Memo fields are converted to Null values.
Version	Indicates the DAO version currently in use.

Documents **Collection,** Document **Object**

The Documents collection contains all the Document objects for a specific type of Microsoft Jet Database object (Database, Table or Query, or Relationship). Table B.8 lists the methods of the Documents collection, and Table B.9 lists its properties. Table B.10 lists the Document object methods, and Table B.11 lists its properties.

Table B.8. Documents collection methods.

METHOD	DESCRIPTION
Refresh	Updates the contents of the collection to reflect the current status of the database.

Table B.9. Documents collection properties.

PROPERTY	DESCRIPTION
Count	Returns the number of objects in the collection.

Table B.10. Document object methods.

METHOD	DESCRIPTION
CreateProperty	Creates a new user-defined Property object.

Table B.11. Document object properties.

PROPERTY	DESCRIPTION
AllPermissions	Indicates all the permissions belonging to the current user of the document that are specific as well as inherited from its group.
Container	Returns the name of the Container object that the current Document object belongs to.
DateCreated	Returns the date and time the current object was created.
LastUpdated	Returns the date and time the current object was last modified.
KeepLocal	Indicates that the current object is not to be replicated.
Name	Sets a user-defined name for the DAO object.
Owner	Returns the user who is considered the owner of the current Document object.
Permissions	Returns the permissions that are specific to the current user of the document.
Replicable	Indicates whether the current Document object can be replicated.
UserName	Returns the name of the current user of the document.

DBEngine **Object**

DBEngine is the only part of the DAO object model that is not a collection; rather it is only an object that contains and controls all the other components of the DAO object model. Table B.12 lists the methods of the DBEngine object; Table B.13 lists the properties.

Table B.12. DBEngine object methods.

METHOD	DESCRIPTION
BeginTrans	Begins transaction for the database engine.
CommitTrans	Commits changes since the last call to the BeginTrans method.
Rollback	Rolls back to the state before the call to the BeginTrans method.
CompactDatabase	Compacts an existing database into a new database.
CreateDatabase	Creates a new Database object, saves it to disk, and returns the opened Database object.
CreateWorkspace	Creates a new Workspace object and appends it to the Workspaces collection.
Idle	Allows the Jet engine to complete any pending tasks by suspending data processing.
OpenConnection	Opens a connection to an ODBC data source.
OpenDatabase	Opens a database and returns a Database object that represents it.
RegisterDatabase	Enters connections information for an ODBC data source in the Windows Registry.
RepairDatabase	Tries to repair a corrupt Jet database.
SetOption	Temporarily overrides values in the Windows Registry for the Microsoft Jet database engine.

Table B.13. DBEngine object properties.

PROPERTY	DESCRIPTION
DefaultType	Sets the type of Workspace object to be used when the next Workspace object is created.
DefaultUser	Sets the user name of the default Workspace object that is to be created.
DefaultPassword	Sets the password used to create the default Workspace object when it is initiated.
IniPath	Indicates the path of the information used from the Windows Registry about the Jet database engine.
LoginTimeout	Returns the number of seconds before an error occurs when attempting to log on to an ODBC database.
SystemDB	Returns the path and name of the current workgroup information file.
Version	Indicates the DAO version currently in use.

Errors **Collection,** Error **Object**

The Errors collection is a collection of Error objects pertaining to individual DAO operation failures. Tables B.14 and B.15 list the methods and properties, respectively, of the Errors collection. Table B.16 lists the properties of the Error object.

Table B.14. Errors collection methods.

METHOD	DESCRIPTION
Refresh	Updates the contents of the collection to reflect the current status of the database.

Table B.15. Errors collection properties.

PROPERTY	DESCRIPTION
Count	Returns the number of objects in the collection.

Table B.16. Error object properties.

PROPERTY	DESCRIPTION
Description	Indicates the description of the current error.
HelpContext	Returns the context ID for a topic in a Windows Help file.
HelpFile	Returns the name of a Windows Help file.
Number	Indicates the number referring to the current error.
Source	Indicates the source of the current error.

Fields **Collection,** Field **Object**

The Fields collection belongs to the Index, QueryDef, Relation, and TableDef objects. The collection is composed of all the Field objects of the corresponding object. The Field object is used to access the value of that field and its definition. Tables B.17 and B.18 list the methods and properties of the Fields collection. Tables B.19 and B.20 list the methods and properties of the Field object.

Table B.17. Fields collection methods.

METHOD	DESCRIPTION
Append	Adds a new object to the collection.
Delete	Removes an object from the collection.
Refresh	Updates the contents of the collection to reflect the current status of the database.

Table B.18. Fields collection properties.

PROPERTY	DESCRIPTION
Count	Indicates the number of objects in the collection.

Table B.19. Field object methods.

METHOD	DESCRIPTION
AppendChunk	Appends a string to a Memo or Long Binary field.
CreateProperty	Creates a new user-defined Property object.
GetChunk	Returns a portion of a Memo or Long Binary field.

Table B.20. Field object properties.

PROPERTY	DESCRIPTION
AllowZeroLength	Indicates whether a zero-length value can be stored in the field.
Attributes	Returns information containing characteristics of an object.
CollatingOrder	Returns the sequence of the sort order in text and string comparison.
DataUpdatable	Indicates whether the object's data is updatable.
DefaultValue	Returns a default value given to the field if no other value is specified.
FieldSize	Indicates the number of bytes used in the database for a Memo or Long Binary field.
ForeignName	Returns the name of a Field object in a foreign table that corresponds to a field in a primary table for a relationship.
Name	Sets a user-defined name for the DAO object.
OrdinalPosition	Indicates a numbered position of the current field in the Fields collection.
OriginalValue	Returns the value of the field when the last batch update began.
Required	Indicates whether the field must be given a value.
Size	Returns the size in length of the field.
SourceField	Indicates the name of the field that is the original source of the data for the current Field object.
SourceTable	Sets the name of the table that is the original source of the data for a Field object.
Type	Returns the operational type of object.
ValidateOnSet	Indicates whether a Field object value is indicated when its Value property is set.
ValidationRule	Returns the value that validates data in a field as it is changed or added to a table.
ValidationText	Indicates the message that your application displays if the value of the Field object does not satisfy the validation rule.
Value	Returns the actual data stored in the field.
VisibleValue	Returns the value that is newer than the OriginalValue property as determined by a batch update conflict.

Groups **Collection,** Group **Object**

The Groups collection contains Group objects of a workspace or user. A Group object is a group of users who have common access permissions. Tables B.21 and B.22 list the methods and properties of the Groups collection, while Tables B.23 and B.24 list the methods and properties of the Group object.

Table B.21. Groups collection methods.

METHOD	DESCRIPTION
Append	Adds a new object to the collection.
Delete	Removes an object from the collection.
Refresh	Updates the contents of the collection to reflect the current status of the database.

Table B.22. Groups collection properties.

PROPERTY	DESCRIPTION
Count	Indicates the number of objects in the collection.

Table B.23. Group object methods.

METHOD	DESCRIPTION
CreateUser	Creates a new user object for the current group.

Table B.24. Group object properties.

PROPERTY	DESCRIPTION
Name	Sets a user-defined name for the DAO object.
PID	Returns a group personal identifier.

Indexes `Collection,` Index `Object`

The `Indexes` collection contains all the `Index` objects pertaining to a particular `TableDef` object. The `Index` object specifies the order of the records in a table. Table B.25 lists the methods of the `Indexes` collection, and Table B.26 lists the `Indexes` collection properties. Table B.27 lists the `Index` object methods, and Table B.28 lists the `Index` object properties.

Table B.25. Indexes collection methods.

METHOD	DESCRIPTION
Append	Adds a new object to the collection.
Delete	Removes an object from the collection.
Refresh	Updates the contents of the collection to reflect the current status of the database.

Table B.26. Indexes collection properties.

PROPERTY	DESCRIPTION
Count	Indicates the number of objects in the collection.

Table B.27. Index object methods.

METHOD	DESCRIPTION
CreateField	Creates a Field object and appends it to the Fields collection.
CreateProperty	Creates a Property object.

Table B.28. Index object properties.

PROPERTY	DESCRIPTION
Clustered	Indicates whether the Index object is a clustered index.
DistinctCount	Indicates the number of unique values for the Index object.
Foreign	Indicates whether the current Index object represents a foreign key.
IgnoreNulls	Indicates whether Null values in the fields of the current Index object are allowed.
Name	Sets a user-defined name for the DAO object.
Primary	Indicates that the current index is the primary key.
Required	Indicates that the values of the Field objects that make up the current Index object must be specified.
Unique	Indicates that the combination of the Field object values that make up the current Index object is unique.

Parameters **Collection,** Parameter **Object**

The Parameters collection contains all the Parameter objects of a QueryDef object. A Parameter object contains a value that is passed to a QueryDef object. Table B.29 lists the Parameters collection methods, and Table B.30 lists its properties. Table B.31 lists the Parameter object properties.

Table B.29. Parameters collection methods.

METHOD	DESCRIPTION
Refresh	Updates the contents of the collection to reflect the current status of the database.

Table B.30. Parameters collection properties.

PROPERTY	DESCRIPTION
Count	Indicates the number of objects in the collection.

Table B.31. Parameter object properties.

PROPERTY	DESCRIPTION
Direction	Indicates whether the object represents an input, an output, both, or the return value from the procedure.
Name	Sets a user-defined name for the DAO object.
Type	Indicates the operational type of object.
Value	Sets the value of the Parameter object.

QueryDefs **Collection,** QueryDef **Object**

The QueryDefs collection holds all QueryDef objects for a database. The QueryDef object is a stored definition of a query in a Jet database file or a temporary definition in an ODBCDirect workspace. Tables B.32 and B.33 list the methods and properties of the QueryDefs collection. Tables B.34 and B.35 list the methods and properties of the QueryDef object.

Table B.32. QueryDefs collection methods.

METHOD	DESCRIPTION
Append	Adds a new object to the collection.
Delete	Removes an object from the collection.
Refresh	Updates the contents of the collection to reflect the current status of the database.

Table B.33. QueryDefs collection properties.

PROPERTY	DESCRIPTION
Count	Indicates the number of objects in the collection.

Table B.34. QueryDef object methods.

METHOD	DESCRIPTION
Cancel	Cancels execution of an asynchronous method call.
Close	Closes the current recordset.
CreateProperty	Creates a new user-defined Property object.
Execute	Executes the current query definition.
OpenRecordset	Creates a new Recordset object and appends it to the Recordsets collection.

Table B.35. QueryDef object properties.

PROPERTY	DESCRIPTION
CacheSize	Returns the number of locally cached records that will be received from an ODBC data source.
Connect	Indicates the information about the source of an open connection.

PROPERTY	DESCRIPTION
DateCreated	Returns the date and time the current object was created.
LastUpdated	Returns the date and time the current object was last modified.
KeepLocal	Indicates that the current object is not to be replicated.
LogMessages	Indicates whether messages from an ODBC data source are recorded.
MaxRecords	Indicates the maximum number of records to return from the query.
Name	Sets a user-defined name for the DAO object.
ODBCTimeout	Returns a number, indicating the number of seconds to wait before a timeout error occurs when a QueryDef is executed on an ODBC database.
Prepare	Indicates whether the query should be prepared on the server as a temporary stored procedure.
RecordsAffected	Indicates the number of records affected by the last call to the Execute method.
Replicable	Indicates whether the current object can be replicated.
ReturnsRecords	Indicates whether a SQL pass-through query returns records.
SQL	Sets the SQL statement that composes the current query.
StillExecuting	Indicates whether an asynchronous operation has finished executing.
Type	Returns the operational type of object.
Updatable	Indicates whether the QueryDef object can be updated.

Recordsets **Collection,** Recordset **Object**

The Recordsets collection contains all open Recordset objects of a database. Through the Recordset object, data can be manipulated and accessed. Recordset types include Table, Dynaset, Snapshot, Forward-only, and Dynamic. All recordsets are accessed by rows (records) and columns (fields). Table B.36 lists the methods of the Recordsets collection, and Table B.37 lists the properties. Table B.38 lists the methods of the Recordset object, and Table B.39 lists the properties.

Table B.36. Recordsets collection methods.

METHOD	DESCRIPTION
Refresh	Updates the contents of the collection to reflect the current status of the database.

Table B.37. Recordsets collection properties.

PROPERTY	DESCRIPTION
Count	Indicates the number of objects in the collection.

Table B.38. Recordset object methods.

METHOD	DESCRIPTION
AddNew	Adds a new record to the current recordset.
Cancel	Cancels operation of an asynchronous operation.
CancelUpdate	Cancels any pending updates.
Clone	Creates a duplicate of the current Recordset object.
Close	Closes the current recordset.
CopyQueryDef	Returns a QueryDef object that is a copy of the QueryDef used to create the current Recordset object.
Delete	Deletes the current record.
Edit	Prepares the current record for editing by Visual Basic code.
FillCache	Fills all or part of a local cache for a Recordset object that contains data from an ODBC data source.
FindFirst	Finds the first record that matches specified criteria.
FindLast	Finds the last record that matches specified criteria.
FindNext	Finds the next record that matches specified criteria.
FindPrevious	Finds the previous record that matches specified criteria.
GetRows	Returns multiple rows from the current Recordset object.
Move	Moves the position of the current record in the current Recordset object.
MoveFirst	Moves to the first record of the recordset.
MoveLast	Moves to the last record of the recordset.
MoveNext	Moves to the next record of the recordset.
MovePrevious	Moves to the previous record of the recordset.
NextRecordset	Returns the next set of records returned by a multipart selection query in an OpenRecordset call.
OpenRecordset	Sets the recordset to a new selection of records.
Requery	Performs the specified query again to update the recordset with the current database information.
Seek	Finds a match to a specific criteria by using an index of the current recordset.
Update	Saves changes specified to the recordset from the AddNew or Edit method.

Table B.39. Recordset object properties.

PROPERTY	DESCRIPTION
AbsolutePosition	Sets the record pointer position within the Recordset object.
BatchCollisionCount	Indicates the number of records that did not complete the last batch update.
BatchCollisions	Returns an array of bookmarks indicating which rows generated collisions in the last batch update operation.
BatchSize	Indicates the number of statements sent back to the server in each batch.

PROPERTY	DESCRIPTION
BOF	Returns the beginning-of-file indicator.
EOF	Returns the end-of-file indicator.
Bookmark	Returns the bookmark for record position.
Bookmarkable	Returns a Boolean stating the capability to create bookmarks.
CacheSize	Indicates the number of locally cached records that will be received from an ODBC data source.
CacheStart	Returns a bookmark to the first record in a Recordset object containing data to be locally cached from an ODBC data source.
Connection	Sets the Connection object that owns the current Recordset object.
DateCreated	Returns the date and time the current object was created.
LastUpdated	Returns the date and time the current object was last modified.
EditMode	Indicates the state of editing for the current record.
Filter	Sets a filter to determine the records included in a subsequently opened Recordset object.
Index	Sets the current index for the Recordset object.
LastModified	Returns a bookmark to the last edited or new record of the current Recordset object.
LockEdits	Indicates the type of locking that is in effect while editing.
Name	Sets a user-defined name for the DAO object.
NoMatch	Indicates whether a record was found after using either the Seek method or a Find method.
PercentPosition	Returns an approximate percentage of the current record position as compared to the entire record population of the current Recordset object.
RecordCount	Indicates the number of records in the current Recordset object.
RecordStatus	Returns the update status of a current record that is part of a batch update.
Restartable	Indicates whether the current object supports the Requery method.
Sort	Sets the order for records in the current Recordset object.
StillExecuting	Indicates whether an asynchronous operation has finished.
Transactions	Indicates whether the object supports transactions.
Type	Indicates the operational type of the object.
Updatable	Indicates whether the current object can be updated.
UpdateOptions	Indicates the way in which batch updates are executed.
ValidationRule	Returns the value that validates data in a field as it is changed or added to a table.
ValidationText	Sets a message that your application displays if the value of the Field object does not satisfy the validation rule.

Relations **Collection,** Relation **Object**

The Relations collection contains all the Relation objects stored in a database. A Relation object indicates the relationship between fields and tables or queries of a Jet database. Tables B.40 and B.41 list the methods and properties of the Relations collection. Tables B.42 and B.43 list the methods and properties of the Relation object.

Table B.40. Relations collection methods.

METHOD	DESCRIPTION
Append	Adds a new object to the collection.
Delete	Removes an object from the collection.
Refresh	Updates the contents of the collection to reflect the current status of the database.

Table B.41. Relations collection properties.

PROPERTY	DESCRIPTION
Count	Indicates the number of objects in the collection.

Table B.42. Relation object methods.

METHOD	DESCRIPTION
CreateField	Creates a Field object and appends it to the Fields collection.

Table B.43. Relation object properties.

PROPERTY	DESCRIPTION
Attributes	Returns characteristics of the current Relation object.
ForeignTable	Sets the name of the current Relation object's foreign table.
Name	Sets a user-defined name for the DAO object.
PartialReplica	Indicates whether the Relation object should be included in a partial replica.
Table	Returns the name of the current Relation object's primary table.
ValidationText	Sets a message that your application displays if the value of the Field object does not satisfy the validation rule.

TableDefs **Collection,** TableDef **Object**

The TableDefs collection contains all TableDef objects for a given database. The TableDef object is used to access and manipulate a table's definition. Tables B.44 and B.45 list the methods and properties of the TableDefs collection. Table B.46 lists the methods of the TableDef object, and Table B.47 lists the properties of the TableDef object.

Table B.44. TableDefs collection methods.

METHOD	DESCRIPTION
Append	Adds a new object to the collection.
Delete	Removes an object from the collection.
Refresh	Updates the contents of the collection to reflect the current status of the database.

Table B.45. `TableDefs` collection properties.

PROPERTY	DESCRIPTION
Count	Indicates the number of objects in the collection.

Table B.46. `TableDef` object methods.

METHOD	DESCRIPTION
CreateField	Creates a new `Field` object for the current `TableDef` and appends it to the `Fields` collection.
CreateIndex	Creates a new `Index` object for the current `TableDef` object and appends it to the `Indexes` collection.
CreateProperty	Creates a new user-defined `Property` object for the current `TableDef` object.
OpenRecordset	Creates a new `Recordset` object and appends it to the `Recordsets` collection.
RefreshLink	Updates the connection information for a linked table.

Table B.47. `TableDef` object properties.

PROPERTY	DESCRIPTION
Attributes	Indicates the characteristics of the current `TableDef` object.
ConflictTable	Returns the name of a conflict table containing the database records that conflicted during the synchronization of two replicas.
Connect	Sets information about the source of an open connection.
DateCreated	Returns the date and time the current object was created.
LastUpdated	Returns the date and time the current object was last modified.
KeepLocal	Indicates that the object is not to be replicated with replication of the database.
Name	Sets a user-defined name for the DAO object.
RecordCount	Indicates the number of records in a table.
Replicable	Indicates whether the object is replicable.
ReplicaFilter	Indicates what subset of records is replicated from a full replica.
SourceTableName	Indicates the name of a linked table or the name of a base table.
Updatable	Indicates whether you can change the DAO object.
ValidationRule	Sets a value that validates data in a field as it is changed or added to a table.
ValidationText	Sets a message that your application displays if the value of the `Field` object does not satisfy the validation rule.

Workspaces **Collection,** Workspace **Object**

The `Workspaces` collection contains all active `Workspace` objects that are not hidden. A `Workspace` object defines how the Visual Basic application interacts with data. Tables B.48

and B.49 list the methods and properties of the Workspaces collection, and Tables B.50 and B.51 list the methods and properties of the Workspace object.

Table B.48. Workspaces collection methods.

METHOD	DESCRIPTION
Append	Adds a new object to the collection.
Delete	Removes an object from the collection.
Refresh	Updates the contents of the collection to reflect the current status of the database.

Table B.49. Workspaces collection properties.

PROPERTY	DESCRIPTION
Count	Indicates the number of objects in the collection.

Table B.50. Workspace object methods.

METHOD	DESCRIPTION
BeginTrans	Begins a transaction for the workspace.
CommitTrans	Commits changes since the last call to the BeginTrans method.
Rollback	Rolls back to the workspace state before the call to the BeginTrans method.
Close	Closes the Workspace object.
CreateDatabase	Creates a new Database object.
CreateGroup	Creates a new Group object.
CreateUser	Creates a new User object.
OpenConnection	Opens a connection object for an ODBC data source.
OpenDatabase	Open a database with the current workspace.

Table B.51. Workspace object properties.

PROPERTY	DESCRIPTION
DefaultCursorDriver	Returns the type of cursor driver used on the connection created by the call to OpenConnection or OpenDatabase.
IsolateODBCTrans	Indicates whether multiple transactions that involve the same Jet-connected ODBC data source are isolated.
LoginTimeout	Indicates the number of seconds before an error occurs while attempting to log on to an ODBC database.
Name	Sets a user-defined name for the DAO object.
Type	Indicates the operational type of the object.
UserName	Returns the owner of the current Workspace object.

Users **Collection,** User **Object**

A Users collection contains all User objects belonging to a particular Workspace or Group object. The User object refers to a specific user account with various permissions. Tables B.52 and B.53 list the methods and properties of the Users collection. Tables B.54 and B.55 list the methods and properties of the User object.

Table B.52. Users collection methods.

METHOD	DESCRIPTION
Append	Adds a new object to the collection.
Delete	Removes an object from the collection.
Refresh	Updates the contents of the collection to reflect the current status of the database.

Table B.53. Users collection properties.

PROPERTY	DESCRIPTION
Count	Indicates the number of objects in the collection.

Table B.54. User object methods.

METHOD	DESCRIPTION
CreateGroup	Creates a new Group object for the current user.
NewPassword	Changes the password of the current user.

Table B.55. User object properties.

PROPERTY	DESCRIPTION
Name	Sets the name of the current User object.
Password	Sets the password for the current User object.
PID	Returns a personal identifier for the current User object.

C

A SHORT INTRODUCTION TO VISUAL BASIC OBJECTS

With the introduction of Visual Basic 5, object-oriented programming has never been easier. In this appendix, we will define and discuss objects, as well as illustrate how to use them.

Object Overview

The biggest selling point of object-oriented programming is *encapsulation*. Encapsulation means that both the data and the means of transforming or altering that data are wrapped up into one easy-to-use shell called an *object*. In its simplest form, an object is a group of data describing a particular thing that cannot be described by a single number or string.

For instance, imagine that you want to take yourself as the object that you need to store in your application. With a single variable, you can give yourself a name. Most likely you need much more information than this to describe yourself. You might want to indicate your age and possibly your address. It is possible to incorporate all of this information into one structure that would represent you. Take, for instance, the following type declaration:

```
Private Type Person
    Name As String
    Age As Integer
    Address As String
    City As String
    State As String
    ZipCode As String
End Type
```

This declaration creates a new data type called Person that can hold a person's name, age, address, city, state, and zip code. To create a new person, we would use something similar to the following declaration:

```
Private Steven As Person
```

This data structure was acceptable to Visual Basic programmers up until version 5, when developers suddenly demanded more (and we have the right!).

Now, in Visual Basic 5, we can include much more in a data structure than just the data. Using encapsulation, we can add methods and events. The data, as we know it, becomes properties. Properties are user-interface variables or variable objects. With these interfaces, we can cleanly access the data for what is now called a class.

The concept of classes was not developed for Visual Basic—it was developed a long time ago for much older languages (if I quote a language that invented classes or object-oriented programming, I know I will receive hate mail telling me of an earlier programming language, so I will be vague in my history). What is important is that we have the ability to use classes now, in Visual Basic.

A class is similar to a type declaration in that it is a framework or a shell used to hold and manipulate data; however, no data manipulation is done in the class itself. For us to work with this structure, we must create an instance of the class by declaring a variable—an object variable:

```
Private m_oNewPerson As New Person
```

Here, **Person** is no longer the name of a data structure, but rather the name of a class that would hold properties called **Name**, **Age**, **Address**, and so on. We would also have methods within this class to manipulate this information. For instance, we might have a method that is part of the **Person** class that would load the person's information from a file. In this case, we might have a **Load** method, as in this example:

```
m_oNewPerson.Load "Steven"
```

This example accepts a string as an argument to determine the name of the person to load.

There have always been objects in Visual Basic, even if you did not realize it. Take, for instance, the text box control. This is an object, an instance of the text box class. We can use object-oriented programming to access the properties of a text box control, as shown in this procedure:

```
Private Sub DoSomethingSenseless()

    Text1.Enabled = True
    Text1.Text = "Hello Mommy!"
    Text1.SelStart = 0
    Text1.SelLength = Len(Text1.Text)

End Sub
```

This example simply sets various properties of the text box control to what we have specified. We also read one of the properties from the text box control (`Text1.Text`), as shown in the last line.

We can also call methods of this control in a fashion similar to this:

```
Text1.SetFocus
```

In this example, we simply called the `SetFocus` method that puts the focus of the window on the text box control.

The `DoSomethingSenseless` routine shown previously takes advantage of a great interface to the text box control. However, there is an even more object-oriented approach we can take, as shown in this newly revised `DoSomethingSenseless` routine:

```
Private Sub DoSomethingSenseless()

    With Text1
        .Enabled = True
        .Text = "Hello Mommy!"
        .SelStart = 0
        .SelLength = Len(.Text)
        .SetFocus
    End With

End Sub
```

This routine uses a statement called `With`. `With` uses the `Text1` control to access its public members.

Many objects have default properties. The text box control's default property is the `Text` property. The following example shows how you can access the default property:

```
Private Sub DoMoreThings()

    ' declare a new object and call it oNewObject
    Dim oNewObject As Object

    ' all objects can be set to the 'root' type of Object
    Set oNewObject = Text1

    ' the following are equivalent
    oNewObject.Text = "Hello Dad!"
    oNewObject = "Hello Dad!"

    Tezt1.Text = "Hello Dad!"
```

continued on next page

continued from previous page

```
    Text1 = "Hello Dad!"

End Sub
```

Notice the declaration of a new object variable in the beginning of this routine. All objects can be assigned to the Object data type. This means that all objects implement the `object` class. After we have our new object, we can set it to the `Text1` control (actually, just give it a reference to the control). This step allows us to access our `Text1` control using the `oNewObject` object variable. Also notice that the `Text` property does not have to be entered to assign the property its value, because it is the object's default value.

Our Own Object

We can create our own object definition, or class, using Visual Basic 5. To do so, first create a new project. Along with `Form1`, which should be part of your new project already, add a class module. Name the class `Person`, and add the following code to the declarations section of the class module:

```
Option Explicit

Private m_sFirstName As String
Private m_sLastName As String
```

These two member variables of the `Person` class are private variables—they cannot be accessed by anybody outside of our class.

Now add our public properties, which serve as our user interface to retrieve information from the user:

```
Public Property Let FirstName(ByVal sNewValue As String)
    m_sFirstName = sNewValue
End Property

Public Property Let LastName(ByVal sNewValue As String)
    m_sLastName = sNewValue
End Property
```

It should be noted that there are no `Property Get` routines for the `FirstName` and `LastName` properties. This means that the properties are write only and cannot be read.

Now create a property that allows the user to retrieve the entire name of the `Person` class as shown here:

```
Public Property Get FullName() As String
    FullName = m_sFirstName & " " & m_sLastName
End Property
```

This is a `Property Get` routine and there is no `Property Let` routine; therefore, this property is read only.

We can now use our new class in a routine to create a new `Person` object:

```
Private Sub CreatePerson()

    Dim oNewPerson As New Person
```

```
    With oNewPerson

        ' retrieve information from the user
        .FirstName = InputBox$("Enter first name:")
        .LastName = InputBox$("Enter last name:")

        ' display the full name for the user
        MsgBox "Person's full name: " & .FullName

    End With

End Sub
```

This routine declares a new instance of the **Person** class that we wrote earlier. The user is then asked for the first and last name of the new person, and both strings are stored in the corresponding property. Finally, the **FullName** property is called to show the user the full name of the new person.

Collections of Objects

Collections are used to group related data objects into a single set. In DAO, we find collections everywhere, from the **Workspaces** collection to the **Fields** and **Indexes** collections.

Collections are good to keep a list of objects. For instance, take the **Person** class shown previously. Suppose we wanted to add many people to a group or list. In this case, it would be good to use the **Collection** class to keep track of our people. Take the following event, for example:

```
Public Persons As New Collection


Private Sub cmdAddPerson_Click()

    ' initiate a new person object
    Dim oNewPerson As New Person

    With oNewPerson

        ' get new name from the user
        .FirstName = InputBox$("Enter first name:")
        .LastName = InputBox$("Enter last name:")

        ' add the person to the persons collection
        Persons.Add .FullName

    End With

End Sub
```

This event is fired when a user presses a command button. First, a new **Person** object is initiated from the **Person** class. Next, the person's first and last names are filled, and finally, the person is added to the collection using the **Add** method of the **Persons** collection.

The `Collection` class stores all items as Variant data types; therefore, you can add any data type to a collection object, with the exception of user-defined types. This also means that you can add different types to the same collection because the `Collection` class cannot tell the difference anyway.

Table C.1 shows the property and three methods of the `Collection` class.

Table C.1. The `Collection` class.

METHOD OR PROPERTY	DESCRIPTION
`Count` property	Returns the number of items belonging to the current collection object
`Add` method	Adds a new item to the current collection object
`Item` method	Returns an item, by an index or a key, from the current collection object
`Remove` method	Removes an item from the current collection, by an index or a key

As you can see, the `Collection` class is pretty straightforward. Although arrays are more efficient memory managers than collection objects, they cannot compete with other advantages. For one, you never need to use `ReDim` with a collection object—it takes care of its size for you. Also, the `Collection` class can access its items very quickly using the `Item` method, whereas an array does not have this built-in functionality.

An item of a collection is retrieved, removed, or added to a collection object using a key and an index. A key is a string used during the `Add` method call, whereas an index is usually determined after each object is added to a collection. An index is a Long value that can be determined by using the `before` and `after` parameters; however, the index can change after another object is added to the collection.

You can use the index to iterate through a collection to access each item as shown in this example:

```
Dim nCount As Integer

With Persons

    For nCount = 1 To .Count
        Debug.Print .Item(nCount).FullName
    Next nCount

End With
```

This code uses the `Count` property of the `Persons` collection to determine an upper bound for the `For...Next` loop. For each item in the collection object `Persons`, the `FullName` property is printed to the immediate window.

An easier and more efficient way to iterate through a collection is to use the `For Each...Next` statement instead of `For...Next`, as shown in this code:

```
Dim oPerson As Person

For Each oPerson In Persons
    Debug.Print oPerson.FullName
Next nCount
```

This code declares a new object variable called oPerson as a Person object. Using this variable, the For Each oPerson In Persons line of code sets oPerson to each Persons.Item(index) object in the collection. Now you can use the oPerson object to access the collection object.

Adding an Item to a Collection Object

To add items to a collection, you would use the Add method with the following syntax:

```
Sub Add (item As Variant [, key As Variant] [, before As Variant]
                                    [, after As Variant])
```

The first parameter to the routine is the actual object you are to add to the collection, and the second is a key that would be used to search quickly for the given object. The following statements demonstrate the use of keys in a collection:

```
Persons.Add oNewPerson, oNewPerson.FullName
Persons.Add oNewPerson, "Jason"
```

The other two parameters for the Add method are the before and after parameters. By using one of these two parameters, you can specify the ordinal position of your item in the collection object as shown in these examples:

```
Persons.Add oNewPerson, "Jason", 1         ' adds as first item
Persons.Add oNewPerson, "John", before:=3  ' adds as second item
Persons.Add oNewPerson, "Kimberly", after:=6  ' adds as seventh item
```

As you can see, the Add method supports named arguments.

Removing an Item from a Collection Object

To delete an item from a collection, you must know the index or the key of the item intended for deletion. The syntax for the Remove method is as follows:

```
Sub Remove (index As Variant)
```

The *index* argument in the Remove method can be either the item's key or the item's index number.

Following are some examples of the Remove method:

```
Persons.Remove 5
Persons.Remove "Jason"
```

Accessing Items in a Collection Object

To access items in a collection, you can use the Item method. The syntax for the Item method is as follows:

```
Function Item (index As Variant) As Variant
```

You must use the Set statement when the Item being returned is an object variable. The *index* argument is either the key or the index of the item in the collection object, as shown in these examples:

```
Set oNewPerson = Persons.Item(6)
Set oNewPerson = Persons.Item("Jason")
Set oNewPerson = Persons(6)
Set oNewPerson = Persons("Jason")
```

Notice the last two statements. The `Item` method is omitted because it is the default method for the `Collection` class.

INDEX

N

O

U

V

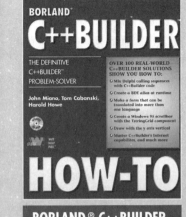

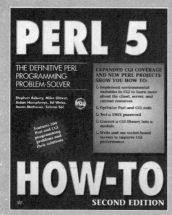

Message from the
Publisher

WELCOME TO OUR NERVOUS SYSTEM

Some people say that the World Wide Web is a graphical extension of the information superhighway, just a network of humans and machines sending each other long lists of the equivalent of digital junk mail.

I think it is much more than that. To me, the Web is nothing less than the nervous system of the entire planet—not just a collection of computer brains connected together, but more like a billion silicon neurons entangled and recirculating electro-chemical signals of information and data, each contributing to the birth of another CPU and another Web site.

Think of each person's hard disk connected at once to every other hard disk on Earth, driven by human navigators searching like Columbus for the New World. Seen this way, the Web is more of a super-entity, a growing, living thing, controlled by the universal human will to expand, to be more. Yet, unlike a purposeful business plan with rigid rules, the Web expands in a nonlinear, unpredictable, creative way that echoes natural evolution.

We created our Web site not just to extend the reach of our computer book products but to be part of this synaptic neural network, to experience, like a nerve in the body, the flow of ideas and then to pass those ideas up the food chain of the mind. Your mind. Even more, we wanted to pump some of our own creative juices into this rich wine of technology.

TASTE OUR DIGITAL WINE

And so we ask you to taste our wine by visiting the body of our business. Begin by understanding the metaphor we have created for our Web site—a universal learning center, situated in outer space in the form of a space station. A place where you can journey to study any topic from the convenience of your own screen. Right now we are focusing on computer topics, but the stars are the limit on the Web.

If you are interested in discussing this Web site or finding out more about the Waite Group, please send me email with your comments, and I will be happy to respond. Being a programmer myself, I love to talk about technology and find out what our readers are looking for.

Sincerely,

Mitchell Waite

Mitchell Waite, CEO and Publisher

200 Tamal Plaza
Corte Madera, CA 94925
415-924-2575
415-924-2576 fax

Website:
http://www.waite.com/waite

CREATING THE HIGHEST QUALITY COMPUTER BOOKS IN THE INDUSTRY

Waite Group Press

Come Visit

WAITE.COM

Waite Group Press
World Wide Web Site

Now find all the latest information on Waite Group books at our new Web site, **http://www.waite.com/waite**. You'll find an online catalog where you can examine and order any title, review upcoming books, and send email to our authors and editors. Our FTP site has all you need to update your book: the latest program listings, errata sheets, most recent versions of Fractint, POV Ray, Polyray, DMorph, and all the programs featured in our books. So download, talk to us, ask questions, on **http://www.waite.com/waite**.

The New Arrivals Room has all our new books listed by month. Just click for a description, Index, Table of Contents, and links to authors.

The Backlist Room has all our books listed alphabetically.

The People Room is where you'll interact with Waite Group employees.

Links to Cyberspace get you in touch with other computer book publishers and other interesting Web sites.

The FTP site contains all program listings, errata sheets, etc.

The Order Room is where you can order any of our books online.

The Subject Room contains typical book pages that show description, Index, Table of Contents, and links to authors.

World Wide Web:

COME SURF OUR TURF—THE WAITE GROUP WEB

http://www.waite.com/waite
Gopher: gopher.waite.com
FTP: ftp.waite.com

LIMITED WARRANTY

The following warranties shall be effective for 90 days from the date of purchase: (i) The Waite Group, Inc., warrants the enclosed disc to be free of defects in materials and workmanship under normal use; and (ii) The Waite Group, Inc., warrants that the programs, unless modified by the purchaser, will substantially perform the functions described in the documentation provided by The Waite Group, Inc., when operated on the designated hardware and operating system. The Waite Group, Inc., does not warrant that the programs will meet purchaser's requirements or that operation of a program will be uninterrupted or error-free. The program warranty does not cover any program that has been altered or changed in any way by anyone other than The Waite Group, Inc. The Waite Group, Inc., is not responsible for problems caused by changes in the operating characteristics of computer hardware or computer operating systems that are made after the release of the programs, nor for problems in the interaction of the programs with each other or other software.

THESE WARRANTIES ARE EXCLUSIVE AND IN LIEU OF ALL OTHER WARRANTIES OF MERCHANTABILITY OR FITNESS FOR A PARTICULAR PURPOSE OR OF ANY OTHER WARRANTY, WHETHER EXPRESSED OR IMPLIED.

EXCLUSIVE REMEDY

The Waite Group, Inc., will replace any defective disk without charge if the defective disc is returned to The Waite Group, Inc., within 90 days from date of purchase.

This is Purchaser's sole and exclusive remedy for any breach of warranty or claim for contract, tort, or damages.

LIMITATION OF LIABILITY

THE WAITE GROUP, INC., AND THE AUTHORS OF THE PROGRAMS SHALL NOT IN ANY CASE BE LIABLE FOR SPECIAL, INCIDENTAL, CONSEQUENTIAL, INDIRECT, OR OTHER SIMILAR DAMAGES ARISING FROM ANY BREACH OF THESE WARRANTIES EVEN IF THE WAITE GROUP, INC., OR ITS AGENT HAS BEEN ADVISED OF THE POSSIBILITY OF SUCH DAMAGES.

THE LIABILITY FOR DAMAGES OF THE WAITE GROUP, INC., AND THE AUTHORS OF THE PROGRAMS UNDER THIS AGREEMENT SHALL IN NO EVENT EXCEED THE PURCHASE PRICE PAID.

COMPLETE AGREEMENT

This Agreement constitutes the complete agreement between The Waite Group, Inc., and the authors of the programs, and you, the purchaser.

Some states do not allow the exclusion or limitation of implied warranties or liability for incidental or consequential damages, so the above exclusions or limitations may not apply to you. This limited warranty gives you specific legal rights; you may have others, which vary from state to state.

MACMILLAN COMPUTER PUBLISHING USA

A VIACOM COMPANY

Technical ┄┄ Support:

If you cannot get the CD/Disk to install properly, or you need assistance with a particular situation in the book, please feel free to check out the Knowledge Base on our Web site at **http://www.superlibrary.com/general/support**. We have answers to our most Frequently Asked Questions listed there. If you do not find your specific question answered, please contact Macmillan Technical Support at **(317) 581-3833**. We can also be reached by email at **support@mcp.com**.

SATISFACTION REPORT CARD

Please fill out this card if you wish to know of future updates to
Visual Basic 5 Database How-To, **or to receive our catalog.**

First Name: _____ **Last Name:** _____

Street Address: _____

City: _____ **State:** _____ **Zip:** _____

Email Address: _____

Daytime Telephone: (_____) _____

Date product was acquired: Month _____ **Day** _____ **Year** _____ **Your Occupation:** _____

Overall, how would you rate *Visual Basic 5 Database How-To*?

☐ Excellent ☐ Very Good ☐ Good
☐ Fair ☐ Below Average ☐ Poor

What did you like MOST about this book? _____

_____

_____

What did you like LEAST about this book? _____

_____

_____

Please describe any problems you may have encountered with installing or using the disc: _____

_____

How did you use this book (problem-solver, tutorial, reference...)?

_____

What is your level of computer expertise?

☐ New ☐ Dabbler ☐ Hacker
☐ Power User ☐ Programmer ☐ Experienced Professional

What computer languages are you familiar with? _____

_____

Please describe your computer hardware:

Computer _____ Hard disk _____

5.25" disk drives _____ 3.5" disk drives _____

Video card _____ Monitor _____

Printer _____ Peripherals _____

Sound Board _____ CD-ROM _____

Where did you buy this book?

☐ Bookstore (name): _____
☐ Discount store (name): _____
☐ Computer store (name): _____
☐ Catalog (name): _____
☐ Direct from WGP ☐ Other _____

What price did you pay for this book? _____

What influenced your purchase of this book?

☐ Recommendation ☐ Advertisement
☐ Magazine review ☐ Store display
☐ Mailing ☐ Book's format
☐ Reputation of Waite Group Press ☐ Other

How many computer books do you buy each year? _____

How many other Waite Group books do you own? _____

What is your favorite Waite Group book? _____

_____

Is there any program or subject you would like to see Waite Group Press cover in a similar approach? _____

_____

Additional comments? _____

_____

_____

Please send to: **Waite Group Press**
200 Tamal Plaza
Corte Madera, CA 94925

☐ **Check here for a free Waite Group catalog**

END-USER LICENSE AGREEMENT FOR MICROSOFT SOFTWARE
Visual Basic 5 Database How-To

IMPORTANT—READ CAREFULLY: This Microsoft End-User License Agreement ("EULA") is a legal agreement between you (either an individual or a single entity) and Microsoft Corporation for the Microsoft software product identified above, which includes computer software and may include associated media, printed materials, and "online" or electronic documentation ("SOFTWARE PRODUCT"). By installing, copying, or otherwise using the SOFTWARE PRODUCT, you agree to be bound by the terms of this EULA. If you do not agree to the terms of this EULA, do not install or use the SOFTWARE PRODUCT; you may, however, return it to your place of purchase for a full refund.

SOFTWARE PRODUCT LICENSE

The SOFTWARE PRODUCT is protected by copyright laws and international copyright treaties, as well as other intellectual property laws and treaties. The SOFTWARE PRODUCT is licensed, not sold.

1. GRANT OF LICENSE. This EULA grants you the following rights:

   a. Software Product. Microsoft grants to you as an individual, a personal, nonexclusive license to make and use copies of the SOFTWARE for the sole purposes of designing, developing, and testing your software product(s) that are designed to operate in conjunction with any Microsoft operating system product. You may install copies of the SOFTWARE on an unlimited number of computers provided that you are the only individual using the SOFTWARE. If you are an entity, Microsoft grants you the right to designate one individual within your organization to have the right to use the SOFTWARE in the manner provided above.

   b. Electronic Documents. Solely with respect to electronic documents included with the SOFTWARE, you may make an unlimited number of copies (either in hardcopy or electronic form), provided that such copies shall be used only for internal purposes and are not republished or distributed to any third party.

   c. Storage/Network Use. You may also store or install a copy of the SOFTWARE PRODUCT on a storage device, such as a network server, used only to install or run the SOFTWARE PRODUCT on your other computers over an internal network; however, you must acquire and dedicate a license for each separate computer on which the SOFTWARE PRODUCT is installed or run from the storage device. A license for the SOFTWARE PRODUCT may not be shared or used concurrently on different computers.

   d. Redistributable Components.

      (i) Sample Code. In addition to the rights granted in Section 1, Microsoft grants you the right to use and modify the source code version of those portions of the SOFTWARE designated as "Sample Code" ("SAMPLE CODE") for the sole purposes of designing, developing, and testing your software product(s), and to reproduce and distribute the SAMPLE CODE, along with any modifications thereof, only in object code form provided that you comply with Section d(iii), below.

      (ii) Redistributable Components. In addition to the rights granted in Section 1, Microsoft grants you a nonexclusive royalty-free right to reproduce and distribute the object code version of any portion of the SOFTWARE listed in the SOFTWARE file REDIST.TXT ("REDISTRIBUTABLE SOFTWARE"), provided you comply with Section d(iii), below.

      (iii) Redistribution Requirements. If you redistribute the SAMPLE CODE or REDISTRIBUTABLE SOFTWARE (collectively, "REDISTRIBUTABLES"), you agree to: (A) distribute the REDISTRIBUTABLES in object code only in conjunction with and as a part of a software application product developed by you that adds significant and primary functionality to the SOFTWARE and that is developed to operate on the Windows or Windows NT environment ("Application"); (B) not use Microsoft's name, logo, or trademarks to market your software application product; (C) include a valid copyright notice on your software product; (D) indemnify, hold harmless, and defend Microsoft from and against any claims or lawsuits, including attorney's fees, that arise or result from the use or distribution of your software application product; (E) not permit further distribution of the REDIS-TRIBUTABLES by your end user. The following exceptions apply to subsection (iii)(E), above: (1) you may permit further redistribution of the REDISTRIBUTABLES by your distributors to your end-user customers if your distributors only distribute the REDISTRIBUTABLES in conjunction with, and as part of, your Application and you and your distributors comply with all other terms of this EULA; and (2) you may permit your end users to reproduce and distribute the object code version of the files designated by ".ocx" file extensions ("Controls") only in conjunction with and as a part of an Application and/or Web page that adds significant and primary functionality to the Controls, and such end user complies with all other terms of this EULA. NOTE: The rights granted in the foregoing subsection (2) DO NOT APPLY to those files identified in the SOFTWARE as Dbgrid.ocx and Graph32.ocx.

2.   DESCRIPTION OF OTHER RIGHTS AND LIMITATIONS.

a. Not for Resale Software. If the SOFTWARE PRODUCT is labeled "Not for Resale" or "NFR," then, notwithstanding other sections of this EULA, you may not resell, or otherwise transfer for value, the SOFTWARE PRODUCT.

b. Limitations on Reverse Engineering, Decompilation, and Disassembly. You may not reverse engineer, decompile, or disassemble the SOFTWARE PRODUCT, except and only to the extent that such activity is expressly permitted by applicable law notwithstanding this limitation.

c. Separation of Components. The SOFTWARE PRODUCT is licensed as a single product. Its component parts may not be separated for use on more than one computer.

d. Rental. You may not rent, lease, or lend the SOFTWARE PRODUCT.

e. Support Services. Microsoft may provide you with support services related to the SOFTWARE PRODUCT ("Support Services"). Use of Support Services is governed by the Microsoft policies and programs described in the user manual, in "online" documentation, and/or in other Microsoft-provided materials. Any supplemental software code provided to you as part of the Support Services shall be considered part of the SOFTWARE PRODUCT and subject to the terms and conditions of this EULA. With respect to technical information you provide to Microsoft as part of the Support Services, Microsoft may use such information for its business purposes, including for product support and development. Microsoft will not utilize such technical information in a form that personally identifies you.

f. Software Transfer. You may permanently transfer all of your rights under this EULA, provided you retain no copies, you transfer all of the SOFTWARE PRODUCT (including all component parts, the media and printed materials, any upgrades, this EULA, and, if applicable, the Certificate of Authenticity), and the recipient agrees to the terms of this EULA. If the SOFTWARE PRODUCT is an upgrade, any transfer must include all prior versions of the SOFTWARE PRODUCT.

g. Termination. Without prejudice to any other rights, Microsoft may terminate this EULA if you fail to comply with the terms and conditions of this EULA. In such event, you must destroy all copies of the SOFTWARE PRODUCT and all of its component parts.

3.   UPGRADES. If the SOFTWARE PRODUCT is labeled as an upgrade, you must be properly licensed to use a product identified by Microsoft as being eligible for the upgrade in order to use the SOFTWARE PRODUCT. A SOFTWARE PRODUCT labeled as an upgrade replaces and/or supplements the product that formed the basis for your eligibility for the upgrade. You may use the resulting upgraded product only in accordance with the terms of this EULA. If the SOFTWARE PRODUCT is an upgrade of a component of a package of software programs that you licensed as a single product, the SOFTWARE PRODUCT may be used and transferred only as part of that single product package and may not be separated for use on more than one computer.

4.   COPYRIGHT. All title and copyrights in and to the SOFTWARE PRODUCT (including but not limited to any images, photographs, animations, video, audio, music, text, and "applets" incorporated into the SOFTWARE PRODUCT), the accompanying printed materials, and any copies of the SOFTWARE PRODUCT are owned by Microsoft or its suppliers. The SOFTWARE PRODUCT is protected by copyright laws and international treaty provisions. Therefore, you must treat the SOFTWARE PRODUCT like any other copyrighted material except that you may install the SOFTWARE PRODUCT on a single computer

provided you keep the original solely for backup or archival purposes. You may not copy the printed materials accompanying the SOFTWARE PRODUCT.

5. DUAL-MEDIA SOFTWARE. You may receive the SOFTWARE PRODUCT in more than one medium. Regardless of the type or size of medium you receive, you may use only one medium that is appropriate for your single computer. You may not use or install the other medium on another computer. You may not loan, rent, lease, or otherwise transfer the other medium to another user, except as part of the permanent transfer (as provided above) of the SOFTWARE PRODUCT.

6. U.S. GOVERNMENT RESTRICTED RIGHTS. The SOFTWARE PRODUCT and documentation are provided with RESTRICTED RIGHTS. Use, duplication, or disclosure by the Government is subject to restrictions as set forth in subparagraph (c)(1)(ii) of the Rights in Technical Data and Computer Software clause at DFARS 252.227-7013 or subparagraphs (c)(1) and (2) of the Commercial Computer Software-Restricted Rights at 48 CFR 52.227-19, as applicable. Manufacturer is Microsoft Corporation/One Microsoft Way/Redmond, WA 98052-6399.

7. EXPORT RESTRICTIONS. You agree that neither you nor your customers intend to or will, directly or indirectly, export or transmit (i) the SOFTWARE or related documentation and technical data or (ii) your software product as described in Section 1(b) of this License (or any part thereof), or process, or service that is the direct product of the SOFTWARE, to any country to which such export or transmission is restricted by any applicable U.S. regulation or statute, without the prior written consent, if required, of the Bureau of Export Administration of the U.S. Department of Commerce, or such other governmental entity as may have jurisdiction over such export or transmission.

MISCELLANEOUS

If you acquired this product in the United States, this EULA is governed by the laws of the State of Washington. If you acquired this product in Canada, this EULA is governed by the laws of the Province of Ontario, Canada. Each of the parties hereto irrevocably attorns to the jurisdiction of the courts of the Province of Ontario and further agrees to commence any litigation which may arise hereunder in the courts located in the Judicial District of York, Province of Ontario. If this product was acquired outside the United States, then local law may apply.

Should you have any questions concerning this EULA, or if you desire to contact Microsoft for any reason, please contact the Microsoft subsidiary serving your country, or write: Microsoft Sales Information Center/One Microsoft Way/Redmond, WA 98052-6399.

LIMITED WARRANTY

NO WARRANTIES. Microsoft expressly disclaims any warranty for the SOFTWARE PRODUCT. The SOFTWARE PRODUCT and any related documentation is provided "as is" without warranty of any kind, either express or implied, including, without limitation, the implied warranties or merchantability, fitness for a particular purpose, or noninfringement. The entire risk arising out of use or performance of the SOFTWARE PRODUCT remains with you.

NO LIABILITY FOR DAMAGES. In no event shall Microsoft or its suppliers be liable for any damages whatsoever (including, without limitation, damages for loss of business profits,business interruption, loss of business information, or any other pecuniary loss) arising out of the use of or inability to use this Microsoft product, even if Microsoft has been advised of the possibility of such damages. Because some states/jurisdictions do not allow the exclusion or limitation of liability for consequential or incidental damages, the above limitation may not apply to you.

INSTALLING
THE CD-ROM

The companion CD-ROM contains all the source code from the book's How-To's, along with third-party utilities that might be useful as you develop for Visual Basic.

Windows 95 and Windows NT 4.0

1. Insert the CD-ROM into your CD-ROM drive. If you have more than one CD-ROM drive, insert the disc into the first drive.

2. From the Start button on your taskbar, choose Run.

3. Type *drive*\WSETUP and press ENTER, where *drive* corresponds to the drive letter of your CD-ROM. For example, if your CD-ROM drive is D:, type **D:\WSETUP** and press ENTER.

4. Follow the on-screen instructions in the installation program.

BEFORE YOU OPEN THE DISK OR CD-ROM PACKAGE ON THE FACING PAGE, CAREFULLY READ THE LICENSE AGREEMENT.

Opening this package indicates that you agree to abide by the license agreement found in the back of this book. If you do not agree with it, promptly return the unopened disk package (including the related book) to the place you obtained it for a refund.